A
HISTORY
— OF —
WESTERN
PHILOSOPHY
Bertrand Russell

UNWIN
PAPERBACKS

LONDON SYDNEY WELLINGTON

First published in Great Britain by George Allen & Unwin 1946
Reprinted five times
Second edition 1961
Reprinted seven times
First published in Unwin® Paperbacks 1979
Reprinted three times
This edition first published in 1984, reprinted 1984, 1985, 1987, 1988,
1989, 1990

Unwin Hyman Limited
15/17 Broadwick Street
London W1V 1FP

Allen & Unwin Australia Pty Ltd
8 Napier Street, North Sydney, NSW 2060, Australia

Allen & Unwin New Zealand Pty Ltd with the Port Nicholson Press
75 Ghuznee Street, Wellington, New Zealand

ISBN 0-04-100045-5

CIP Data

Russell, Bertrand
    A history of Western philosophy and its connection with political
and social circumstances from the earliest times to the present
day. ___
1. Philosophy ___ History
I. Title   II. Series
190′.9   B72

Printed in Finland by Werner Söderström Oy.

PREFACE

A FEW words of apology and explanation are called for if this book is to escape even more severe censure than it doubtless deserves.

Apology is due to the specialists on various schools and individual philosophers. With the possible exception of Leibniz, every philosopher of whom I treat is better known to some others than to me. If, however, books covering a wide field are to be written at all, it is inevitable, since we are not immortal, that those who write such books should spend less time on any one part than can be spent by a man who concentrates on a single author or a brief period. Some, whose scholarly austerity is unbending, will conclude that books covering a wide field should not be written at all, or, if written, should consist of monographs by a multitude of authors. There is, however, something lost when many authors co-operate. If there is any unity in the movement of history, if there is any intimate relation between what goes before and what comes later, it is necessary, for setting this forth, that earlier and later periods should be synthesized in a single mind. The student of Rousseau may have difficulty in doing justice to his connection with the Sparta of Plato and Plutarch; the historian of Sparta may not be prophetically conscious of Hobbes and Fichte and Lenin. To bring out such relations is one of the purposes of this book, and it is a purpose which only a wide survey can fulfil.

There are many histories of philosophy, but none of them, so far as I know, has quite the purpose that I have set myself. Philosophers are both effects and causes: effects of their social circumstances and of the politics and institutions of their time; causes (if they are fortunate) of beliefs which mould the politics and institutions of later ages. In most histories of philosophy, each philosopher appears as in a vacuum; his opinions are set forth unrelated except, at most, to those of earlier philosophers. I have tried, on the contrary, to exhibit each philosopher, as far as truth permits, as an outcome of his *milieu*, a man in whom were crystallized and concentrated thoughts and feelings which, in a vague and diffused form, were common to the community of which he was a part.

This has required the insertion of certain chapters of purely social history. No one can understand the Stoics and Epicureans without some knowledge of the Hellenistic age, or the scholastics without a modicum of understanding of the growth of the Church from the fifth to the thirteenth centuries. I have therefore set forth briefly those parts of the main historical outlines that seemed to me to

7

have had most influence on philosophical thought, and I have done this with most fullness where the history may be expected to be unfamiliar to some readers—for example, in regard to the early Middle Ages. But in these historical chapters I have rigidly excluded whatever seemed to have little or no bearing on contemporary or subsequent philosophy.

The problem of selection, in such a book as the present, is very difficult. Without detail, a book becomes jejune and uninteresting; with detail, it is in danger of becoming intolerably lengthy. I have sought a compromise, by treating only those philosophers who seem to me to have considerable importance, and mentioning, in connection with them, such details as, even if not of fundamental importance, have value on account of some illustrative or vivifying quality.

Philosophy, from the earliest times, has been not merely an affair of the schools, or of disputation between a handful of learned men. It has been an integral part of the life of the community, and as such I have tried to consider it. If there is any merit in this book, it is from this point of view that it is derived.

This book owes its existence to Dr Albert C. Barnes, having been originally designed and partly delivered as lectures at the Barnes Foundation in Pennsylvania.

As in most of my work during the years since 1932, I have been greatly assisted in research and in many other ways by my wife, Patricia Russell.

CONTENTS

CONTENTS

BOOK THREE
MODERN PHILOSOPHY

Part 1
From the Renaissance to Hume

Part 2
From Rousseau to the Present Day

INTRODUCTION

T HE conceptions of life and the world which we call 'philosophical' are a product of two factors: one, inherited religious
and ethical conceptions; the other, the sort of investigation
which may be called 'scientific', using this word in its broadest
sense. Individual philosophers have differed widely in regard to the
proportions in which these two factors entered into their systems,
but it is the presence of both, in some degree, that characterizes
philosophy.

'Philosophy' is a word which has been used in many ways, some
wider, some narrower. I propose to use it in a very wide sense,
which I will now try to explain.

Philosophy, as I shall understand the word, is something intermediate between theology and science. Like theology, it consists
of speculations on matters as to which definite knowledge has, so
far, been unascertainable; but like science, it appeals to human
reason rather than to authority, whether that of tradition or that
of revelation. All *definite* knowledge—so I should contend— belongs to science; all *dogma* as to what surpasses definite knowledge
belongs to theology. But between theology and science there is a No
Man's Land, exposed to attack from both sides; this No Man's Land
is philosophy. Almost all the questions of most interest to speculative minds are such as science cannot answer, and the confident
answers of theologians no longer seem so convincing as they did
in former centuries. Is the world divided into mind and matter, and,
if so, what is mind and what is matter? Is mind subject to matter,
or is it possessed of independent powers? Has the universe any
unity or purpose? Is it evolving towards some goal? Are there
really laws of nature, or do we believe in them only because of our
innate love of order? Is man what he seems to the astronomer, a
tiny lump of impure carbon and water impotently crawling on a
small and unimportant planet? Or is he what he appears to Hamlet? Is he perhaps both at once? Is there a way of living that is
noble and another that is base, or are all ways of living merely
futile? If there is a way of living that is noble, in what does it
consist, and how shall we achieve it? Must the good be eternal in
order to deserve to be valued, or is it worth seeking even if the
universe is inexorably moving towards death? Is there such a thing
as wisdom, or is what seems such merely the ultimate refinement
of folly? To such questions no answer can be found in the labora-

tory. Theologies have professed to give answers, all too definite; but their very definiteness causes modern minds to view them with suspicion. The studying of these questions, if not the answering of them, is the business of philosophy.

Why, then, you may ask, waste time on such insoluble problems? To this one may answer as a historian, or as an individual facing the terror of cosmic loneliness.

The answer of the historian, in so far as I am capable of giving it, will appear in the course of this work. Ever since men became capable of free speculation, their actions, in innumerable important respects, have depended upon their theories as to the world and human life, as to what is good and what is evil. This is as true in the present day as at any former time. To understand an age or a nation, we must understand its philosophy, and to understand its philosophy we must ourselves be in some degree philosophers. There is here a reciprocal causation: the circumstances of men's lives do much to determine their philosophy, but, conversely, their philosophy does much to determine their circumstances. This inter-action throughout the centuries will be the topic of the following pages.

There is also, however, a more personal answer. Science tells us what we can know, but what we can know is little, and if we forget how much we cannot know we become insensitive to many things of very great importance. Theology, on the other hand, induces a dogmatic belief that we have knowledge where in fact we have ignorance, and by doing so generates a kind of impertinent in-solence towards the universe. Uncertainty, in the presence of vivid hopes and fears, is painful, but must be endured if we wish to live without the support of comforting fairy tales. It is not good either to forget the questions that philosophy asks, or to persuade our-selves that we have found indubitable answers to them. To teach how to live without certainty, and yet without being paralysed by hesitation, is perhaps the chief thing that philosophy, in our age, can still do for those who study it.

Philosophy, as distinct from theology, began in Greece in the sixth century B.C. After running its course in antiquity, it was again submerged by theology as Christianity rose and Rome fell. Its second great period, from the eleventh to the fourteenth centuries, was dominated by the Catholic Church, except for a few great rebels, such as the Emperor Frederick II (1195-1250). This period was brought to an end by the confusions that culminated in the Reformation. The third period, from the seventeenth century to the present day, is dominated, more than either of its predecessors, by science; traditional religious beliefs remain important, but are felt to need justification, and are modified wherever science seems to make this imperative. Few of the philosophers of this period are orthodox from a Catholic standpoint, and the secular State is more important in their speculations than the Church.

Social cohesion and individual liberty, like religion and science, are in a state of conflict or uneasy compromise throughout the whole period. In Greece, social cohesion was secured by loyalty to the City State; even Aristotle, though in his time Alexander was making the City State obsolete, could see no merit in any other kind of polity. The degree to which the individual's liberty was curtailed by his duty to the City varied widely. In Sparta he had as little liberty as in modern Germany or Russia; in Athens, in spite of occasional persecutions, citizens had, in the best period, a very extraordinary freedom from restrictions imposed by the State. Greek thought down to Aristotle is dominated by religious and patriotic devotion to the City; its ethical systems are adapted to the lives of *citizens* and have a large political element. When the Greeks became subject, first to the Macedonians, and then to the Romans, the conceptions appropriate to their days of independence were no longer applicable. This produced, on the one hand, a loss of vigour through the breach with tradition, and, on the other hand, a more individual and less social ethic. The Stoics thought of the virtuous life as a relation of the soul to God, rather than as a relation of the citizen to the State. They thus prepared the way for Christianity, which, like Stoicism, was originally unpolitical, since, during its first three centuries, its adherents were devoid of influence on government. Social cohesion, during the six and a half centuries from Alexander to Constantine, was secured, not by philosophy and not by ancient loyalties, but by force, first that of armies and then that of civil administration. Roman armies, Roman roads, Roman law, and Roman officials first created and then preserved a powerful centralized State. Nothing was attributable to Roman philosophy, since there was none.

During this long period, the Greek ideas inherited from the age of freedom underwent a gradual process of transformation. Some of the old ideas, notably those which we should regard as specifically religious, gained in relative importance; others, more rationalistic, were discarded because they no longer suited the spirit of the age. In this way the later pagans trimmed the Greek tradition until it became suitable for incorporation in Christian doctrine.

Christianity popularized an important opinion, already implicit in the teaching of the Stoics, but foreign to the general spirit of antiquity—I mean, the opinion that a man's duty to God is more imperative than his duty to the State.[1] This opinion—that 'we ought to obey God rather than Man', as Socrates and the Apostles said—survived the conversion of Constantine, because the early Christian emperors were Arians or inclined to Arianism. When the emperors became orthodox, it fell into abeyance. In the Byzantine Empire it remained latent, as also in the subsequent Russian Empire, which derived its Christianity from Constantinople.[2] But in the West, where the Catholic emperors were almost immediately replaced (except in parts of Gaul) by heretical barbarian conquerors, the superiority of religious to political allegiance survived, and to some extent still survives.

The barbarian invasion put an end, for six centuries, to the civilization of western Europe. It lingered in Ireland until the Danes destroyed it in the ninth century; before its extinction there it produced one notable figure, Scotus Erigena. In the Eastern Empire, Greek civilization, in a desiccated form, survived, as in a museum, till the fall of Constantinople in 1453, but nothing of importance to the world came out of Constantinople except an artistic tradition and Justinian's Codes of Roman law.

During the period of darkness, from the end of the fifth century to the middle of the eleventh, the western Roman world underwent some very interesting changes. The conflict between duty to God and duty to the State, which Christianity had introduced, took the form of a conflict between Church and king. The ecclesiastical jurisdiction of the Pope extended over Italy, France, and Spain, Great Britain and Ireland, Germany, Scandinavia, and Poland. At first, outside Italy and southern France, his control over bishops and abbots was very slight, but from the time of Gregory VII (late eleventh century) it became real and effective. From that time on, the clergy, throughout western Europe, formed a single organization directed from Rome, seeking power intelligently and relentlessly, and usually victorious, until after the year 1300, in their conflicts with secular rulers. The conflict between Church and State was not only a conflict between clergy and laity; it was also a renewal of the conflict between the Mediterranean world and the northern barbarians. The unity of the Church echoed the unity of the Roman Empire; its liturgy was Latin, and its dominant men were mostly Italian, Spanish, or southern French. Their education, when education revived, was classical; their conceptions of law and government would have been more intelligible to Marcus Aurelius

---

[1] This opinion was not unknown in earlier times: it is stated, for example, in the *Antigone* of Sophocles. But before the Stoics those who held it were few.

[2] That is why the modern Russian does not think that we ought to obey dialectical materialism rather than Stalin.

than they were to contemporary monarchs. The Church represented at once continuity with the past and what was most civilized in the present.

The secular power, on the contrary, was in the hands of kings and barons of Teutonic descent, who endeavoured to preserve what they could of the institutions that they had brought out of the forests of Germany. Absolute power was alien to those institutions, and so was what appeared to these vigorous conquerors as a dull and spiritless legality. The king had to share his power with the feudal aristocracy, but all alike expected to be allowed occasional outbursts of passion in the form of war, murder, pillage, or rape. Monarchs might repent, for they were sincerely pious, and, after all, repentance was itself a form of passion. But the Church could never produce in them the quiet regularity of good behaviour which a modern employer demands, and usually obtains, of his employees. What was the use of conquering the world if they could not drink and murder and love as the spirit moved them? And why should they, with their armies of proud knights, submit to the orders of bookish men, vowed to celibacy and destitute of armed force? In spite of ecclesiastical disapproval, they preserved the duel and trial by battle, and they developed tournaments and courtly love. Occasionally, in a fit of rage, they would even murder eminent churchmen.

All the armed force was on the side of the kings, and yet the Church was victorious. The Church won, partly because it had almost a monopoly of education, partly because the kings were perpetually at war with each other, but mainly because, with very few exceptions, rulers and people alike profoundly believed that the Church possessed the power of the keys. The Church could decide whether a king should spend eternity in heaven or in hell; the Church could absolve subjects from the duty of allegiance, and so stimulate rebellion. The Church, moreover, represented order in place of anarchy, and consequently won the support of the rising mercantile class. In Italy, especially, this last consideration was decisive.

The Teutonic attempt to preserve at least a partial independence of the Church expressed itself not only in politics, but also in art, romance, chivalry, and war. It expressed itself very little in the intellectual world, because education was almost wholly confined to the clergy. The explicit philosophy of the Middle Ages is not an accurate mirror of the times, but only of what was thought by one party. Among ecclesiastics, however—especially among the Franciscan friars—a certain number, for various reasons, were at variance with the Pope. In Italy, moreover, culture spread to the laity some centuries sooner than it did north of the Alps. Frederick II, who tried to found a new religion, represents the extreme of anti-papal culture; Thomas Aquinas, who was born in the kingdom of Naples where Frederick II was supreme, remains to this day the classic exponent of papal philosophy. Dante, some fifty years later, achieved a synthesis, and gave the only balanced exposition of the complete medieval world of ideas.

After Dante, both for political and for intellectual reasons, the medieval philosophical synthesis broke down. It had, while it lasted, a quality of tidiness and miniature completeness; whatever the system took account of was placed with precision with relation to the other contents of its very finite cosmos. But the Great Schism, the conciliar movement, and the Renaissance papacy led up to the Reformation, which destroyed the unity of Christendom and the scholastic theory of government that centred round the Pope. In the Renaissance period new knowledge, both of antiquity and of the earth's surface, made men tired of systems, which were felt to be mental prisons. The Copernican astronomy assigned to the earth and to man a humbler position than they had enjoyed in the Ptolemaic theory. Pleasure in new facts took the place, among intelligent men, of pleasure in reasoning, analysing, and systematizing. Although in art the Renaissance is still orderly, in thought it prefers a large and fruitful disorder. In this respect, Montaigne is the most typical exponent of the age.

In the theory of politics, as in everything except art, there was a collapse of order. The Middle Ages, though turbulent in practice, were dominated in thought by a passion for legality and by a very precise theory of political power. All power is ultimately from God; He has delegated power to the Pope in sacred things and to the Emperor in secular matters. But Pope and Emperor alike lost their importance during the fifteenth century. The Pope became merely one of the Italian princes, engaged in the incredibly complicated and unscrupulous game of Italian power politics. The new national monarchies in France, Spain, and England had, in their own territories, a power with which neither Pope nor Emperor could interfere. The national State, largely owing to gunpowder, acquired an influence over men's thoughts and feelings which it had not had before, and which progressively destroyed what remained of the Roman belief in the unity of civilization.

This political disorder found expression in Machiavelli's *Prince*. In the absence of any guiding principle, politics becomes a naked struggle for power; *The Prince* gives shrewd advice as to how to play this game successfully. What had happened in the great age of Greece happened again in Renaissance Italy: traditional moral restraints disappeared, because they were seen to be associated with superstition; the liberation from fetters made individuals energetic and creative, producing a rare florescence of genius; but the anarchy and treachery which inevitably resulted from the decay of morals made Italians collectively impotent, and they fell, like the Greeks, under the domination of nations less civilized than themselves but not so destitute of social cohesion.

The result, however, was less disastrous than in the case of Greece, because the newly powerful nations, with the exception of Spain, showed themselves as capable of great achievement as the Italians had been.

From the sixteenth century onward, the history of European thought is dominated by the Reformation. The Reformation was a complex many-sided movement, and owed its success to a variety of causes. In the main, it was a revolt of the northern nations against the renewed dominion of Rome. Religion was the force that had subdued the North, but religion in Italy had decayed: the papacy remained as an institution, and extracted a huge tribute from Germany and England, but these nations, which were still pious, could feel no reverence for the Borgias and Medicis, who professed to save souls from purgatory in return for cash which they squandered on luxury and immorality. National motives, economic motives, and moral motives all combined to strengthen the revolt against Rome. Moreover the Princes soon perceived that, if the Church in their territories became merely national, they would be able to dominate it, and would thus become much more powerful at home than they had been while sharing dominion with the Pope. For all these reasons, Luther's theological innovations were welcomed by rulers and peoples alike throughout the greater part of northern Europe.

The Catholic Church was derived from three sources. Its sacred history was Jewish, its theology was Greek, its government and canon law were, at least indirectly, Roman. The Reformation rejected the Roman elements, softened the Greek elements, and greatly strengthened the Judaic elements. It thus co-operated with the nationalist forces which were undoing the work of social cohesion which had been effected first by the Roman Empire and then by the Roman Church. In Catholic doctrine, divine revelation did not end with the scriptures, but continued from age to age through the medium of the Church, to which, therefore, it was the duty of the individual to submit his private opinions. Protestants, on the contrary, rejected the Church as a vehicle of revelation; truth was to be sought only in the Bible, which each man could interpret for himself. If men differed in their interpretation, there was no divinely appointed authority to decide the dispute. In practice, the State claimed the right that had formerly belonged to the Church, but this was a usurpation. In Protestant theory, there should be no earthly intermediary between the soul and God.

The effects of this change were momentous. Truth was no longer to be ascertained by consulting authority, but by inward meditation. There was a tendency, quickly developed, towards anarchism in politics, and, in religion, towards mysticism, which had always fitted with difficulty into the framework of Catholic orthodoxy. There came to be not one Protestantism, but a multitude of sects; not one philosophy opposed to scholasticism, but as many as there were philosophers; not, as in the thirteenth century, one Emperor opposed to the Pope, but a large number of heretical kings. The result, in thought as in literature, was a continually deepening subjectivism, operating at first as a wholesome liberation from spiritual slavery, but advancing steadily towards a personal isolation inimical to social sanity.

Modern philosophy begins with Descartes, whose fundamental certainty is the existence of himself and his thoughts, from which the external world is to be inferred. This was only the first stage in a development, through Berkeley and Kant, to Fichte, for whom everything is only an emanation of the ego. This was insanity, and, from this extreme, philosophy has been attempting, ever since, to escape into the world of everyday common sense.

With subjectivism in philosophy, anarchism in politics goes hand in hand. Already during Luther's lifetime, unwelcome and unacknowledged disciples had developed the doctrine of Anabaptism, which, for a time, dominated the city of Münster. The Anabaptists repudiated all law, since they held that the good man will be guided at every moment by the Holy Spirit, who cannot be bound by formulas. From this premiss they arrive at communism and sexual promiscuity; they were therefore exterminated after a heroic resistance. But their doctrine, in softened forms, spread to Holland, England and America; historically, it is the source of Quakerism. A fiercer form of anarchism, no longer connected with religion, arose in the nineteenth century. In Russia, in Spain, and to a lesser degree in Italy, it had considerable success, and to this day it remains a bugbear of the American immigration authorities. This modern form, though anti-religious, has still much of the spirit of early Protestantism; it differs mainly in directing against secular governments the hostility that Luther directed against popes.

Subjectivity, once let loose, could not be confined within limits until it had run its course. In morals, the Protestant emphasis on the individual conscience was essentially anarchic. Habit and custom were so strong that, except in occasional outbreaks such as that of Münster, the disciples of individualism in ethics continued to act in a manner which was conventionally virtuous. But this was a precarious equilibrium. The eighteenth-century cult of 'sensibility' began to break it down: an act was admired, not for its good consequences, or for its conformity to a moral code, but for the emotion that inspired it. Out of this attitude developed the cult of the hero, as it is expressed by Carlyle and Nietzsche, and the Byronic cult of violent passion of no matter what kind.

The romantic movement, in art, in literature, and in politics, is bound up with this subjective way of judging men, not as members of a community, but as aesthetically delightful objects of contemplation. Tigers are more beautiful than sheep, but we prefer them behind bars. The typical romantic removes the bars and enjoys the magnificent leaps with which the tiger annihilates the sheep. He exhorts men to imagine themselves tigers, and when he succeeds the results are not wholly pleasant.

Against the more insane forms of subjectivism in modern times there have been various reactions. First, a half-way compromise philosophy, the doctrine of liberalism, which attempted to assign the respective spheres of government and the individual. This begins, in its modern form, with Locke, who is as much opposed to 'enthusiasm'—the individualism of the Anabaptists—as to absolute authority and blind subservience to tradition. A more thorough-going revolt leads to the doctrine of State worship, which assigns to the State the position that Catholicism gave to the Church, or even sometimes, to God. Hobbes, Rousseau, and Hegel represent different phases of this theory, and their doctrines are embodied practically in Cromwell, Napoleon, and modern Germany. Communism, in theory, is far removed from such philosophies, but is driven, in practice, to a type of community very similar to that which results from State worship.

Throughout this long development, from 600 B.C. to the present day, philosophers have been divided into those who wished to tighten social bonds and those who wished to relax them. With this difference others have been associated. The disciplinarians have advocated some system of dogma, either old or new, and have therefore been compelled to be, in a greater or less degree, hostile to science, since their dogmas could not be proved empirically. They have almost invariably taught that happiness is not the good, but that 'nobility' or 'heroism' is to be preferred. They have had a sympathy with the irrational parts of human nature, since they have felt reason to be inimical to social cohesion. The libertarians, on the other hand, with the exception of the extreme anarchists, have tended to be scientific, utilitarian, rationalistic, hostile to violent passion, and enemies of all the more profound forms of religion. This conflict existed in Greece before the rise of what we recognize as philosophy, and is already quite explicit in the earliest Greek thought. In changing forms, it has persisted down to the present day, and no doubt will persist for many ages to come.

It is clear that each party to this dispute—as to all that persist through long periods of time—is partly right and partly wrong. Social cohesion is a necessity, and mankind has never yet succeeded in enforcing cohesion by merely rational arguments. Every community is exposed to two opposite dangers; ossification through too much discipline and reverence for tradition, on the one hand; on the other hand, dissolution, or subjection to foreign conquest, through the growth of an individualism and personal independence that makes co-operation impossible. In general, important civilizations start with a rigid and superstitious system, gradually relaxed, and leading, at a certain stage, to a period of brilliant genius, while the good of the old tradition remains and the evil inherent in its dissolution has not yet developed. But as the evil unfolds, it leads to anarchy, thence, inevitably, to a new tyranny, producing a new synthesis secured by a new system of dogma. The doctrine of liberalism is an attempt to escape from this endless oscillation. The essence of liberalism is an attempt to secure a social order not based on irrational dogma, and insuring stability without involving more restraints than are necessary for the preservation of the community. Whether this attempt can succeed only the future can determine.

BOOK ONE

ANCIENT PHILOSOPHY

PART I

THE PRE-SOCRATICS

Chapter I

THE RISE OF GREEK CIVILIZATION

IN all history, nothing is so surprising or so difficult to account for as the sudden rise of civilization in Greece. Much of what makes civilization had already existed for thousands of years in Egypt and in Mesopotamia, and had spread thence to neighbouring countries. But certain elements had been lacking until the Greeks supplied them. What they achieved in art and literature is familiar to everybody, but what they did in the purely intellectual realm is even more exceptional. They invented mathematics[1] and science and philosophy; they first wrote history as opposed to mere annals; they speculated freely about the nature of the world and the ends of life, without being bound in the fetters of any inherited orthodoxy. What occurred was so astonishing that, until very recent times, men were content to gape and talk mystically about the Greek genius. It is possible, however, to understand the development of Greece in scientific terms, and it is well worth while to do so.

Philosophy begins with Thales, who, fortunately, can be dated by the fact that he predicted an eclipse which, according to the astronomers, occurred in the year 585 B.C. Philosophy and science —which were not originally separate—were therefore born together at the beginning of the sixth century. What had been happening in Greece and neighbouring countries before this time? Any answer must be in part conjectural, but archaeology, during the present century, has given us much more knowledge than was possessed by our grandfathers.

The art of writing was invented in Egypt about the year 4000 B.C., and in Mesopotamia not much later. In each country writing began with pictures of the objects intended. These pictures quickly became conventionalized, so that words were represented by ideograms, as they still are in China. In the course of thousands of years, this cumbrous system developed into alphabetic writing.

The early development of civilization in Egypt and Mesopotamia was due to the Nile, the Tigris, and the Euphrates, which made agriculture very easy and very productive. The civilization was in

[1] Arithmetic and some geometry existed among the Egyptians and Babylonians, but mainly in the form of rules of thumb. Deductive reasoning from general premises was a Greek innovation.

25

many ways similar to that which the Spaniards found in Mexico and Peru. There was a divine king, with despotic powers; in Egypt, he owned all the land. There was a polytheistic religion, with a supreme god to whom the king had a specially intimate relation. There was a military aristocracy, and also a priestly aristocracy. The latter was often able to encroach on the royal power if the king was weak or if he was engaged in a difficult war. The cultivators of the soil were serfs, belonging to the king, the aristocracy, or the priesthood.

There was a considerable difference between Egyptian and Babylonian theology. The Egyptians were preoccupied with death, and believed that the souls of the dead descend into the underworld, where they are judged by Osiris according to the manner of their life on earth. They thought that the soul would ultimately return to the body; this led to mummification and to the construction of splendid tombs. The pyramids were built by various kings at the end of the fourth millennium B.C. and the beginning of the third. After this time, Egyptian civilization became more and more stereotyped, and religious conservatism made progress impossible. About 1800 B.C. Egypt was conquered by Semites named Hyksos, who ruled the country for about two centuries. They left no permanent mark on Egypt, but their presence there must have helped to spread Egyptian civilization in Syria and Palestine.

Babylonia had a more warlike development than Egypt. At first, the ruling race were not Semites, but 'Sumerians', whose origin is unknown. They invented cuneiform writing, which the conquering Semites took over from them. There was a period when there were various independent cities which fought with each other, but in the end Babylon became supreme and established an empire. The gods of other cities became subordinate, and Marduk, the god of Babylon, acquired a position like that later held by Zeus in the Greek pantheon. The same sort of thing had happened in Egypt, but at a much earlier time.

The religions of Egypt and Babylonia, like other ancient religions, were originally fertility cults. The earth was female, the sun male. The bull was usually regarded as an embodiment of male fertility, and bull-gods were common. In Babylon, Ishtar, the earth-goddess, was supreme among female divinities. Throughout western Asia, the Great Mother was worshipped under various names. When Greek colonists in Asia Minor found temples to her, they named her Artemis and took over the existing cult. This is the origin of 'Diana of the Ephesians'.[1] Christianity transformed her into the

[1] Diana was the Latin equivalent of Artemis. It is Artemis who is mentioned in the Greek Testament where our translation speaks of Diana.

Virgin Mary, and it was a Council at Ephesus that legitimated the title 'Mother of God' as applied to Our Lady.

Where a religion was bound up with the government of an empire, political motives did much to transform its primitive features. A god or goddess became associated with the State, and had to give, not only an abundant harvest, but victory in war. A rich priestly caste elaborated the ritual and the theology, and fitted together into a pantheon the several divinities of the component parts of the empire.

Through association with government, the gods also became associated with morality. Lawgivers received their codes from a god; thus a breach of the law became an impiety. The oldest legal code still known is that of Hammurabi, king of Babylon, (2067-2025 B.C.); this code was asserted by the king to have been delivered to him by Marduk. The connection between religion and morality became continually closer throughout ancient times.

Babylonian religion, unlike that of Egypt, was more concerned with prosperity in this world than with happiness in the next. Magic, divination, and astrology, though not peculiar to Babylonia, were more developed there than elsewhere, and it was chiefly through Babylon that they acquired their hold on later antiquity. From Babylon come some things that belong to science: the division of the day into twenty-four hours, and of the circle into 360 degrees; also the discovery of a cycle in eclipses, which enabled lunar eclipses to be predicted with certainty, and solar eclipses with some probability. This Babylonian knowledge, as we shall see, was acquired by Thales.

The civilizations of Egypt and Mesopotamia were agricultural, and those of surrounding nations, at first, were pastoral. A new element came with the development of commerce, which was at first almost entirely maritime. Weapons, until about 1000 B.C., were made of bronze, and nations which did not have the necessary metals on their own territory were obliged to obtain them by trade or piracy. Piracy was a temporary expedient, and where social and political conditions were fairly stable, commerce was found to be more profitable. In commerce, the island of Crete seems to have been the pioneer. For about eleven centuries, say from 2500 B.C. to 1400 B.C., an artistically advanced culture, called the Minoan, existed in Crete. What survives of Cretan art gives an impression of cheerfulness and almost decadent luxury, very different from the terrifying gloom of Egyptian temples.

Of this important civilization almost nothing was known until the excavations of Sir Arthur Evans and others. It was a maritime civilization, in close touch with Egypt (except during the time of the Hyksos). From Egyptian pictures it is evident that the very considerable commerce between Egypt and Crete was carried on by Cretan sailors; this commerce reached its maximum about 1500 B.C. The Cretan religion appears to have had some affinities with the religions of Syria and Asia Minor, but in art there was more affinity with Egypt, though Cretan art was very original and amazingly full of life. The centre of the Cretan civilization was the so-called 'palace of Minos' at Knossos, of which memories lingered in the traditions of classical Greece. The palaces of Crete were very magnificent, but were destroyed about the end of the fourteenth century B.C., probably by invaders from Greece. The chronology of Cretan history is derived from Egyptian objects found in Crete, and Cretan objects found in Egypt; throughout, our knowledge is dependent on archaeological evidence.

The Cretans worshipped a goddess, or perhaps several goddesses. The most indubitable goddess was the 'Mistress of Animals', who was a huntress, and probably the source of the classical Artemis.[1] She apparently was also a mother; the only male deity, apart from the 'Master of Animals', is her young son. There is some evidence of belief in an after life, in which, as in Egyptian belief, deeds on earth receive reward or retribution. But on the whole the Cretans appear, from their art, to have been cheerful people, not much oppressed by gloomy superstitions. They were fond of bull-fights, at which female as well as male toreadors performed amazing acrobatic feats. Sir Arthur Evans thinks that the bull-fights were religious celebrations, and that the performers belonged to the highest nobility, but this view is not generally accepted. The surviving pictures are full of movement and realism.

The Cretans had a linear script, but it has not been deciphered. At home they were peaceful, and their cities were unwalled; no doubt they were defended by sea power.

Before the destruction of the Minoan culture, it spread, about 1600 B.C., to the mainland of Greece, where it survived, through gradual stages of modification, until about 900 B.C. This mainland civilization is called the Mycenaean; it is known through the tombs of kings, and also through fortresses on hill-tops, which show more fear of war than had existed in Crete. Both tombs and fortresses remained to impress the imagination of classical Greece. The older art products in the palaces are either actually of Cretan workmanship or closely akin to those of Crete. The Mycenaean civilization, seen through a haze of legend, is that which is depicted in Homer.

---

[1] She has a male twin or consort, the 'Master of Animals', but he is less prominent. It was at a later date that Artemis was identified with the Great Mother of Asia Minor.

There is much uncertainty concerning the Mycenaeans. Did they owe their civilization to being conquered by the Cretans? Did they speak Greek, or were they an earlier indigenous race? No certain answer to these questions is possible, but there is evidence which makes it probable that they were conquerors who spoke Greek, and that at least the aristocracy consisted of fair-haired invaders from the North, who brought the Greek language with them.[1] The Greeks came to Greece in three successive waves, first the Ionians, then the Achaeans, and last the Dorians. The Ionians appear, though con-querors, to have adopted the Cretan civilization pretty completely, as, later, the Romans adopted the civilization of Greece. But the Ionians were disturbed, and largely dispossessed, by their successors, the Achaeans. The Achaeans are known, from the Hittite tablets found at Boghaz-Keui, to have had a large organized empire in the fourteenth century B.C. The Mycenaean civilization, which had been weakened by the warfare of the Ionians and Achaeans, was practic-ally destroyed by the Dorians, the last Greek invaders. Whereas pre-vious invaders had largely adopted the Minoan religion, the Dorians retained the original Indo-European religion of their ancestors. The religion of Mycenaean times, however, lingered on, especially in the lower classes, and the religion of classical Greece was a blend of the two. In fact some of the classical goddesses were of Mycenaean origin.

Although the above account seems probable, it must be remem-bered that we do not *know* whether the Mycenaeans were Greeks or not. What we do know is that their civilization decayed, that about the time when it ended iron superseded bronze, and that for some time sea supremacy passed to the Phoenicians.

Both during the later part of the Mycenaean age and after its end, some of the invaders settled down and became agriculturists, while some pushed on, first into the islands and Asia Minor, then into Sicily and southern Italy, where they founded cities that lived by maritime commerce. It was in these maritime cities that the Greeks first made qualitatively new contributions to civilization; the sup-remacy of Athens came later, and was equally associated, when it came, with naval power.

The mainland of Greece is mountainous and largely infertile. There are, however, many fertile valleys, with easy access to the sea, but cut off by the mountains from easy land communication with each other. In these valleys little separate communities grew up, living by agriculture, and centring round a town, generally close to the sea. In such circumstances it was natural that, as soon as the

---

[1] See *The Minoan-Mycenaean Religion and Its Survival in Greek Religion,* by Martin P. Nilsson, p. 11 ff.

population of any community grew too great for its internal resources, those who could not live on the land should take to seafaring. The cities of the mainland founded colonies, often in places where it was much easier to find subsistence than it had been at home. Thus in the earliest historical period the Greeks of Asia Minor, Sicily, and Italy were much richer than those of the Greek mainland.

The social system was very different in different parts of Greece. In Sparta, a small aristocracy subsisted on the labour of oppressed serfs of a different race; in the poorer agricultural regions, the population consisted mainly of farmers cultivating their own land with the help of their families. But where commerce and industry flourished, the free citizens grew rich by the employment of slaves—male in the mines, female in the textile industry. These slaves were, in Ionia, of the surrounding barbarian population, and were, as a rule, first acquired in war. With increasing wealth went increasing isolation of respectable women, who in later times had little part in the civilized aspects of Greek life except in Sparta and Lesbos.

There was a very general development, first from monarchy to aristocracy, then to an alternation of tyranny and democracy. The kings were not absolute, like those of Egypt and Babylonia; they were advised by a Council of Elders, and could not transgress custom with impunity. 'Tyranny' did not mean necessarily bad government, but only the rule of a man whose claim to power was not hereditary. 'Democracy' meant government by all the citizens, among whom slaves and women were not included. The early tyrants, like the Medici, acquired their power through being the richest members of their respective plutocracies. Often the source of their wealth was the ownership of gold and silver mines, made the more profitable by the new institution of coinage, which came from the kingdom of Lydia, adjacent to Ionia.[1] Coinage seems to have been invented shortly before 700 B.C.

One of the most important results, to the Greeks, of commerce or piracy—at first the two are scarcely distinct—was the acquisition of the art of writing. Although writing had existed for thousands of years in Egypt and Babylonia, and the Minoan Cretans had a script now known to be a form of Greek, the date when the Greeks acquired alphabetic writing is uncertain. They learnt the art from the Phoenicians, who, like the other inhabitants of Syria, were exposed to both Egyptian and Babylonian influences, and who held the supremacy in maritime commerce until the rise of the Greek cities of Ionia, Italy, and Sicily. In the fourteenth century, writing to Ikhnaton (the heretic king of Egypt), Syrians still used the Babylonian cuneiform; but Hiram of Tyre (969-936) used the Phoenician

[1] See P. N. Ure, *The Origin of Tyranny*.

alphabet, which probably devoloped out of the Egyptian script. The Egyptians used, at first, a pure picture writing; gradually the pictures, much conventionalized, came to represent syllables (the first syllables of the names of the things pictured), and at last single letters, on the principle of 'A was an Archer who shot at a frog.'[1] This last step, which was not taken with any completeness by the Egyptians themselves, but by the Phoenicians, gave the alphabet with all its advantages. The Greeks, borrowing from the Phoenicians, altered the alphabet to suit their language, and made the important innovation of adding vowels instead of having only consonants. There can be no doubt that the acquisition of this convenient method of writing greatly hastened the rise of Greek civilization.

The first notable product of the Hellenic civilization was Homer. Everything about Homer is conjectural, but there is a widely held opinion that he was a series of poets rather than an individual. According to those who hold this opinion, the Iliad and the Odyssey between them took about two hundred years to complete, some say from 750 to 550 B.C.,[2] while others hold that 'Homer' was nearly complete at the end of the eighth century.[3] The Homeric poems, in their present form, were brought to Athens by Peisistratus, who reigned (with intermissions) from 560 to 527 B.C. From his time onward, the Athenian youth learnt Homer by heart, and this was the most important part of their education. In some part of Greece, notably in Sparta, Homer had not the same prestige until a later date.

The Homeric poems, like the courtly romances of the later Middle Ages, represent the point of view of a civilized aristocracy, which ignores as plebeian various superstitions that are still rampant among the populace. In much later times, many of these superstitions rose again to the light of day. Guided by anthropology, many modern writers have come to the conclusion that Homer, so far from being primitive, was an expurgator, a kind of eighteenth century rationalizer of ancient myths, holding up an upper-class ideal of urbane enlightenment. The Olympian gods, who represent religion in Homer, were not the only objects of worship among the Greeks, either in his time or later. There were other darker and more savage elements in popular religion, which were kept at bay by the Greek intellect at its best, but lay in wait to pounce in moments of weakness or terror. In the time of decadence, beliefs which Homer had discarded proved to have persisted, half buried, throughout the classical period. This fact explains many things that would otherwise seem inconsistent and surprising.

[1] For instance, 'Gimel', the third letter of the Hebrew alphabet, means 'camel', and the sign for it is a conventionalized picture of a camel.
[2] Beloch, *Griechische Geschichte*, chap. xii.
[3] Rostovtseff, *History of the Ancient World*, Vol. I, p. 399.

Primitive religion, everywhere, was tribal rather than personal. Certain rites were performed, which were intended, by sympathetic magic, to further the interests of the tribe, especially in respect of fertility, vegetable, animal, and human. The winter solstice was a time when the sun had to be encouraged not to go on diminishing in strength; spring and harvest also called for appropriate ceremonies. These were often such as to generate a great collective excitement, in which individuals lost their sense of separateness and felt themselves at one with the whole tribe. All over the world, at a certain stage of religious evolution, sacred animals and human beings were ceremonially killed and eaten. In different regions, this stage occurred at very different dates. Human sacrifice usually lasted longer than the sacrificial eating of human victims; in Greece it was not yet extinct at the beginning of historical times. Fertility rites without such cruel aspects were common throughout Greece; the Eleusinian mysteries, in particular, were essentially agricultural in their symbolism.

It must be admitted that religion, in Homer, is not very religious. The gods are completely human, differing from men only in being immortal and possessed of superhuman powers. Morally, there is nothing to be said for them, and it is difficult to see how they can have inspired much awe. In some passages, supposed to be late, they are treated with Voltairean irreverence. Such genuine religious feeling as is to be found in Homer is less concerned with the gods of Olympus than with more shadowy beings such as Fate or Necessity or Destiny, to whom even Zeus is subject. Fate exercised a great influence on all Greek thought, and perhaps was one of the sources from which science derived the belief in natural law.

The Homeric gods were the gods of a conquering aristocracy, not the useful fertility gods of those who actually tilled the soil. As Gilbert Murray says:[1]

'The gods of most nations claim to have created the world. The Olympians make no such claim. The most they ever did was to conquer it. . . . And when they have conquered their kingdoms, what do they do? Do they attend to the government? Do they promote agriculture? Do they practise trades and industries? Not a bit of it. Why should they do any honest work? They find it easier to live on the revenues and blast with thunderbolts the people who do not pay. They are conquering chieftains, royal buccaneers. They fight, and feast, and play, and make music; they drink deep, and roar with laughter at the lame smith who waits on them. They are never afraid, except of their own king. They never tell lies, except in love and war.'

[1] *Five Stages of Greek Religion*, p. 67.

Homer's human heroes, equally, are not very well behaved. The leading family is the House of Pelops, but it did not succeed in setting a pattern of happy family life.

'Tantalos, the Asiatic founder of the dynasty, began its career by a direct offence against the gods; some said, by trying to cheat them into eating human flesh, that of his own son Pelops. Pelops, having been miraculously restored to life, offended in his turn. He won his famous chariot-race against Oinomaos, king of Pisa, by the connivance of the latter's charioteer, Myrtilos, and then got rid of his confederate, whom he had promised to reward, by flinging him into the sea. The curse descended to his sons, Atreus and Thyestes, in the form of what the Greeks called *ate*, a strong if not actually irresistible impulse to crime. Thyestes corrupted his brother's wife and thereby managed to steal the "luck" of the family, the famous golden-fleeced ram. Atreus in turn secured his brother's banishment, and recalling him under pretext of a reconciliation, feasted him on the flesh of his own children. The curse was now inherited by Atreus' son Agamemnon, who offended Artemis by killing a sacred stag, sacrificed his own daughter Iphigenia to appease the goddess and obtain a safe passage to Troy for his fleet, and was in turn murdered by his faithless wife Klytaimnestra and her paramour Aigisthos, a surviving son of Thyestes. Orestes, Agamemnon's son, in turn avenged his father by killing his mother and Aigisthos.'[1]

Homer as a finished achievement was a product of Ionia, i.e. of a part of Hellenic Asia Minor and the adjacent islands. Some time during the sixth century at latest, the Homeric poems became fixed in their present form. It was also during this century that Greek science and philosophy and mathematics began. At the same time events of fundamental importance were happening in other parts of the world. Confucius, Buddha, and Zoroaster, if they existed, probably belong to the same century.[2] In the middle of the century the Persian Empire was established by Cyrus; towards its close the Greek cities of Ionia, to which the Persians had allowed a limited autonomy, made a fruitless rebellion, which was put down by Darius, and their best men became exiles. Several of the philosophers of this period were refugees, who wandered from city to city in the still unenslaved parts of the Hellenic world, spreading the civilization that, until then, had been mainly confined to Ionia. They were kindly treated in their wanderings. Xenophanes, who flourished in the later part of the sixth century, and who was one of the refugees, says: 'This is the sort of thing we should say by the

[1] *Primitive Culture in Greece*, H. J. Rose, 1925, p. 193.
[2] Zoroaster's date, however, is very conjectural. Some place it as early as 1000 B.C. See *Cambridge Ancient History*, Vol. IV, p. 207.

fireside in the winter-time, as we lie on soft couches, after a good meal, drinking sweet wine and crunching chickpeas: "Of what country are you, and how old are you, good Sir? And how old were you when the Mede appeared?" ' The rest of Greece succeeded in preserving its independence at the battles of Salamis and Plataea, after which Ionia was liberated for a time.[1]

Greece was divided into a large number of small independent states, each consisting of a city with some agricultural territory surrounding it. The level of civilization was very different in different parts of the Greek world, and only a minority of cities contributed to the total of Hellenic achievement. Sparta, of which I shall have much to say later, was important in a military sense, but not culturally. Corinth was rich and prosperous, a great commercial centre, but not prolific in great men.

Then there were purely agricultural rural communities, such as the proverbial Arcadia, which townsmen imagined to be idyllic, but which really was full of ancient barbaric horrors.

The inhabitants worshipped Hermes and Pan, and had a multitude of fertility cults, in which, often, a mere square pillar did duty in place of a statue of the god. The goat was the symbol of fertility, because the peasants were too poor to possess bulls. When food was scarce, the statue of Pan was beaten. (Similar things are still done in remote Chinese villages.) There was a clan of supposed were-wolves, associated, probably, with human sacrifice and cannibalism. It was thought that whoever tasted the flesh of a sacrificed human victim became a were-wolf. There was a cave sacred to Zeus Lykaios (the wolf-Zeus); in this cave no one had a shadow, and whoever entered it died within a year. All this superstition was still flourishing in classical times.[2]

Pan, whose original name (some say) was 'Paon', meaning the feeder or shepherd, acquired his better-known title, interpreted as meaning the All-God, when his worship was adopted by Athens in the fifth century, after the Persian war.[3]

There was, however, in ancient Greece, much that we can feel to have been religion as we understand the term. This was connected, not with the Olympians, but with Dionysus, or Bacchus, whom we think of most naturally as the somewhat disreputable god of wine and drunkenness. The way in which, out of his worship, there arose a profound mysticism, which greatly influenced

---

[1] As a result of the defeat of Athens by Sparta, the Persians regained the whole coast of Asia Minor, to which their right was acknowledged in the Peace of Antalcidas (387-6 B.C.). About fifty years later, they were incorporated in Alexander's empire.

[2] Rose, *Primitive Greece*, p. 65 ff.

[3] J. E. Harrison, *Prolegomena to the Study of Greek Religion*, p. 651.

many of the philosophers, and even had a part in shaping Christian theology, is very remarkable, and must be understood by anyone who wishes to study the development of Greek thought.

Dionysus, or Bacchus, was originally a Thracian god. The Thracians were very much less civilized than the Greeks, who regarded them as barbarians. Like all primitive agriculturists, they had fertility cults, and a god who promoted fertility. His name was Bacchus. It was never quite clear whether Bacchus had the shape of a man or of a bull. When they discovered how to make beer, they thought intoxication divine, and gave honour to Bacchus. When, later, they came to know the vine and to learn to drink wine, they thought even better of him. His functions in promoting fertility in general became somewhat subordinate to his functions in relation to the grape and the divine madness produced by wine.

At what date his worship migrated from Thrace to Greece is not known, but it seems to have been just before the beginning of historical times. The cult of Bacchus was met with hostility by the orthodox, but nevertheless it established itself. It contained many barbaric elements, such as tearing wild animals to pieces and eating the whole of them raw. It had a curious element of feminism. Respectable matrons and maids, in large companies, would spend whole nights on the bare hills in dances which stimulated ecstasy, and in an intoxication perhaps partly alcoholic, but mainly mystical. Husbands found the practice annoying, but did not dare to oppose religion. Both the beauty and the savagery of the cult are set forth in the *Bacchae* of Euripides.

The success of Dionysus in Greece is not surprising. Like all communities that have been civilized quickly, the Greeks, or at least a certain proportion of them, developed a love of the primitive, and a hankering after a more instinctive and passionate way of life than that sanctioned by current morals. To the man or woman who, by compulsion, is more civilized in behaviour than in feeling, rationality is irksome and virtue is felt as a burden and a slavery. This leads to a reaction in thought, in feeling, and in conduct. It is the reaction in thought that will specially concern us, but something must first be said about the reaction in feeling and conduct.

The civilized man is distinguished from the savage mainly by *prudence*, or, to use a slightly wider term, *forethought*. He is willing to endure present pains for the sake of future pleasures, even if the future pleasures are rather distant. This habit began to be important with the rise of agriculture; no animal and no savage would work in the spring in order to have food next winter, except for a few purely instinctive forms of action, such as bees making honey or squirrels burying nuts. In these cases, there is no forethought;

there is a direct impulse to an act which, to the human spectator, is obviously going to prove useful later on. True forethought only arises when a man does something towards which no impulse urges him, because his reason tells him that he will profit by it at some future date. Hunting requires no forethought, because it is pleasurable; but tilling the soil is labour, and cannot be done from spontaneous impulse.

Civilization checks impulse not only through forethought, which is a self-administered check, but also through law, custom, and religion. This check it inherits from barbarism, but it makes it less instinctive and more systematic. Certain acts are labelled criminal, and are punished, certain others, thought not punished by law, are labelled wicked, and expose those who are guilty of them to social disapproval. The institution of private property brings with it the subjection of women, and usually the creation of a slave class. On the one hand the purposes of the community are enforced upon the individual, and, on the other hand the individual, having acquired the habit of viewing his life as a whole, increasingly sacrifices his present to his future.

It is evident that this process can be carried too far, as it is, for instance, by the miser. But without going to such extremes prudence may easily involve the loss of some of the best things in life. The worshipper of Dionysus reacts against prudence. In intoxication, physical or spiritual, he recovers an intensity of feeling which prudence had destroyed; he finds the world full of delight and beauty, and his imagination is suddenly liberated from the prison of every-day preoccupations. The Bacchic ritual produced what was called 'enthusiasm', which means, etymologically, having the god enter into the worshipper, who believed that he became one with the god. Much of what is greatest in human achievement involves some element of intoxication,[1] some sweeping away of prudence by passion. Without the Bacchic element, life would be uninteresting; with it, it is dangerous. Prudence versus passion is a conflict that runs through history. It is not a conflict in which we ought to side wholly with either party.

In the sphere of thought, sober civilization is roughly synonymous with science. But science, unadulterated, is not satisfying; men need also passion and art and religion. Science may set limits to knowledge, but should not set limits to imagination. Among Greek philosophers, as among those of later times, there were those who were primarily scientific and those who were primarily religious; the latter owed much, directly or indirectly, to the religion of Bacchus. This applies especially to Plato, and through him to

[1] I mean mental intoxication, not intoxication by alcohol.

those later developments which were ultimately embodied in Christian theology.

The worship of Dionysus in its original form was savage, and in many ways repulsive. It was not in this form that it influenced the philosophers, but in the spiritualized form attributed to Orpheus, which was ascetic, and substituted mental for physical intoxication.

Orpheus is a dim but interesting figure. Some hold that he was an actual man, others that he was a god or an imaginary hero. Traditionally, he came from Thrace, like Bacchus, but it seems more probable that he (or the movement associated with his name) came from Crete. It is certain that Orphic doctrines contain much that seems to have it first source in Egypt, and it was chiefly through Crete that Egypt influenced Greece. Orpheus is said to have been a reformer who was torn to pieces by frenzied Maenads actuated by Bacchic orthodoxy. His addiction to music is not so prominent in the older forms of the legend as it became later. Primarily he was a priest and a philosopher.

Whatever may have been the teaching of Orpheus (if he existed), the teaching of the Orphics is well known. They believed in the transmigration of souls; they taught that the soul hereafter might achieve eternal bliss or suffer eternal or temporary torment according to its way of life here on earth. They aimed at becoming 'pure', partly by ceremonies of purification, partly by avoiding certain kinds of contamination. The most orthodox among them abstained from animal food, except on ritual occasions when they ate it sacramentally. Man, they held, is partly of earth, partly of heaven; by a pure life the heavenly part is increased and the earthly part diminished. In the end a man may become one with Bacchus, and is called 'a Bacchus'. There was an elaborate theology, according to which Bacchus was twice born, once of his mother Semele, and once from the thigh of his father Zeus.

There are many forms of the Dionysus myth. In one of them, Dionysus is the son of Zeus and Persephone; while still a boy, he is torn to pieces by Titans, who eat his flesh, all but the heart. Some say that the heart was given by Zeus to Semele, others that Zeus swallowed it; in either case, it gave rise to the second birth of Dionysus. The tearing of a wild animal and the devouring of its raw flesh by Bacchae was supposed to re-enact the tearing and eating of Dionysus by the Titans, and the animal, in some sense, was an incarnation of the god. The Titans were earth-born, but after eating the god they had a spark of divinity. So man is partly of earth, partly divine, and Bacchic rites sought to make him more nearly completely divine.

Euripides puts a confession into the mouth of an Orphic priest, which is instructive:[1]

> Lord of Europa's Tyrian line,
>   Zeus-born, who holdest at thy feet
>   The hundred citadels of Crete,
> I seek to Thee from that dim shrine,
>
> Roofed by the Quick and Carven Beam,
>   By Chalyb steel and wild bull's blood,
>   In flawless joints of Cypress wood
> Made steadfast. There is one pure stream
>
> My days have run. The servant I,
>   Initiate, of Idaean Jove;[2]
>   Where midnight Zagreus[3] roves, I rove;
> I have endured his thunder-cry;
>
> Fulfilled his red and bleeding feasts;
>   Held the Great Mother's mountain flame,
>   I am set free and named by name
> A Bacchos of the Mailed Priests.
>
> Robed in pure white I have borne me clean
>   From man's vile birth and coffined clay,
>   And exiled from my lip alway
> Touch of all meat where Life hath been.

Orphic tablets have been found in tombs, giving instructions to the soul of the dead person as to how to find his way in the next world, and what to say in order to prove himself worthy of salvation. They are broken and incomplete; the most nearly complete (the Petelia tablet) is as follows:

Thou shalt find on the left of the House of Hades a Well-spring,
And by the side thereof standing a white cypress.
To this well-spring approach not near.
But thou shalt find another by the Lake of Memory,
Cold water flowing forth, and there are Guardians before it,
Say: 'I am a child of Earth and of Starry Heaven;
But my race is of Heaven (alone). This ye know yourselves.

[1] The verse translations in this chapter are by Professor Gilbert Murray.
[2] Mystically indentified with Dionysus.
[3] One of the many names of Dionysus.

38

And lo, I am parched with thirst and I perish. Give me quickly
The cold water flowing forth from the Lake of Memory.'
And of themselves they will give thee to drink from the holy well-
  spring,
And thereafter among the other heroes thou shalt have lordship. . . .

Another tablet says:—'Hail, Thou who hast suffered the suffering . . . Thou art become God from Man.' And yet in another:—
'Happy and Blessed One, thou shalt be God instead of mortal.'

The well-spring of which the soul is not to drink is Lethe, which
brings forgetfulness; the other well-spring is Mnemosyne, remem-
brance. The soul in the next world, if it is to achieve salvation, is
not to forget, but, on the contrary, to acquire a memory surpassing
what is natural.

The Orphics were an ascetic sect; wine, to them, was only a
symbol, as, later, in the Christian sacrament. The intoxication that
they sought was that of 'enthusiasm', of union with the god. They
believed themselves, in this way, to acquire mystic knowledge not
obtainable by ordinary means. This mystical element entered into
Greek philosophy with Pythagoras, who was a reformer of Orphism
as Orpheus was a reformer of the religion of Dionysus. From
Pythagoras Orphic elements entered into the philosophy of Plato,
and from Plato into most later philosophy that was in any degree
religious.

Certain definitely Bacchic elements survived wherever Orphism
had influence. One of these was feminism, of which there was much
in Pythagoras, and which, in Plato, went so far as to claim complete political equality for women. 'Women as a sex,' says Pythagoras, 'are more naturally akin to piety.' Another Bacchic element
was respect for violent emotion. Greek tragedy grew out of the
rites of Dionysus. Euripides, especially, honoured the two chief gods
of Orphism, Dionysus and Eros. He has no respect for the coldly
self-righteous well-behaved man, who, in his tragedies, is apt to be
driven mad or otherwise brought to grief by the gods in resentment
of his blasphemy.

The conventional tradition concerning the Greeks is that they
exhibited an admirable serenity, which enabled them to contemplate passion from without, perceiving whatever beauty it exhibited
but themselves calm and Olympian. This is a very one-sided view.
It is true, perhaps, of Homer, Sophocles, and Aristotle, but it is
emphatically not true of those Greeks who were touched, directly
or indirectly, by Bacchic or Orphic influences. At Eleusis, where
the Eleusinian mysteries formed the most sacred part of Athenian
State religion, a hymn was sung, saying:

39

With Thy wine-cup waving high,
With Thy maddening revelry,
To Eleusis' flowery vale,
Comest Thou—Bacchus, Paean, hail!

In the *Bacchae* of Euripides, the chorus of Maenads displays a combination of poetry and savagery which is the very reverse of serene. They celebrate the delight in tearing a wild animal limb from limb, and eating it raw then and there:

O glad, glad on the Mountains
To swoon in the race outworn,
When the holy fawn-skin clings
And all else sweeps away,
To the joy of the quick red fountains,
The blood of the hill-goat torn,
The glory of wild-beast ravenings
Where the hill-top catches the day,
To the Phrygian, Lydian mountains
'Tis Bromios leads the way.

(Bromios was another of the many names of Dionysus.) The dance of the Maenads on the mountain side was not only fierce; it was an escape from the burdens and cares of civilization into the world of non-human beauty and the freedom of wind and stars. In a less frenzied mood they sing:

Will they ever come to me, ever again,
The long, long dances,
On through the dark till the dim stars wane?
Shall I feel the dew on my throat, and the stream
Of wind in my hair? Shall our white feet gleam
In the dim expanses?
O feet of the fawn to the greenwood fled,
Alone in the grass and the loveliness;
Leap of the hunted, no more in dread,
Beyond the snares and the deadly press.
Yet a voice still in the distance sounds,
A voice and a fear and a haste of hounds,
O wildly labouring, fiercely fleet,
Onward yet by river and glen—
Is it joy or terror, ye storm-swift feet?
To the dear lone lands untroubled of men,
Where no voice sounds, and amid the shadowy green
The little things of the woodland live unseen.

Before repeating that the Greeks were 'serene', try to imagine the matrons of Philadelphia behaving in this manner, even in a play by Eugene O'Neill.

The Orphic is no more 'serene' than the unreformed worshipper of Dionysus. To the Orphic, life in this world is pain and weariness. We are bound to a wheel which turns through endless cycles of birth and death; our true life is the stars, but we are tied to earth. Only by purification and renunciation and an ascetic life can we escape from the wheel and attain at last to the ecstasy of union with God. This is not the view of men to whom life is easy and pleasant. It is more like the Negro spiritual:

> I'm going to tell God all of my troubles
> When I get home.

Not all of the Greeks, but a large proportion of them, were passionate, unhappy, at war with themselves, driven along one road by the intellect and along another by the passions, with the imagination to conceive heaven and the wilful self-assertion that creates hell. They had a maxim 'nothing too much', but they were in fact excessive in everything—in pure thought, in poetry, in religion, and in sin. It was the combination of passion and intellect that made them great, while they were great. Neither alone would have transformed the world for all future time as they transformed it. Their prototype in mythology is not Olympian Zeus, but Prometheus, who brought fire from heaven and was rewarded with eternal torment.

If taken as characterizing the Greeks as a whole, however, what has just been said would be as one-sided as the view that the Greeks were characterized by 'serenity'. There were, in fact, two tendencies in Greece, one passionate, religious, mystical, otherworldly, the other cheerful, empirical, rationalistic, and interested in acquiring knowledge of a diversity of facts. Herodotus represents this latter tendency; so do the earliest Ionian philosophers; so, up to a point, does Aristotle. Beloch (*op. cit.*, I, 1, p. 434), after describing Orphism, says:

'But the Greek nation was too full of youthful vigour for the general acceptance of a belief which denies this world and transfers real life to the Beyond. Accordingly the Orphic doctrine remained confined to the relatively narrow circle of the initiate, without acquiring the smallest influence on the State religion, not even in communities which, like Athens, had taken up the celebration of the mysteries into the State ritual and placed it under legal protection. A full millennium was to pass before these ideas—in a quite different theological dress, it is true—achieved victory in the Greek world.'

It would seem that this is an overstatement, particularly as regards the Eleusinian mysteries, which were impregnated with Orphism. Broadly speaking, those who were of a religious temperament turned to Orphism, while rationalists despised it. One might compare its status to that of Methodism in England in the late eighteenth and early nineteenth centuries.

We know more or less what an educated Greek learnt from his father, but we know very little of what, in his earliest years, he learnt from his mother, who was, to a great extent, shut out from the civilization in which the men took delight. It seems probable that educated Athenians, even in the best period, however rationalistic they may have been in their explicitly conscious mental processes, retained from tradition and from childhood a more primitive way of thinking and feeling, which was always liable to prove victorious in times of stress. For this reason, no simple analysis of the Greek outlook is likely to be adequate.

The influence of religion, more particularly of non-Olympian religion, on Greek thought was not adequately recognized until recent times. A revolutionary book, Jane Harrison's *Prolegomena to the Study of Greek Religion*, emphasized both the primitive and the Dionysiac elements in the religion of ordinary Greeks; F. M. Cornford's *From Religion to Philosophy* tried to make students of Greek philosophy aware of the influence of religion on the philosophers, but cannot be wholly accepted as trustworthy in many of its interpretations, or, for that matter, in its anthropology.[1] The most balanced statement known to me is in John Burnet's *Early Greek Philosophy*, especially chapter ii, 'Science and Religion'. A conflict between science and religion arose, he says, out of 'the religious revival which swept over Hellas in the sixth century B.C.,' together with the shifting of the scene from Ionia to the West. 'The religion of continental Hellas,' he says, 'had developed in a very different way from that of Ionia. In particular, the worship of Dionysus, which came from Thrace, and is barely mentioned in Homer, contained in germ a wholly new way of looking at man's relation to the world. It would certainly be wrong to credit the Thracians themselves with any very exalted views; but there can be no doubt that, to the Greeks, the phenomenon of ecstasy suggested that the soul was something more than a feeble double of the self, and that it was only when "out of the body" that it could show its true nature. . . .

[1] On the other hand Cornford's books on various Platonic dialogues seem to me wholly admirable.

'It looked as if Greek religion were about to enter on the same stage as that already reached by the religions of the East; and, but for the rise of science, it is hard to see what could have checked this tendency. It is usual to say that the Greeks were saved from a religion of the Oriental type by their having no priesthood; but this is to mistake the effect for the cause. Priesthoods do not make dogmas, though they preserve them once they are made; and in the earlier stages of their development, the Oriental peoples had no priesthoods either in the sense intended. It was not so much the absence of a priesthood as the existence of the scientific schools that saved Greece.

'The new religion—for in one sense it was new, though in another as old as mankind—reached its highest point of development with the foundation of the Orphic communities. So far as we can see, the original home of these was Attica; but they spread with extraordinary rapidity, especially in Southern Italy and Sicily. They were first of all associations for the worship of Dionysus; but they were distinguished by two features which were new among the Hellenes. They looked to a revelation as the source of religious authority, and they were organized as artificial communities. The poems which contained their theology were ascribed to the Thracian Orpheus, who had himself descended into Hades, and was therefore a safe guide through the perils which beset the disembodied soul in the next world.'

Burnet goes on to state that there is a striking similarity between Orphic beliefs and those prevalent in India at about the same time, though he holds that there cannot have been any contact. He then comes on to the original meaning of the word 'orgy', which was used by the Orphics to mean 'sacrament', and was intended to purify the believer's soul and enable it to escape from the wheel of birth. The Orphics, unlike the priests of Olympian cults, founded what we may call 'churches', i.e. religious communities to which anybody, without distinction of race or sex, could be admitted by initiation, and from their influence arose the conception of philosophy as a way of life.

Chapter II

THE MILESIAN SCHOOL

IN every history of philosophy for students, the first thing mentioned is that philosophy began with Thales, who said that everything is made of water. This is discouraging to the beginner, who is struggling—perhaps not very hard—to feel that respect for philosophy which the curriculum seems to expect. There is, however, ample reason to feel respect for Thales, though perhaps rather as a man of science than as a philosopher in the modern sense of the word.

Thales was a native of Miletus, in Asia Minor, a flourishing commercial city, in which there was a large slave population, and a bitter class struggle between the rich and poor among the free population. 'At Miletus the people were at first victorious and murdered the wives and children of the aristocrats; then the aristocrats prevailed and burned their opponents alive, lighting up the open spaces of the city with live torches.'[1] Similar conditions prevailed in most of the cities of Asia Minor at the time of Thales.

Miletus, like other commercial cities of Ionia, underwent important economic and political developments during the seventh and sixth centuries. At first, political power belonged to a landowning aristocracy, but this was gradually replaced by a plutocracy of merchants. They, in turn, were replaced by a tyrant, who (as was usual) achieved power by the support of the democratic party. The kingdom of Lydia lay to the east of the Greek coast towns, but remained on friendly terms with them until the fall of Nineveh (606 B.C.). This left Lydia free to turn its attention to the West, but Miletus usually succeeded in preserving friendly relations, especially with Croesus, the last Lydian king, who was conquered by Cyrus in 546 B.C. There were also important relations with Egypt, where the king depended upon Greek mercenaries, and had opened certain cities to Greek trade. The first Greek settlement in Egypt was a fort occupied by a Milesian garrison; but the most important, during the period 610-560 B.C., was Daphnae. Here Jeremiah and many other Jewish fugitives took refuge from Nebuchadrezzar (*Jeremiah* xliii, 5 ff); but while Egypt undoubtedly influenced the Greeks, the Jews did not, nor can we suppose that Jeremiah felt anything but horror towards the sceptical Ionians.

[1] Rostovtsev, *History of the Ancient World*, Vol. I, p. 204.

As regards the date of Thales, the best evidence, as we saw, is that he was famous for predicting an eclipse which, according to the astronomers, must have taken place in 585 B.C. Other evidence, such as it is, agrees in placing his activities at about this time. It is no proof of extraordinary genius on his part to have predicted an eclipse. Miletus was allied with Lydia, and Lydia had cultural relations with Babylonia, and Babylonian astronomers had discovered that eclipses recur in a cycle of about nineteen years. They could predict eclipses of the moon with pretty complete success, but as regards solar eclipses they were hampered by the fact that an eclipse may be visible in one place and not in another. Consequently they could only know that at such and such a date it was worth while to look out for an eclipse, and this is probably all that Thales knew. Neither he nor they knew why there is this cycle.

Thales is said to have travelled in Egypt, and to have thence brought to the Greeks the science of geometry. What the Egyptians knew of geometry was mainly rules of thumb, and there is no reason to believe that Thales arrived at deductive proofs, such as later Greeks discovered. He seems to have discovered how to calculate the distance of a ship at sea from observations taken at two points on land, and how to estimate the height of a pyramid from the length of its shadow. Many other geometrical theorems are attributed to him, but probably wrongly.

He was one of the Seven Wise men of Greece, each of whom was specially noted for one wise saying; his it is a mistake to suppose was 'water is best'.

According to Aristotle, he thought that water is the original substance, out of which all others are formed; and he maintained that the earth rests on water. Aristotle also says of him that he said the magnet has a soul in it, because it moves the iron; further, that all things are full of gods.[1]

The statement that everything is made of water is to be regarded as a scientific hypothesis, and by no means a foolish one. Twenty years ago, the received view was that everything is made of hydrogen, which is two thirds of water. The Greeks were rash in their hypotheses, but the Milesian school, at least, was prepared to test them empirically. Too little is known of Thales to make it possible to reconstruct him at all satisfactorily, but of his successors in Miletus much more is known, and it is reasonable to suppose that something of their outlook came from him. His science and his philosophy were both crude, but they were such as to stimulate both thought and observation.

There are many legends about him, but I do not think more is

[1] Burnet (*Early Greek Philosophy*, p.51) questions this last saying.

known than the few facts I have mentioned. Some of the stories are pleasant, for instance, the one told by Aristotle in his *Politics* (1259ᵇ): 'He was reproached for his poverty, which was supposed to show that philosophy is of no use. According to the story, he knew by his skill in the stars while it was yet winter that there would be a great harvest of olives in the coming year; so, having a little money, he gave deposits for the use of all the olive-presses in Chios and Miletus, which he hired at a low price because no one bid against him. When the harvest time came, and many were wanted all at once and of a sudden, he let them out at any rate which he pleased, and made a quantity of money. Thus he showed the world that philosophers can easily be rich if they like, but that their ambition is of another sort.'

Anaximander, the second philosopher of the Milesian school, is much more interesting than Thales. His dates are uncertain, but he was said to have been sixty-four years old in 546 B.C., and there is reason to suppose that this is somewhere near the truth. He held that all things come from a single primal substance, but that it is not water, as Thales held, or any other of the substances that we know. It is infinite, eternal and ageless, and 'it encompasses all the worlds'—for he thought our world only one of many. The primal substance is transformed into the various substances with which we are familiar, and these are transformed into each other. As to this, he makes an important and remarkable statement:

'Into that from which things take their rise they pass away once more, as is ordained, for they make reparation and satisfaction to one another for their injustice according to the ordering of time.'

The idea of justice, both cosmic and human, played a part in Greek religion and philosophy which is not altogether easy for a modern to understand; indeed our word 'justice' hardly expresses what is meant, but it is difficult to find any other word that would be preferable. The thought which Anaximander is expressing seems to be this: there should be a certain proportion of fire, of earth, and of water in the world, but each element (conceived as a god) is perpetually attempting to enlarge its empire. But there is a kind of necessity or natural law which perpetually redresses the balance; where there has been fire, for example, there are ashes, which are earth. This conception of justice—of not overstepping eternally fixed bounds—was one of the most profound of Greek beliefs. The gods were subject to justice just as much as men were, but this supreme power was not itself personal, and was not a supreme God.

Anaximander had an argument to prove that the primal substance could not be water, or any other known element. If one of these were primal, it would conquer the others. Aristotle reports

46

him as saying that these known elements are in opposition to one another. Air is cold, water is moist, and fire is hot. 'And therefore, if any one of them were infinite, the rest would have ceased to be by this time.' The primal substance, therefore, must be neutral in this cosmic strife.

There was an eternal motion, in the course of which was brought about the origin of the worlds. The worlds were not created, as in Jewish or Christian theology, but evolved. There was evolution also in the animal kingdom. Living creatures arose from the moist element as it was evaporated by the sun. Man, like every other animal, was descended from fishes. He must be derived from animals of a different sort, because, owing to his long infancy, he could not have survived, originally, as he is now.

Anaximander was full of scientific curiosity. He is said to have been the first man who made a map. He held that the earth is shaped like a cylinder. He is variously reported as saying the sun is as large as the earth, or twenty-seven times as large, or twenty-eight times as large.

Wherever he is original, he is scientific and rationalistic.

Anaximenes, the last of the Milesian triad, is not quite so interesting as Anaximander, but makes some important advances. His dates are very uncertain. He was certainly subsequent to Anaximander, and he certainly flourished before 494 B.C., since in that year Miletus was destroyed by the Persians in the course of their suppression of the Ionian revolt.

The fundamental substance, he said, is air. The soul is air; fire is rarefied air; when condensed, air becomes first water, then, if further condensed, earth, and finally stone. This theory has the merit of making all the differences between different substances quantitative, depending entirely upon the degree of condensation.

He thought that the earth is shaped like a round table, and that air encompasses everything: 'Just as our soul, being air, holds us together, so do breath and air encompass the whole world.' It seems that the world breathes.

Anaximenes was more admired in antiquity than Anaximander, though almost any modern world would make the opposite valuation. He had an important influence on Pythagoras and on much subsequent speculation. The Pythagoreans discovered that the earth is spherical, but the atomists adhered to the view of Anaximenes, that it is shaped like a disc.

The Milesian school is important, not for what it achieved, but for what it attempted. It was brought into existence by the contact of the Greek mind with Babylonia and Egypt. Miletus was a rich commercial city, in which primitive prejudices and superstitions were softened by intercourse with many nations, Ionia, until its subjugation by Darius at the beginning of the fifth century, was culturally the most important part of the Hellenic world. It was almost untouched by the religious movement connected with Dionysus and Orpheus; its religion was Olympic, but seems to have been not taken very seriously. The speculations of Thales, Anaximander, and Anaximenes are to be regarded as scientific hypotheses, and seldom show any undue intrusion of anthropomorphic desires and moral ideas. The question they asked were good questions, and their vigour inspired subsequent investigators.

The next stage in Greek philosophy, which is associated with the Greek cities in southern Italy, is more religious, and, in particular, more Orphic—in some ways more interesting, admirable in achievement, but in spirit less scientific than that of the Milesians.

Chapter III

PYTHAGORAS

PYTHAGORAS, whose influence in ancient and modern times is my subject in this chapter, was intellectually one of the most important men that ever lived, both when he was wise and when he was unwise. Mathematics, in the sense of demonstrative deductive argument, begins with him, and in him is intimately connected with a peculiar form of mysticism. The influence of mathematics on philosophy, partly owing to him, has, ever since his time, been both profound and unfortunate.

Let us begin with what little is known of his life. He was a native of the island of Samos, and flourished about 532 B.C. Some say he was the son of a substantial citizen named Mnesarchos, others that he was the son of the god Apollo; I leave the reader to take his choice between these alternatives. In his time Samos was ruled by the tyrant Polycrates, an old ruffian who became immensely rich, and had a vast navy.

Samos was a commercial rival of Miletus; its traders went as far afield as Tartessus in Spain, which was famous for its mines. Polycrates became tyrant of Samos about 535 B.C., and reigned until 515 B.C. He was not much troubled by moral scruples; he got rid of his two brothers, who were at first associated with him in the tyranny, and he used his navy largely for piracy. He profited by the fact that Miletus had recently submitted to Persia. In order to obstruct any further westward expansion of the Persians, he allied himself with Amasis, king of Egypt. But when Cambyses, king of Persia, devoted his full energies to the conquest of Egypt, Polycrates realized that he was likely to win, and changed sides. He sent a fleet, composed of his political enemies, to attack Egypt; but the crews mutinied and returned to Samos to attack him. He got the better of them, however, but fell at last by a treacherous appeal to his avarice. The Persian satrap at Sardes represented that he intended to rebel against the Great King, and would pay vast sums for the help of Polycrates, who went to the mainland for an interview, was captured and crucified.

Polycrates was a patron of the arts, and beautified Samos with remarkable public works. Anacreon was his court poet. Pythagoras, however, disliked his government, and therefore left Samos. It is said, and is not improbable, that Pythagoras visited Egypt, and learnt much of his wisdom there; however that may be, it is certain that he ultimately established himself at Croton, in southern Italy.

The Greek cities of southern Italy, like Samos and Miletus, were rich and prosperous; moreover they were not exposed to danger from the Persians.[1] The two greatest were Sybaris and Croton. Sybaris has remained proverbial for luxury; its population, in its greatest days, is said by Diodorus to have amounted to 300,000, though this is no doubt an exaggeration. Croton was about equal in size to Sybaris. Both cities lived by importing Ionian wares into Italy, partly for consumption in that country, partly for re-export from the western coast to Gaul and Spain. The various Greek cities of Italy fought each other fiercely; when Pythagoras arrived in Croton, it had just been defeated by Locri. Soon after his arrival, however, Croton was completely victorious in a war against Sybaris, which was utterly destroyed (510 B.C.). Sybaris had been closely linked in commerce with Miletus. Croton was famous for medicine; a certain Democedes of Croton became physician to Polycrates and then to Darius.

At Croton Pythagoras founded a society of disciples, which for a time was influential in that city. But in the end the citizens turned against him, and he moved to Metapontion (also in southern Italy), where he died. He soon became a mythical figure, credited with miracles and magic powers, but he was also the founder of a school of mathematicians.[2] Thus two opposing traditions disputed his memory, and the truth is hard to disentangle.

Pythagoras is one of the most interesting and puzzling men in history. Not only are the traditions concerning him an almost inextricable mixture of truth and falsehood, but even in their barest and least disputable form they present us with a very curious psychology. He may be described, briefly, as a combination of Einstein and Mrs Eddy. He founded a religion, of which the main tenets were the transmigration of souls[3] and the sinfulness of eating beans. His religion was embodied in a religious order, which, here and there, acquired control of the State and established a rule of the

---

[1] The Greek cities of Sicily were in danger from the Carthaginians, but in Italy this danger was not felt to be imminent.

[2] Aristotle says of him that he 'first worked at mathematics and arithmetic, and afterwards, at one time, condescended to the wonder-working practised by Pherecydes.'

[3] *Clown*: What is the opinion of Pythagoras concerning wildfowl?
Malvolio: That the soul of our grandam might haply inhabit a bird.
Clown: What thinkest thou of his opinion?
Malvolio: I think nobly of the soul, and no way approve his opinion.
Clown: Fare thee well; remain thou still in darkness; thou shalt hold the opinion of Pythagoras ere I will allow of thy wits. (*Twelfth Night*.)

saints. But the unregenerate hankered after beans, and sooner or later rebelled.

Some of the rules of the Pythagorean order were:

1. To abstain from beans.
2. Not to pick up what was fallen.
3. Not to touch a white cock.
4. Not to break bread.
5. Not to step over a crossbar.
6. Not to stir the fire with iron.
7. Not to eat from a whole loaf.
8. Not to pluck a garland.
9. Not to sit on a quart measure.
10. Not to eat the heart.
11. Not to walk on highways.
12. Not to let swallows share one's roof.
13. When the pot is taken off the fire, not to leave the mark of it in the ashes, but to stir them together.
14. Do not look in a mirror beside a light.
15. When you rise from the bedclothes, roll them together and smooth out the impress of the body.[1]

All these precepts belong to primitive tabu-conceptions.

Cornford (*From Religion to Philosophy*) says that, in his opinion, 'The School of Pythagoras represents the main current of that mystical tradition which we have set in contrast with the scientific tendency.' He regards Parmenides, whom he calls 'the discoverer of logic', as 'an offshoot of Pythagoreanism, and Plato himself as finding in the Italian philosophy the chief source of his inspiration.' Pythagoreanism, he says, was a movement of reform in Orphism, and Orphism was a movement of reform in the worship of Dionysus. The opposition of the rational and the mystical, which runs all through history, first appears, among the Greeks, as an opposition between the Olympic gods and those other less civilized gods who had more affinity with the primitive beliefs dealt with by anthropologists. In this division, Pythagoras was on the side of mysticism, though his mysticism was of a peculiarly intellectual sort. He attributed to himself a semi-divine character, and appears to have said: 'There are men and gods, and beings like Pythagoras.' All the systems that he inspired, Cornford says, 'tend to be otherworldly, putting all value in the unseen unity of God, and condemning the visible world as false and illusive, a turbid medium in which

[1] Quoted from Burnet's *Early Greek Philosophy*.

the rays of heavenly light are broken and obscured in mist and darkness.'

Dikaiarchos says that Pythagoras taught 'first, that the soul is an immortal thing, and that it is transformed into other kinds of living things; further, that whatever comes into existence is born again in the revolutions of a certain cycle, nothing being absolutely new; and that all things that are born with life in them ought to be treated as kindred.'[1] It is said that Pythagoras, like St Francis, preached to animals.

In the society that he founded, men and women were admitted on equal terms; property was held in common, and there was a common way of life. Even scientific and mathematical discoveries were deemed collective, and in a mystical sense due to Pythagoras even after his death. Hippasos of Metapontion, who violated this rule, was shipwrecked as a result of divine wrath at his impiety.

But what has all this to do with mathematics? It is connected by means of an ethic which praised the contemplative life. Burnet sums up this ethic as follows:

We are strangers in this world, and the body is the tomb of the soul, and yet we must not seek to escape by self-murder; for we are the chattels of God who is our herdsman, and without His command we have no right to make our escape. In this life, there are three kinds of men, just as there are three sorts of people who come to the Olympic Games. The lowest class is made up of those who come to buy and sell, the next above them are those who compete. Best of all, however, are those who come simply to look on. The greatest purification of all is, therefore, disinterested science, and it is the man who devotes himself to that, the true philosopher, who has most effectually released himself from the 'wheel of birth.'[2]

The changes in the meanings of words are often very instructive. I spoke above about the word 'orgy'; now I want to speak about the word 'theory'. This was originally an Orphic word, which Cornford interprets as 'passionate sympathetic contemplation'. In this state, he says, 'The spectator is identified with the suffering God, dies in his death, and rises again in his new birth.' For Pythagoras, the 'passionate sympathetic contemplation' was intellectual, and issued in mathematical knowledge. In this way, through Pythagoreanism, 'theory' gradually acquired its modern meaning; but for all who were inspired by Pythagoras it retained an element of ecstatic revelation. To those who have reluctantly learnt a little mathematics in school this may seem strange; but to those who have

[1] Cornford, *op. cit.*, p. 201.   [2] *Early Greek Philosophy*, p. 108.

experienced the intoxicating delight of sudden understanding that mathematics gives, from time to time, to those who love it, the Pythagorean view will seem completely natural even if untrue. It might seem that the empirical philosopher is the slave of his material, but that the pure mathematician, like the musician, is a free creator of his world of ordered beauty.

It is interesting to observe, in Burnet's account of the Pythagorean ethic, the opposition to modern values. In connection with a football match, modern-minded men think the players grander than the mere spectators. Similarly as regards the State: they admire more the politicians who are the contestants in the game than those who are only onlookers. This change of values is connected with a change in the social system—the warrior, the gentleman, the plutocrat, and the dictator, each has his own standard of the good and the true. The gentleman has had a long innings in philosophical theory, because he is associated with the Greek genius, because the virtue of contemplation acquired theological endorsement, and because the ideal of disinterested truth dignified the academic life. The gentleman is to be defined as one of a society of equals who live on slave labour, or at any rate upon the labour of men whose inferiority is unquestioned. It should be observed that this definition includes the saint and the sage, insofar as these men's lives are contemplative rather than active

Modern definitions of truth, such as those of pragmatism and instrumentalism, which are practical rather than contemplative, are inspired by industrialism as opposed to aristocracy.

Whatever may be thought of a social system which tolerates slavery, it is to gentlemen in the above sense that we owe pure mathematics. The contemplative ideal, since it lead to the creation of pure mathematics, was the source of a useful activity; this increased its prestige, and gave it a success in theology, in ethics, and in philosophy, which it might not otherwise have enjoyed.

So much by way of explanation of the two aspects of Pythagoras: as religious prophet and as pure mathematician. In both respects he was immeasurably influential, and the two were not so separate as they seem to a modern mind.

Most sciences, at their inception, have been connected with some form of false belief, which gave them a fictitious value. Astronomy was connected with astrology, chemistry with alchemy. Mathematics was associated with a more refined type of error. Mathematical knowledge appeared to be certain, exact, and applicable to the real world; moreover it was obtained by mere thinking, without the need of observation. Consequently, it was thought to supply an ideal, from which every-day empirical knowledge fell short. It was supposed, on the basis of mathematics, that thought is superior to sense, intuition to observation. If the world of sense does not fit mathematics, so much the worse for the world of sense. In various ways, methods of approaching nearer to the mathematician's ideal were sought, and the resulting suggestions were the source of much that was mistaken in metaphysics and theory of knowledge. This form of philosophy begins with Pythagoras.

Pythagoras, as everyone knows, said that 'all things are numbers'. This statement, interpreted in a modern way, is logically nonsense, but what he meant was not exactly nonsense. He discovered the importance of numbers in music, and the connection which he established between music and arithmetic survives in the mathematical terms 'harmonic mean' and 'harmonic progression'. He thought of numbers as shapes, as they appear on dice or playing cards. We still speak of squares and cubes of numbers, which are terms that we owe to him. He also spoke of oblong numbers, triangular numbers, pyramidal numbers, and so on. These were the numbers of pebbles (or, as we should more naturally say, shot) required to make the shapes in question. He presumably thought of the world as atomic, and of bodies as built up of molecules composed of atoms arranged in various shapes. In this way he hoped to make arithmetic the fundamental study in physics as in aesthetics.

The greatest discovery of Pythagoras, or of his immediate disciples, was the proposition about right-angled triangles, that the sum of the squares on the sides adjoining the right angle is equal to the square on the remaining side, the hypotenuse. The Egyptians had known that a triangle whose sides are 3, 4, 5 has a right angle, but apparently the Greeks were the first to observe that $3^2 + 4^2 = 5^2$, and, acting on this suggestion, to discover a proof of the general proposition.

Unfortunately for Pythagoras, his theorem led at once to the discovery of incommensurables, which appeared to disprove his whole philosophy. In a right-angled isosceles triangle, the square on the hypotenuse is double of the square on either side. Let us suppose each side an inch long; then how long is the hypotenuse? Let us suppose its length is m/n inches. Then $m^2/n^2 = 2$. If m and n have a common factor, divide it out, then either m or n must be odd. Now $m^2 = 2n^2$, therefore m^2 is even, therefore m is even, therefore n is odd. Suppose $m = 2p$. Then $4p^2 = 2n^2$, therefore, $n^2 = 2p^2$ and therefore n is even, *contra hyp*. Therefore no fraction m/n will measure the hypotenuse. The above proof is substantially that in Euclid, Book X.[1]

[1] But not by Euclid. See Heath, *Greek Mathematics*. The above proof was probably known to Plato.

This argument proved that, whatever unit of length we may adopt, there are lengths which bear no exact numerical relation to the unit, in the sense that there are no two integers m, n, such that m times the length in question is n times the unit. This convinced the Greek mathematicians that geometry must be established independently of arithmetic. There are passages in Plato's dialogues which prove that the independent treatment of geometry was well under way in his day; it is perfected in Euclid. Euclid, in Book II, proves geometrically many things which we should naturally prove by algebra, such as $(a + b)^2 = a^2 + 2ab + b^2$. It was because of the difficulty about incommensurables that he considered this course necessary. The same applies to his treatment of proportion in Books V and VI. The whole system is logically delightful, and anticipates the rigour of nineteenth-century mathematicians. So long as no adequate arithmetical theory of incommensurables existed, the method of Euclid was the best that was possible in geometry. When Descartes introduced co-ordinate geometry, thereby again making arithmetic supreme, he assumed the possibility of a solution of the problem of incommensurables, though in his day no such solution had been found.

The influence of geometry upon philosophy and scientific method has been profound. Geometry, as established by the Greeks, starts with axioms which are (or are deemed to be) self-evident, and proceeds, by deductive reasoning, to arrive at theorems that are very far from self-evident. The axioms and theorems are held to be true of actual space, which is something given in experience. It thus appeared to be possible to discover things about the actual world by first noticing what is self-evident and then using deduction. This view influenced Plato and Kant, and most of the intermediate philosophers. When the Declaration of Independence says 'we hold these truths to be self-evident', it is modelling itself on Euclid. The eighteenth-century doctrine of natural rights is a search for Euclidean axioms in politics.[1] The form of Newton's *Principia*, in spite of its admittedly empirical material, is entirely dominated by Euclid. Theology, in its exact scholastic forms, takes its style from the same source. Personal religion is derived from ecstasy, theology from mathematics; and both are to be found in Pythagoras.

Mathematics is, I believe, the chief source of the belief in eternal and exact truth, as well as in a super-sensible intelligible world. Geometry deals with exact circles, but no sensible object is *exactly* circular; however carefully we may use our compasses, there will be some imperfections and irregularities. This suggests the view

[1] 'Self-evident' was substituted by Franklin for Jefferson's 'sacred and undeniable.'

that all exact reasoning applies to ideal as opposed to sensible objects; it is natural to go further, and to argue that thought is nobler than sense, and the objects of thought more real than those of sense-perception. Mystical doctrines as to the relation of time to eternity are also reinforced by pure mathematics, for mathematical objects, such as numbers, if real at all, are eternal and not in time. Such eternal objects can be conceived as God's thoughts. Hence Plato's doctrine that God is a geometer, and Sir James Jeans' belief that He is addicted to arithmetic. Rationalistic as opposed to apocalyptic religion has been, ever since Pythagoras, and notably ever since Plato, very completely dominated by mathematics and mathematical method.

The combination of mathematics and theology, which began with Pythagoras, characterized religious philosophy in Greece, in the Middle Ages, and in modern times down to Kant. Orphism before Pythagoras was analogous to Asiatic mystery religions. But in Plato, St Augustine, Thomas Aquinas, Descartes, Spinoza, and Leibniz there is an intimate blending of religion and reasoning, of moral aspiration with logical admiration of what is timeless, which comes from Pythagoras, and distinguishes the intellectualized theology of Europe from the more straightforward mysticism of Asia. It is only in quite recent times that it has been possible to say clearly where Pythagoras was wrong. I do not know of any other man who has been as influential as he was in the sphere of thought. I say this because what appears as Platonism is, when analysed, found to be in essence Pythagoreanism. The whole conception of an eternal world, revealed to the intellect but not to the senses, is derived from him. But for him, Christians would not have thought of Christ as the Word; but for him, theologians would not have sought logical *proofs* of God and immortality. But in him all this is still implicit. How it became explicit will appear as we proceed.

Chapter IV

HERACLITUS

Two opposite attitudes towards the Greeks are common at the present day. One, which was practically universal from the Renaissance until very recent times, views the Greeks with almost superstitious reverence, as the inventors of all that is best, and as men of superhuman genius whom the moderns cannot hope to equal. The other attitude, inspired by the triumphs of science and by an optimistic belief in progress, considers the authority of the ancients an incubus, and maintains that most of their contributions to thought are now best forgotten. I cannot myself take either of these extreme views; each, I should say, is partly right and partly wrong. Before entering upon any detail, I shall try to say what sort of wisdom we can still derive from the study of Greek thought.

As to the nature and structure of the world, various hypotheses are possible. Progress in metaphysics, so far as it has existed, has consisted in a gradual refinement of all these hypotheses, a development of their implications, and a reformulation of each to meet the objections urged by adherents of rival hypotheses. To learn to conceive the universe according to each of these systems is an imaginative delight and an antidote to dogmatism. Moreover, even if no one of the hypotheses can be demonstrated, there is genuine knowledge in the discovery of what is involved in making each of them consistent with itself and with known facts. Now almost all the hypotheses that have dominated modern philosophy were first thought of by the Greeks; their imaginative inventiveness in abstract matters can hardly be too highly praised. What I shall have to say about the Greeks will be said mainly from this point of view; I shall regard them as giving birth to theories which have had an independent life and growth, and which, though at first somewhat infantile, have proved capable of surviving and developing throughout more than two thousand years.

The Greeks contributed, it is true, something else which proved of more permanent value to abstract thought: they discovered mathematics and the art of deductive reasoning. Geometry, in particular, is a Greek invention, without which modern science would have been impossible. But in connection with mathematics the one-sidedness of the Greek genius appears: it reasoned deductively from what appeared self-evident, not inductively from what had been

57

observed. Its amazing successes in the employment of this method misled not only the ancient world, but the greater part of the modern world also. It has only been very slowly that scientific method, which seeks to reach principles inductively from observations of particular facts, has replaced the Hellenic belief in deduction from luminous axioms derived from the mind of the philosopher. For this reason, apart from others, it is a mistake to treat the Greeks with superstitious reverence. Scientific method, though some few among them were the first men who had an inkling of it, is, on the whole, alien to their temper of mind, and the attempt to glorify them by belittling the intellectual progress of the last four centuries has a cramping effect upon modern thought.

There is, however, a more general argument against reverence, whether for the Greeks or for anyone else. In studying a philosopher, the right attitude is neither reverence nor contempt, but first a kind of hypothetical sympathy, until it is possible to know what it feels like to believe in his theories, and only then a revival of the critical attitude, which should resemble, as far as possible, the state of mind of a person abandoning opinions which he has hitherto held. Contempt interferes with the first part of this process, and reverence with the second. Two things are to be remembered : that a man whose opinions and theories are worth studying may be presumed to have had some intelligence, but that no man is likely to have arrived at complete and final truth on any subject whatever. When an intelligent man expresses a view which seems to us obviously absurd, we should not attempt to prove that it is somehow true, but we should try to understand how it ever came to *seem* true. This exercise of historical and psychological imagination at once enlarges the scope of our thinking, and helps us to realize how foolish many of our own cherished prejudices will seem to an age which has a different temper of mind.

Between Pythagoras and Heraclitus, with whom we shall be concerned in this chapter, there was another philosopher, of less importance, namely Xenophanes. His date is uncertain, and is mainly determined by the fact that he alludes to Pythagoras and Heraclitus alludes to him. He was an Ionian by birth, but lived most of his life in southern Italy. He believed all things to be made out of earth and water. As regards the gods he was a very emphatic free thinker. 'Homer and Hesiod have ascribed to the gods all things that are a shame and a disgrace among mortals, stealings and adulteries and deceivings of one another. . . . Mortals deem that gods are begotten as they are, and have clothes like theirs, and voice and form . . . yes. and if oxen and horses or lions had hands, and could paint with their hands, and produce works of art as men do, horses would paint the forms of gods like horses, and oxen like oxen, and make their bodies in the image of their several kinds. . . . The Ethiopians make their gods black and snub-nosed; the Thracians say theirs have blue eyes and red hair.' He believed in one God, unlike men in form and thought, who 'without toil swayeth all things by the force of his mind'. Xenophanes made fun of the Pythagorean doctrine of transmigration. 'Once, they say, he (Pythagoras) was passing by when a dog was being ill-treated. "Stop," he said, "don't hit it! It is the soul of a friend! I knew it when I heard its voice".' He believed it impossible to ascertain the truth in matters of theology. 'The certain truth there is no man who knows, nor ever shall be, about the gods and all the things whereof I speak. Yea, even if a man should chance to say something utterly right, still he himself knows it not—there is nowhere anything but guessing.'[1]

Xenophanes has his place in the succession of rationalists, who were opposed to the mystical tendencies of Pythagoras and others, but as an independent thinker he is not in the first rank.

The doctrine of Pythagoras, as we saw, is very difficult to disentangle from that of his disciples, and although Pythagoras himself is very early, the influence of his school is mainly subsequent to that of various other philosophers. The first of these to invent a theory which is still influential was Heraclitus, who flourished about 500 B.C. Of his life very little is known, except that he was an aristocratic citizen of Ephesus. He was chiefly famous in antiquity for his doctrine that everything is in a state of flux, but this, as we shall see, is only one aspect of his metaphysics.

Heraclitus, though an Ionian, was not in the scientific tradition of the Milesians.[2] He was a mystic, but of a peculiar kind. He regarded fire as the fundamental substance; everything, like flame in a fire, is born by the death of something else. 'Mortals are immortals, and immortals are mortals, the one living the other's death and dying the other's life.' There is unity in the world, but it is a unity formed by the combination of opposites. 'All things come out of the one, and the one out of all things'; but the many have less reality than the one, which is God.

From what survives of his writings he does not appear as an amiable character. He was much addicted to contempt, and was the reverse of a democrat. Concerning his fellow-citizens, he says: 'The Ephesians would do well to hang themselves, every grown man of them, and leave the city to beardless lads; for they have cast out Hermodorus, the best man among them, saying "We will

---

[1] Quoted from Edwyn Bevan, *Stoics and Sceptics*, Oxford, 1913, p. 121.
[2] Cornford, *op. cit.* (p. 184), emphasizes this, I think rightly. Heraclitus is often misunderstood through being assimilated to other Ionians.

have none who is best among us; if there be any such, let him be so elsewhere and among others".' He speaks ill of all his eminent pre-decessors, with a single exception. 'Homer should be turned out of the lists and whipped.' 'Of all whose discourses I have heard, there is not one who attains to understanding that wisdom is apart from all.' 'The learning of many things teacheth not understanding, else would it have taught Hesiod and Pythagoras, and again Xenophanes and Hecataeus.' 'Pythagoras . . . claimed for his own wisdom what was but a knowledge of many things and an art of mischief.' The one exception to his condemnations is Teutamus, who is signalled out as 'of more account than the rest'. When we inquire the reason for this praise, we find that Teutamus said 'most men are bad'.

His contempt for mankind leads him to think that only force will compel them to act for their own good. He says: 'Every beast is driven to the pasture with blows'; and again: 'Asses would rather have straw than gold.'

As might be expected, Heraclitus believes in war. 'War,' he says, 'is the father of all and the king of all; and some he has made gods and some men, some bond and some free.' Again: 'Homer was wrong in saying: "Would that strife might perish from among gods and men!" He did not see that he was praying for the destruction of the universe; for, if his prayer were heard, all things would pass away.' And yet again: 'We must know that war is common to all and strife is justice, and that all things come into being and pass away through strife.'

His ethic is a kind of proud asceticism, very similar to Nietzsche's. He regards the soul as a mixture of fire and water, the fire being noble and the water ignoble. The soul that has most fire he calls 'dry'. 'The dry soul is the wisest and best.' 'It is pleasure to souls to become moist.' 'A man, when he gets drunk, is lead by a beardless lad, tripping, knowing not where he steps, having his soul moist.' 'It is death to souls to become water.' 'It is hard to fight with one's heart's desire. Whatever it wishes to get, it purchases at the cost of soul.' 'It is not good for men to get all that they wish to get.' One may say that Heraclitus values power obtained through self-mastery, and despises the passions that distract men from their central ambitions.

The attitude of Heraclitus to the religions of his time, at any rate the Bacchic religion, is largely hostile, but not with the hostility of a scientific rationalist. He has his own religion, and in part interprets current theology to fit his doctrine, in part rejects it with consider-able scorn. He has been called Bacchic (by Cornford), and regarded as an interpreter of the mysteries (by Pfleiderer). I do not think the relevant fragments bear out this view. He says, for example: 'The mysteries practised among men are unholy mysteries.' This suggests that he had in mind possible mysteries that would not be 'unholy', but would be quite different from those that existed. He would have been a religious reformer, if he had not been too scornful of the vulgar to engage in propaganda.

The following are all the extant sayings of Heraclitus that bear on his attitude to the theology of his day.

The Lord whose is the oracle of Delphi neither utters nor hides his meaning, but shows it by a sign.

And the Sibyl, with raving lips uttering things mirthless, un-bedizened and unperfumed, reaches over a thousand years with her voice, thanks to the god in her.

Souls smell in Hades.

Greater deaths win greater portions. (Those who die them become gods.)

Night-walkers, magicians, priests of Bacchus, and priestesses of the wine-vat, mystery-mongers.

The mysteries practised among men are unholy mysteries.

And they pray to these images, as if one were to talk with a man's house, knowing not what gods or heroes are.

For if it were not to Dionysus that they made a procession and sang the shameful phallic hymn, they would be acting most shamelessly. But Hades is the same as Dionysus in whose honour they go mad and keep the feast of the wine-vat.

They vainly purify themselves by defiling themselves with blood, just as if one who had stepped into the mud were to wash his feet in mud. Any man who marked him doing this, would deem him mad.

Heraclitus believed fire to be the primordial element, out of which everything else had arisen. Thales, the reader will remember, thought everything was made of water; Anaximenes thought air was the primitive element; Heraclitus preferred fire. At last Empedocles suggested a statesmanlike compromise by allowing four elements, earth, air, fire and water. The chemistry of the ancients stopped dead at this point. No further progress was made in this science until the Mohammedan alchemists embarked upon their search for the philosopher's stone, the elixir of life, and a method of transmuting base metals into gold.

The metaphysics of Heraclitus are sufficiently dynamic to satisfy the most hustling of moderns:

'This world, which is the same for all, no one of gods or men has made; but it was ever, is now, and ever shall be an ever-living Fire, with measures kindling and measures going out.'

'The transformations of Fire are, first of all, sea; and half of the sea is earth, half whirlwind.'

In such a world, perpetual change was to be expected, and perpetual change was what Heraclitus believed in.

He had, however, another doctrine on which he set even more store than on the perpetual flux; this was the doctrine of the mingling of opposites. 'Men do not know,' he says, 'how what is at variance agrees with itself. It is an attunement of opposite tensions, like that of the bow and the lyre.' His belief in strife is connected with this theory, for in strife opposites combine to produce a motion which is a harmony. There is a unity in the world, but it is a unity resulting from diversity:

'Couples are things whole and things not whole, what is drawn together and what is drawn asunder, the harmonious and the discordant. The one is made up of all things, and all things issue from the one."

Sometimes he speaks as if the unity were more fundamental than the diversity:

'Good and ill are one.'

'To God all things are fair and good and right, but men hold some things wrong and some right.'

'The way up and the way down is one and the same.'

'God is day and night, winter and summer, war and peace, surfeit and hunger; but he takes various shapes, just as fire, when it is mingled with spices, is named according to the savour of each.'

Nevertheless there would be no unity if there were not opposites to combine: 'It is the opposite which is good for us.'

This doctrine contains the germ of Hegel's philosophy, which proceeds by a synthesizing of opposites.

The metaphysics of Heraclitus, like that of Anaximander, is dominated by a conception of cosmic justice, which prevents the strife of opposites from ever issuing in the complete victory of either.

'All things are an exchange for Fire, and Fire for all things, even as wares for gold and gold for wares.'

'Fire lives the death of air, and air lives the death of fire; water lives the death of earth, earth that of water.'

'The sun will not overstep his measures; if he does, the Erinyes, the handmaids of Justice, will find him out.'

'We must know that war is common to all, and strife is justice.'

Heraclitus repeatedly speaks of 'God' as distinct from 'the gods'. 'The way of man has no wisdom, but that of God has. . . . Man is called a baby by God, even as a child by a man. . . . The wisest man is an ape compared to God, just as the most beautiful ape is ugly compared to man.'

God, no doubt, is the embodiment of cosmic justice.

The doctrine that everything is in a state of flux is the most famous of the opinions of Heraclitus, and the one most emphasized by his disciples, as described in Plato's *Theaetetus*.

'You cannot step twice into the same river; for fresh waters are ever flowing in upon you.'[1]

'The sun is new every day.'

His belief in universal change is commonly supposed to have been expressed in the phrase 'all things are flowing', but this is probably apocryphal, like Washington's 'Father, I cannot tell a lie' and Wellington's 'Up Guards and at 'em.' His words, like those of all the philosophers before Plato, are only known through quota-tions, largely made by Plato and Aristotle for the sake of refutation. When one thinks what would become of any modern philosopher if he were only known through the polemics of his rivals, one can see how admirable the pre-Socratics must have been, since even through the mist of malice spread by their enemies they still appear great. However this may be, Plato and Aristotle agree that Hera-clitus taught that 'nothing ever is, everything is becoming' (Plato), and that 'nothing steadfastly is' (Aristotle).

I shall return to the consideration of this doctrine in connection with Plato, who is much concerned to refute it. For the present, I shall not investigate what philosophy has to say about it, but only what the poets have felt and the men of science have taught.

The search for something permanent is one of the deepest of the instincts leading men to philosophy. It is derived, no doubt, from love of home and desire for a refuge from danger; we find, accord-ingly, that it is most passionate in those whose lives are most exposed to catastrophe. Religion seeks permanence in two forms, God and immortality. In God is no variableness neither shadow of turning; the life after death is eternal and unchanging. The cheer-fulness of the nineteenth century turned men against these static conceptions, and modern liberal theology believes that there is pro-gress in heaven and evolution in the Godhead. But even in this con-ception there is something permanent, namely progress itself and its immanent goal. And a dose of disaster is likely to bring men's hopes back to their older super-terrestrial forms : if life on earth is despaired of, it is only in heaven that peace can be sought.

[1] But cf. 'We step and do not step into the same rivers : we are, and are not.'

The poets have lamented the power of Time to sweep away every object of their love.

> Time doth transfix the flourish set on youth,
> And delves the parallels in beauty's brow,
> Feeds on the rarities of nature's truth,
> And nothing stands but for his scythe to mow.

They generally add that their own verses are indestructible:

> And yet to times in hope my verse shall stand,
> Praising thy worth, despite his cruel hand.

But this is only a conventional literary conceit.

Philosophically inclined mystics, unable to deny that whatever is in time is transitory, have invented a conception of eternity as not persistence through endless time, but existence outside the whole temporal process. Eternal life, according to some theologians, for example, Dean Inge, does not mean existence throughout every moment of future time, but a mode of being wholly independent of time, in which there is no before and after, and therefore no logical possibility of change. This view has been poetically expressed by Vaughan :

> I saw Eternity the other night,
> Like a great ring of pure and endless light,
>   All calm, as it was bright;
> And round beneath it, Time in hours, days, years,
>   Driven by the spheres
> Like a vast shadow moved; in which the world
>   And all her train were hurled.

Several of the most famous systems of philosophy have tried to state this conception in sober prose, as expressing what reason, patiently pursued, will ultimately compel us to believe.

Heraclitus himself, for all his belief in change, allowed *something* everlasting. The conception of eternity (as opposed to endless duration), which comes from Parmenides, is not to be found in Heraclitus, but in his philosophy the central fire never dies: the world 'was ever, is now, and ever shall be, an ever-living Fire'. But fire is something continually changing, and its permanence is rather that of a process than that of a substance—though this view should not be attributed to Heraclitus.

Science, like philosophy, has sought to escape from the doctrine of perpetual flux by finding some permanent substratum amid changing phenomena. Chemistry seemed to satisfy this desire. It was found that fire, which appears to destroy, only transmutes : elements are recombined, but each atom that existed before combustion still exists when the process is completed. Accordingly it was supposed that atoms are indestructible, and that all change in the physical world consists merely in re-arrangement of persistent elements. This view prevailed until the discovery of radio-activity, when it was found that atoms could disintegrate.

Nothing daunted, the physicists invented new and smaller units, called electrons and protons, out of which atoms were composed; and these units were supposed, for a few years, to have the indestructibility formerly attributed to atoms. Unfortunately it seemed that protons and electrons could meet and explode, forming, not new matter, but a wave of energy spreading through the universe with the velocity of light. Energy had to replace matter as what is permanent. But energy, unlike matter, is not a refinement of the common-sense notion of a 'thing'; it is merely a characteristic of physical processes. It might be fancifully identified with the Heraclitean Fire, but it is the burning, not what burns. 'What burns' has disappeared from modern physics.

Passing from the small to the large, astronomy no longer allows us to regard the heavenly bodies as everlasting. The planets came out of the sun, and the sun came out of a nebula. It has lasted some time, and will last some time longer; but sooner or later—probably in about a million million years—it will explode, destroying all the planets. So at least the astronomers say; perhaps as the fatal day draws nearer they will find some mistake in their calculations.

The doctrine of the perpetual flux, as taught by Heraclitus, is painful, and science, as we have seen, can do nothing to refute it. One of the main ambitions of philosophers has been to revive hopes that science seemed to have killed. Philosophers, accordingly, have sought, with great persistence, for something not subject to the empire of Time. This search begins with Parmenides.

Chapter V

PARMENIDES

THE Greeks were not addicted to moderation, either in their theories or in their practice. Heraclitus maintained that *everything* changes: Parmenides retorted that *nothing* changes.

Parmenides was a native of Elea, in the south of Italy, and flourished in the first half of the fifth century B.C. According to Plato, Socrates in his youth (say about the year 450 B.C.) had an interview with Parmenides, then an old man, and learnt much from him. Whether or not this interview is historical, we may at least infer, what is otherwise evident, that Plato himself was influenced by the doctrines of Parmenides. The south Italian and Sicilian philosophers were more inclined to mysticism and religion than those of Ionia, who were on the whole scientific and sceptical in their tendencies. But mathematics, under the influence of Pythagoras, flourished more in Magna Graecia than in Ionia; mathematics at that time, however, was entangled with mysticism. Parmenides was influenced by Pythagoras, but the extent of this influence is conjectural. What makes Parmenides historically important is that he invented a form of metaphysical argument that, in one form or another, is to be found in most subsequent metaphysicians down to and including Hegel. He is often said to have invented logic, but what he really invented was metaphysics based on logic.

The doctrine of Parmenides was set forth in a poem *On Nature*. He considered the senses deceptive, and condemned the multitude of sensible things as mere illusion. The only true being is 'the One', which is infinite and indivisible. It is not, as in Heraclitus, a union of opposites, since there are no opposites. He apparently thought, for instance, that 'cold' means only 'not hot', and 'dark' means only 'not light'. 'The One' is not conceived by Parmenides as we conceive God; he seems to think of it as material and extended, for he speaks of it as a sphere. But it cannot be divided, because the whole of it is present everywhere.

Parmenides divides his teaching into two parts, called respectively 'the way of truth' and 'the way of opinion'. We need not concern ourselves with the latter. What he says about the way of truth, so far as it has survived, is, in its essential points, as follows:

'Thou canst not know what is not—that is impossible—nor utter it; for it is the same thing that can be thought and that can be."

66

'How, then, can what *is* be going to be in the future? Or how could it come into being? If it came into being, it is not; nor is it if it is going to be in the future. Thus is *becoming* extinguished and *passing away* not to be heard of.

'The thing that can be thought and that for the sake of which the thought exists is the same; for you cannot find thought without something that is, as to which it is uttered.'[1]

The essence of this argument is: When you think, you think *of* something; when you use a name, it must be the name *of* something. Therefore both thought and language require objects outside themselves. And since you can think of a thing or speak of it at one time as well as at another, whatever can be thought of or spoken of must exist at all times. Consequently there can be no change, since change consists in things coming into being or ceasing to be.

This is the first example in philosophy of an argument from thought and language to the world at large. It cannot of course be accepted as valid, but it is worth while to see what element of truth it contains.

We can put the argument in this way: if language is not just nonsense, words must mean something, and in general they must not mean just other words, but something that is there whether we talk of it or not. Suppose, for example, that you talk of George Washington. Unless there were a historical person who had that name, the name (it would seem) would be meaningless, and sentences containing the name would be nonsense. Parmenides maintains that not only must George Washington have existed in the past, but in some sense he must still exist, since we can still use his name significantly. This seems obviously untrue, but how are we to get round the argument?

Let us take an imaginary person, say Hamlet. Consider the statement 'Hamlet was Prince of Denmark.' In some sense this is true, but not in the plain historical sense. The true statement is 'Shakespeare says that Hamlet was Prince of Denmark,' or, more explicitly, 'Shakespeare says there was a Prince of Denmark called "Hamlet".' Here there is no longer anything imaginary. Shakespeare and Denmark and the noise 'Hamlet' are all real, but the noise 'Hamlet' is not really a name, since nobody is really called 'Hamlet'. If you say ' "Hamlet" is the name of an imaginary person,' that is not strictly correct; you ought to say 'It is imagined that "Hamlet" is the name of a real person.'

Hamlet is an imagined individual; unicorns are an imagined species. Some sentences in which the word 'unicorn' occurs are

---

[1] Burnet's note: 'The meaning, I think, is this. . . . There can be no thought corresponding to a name that is not the name of something real.'

true, and some are false, but in each case not directly. Consider 'a unicorn has one horn' and 'a cow has two horns'. To prove the latter you have to look at a cow; it is not enough to say that in some book cows are said to have two horns. But the evidence that unicorns have one horn is only to be found in books, and in fact the correct statement is: 'Certain books assert that there are animals with one horn called "unicorns".' All statements about unicorns are really about the *word* 'unicorn', just as all statements about Hamlet are really about the *word* 'Hamlet'.

But it is obvious that, in most cases, we are not speaking of words, but of what the words mean. And this brings us back to the argument of Parmenides, that if a word can be used significantly it must mean *something*, not nothing, and therefore what the word means must in some sense exist.

What, then, are we to say about George Washington? It seems we have only two alternatives: one is to say that he still exists; the other is to say that, when *we* use the words 'George Washington', we are not really speaking of the man who bore that name. Either seems a paradox, but the latter is less of a paradox, and I shall try to show a sense in which it is true.

Parmenides assumes that words have a constant meaning; this is really the basis of his argument, which he supposes unquestionable. But although the dictionary or the encyclopaedia gives what may be called the official and socially sanctioned meaning of a word, no two people who use the same word have just the same thought in their minds.

George Washington himself could use his name and the word 'I' as synonyms. He could perceive his own thoughts and the movements of his body, and could therefore use his name with a fuller meaning than was possible for any one else. His friends, when in his presence, could perceive the movements of his body, and could divine his thoughts; to them, the name 'George Washington' still denoted something concrete in their own experience. After his death they had to substitute memories for perceptions, which involved a change in the mental processes taking place when they used his name. For us, who never knew him, the mental processes are again different. We may think of his picture, and say to ourselves 'yes, that man'. We may think 'the first President of the United States'. If we are very ignorant, he may be to us merely 'The man who was called "George Washington".' Whatever the name suggests to us, it must be not the man himself, since we never knew him, but something now present to sense or memory or thought. This shows the fallacy of the argument of Parmenides.

This perpetual change in the meanings of words is concealed by the fact that, in general, the change makes no difference to the truth or falsehood of the propositions in which the words occur. If you take any true sentence in which the name 'George Washington' occurs, it will, as a rule, remain true if you substitute the phrase 'the first President of the United States'. There are exceptions to this rule. Before Washington's election, a man might say 'I hope George Washington will be the first President of the United States,' but he would not say 'I hope the first President of the United States will be the first President of the United States' unless he had an unusual passion for the law of identity. But it is easy to make a rule for excluding these exceptional cases, and in those that remain you may substitute for 'George Washington' any descriptive phrase that applies to him alone. And it is only by means of such phrases that we know what we know about him.

Parmenides contends that, since we can now know what is commonly regarded as past, it cannot really be past, but must, in some sense, exist now. Hence he infers that there is no such thing as change. What we have been saying about George Washington meets this argument. It may be said, in a sense, that we have no knowledge of the past. When you recollect, the recollection occurs now, and is not identical with the event recollected. But the recollection affords a *description* of the past event, and for most practical purposes it is unnecessary to distinguish between the description and what it describes.

This whole argument shows how easy it is to draw metaphysical conclusions from language, and how the only way to avoid fallacious arguments of this kind is to push the logical and psychological study of language further than has been done by most metaphysicians.

I think, however, that, if Parmenides could return from the dead and read what I have been saying, he would regard it as very superficial. 'How do you know,' he would ask, 'that your statements about George Washington refer to a past time? By your own account, the direct reference is to things now present; your recollections, for instance, happen now, not at the time that you think you recollect. If memory is to be accepted as a source of knowledge, the past must be before the mind *now*, and must therefore in some sense still exist.'

I will not attempt to meet this argument now; it requires a discussion of memory, which is a difficult subject. I have put the argument here to remind the reader that philosophical theories, if they are important, can generally be revived in a new form after being refuted as originally stated. Refutations are seldom final; in most cases, they are only a prelude to further refinements.

What subsequent philosophy, down to quite modern times, accepted from Parmenides, was not the impossibility of all change, which was too violent a paradox, but the indestructibility of *substance*. The word 'substance' did not occur in his immediate successors, but the *concept* is already present in their speculations. A substance was supposed to be the persistent subject of varying predicates. As such it became, and remained for more than two thousand years, one of the fundamental concepts of philosophy, psychology, physics, and theology. I shall have much to say about it at a later stage. For the present, I am merely concerned to note that it was introduced as a way of doing justice to the arguments of Parmenides without denying obvious facts.

Chapter VI

EMPEDOCLES

THE mixture of philosopher, prophet, man of science, and charlatan, which we found already in Pythagoras, was exemplified very completely in Empedocles, who flourished about 440 B.C., and was thus a younger contemporary of Parmenides, though his doctrine had in some ways more affinity with that of Heraclitus. He was a citizen of Acragas, on the south coast of Sicily; he was a democratic politician, who at the same time claimed to be a god. In most Greek cities, and especially in those of Sicily, there was a constant conflict between democracy and tyranny; the leaders of whichever party was at the moment defeated were executed or exiled. Those who were exiled seldom scrupled to enter into negotiations with the enemies of Greece—Persia in the East, Carthage in the West. Empedocles, in due course, was banished, but he appears, after his banishment, to have preferred the career of a sage to that of an intriguing refugee. It seems probable that in youth he was more or less Orphic; that before his exile he combined politics and science; and that it was only in later life, as an exile, that he became a prophet.

Legend had much to say about Empedocles. He was supposed to have worked miracles, or what seemed such, sometimes by magic, sometimes by means of his scientific knowledge. He could control the winds, we are told; he restored to life a woman who had seemed dead for thirty days; finally, it is said, he died by leaping into th∴ crater of Etna to prove that he was a god. In the words of the poet:

> Great Empedocles, that ardent soul,
> Leapt into Etna, and was roasted whole.

Matthew Arnold wrote a poem on this subject, but, although one of his worst, it does not contain the above couplet.

Like Parmenides, Empedocles wrote in verse. Lucretius, who was influenced by him, praised him highly as a poet, but on this subject opinions were divided. Since only fragments of his writings have survived, his poetic merit must remain in doubt.

It is necessary to deal separately with his science and his religion, as they are not consistent with each other. I shall consider first his science, then his philosophy, and finally his religion.

71

His most important contribution to science was his discovery of air as a separate substance This he proved by the observation that when a bucket or any similar vessel is put upside down into water, the water does not enter into the bucket. He says:

'When a girl, playing with a water-clock of shining brass, puts the orifice of the pipe upon her comely hand, and dips the water-clock into the yielding mass of silvery water, the stream does not then flow into the vessel, but the bulk of the air inside, pressing upon the close-packed perforations, keeps it out till she uncovers the compressed stream; but then air escapes and an equal volume of water runs in.'

This passage occurs in an explanation of respiration.

He also discovered at least one example of centrifugal force: that if a cup of water is whirled round at the end of a string, the water does not come out.

He knew that there is sex in plants, and he had a theory (somewhat fantastic, it must be admitted) of evolution and the survival of the fittest. Originally, 'countless tribes of mortal creatures were scattered abroad endowed with all manner of forms, a wonder to behold.' There were heads without necks, arms without shoulders, eyes without foreheads, solitary limbs seeking for union. These things joined together as each might chance; there were shambling creatures with countless hands, creatures with faces and breasts looking in different directions, creatures with the bodies of oxen and the faces of men, and others with the faces of oxen and the bodies of men. There were hermaphrodites combining the natures of men and women, but sterile. In the end, only certain forms survived.

As regards astronomy : he knew that the moon shines by reflected light, and thought that this is also true of the sun; he said that light takes time to travel, but so little time that we cannot observe it; he knew that solar eclipses are caused by the interposition of the moon, a fact which he seems to have learnt from Anaxagoras.

He was the founder of the Italian school of medicine, and the medical school which sprang from him influenced both Plato and Aristotle. According to Burnet (p. 234), it affected the whole tendency of scientific and philosophical thinking.

All this shows the scientific vigour of his time, which was not equalled in the later ages of Greece.

I come now to his cosmology. It was he, as already mentioned, who established earth, air, fire, and water as the four elements (though the word 'element' was not used by him). Each of these was everlasting, but they could be mixed in different proportions and thus produce the changing complex substances that we find in the world. They were combined by Love and separated by Strife. Love and Strife were, for Empedocles, primitive substances on a level with earth, air, fire, and water. There were periods when Love was in the ascendant, and others when Strife was the stronger. There had been a golden age when Love was completely victorious. In that age, men worshipped only the Cyprian Aphrodite (fr. 128). The changes in the world are not governed by any purpose, but only by Chance and Necessity. There is a cycle: when the elements have been thoroughly mixed by Love, Strife gradually sorts them out again; when Strife has separated them, Love gradually reunites them. Thus every compound substance is temporary; only the elements, together with Love and Strife, are everlasting.

There is a similarity to Heraclitus, but a softening, since it is not Strife alone, but Strife and Love together, that produce change. Plato couples Heraclitus and Empedocles in the *Sophist* (242):

There are Ionian, and in more recent time Sicilian, muses, who have arrived at the conclusion that to unite the two principles (of the One and the Many), is safer, and to say that being is one and many, and that these are held together by enmity and friendship, ever parting, ever meeting, as the severer Muses assert, while the gentler ones do not insist on the perpetual strife and peace, but admit a relaxation and alternation of them; peace and unity sometimes prevailing under the sway of Aphrodite, and then again plurality and war, by reason of a principle of strife.

Empedocles held that the material world is a sphere; that in the Golden Age Strife was outside and Love inside; then, gradually, Strife entered and Love was expelled, until, at the worst, Strife will be wholly within and Love wholly without the sphere. Then—though for what reason is not clear—an opposite movement begins, until the Golden Age returns, but not for ever. The whole cycle is then repeated. One might have supposed that either extreme could be stable, but that is not the view of Empedocles. He wished to explain motion while taking account of the arguments of Parmenides, and he had no wish to arrive, at any stage, at an unchanging universe.

The views of Empedocles on religion are, in the main, Pythagorean. In a fragment which, in all likelihood, refers to Pythagoras, he says: 'There was among them a man of rare knowledge, most skilled in all manner of wise works, a man who had won the utmost wealth of wisdom; for whensoever he strained with all his mind, he easily saw everything of all the things that are, in ten, yea twenty lifetimes of men.' In the Golden Age, as already mentioned, men worshipped only Aphrodite, 'and the altar did not reek with pure bull's blood, but this was held in the greatest abomination among men, to eat the goodly limbs after tearing out the life'.

At one time he speaks of himself exuberantly as a god:

Friends, that inhabit the great city looking down on the yellow rock of Acragas, up by the citadel, busy in goodly works, harbour of honour for the stranger, men unskilled in meanness, all hail. I go about among you an immortal god, no mortal now, honoured among all as is meet, crowned with fillets and flowery garlands. Straightway, whenever I enter with these in my train, both men and women, into the flourishing towns, is reverence done me; they go after me in countless throngs, asking of me what is the way to gain; some desiring oracles, while some, who for many a weary day have been pierced by the grievous pangs of all manner of sickness, beg to hear from me the word of healing. . . . But why do I harp on these things, as if it were any great matter that I should surpass mortal, perishable men?'

At another time he feels himself a great sinner, undergoing expiation for his impiety:

There is an oracle of Necessity, an ancient ordinance of the gods, eternal and sealed fast by broad oaths, that whenever one of the daemons, whose portion is length of days, has sinfully polluted his hands with blood, or followed strife and forsworn himself, he must wander thrice ten thousand years from the abodes of the blessed, being born throughout the time in all manners of mortal forms, changing one toilsome path of life for another. For the mighty Air drives him into the Sea, and the Sea spews him forth upon the dry Earth; Earth tosses him into the beams of the blazing Sun, and he flings him back to the eddies of Air. One takes him from the other, and all reject him. One of these I now am, an exile and a wanderer from the gods, for that I put my trust in an insensate strife.

What his sin had been, we do not know; perhaps nothing that we should think very grievous. For he says:

'Ah, woe is me that the pitiless day of death did not destroy me ere ever I wrought evil deeds of devouring with my lips! . . .

'Abstain wholly from laurel leaves . . .

'Wretches, utter wretches, keep your hands from beans!'

So perhaps he had done nothing worse than munching laurel leaves or guzzling beans.

The most famous passage in Plato, in which he compares this world to a cave, in which we see only shadows of the realities in the bright world above, is anticipated by Empedocles; its origin is in the teaching of the Orphics.

There are some—presumably those who abstain from sin through many incarnations—who at last achieve immortal bliss in the company of the gods:

But at the last, they[1] appear among mortal men as prophets, song-writers, physicians, and princes; and thence they rise up as gods exalted in honour, sharing the hearth of the other gods and the same table, free from human woes, safe from destiny, and incapable of hurt.

In all this, it would seem, there is very little that was not already contained in the teaching of Orphism and Pythagoreanism.

The originality of Empedocles, outside science, consists in the doctrine of the four elements, and in the use of the two principles of Love and Strife to explain change.

He rejected monism, and regarded the course of nature as regulated by chance and necessity rather than by purpose. In these respects his philosophy was more scientific than those of Parmenides, Plato, and Aristotle. In other respects, it is true, he acquiesced in current superstitions; but in this he was no worse than many more recent men of science.

---

[1] It does not appear who 'they' are, but one may assume that they are those who have preserved purity.

Chapter VII

ATHENS IN RELATION TO CULTURE

THE greatness of Athens begins at the time of the two Persian wars (490 B.C. and 480-79 B.C.). Before that time Ionia and Magna Graecia (the Greek cities of south Italy and Sicily) produced the great men. The victory of Athens against the Persian king Darius at Marathon (490), and of the combined Greek fleets against his son and successor Xerxes (480) under Athenian leadership, gave Athens great prestige. The Ionians in the islands and on part of the mainland of Asia Minor had rebelled against Persia, and their liberation was effected by Athens after the Persians had been driven from the mainland of Greece. In this operation the Spartans, who cared only about their own territory, took no part. Thus Athens became the predominant partner in an alliance against Persia. By the constitution of the alliance, any constituent State was bound to contribute either a specified number of ships, or the cost of them. Most chose the latter, and thus Athens acquired naval supremacy over the other allies, and gradually transformed the alliance into an Athenian Empire. Athens became rich, and prospered under the wise leadership of Pericles, who governed, by the free choice of the citizens, for about thirty years, until his fall in 430 B.C.

The age of Pericles was the happiest and most glorious time in the history of Athens. Aeschylus, who had fought in the Persian wars, inaugurated Greek tragedy; one of his tragedies, the *Persae*, departing from the custom of choosing Homeric subjects, deals with the defeat of Xerxes. He was quickly followed by Sophocles, and Sophocles by Euripides. Both extend into the dark days of the Peloponnesian War that followed the fall and death of Pericles, and Euripides reflects in his plays the scepticism of the later period. His contemporary Aristophanes, the comic poet, makes fun of all isms from the standpoint of robust and limited common sense; more particularly, he holds up Socrates to obloquy as one who denies the existence of Zeus and dabbles in unholy pseudo-scientific mysteries.

Athens had been captured by Xerxes, and the temples on the Acropolis had been destroyed by fire. Pericles devoted himself to their reconstruction. The Parthenon and the other temples whose ruins remain to impress our age were built by him. Pheidias the sculptor was employed by the State to make colossal statues of gods

76

and goddesses. At the end of this period, Athens was the most beautiful and splendid city of the Hellenic world.

Herodotus, the father of history, was a native of Halicarnassus, in Asia Minor, but lived in Athens, was encouraged by the Athenian State, and wrote his account of the Persian wars from the Athenian point of view.

The achievements of Athens in the time of Pericles are perhaps the most astonishing thing in all history. Until that time, Athens had lagged behind many other Greek cities; neither in art nor in literature had it produced any great man (except Solon, who was primarily a lawgiver). Suddenly, under the stimulus of victory and wealth and the need of reconstruction, architects, sculptors, and dramatists, who remain unsurpassed to the present day, produced works which dominated the future down to modern times. This is the more surprising when we consider the smallness of the population involved. Athens at its maximum, about 430 B.C., is estimated to have numbered about 230,000 (including slaves), and the surrounding territory of rural Attica probably contained a rather smaller population. Never before or since has anything approaching the same proportion of the inhabitants of any area shown itself capable of work of the highest excellence.

In philosophy, Athens contributes only two great names, Socrates and Plato. Plato belongs to a somewhat later period, but Socrates passed his youth and early manhood under Pericles. The Athenians were sufficiently interested in philosophy to listen eagerly to teachers from other cities. The Sophists were sought after by young men who wished to learn the art of disputation; in the *Protagoras*, the Platonic Socrates gives an amusing satirical description of the ardent disciples hanging on the words of the eminent visitor. Pericles, as we shall see, imported Anaxagoras, from whom Socrates professed to have learned the pre-eminence of mind in creation.

Most of Plato's dialogues are supposed by him to take place during the time of Pericles, and they give an agreeable picture of life among the rich. Plato belonged to an aristocratic Athenian family, and grew up in the tradition of the period before war and democracy had destroyed the wealth and security of the upper classes. His young men, who have no need to work, spend most of their leisure in the pursuit of science and mathematics and philosophy; they know Homer almost by heart, and are critical judges of the merits of professional reciters of poetry. The art of deductive reasoning had been lately discovered, and afforded the excitement of new theories, both true and false, over the whole field of knowledge. It was possible in that age, as in few others, to be both intelligent and happy, and happy through intelligence.

But the balance of forces which produced this golden age was precarious. It was threatened both from within and from without —from within by the democracy, and from without by Sparta. To understand what happened after Pericles, we must consider briefly the earlier history of Attica.

Attica, at the beginning of the historical period, was a self-supporting little agricultural region; Athens, its capital, was not large, but contained a growing population of artisans and skilled artificers who desired to dispose of their produce abroad. Gradually it was found more profitable to cultivate vines and olives rather than grain, and to import grain, chiefly from the coast of the Black Sea. This form of cultivation required more capital than the cultivation of grain, and the small farmers got into debt. Attica, like other Greek states, had been a monarchy in the Homeric age, but the king became a merely religious official without political power. The government fell into the hands of the aristocracy, who oppressed both the country farmers and the urban artisans. A compromise in the direction of democracy was effected by Solon early in the sixth century, and much of his work survived through a subsequent period of tyranny under Peisistratus and his sons. When this period came to an end, the aristocrats, as the opponents of tyranny, were able to recommend themselves to the democracy. Until the fall of Pericles, democratic processes gave power to the aristocracy, as in nineteenth-century England. But towards the end of his life the leaders of the Athenian democracy began to demand a larger share of political power. At the same time, his imperialist policy, with which the economic prosperity of Athens was bound up, caused increasing friction with Sparta, leading at last to the Peloponnesian War (431-404), in which Athens was completely defeated.

In spite of political collapse, the prestige of Athens survived, and throughout almost a millennium philosophy was centred there. Alexandria eclipsed Athens in mathematics and science, but Plato and Aristotle had made Athens philosophically supreme. The Academy, where Plato had taught, survived all other schools, and persisted, as an island of paganism, for two centuries after the conversion of the Roman Empire to Christianity. At last, in A.D. 529, it was closed by Justinian because of his religious bigotry, and the Dark Ages descended upon Europe.

Chapter VIII

ANAXAGORAS

THE philosopher Anaxagoras, though not the equal of Pythagoras, Heraclitus, or Parmenides, has nevertheless a considerable historical importance. He was an Ionian, and carried on the scientific, rationalist tradition of Ionia. He was the first to introduce philosophy to the Athenians, and the first to suggest mind as the primary cause of physical changes.

He was born at Clazomenae, in Ionia, about the year 500 B.C., but he spent about thirty years of his life in Athens, approximately from 462 to 432 B.C. He was probably induced to come by Pericles, who was bent on civilizing his fellow-townsmen. Perhaps Aspasia, who came from Miletus, introduced him to Pericles. Plato, in the *Phaedrus*, says:

Pericles 'fell in, it seems with Anaxagoras, who was a scientific man; and satiating himself with the theory of things on high, and having attained to a knowledge of the true nature of intellect and folly, which were just what the discourses of Anaxagoras were mainly about, he drew from that source whatever was of a nature to further him in the art of speech.'

It is said that Anaxagoras also influenced Euripides, but this is more doubtful.

The citizens of Athens, like those of other cities in other ages and continents, showed a certain hostility to those who attempted to introduce a higher level of culture than that to which they were accustomed. When Pericles was growing old, his opponents began a campaign against him by attacking his friends. They accused Pheidias of embezzling some of the gold that was to be employed on his statues. They passed a law permitting impeachment of those who did not practise religion and taught theories about 'the things on high'. Under this law, they prosecuted Anaxagoras, who was accused of teaching that the sun was a red-hot stone and the moon was earth. (The same accusation was repeated by the prosecutors of Socrates, who made fun of them for being out of date.) What happened is not certain, except that Anaxagoras had to leave Athens. It seems probable that Pericles got him out of prison and managed to get him away. He returned to Ionia, where he founded a school.

In accordance with his will, the anniversary of his death was kept as a schoolchildren's holiday.

Anaxagoras held that everything is infinitely divisible, and that even the smallest portion of matter contains some of each element. Things appear to be that of which they contain most. Thus, for example, everything contains some fire, but we only call it fire if that element preponderates. Like Empedocles, he argues against the void, saying that the clepsydra or an inflated skin shows that there is air where there seems to be nothing.

He differed from his predecessors in regarding mind (*nous*) as a substance which enters into the composition of living things, and distinguishes them from dead matter. In everything, he says, there is a portion of everything except mind, and some things contain mind also. Mind has power over all things that have life; it is infinite and self-ruled, and is mixed with nothing. Except as regards mind, everything, however small, contains portions of all opposites, such as hot and cold, white and black. He maintained that snow is black (in part).

Mind is the source of all motion. It causes a rotation, which is gradually spreading throughout the world, and is causing the lightest things to go to the circumference, and the heaviest to fall towards the centre. Mind is uniform, and is just as good in animals as in man. Man's apparent superiority is due to the fact that he has hands; all seeming differences of intelligence are really due to bodily differences.

Both Aristotle and the Platonic Socrates complain that Anaxagoras, after introducing mind, makes very little use of it. Aristotle points out that he only introduces mind as a cause when he knows no other. Whenever he can, he gives a mechanical explanation He rejected necessity and chance as giving the origins of things; nevertheless, there was no 'Providence' in his cosmology. He does not seem to have thought much about ethics or religion; probably he was an atheist, as his prosecutors maintained. All his predecessors influenced him, except Pythagoras. The influence of Parmenides was the same in his case as in that of Empedocles.

In science he had great merit. It was he who first explained that the moon shines by reflected light, though there is a cryptic fragment in Parmenides suggesting that he also knew this. Anaxagoras gave the correct theory of eclipses, and knew that the moon is below the sun. The sun and stars, he said, are fiery stones, but we do not feel the heat of the stars because they are too distant. The sun is larger than the Peloponnesus. The moon has mountains, and (he thought) inhabitants.

Anaxagoras is said to have been of the school of Anaximenes;

certainly he kept alive the rationalist and scientific tradition of the Ionians. One does not find in him the ethical and religious pre-occupations which, passing from the Pythagoreans to Socrates and from Socrates to Plato, brought an obscurantist bias into Greek philosophy. He is not quite in the first rank, but he is important as the first to bring philosophy to Athens, and as one of the influences that helped to form Socrates.

Chapter IX

THE ATOMISTS

THE founders of atomism were two, Leucippus and Democritus. It is difficult to disentangle them, because they are generally mentioned together, and apparently some of the works of Leucippus were subsequently attributed to Democritus.

Leucippus, who seems to have flourished about 440 B.C.,[1] came from Miletus, and carried on the scientific rationalist philosophy associated with that city. He was much influenced by Parmenides and Zeno. So little is known of him that Epicurus (a later follower of Democritus) was thought to have denied his existence altogether, and some moderns have revived this theory. There are, however, a number of allusions to him in Aristotle, and it seems incredible that these (which include textual quotations) would have occurred if he had been merely a myth.

Democritus is a much more definite figure. He was a native of Abdera in Thrace; as for his date, he stated that he was young when Anaxagoras was old, say about 432 B.C., and he is taken to have flourished about 420 B.C. He travelled widely in southern and eastern lands in search of knowledge; he perhaps spent a considerable time in Egypt, and he certainly visited Persia. He then returned to Abdera, where he remained. Zeller calls him 'superior to all earlier and contemporary philosophers in wealth of knowledge, and to most in acuteness and logical correctness of thinking'.

Democritus was a contemporary of Socrates and the Sophists, and should, on purely chronological grounds, be treated somewhat later in our history. The difficulty is that he is so hard to separate from Leucippus. On this ground, I am considering him before Socrates and the Sophists, although part of his philosophy was intended as an answer to Protagoras, his fellow-townsman and the most eminent of the Sophists. Protagoras, when he visited Athens, was received enthusiastically; Democritus, on the other hand, says: 'I went to Athens, and no one knew me.' For a long time, his philosophy was ignored in Athens; 'It is not clear,' says Burnet, 'that Plato knew anything about Democritus. . . . Aristotle, on the other hand, knows Democritus well; for he too was an Ionian from the North.'[2]

[1] Cyril Bailey, *The Greek Atomists and Epicurus*, estimates that he flourished about 430 B.C. or a little earlier.   [2] *From Thales to Plato*, p. 193.

Plato never mentions him in the Dialogues, but is said by Diogenes Laertius to have disliked him so much that he wished all his books burnt. Heath esteems him highly as a mathematician.[1]

The fundamental ideas of the common philosophy of Leucippus and Democritus were due to the former, but as regards the working out it is hardly possible to disentangle them, nor is it, for our purposes, important to make the attempt. Leucippus, if not Democritus, was led to atomism in the attempt to mediate between monism and pluralism, as represented by Parmenides and Empedocles respectively. Their point of view was remarkably like that of modern science, and avoided most of the faults to which Greek speculation was prone. They believed that everything is composed of atoms, which are physically, but not geometrically, indivisible; that between the atoms there is empty space; that atoms are indestructible; that they always have been, and always will be, in motion; that there are an infinite number of atoms, and even of kinds of atoms, the differences being as regards shape and size. Aristotle[2] asserts that, according to the atomists, atoms also differ as regards heat, the spherical atoms, which compose fire, being the hottest; and as regards weight, he quotes Democritus as saying 'The more any indivisible exceeds, the heavier it is.' But the question whether atoms are originally possessed of weight in the theories of the atomists is a controversial one.

The atoms were always in motion, but there is disagreement among commentators as to the character of the original motion. Some, especially Zeller, hold that the atoms were thought to be always falling, and that the heavier ones fell faster; they thus caught up the lighter ones, there were impacts, and the atoms were deflected like billiard balls. This was certainly the view of Epicurus, who in most respects based his theories on those of Democritus, while trying, rather unintelligently, to take account of Aristotle's criticisms. But there is considerable reason to think that weight was not an original property of the atoms of Leucippus and Democritus. It seems more probable that, on their view, atoms were originally moving at random, as in the modern kinetic theory of gases. Democritus said there was neither up nor down in the infinite void, and compared the movement of atoms in the soul to that of motes in a sunbeam when there is no wind. This is a much more intelligent view than that of Epicurus, and I think we may assume it to have been that of Leucippus and Democritus.[3]

[1] *Greek Mathematics*, Vol. I, p. 176.
[2] On *Generation and Corruption*, 316ᵃ.
[3] This interpretation is adopted by Burnet, and also, at least as regards Leucippus, by Bailey (*op. cit.*, p. 83).

As a result of collisions, collections of atoms came to form vortices. The rest proceeded much as in Anaxagoras, but it was an advance to explain the vortices mechanically rather than as due to the action of mind.

It was common in antiquity to reproach the atomists with attributing everything to chance. They were, on the contrary, strict determinists, who believed that everything happens in accordance with natural laws. Democritus explicity denied that anything can happen by chance.[1] Leucippus, though his existence is questioned, is known to have said one thing: 'Naught happens for nothing, but everything from a ground and of necessity.' It is true that he gave no reason why the world should originally have been as it was; this, perhaps, might have been attributed to chance. But when once the world existed, its further development was unalterably fixed by mechanical principles. Aristotle and others reproached him and Democritus for not accounting for the original motion of the atoms, but in this the atomists were more scientific than their critics. Causation must start from something, and wherever it starts no cause can be assigned for the initial datum. The world may be attributed to a Creator, but even then the Creator Himself is unaccounted for. The theory of the atomists, in fact, was more nearly that of modern science than any other theory propounded in antiquity.

The atomists, unlike Socrates, Plato, and Aristotle, sought to explain the world without introducing the notion of *purpose* or *final cause*. The 'final cause' of an occurrence is an event in the future for the sake of which the occurrence takes place. In human affairs, this conception is applicable. Why does the baker make bread? Because people will be hungry. Why are railways built? Because people will wish to travel. In such cases, things are explained by the purpose they serve. When we ask 'why?' concerning an event, we may mean either of two things. We may mean: 'What purpose did this event serve?' or we may mean: 'What earlier circumstances caused this event?' The answer to the former question is a teleological explanation, or an explanation by final causes; the answer to the latter question is a mechanistic explanation. I do not see how it could have been known in advance which of these two questions science ought to ask, or whether it ought to ask both. But experience has shown that the mechanistic question leads to scientific knowledge, while the teleological question does not. The atomists asked the mechanistic question, and gave a mechanistic answer. Their successors, until the Renaissance, were

---

[1] See Bailey, *op. cit.*, p. 121, on the determinism of Democritus.

more interested in the teleological question, and thus led science up a blind alley.

In regard to both questions alike, there is a limitation which is often ignored, both in popular thought and in philosophy. Neither question can be asked intelligibly about reality as a whole (including God), but only about parts of it. As regards the teleological explanation, it usually arrives, before long, at a Creator, or at least an Artificer, whose purposes are realized in the course of nature. But if a man is so obstinately teleological as to continue to ask what purpose is served by the Creator, it becomes obvious that his question is impious. It is, moreover, unmeaning, since, to make it significant, we should have to suppose the Creator created by some super-Creator whose purposes He served. The conception of purpose, therefore, is only applicable within reality, not to reality as a whole.

A not dissimilar argument applies to mechanistic explanations. One event is caused by another, the other by a third, and so on. But if we ask for a cause of the whole, we are driven again to the Creator, who must Himself be uncaused. All causal explanations, therefore must have an arbitrary beginning. That is why it is no defect in the theory of the atomists to have left the original movements of the atoms unaccounted for.

It must not be supposed that their reasons for their theories were *wholly* empirical. The atomic theory was revived in modern times to explain the facts of chemistry, but these facts were not known to the Greeks. There was no very sharp distinction, in ancient times, between empirical observation and logical argument. Parmenides, it is true, treated observed facts with contempt, but Empedocles and Anaxagoras would combine much of their metaphysics with observations on water-clocks and whirling buckets. Until the Sophists, no philosopher seems to have doubted that a complete metaphysic and cosmology could be established by a combination of much reasoning and some observation. By good luck, the atomists hit on a hypothesis for which, more than two thousand years later, some evidence was found, but their belief, in their day, was none the less destitute of any solid foundation.[1]

Like the other philosophers of his time, Leucippus was concerned to find a way of reconciling the arguments of Parmenides with the obvious fact of motion and change. As Aristotle says:[2]

'Although these opinions [those of Parmenides] appear to follow logically in a dialectical discussion, yet to believe them seems next door to madness when one considers the facts. For indeed no lunatic

---

[1] On the logical and mathematical grounds for the theories of the atomists, see Gaston Milhand, *Les Philosophes Géomètres de la Grèce*, chap. iv.

[2] *On Generation and Corruption*, 325ᵃ.

seems to be so far out of his senses as to suppose that fire and ice are "one"; it is only between what *is* right and what *seems* right from habit that some people are mad enough to see no difference.'

Leucippus, however, thought he had a theory which harmonized with sense-perception and would not abolish either coming-to-be and passing-away or motion and the multiplicity of things. He made these concessions to the facts of perception: on the other hand, he conceded to the Monists that there could be no motion without a void. The result is a theory which he states as follows: 'The void is a *not-being*, and no part of what *is* is a *not-being*; for what *is* in the strict sense of the term is an absolute plenum. This plenum, however, is not *one*; on the contrary, it is a *many* infinite in number and invisible owing to the minuteness of their bulk. The *many* move in the void (for there is a void): and by coming together they produce *coming-to-be*, while by separating they produce *passing-away*. Moreover, they act and suffer action whenever they chance to be in contact (for there they are not *one*), and they generate by being put together and become intertwined. From the genuinely *one*, on the other hand, there could never have come to be a multiplicity, nor from the genuinely many a *one*: that is impossible.'

It will be seen that there was one point on which everybody so far was agreed, namely that there could be no motion in a plenum. In this, all alike were mistaken. There can be *cyclic* motion in a plenum, provided it has always existed. The idea was that a thing could only move into an empty place, and that, in a plenum, there are no empty places. It might be contended, perhaps validly, that motion could never *begin* in a plenum, but it cannot be validly maintained that it could not occur at all. To the Greeks, however, it seemed that one must either acquiesce in the unchanging world of Parmenides, or admit the void.

Now the arguments of Parmenides against not-being seemed logically irrefutable against the void, and they were reinforced by the discovery that where there seems to be nothing there is air. (This is an example of the confused mixture of logic and observation that was common.) We may put the Parmenidean position in this way: 'You say there *is* the void; therefore the void is not nothing; therefore it is not the void.' It cannot be said that the atomists *answered* this argument; they merely proclaimed that they proposed to ignore it, on the ground that motion is a fact of experience, and therefore there *must* be a void, however difficult it may be to conceive.[1]

[1] Bailey (*op. cit.*, p. 75) maintains, on the contrary, that Leucippus had an answer, which was 'extremely subtle'. It consisted essentially in admitting the existence of something (the void) which was not corporeal. Similarly Burnet says: 'It is a curious fact that the Atomists, who are commonly

Let us consider the subsequent history of this problem. The first and most obvious way of avoiding the logical difficulty is to distinguish between *matter* and *space*. According to this view, space is not nothing, but is of the nature of a receptacle, which may or may not have any given part filled with matter. Aristotle say; (*Physics*, 208*b*): 'The theory that the void exists involves the existence of place: for one would define void as place bereft of body.' This view is set forth with the utmost explicitness by Newton, who asserts the existence of absolute space, and accordingly distinguishes absolute from relative motion. In the Copernican controversy, both sides (however little they may have realized it) were committed to this view, since they thought there was a difference between saying 'the heavens revolve from east to west' and saying 'the earth rotates from west to east.' If all motion is relative, these two statements are merely different ways of saying the same thing, like 'John is the father of James' and 'James is the son of John.' But if all motion is relative, and space is not substantial, we are left with the Parmenidean arguments against the void on our hands.

Descartes, whose arguments are of just the same sort as those of early Greek philosophers, said that extension is the essence of matter, and therefore there is matter everywhere. For him, extension is an adjective, not a substantive; its substantive is matter, and without its substantive it cannot exist. Empty space, to him, is as absurd as happiness without a sentient being who is happy. Leibniz, on somewhat different grounds, also believed in the plenum, but he maintained that space is merely a system of relations. On this subject there was a famous controversy between him and Newton, the latter represented by Clarke. The controversy remained undecided until the time of Einstein, whose theory conclusively gave the victory to Leibniz.

The modern physicist, while he still believes that matter is in some sense atomic, does not believe in empty space. Where there is not matter, there is still *something*, notably light-waves. Matter no longer has the lofty status that it acquired in philosophy through the arguments of Parmenides. It is not unchanging substance, but merely a way of grouping events. Some events belong to groups that can be regarded as material things; others, such as light-waves, do not. It is the events that are the *stuff* of the world, and each of them is of brief duration. In this respect, modern physics is on the side of Heraclitus as against Parmenides. But it was on the side of Parmenides until Einstein and quantum theory.

As regards space, the modern view is that it is neither a sub-

regarded as the great materialists of antiquity, were actually the first to say distinctly that a thing might be real without being a body.'

stance, as Newton maintained, and as Leucippus and Democritus ought to have said, nor an adjective of extended bodies, as Descartes thought, but a system of relations, as Leibniz held. It is not by any means clear whether this view is compatible with the existence of the void. Perhaps, as a matter of abstract logic, it can be reconciled with the void. We might say that, between any two things, there is a certain greater or smaller *distance*, and that distance does not imply the existence of intermediate things. Such a point of view, however, would be impossible to utilize in modern physics. Since Einstein, distance is between *events*, not between *things*, and involves time as well as space. It is essentially a causal conception, and in modern physics there is no action at a distance. All this, however, is based upon empirical rather than logical grounds. Moreover the modern view cannot be stated except in terms of differential equations, and would therefore be unintelligible to the philosophers of antiquity.

It would seem, accordingly, that the logical development of the views of the atomists is the Newtonian theory of absolute space, which meets the difficulty of attributing reality to not-being. To this theory there are no *logical* objections. The chief objection is that absolute space is absolutely unknowable, and cannot therefore be a necessary hypothesis in an empirical science. The more practical objection is that physics can get on without it. But the world of the atomists remains logically possible, and is more akin to the actual world than is the world of any other of the ancient philosophers.

Democritus worked out his theories in considerable detail, and some of the working-out is interesting. Each atom, he said, was impenetrable and indivisible because it contained no void. When you use a knife to cut an apple, the knife has to find empty places where it can penetrate; if the apple contained no void, it would be infinitely hard and therefore physically indivisible. Each atom is internally unchanging, and in fact a Parmenidean One. The only things that atoms do are to move and hit each other, and sometimes to combine when they happen to have shapes that are capable of interlocking. They are of all sorts of shapes; fire is composed of small spherical atoms, and so is the soul. Atoms, by collision, produce vortices, which generate bodies and ultimately worlds.[1] There are many worlds, some growing, some decaying; some may have no sun or moon, some several. Every world has a beginning and an end. A world may be destroyed by collision with a larger world. This cosmology may be summarized in Shelley's words:

[1] On the way in which this was supposed to happen, see Bailey, *op. cit.*, p. 138 ff.

Worlds on worlds are rolling ever
From creation to decay,
Like the bubbles on a river
Sparkling, bursting, borne away.

Life developed out of the primeval slime. There is some fire everywhere in a living body, but most in the brain or in the breast. (On
this, authorities differ.) Thought is a kind of motion, and is thus
able to cause motion elsewhere. Perception and thought are physical
processes. Perception is of two sorts, one of the senses, one of the
understanding. Perceptions of the latter sort depend only on the
things perceived, while those of the former sort depend also on our
senses, and are therefore apt to be deceptive. Like Locke, Democritus held that such qualities as warmth, taste, and colour are not
really in the object, but are due to our sense-organs, while such
qualities as weight, density, and hardness are really in the object.

Democritus was a thorough-going materialist; for him, as we
have seen, the soul was composed of atoms, and thought was a
physical process. There was no purpose in the universe; there were
only atoms governed by mechanical laws. He disbelieved in popular
religion, and he argued against the *nous* of Anaxagoras. In ethics
he considered cheerfulness the goal of life, and regarded moderation
and culture as the best means to it. He disliked everything violent
and passionate; he disapproved of sex, because, he said, it involved
the overwhelming of consciousness by pleasure. He valued friendship, but thought ill of women, and did not desire children, because
their education interferes with philosophy. In all this, he was very
like Jeremy Bentham; he was equally so in his love of what the
Greeks called democracy.[1]

Democritus—such, at least, is my opinion—is the last of the
Greek philosophers to be free from a certain fault which vitiated
all later ancient and medieval thought. All the philosophers we have
been considering so far were engaged in a disinterested effort to
understand the world. They thought it easier to understand than it
is, but without this optimism they would not have had the courage
to make a beginning. Their attitude, in the main, was genuinely
scientific whenever it did not merely embody the prejudices of
their age. But it was not *only* scientific; it was imaginative and
vigorous and filled with the delight of adventure. They were interested in everything—meteors and eclipses, fishes and whirlwinds,
religion and morality; with a penetrating intellect they combined
the zest of children.

[1] 'Poverty in a democracy is as much to be preferred to what is called
prosperity under despots as freedom is to slavery,' he says.

From this point onwards, there are first certain seeds of decay, in spite of previously unmatched achievement, and then a gradual decadence. What is amiss, even in the best philosophy after Democritus, is an undue emphasis on man as compared with the universe. First comes scepticism, with the Sophists, leading to a study of *how* we know rather than to the attempt to acquire fresh knowledge. Then comes, with Socrates, the emphasis on ethics; with Plato, the rejection of the world of sense in favour of the self-created world of pure thought; with Aristotle, the belief in purpose as the fundamental concept in science. In spite of the genius of Plato and Aristotle, their thought has vices which proved infinitely harmful. After their time, there was a decay of vigour, and a gradual recrudescence of popular superstition. A partially new outlook arose as a result of the victory of Catholic orthodoxy; but it was not until the Renaissance that philosophy regained the vigour and independence that characterize the predecessors of Socrates.

Chapter X

PROTAGORAS

T HE great pre-Socratic systems that we have been considering were confronted, in the latter half of the fifth century, by a sceptical movement, in which the most important figure was Protagoras, chief of the Sophists. The word 'Sophist' had originally no bad connotation; it meant, as nearly as may be, what we mean by 'professor'. A Sophist was a man who made his living by teaching young men certain things that, it was thought, would be useful to them in practical life. As there was no public provision for such education, the Sophists taught only those who had private means, or whose parents had. This tended to give them a certain class bias, which was increased by the political circumstances of the time. In Athens and many other cities, democracy was politically triumphant, but nothing had been done to diminish the wealth of those who belonged to the old aristocratic families. It was, in the main, the rich who embodied what appears to us as Hellenic culture: they had education and leisure, travel had taken the edge off their traditional prejudices, and the time that they spent in discussion sharpened their wits. What was called democracy did not touch the institution of slavery, which enabled the rich to enjoy their wealth without oppressing free citizens.

In many cities, however, and especially in Athens, the poorer citizens had towards the rich a double hostility, that of envy, and that of traditionalism. The rich were supposed—often with justice —to be impious and immoral; they were subverting ancient beliefs, and probably trying to destroy democracy. It thus happened that political democracy was associated with cultural conservatism, while those who were cultural innovators tended to be political reactionaries. Somewhat the same situation exists in modern America, where Tammany, as a mainly Catholic organization, is engaged in defending traditional theological and ethical dogmas against the assaults of enlightenment. But the enlightened are politically weaker in America than they were in Athens, because they have failed to make common cause with the plutocracy. There is, however, one important and highly intellectual class which is concerned with the defence of the plutocracy, namely the class of corporation lawyers. In *some* respects, their functions are similar to those that were performed in Athens by the Sophists.

Athenian democracy, though it had the grave limitation of not including slaves or women, was in some respects more democratic than any modern system. Judges and most executive officers were chosen by lot, and served for short periods; they were thus average citizens, like our jurymen, with the prejudices and lack of professionalism characteristic of average citizens. In general, there were a large number of judges to hear each case. The plaintiff and defendant, or prosecutor and accused, appeared in person, not through professional lawyers. Naturally, success or failure depended largely on oratorical skill in appealing to popular prejudices. Although a man had to deliver his own speech, he could hire an expert to write the speech for him, or, as many preferred, he could pay for instruction in the arts required for success in the law courts. These arts the Sophists were supposed to teach.

The age of Pericles is analogous, in Athenian history to the Victorian age in the history of England. Athens was rich and powerful, not much troubled by wars, and possessed of a democratic constitution administered by aristocrats. As we have seen, in connection with Anaxagoras, a democratic opposition to Pericles gradually gathered strength, and attacked his friends one by one. The Peloponnesian War broke out in 431 B.C.;[1] Athens (in common with many other places) was ravaged by the plague; the population, which had been about 230,000, was greatly reduced, and never rose again to its former level (Bury, *History of Greece*, I, p. 444). Pericles himself, in 430 B.C., was deposed from the office of general and fined for misappropriation of public money, but soon reinstated. His two legitimate sons died of the plague, and he himself died in the following year (429). Pheidias and Anaxagoras were condemned; Aspasia was prosecuted for impiety and for keeping a disorderly house, but acquitted.

In such a community, it was natural that men who were likely to incur the hostility of democratic politicians should wish to acquire forensic skill. For Athens, though much addicted to persecution, was in one respect less illiberal than modern America, since those accused of impiety and corrupting the young were allowed to plead in their own defence.

This explains the popularity of the Sophists with one class and their unpopularity with another. But in their own minds they served more impersonal purposes, and it is clear that many of them were genuinely concerned with philosophy. Plato devoted himself to caricaturing and vilifying them, but they must not be judged by his polemics. In his lighter vein, take the following passage from the *Euthydemus*, in which two Sophists, Dionysodorus and Euthydemus,

---

[1] It ended in 404 B.C. with the complete overthrow of Athens.

set to work to puzzle a simple-minded person named Clesippus.
Dionysodorus begins:

> You say that you have a dog?
> Yes, a villain of a one, said Clesippus.
> And he has puppies?
> Yes, and they are very like himself.
> And the dog is the father of them?
> Yes, he said, I certainly saw him and the mother of the
>   puppies come together.
> And is he not yours?
> To be sure he is.
> Then he is a father, and he is yours; ergo, he is your father,
>   and the puppies are your brothers.

In a more serious vein, take the dialogue called *The Sophist*. This
is a logical discussion of definition, which uses the sophist as an
illustration. With its logic we are not at present concerned; the only
thing I wish to mention at the moment as regards this dialogue is
the final conclusion:

'The art of contradiction-making, descended from an insincere
kind of conceited mimicry, of the semblance-making breed, derived
from image-making, distinguished as a portion, not divine but
human, of production, that presents a shadow-play of words—such
is the blood and lineage which can, with perfect truth, be assigned
to the authentic Sophist.' (Cornford's translation.)

There is a story about Protagoras, no doubt apocryphal, which
illustrates the connection of the Sophists with the law-courts in the
popular mind. It is said that he taught a young man on the terms
that he should be paid his fee if the young man won his first law-
suit, but not otherwise, and that the young man's first law-suit was
one brought by Protagoras for recovery of his fee.

However, it is time to leave these preliminaries and see what is
really known about Protagoras.

Protagoras was born about 500 B.C., at Abdera, the city from
which Democritus came. He twice visited Athens, his second visit
being not later than 432 B.C. He made a code of laws for the city of
Thurii in 444-3 B.C. There is a tradition that he was prosecuted for
impiety, but this seems to be untrue, in spite of the fact that he
wrote a book *On the Gods*, which began: 'With regard to the gods,
I cannot feel sure either that they are or that they are not, nor what
they are like in figure; for there are many things that hinder sure
knowledge, the obscurity of the subject and the shortness of human
life.'

His second visit to Athens is described somewhat satirically in

Plato's *Protagoras*, and his doctrines are discussed seriously in the *Theaetetus*. He is chiefly noted for his doctrine that 'Man is the measure of all things, of things that are that they are, and of things that are not that they are not.' This is interpreted as meaning that *each* man is the measure of all things, and that, when men differ, there is no objective truth in virtue of which one is right and the other wrong. The doctrine is essentially sceptical, and is presumably based on the 'deceitfulness' of the senses.

One of the three founders of pragmatism, F. C. S. Schiller, was in the habit of calling himself a disciple of Protagoras. This was, I think, because Plato, in the *Theaetetus*, suggests, as an interpretation of Protagoras, that one opinion can be *better* than another, though it cannot be *truer*. For example, when a man has jaundice everything looks yellow. There is no sense in saying that things are really not yellow, but the colour they look to a man in health; we can say, however, that, since health is better than sickness, the opinion of the man in health is better than that of the man who has jaundice. This point of view, obviously, is akin to pragmatism.

The disbelief in objective truth makes the majority, for practical purposes, the arbiters as to what to believe. Hence Protagoras was led to a defence of law and convention and traditional morality. While, as we saw, he did not know whether the gods existed, he was sure they ought to be worshipped. This point of view is obviously the right one for a man whose theoretical scepticism is thoroughgoing and logical.

Protagoras spent his adult life in a sort of perpetual lecture tour through the cities of Greece, teaching, for a fee, 'any one who desired practical efficiency and higher mental culture' (Zeller, p. 1299). Plato objects—somewhat snobbishly, according to modern notions—to the Sophists' practice of charging money for instruction. Plato himself had adequate private means, and was unable, apparently, to realize the necessities of those who had not his good fortune. It is odd that modern professors, who see no reason to refuse a salary, have so frequently repeated Plato's strictures.

There was, however, another point in which the Sophists differed from most contemporary philosophers. It was usual, except among the Sophists, for a teacher to found a school, which had some of the properties of a brotherhood; there was a greater or smaller amount of common life, there was often something analogous to a monastic rule, and there was usually an esoteric doctrine not proclaimed to the public. All this was natural wherever philosophy had arisen out of Orphism. Among the Sophists there was none of this. What they had to teach was not, in their minds, connected with religion or virtue. They taught the art of arguing, and as much

94

knowledge as would help in this art. Broadly speaking, they were prepared, like modern lawyers, to show how to argue for or against any opinion, and were not concerned to advocate conclusions of their own. Those to whom philosophy was a way of life, closely bound up with religion, were naturally shocked; to them, the Sophists appeared frivolous and immoral.

To some extent—though it is impossible to say how far—the odium which the Sophists incurred, not only with the general public, but with Plato and subsequent philosophers, was due to their intellectual merit. The pursuit of truth, when it is whole-hearted, must ignore moral considerations; we cannot know in advance that the truth will turn out to be what is thought edifying in a given society. The Sophists were prepared to follow an argument wherever it might lead them. Often it led them to scepticism. One of them, Gorgias, maintained that nothing exists; that if any-things exists, it is unknowable; and granting it even to exist and to be knowable by any one man, he could never communicate it to others. We do not know what his arguments were, but I can well imagine that they had a logical force which compelled his opponents to take refuge in edification. Plato is always concerned to advocate views that will make people what he thinks virtuous; he is hardly ever intellectually honest, because he allows himself to judge doctrines by their social consequences. Even about this, he is not honest; he pretends to follow the argument and to be judging by purely theoretical standards, when in fact he is twisting the discussion so as to lead to a virtuous result. He introduced this vice into philosophy, where it has persisted ever since. It was probably largely hostility to the Sophists that gave this character to his dialogues. One of the defects of all philosophers since Plato is that their inquiries into ethics proceed on the assumption that they already know the conclusions to be reached.

It seems that there were men, in the Athens of the late fifth century, who taught political doctrines which seemed immoral to their contemporaries, and seem so to the democratic nations of the present day. Thrasymachus, in the first book of the *Republic*, argues that there is no justice except the interest of the stronger; that laws are made by governments for their own advantage; and that there is no impersonal standard to which to appeal in contests for power. Callicles, according to Plato (in the *Gorgias*), maintained a similar doctrine. The law of nature, he said, is the law of the stronger; but for convenience men have established institutions and moral precepts to restrain the strong. Such doctrines have won much wider assent in our day than they did in antiquity. And whatever may be thought of them, they are not characteristic of the Sophists.

During the fifth century—whatever part the Sophists may have had in the change—there was in Athens a transformation from a certain stiff Puritan simplicity to a quick-witted and rather cruel cynicism in conflict with a slow-witted and equally cruel defence of crumbling orthodoxy. At the beginning of the century comes the Athenian championship of the cities of Ionia against the Persians, and the victory of Marathon in 490 B.C. At the end comes the defeat of Athens by Sparta in 404 B.C., and the execution of Socrates in 399 B.C. After this time Athens ceased to be politically important, but acquired undoubted cultural supremacy, which it retained until the victory of Christianity.

Something of the history of fifth-century Athens is essential to the understanding of Plato and of all subsequent Greek thought. In the first Persian war, the chief glory went to the Athenians, owing to the decisive victory at Marathon. In the second war, ten years later, the Athenians still were the best of the Greeks at sea, but on land victory was mainly due to the Spartans, who were the acknowledged leaders of the Hellenic world. The Spartans, however, were narrowly provincial in their outlook, and ceased to oppose the Persians when they had been chased out of European Greece. The championship of the Asiatic Greeks, and the liberation of the islands that had been conquered by the Persians, was undertaken, with great success, by Athens. Athens became the leading sea power, and acquired a considerable imperialist control over the Ionian islands. Under the leadership of Pericles, who was a moderate democrat and a moderate imperialist, Athens prospered. The great temples, whose ruins are still the glory of Athens, were built by his initiative, to replace those destroyed by Xerxes. The city increased very rapidly in wealth, and also in culture, and, as invariably happens at such times, particularly when wealth is due to foreign commerce, traditional morality and traditional beliefs decayed.

There was at this time in Athens an extraordinarily large number of men of genius. The three great dramatists, Aeschylus, Sophocles, and Euripides, all belong to the fifth century. Aeschylus fought at Marathon and saw the battle of Salamis. Sophocles was still religiously orthodox. But Euripides was influenced by Protagoras and by the free-thinking spirit of the time, and his treatment of the myths is sceptical and subversive. Aristophanes, the comic poet, made fun of Socrates, Sophists, and philosophers, but, nevertheless, belonged to their circle; in the *Symposium* Plato represents him as on very friendly terms with Socrates. Pheidias the sculptor, as we have seen, belonged to the circle of Pericles.

The excellence of Athens, at this period, was artistic rather than intellectual. None of the great mathematicians or philosophers of the fifth century were Athenians, with the exception of Socrates; and Socrates was not a writer, but a man who confined himself to oral discussion.

The outbreak of the Peloponnesian War in 431 B.C. and the death of Pericles in 429 B.C. introduced a darker period in Athenian history. The Athenians were superior at sea, but the Spartans had supremacy on land, and repeatedly occupied Attica (except Athens) during the summer. The result was that Athens was over-crowded, and suffered severely from the plague. In 414 B.C. the Athenians sent a large expedition to Sicily, in the hope of capturing Syracuse, which was allied with Sparta; but the attempt was a failure. War made the Athenians fierce and persecuting. In 416 B.C. they conquered the island of Melos, put to death all men of military age and enslaved the other inhabitants. *The Trojan Women* of Euripides is a protest against such barbarism. The conflict had an ideological aspect, since Sparta was the champion of oligarchy and Athens of democracy. The Athenians had reason to suspect some of their own aristocrats of treachery, which was generally thought to have had a part in the final naval defeat at the battle of Aegospotami in 405 B.C.

At the end of the war, the Spartans established in Athens an oligarchical government, known as the Thirty Tyrants. Some of the Thirty, including Critias, their chief, had been pupils of Socrates. They were deservedly unpopular, and were overthrown within a year. With the compliance of Sparta, democracy was restored, but it was an embittered democracy, precluded by an amnesty from direct vengeance against its internal enemies, but glad of any pretext, not covered by the amnesty, for prosecuting them. It was in this atmosphere that the trial and death of Socrates took place (399 B.C.).

PART 2

SOCRATES, PLATO, AND ARISTOTLE

Chapter XI

SOCRATES

SOCRATES is a very difficult subject for the historian. There are many men concerning whom it is certain that very little is known, and other men concerning whom it is certain that a great deal is known; but in the case of Socrates the uncertainty is as to whether we know very little or a great deal. He was undoubtedly an Athenian citizen of moderate means, who spent his time in disputation, and taught philosophy to the young, but not for money, like the Sophists. He was certainly tried, condemned to death, and executed in 399 B.C., at about the age of seventy. He was unquestionably a well-known figure in Athens, since Aristophanes caricatured him in *The Clouds*. But beyond this point we become involved in controversy. Two of his pupils, Xenophon and Plato, wrote voluminously about him, but they said very different things. Even when they agree, it has been suggested by Burnet that Xenophon is copying Plato. Where they disagree, some believe the one, some the other, some neither. In such a dangerous dispute, I shall not venture to take sides, but I will set out briefly the various points of view.

Let us begin with Xenophon, a military man, not very liberally endowed with brains, and on the whole conventional in his outlook. Xenophon is pained that Socrates should have been accused of impiety and of corrupting the youth; he contends that, on the contrary, Socrates was eminently pious and had a thoroughly wholesome effect upon those who came under his influence. His ideas, it appears, so far from being subversive, were rather dull and commonplace. This defence goes too far, since it leaves the hostility to Socrates unexplained. As Burnet says (*Thales to Plato*, p. 149): 'Xenophon's defence of Socrates is too successful. He would never have been put to death if he had been like that.'

There has been a tendency to think that everything Xenophon says must be true, because he had not the wits to think of anything untrue. This is a very invalid line of argument. A stupid man's report of what a clever man says is never accurate, because he unconsciously translates what he hears into something that he can understand. I would rather be reported by my bitterest enemy among philosophers than by a friend innocent of philosophy. We cannot therefore accept what Xenophon says if it either involves any difficult point in philosophy or is part of an argument to prove that Socrates was unjustly condemned.

Nevertheless, some of Xenophon's reminiscences are very convincing. He tells (as Plato also does) how Socrates was continually occupied with the problem of getting competent men into positions of power. He would ask such questions as: 'If I wanted a shoe-mended, whom should I employ?' To which some ingenuous youth would answer: 'A shoemaker, O Socrates.' He would go on to carpenters, coppersmiths, etc., and finally ask some such question as 'who should mend the Ship of State?' When he fell into conflict with the Thirty Tyrants, Critias, their chief, who knew his ways from having studied under him, forbade him to continue teaching the young, and added: 'You had better be done with your shoe-makers, carpenters, and coppersmiths. These must be pretty well trodden out at heel by this time, considering the circulation you have given them' (Xenophon, *Memorabilia*, Bk. I. chap. ii). This happened during the brief oligarchic government established by the Spartans at the end of the Peloponnesian War. But at most times Athens was democratic, so much so that even generals were elected or chosen by lot. Socrates came across a young man who wished to become a general, and persuaded him that it would be well to know something of the art of war. The young man accordingly went away and took a brief course in tactics. When he returned, Socrates, after some satirical praise, sent him back for further in-struction (*ibid.*, Bk. III, chap. i). Another young man he set to learn-ing the principles of finance. He tried the same sort of plan on many people, including the war minister; but it was decided that it was easier to silence him by means of the hemlock than to cure the evils of which he complained.

With Plato's account of Socrates, the difficulty is quite a different one from what it is in the case of Xenophon, namely, that it is very hard to judge how far Plato means to portray the historical Socrates, and how far he intends the person called 'Socrates' in his dialogues to be merely the mouthpiece of his own opinions. Plato, in addition to being a philosopher, is an imaginative writer of great genius and charm. No one supposes, and he himself does not seriously pretend, that the conversations in his dialogues took place just as he records them. Nevertheless, at any rate in the earlier dialogues, the con-versation is completely natural and the characters quite convincing. It is the excellence of Plato as a writer of fiction that throws doubt on him as a historian. His Socrates is a consistent and extraordin-arily interesting character, far beyond the power of most men to invent; but I think Plato *could* have invented him. Whether he did so is of course another question.

The dialogue which is most generally regarded as historical is the *Apology*. This professes to be the speech that Socrates made in his own defence at his trial—not, of course, a stenographic report, but what remained in Plato's memory some years after the event, put together and elaborated with literary art. Plato was present at the trial, and it certainly seems fairly clear that what is set down is the *sort* of thing that Plato remembered Socrates as saying, and that the intention is, broadly speaking, historical. This, with all its limitations, is enough to give a fairly definite picture of the character of Socrates.

The main facts of the trial of Socrates are not open to doubt. The prosecution was based upon the charge that 'Socrates is an evil-doer and a curious person, searching into things under the earth and above the heaven; and making the worse appear the better cause, and teaching all this to others.' The real ground of hostility to him was, almost certainly, that he was supposed to be connected with the aristocratic party; most of his pupils belonged to this faction, and some, in positions of power, had proved themselves very pernicious. But this ground could not be made evident, on account of the amnesty. He was found guilty by a majority, and it was then open to him, by Athenian law, to propose some lesser penalty than death. The judges had to choose, if they had found the accused guilty, between the penalty demanded by the prosecution and that suggested by the defence. It was therefore to the interest of Socrates to suggest a substantial penalty, which the court might have accepted as adequate. He, however, proposed a fine of thirty minae, for which some of his friends (including Plato) were willing to go surety. This was so small a punishment that the court was annoyed, and condemned him to death by a larger majority than that which had found him guilty. Undoubtedly he foresaw the result. It is clear that he had no wish to avoid the death penalty by concessions which might seem to acknowledge his guilt.

The prosecutors were Anytus, a democratic politician; Meletus, a tragic poet, 'youthful and unknown, with lanky hair, and scanty beard and a hooked nose'; and Lykon, an obscure rhetorician. (See Burnet, *Thales to Plato*, p. 180.) They maintained that Socrates was guilty of not worshipping the gods the State worshipped but introducing other new divinities, and further that he was guilty of corrupting the young by teaching them accordingly.

Without further troubling ourselves with the insoluble question of the relation of the Platonic Socrates to the real man, let us see what Plato makes him say in answer to this charge.

Socrates begins by accusing his prosecutors of eloquence, and rebutting the charge of eloquence as applied to himself. The only eloquence of which he is capable, he says, is that of truth. And they must not be angry with him if he speaks in his accustomed manner, not in 'a set oration, duly ornamented with words and phrases'.[1] He is over seventy, and has never appeared in a court of law until now; they must therefore pardon his un-forensic way of speaking.

He goes on to say that, in addition to his formal accusers, he has a large body of informal accusers, who, ever since the judges were children, have gone about 'telling of one Socrates, a wise man, who speculated about the heavens above, and searched into the earth beneath, and made the worse appear the better cause'. Such men, he says, are supposed not to believe in the existence of the gods. This old accusation by public opinion is more dangerous than the formal indictment, the more so as he does not know who are the men from whom it comes, except in the case of Aristophanes.[2] He points out, in reply to these older grounds of hostility, that he is not a man of science—'I have nothing to do with physical speculations' —that he is not a teacher, and does not take money for teaching. He goes on to make fun of the Sophists, and to disclaim the knowledge that they profess to have. What, then, is 'the reason why I am called wise and have such an evil fame?'

The oracle of Delphi, it appears, was once asked if there were any man wiser than Socrates, and replied that there was not. Socrates professes to have been completely puzzled, since he knew nothing, and yet a god cannot lie. He therefore went about among men reputed wise, to see whether he could convict the god of error. First he went to a politician, who 'was thought wise by many, and still wiser by himself'. He soon found that the man was not wise, and explained this to him, kindly but firmly, 'and the consequence was that he hated me'. He then went to the poets, and asked them to explain passages in their writings, but they were unable to do so. 'Then I knew that not by wisdom do poets write poetry, but by a sort of genius and inspiration.' Then he went to the artisans, but found them equally disappointing. In the process, he says, he made many dangerous enemies. Finally he concluded that 'God only is wise; and by his answer he intends to show that the wisdom of men is worth little or nothing; he is not speaking of Socrates, he is only using my name by way of illustration, as if he said, He, O men, is the wisest, who, like Socrates, knows that his wisdom is in truth worth nothing.' This business of showing up pretenders to wisdom takes up all his time, and has left him in utter poverty, but he feels it a duty to vindicate the oracle.

[1] In quotations from Plato, I have generally used Jowett's translation.
[2] In *The Clouds*, Socrates is represented as denying the existence of Zeus.

Young men of the richer classes, he says, having not much to do, enjoy listening to him exposing people, and proceed to do likewise, thus increasing the number of his enemies. 'For they do not like to confess that their pretence of knowledge has been detected.'

So much for the first class of accusers.

Socrates now proceeds to examine his prosecutor Meletus, 'that good man and true lover of his country, as he calls himself'. He asks who are the people who *improve* the young. Meletus first mentions the judges; then, under pressure, is driven, step by step, to say that every Athenian except Socrates improves the young; whereupon Socrates congratulates the city on its good fortune. Next, he points out that good men are better to live among than bad men, and therefore he cannot be so foolish as to corrupt his fellow-citizens *intentionally*; but if unintentionally, then Meletus should instruct him, not prosecute him.

The indictment had said that Socrates not only denied the gods of the State, but introduced other gods of his own; Meletus, however, says that Socrates is a complete atheist, and adds: 'He says that the sun is stone and the moon earth.' Socrates replies that Meletus seems to think he is prosecuting Anaxagoras, whose views may be heard in the theatre for one drachma (presumably in the plays of Euripides). Socrates of course points out that this new accusation of complete atheism contradicts the indictment, and then passes on to more general considerations.

The rest of the *Apology* is essentially religious in tone. He has been a soldier, and has remained at his post, as he was ordered to do. Now 'God orders me to fulfil the philosopher's mission of searching into myself and other men,' and it would be as shameful to desert his post now as in time of battle. Fear of death is not wisdom, since no one knows whether death may not be the greater good. If he were offered his life on condition of ceasing to speculate as he has done hitherto, he would reply: 'Men of Athens, I honour and love you; but I shall obey God rather than you,[1] and while I have life and strength I shall never cease from the practice and teaching of philosophy, exhorting any one whom I meet. . . . For know that this is the command of God; and I believe that no greater good has ever happened in the State than my service to the God.' He goes on:

I have something more to say, at which you may be inclined to cry out; but I believe that to hear me will be good for you, and therefore I beg that you will not cry out. I would have you know, that if you kill such a one as I am, you will injure yourselves more

[1] Cf. *Acts*, v. 29.

than you will injure me. Nothing will injure me, not Meletus nor yet Anytus—they cannot, for a bad man is not permitted to injure a better than himself. I do not deny that Anytus may perhaps kill him, or drive him into exile, or deprive him of civil rights; and he may imagine, and others may imagine, that he is inflicting a great injury upon him: but there I do not agree. For the evil of doing as he is doing—the evil of unjustly taking away the life of another—is greater far.

It is for the sake of his judges, he says, not for his own sake, that he is pleading. He is a gad-fly, given to the State by God, and it will not be easy to find another like him. 'I dare say you may feel out of temper (like a person who is suddenly awakened from sleep), and you think that you might easily strike me dead as Anytus advises, and then you would sleep on for the remainder of your lives, unless God in his care of you sent you another gad-fly.'

Why has he only gone about in private, and not given advice on public affairs? 'You have heard me speak at sundry times and in diverse places of an oracle or sign which comes to me, and is the divinity which Meletus ridicules in the indictment. This sign, which is a kind of voice, first began to come to me when I was a child; it always forbids but never commands me to do anything which I am going to do. This is what deters me from being a politician.' He goes on to say that in politics no honest man can live long. He gives two instances in which he was unavoidably mixed up in public affairs: in the first, he resisted the democracy; in the second, the Thirty Tyrants, in each case when the authorities were acting illegally.

He points out that among those present are many former pupils of his, and fathers and brothers of pupils; not one of these has been produced by the prosecution to testify that he corrupts the young. (This is almost the only argument in the *Apology* that a lawyer for the defence would sanction.) He refuses to follow the custom of producing his weeping children in court, to soften the hearts of the judges; such scenes, he says, make the accused and the city alike ridiculous. It is his business to convince the judges, not to ask a favour of them.

After the verdict, and the rejection of the alternative penalty of thirty minae (in connection with which Socrates names Plato as one among his sureties, and present in court), he makes one final speech.

And now, O men who have condemned me, I would fain prophesy to you; for I am about to die, and in the hour of death men are gifted with prophetic power. And I prophesy to you, who are my murderers, that immediately after my departure punishment far heavier than you have inflicted on me will surely await you. . . . If you think that by killing men you can prevent some one from censuring your evil lives, you are mistaken; that is not a way of escape which is either possible or honourable; the easiest and the noblest way is not to be disabling others, but to be improving yourselves.

He then turns to those of his judges who have voted for acquittal, and tells them that, in all that he has done that day, his oracle has never opposed him, though on other occasions it has often stopped him in the middle of a speech. This, he says, 'is an intimation that what has happened to me is a good, and that those of us who think death is an evil are in error'. For either death is a dreamless sleep—which is plainly good—or the soul migrates to another world. And 'what would not a man give if he might converse with Orpheus and Musaeus and Hesiod and Homer? Nay, if this be true, let me die and die again.' In the next world, he will converse with others who have suffered death unjustly, and, above all, he will continue his search after knowledge. 'In another world they do not put a man to death for asking questions: assuredly not. For besides being happier than we are, they will be immortal, if what is said is true. . . .

'The hour of departure has arrived, and we go our ways—I to die, and you to live. Which is better God only knows.'

The *Apology* gives a clear picture of a man of a certain type: a man very sure of himself, high-minded, indifferent to worldly success, believing that he is guided by a divine voice, and persuaded that clear thinking is the most important requisite for right living. Except in this last point, he resembles a Christian martyr or a Puritan. In the final passage, where he considers what happens after death, it is impossible not to feel that he firmly believes in immortality, and that his professed uncertainty is only assumed. He is not troubled, like the Christians, by fears of eternal torment: he has no doubt that his life in the next world will be a happy one. In the *Phaedo*, the Platonic Socrates gives reasons for the belief in immortality; whether these were the reasons that influenced the historical Socrates, it is impossible to say.

There seems hardly any doubt that the historical Socrates claimed to be guided by an oracle or *daimon*. Whether this was analogous to what a Christian would call the voice of conscience, or whether it appeared to him as an *actual* voice, it is impossible to know. Joan of Arc was inspired by voices, which are a common symptom of insanity. Socrates was liable to cataleptic trances; at least, that seems the natural explanation of such an incident as occurred once when he was on military service:

One morning he was thinking about something which he could not resolve; he would not give it up, but continued thinking from early dawn until noon—there he stood fixed in thought; and at noon attention was drawn to him, and the rumour ran through the wondering crowd that Socrates had been standing and thinking about something ever since the break of day. At last, in the evening after supper, some Ionians out of curiosity (I should explain that this occurred not in winter but in summer), brought out their mats and slept in the open air that they might watch him and see whether he would stand all night. There he stood until the following morning; and with the return of light he offered up a prayer to the sun, and went his way (*Symposium*, 220).

This sort of thing, in a lesser degree, was a common occurrence with Socrates. At the beginning of the *Symposium*, Socrates and Aristodemus go together to the banquet, but Socrates drops behind in a fit of abstraction. When Aristodemus arrives, Agathon, the host, says, 'what have you done with Socrates?' Aristodemus is astonished to find Socrates not with him; a slave is sent to look for him, and finds him in the portico of a neighbouring house. 'There he is fixed,' says the slave on his return, 'and when I call to him he will not stir.' Those who know him well explain that 'he has a way of stopping anywhere and losing himself without any reason'. They leave him alone, and he enters when the feast is half over.

Every one is agreed that Socrates was very ugly; he had a snub nose and a considerable paunch; he was 'uglier than all the Silenuses in the Satyric drama' (Xenophon, *Symposium*). He was always dressed in shabby old clothes, and went barefoot everywhere. His indifference to heat and cold, hunger and thirst, amazed every one. Alcibiades in the *Symposium*, describing Socrates on military service, says:

His endurance was simply marvellous when, being cut off from our supplies, we were compelled to go without food—on such occasions, which often happen in time of war, he was superior not only to me but to everybody: there was no one to be compared to him. . . . His fortitude in enduring cold was also surprising. There was a severe frost, for the winter in that region is really tremendous, and everybody else either remained indoors or if they went out had on an amazing quantity of clothes, and were all well shod, and had their feet swathed in felt and fleeces: in the midst of this, Socrates with his bare feet on the ice and in his ordinary dress marched better than the other soldiers who had shoes and they looked daggers at him because he seemed to despise them.

His mastery over all bodily passions is constantly stressed. He seldom drank wine, but when he did, he could out-drink anybody; no one had ever seen him drunk. In love, even under the strongest temptations, he remained 'Platonic', if Plato is speaking the truth. He was the perfect Orphic saint: in the dualism of heavenly soul and earthly body, he had achieved the complete mastery of the soul over the body. His indifference to death at the last is the final proof of this mastery. At the same time, he is not an orthodox Orphic; it is only the fundamental doctrines that he accepts, not the superstitions and ceremonies of purification.

The Platonic Socrates anticipates both the Stoics and the Cynics. The Stoics held that the supreme good is virtue, and that a man cannot be deprived of virtue by outside causes; this doctrine is implicit in the contention of Socrates that his judges cannot harm him. The Cynics despised worldly goods, and showed their contempt by eschewing the comforts of civilization; this is the same point of view that led Socrates to go barefoot and ill-clad.

It seems fairly certain that the preoccupations of Socrates were ethical rather than scientific. In the *Apology*, as we saw, he says: 'I have nothing to do with physical speculations.' The earliest of the Platonic dialogues, which are generally supposed to be the most Socratic, are mainly occupied with the search for definitions of ethical terms. The *Charmides* is concerned with the definition of temperance or moderation; the *Lysis* with friendship; the *Laches* with courage. In all of these, no conclusion is arrived at, but Socrates makes it clear that he thinks it important to examine such questions. The Platonic Socrates consistently maintains that he knows nothing, and is only wiser than others in knowing that he knows nothing; but he does not think knowledge unobtainable. On the contrary, he thinks the search for knowledge of the utmost importance. He maintains that no man sins wittingly, and therefore only knowledge is needed to make all men perfectly virtuous.

The close connection between virtue and knowledge is characteristic of Socrates and Plato. To some degree, it exists in all Greek thought, as opposed to that of Christianity. In Christian ethics, a pure heart is the essential, and is at least as likely to be found among the ignorant as among the learned. This difference between Greek and Christian ethics has persisted down to the present day.

Dialectic, that is to say, the method of seeking knowledge by question and answer, was not invented by Socrates. It seems to have been first practised systematically by Zeno, the disciple of Parmenides; in Plato's dialogue *Parmenides*, Zeno subjects Socrates to the same kind of treatment to which, elsewhere in Plato, Socrates subjects others. But there is every reason to suppose that Socrates practised and developed the method. As we saw, when Socrates is condemned to death he reflects happily that in the next world he can go on asking questions for ever, and cannot be put to death, as he will be immortal. Certainly, if he practised dialectic in the way described in the *Apology*, the hostility to him is easily explained: all the humbugs in Athens would combine against him.

The dialectic method is suitable for some questions, and unsuitable for others. Perhaps this helped to determine the character of Plato's inquiries, which were, for the most part, such as could be dealt with in this way. And through Plato's influence, most subsequent philosophy has been bounded by the limitations resulting from his method.

Some matters are obviously unsuitable for treatment in this way —empirical science, for example. It is true that Galileo used dialogues to advocate his theories, but that was only in order to overcome prejudice—the positive grounds for his discoveries could not be inserted in a dialogue without great artificiality. Socrates, in Plato's works, always pretends that he is only eliciting knowledge already possessed by the man he is questioning; on this ground, he compares himself to a midwife. When, in the *Phaedo* and the *Meno*, he applies his method to geometrical problems, he has to ask leading questions which any judge would disallow. The method is in harmony with the doctrine of reminiscence, according to which we learn by remembering that we knew in a former existence. As against this view, consider any discovery that has been made by means of the microscope, say the spread of diseases by bacteria; it can hardly be maintained that such knowledge can be elicited from a previously ignorant person by the method of question and answer.

The matters that are suitable for treatment by the Socratic method are those as to which we have already enough knowledge to come to a right conclusion, but have failed, through confusion of thought or lack of analysis, to make the best logical use of what we know. A question such as 'what is justice?' is eminently suited for discussion in a Platonic dialogue. We all freely use the words 'just' and 'unjust', and, by examining the ways in which we use them, we can arrive inductively at the definition that will best suit with usage. All that is needed is knowledge of how the words in question are used. But when our inquiry is concluded, we have made only a linguistic discovery, not a discovery in ethics.

We can, however, apply the method profitably to a somewhat larger class of cases. Wherever what is being debated is logical rather than factual, discussion is a good method of eliciting truth. Suppose someone maintains, for example, that democracy is good, but persons holding certain opinions should not be allowed to vote, we may convict him of inconsistency, and prove to him that at least one of his two assertions must be more or less erroneous. Logical errors are, I think, of greater practical importance than many people believe; they enable their perpetrators to hold the comfortable opinion on every subject in turn. Any logically coherent body of doctrine is sure to be in part painful and contrary to current prejudices. The dialectic method—or, more generally, the habit of unfettered discussion—tends to promote logical consistency, and is in this way useful. But it is quite unavailing when the object is to discover new facts. Perhaps 'philosophy' might be defined as the sum-total of those inquiries that can be pursued by Plato's methods. But if this definition is appropriate, that is because of Plato's influence upon subsequent philosophers.

Chapter XII

THE INFLUENCE OF SPARTA

To understand Plato, and indeed many later philosophers, it is necessary to know something of Sparta. Sparta had a double effect on Greek thought: through the reality, and through the myth. Each is important. The reality enabled the Spartans to defeat Athens in war; the myth influenced Plato's political theory, and that of countless subsequent writers. The myth, fully developed, is to be found in Plutarch's *Life of Lycurgus*; the ideals that it favours have had a great part in framing the doctrines of Rousseau, Nietzsche, and National Socialism.[1] The myth is of even more importance, historically, than the reality; nevertheless, we will begin with the latter. For the reality was the source of the myth.

Laconia, of which Sparta, or Lacedaemon was the capital, occupied the south-east of the Peloponnesus. The Spartans, who were the ruling race, had conquered the country at the time of the Dorian invasion from the north, and had reduced the population that they found there to the condition of serfs. These serfs were called helots. In historical times, all the land belonged to the Spartans, who, however, were forbidden by law and custom to cultivate it themselves, both on the ground that such labour was degrading, and in order that they might always be free for military service. The serfs were not bought and sold, but remained attached to the land, which was divided into lots, one or more for each adult male Spartan. These lots, like the helots, could not be bought or sold, and passed, by law, from father to son. (They could, however, be bequeathed.) The land-owner received from the helot who cultivated the lot seventy medimni (about 105 bushels) of grain for himself, twelve for his wife, and a stated portion of wine and fruit annually.[2] Anything beyond this amount was the property of the helot. The helots were Greeks, like the Spartans, and bitterly resented their servile condition. When they could, they rebelled. The Spartans had a body of secret police to deal with this danger, but to supplement this precaution they had another: once a year, they declared war on the helots, so that their young men could kill any who seemed insubordinate without incurring the legal guilt of homicide. Helots could be emancipated by the State, but not by their masters; they were

[1] Not to mention Dr. Thomas Arnold and the English public schools.

[2] Bury, *History of Greece*, Vol. I, p. 138. It seems that Spartan men ate nearly six times as much as their wives.

emancipated, rather rarely, for exceptional bravery in battle.

At some time during the eighth century B.C. the Spartans conquered the neighbouring country of Messenia, and reduced most of its inhabitants to the condition of helots. There had been a lack of *Lebensraum* in Sparta, but the new territory, for a time, removed this source of discontent.

Lots were for the common run of Spartans; the aristocracy had estates of their own, whereas the lots were portions of common land assigned by the State.

The free inhabitants of other parts of Laconia, called 'perioeci', had no share of political power.

The sole business of a Spartan citizen was war, to which he was trained from birth. Sickly children were exposed after inspection by the heads of the tribe; only those judged vigorous were allowed to be reared. Up to the age of twenty, all the boys were trained in one big school; the purpose of the training was to make them hardy, indifferent to pain, and submissive to discipline. There was no nonsense about cultural or scientific education; the sole aim was to produce good soldiers, wholly devoted to the State.

At the age of twenty, actual military service began. Marriage was permitted to anyone over the age of twenty, but until the age of thirty a man had to live in the 'men's house', and had to manage his marriage as if it were an illicit and secret affair. After thirty, he was a full-fledged citizen. Every citizen belonged to a mess, and dined with the other members; he had to make a contribution in kind from the produce of his lot. It was the theory of the State that no Spartan citizen should be destitute, and none should be rich. Each was expected to live on the produce of his lot, which he could not alienate except by free gift. None was allowed to own gold or silver, and the money was made of iron. Spartan simplicity became proverbial.

The position of women in Sparta was peculiar. They were not secluded, like respectable women elsewhere in Greece. Girls went through the same physical training as was given to boys; what is more remarkable, boys and girls did their gymnastics together, all being naked. It was desired (I quote Plutarch's *Lycurgus* in North's translation):

that the maidens should harden their bodies with exercise of running, wrestling, throwing the bar, and casting the dart, to the end that the fruit wherewith they might be afterwards conceived, taking nourishment of a strong and lusty body, should shoot out and spread the better: and that they by gathering strength thus by exercises, should more easily away with the pains of child bearing. . . . And though the maidens did show themselves thus naked openly, yet was there no dishonesty seen nor offered, but all this sport was full of play and toys, without any youthful part or wantonness.

Men who would not marry were made 'infamous by law', and compelled, even in the coldest weather, to walk up and down naked *outside* the place where the young people were doing their exercises and dances.

Women were not allowed to exhibit any emotion not profitable to the State. They might display contempt for a coward, and would be praised if he were their son; but they might not show grief if their new-born child was condemned to death as a weakling, or if their sons were killed in battle. They were considered, by other Greeks, exceptionally chaste; at the same time, a childless married woman would raise no objection if the State ordered her to find out whether some other man would be more successful than her husband in begetting citizens. Children were encouraged by legislation. According to Aristotle, the father of three sons was exempt from military service, and the father of four from all the burdens of the State.

The constitution of Sparta was complicated. There were two kings, belonging to two different families, and succeeding by heredity. One or other of the kings commanded the army in time of war, but in time of peace their powers were limited. At communal feasts they got twice as much to eat as any one else, and there was general mourning when one of them died. They were members of the Council of Elders, a body consisting of thirty men (including the kings); the other twenty-eight must be over sixty, and were chosen for life by the whole body of the citizens, but only from aristocratic families. The Council tried criminal cases, and prepared matters which were to come before the Assembly. This body (the Assembly) consisted of all the citizens; it could not initiate anything, but could vote yes or no to any proposal brought before it. No law could be enacted without its consent. But its consent, though necessary, was not sufficient; the elders and magistrates must proclaim the decision before it became valid.

In addition to the kings, the Council of Elders, and the Assembly, there was a fourth branch of the government, peculiar to Sparta. This was the five ephors. These were chosen out of the whole body of the citizens, by a method which Aristotle says was 'too childish', and which Bury says was virtually by lot. They were a 'democratic' element in the constitution,[1] apparently intended to balance the

[1] In speaking of 'democratic' elements in the Spartan constitution, one must of course remember that the citizens as a whole were a ruling class fiercely tyrannizing over the helots, and allowing no power to the perioeci.

kings. Every month the kings swore to uphold the constitution, and the ephors then swore to uphold the kings so long as they remained true to their oath. When either king went on a warlike expedition, two ephors accompanied him to watch his behaviour. The ephors were the supreme civil court, but over the kings they had criminal jurisdiction.

The Spartan constitution was supposed, in later antiquity, to have been due to a legislator named Lycurgus, who was said to have promulgated his laws in 885 B.C. In fact, the Spartan system grew up gradually, and Lycurgus was a mythical person, originally a god. His name meant 'wolf-repeller', and his origin was Arcadian.

Sparta aroused among the other Greeks an admiration which is to us somewhat surprising. Originally, it had been much less different from other Greek cities than it became later; in early days it produced poets and artists as good as those elsewhere. But about the seventh century B.C., or perhaps even later, its constitution (falsely attributed to Lycurgus) crystallized into the form we have been considering; everything else was sacrificed to success in war, and Sparta ceased to have any part whatever in what Greece contributed to the civilization of the world. To us, the Spartan State appears as a model, in miniature, of the State that the Nazis would establish if victorious. To the Greeks it seemed otherwise. As Bury says:

A stranger from Athens or Miletus in the fifth century visiting the straggling villages which formed her unwalled unpretentious city must have had a feeling of being transported into an age long past, when men were braver, better and simpler, unspoiled by wealth, undisturbed by ideas. To a philosopher, like Plato, speculating in political science, the Spartan State seemed the nearest approach to the ideal. The ordinary Greek looked upon it as a structure of severe and simple beauty, a Dorian city stately as a Dorian temple, far nobler than his own abode but not so comfortable to dwell in.[1]

One reason for the admiration felt for Sparta by other Greeks was it stability. All other Greek cities had revolutions, but the Spartan constitution remained unchanged for centuries, except for a gradual increase in the powers of the ephors, which occurred by legal means, without violence.

It cannot be denied that, for a long period, the Spartans were successful in their main purpose, the creation of a race of invincible warriors. The battle of Thermopylae (480 B.C.), though technically a defeat, is perhaps the best example of their valour. Ther-

[1] *History of Greece*, Vol. I, p. 141.

mopylae was a narrow pass through the mountains, where it was hoped that the Persian army could be held. Three hundred Spartans, with auxiliaries, repulsed all frontal attacks. But at last the Persians discovered a detour through the hills, and succeeded in attacking the Greeks on both sides at once. Every single Spartan was killed at his post. Two men had been absent on sick leave, suffering from a disease of the eyes amounting almost to temporary blindness. One of them insisted on being led by his helot to the battle, where he perished; the other, Aristodemus, decided that he was too ill to fight, and remained absent. When he returned to Sparta, no one would speak to him; he was called 'the coward Aristodemus'. A year later, he wiped out his disgrace by dying bravely at the battle of Plataea, where the Spartans were victorious.

After the war, the Spartans erected a memorial on the battlefield of Thermopylae, saying only: 'Stranger, tell the Lacedaemonians that we lie here, in obedience to their orders.'

For a long time, the Spartans proved themselves invincible on land. They retained their supremacy until the year 371 B.C., when they were defeated by the Thebans at the battle of Leuctra. This was the end of their military greatness.

Apart from war, the reality of Sparta was never quite the same as the theory. Herodotus, who lived at its great period, remarks, surprisingly, that no Spartan could resist a bribe. This was in spite of the fact that contempt for riches and love of the simple life was one of the main things inculcated in Spartan education. We are told that the Spartan women were chaste, yet it happened several times that a reputed heir to the kingship was set aside on the ground of not being the son of his mother's husband. We are told that the Spartans were inflexibly patriotic, yet the king Pausanias, the victor of Plataea, ended as a traitor in the pay of Xerxes. Apart from such flagrant matters, the policy of Sparta was always petty and provincial. When Athens liberated the Greeks of Asia Minor and the adjacent islands from the Persians, Sparta held aloof; so long as the Peloponnesus was deemed safe, the fate of other Greeks was a matter of indifference. Every attempt at a confederation of the Hellenic world was defeated by Spartan particularism.

Aristotle, who lived after the downfall of Sparta, gives a very hostile account of its constitution.[1] What he says is so different from what other people say that it is difficult to believe he is speaking of the same place, e.g. 'The legislator wanted to make the whole State hardy and temperate, and he has carried out his intention in the case of men, but he has neglected the women, who live in every

---

[1] *Politics*, Vol. II, 9 (1269B-1270A).

sort of intemperance and luxury. The consequence is that in such a State wealth is too highly valued, especially if the citizens fall under the dominion of their wives, after the manner of most warlike races. . . . Even in regard to courage, which is of no use in daily life, and is needed only in war, the influence of the Lacedaemonian women has been most mischievous. . . . This license of the Lacedaemonian women existed from the earliest times, and was only what might be expected. For . . . when Lycurgus, as tradition says, wanted to bring the women under his laws, they resisted, and he gave up the attempt.'

He goes on to accuse Spartans of avarice, which he attributes to the unequal distribution of property. Although lots cannot be sold, he says, they can be given or bequeathed. Two-fifths of all the land, he adds, belongs to women. The consequence is a great diminution in the number of citizens: it is said that once there were ten thousand, but at the time of the defeat by Thebes there were less than one thousand.

Aristotle criticizes every point of the Spartan constitution. He says that the ephors are often very poor, and therefore easy to bribe; and their power is so great that even kings are compelled to court them, so that the constitution has been turned into a democracy. The ephors, we are told, have too much licence, and live in a manner contrary to the spirit of the constitution, while the strictness in relation to ordinary citizens is so intolerable that they take refuge in the secret illegal indulgence of sensual pleasures.

Aristotle wrote when Sparta was decadent, but on some points he expressly says that the evil he is mentioning has existed from early times. His tone is so dry and realistic that it is difficult to disbelieve him, and it is in line with all modern experience of the results of excessive severity in the laws. But it was not Aristotle's Sparta that persisted in men's imagination; it was the mythical Sparta of Plutarch and the philosophic idealization of Sparta in Plato's *Republic*. Century after century, young men read these works, and were fired with the ambition to become Lycurguses or philosopher-kings. The resulting union of idealism and love of power has led men astray over and over again, and is still doing so in the present day.

The myth of Sparta, for medieval and modern readers, was mainly fixed by Plutarch. When he wrote, Sparta belonged to the romantic past; its great period was as far removed from his time as Columbus is from ours. What he says must be treated with great caution by the historian of institutions, but to the historian of myth it is of the utmost importance. Greece has influenced the world, always, through its effect on men's imaginations, ideals, and hopes, not directly through political power. Rome made roads which largely still survive, and laws which are the source of many modern legal codes, but it was the armies of Rome that made these things important. The Greeks, though admirable fighters, made few conquests, because they expended their military fury mainly on each other. It was left to the semi-barbarian Alexander to spread Hellenism throughout the Near East, and to make Greek the literary language in Egypt and Syria and the inland parts of Asia Minor. The Greeks could never have accomplished this task, not for lack of military force, but owing to their incapacity for political cohesion. The political vehicles of Hellenism have always been non-Hellenic; but it was the Greek genius that so inspired alien nations as to cause them to spread the culture of those whom they had conquered.

What is important to the historian of the world is not the petty wars between Greek cities, or the sordid squabbles for party ascendancy, but the memories retained by mankind when the brief episode was ended—like the recollection of a brilliant sunrise in the Alps, while the mountaineer struggles through an arduous day of wind and snow. These memories, as they gradually faded, left in men's minds the images of certain peaks that had shone with peculiar brightness in the early light, keeping alive the knowledge that behind the clouds a splendour still survived, and might at any moment become manifest. Of these, Plato was the most important in early Christianity, Aristotle in the medieval Church; but when, after the Renaissance, men began to value political freedom, it was above all to Plutarch that they turned. He influenced profoundly the English and French liberals of the eighteenth century, and the founders of the United States; he influenced the romantic movement in Germany, and has continued, mainly by indirect channels, to influence German thought down to the present day. In some ways his influence was good, in some bad; as regards Lycurgus and Sparta, it was bad. What he has to say about Lycurgus is important, and I shall give a brief account of it, even at the cost of some repetition.

Lycurgus—so Plutarch says—having resolved to give laws to Sparta, travelled widely in order to study different institutions. He liked the laws of Crete, which were 'very straight and severe',[1] but disliked those of Ionia, where there were 'superfluities and vanities'. In Egypt he learned the advantage of separating the soldiers from the rest of the people, and afterwards, having returned from his travels, 'brought the practice of it into Sparta: where setting the merchants, artificers, and labourers every one a part by themselves, he did establish a noble Commonwealth'. He made an equal division

[1] In quoting Plutarch I use North's translation.

of lands among all the citizens of Sparta in order to 'banish out of
the city all insolvency, envy, covetousness, and deliciousness, and
also all riches and poverty'. He forbade gold and silver money,
allowing only iron coinage, of so little value that 'to lay up thereof
the value of ten minas, it would have occupied a whole cellar in a
house'. By this means he banished 'all superfluous and unprofitable
sciences', since there was not enough money to pay their practitioners; and by the same law he made all external commerce impossible. Rhetoricians, panders, and jewellers, not liking the iron
money, avoided Sparta. He next ordained that all the citizens should
eat together, and all should have the same food.

Lycurgus, like other reformers, thought the education of children
'the chiefest and greatest matter, that a reformer of laws should
establish'; and like all who aim chiefly at military power, he was
anxious to keep up the birth rate. The 'plays, sports, and dances
the maids did naked before young men, were provocations to draw
and allure the young men to marry: not as persuaded by geometrical reasons, as saith Plato, but brought to it by liking, and of
very love'. The habit of treating a marriage, for the first few years,
as if it were a clandestine affair, 'continued in both parties a still
burning love, and a new desire of the one to the other'—such, at
least, is the opinion of Plutarch. He goes on to explain that a man
was not thought ill of if, being old and having a young wife, he
allowed a younger man to have children by her. 'It was lawful
also for an honest man that loved another man's wife . . . to in-
treat her husband to suffer him to lie with her, and that he might
also plough in that lusty ground, and cast abroad the seed of well-
favoured children'. There was to be no foolish jealousy, for 'Lycurgus did not like that children should be private to any men, but that
they should be common to the common weal: by which reason
he would also, that such as should become citizens should not be
begotten of every man, but of the most honest men only.' He goes
on to explain that this is the principle that farmers apply to their
live-stock.

When a child was born, the father brought him before the elders
of his family to be examined: if he was healthy, he was given back
to the father to be reared; if not, he was thrown into a deep pit of
water. Children, from the first, were subjected to a severe hardening
process, in some respects good—for example, they were not put in
swaddling clothes. At the age of seven, boys were taken away from
home and put in a boarding school, where they were divided into
companies, each under the orders of one of their number, chosen
for sense and courage. 'Touching learning they had as much as
served their turn: for the rest of their time they spent in learning

how to obey, to away with pain, to endure labour, to overcome still in fight.' They played naked together most of the time; after twelve years old, they wore no coats; they were always 'nasty and sluttish', and they never bathed except on certain days in the year. They slept on beds of straw, which in winter they mixed with thistle. They were taught to steal, and were punished if caught— not for stealing, but for stupidity.

Homosexual love, male if not female, was a recognized custom in Sparta, and had an acknowledged part in the education of adolescent boys. A boy's lover suffered credit or discredit by the boys actions; Plutarch states that once, when a boy cried out because he was hurt in fighting, his lover was fined for the boy's cowardice.

There was little liberty at any stage in the life of a Spartan.

Their discipline and order of life continued still, after they were full grown men, For it was not lawful for any man to live as he listed, but they were within their city, as if they had been in a camp, where every man knoweth what allowance he hath to live withal, and what business he hath else to do in his calling. To be short, they were all of this mind, that they were not born to serve themselves, but to serve their country. . . . One of the best and happiest things which Lycurgus ever brought into his city, was the great rest and leisure which he made his citizens to have, only forbidding them that they should not profess any vile or base occupation: and they needed not also to be careful to get great riches, in a place where goods were nothing profitable nor esteemed. For the Helots, which were bond men made by the wars, did till their grounds, and yielded them a certain revenue every year.

Plutarch goes on to tell a story of an Athenian condemned for idleness, upon hearing of which a Spartan exclaimed: 'show me the man condemned for living nobly and like a gentleman.'

Lycurgus (Plutarch continues) 'did accustom his citizens so, that they neither would nor could live alone, but were in manner as men incorporated one with another, and were always in company together, as the bees be about their master bee'.

Spartans were not allowed to travel, nor were foreigners admitted to Sparta, except on business; for it was feared that alien customs would corrupt Lacedaemonian virtue.

Plutarch relates the law that allowed Spartans to kill helots whenever they felt so disposed, but refuses to believe that anything so abominable can have been due to Lycurgus. 'For I cannot be persuaded, that ever Lycurgus invented, or instituted so wicked and mischievous an act, as that kind of ordinance was: because I imagine his nature was gentle and merciful, by the clemency and justice we see he used in all his other doings.' Except in this matter Plutarch has nothing but praise for the constitution of Sparta.

The effect of Sparta on Plato, with whom, at the moment, we shall be specially concerned, will be evident from the account of his Utopia, which will occupy the next chapter.

Chapter XIII

THE SOURCES OF PLATO'S OPINIONS

Plato and Aristotle were the most influential of all philosophers, ancient, medieval, or modern; and of the two, it was Plato who had the greater effect upon subsequent ages. I say this for two reasons: first, that Aristotle himself is an outcome of Plato; second, that Christian theology and philosophy, at any rate until the thirteenth century, was much more Platonic than Aristotelian. It is necessary therefore, in a history of philosophic thought, to treat Plato, and to a lesser degree Aristotle, more fully than any of their predecessors or successors.

The most important matters in Plato's philosophy are: first, his Utopia, which was the earliest of a long series; second, his theory of ideas, which was a pioneer attempt to deal with the still unsolved problem of universals; third, his arguments in favour of immortality; fourth, his cosmogony; fifth, his conception of knowledge as reminiscence rather than perception. But before dealing with any of these topics, I shall say a few words about the circumstances of his life and the influences which determined his political and philosophical opinions.

Plato was born in 428-7 B.C., in the early years of the Peloponnesian War. He was a well-to-do aristocrat, related to various people who were concerned in the rule of the Thirty Tyrants. He was a young man when Athens was defeated, and he could attribute the defeat to democracy, which his social position and his family connections were likely to make him despise. He was a pupil of Socrates, for whom he had a profound affection and respect; and Socrates was put to death by the democracy. It is not, therefore, surprising that he should turn to Sparta for an adumbration of his ideal commonwealth. Plato possessed the art to dress up illiberal suggestions in such a way that they deceived future ages, which admired the *Republic* without ever becoming aware of what was involved in its proposals. It has always been correct to praise Plato, but not to understand him. This is the common fate of great men. My object is the opposite. I wish to understand him, but to treat him with as little reverence as if he were a contemporary English or American advocate of totalitarianism.

The purely philosophical influences on Plato were also such as to predispose him in favour of Sparta. These influences, speaking broadly, were: Pythagoras, Parmenides, Heraclitus, and Socrates.

From Pythagoras (whether by way of Socrates or not) Plato derived the Orphic elements in his philosophy: the religious trend, the belief in immortality, the other-worldliness, the priestly tone, and all that is involved in the simile of the cave; also his respect for mathematics, and his intimate intermingling of intellect and mysticism.

From Parmenides he derived the belief that reality is eternal and timeless, and that, on logical grounds, all change must be illusory.

From Heraclitus he derived the negative doctrine that there is nothing permanent in the sensible world. This, combined with the doctrine of Parmenides, led to the conclusion that knowledge is not to be derived from the senses, but is only to be achieved by the intellect. This, in turn, fitted in well with Pythagoreanism.

From Socrates he probably learnt his preoccupation with ethical problems, and his tendency to seek teleological rather than mechanical explanations of the world. 'The Good' dominated his thought more than that of the pre-Socratics, and it is difficult not to attribute this fact to the influence of Socrates.

How is all this connected with authoritarianism in politics?

In the first place: Goodness and Reality being timeless, the best State will be the one which most nearly copies the heavenly model, by having a minimum of change and a maximum of static perfection, and its rulers should be those who best understand the eternal Good.

In the second place: Plato, like all mystics, has, in his beliefs, a core of certainty which is essentially incommunicable except by a way of life. The Pythagoreans had endeavoured to set up a rule of the initiate, and this is, at bottom, what Plato desires. If a man is to be a good statesman, he must know the Good; this he can only do by a combination of intellectual and moral discipline. If those who have not gone through this discipline are allowed a share in the government, they will inevitably corrupt it.

In the third place: much education is needed to make a good ruler on Plato's principles. It seems to us unwise to have insisted on teaching geometry to the younger Dionysius, tyrant of Syracuse, in order to make him a good king, but from Plato's point of view it was essential. He was sufficiently Pythagorean to think that without mathematics no true wisdom is possible. This view implies an oligarchy.

In the fourth place: Plato, in common with most Greek philosophers, took the view that leisure is essential to wisdom, which will therefore not be found among those who have to work for their living, but only among those who have independent means or who are relieved by the State from anxieties as to their subsistence. This point of view is essentially aristocratic.

Two general questions arise in confronting Plato with modern ideas. The first is: is there such a thing as 'wisdom'? The second is: granted that there is such a thing, can any constitution be devised that will give it political power?

'Wisdom', in the sense supposed, would not be any kind of specialized skill, such as is possessed by the shoemaker or the physician or the military tactician. It must be something more generalized than this, since its possession is supposed to make a man capable of governing wisely. I think Plato would have said that it consists in knowledge of the good, and would have supplemented this definition with the Socratic doctrine that no man sins wittingly, from which it follows that whoever knows what is good does what is right. To us, such a view seems remote from reality. We should more naturally say that there are divergent interests, and that the statesman should arrive at the best available compromise. The members of a class or a nation may have a common interest, but it will usually conflict with the interests of other classes or other nations. There are, no doubt, some interests of mankind as a whole, but they do not suffice to determine political action. Perhaps they will do so at some future date, but certainly not so long as there are many sovereign States. And even then the most difficult part of the pursuit of the general interest would consist in arriving at compromises among mutually hostile special interests.

But even if we suppose that there is such a thing as 'wisdom', is there any form of constitution which will give the government to the wise? It is clear that majorities, like general councils, may err, and in fact have erred. Aristocracies are not always wise; kings are often foolish; Popes, in spite of infallibility, have committed grievous errors. Would anybody advocate entrusting the government to university graduates, or even to doctors of divinity? Or to men who, having been born poor, have made great fortunes? It is clear that no legally definable selection of citizens is likely to be wiser, in practice, than the whole body.

It might be suggested that men could be given political wisdom by a suitable training. But the question would arise: what is a suitable training? And this would turn out to be a party question.

The problem of finding a collection of 'wise' men and leaving the government to them is thus an insoluble one. That is the ultimate reason for democracy.

Chapter XIV

PLATO'S UTOPIA

PLATO'S most important dialogue, the *Republic*, consists, broadly, of three parts. The first (to near the end of Book V) consists in the construction of an ideal commonwealth; it is the earliest of Utopias.

One of the conclusions arrived at is that rulers must be philosophers. Books VI and VII are concerned to define the word 'philosopher'. This discussion constitutes the second section.

The third section consists mainly of a discussion of various kinds of actual constitutions and of their merits and defects.

The nominal purpose of the *Republic* is to define 'justice'. But at an early stage it is decided that, since everything is easier to see in the large than in the small, it will be better to inquire what makes a just State than what makes a just individual. And since justice must be among the attributes of the best imaginable State, such a State is first delineated, and then it is decided which of its perfections is to be called 'justice'.

Let us first describe Plato's Utopia in its broad outlines, and then consider points that arise by the way.

Plato begins by deciding that the citizens are to be divided into three classes: the common people, the soldiers, and the guardians. The last, alone, are to have political power. There are to be much fewer of them than of the other two classes. In the first instance, it seems, they are to be chosen by the legislator; after that, they will usually succeed by heredity, but in exceptional cases a promising child may be promoted from one of the inferior classes, while among the children of guardians a child or young man who is unsatisfactory may be degraded.

The main problem, as Plato perceives, is to insure that the guardians shall carry out the intentions of the legislator. For this purpose he has various proposals, educational, economic, biological, and religious. It is not always clear how far these proposals apply to other classes than the guardians; it is clear that some of them apply to the soldiers, but in the main Plato is concerned only with the guardians, who are to be a class apart, like the Jesuits in old Paraguay, the ecclesiastics in the States of the Church until 1870, and the Communist Party in the U.S.S.R. at the present day.

The first thing to consider is education. This is divided into two parts, music and gymnastics. Each has a wider meaning than at present: 'music' means everything that is in the province of the muses, and 'gymnastics' means everything concerned with physical training and fitness. 'Music' is almost as wide as what we should call 'culture', and 'gymnastics' is somewhat wider than what we call 'athletics'.

Culture is to be devoted to making men *gentlemen*, in the sense which, largely owing to Plato, is familiar in England. The Athens of his day was, in one respect, analogous to England in the nineteenth century: there was in each an aristocracy enjoying wealth and social prestige, but having no monopoly of political power; and in each the aristocracy had to secure as much power as it could by means of impressive behaviour. In Plato's Utopia, however, the aristocracy rules unchecked.

Gravity, decorum and courage seem to be the qualities mainly to be cultivated in education. There is to be a rigid censorship from very early years over the literature to which the young have access and the music they are allowed to hear. Mothers and nurses are to tell their children only authorized stories. Homer and Hesiod are not to be allowed, for a number of reasons. First they represent the gods as behaving badly on occasion, which is unedifying; the young must be taught that evils never come from the gods, for God is not the author of all things, but only of good things. Second, there are things in Homer and Hesiod which are calculated to make their readers fear death, whereas everything ought to be done in education to make young people willing to die in battle. Our boys must be taught to consider slavery worse than death, and therefore they must have no stories of good men weeping and wailing, even for the death of friends. Third, decorum demands that there should never be loud laughter, and yet Homer speaks of 'inextinguishable laughter among the blessed gods'. How is a schoolmaster to reprove mirth effectively, if boys can quote this passage? Fourth, there are passages in Homer praising rich feasts, and others describing the lusts of the gods; such passages discourage temperance. (Dean Inge, a true Platonist, objected to a line in a well-known hymn: 'The shout of them that triumph, the song of them that feast,' which occurs in a description of the joys of heaven.) Then there must be no stories in which the wicked are happy or the good unhappy; the moral effect on tender minds might be most unfortunate. On all these counts, the poets are to be condemned.

Plato passes on to a curious argument about the drama. The good man, he says, ought to be unwilling to imitate a bad man; now most plays contain villains; therefore the dramatist, and the actor who plays the villain's part, have to imitate people guilty of various crimes. Not only criminals, but women, slaves, and inferiors generally, ought not to be imitated by superior men. (In Greece, as in Elizabethan England, women's parts were acted by men.) Plays, therefore, if permissible at all, must contain no characters except faultless male heroes of good birth. The impossibility of this is so evident that Plato decides to banish all dramatists from his city:

When any of these pantomimic gentlemen, who are so clever that they can imitate anything, comes to us, and makes a proposal to exhibit himself and his poetry, we will fall down and worship him as a sweet and holy and wonderful being; but we must also inform him that in our State such as he are not permitted to exist; the law will not allow them. And so when we have anointed him with myrrh, and set a garland of wool upon his head, we shall send him away to another city.

Next we come to the censorship of music (in the modern sense). The Lydian and Ionian harmonies are to be forbidden, the first because it expresses sorrow, the second because it is relaxed. Only the Dorian (for courage) and the Phrygian (for temperance) are to be allowed. Permissible rhythms must be simple, and such as are expressive of a courageous and harmonious life.

The training of the body is to be very austere. No one is to eat fish, or meat cooked otherwise than roasted, and there must be no sauces or confectionery. People brought up on his regimen, he says, will have no need of doctors.

Up to a certain age, the young are to see no ugliness or vice. But at a suitable moment, they must be exposed to 'enchantments', both in the shape of terrors that must not terrify, and of bad pleasures that must not seduce the will. Only after they have withstood these tests will they be judged fit to be guardians.

Young boys, before they are grown up, should see war, though they should not themselves fight.

As for economics: Plato proposes a thoroughgoing communism for the guardians, and (I think) also for the soldiers, though this is not very clear. The guardians are to have small houses and simple food; they are to live as in a camp, dining together in companies; they are to have no private property beyond what is absolutely necessary. Gold and silver are to be forbidden. Though not rich, there is no reason why they should not be happy; but the purpose of the city is the good of the whole, not the happiness of one class. Both wealth and poverty are harmful, and in Plato's city neither will exist. There is a curious argument about war, that it will be easy to purchase allies, since our city will not want any share in the spoils of victory.

With feigned unwillingness, the Platonic Socrates proceeds to apply his communism to the family. Friends, he says, should have all things in common, including women and children. He admits that this presents difficulties, but thinks them not insuperable. First of all, girls are to have exactly the same education as boys, learning music, gymnastics, and the art of war along with the boys. Women are to have complete equality with men in all respects. 'The same education which makes a man a good guardian will make a woman a good guardian; for their original nature is the same.' No doubt there are differences between men and women, but they have nothing to do with politics. Some women are philosophic, and suitable as guardians; some are warlike, and could make good soldiers.

The legislator, having selected the guardians, some men and some women, will ordain that they shall all share common houses and common meals. Marriage, as we know it, will be radically transformed.[1] At certain festivals, brides and bridegrooms, in such numbers as are required to keep the population constant, will be brought together, by lot, as they will be taught to believe; but in fact the rulers of the city will manipulate the lots on eugenic principles. They will arrange that the best sires shall have the most children. All children will be taken away from their parents at birth, and great care will be taken that no parents shall know who are their children, and no children shall know who are their parents. Deformed children, and children of inferior parents, 'will be put away in some mysterious unknown place, as they ought to be'. Children arising from unions not sanctioned by the State are to be considered illegitimate. Mothers are to be between twenty and forty, fathers between twenty-five and fifty-five. Outside these ages, intercourse is to be free, but abortion or infanticide is to be compulsory. In the 'marriages' arranged by the State, the people concerned have no voice; they are to be actuated by the thought of their duty to the State, not by any of those common emotions that the banished poets used to celebrate.

Since no one knows who his parents are, he is to call every one 'father' whose age is such that he might be his father, and similarly as regards 'mother' and 'brother' and 'sister'. (This sort of thing happens among some savages, and used to puzzle missionaries.) There is to be no marriage between a 'father' and 'daughter' or 'mother' and 'son'; in general, but not absolutely, marriages of 'brother' and 'sister' are to be prevented. (I think if Plato had

---

[1] "These women shall be, without exception, the common wives of these men, and no one shall have a wife of his own."

thought this out more carefully he would have found that he had prohibited *all* marriages, except the 'brother-sister' marriages which he regards as rare exceptions.)

It is supposed that the sentiments at present attached to the words 'father', 'mother', 'son', and 'daughter' will still attach to them under Plato's new arrangements; a young man, for instance, will not strike an old man, because he might be striking his father.

The advantage sought is, of course, to minimize private possessive emotions, and so remove obstacles to the domination of public spirit, as well as to acquiescence in the absence of private property. It was largely motives of a similar kind that led to the celibacy of the clergy.[1]

I come last to the theological aspect of the system. I am not thinking of the accepted Greek gods, but of certain myths which the government is to inculcate. Lying, Plato says explicitly, is to be a prerogative of the government, just as giving medicine is of physicians. The government, as we have already seen, is to deceive people in pretending to arrange marriages by lot, but this is not a religious matter.

There is to be 'one royal lie,' which, Plato hopes, may deceive the rulers, but will at any rate deceive the rest of the city. This 'lie' is set forth in considerable detail. The most important part of it is the dogma that God has created men of three kinds, the best made of gold, the second best of silver, and the common herd of brass and iron. Those made of gold are fit to be guardians; those made of silver should be soldiers; the others should do the manual work. Usually, but by no means always, children will belong to the same grade as their parents; when they do not, they must be promoted or degraded accordingly. It is thought hardly possible to make the present generation believe this myth, but the next, and all subsequent generations, can be so educated as not to doubt it.

Plato is right in thinking that belief in this myth could be generated in two generations. The Japanese have been taught since 1868 that the Mikado is descended from the sun-goddess, and that Japan was created earlier than the rest of the world. Any university professor, who, even in a learned work, throws doubt on these dogmas, is dismissed for un-Japanese activities. What Plato does not seem to realize is that the compulsory acceptance of such myths is incompatible with philosophy, and involves a kind of education which stunts intelligence.

The definition of 'justice', which is the nominal goal of the whole discussion, is reached in Book IV. It consists, we are told, in everybody doing his own work and not being a busybody: the city is

[1] See Henry C. Lea, *A History of Sacerdotal Celibacy.*

just when trader, auxiliary, and guardian, each does his own job without interfering with that of other classes.

That everybody should mind his own business is no doubt an admirable precept, but it hardly corresponds to what a modern would naturally call 'justice'. The Greek word so translated corresponded to a concept which was very important in Greek thought, but for which we have no exact equivalent. It is worth while to recall that Anaximander said:

Into that from which things take their rise they pass away once more, as is ordained; for they make reparation and satisfaction to one another for their injustice according to the appointed time.

Before philosophy began, the Greeks had a theory or feeling about the universe, which may be called religious or ethical. According to this theory, every person and every thing has his or its appointed place and appointed function. This does not depend upon the fiat of Zeus, for Zeus himself is subject to the same kind of law as governs others. The theory is connected with the idea of fate or necessity. It applies emphatically to the heavenly bodies. But where there is vigour, there is a tendency to overstep just bounds; hence arises strife. Some kind of impersonal super-Olympian law punishes *hubris*, and restores the eternal order which the aggressor sought to violate. This whole outlook, originally, perhaps, scarcely conscious, passed over into philosophy; it is to be found alike in cosmologies of strife, such as those of Heraclitus and Empedocles, and in monistic doctrines such as that of Parmenides. It is the source of the belief both in natural and in human law, and it clearly underlies Plato's conception of justice.

The word 'justice', as still used in the law, is more similar to Plato's conception than it is as used in political speculation. Under the influence of democratic theory, we have come to associate justice with equality, while for Plato it has no such implication. 'Justice', in the sense in which it is almost synonymous with 'law' —as when we speak of 'courts of justice'—is concerned mainly with property rights, which have nothing to do with equality. The first suggested definition of 'justice', at the beginning of the *Republic*, is that it consists in paying debts. This definition is soon abandoned as inadequate, but something of it remains at the end.

There are several points to be noted about Plato's definition. First, it makes it possible to have inequalities of power and privilege without justice. The guardians are to have all the power, because they are the wisest members of the community; injustice would only occur, on Plato's definition, if there were men in the other classes who were wiser than some of the guardians. That is why Plato provides for promotion and degradation of citizens, although he thinks that the double advantage of birth and education will, in most cases, make the children of guardians superior to the children of others. If there were a more exact science of government, and more certainty of men following its precepts, there would be much to be said for Plato's system. No one thinks it unjust to put the best men into a football team, although they acquire thereby a great superiority. If football were managed as democratically as the Athenian government the students to play for their university would be chosen by lot. But in matters of government it is difficult to know who has the most skill, and very far from certain that a politician will use his skill in the public interest rather than in his own or in that of his class or party or creed.

The next point is that Plato's definition of 'justice' presupposes a State organized either on traditional lines, or, like his own, so as to realize, in its totality, some ethical ideal. Justice, we are told, consists in every man doing his own job. But what is a man's job? In a State which, like ancient Egypt or the kingdom of the Incas, remains unchanged generation after generation, a man's job is his father's job, and no question arises. But in Plato's State no man has any legal father. His job, therefore, must be decided either by his own tastes or by the State's judgment as to his aptitudes. The latter is obviously what Plato would desire. But some kinds of work, though highly skilled, may be deemed pernicious; Plato takes this view of poetry, and I should take it of the work of Napoleon. The purposes of the Government, therefore, are essential in determining what is a man's job. Although all the rulers are to be philosophers, there are to be no innovations: a philosopher is to be, for all time, a man who understands and agrees with Plato.

When we ask: what will Plato's Republic achieve? the answer is rather humdrum. It will achieve success in wars against roughly equal populations, and it will secure a livelihood for a certain small number of people. It will almost certainly produce no art or science, because of its rigidity; in this respect, as in others, it will be like Sparta. In spite of all the fine talk, skill in war and enough to eat is all that will be achieved. Plato had lived through famine and defeat in Athens; perhaps, subconsciously, he thought the avoidance of these evils the best that statesmanship could accomplish.

A Utopia, if seriously intended, obviously must embody the ideals of its creator. Let us consider, for a moment, what we can mean by 'ideals'. In the first place, they are desired by those who believe in them; but they are not desired quite in the same way as a man desires personal comforts, such as food and shelter. What makes the difference between an 'ideal' and an ordinary object of desire is that the former is impersonal; it is something having (at least ostensibly) no special reference to the ego of the man who feels the desire, and therefore capable, theoretically, of being desired by everybody. Thus we might define an 'ideal' as something desired, not egocentric, and such that the person desiring it wishes that every one else also desired it. I may wish that everybody had enough to eat, that everybody felt kindly towards everybody, and so on, and if I wish anything of this kind I shall also wish others to wish it. In this way, I can build up what looks like an impersonal ethic, although in fact it rests upon the personal basis of my own desires—for the desire remains mine, even when what is desired has no reference to myself. For example, one man may wish that everybody understood science, and another that everybody appreciated art; it is a personal difference between the two men that produces this difference in their desires.

The personal element becomes apparent as soon as controversy is involved. Suppose some man says : 'You are wrong to wish everybody to be happy; you ought to desire the happiness of Germans and the unhappiness of everyone else.' Here 'ought' may be taken to mean that that is what the speaker wishes me to desire. I might retort that, not being German, it is psychologically impossible for me to desire the unhappiness of all non-Germans; but this answer seems inadequate.

Again, there may be a conflict of purely impersonal ideals. Nietzsche's hero differs from a Christian saint, yet both are impersonally admired, the one by Nietzscheans, the other by Christians. How are we to decide between the two except by means of our own desires? Yet, if there is nothing further, an ethical disagreement can only be decided by emotional appeals, or by force—in the ultimate resort, by war. On questions of fact, we can appeal to science and scientific methods of observation; but on ultimate questions of ethics there seems to be nothing analogous. Yet, if this is really the case, ethical disputes resolve themselves into contests for power—including propaganda power.

This point of view, in a crude form, is put forth in the first book of the *Republic* by Thrasymachus, who, like almost all the characters in Plato's dialogues, was a real person. He was a Sophist from Chalcedon, and a famous teacher of rhetoric; he appeared in the first comedy of Aristophanes, 427 B.C. After Socrates has, for some time, been amiably discussing justice with an old man named Cephalus, and with Plato's elder brothers Glaucon and Adeimantus, Thrasymachus, who has been listening with growing impatience, breaks in with a vehement protest against such childish nonsense.

He proclaims emphatically that 'justice is nothing else than the interest of the stronger'.

This point of view is refuted by Socrates with quibbles; it is never fairly faced. It raises the fundamental question in ethics and politics, namely: Is there any standard of 'good' and 'bad', except what the man using these words desires? If there is not, many of the consequences drawn by Thrasymachus seem unescapable. Yet how are we to say that there is?

At this point, religion has, at first sight, a simple answer. God determines what is good and what bad; the man whose will is in harmony with the will of God is a good man. Yet this answer is not quite orthodox. Theologians say that God is good, and this implies that there is a standard of goodness which is independent of God's will. We are thus forced to face the question: Is there objective truth or falsehood in such a statement as 'pleasure is good', in the same sense as in such a statement as 'snow is white'?

To answer this question, a very long discussion would be necessary. Some may think that we can, for practical purposes, evade the fundamental issue, and say: 'I do not know what is meant by "objective truth", but I shall consider a statement "true" if all, or virtually all, of those who have investigated it are agreed in upholding it.' In this sense, it is 'true' that snow is white, that Caesar was assassinated, that water is composed of hydrogen and oxygen, and so on. We are then faced with a question of fact: are there any similarly agreed statements in ethics? If there are, they can be made the basis both for rules of private conduct, and for a theory of politics. If there are not, we are driven in practice, whatever may be the philosophic truth, to a contest by force or propaganda or both, whenever an irreconcilable ethical difference exists between powerful groups.

For Plato, this question does not really exist. Although his dramatic sense leads him to state the position of Thrasymachus forcibly, he is quite unaware of its strength, and allows himself to be grossly unfair in arguing against it. Plato is convinced that there is 'the Good', and that its nature can be ascertained; when people disagree about it, one, at least, is making an intellectual error, just as much as if the disagreement were a scientific one on some matter of fact.

The difference between Plato and Thrasymachus is very important, but for the historian of philosophy it is one to be only noted, not decided. Plato thinks he can *prove* that his ideal Republic is good; a democrat who accepts the objectivity of ethics may think that he can *prove* the Republic bad; but anyone who agrees with Thrasymachus will say: 'There is no question of proving or disproving; the only question is whether you *like* the kind of State that Plato desires. If you do, it is good for you; if you do not, it is bad for you. If many do and many do not, the decision cannot be made by reason, but only by force, actual or concealed.' This is one of the issues in philosophy that are still open; on each side there are men who command respect. But for a very long time the opinion that Plato advocated remained almost undisputed.

It should be observed, further, that the view which substitutes the consensus of opinion for an objective standard has certain consequences that few would accept. What are we to say of scientific innovators like Galileo, who advocate an opinion with which few agree, but finally win the support of almost everybody? They do so by means of arguments, not by emotional appeals or state propaganda or the use of force. This implies a criterion other than the general opinion. In ethical matters, there is something analogous in the case of the great religious teachers. Christ taught that it is not wrong to pluck ears of corn on the Sabbath, but that it is wrong to hate your enemies. Such ethical innovations obviously imply some standard other than majority opinion, but the standard, whatever it is, is not objective fact, as in a scientific question. This problem is a difficult one, and I do not profess to be able to solve it. For the present, let us be content to note it.

Plato's Republic, unlike modern Utopias, was perhaps intended to be actually founded. This was not so fantastic or impossible as it might naturally seem to us. Many of its provisions, including some that we should have thought quite impracticable, were actually realized at Sparta. The rule of philosophers had been attempted by Pythagoras, and in Plato's time Archytas the Pythagorean was politically influential in Taras (the modern Taranto) when Plato visited Sicily and southern Italy. It was a common practice for cities to employ a sage to draw up their laws; Solon had done this for Athens, and Protagoras for Thurii. Colonies, in those days, were completely free from control by their parent cities, and it would have been quite feasible for a band of Platonists to establish the Republic on the shores of Spain or Gaul. Unfortunately chance led Plato to Syracuse, a great commercial city engaged in desperate wars with Carthage; in such an atmosphere, no philosopher could have achieved much. In the next generation, the rise of Macedonia had made all small States antiquated, and had brought about the futility of all political experiments in miniature.

Chapter XV

THE THEORY OF IDEAS

THE middle of the *Republic*, from the later part of Book V to the end of Book VII, is occupied mainly with questions of pure philosophy, as opposed to politics. These questions are introduced by a somewhat abrupt statement:

Until philosophers are kings, or the kings and princes of this world have the spirit and power of philosophy, and political greatness and wisdom meet in one, and those commoner natures who pursue either to the exclusion of the other are compelled to stand aside, cities will never have rest from these evils—no, nor the human race, as I believe—and then only will this our State have a possibility of life and behold the light of day.

If this is true, we must decide what constitutes a philosopher, and what we mean by 'philosophy'. The consequent discussion is the most famous part of the *Republic*, and has perhaps been the most influential. It has, in parts, extraordinary literary beauty; the reader may disagree (as I do) with what is said, but cannot help being moved by it.

Plato's philosophy rests on the distinction between reality and appearance, which was first set forth by Parmenides; throughout the discussion with which we are now concerned, Parmenidean phrases and arguments are constantly recurring. There is, however, a religious tone about reality, which is rather Pythagorean than Parmenidean; and there is much about mathematics and music which is directly traceable to the disciples of Pythagoras. This combination of the logic of Parmenides with the other-worldliness of Pythagoras and the Orphics produced a doctrine which was felt to be satisfying to both the intellect and the religious emotions; the result was a very powerful synthesis, which, with various modifications, influenced most of the great philosophers, down to and including Hegel. But not only philosophers were influenced by Plato. Why did the Puritans object to the music and painting and gorgeous ritual of the Catholic Church? You will find the answer in the tenth book of the *Republic*. Why are children in school compelled to learn arithmetic? The reasons are given in the seventh book.

The following paragraphs summarize Plato's theory of ideas.

Our question is: What is a philosopher? The first answer is in accordance with the etymology: a philosopher is a lover of wisdom. But this is not the same thing as a lover of knowledge, in the sense in which an inquisitive man may be said to love knowledge; vulgar curiosity does not make a philosopher. The definition is therefore amended: the philosopher is a man who loves the 'vision of truth'. But what is this vision?

Consider a man who loves beautiful things, who makes a point of being present at new tragedies, seeing new pictures, and hearing new music. Such a man is not a philosopher, because he loves only beautiful things, whereas the philosopher loves beauty in itself. The man who only loves beautiful things is dreaming, whereas the man who knows absolute beauty is wide awake. The former has only opinion; the latter has knowledge.

What is the difference between 'knowledge' and 'opinion'? The man who has knowledge has knowledge of *something*, that is to say, of something that exists, for what does not exist is nothing. (This is reminiscent of Parmenides.) Thus knowledge is infallible, since it is logically impossible for it to be mistaken. But opinion can be mistaken. How can this be? Opinion cannot be of what is not, for that is impossible; nor of what is, for then it would be knowledge. Therefore opinion must be of what both is and is not.

But how is this possible? The answer is that particular things always partake of opposite characters: what is beautiful is also, in some respects, ugly; what is just is, in some respects, unjust; and so on. All particular sensible objects, so Plato contends, have this contradictory character; they are thus intermediate between being and not-being, and are suitable as objects of opinion, but not of knowledge. 'But those who see the absolute and eternal and immutable may be said to know, and not to have opinion only.'

Thus we arrive at the conclusion that opinion is of the world presented to the senses, whereas knowledge is of a super-sensible eternal world; for instance, opinion is concerned with particular beautiful things, but knowledge is concerned with beauty in itself.

The only argument advanced is that it is self-contradictory to suppose that a thing can be both beautiful and not beautiful, or both just and not just, and that nevertheless particular things seem to combine such contradictory characters. Therefore particular things are not real. Heraclitus had said 'We step and do not step into the same rivers; we are and are not.' But combining this with Parmenides we arrive at Plato's result.

There is, however, something of great importance in Plato's doctrine which is not traceable to his predecessors, and that is the theory of 'ideas' or 'forms'. This theory is partly logical, partly metaphysical. The logical part has to do with the meaning of general words. There are many individual animals of whom we can truly say 'this is a cat'. What do we mean by the word 'cat'? Obviously something different from each particular cat. An animal is a cat, it would seem, because it participates in a general nature common to all cats. Language cannot get on without general words such as 'cat', and such words are evidently not meaningless. But if the word 'cat' means anything, it means something which is not this or that cat, but some kind of universal cattiness. This is not born when a particular cat is born, and does not die when it dies. In fact, it has no position in space or time; it is 'eternal'. This is the logical part of the doctrine. The arguments in its favour, whether ultimately valid or not, are strong, and quite independent of the metaphysical part of the doctrine.

According to the metaphysical part of the doctrine, the word 'cat' means a certain ideal cat, 'the cat', created by God, and unique. Particular cats partake of the nature of the cat, but more or less imperfectly; it is only owing to this imperfection that there can be many of them. The cat is real; particular cats are only apparent.

In the last book of the Republic, as a preliminary to a condemnation of painters, there is a very clear exposition of the doctrine of ideas or forms.

Here Plato explains that, whenever a number of individuals have a common name, they have also a common 'idea' or 'form'. For instance, though there are many beds, there is only one 'idea' or 'form' of a bed. Just as a reflection of a bed in a mirror is only apparent and not 'real', so the various particular beds are unreal, being only copies of the 'idea', which is the one real bed, and is made by God. Of this one bed, made by God, there can be knowledge, but in respect of the many beds made by carpenters there can be only opinion. The philosopher, as such, will be interested only in the one ideal bed, not in the many beds found in the sensible world. He will have a certain indifference to ordinary mundane affairs: 'how can he who has magnificence of mind and is the spectator of all time and all existence, think much of human life?' The youth who is capable of becoming a philosopher will be distinguished among his fellows as just and gentle, fond of learning, possessed of a good memory and a naturally harmonious mind. Such a one shall be educated into a philosopher and a guardian.

At this point Adeimantus breaks in with a protest. When he tries to argue with Socrates, he says, he feels himself led a little astray at each step, until, in the end, all his former notions are turned upside down. But whatever Socrates may say, it remains the case, as any one can see, that people who stick to philosophy become strange monsters, not to say utter rogues; even the best of them are made useless by philosophy.

Socrates admits that this is true in the world as it is, but maintains that it is the other people who are to blame, not the philosophers; in a wise community the philosophers would not seem foolish; it is only among fools that the wise are judged to be destitute of wisdom.

What are we to do in this dilemma? There were to have been two ways of inaugurating our Republic: by philosophers becoming rulers, or by rulers becoming philosophers. The first way seems impossible as a beginning, because in a city not already philosophic the philosophers are unpopular. But a born prince *might* be a philosopher, and 'one is enough; let there be one man who has a city obedient to his will, and he might bring into existence the ideal polity about which the world is so incredulous.' Plato hoped that he had found such a prince in the younger Dionysius, tyrant of Syracuse, but the young man turned out disappointingly.

In the sixth and seventh books of the *Republic*, Plato is concerned with two questions: First, what is philosophy? Second, how can a young man or woman, of suitable temperament, be so educated as to become a philosopher?

Philosophy, for Plato, is a kind of vision, the 'vision of truth'. It is not *purely* intellectual; it is not merely wisdom, but *love* of wisdom. Spinoza's 'intellectual love of God' is much the same intimate union of thought and feeling. Every one who has done any kind of creative work has experienced, in a greater or less degree, the state of mind in which, after long labour, truth or beauty appears, or seems to appear, in a sudden glory—it may be only about some small matter, or it may be about the universe. The experience is, at the moment, very convincing; doubt may come later, but at the time there is utter certainty. I think most of the best creative work, in art, in science, in literature, and in philosophy, has been the result of such a moment. Whether it comes to others as to me, I cannot say. For my part, I have found that, when I wish to write a book on some subject, I must first soak myself in detail, until all the separate parts of the subject-matter are familiar; then, some day, if I am fortunate, I perceive the whole, with all its parts duly interrelated. After that, I only have to write down what I have seen. The nearest analogy is first walking all over a mountain in a mist, until every path and ridge and valley is separately familiar, and then, from a distance, seeing the mountain whole and clear in bright sunshine.

This experience, I believe, is necessary to good creative work, but it is not sufficient; indeed the subjective certainty that it brings with it may be fatally misleading. William James describes a man who got the experience from laughing-gas; whenever he was under its influence, he knew the secret of the universe, but when he came to, he had forgotten it. At last, with immense effort, he wrote down the secret before the vision had faded. When completely recovered, he rushed to see what he had written. It was: 'A smell of petroleum prevails throughout.' What seems like sudden insight may be misleading, and must be tested soberly, when the divine intoxication has passed.

Plato's vision, which he completely trusted at the time when he wrote the *Republic*, needs ultimately the help of a parable, the parable of the cave, in order to convey its nature to the reader. But it is led up to by various preliminary discussions, designed to make the reader see the necessity of the world of ideas.

First, the world of the intellect is distinguished from the world of the senses; then intellect and sense-perception are in turn each divided into two kinds. The two kinds of sense-perception need not concern us; the two kinds of intellect are called, respectively, 'reason' and 'understanding'. Of these, reason is the higher kind; it is concerned with pure ideas, and its method is dialectic. Understanding is the kind of intellect that is used in mathematics; it is inferior to reason in that it uses hypotheses which it cannot test. In geometry, for example, we say: 'Let ABC be a rectilinear triangle.' It is against the rules to ask whether ABC really *is* a rectilinear triangle, although, if it is a figure that we have drawn, we may be sure that it is not, because we can't draw absolutely straight lines. Accordingly, mathematics can never tell us what *is*, but only what *would* be if. . . . There are no straight lines in the sensible world; therefore, if mathematics is to have more than hypothetical truth, we must find evidence for the existence of super-sensible straight lines in a super-sensible world. This cannot be done by the understanding, but according to Plato it can be done by reason, which shows that there is a rectilinear triangle in heaven, of which geometrical propositions can be affirmed categorically, not hypothetically.

There is, at this point, a difficulty which did not escape Plato's notice, and was evident to modern idealistic philosophers. We saw that God made only one bed, and it would be natural to suppose that he made only one straight line. But if there is a heavenly triangle, he must have made at least three straight lines. The objects of geometry, though ideal, must exist in many examples; we need the possibility of *two* intersecting circles, and so on. This suggests that geometry, on Plato's theory, should not be capable of ultimate truth, but should be condemned as part of the study of appearance. We will, however, ignore this point, as to which Plato's answer is somewhat obscure

Plato seeks to explain the difference between clear intellectual vision and the confused vision of sense-perception by an analogy from the sense of sight. Sight, he says, differs from the other senses, since it requires not only the eye and the object, but also light. We see clearly objects on which the sun shines: in twilight we see confusedly, and in pitch-darkness not at all. Now the world of ideas is what we see when the object is illumined by the sun, while the world of passing things is a confused twilight world. The eye is compared to the soul, and the sun, as the source of light, to truth or goodness.

The soul is like an eye: when resting upon that on which truth and being shine, the soul perceives and understands, and is radiant with intelligence; but when turned towards the twilight of becoming and perishing, then she has opinion only, and goes blinking about, and is first of one opinion and then of another, and seems to have no intelligence. . . . Now what imparts truth to the known and the power of knowing to the knower is what I would have you term the idea of good, and this you will deem to be the cause of science.

This leads up to the famous simile of the cave or den, according to which those who are destitute of philosophy may be compared to prisoners in a cave, who are only able to look in one direction because they are bound, and who have a fire behind them and a wall in front. Between them and the wall there is nothing; all that they see are shadows of themselves, and of objects behind them, cast on the wall by the light of the fire. Inevitably they regard these shadows as real, and have no notion of the objects to which they are due. At last some man succeeds in escaping from the cave to the light of the sun; for the first time he sees real things, and becomes aware that he had hitherto been deceived by shadows. If he is the sort of philosopher who is fit to become a guardian, he will feel it is his duty to those who were formerly his fellow-prisoners to go down again into the cave, instruct them as to the truth, and show them the way up. But he will have difficulty in persuading them, because, coming out of the sunlight, he will see shadows less clearly than they do, and will seem to them stupider than before his escape.

'And now, I said, let me show in a figure how far our nature is enlightened or unenlightened:—Behold! human beings living in an underground den, which has a mouth open toward the light and reaching all along the den; here they have been from their childhood, and have their legs and necks chained so that they cannot move, and can only see before them, being prevented by the chains from turning round their heads. Above and behind them a fire is blazing at a distance, and between the fire and the prisoners there is a raised way; and you will see, if you look, a low wall built along the way, like the screen which marionette players have in front of them, over which they show the puppets.

'I see.

'And do you see, I said, men passing along the wall carrying all sorts of vessels, and statues and figures of animals made of wood and stone and various materials, which appear over the wall? Some of them are talking, others silent.

'You have shown me a strange image, and they are strange prisoners.

'Like ourselves, I replied; and they see only their own shadows, or the shadows of one another, which the fire throws on the opposite wall of the cave.'

The position of the good in Plato's philosophy is peculiar. Science and truth, he says, are *like* the good, but the good has a higher place. 'The good is not essence, but far exceeds essence in dignity and power.' Dialectic leads to the end of the intellectual world in the perception of the absolute good. It is by means of the good that dialectic is able to dispense with the hypotheses of the mathematician. The underlying assumption is that reality, as opposed to appearance, is completely and perfectly good; to perceive the good, therefore, is to perceive reality. Throughout Plato's philosophy there is the same fusion of intellect and mysticism as in Pythagoreanism, but at this final culmination mysticism clearly has the upper hand.

Plato's doctrine of ideas contains a number of obvious errors. But in spite of these it marks a very important advance in philosophy, since it is the first theory to emphasize the problem of universals, which, in varying forms, has persisted to the present day. Beginnings are apt to be crude, but their originality should not be overlooked on this account. Something remains of what Plato had to say, even after all necessary corrections have been made. The absolute minimum of what remains, even in the view of those most hostile to Plato, is this: that we cannot express ourselves in a language composed wholly of proper names, but must have also general words such as 'man', 'dog', 'cat'; or, if not these, then relational words such as 'similar', 'before', and so on. Such words are not meaningless noises, and it is difficult to see how they can have meaning if the world consists entirely of particular things, such as are designated by proper names. There may be ways of getting round this argument, but at any rate it affords a *prima facie* case in favour of universals. I shall provisionally accept it as in some degree valid. But when so much is granted, the rest of what Plato says by no means follows.

In the first place, Plato has no understanding of philosophical syntax. I can say 'Socrates is human', 'Plato is human', and so on. In all these statements, it may be assumed that the word 'human' has exactly the same meaning. But whatever it means, it means something which is not of the same kind as Socrates, Plato, and the rest of the individuals who compose the human race. 'Human' is an adjective; it would be nonsense to say 'human is human'. Plato makes a mistake analogous to saying 'human is human'. He thinks that beauty is beautiful; he thinks that the universal 'man' is the name of a pattern man created by God, of whom actual men are imperfect and somewhat unreal copies: He fails altogether to realize how great is the gap between universals and particulars; his 'ideas' are really just other particulars, ethically and aesthetically superior to the ordinary kind. He himself, at a later date, began to see this difficulty, as appears in the *Parmenides*, which contains one of the most remarkable cases in history of self-criticism by a philosopher.

The *Parmenides* is supposed to be related by Antiphon (Plato's half-brother), who alone remembers the conversation, but is now only interested in horses. They find him carrying a bridle, and with difficulty persuade him to relate the famous discussion between Parmenides, Zeno, and Socrates. This, we are told, took place when Parmenides was old (about sixty-five), Zeno in middle life (about forty), and Socrates quite a young man. Socrates expounds the theory of ideas; he is sure that there are ideas of likeness, justice, beauty, and goodness; he is not sure that there is an idea of man; and he rejects with indignation the suggestion that there could be ideas of such things as hair and mud and dirt—though, he adds, there are times when he thinks that there is nothing without an idea. He runs away from this view because he is afraid of falling into a bottomless pit of nonsense.

'Yes, Socrates, said Parmenides; that is because you are still young; the time will come, if I am not mistaken, when philosophy will have a firmer grasp of you, and then you will not despise even the meanest things.'

Socrates agrees that, in his view, 'There are certain ideas of which all other things partake, and from which they derive their names; that similars, for example, become similar, because they partake of similarity; and great things become great, because they partake of greatness; and that just and beautiful things become just and beautiful, because they partake of justice and beauty.'

Parmenides proceeds to raise difficulties. (a) Does the individual partake of the whole idea, or only of a part? To either view there are objections. If the former, one thing is in many places at once; if the latter, the idea is divisible, and a thing which has a part of smallness will be smaller than absolute smallness, which is absurd. (b) When an individual partakes of an idea, the individual and the idea are similar; therefore there will have to be another idea, embracing both the particulars and the original idea. And there will have to be yet another, embracing the particulars and the two ideas, and so on *ad infinitum*. Thus every idea, instead of being one, becomes an infinited series of ideas. (This is the same as Aristotle's argument of the 'third man'.) (c) Socrates suggests that perhaps ideas are only thoughts, but Parmenides points out that thoughts must be of something. (d) Ideas cannot resemble the particulars that partake of them, for the reason given in (b) above. (e) Ideas, if there are any, must be unknown to us, because our knowledge is not absolute. (f) If God's knowledge is absolute, He will not know us, and therefore cannot rule us.

Nevertheless, the theory of ideas is not wholly abandoned. Without ideas, Socrates says, there will be nothing on which the mind can rest, and therefore reasoning will be destroyed. Parmenides tells him that his troubles come of lack of previous training, but no definite conclusion is reached.

I do not think that Plato's logical objections to the reality of sensible particulars will bear examination. He says, for example, that whatever is beautiful is also in some respects ugly; what is double is also half; and so on. But when we say of some work of art that it is beautiful in some respects and ugly in others, analysis will always (at least theoretically) enable us to say 'this part or aspect is beautiful, while that part or aspect is ugly.' And as regards 'double' and 'half', these are relative terms; there is no contradiction in the fact that 2 is double of 1 and half of 4. Plato is perpetually getting into trouble through not understanding relative terms. He thinks that if A is greater than B and less than C, then A is at once great and small, which seems to him a contradiction. Such troubles are among the infantile diseases of philosophy.

The distinction between reality and appearance cannot have the consequences attributed to it by Parmenides and Plato and Hegel. If appearance really appears, it is not nothing, and is therefore part of reality; this is an argument of the correct Parmenidean sort. If appearance does not really appear, why trouble our heads about it? But perhaps some one will say: 'Appearance does not really appear, but it appears to appear.' This will not help, for we shall ask again:

'Does it really appear to appear, or only *apparently* appear to appear?' Sooner or later, if appearance is even to appear to appear, we must reach something that *really* appears, and is therefore part of reality. Plato would not dream of denying that there appear to be many beds, although there is only one real bed, namely the one made by God. But he does not seem to have faced the implications of the fact that there are many appearances, and that this many-ness is part of reality. Any attempt to divide the world into por-tions, of which one is more 'real' than the other, is doomed to failure.

Connected with this is another curious view of Plato's, that knowledge and opinion must be concerned with different subject-matters. *We* should say: If I think it is going to snow, that is opinion; if later I see it snowing, that is knowledge; but the subject-matter is the same on both occasions. Plato, however, thinks that what can at any time be a matter of opinion can never be a matter of knowledge. Knowledge is certain and infallible; opinion is not merely fallible, but is necessarily mistaken, since it assumes the reality of what is only appearance. All this repeats what had been said by Parmenides.

There is one respect in which Plato's metaphysic is apparently different from that of Parmenides. For Parmenides there is only the One; for Plato, there are many ideas. There are not only beauty, truth, and goodness, but, as we saw, there is the heavenly bed, created by God; there is a heavenly man, a heavenly dog, a heavenly cat, and so on through a whole Noah's ark. All this however, seems, in the *Republic*, to have been not adequately thought out. A Platonic idea or form is not a thought, though it may be the object of a thought. It is difficult to see how God can have created it, since its being is timeless, and he could not have decided to create a bed unless his thought, when he decided, had had for its object that very Platonic bed which we are told he brought into existence. What is timeless must be uncreated. We come here to a difficulty which has troubled many philosophic theologians. Only the con-tingent world, the world in space and time, can have been created; but this is the everyday world which has been condemned as illusory and also bad. Therefore the Creator, it would seem, created only illusion and evil. Some Gnostics were so consistent as to adopt this view; but in Plato the difficulty is still below the surface, and he seems, in the *Republic*, to have never become aware of it.

The philosopher who is to be a guardian must, according to Plato, return into the cave, and live among those who have never seen the sun of truth. It would seem that God Himself, if He wishes to amend His creation, must do likewise; a Christian Platonist might so interpret the Incarnation. But it remains completely impossible to explain why God was not content with the world of ideas. The philosopher finds the cave in existence, and is actuated by benevolence in returning to it; but the Creator, if He created everything, might, one would think, have avoided the cave altogether.

Perhaps this difficulty arises only from the Christian notion of a Creator, and is not chargeable to Plato, who says that God did not create everything, but only what is good. The multiplicity of the sensible world, on this view, would have some other source than God. And the ideas would, perhaps, be not so much *created* by God as constituents of His essence. The apparent pluralism involved in the multiplicity of ideas would thus not be ultimate. Ultimately there is only God, or the Good, to whom the ideas are adjectival. This, at any rate, is a possible interpretation of Plato.

Plato proceeds to an interesting sketch of the education proper to a young man who is to be a guardian. We saw that the young man is selected for this honour on the ground of a combination of intellectual and moral qualities; he must be just and gentle, fond of learning, with a good memory and a harmonious mind. The young man who has been chosen for these merits will spend the years from twenty to thirty on the four Pythagorean studies: arithmetic, geometry (plane and solid), astronomy, and harmony. These studies are not to be pursued in any utilitarian spirit, but in order to prepare his mind for the vision of eternal things. In astronomy, for example, he is not to trouble himself too much about the actual heavenly bodies, but rather with the mathematics of the motion of ideal heavenly bodies. This may sound absurd to modern ears, but strange to say, it proved to be a fruitful point of view in connection with empirical astronomy. The way this came about is curious, and worth considering.

The apparent motions of the planets, until they have been very profoundly analysed, appear to be irregular and complicated, and not at all such as a Pythagorean Creator would have chosen. It was obvious to every Greek that the heavens ought to exemplify mathematical beauty, which would only be the case if the planets moved in circles. This would be especially evident to Plato, owing to his emphasis on the good. The problem thus arose: is there any hypothesis which will reduce the apparent disorderliness of planetary motions to order and beauty and simplicity? If there is, the idea of the good will justify us in asserting this hypothesis. Aristarchus of Samos found such a hypothesis: that all the planets, including the earth, go round the sun in circles. This view was rejected for two thousand years, partly on the authority of Aristotle, who attributes a rather similar hypothesis to 'the Pythagoreans' (*De Coelo*, 293 *a*).

It was revived by Copernicus, and its success might seem to justify Plato's aesthetic bias in astronomy. Unfortunately, however, Kepler discovered that the planets move in ellipses, not in circles, with the sun at a focus, not at the centre; then Newton discovered that they do not move even in exact ellipses. And so the geometrical simplicity sought by Plato, and apparently found by Aristarchus of Samos, proved in the end illusory.

This piece of scientific history illustrates a general maxim: that any hypothesis, however absurd, *may* be useful in science, if it enables a discoverer to conceive things in a new way; but that, when it has served this purpose by luck, it is likely to become an obstacle to further advance. The belief in the good as the key to the scientific understanding of the world was useful, at a certain stage, in astronomy, but at every later stage it was harmful. The ethical and aesthetic bias of Plato, and still more of Aristotle, did much to kill Greek science.

It is noteworthy that modern Platonists, with few exceptions, are ignorant of mathematics, in spite of the immense importance that Plato attached to arithmetic and geometry, and the immense influence that they had on his philosophy. This is an example of the evils of specialization: a man must not write on Plato unless he has spent so much of his youth on Greek as to have had no time for the things that Plato thought important.

Chapter XVI

PLATO'S THEORY OF IMMORTALITY

THE dialogue called after Phaedo is interesting in several respects. It purports to describe the last moments in the life of Socrates: his conversation immediately before drinking the hemlock, and after, until he loses consciousness. This presents Plato's ideal of a man who is both wise and good in the highest degree, and who is totally without fear of death. Socrates in face of death, as represented by Plato, was important ethically, both in ancient and in modern times. What the gospel account of the Passion and the Crucifixion was for Christians, the *Phaedo* was for pagan or free-thinking philosophers.[1] But the imperturbability of Socrates in his last hour is bound up with his belief in immortality, and the *Phaedo* is important as setting forth, not only the death of a martyr, but also many doctrines which were afterwards Christian. The theology of St Paul and of the Fathers was largely derived from it, directly or indirectly, and can hardly be understood if Plato is ignored.

An earlier dialogue, the *Crito*, tells how certain friends and disciples of Socrates arranged a plan by which he could escape to Thessaly. Probably the Athenian authorities would have been quite glad if he had escaped, and the scheme suggested may be assumed to have been very likely to succeed. Socrates, however, would have none of it. He contended that he had been condemned by due process of law, and that it would be wrong to do anything illegal to avoid punishment. He first proclaimed the principle which we associate with the Sermon on the Mount, that 'we ought not to retaliate evil for evil to any one, whatever evil we may have suffered from him'. He then imagines himself engaged in a dialogue with the laws of Athens, in which they point out that he owes them the kind of respect that a son owes to a father or a slave to his master, but in an even higher degree; and that, moreover, every Athenian citizen is free to emigrate if he dislikes the Athenian state. The laws end a long speech with the words:

Listen, then, Socrates, to us who have brought you up. Think not

[1] Even for many Christians, it is second only to the death of Christ. "There is nothing in any tragedy, ancient or modern, nothing in poetry or history (with one exception), like the last hours of Socrates in Plato." These are the words of the Rev. Benjamin Jowett.

of life and children first, and of justice afterwards, but of justice first, that you may be justified before the princes of the world below. For neither will you nor any that belong to you be happier or holier or juster in this life, or happier in another, if you do as Crito bids. Now you depart in innocence, a sufferer and not a doer of evil; a victim, not of the laws, but of men. But if you go forth, returning evil for evil, and injury for injury, breaking the covenants and agreements which you have made with us, and wronging those whom you ought least of all to wrong, that is to say, yourself, your friends, your country, and us, we shall be angry with you while you live, and our brethren, the laws in the world below, will receive you as an enemy; for they will know that you have done your best to destroy us.

This voice, Socrates says, 'I seem to hear humming in my ears like the sound of the flute in the ears of the mystic.' He decides accordingly, that it is his duty to stay and abide the death sentence.

In the *Phaedo*, the last hour has come; his chains are taken off, and he is allowed to converse freely with his friends. He sends away his weeping wife, in order that her grief may not interfere with the discussion.

Socrates begins by maintaining that, though any one who has the spirit of philosophy will not fear death, but, on the contrary, will welcome it, yet he will not take his own life, for that is held to be unlawful. His friends inquire why suicide is held to be unlawful, and his answer, which is in accordance with Orphic doctrine is almost exactly what a Christian might say. 'There is a doctrine whispered in secret that man is a prisoner who has no right to open the door and run away; this is a great mystery which I do not quite understand.' He compares the relation of man to God with that of cattle to their owner; you would be angry, he says, if your ox took the liberty of putting himself out of the way, and so 'there may be reason in saying that a man should wait, and not take his own life until God summons him, as He is now summoning me'. He is not grieved at death, because he is convinced 'in the first place that I am going to other gods who are wise and good (of which I am as certain as I can be of any such matters) and secondly (though I am not so sure of this last) to men departed, better than those whom I leave behind. I have good hope that there is yet something remaining for the dead, some far better thing for the good than for the evil'.

Death, says Socrates, is the separation of soul and body. Here we come under Plato's dualism: between reality and appearance, ideas and sensible objects, reason and sense-perception, soul and body. These pairs are connected: the first in each pair is superior to the second both in reality and in goodness. An ascetic morality was the natural consequence of this dualism. Christianity adopted this doctrine in part, but never wholly. There were two obstacles. The first was that the creation of the visible world, if Plato was right, might seem to have been an evil deed, and therefore the Creator could not be good. The second was that orthodox Christianity could never bring itself to condemn marriage, though it held celibacy to be nobler. The Manichaeans were more consistent in both respects.

The distinction between mind and matter, which has become a commonplace in philosophy and science and popular thought, has a religious origin, and began as the distinction of soul and body. The Orphic, as we saw, proclaims himself the child of earth and of the starry heaven; from earth comes the body, from heaven the soul. It is this theory that Plato seeks to express in the language of philosophy.

Socrates, in the *Phaedo*, proceeds at once to develop the ascetic implications of his doctrine, but his asceticism is of a moderate and gentlemanly sort. He does not say that the philosopher should wholly abstain from ordinary pleasures, but only that he should not be a slave to them. The philosopher should not care about eating and drinking, but of course he should eat as much as is necessary; there is no suggestion of fasting. And we are told that Socrates, though indifferent to wine, could, on occasion, drink more than anybody else, without ever becoming intoxicated. It was not drinking that he condemned, but pleasure in drinking. In like manner, the philosopher must not care for the pleasures of love, or for costly raiment, or sandals, or other adornments of the person. He must be entirely concerned with the soul, and not with the body. 'He would like, as far as he can, to get away from the body and to turn to the soul.'

It is obvious that this doctrine, popularized, would become ascetic, but in intention it is not, properly speaking, ascetic. The philosopher will not abstain with an effort from the pleasures of sense, but will be thinking of other things. I have known many philosophers who forgot their meals, and read a book when at last they did eat. These men were acting as Plato says they should: they were not abstaining from gluttony by means of a moral effort, but were more interested in other matters. Apparently the philosopher should marry, and beget and rear children, in the same absent-minded way, but since the emancipation of women this has become more difficult. No wonder Xanthippe was a shrew.

Philosophers, Socrates continues, try to dissever the soul from communion with the body, whereas other people think that life is not worth living for a man who has 'no sense of pleasure and no part in bodily pleasure'. In this phrase, Plato seems—perhaps in-advertently—to countenance the view of a certain class of moral-ists, that bodily pleasures are the only ones that count. These moralists hold that the man who does not seek the pleasures of sense must be eschewing pleasure altogether, and living virtuously. This is an error which has done untold harm. In so far as the divi-sion of mind and body can be accepted, the worst pleasures, as well as the best, are mental—for example, envy, and many forms of cruelty and love of power. Milton's Satan rises superior to physical torment, and devotes himself to a work of destruction from which he derives a pleasure that is wholly of the mind. Many eminent ecclesiastics, having renounced the pleasures of sense, and not being on their guard against others, became dominated by love of power, which led them to appalling cruelties and persecutions, nominally for the sake of religion. In our own day, Hitler belonged to this type; by all accounts, the pleasures of sense were of very little importance to him. Liberation from the tyranny of the body contributes to greatness, but just as much to greatness in sin as to greatness in virtue.

This, however, is a digression, from which we must return to Socrates.

We come now to the intellectual aspect of the religion which Plato (rightly or wrongly) attributes to Socrates. We are told that the body is a hindrance in the acquisition of knowledge, and that sight and hearing are inaccurate witnesses: true existence, if re-vealed to the soul at all, is revealed in thought, not in sense. Let us consider, for a moment, the implications of this doctrine. It in-volves a complete rejection of empirical knowledge, including all history and geography. We cannot know that there was such a place as Athens, or such a man as Socrates; his death, and his courage in dying, belong to the world of appearance. It is only through sight and hearing that we know anything about all this, and the true philosopher ignores sight and hearing. What, then, is left to him? First, logic and mathematics; but these are hypothetical and do not justify any categorical assertion about the real world. The next step—and this is the crucial one—depends upon the idea of the good. Having arrived at this idea, the philosopher is supposed to know that the good is the real, and thus to be able to infer that the world of ideas is the real world. Later philosophers had arguments to prove the identity of the real and the good, but Plato seems to have assumed it as self-evident. If we wish to understand him, we must, hypothetically, suppose this assumption justified.

Thought is best, Socrates says, when the mind is gathered into itself, and is not troubled by sounds or sights or pain or pleasure but takes leave of the body and aspires after true being; 'and in this the philosopher dishonours the body'. From this point, Socrates goes on to the ideas or forms or essences. There is absolute justice, absolute beauty, and absolute good, but they are not visible to the eye. 'And I speak not of these alone, but of absolute greatness, and health, and strength, and of the essence or true nature of everything.' All these are only to be seen by intellectual vision. Therefore while we are in the body, and while the soul is infected with the evils of the body, our desire for truth will not be satisfied.

This point of view excludes scientific observation and experiment as methods for the attainment of knowledge. The experimenter's mind is not 'gathered into itself', and does not aim at avoiding sounds or sights. The two kinds of mental activity that can be pursued by the method that Plato recommends are mathematics and mystic insight. This explains how these two come to be so intimately combined in Plato and the Pythagoreans.

To the empiricist, the body is what brings us into touch with the world of external reality, but to Plato it is doubly evil, as a distorting medium, causing us to see as through a glass darkly, and as a source of lusts which distract us from the pursuit of knowledge and the vision of truth. Some quotations will make this clear.

The body is the source of endless trouble to us by reason of the mere requirement of food; and is liable also to diseases which overtake and impede us in the search after true being: it fills us full of loves, and lusts, and fears, and fancies of all kinds, and endless foolery, and in fact, as men say, takes away from us all power of thinking at all. Whence come wars, and fightings and factions? Whence but from the body and the lusts of the body? Wars are occasioned by the love of money, and money has to be acquired for the sake and in the service of the body; and by reason of all these impediments we have no time to give to philosophy; and, last and worst of all, even if we are at leisure to betake ourselves to some speculation, the body is always breaking in upon us, causing turmoil and confusion in our inquiries, and so amazing us that we are prevented from seeing the truth. It has been proved to us by experience that if we would have true knowledge of anything we must be quit of the body—the soul in herself must behold things in themselves: and then we shall attain the wisdom which we desire, and of which we say we are lovers; not while we live, but after death; for if while in company with the body the soul cannot have pure knowledge, knowledge must be attained after death, if at all.

And thus having got rid of the foolishness of the body we shall be pure and have converse with the pure, and know of ourselves the clear light everywhere, which is no other than the light of truth. For the impure are not permitted to approach the pure. . . . And

what is purification but the separation of the soul from the body?
. . . And this separation and release of the soul from the body is
termed death. . . . And the true philosophers, and they only, are
ever seeking to release the soul.

There is one true coin for which all things ought to be exchanged,
and that is wisdom.

The founders of the mysteries would appear to have had a real
meaning, and were not talking nonsense when they intimated in a
figure long ago that he who passes unsanctified and uninitiated into
the world below will lie on a slough, but that he who arrives there
after initiation and purification will dwell with the gods. For many,
as they say in the mysteries, are the thyrsus-bearers, but few are the
mystics, meaning, as I interpret the words, the true philosophers.

All this language is mystical, and is derived from the mysteries.
'Purity' is an Orphic conception, having primarily a ritual meaning,
but for Plato it means freedom from slavery to the body and its
needs. It is interesting to find him saying that wars are caused by
love of money, and that money is only needed for the service of
the body. The first half of this opinion is the same as that held by
Marx, but the second belongs to a very different outlook. Plato
thinks that a man could live on very little money if his wants were
reduced to a minimum, and this no doubt is true. But he also thinks
that a philosopher should be exempt from manual labour; he must
therefore live on wealth created by others. In a very poor State
there are likely to be no philosophers. It was the imperialism of
Athens in the age of Pericles that made it possible for Athenians to
study philosophy. Speaking broadly, intellectual goods are just as
expensive as more material commodities, and just as little independent of economic conditions. Science requires libraries, laboratories,
telescopes, microscopes, and so on, and men of science have to be
supported by the labour of others. But to the mystic all this is
foolishness. A holy man in India or Tibet needs no apparatus, wears
only a loin cloth, eats only rice, and is supported by very meagre
charity because he is thought wise. This is the logical development
of Plato's point of view.

To return to the *Phaedo*: Cebes expresses doubt as to the survival
of the soul after death, and urges Socrates to offer arguments. This
he proceeds to do, but it must be said that the arguments are very
poor.

The first argument is that all things which have opposites are
generated from their opposites—a statement which reminds us of
Anaximander's views on cosmic justice. Now life and death are
opposites, and therefore each must generate the other. It follows
that the souls of the dead exist somewhere, and come back to earth

in due course. St Paul's statement, 'the seed is not quickened except it die,' seems to belong to some such theory as this.

The second argument is that knowledge is recollection, and therefore the soul must have existed before birth. The theory that knowledge is recollection is supported chiefly by the fact that we have ideas, such as exact equality, which cannot be derived from experience. We have experience of approximate equality, but absolute equality is never found among sensible objects, and yet we know what we mean by 'absolute equality'. Since we have not learnt this from experience, we must have brought the knowledge with us from a previous existence. A similar argument, he says, applies to all other ideas. Thus the existence of essences, and our capacity to apprehend them, proves the pre-existence of the soul with knowledge.

The contention that all knowledge is reminiscence is developed at greater length in the *Meno* (82 ff.). Here Socrates says 'there is no teaching, but only recollection.' He professes to prove his point by having Meno call in a slave-boy whom Socrates proceeds to question on geometrical problems. The boy's answers are supposed to show that he really knows geometry, although he has hitherto been unaware of possessing this knowledge. The same conclusion is drawn in the *Meno* as in the *Phaedo*, that knowledge is brought by the soul from a previous existence.

As to this, one may observe, in the first place, that the argument is wholly inapplicable to empirical knowledge. The slave-boy could not have been led to 'remember' when the Pyramids were built, or whether the siege of Troy really occurred, unless he had happened to be present at these events. Only the sort of knowledge that is called *a priori*—especially logic and mathematics—can be possibly supposed to exist in every one independently of experience. In fact, this is the only sort of knowledge (apart from mystic insight) that Plato admits to be really knowledge. Let us see how the argument can be met in regard to mathematics.

Take the concept of equality. We must admit that we have no experience, among sensible objects, of exact equality; we see only approximate equality. How, then, do we arrive at the idea of absolute equality? Or do we, perhaps, have no such idea?

Let us take a concrete case. The metre is defined as the length of a certain rod in Paris at a certain temperature. What should we mean if we said, of some other rod, that its length was exactly one metre? I don't think we should mean anything. We could say: That most accurate processes of measurement known to science at the present day fail to show that our rod is either longer or shorter than the standard metre in Paris. We might, if we were sufficiently rash, add a prophecy that no subsequent refinements in the technique of measurement will alter this result. But this is still an empirical statement, in the sense that empirical evidence may at any moment *dis*prove it. I do not think we really possess the idea of *absolute* equality that Plato supposes us to possess.

But even if we do, it is clear that no child possesses it until it reaches a certain age, and that the idea is *elicited* by experience, although not directly derived from experience. Moreover, unless our existence before birth was not one of sense-perception, it would have been as incapable of generating the idea as this life is; and if our previous existence is supposed to have been partly super-sensible, why not make the same supposition concerning our present existence? On all these grounds, the argument fails.

The doctrine of reminiscence being considered established, Cebes says: 'About half of what was required has been proven; to wit, that our souls existed before we were born:—that the soul will exist after death as well as before birth is the other half of which the proof is still wanting.' Socrates accordingly applies himself to this. He says that it follows from what was said about everything being generated from its opposite, according to which death must generate life just as much as life generates death. But he adds another argument, which had a longer history in philosophy: that only what is complex can be dissolved, and that the soul, like the ideas, is simple and not compounded of parts. What is simple, it is thought, cannot begin or end or change. Now essences are unchanging: absolute beauty, for example, is always the same, whereas beautiful things continually change. Thus things seen are temporal, but things unseen are eternal. The body is seen, but the soul is unseen; therefore the soul is to be classified in the group of things that are eternal.

The soul, being eternal, is at home in the contemplation of eternal things, that is, essences, but is lost and confused when, as in sense-perception, it contemplates the world of changing things.

The soul, when using the body as an instrument of perception, that is to say, when using the sense of sight or hearing or some other sense (for the meaning of perceiving through the body is per-ceiving through the senses) . . . is then dragged by the body into the region of the changeable, and wanders and is confused; the world spins round her, and she is like a drunkard, when she touches change. . . . But when returning into herself she reflects, then she passes into the other world, the region of purity, and eternity, and immortality, and unchangeableness, which are her kindred, and with them she ever lives, when she is by herself, and is not let or hindered; then she ceases from her erring ways, and being in communion with the unchanging is unchanging. And this state of the soul is called wisdom.

The soul of the true philosopher, which has, in life, been liberated from thraldom to the flesh, will, after death, depart to the invisible world, to live in bliss in the company of the gods. But the impure soul, which has loved the body, will become a ghost haunting the sepulchre, or will enter into the body of an animal, such as an ass or wolf or hawk, according to its character. A man who has been virtuous without being a philosopher will become a bee or wasp or ant, or some other animal of a gregarious and social sort.

Only the true philosopher goes to heaven when he dies. 'No one who has not studied philosophy and who is not entirely pure at the time of his departure is allowed to enter the company of the Gods, but the lover of knowledge only.' That is why the true votaries of philosophy abstain from fleshly lusts: not that they fear poverty or disgrace, but because they 'are conscious that the soul was simply fastened or glued to the body—until philosophy received her, she could only view real existence through the bars of a prison, not in and through herself, . . . and by reason of lust had become the principal accomplice in her own captivity'. The philosopher will be temperate because 'each pleasure and pain is a sort of nail which nails and rivets the soul to the body, until she becomes like the body, and believes that to be true which the body affirms to be true'.

At this point, Simmias brings up the Pythagorean opinion that the soul is a harmony, and urges: if the lyre is broken, can the harmony survive? Socrates replies that the soul is not a harmony, for a harmony is complex, but the soul is simple. Moreover, he says, the view that the soul is a harmony is incompatible with its pre-existence, which was proved by the doctrine of reminiscence; for the harmony does not exist before the lyre.

Socrates proceeds to give an account of his own philosophical development, which is very interesting, but not germane to the main argument. He goes on to expound the doctrine of ideas, leading to the conclusion 'that ideas exist, and that other things participate in them and derive their names from them'. At last he describes the fate of souls after death: the good go to heaven, the bad to hell, the intermediate to purgatory.

His end, and his farewells, are described. His last words are: 'Crito, I owe a cock to Asclepius; will you remember to pay the debt?' Men paid a cock to Asclepius when they recovered from an illness, and Socrates has recovered from life's fitful fever.

'Of all the men of his time,' Phaedo concludes, 'he was the wisest and justest and best.'

The Platonic Socrates was a pattern to subsequent philosophers for many ages. What are we to think of him ethically? (I am concerned only with the man as Plato portrays him.) His merits are obvious. He is indifferent to worldly success, so devoid of fear that he remains calm and urbane and humorous to the last moment, caring more for what he believes to be truth than for anything else whatever. He has, however, some very grave defects. He is dishonest and sophistical in argument, and in his private thinking he uses intellect to prove conclusions that are to him agreeable, rather than in a disinterested search for knowledge. There is something smug and unctuous about him, which reminds one of a bad type of cleric. His courage in the face of death would have been more remarkable if he had not believed that he was going to enjoy eternal bliss in the company of the gods. Unlike some of his predecessors, he was not scientific in his thinking, but was determined to prove the universe agreeable to his ethical standards. This is treachery to truth, and the worst of philosophic sins. As a man, we may believe him admitted to the communion of saints; but as a philosopher he needs a long residence in a scientific purgatory.

Chapter XVII

PLATO'S COSMOGONY

PLATO'S cosmogony is set forth in the *Timaeus*,[1] which was translated into Latin by Cicero, and was, moreover, the only one of the dialogues that was known in the West in the Middle Ages. Both then, and earlier in Neoplatonism, it had more influence than anything else in Plato, which is curious, as it certainly contains more that is simply silly than is to be found in his other writings. As philosophy, it is unimportant, but historically it was so influential that it must be considered in some detail.

The place occupied by Socrates in the earlier dialogues is taken, in the *Timaeus*, by a Pythagorean, and the doctrines of that school are in the main adopted, including (up to a point) the view that number is the explanation of the world. There is first a summary of the first five books of the *Republic*, then the myth of Atlantis, which is said to have been an island off the Pillars of Hercules, larger than Libya and Asia put together. Then Timaeus, who is a Pythagorean astronomer, proceeds to tell the history of the world down to the creation of man. What he says is, in outline, as follows.

What is unchanging is apprehended by intelligence and reason; what is changing is apprehended by opinion. The world being sensible, cannot be eternal, and must have been created by God. Since God is good, He made the world after the pattern of the eternal; being without jealousy, He wanted everything as like Himself as possible. 'God desired that all things should be good, and nothing bad, as far as possible.' 'Finding the whole visible sphere not at rest, but moving in an irregular and disorderly fashion, out of disorder he brought order.' (Thus it appears that Plato's God, unlike the Jewish and Christian God, did not create the world out of nothing, but rearranged pre-existing material.) He put intelligence in the soul, and the soul in the body. He made the world as a whole a living creature having soul and intelligence. There is only *one* world, not many, as various pre-Socratics had taught; there cannot be more than one, since it is a created copy designed to accord as closely as possible with the eternal original apprehended by God. The world in its entirety is one visible animal, comprehending within itself all

---

[1] This dialogue contains much that is obscure and has given rise to controversies among commentators. On the whole, I find myself in most agreement with Cornford's admirable book, *Plato's Cosmology*.

other animals. It is a globe, because *like* is fairer than *unlike*, and only a globe is alike everywhere. It rotates, because circular motion is the most perfect; and since this is its only motion it needs no feet or hands.

The four elements, fire, air, water, and earth, each of which apparently is represented by a number, are in continued proportion, i.e. fire is to air as air is to water and as water is to earth. God used all the elements in making the world, and therefore it is perfect, and not liable to old age or disease. It is harmonized by proportion, which causes it to have the spirit of friendship, and therefore to be indissoluble except by God.

God made first the soul, then the body. The soul is compounded of the indivisible-unchangeable and the divisible-changeable; it is a third and intermediate kind of essence.

Here follows a Pythagorean account of the planets, leading to an explanation of the origin of time:

When the father and creator saw the creature which he had made moving and living, the created image of the eternal gods, he rejoiced, and in his joy determined to make the copy still more like the original; and as this was eternal, he sought to make the universe eternal, so far as might be. Now the nature of the ideal being was everlasting, but to bestow this attribute in its fulness upon a creature was impossible. Wherefore he resolved to have a moving image of eternity, and when he set in order the heaven, he made this image eternal but moving, according to number, while eternity itself rests in unity; and this image we call Time.[1]

Before this, there were no days or nights. Of the eternal essence we must not say that it *was* or *will be*; only *is* is correct. It is implied that of the 'moving image of eternity' it is correct to say that it was and will be.

Time and the heavens came into existence at the same instant. God made the sun so that animals could learn arithmetic—without the succession of days and nights, one supposes, we should not have thought of numbers. The sight of day and night, months and years, has created knowledge of number and given us the conception of time, and hence came philosophy. This is the greatest boon we owe to sight.

There are (apart from the world as a whole) four kinds of animals: gods, birds, fishes, and land animals. The gods are mainly fire; the fixed stars are divine and eternal animals. The Creator told the gods that he *could* destroy them, but would not do so. He left it to them to make the mortal part of all other animals, after he

[1] Vaughan must have been reading this passage when he wrote the poem beginning 'I saw eternity the other night.'

had made the immortal and divine part. (This, like other passages about the gods in Plato, is perhaps not to be taken very seriously. At the beginning, Timaeus says he seeks only probability, and cannot be sure. Many details are obviously imaginative, and not meant literally.)

The Creator, Timaeus says, made one soul for each star. Souls have sensation, love, fear, and anger; if they overcome these, they live righteously, but if not, not. If a man lives well, he goes, after death, to live happily for ever in his star. But if he lives badly, he will, in the next life, be a woman; if he (or she) persists in evil-doing, he (or she) will become a brute, and go on through trans-migrations until at last reason conquers. God put some souls on earth, some on the moon, some on other planets and stars, and left it to the gods to fashion their bodies.

There are two kinds of causes, those that are intelligent, and those that, being moved by others, are, in turn, compelled to move others. The former are endowed with mind, and are the workers of things fair and good, while the latter produce chance effects with-out order or design. Both sorts ought to be studied, for the creation is mixed, being made up of necessity and mind. (It will be observed that necessity is not subject to God's power.) Timaeus now pro-ceeds to deal with the part contributed by necessity.[1]

Earth, air, fire, and water are not the first principles or letters or elements; they are not even syllables or first compounds. Fire, for instance, should not be called *this*, but *such*—that is to say, it is not a substance, but rather a state of substance. At this point, the question is raised : are intelligible essences only names? The answer turns, we are told, on whether mind is or is not the same thing as true opinion. If it is not, knowledge must be knowledge of essences, and therefore essences cannot be mere names. Now mind and true opinion certainly differ, for the one is implanted by instruction, the other by persuasion; one is accompanied by true reason, the other is not; all men share in true opinion, but mind is the attribute of the gods and of a very few among men.

This leads to a somewhat curious theory of space, as something intermediate between the world of essence and the world of transient sensible things.

There is one kind of being which is always the same, uncreated and indestructible, never receiving anything into itself from with-out, nor itself going out to any other, but invisible and imper-

[1] Cornford (*op. cit.*) points out that 'necessity' is not to be confounded with the modern conception of a deterministic reign of law. The things that happen through 'necessity' are those not brought about by a purpose : they are chaotic and not subject to laws.

ceptible by any sense, and of which the contemplation is granted to intelligence only. And there is another nature of the same name with it, and like to it, perceived by sense, created, always in motion, becoming in place and again vanishing out of place, which is apprehended by opinion and sense. And there is a third nature, which is space, and is eternal, and admits not of destruction and provides a home for all created things, and is apprehended without the help of sense, by a kind of spurious reason, and is hardly real; which we beholding as in a dream, say of all existence of necessity be in some place and occupy a space, but that what is neither in heaven nor on earth has no existence.

This is a very difficult passage, which I do not pretend to understand at all fully. The theory expressed must, I think, have arisen from reflection on geometry, which appeared to be a matter of pure reason, like arithmetic, and yet had to do with space, which was an aspect of the sensible world. In general it is fanciful to find analogies with later philosophers, but I cannot help thinking that Kant must have liked this view of space, as one having an affinity with his own.

The true elements of the material world, Timaeus says, are not earth, air, fire, and water, but two sorts of right-angled triangles, the one which is half a square and the one which is half an equilateral triangle. Originally everything was in confusion, and 'the various elements had different places before they were arranged so as to form the universe'. But then God fashioned them by form and number, and 'made them as far as possible the fairest and best, out of things which were not fair and good'. The above two sorts of triangles, we are told, are the most beautiful forms, and therefore God used them in constructing matter. By means of these two triangles, it is possible to construct four of the five regular solids, and each atom of one of the four elements is a regular solid. Atoms of earth are cubes; of fire, tetrahedra; of air, octahedra; and of water, icosahedra. (I shall come to the dodecahedron presently.)

The theory of the regular solids, which is set forth in the thirteenth book of Euclid, was, in Plato's day, a recent discovery; it was completed by Theaetetus, who appears as a very young man in the dialogue that bears his name. It was, according to tradition, he who first proved that there are only five kinds of regular solids, and discovered the octahedron and the icosahedron.[1] The regular tetrahedron, octahedron, and icosahedron, have equilateral triangles for their faces; the dodecahedron has regular pentagons, and cannot therefore be constructed out of Plato's two triangles. For this reason he does not use it in connection with the four elements.

[1] See Heath, *Greek Mathematics*, Vol. I, pp. 159, 162, 294-296.

As for the dodecahedron, Plato says only 'there was yet a fifth combination which God used in the delineation of the universe'. This is obscure, and suggests that the universe is a dodecahedron; but elsewhere it is said to be a sphere.[1] The pentagram has always been prominent in magic, and apparently owes this position to the Pythagoreans, who called it 'Health' and used it as a symbol of recognition of members of the brotherhood:[2] It seems that it owed its properties to the fact that the dodecahedron has pentagons for its faces, and is, in some sense, a symbol of the universe. This topic is attractive, but it is difficult to ascertain much that is definite about it.

After a discussion of sensation, Timaeus proceeds to explain the two souls in man, one immortal, the other mortal, one created by God, the other by the gods. The mortal soul is 'subject to terrible and irresistible affections—first of all, pleasure, the greatest incitement to evil; then pain, which deters from good; also rashness and fear, two foolish counsellors, anger hard to be appeased, and hope easily led astray; these they (the gods) mingled with irrational sense and with all-daring love according to necessary laws, and so framed men'.

The immortal soul is in the head, the mortal in the breast.

There is some curious physiology, as, that the purpose of the intestines is to prevent gluttony by keeping the food in, and then there is another account of transmigration. Cowardly or unrighteous men will, in the next life, be women. Innocent light-minded men, who think that astronomy can be learnt by looking at the stars without knowledge of mathematics, will become birds; those who have no philosophy will become wild land-animals; the very stupidest will become fishes.

The last paragraph of the dialogue sums it up:

We may now say that our discourse about the nature of the universe has an end. The world has received animals, mortal and immortal, and is fulfilled with them, and has become a visible animal containing the visible—the sensible God who is the image of the intellectual, the greatest, best, fairest, most perfect—the one only-begotten heaven.

It is difficult to know what to take seriously in the *Timaeus*, and what to regard as play of fancy. I think the account of the creation as bringing order out of chaos is to be taken quite seriously; so also is the proportion between the four elements, and their relation to

---

[1] For a reconciliation of the two statements, see Cornford, *op. cit.*, p. 219.
[2] Heath, *op. cit.*, p. 161.

the regular solids and their constituent triangles. The accounts of time and space are obviously what Plato believes, and so is the view of the created world as a copy of an eternal archetype. The mixture of necessity and purpose in the world is a belief common to practically all Greeks, long antedating the rise of philosophy; Plato accepted it, and thus avoided the problem of evil, which troubles Christian theology. I think his world-animal is seriously meant. But the details about transmigration, and the part attributed to the gods, and other inessentials, are, I think, only put in to give a possible concreteness.

The whole dialogue, as I said before, deserves to be studied because of its great influence on ancient and medieval thought; and this influence is not confined to what is least fantastic.

Chapter XVIII

KNOWLEDGE AND PERCEPTION IN PLATO

Most modern men take it for granted that empirical knowledge is dependent upon, or derived from, perception. There is however in Plato and among philosophers of certain other schools a very different doctrine, to the effect that there is nothing worthy to be called 'knowledge' to be derived from the senses, and that the only real knowledge has to do with concepts. In this view, '2 + 2 = 4' is genuine knowledge, but such a statement as 'snow is white' is so full of ambiguity and uncertainty that it cannot find a place in the philosopher's corpus of truths.

This view is perhaps traceable to Parmenides, but in its explicit form the philosophic world owes it to Plato. I propose, in this chapter, to deal with Plato's criticism of the view that knowledge is the same thing as perception, which occupies the first half of the *Theaetetus*.

This dialogue is concerned to find a definition of 'knowledge', but ends without arriving at any but a negative conclusion; several definitions are proposed and rejected, but no definition that is considered satisfactory is suggested.

The first of the suggested definitions, and the only one that I shall consider, is set forth by Theaetetus in the words:

'It seems to me that one who knows something is perceiving the thing that he knows, and, so far as I can see at present, knowledge is nothing but perception.'

Socrates identifies this doctrine with that of Protagoras, that 'man is the measure of all things', i.e. that any given thing 'is to me such as it appears to me, and is to you such as it appears to you.' Socrates adds: 'Perception, then, is always something that *is*, and, as being knowledge, it is infallible.'

A large part of the argument that follows is concerned with the characterization of perception; when once this is completed, it does not take long to prove that such a thing as perception has turned out to be cannot be knowledge.

Socrates adds to the doctrine of Protagoras the doctrine of Heraclitus, that everything is always changing, i.e. that 'all the things we are pleased to say "are" really are in process of becoming'. Plato believes this to be true of objects of sense, but not of the objects of real knowledge. Throughout the dialogue, however, his positive doctrines remain in the background.

From the doctrine of Heraclitus, even if it be only applicable to objects of sense, together with the definition of knowledge as perception, it follows that knowledge is of what *becomes*, not of what *is*.

There are, at this point, some puzzles of a very elementary character. We are told that, since 6 is greater than 4 but less than 12, 6 is both great and small, which is a contradiction. Again, Socrates is now taller than Theaetetus, who is a youth not yet full grown; but in a few years Socrates will be shorter than Theaetetus. Therefore Socrates is both tall and short. The idea of a relational proposition seems to have puzzled Plato, as it did most of the great philosophers down to Hegel (inclusive). These puzzles, however, are not very germane to the argument, and may be ignored.

Returning to perception, it is regarded as due to an interaction between the object and the sense-organ, both of which, according to the doctrine of Heraclitus, are always changing, and both of which, in changing, change the percept. Socrates remarks that when he is well he finds wine sweet, but when ill, sour. Here it is a change in the percipient that causes the change in the percept.

Certain objections to the doctrine of Protagoras are advanced, and some of these are subsequently withdrawn. It is urged that Protagoras ought equally to have admitted pigs and baboons as measures of all things, since they also are percipients. Questions are raised as to the validity of perception in dreams and in madness. It is suggested that, if Protagoras is right, one man knows no more than another: not only is Protagoras as wise as the gods, but, what is more serious, he is no wiser than a fool. Further, if one man's judgments are as correct as another's, the people who judge that Protagoras is mistaken have the same reason to be thought right as he has.

Socrates undertakes to find an answer to many of these objections, putting himself, for the moment, in the place of Protagoras. As for dreams, the percepts are true as percepts. As for the argument about pigs and baboons, this is dismissed as vulgar abuse. As for the argument that, if each man is the measure of all things, one man is as wise as another, Socrates suggests, on behalf of Protagoras, a very interesting answer, namely that, while one judgment cannot be *truer* than another, it can be *better*, in the sense of having better consequences. This suggests pragmatism.[1]

This answer, however, though Socrates has invented it, does not

[1] It was presumably this passage that first suggested to F. C. S. Schiller his admiration of Protagoras.

satisfy him. He urges, for example, that when a doctor foretells the course of my illness, he actually *knows* more of my future than I do. And when men differ as to what it is wise for the State to decree, the issue shows that some men had a greater knowledge as to the future than others had. Thus we cannot escape the conclusion that a wise man is a better measure of things than a fool.

All these are objections to the doctrine that each man is the measure of all things, and only indirectly to the doctrine that 'knowledge' means 'perception', in so far as this doctrine leads to the other. There is, however, a direct argument, namely that memory must be allowed as well as perception. This is admitted, and to this extent the proposed definition is amended.

We come next to criticisms of the doctrine of Heraclitus. This is first pushed to extremes, in accordance, we are told, with the practice of his disciples among the bright youths of Ephesus. A thing may change in two ways, by locomotion, and by a change of quality, and the doctrine of flux is held to state that everything is always changing in both respects.[1] And not only is everything always undergoing *some* qualitative change, but everything is always changing *all* its qualities—so, we are told, clever people think at Ephesus. This has awkward consequences. We cannot say 'this is white', for if it was white when we began speaking it will have ceased to be white before we end our sentence. We cannot be right in saying we are seeing a thing, for seeing is perpetually changing into not-seeing.[2] If everything is changing in every kind of way, seeing has no right to be called seeing rather than not-seeing, or perception to be called perception rather than not-perception. And when we say 'perception is knowledge', we might just as well say 'perception is not-knowledge.'

What the above argument amounts to is that, whatever else may be in perpetual flux, the meanings of words must be fixed, at least for a time, since otherwise no assertion is definite, and no assertion is true rather than false. There must be *something* more or less constant, if discourse and knowledge are to be possible. This, I think, should be admitted. But a great deal of flux is compatible with this admission.

There is, at this point, a refusal to discuss Parmenides, on the

[1] It seems that neither Plato nor the dynamic youths of Ephesus had noticed that locomotion is impossible on the extreme Heraclitean doctrine. Motion demands that a given thing A should be now here, now there: it must remain the *same* thing while it moves. In the doctrine that Plato examines there is change of quality and change of place, but not change of substance. In this respect, modern quantum physics goes further than the most extreme disciples of Heraclitus went in Plato's time. Plato would have thought this fatal to science, but it has not proved so.

[2] Compare the advertisement: 'That's Shell, that was.'

ground that he is too great and grand. He is a 'reverend and awful figure'. 'There was a sort of depth in him that was altogether noble.' He is 'one being whom I respect above all'. In these remarks Plato shows his love for a static universe, and his dislike of the Heraclitean flux which he has been admitting for the sake of argument. But after this expression of reverence he abstains from developing the Parmenidean alternative to Heraclitus.

We now reach Plato's final argument against the identification of knowledge with perception. He begins by pointing out that we perceive *through* eyes and ears, rather than *with* them, and he goes on to point out that some of our knowledge is not connected with any sense-organ. We can know, for instance, that sounds and colours are unlike, though no organ of sense can perceive both. There is no special organ for 'existence and non-existence, likeness and unlikeness, sameness and differences, and also unity and numbers in general'. The same applies to honourable and dishonourable, and good and bad. 'The mind contemplates some things through its own instrumentality, others through the bodily faculties.' We perceive hard and soft through touch, but it is the mind that judges that they exist and that they are contraries. Only the mind can reach existence, and we cannot reach truth if we do not reach existence. It follows that we cannot know things through the senses alone, since through the senses alone we cannot know that things exist. Therefore knowledge consists in reflection, not in impressions, and perception is not knowledge, because it 'has no part in apprehending truth, since it has none in apprehending existence'.

To disentangle what can be accepted from what must be rejected in this argument against the identification of knowledge with perception is by no means easy. There are three inter-connected theses that Plato discusses, namely:

(1) Knowledge is perception;
(2) Man is the measure of all things;
(3) Everything is in a state of flux.

(1) The first of these, with which alone the argument is primarily concerned, is hardly discussed on its own account except in the final passage with which we have just been concerned. Here it is argued that comparison, knowledge of existence, and understanding of number, are essential to knowledge, but cannot be included in perception since they are not effected through any sense-organ. The things to be said about these are different. Let us begin with likeness and unlikeness.

That two shades of colour, both of which I am seeing, are

similar or dissimilar as the case may be, is something which I, for my part, should accept, not indeed as a 'percept', but as a 'judgment of perception'. A percept, I should say, is not knowledge, but merely something that happens, and that belongs equally to the world of physics and to the world of psychology. We naturally think of perception, as Plato does, as a relation between a percipient and an object: we say 'I see a table.' But here 'I' and 'table' are logical constructions. The core of crude occurrence is merely certain patches of colour. These are associated with images of touch, they may cause words, and they may become a source of memories. The percept as filled out with images of touch becomes an 'object', which is supposed physical; the percept as filled out with words and memories becomes a 'perception', which is part of a 'subject' and is considered mental. The percept is just an occurrence, and neither true nor false; the percept as filled out with words is a judgment, and capable of truth or falsehood. This judgment I call a 'judgment of perception'. The proposition 'knowledge is perception' must be interpreted as meaning 'knowledge is judgments of perception'. It is only in this form that it is grammatically capable of being correct.

To return to likeness and unlikeness, it is quite possible, when I perceive two colours simultaneously, for their likeness or unlikeness to be part of the datum, and to be asserted in a judgment of perception. Plato's argument that we have no sense-organ for perceiving likeness and unlikeness ignores the cortex and assumes that all sense-organs must be at the surface of the body.

The argument for including likeness and unlikeness as possible perceptive data is as follows. Let us assume that we see two shades of colour A and B, and that we judge 'A is like B'. Let us assume further, as Plato does, that such a judgment is in general correct, and, in particular, is correct in the case we are considering. There is, then, a relation of likeness between A and B, and not merely a judgment on our part asserting likeness. If there were only our judgment, it would be an arbitrary judgment, incapable of truth or falsehood. Since it obviously is capable of truth or falsehood, the likeness can subsist between A and B, and cannot be merely something 'mental'. The judgment 'A is like B' is true (if it is true) in virtue of a 'fact', just as much as the judgment 'A is red' or 'A is round'. The mind is no *more* involved in the perception of likeness than in the perception of colour.

I come now to *existence*, on which Plato lays great stress. We have, he says, as regards sound and colour, a thought which includes both at once, namely that they exist. Existence belongs to everything, and is among the things that the mind apprehends by itself; without reaching existence, it is impossible to reach truth.

The argument against Plato here is quite different from that in the case of likeness and unlikeness. The argument here is that all that Plato says about existence is bad grammar, or rather bad syntax. This point is important, not only in connection with Plato, but also with other matters such as the ontological argument for the existence of the Deity.

Suppose you say to a child 'lions exist, but unicorns don't', you can prove your point so far as lions are concerned by taking him to the Zoo and saying 'look, that's a lion'. You will not, unless you are a philosopher, add 'And you can see that that exists.' If, being a philosopher, you do add this, you are uttering nonsense. To say 'lions exist' means 'there are lions', i.e. ' "x is a lion" is true for a suitable x.' But we cannot say of the suitable x that it 'exists'; we can only apply this verb to a description, complete or incomplete. 'Lion' is an incomplete description, because it applies to many objects: 'The largest lion in the Zoo' is complete, because it applies to only one object.

Now suppose that I am looking at a bright red patch. I may say 'this is my present percept'; I may also say 'my present percept exists'; but I must not say 'this exists', because the word 'exists' is only significant when applied to a description as opposed to a name.[1] This disposes of *existence* as one of the things that the mind is aware of in objects.

I come now to understanding of numbers. Here there are two very different things to be considered: on the one hand, the propositions of arithmetic, and on the other hand, empirical propositions of enumeration. '$2 + 2 = 4$' is of the former kind; 'I have ten fingers' is of the latter.

I should agree with Plato that arithmetic, and pure mathematics generally, is not derived from perception. Pure mathematics consists of tautologies, analogous to 'men are men', but usually more complicated. To know that a mathematical proposition is correct, we do not have to study the world, but only the meanings of the symbols; and the symbols, when we dispense with definitions (of which the purpose is merely abbreviation), are found to be such words as 'or' and 'not', and 'all' and 'some', which do not, like 'Socrates', denote anything in the actual world. A mathematical equation asserts that two groups of symbols have the same meaning; and so long as we confine ourselves to pure mathematics, this meaning must be one that can be understood without knowing anything about what can be perceived. Mathematical truth, therefore, is, as Plato contends, independent of perception; but it is truth of a very peculiar sort, and is concerned only with symbols.

[1] On this subject see the last chapter of the present work.

Propositions of enumeration, such as 'I have ten fingers', are in quite a different category, and are obviously, at least in part, dependent on perception. Clearly the concept 'finger' is abstracted from perception; but how about the concept 'ten'? Here we may seem to have arrived at a true universal or Platonic idea. We cannot say that 'ten' is abstracted from perception, for any percept which can be viewed as ten of some kind of thing can equally well be viewed otherwise. Suppose I give the name 'digitary' to all the fingers of one hand taken together; then I can say 'I have two digitaries', and this describes the same fact of perception as I formerly described by the help of the number ten. Thus in the statement 'I have ten fingers' perception plays a smaller part, and conception a larger part, than in such a statement as 'this is red'. The matter, however, is only one of degree.

The complete answer, as regards propositions in which the word 'ten' occurs, is that, when these propositions are correctly analysed, they are found to contain no constituent corresponding to the word 'ten'. To explain this in the case of such a large number as ten would be complicated; let us, therefore, substitute 'I have two hands.' This means:

'There is an a such that there is a b such that a and b are not identical and whatever x may be, "x is a hand of mine" is true when, and only when, x is a or x is b.'

Here the word 'two' does not occur. It is true that two letters a and b occur, but we do not need to *know* that they are two, any more than we need to know that they are black, or white, or whatever colour they may happen to be.

Thus numbers are, in a certain precise sense, *formal*. The facts which verify various propositions asserting that various collections each have two members, have in common, not a constituent, but a form. In this they differ from propositions about the Statue of Liberty, or the moon, or George Washington. Such propositions refer to a particular portion of space-time; it is this that is in common between all the statements that can be made about the Statue of Liberty. But there is nothing in common among propositions 'there are two so-and-so's' except a common form. The relation of the symbol 'two' to the meaning of a proposition in which it occurs is far more complicated than the relation of the symbol 'red' to the meaning of a proposition in which it occurs. We may say, in a certain sense, that the symbol 'two' means nothing, for, when it occurs in a true statement, there is no corresponding constituent in the meaning of the statement. We may continue, if we like, to say that numbers are eternal, immutable, and so on, but we must add that they are logical fictions.

There is a further point. Concerning sound and colour, Plato says 'both together are *two*, and each of them is *one*'. We have considered the *two*; now we must consider the *one*. There is here a mistake very analogous to that concerning existence. The predicate 'one' is not applicable to things, but only to unit classes. We can say 'the earth has one satellite', but it is a syntactical error to say 'the moon is one'. For what can such an assertion mean? You may just as well say 'the moon is many', since it has many parts. To say 'the earth has one satellite' is to give a property of the concept 'earth's satellite', namely the following property:

'There is a *c* such that "*x* is a satellite of the earth" is true when, and only when, *x* is *c*.'

This is an astronomical truth; but if, for 'a satellite of the earth', you substitute 'the moon' or any other proper name, the result is either meaningless or a mere tautology. 'One', therefore is a property of certain concepts, just as 'ten' is a property of the concept 'my finger'. But to argue, 'the earth has one satellite, namely the moon, therefore the moon is one' is as bad as to argue 'The Apostles were twelve; Peter was an apostle; therefore Peter was twelve,' which would be valid if for 'twelve' we substituted 'white'.

The above considerations have shown that, while there is a formal kind of knowledge, namely logic and mathematics, which is not derived from perception, Plato's arguments as regards all other knowledge are fallacious. This does not, of course, prove that his conclusion is false; it proves only that he has given no valid reason for supposing it true.

(2) I come now to the position of Protagoras, that man is the measure of all things, or, as it is interpreted, that *each* man is the measure of all things. Here it is essential to decide the level upon which the discussion is to proceed. It is obvious that, to begin with, we must distinguish between percepts and inferences. Among percepts, each man is inevitably confined to his own; what he knows of the percepts of others he knows by inference from his own percepts in hearing and reading. The percepts of dreamers and madmen, *as* percepts, are just as good as those of others; the only objection to them is that, as their context is unusual, they are apt to give rise to fallacious inferences.

But how about inferences? Are they equally personal and private? In a sense, we must admit that they are. What I am to believe, I must believe because of some reason that appeals to me. It is true that my reason may be some one else's assertion, but that may be a perfectly adequate reason—for instance, if I am a judge listening to evidence. And however Protagorean I may be, it is reasonable to accept the opinion of an accountant about a set of figures in preference to my own, for I may have repeatedly found that if, at first, I disagree with him, a little more care shows me that he was right. In this sense I may admit that another man is wiser than I am. The Protagorean position, rightly interpreted, does not involve the view that I never make mistakes, but only that the evidence of my mistakes must appear to *me*. My past self can be judged just as another person can be judged. But all this presupposes that, as regards inferences as opposed to percepts, there is some impersonal standard of correctness. If any inference that I happen to draw is just as good as any other, then the intellectual anarchy that Plato deduces from Protagoras does in fact follow. On this point, therefore, which is an important one, Plato seems to be in the right. But the empiricist would say that perceptions are the test of correctness in inference in empirical material.

(3) The doctrine of universal flux is caricatured by Plato, and it is difficult to suppose that any one ever held it in the extreme form that he gives to it. Let us suppose, for example, that the colours we see are continually changing. Such a word as 'red' applies to many shades of colour, and if we say 'I see red', there is no reason why this should not remain true throughout the time that it takes to say it. Plato gets his results by applying to processes of continuous change such logical oppositions as perceiving and not-perceiving, knowing and not-knowing. Such oppositions, however, are not suitable for describing such processes. Suppose, on a foggy day, you watch a man walking away from you along a road: he grows dimmer and dimmer, and there comes a moment when you are sure that you no longer see him, but there is an intermediate period of doubt. Logical oppositions have been invented for our convenience, but continuous change requires a quantitative apparatus, the possibility of which Plato ignores. What he says on this subject, therefore, is largely beside the mark.

At the same time, it must be admitted that, unless words, to some extent, had fixed meanings, discourse would be impossible. Here again, however, it is easy to be too absolute. Words do change their meanings; take, for example, the word 'idea'. It is only by a considerable process of education that we learn to give to this word something like the meaning which Plato gave to it. It is necessary that the changes in the meanings of words should be slower than the changes that the words describe; but it is not necessary that there should be *no* changes in the meanings of words. Perhaps this does not apply to the abstract words of logic and mathematics, but these words, as we have seen, apply only to the form, not to the matter, of propositions. Here, again, we find that logic and mathematics are peculiar. Plato, under the influence of the Pythagoreans, assimilated other knowledge too much to mathematics. He shared this mistake with many of the greatest philosophers, but it was a mistake none the less.

Chapter XIX

ARISTOTLE'S METAPHYSICS

IN reading any important philosopher, but most of all in reading Aristotle, it is necessary to study him in two ways: with reference to his predecessors, and with reference to his successors. In the former aspect, Aristotle's merits are enormous; in the latter, his demerits are equally enormous. For his demerits, however, his successors are more responsible than he is. He came at the end of the creative period in Greek thought, and after his death it was two thousand years before the world produced any philosopher who could be regarded as approximately his equal. Towards the end of this long period his authority had become almost as unquestioned as that of the Church, and in science, as well as in philosophy, had become a serious obstacle to progress. Ever since the beginning of the seventeenth century, almost every serious intellectual advance has had to begin with an attack on some Aristotelian doctrine; in logic, this is still true at the present day. But it would have been at least as disastrous if any of his predecessors (except perhaps Democritus) had acquired equal authority. To do him justice, we must, to begin with, forget his excessive posthumous fame, and the equally excessive posthumous condemnation to which it led.

Aristotle was born, probably in 384 B.C., at Stagira in Thrace. His father had inherited the position of family physician to the king of Macedonia. At about the age of eighteen Aristotle came to Athens and became a pupil of Plato; he remained in the Academy for nearly twenty years, until the death of Plato in 348-7 B.C. He then travelled for a time, and married either the sister or the niece of a tyrant named Hermias. (Scandal said she was the daughter or concubine of Hermias, but both stories are disproved by the fact that he was a eunuch.) In 343 B.C. he became tutor to Alexander, then thirteen years old, and continued in that position until, at the age of sixteen, Alexander was pronounced by his father to be of age, and was appointed regent during Philip's absence. Everything one would wish to know of the relations of Aristotle and Alexander is unascertainable, the more so as legends were soon invented on the subject. There are letters between them which are generally regarded as forgeries. People who admire both men suppose that the tutor influenced the pupil. Hegel thinks that Alexander's career shows the practical usefulness of philosophy. As to this, A. W. Benn says: 'It would be unfortunate if philosophy had no better testimonial to show for herself than the character of Alexander. . . . Arrogant, drunken, cruel, vindictive, and grossly superstitious, he united the vices of a Highland chieftain to the frenzy of an Oriental despot.'[1]

For my part, while I agree with Benn about the character of Alexander, I nevertheless think that his work was enormously important and enormously beneficial, since, but for him, the whole tradition of Hellenic civilization might well have perished. As to Aristotle's influence on him, we are left free to conjecture whatever seems to us most plausible. For my part, I should suppose it *nil*. Alexander was an ambitious and passionate boy, on bad terms with his father, and presumably impatient of schooling. Aristotle thought no State should have as many as one hundred thousand citizens,[2] and preached the doctrine of the golden mean. I cannot imagine his pupil regarding him as anything but a prosy old pedant, set over him by his father to keep him out of mischief. Alexander, it is true, had a certain snobbish respect for Athenian civilization, but this was common to his whole dynasty who wished to prove that they were not barbarians. It was analogous to the feeling of nineteenth-century Russian aristocrats for Paris. This, therefore, was not attributable to Aristotle's influence. And I do not see anything else in Alexander that could possibly have come from this source.

It is more surprising that Alexander had so little influence on Aristotle, whose speculations on politics were blandly oblivious of the fact that the era of City States had given way to the era of empires. I suspect that Aristotle, to the end, thought of him as 'that idle and headstrong boy, who never could understand anything of philosophy'. On the whole, the contacts of these two great men seem to have been as unfruitful as if they had lived in different worlds.

From 335 B.C. to 323 B.C. (in which latter year Alexander died), Aristotle lived at Athens. It was during these twelve years that he founded his school and wrote most of his books. At the death of Alexander, the Athenians rebelled, and turned on his friends, including Aristotle, who was indicted for impiety, but, unlike Socrates, fled to avoid punishment. In the next year (322) he died.

Aristotle, as a philosopher, is in many ways very different from all his predecessors. He is the first to write like a professor: his treatises are systematic, his discussions are divided into heads, he is a professional teacher, not an inspired prophet. His work is critical, careful, pedestrian, without any trace of Bacchic enthusiasm. The Orphic elements in Plato are watered down in Aristotle, and mixed

[1] *The Greek Philosophers*, Vol. I, p. 285.   [2] *Ethics*, 1170B.

with a strong dose of common sense; where he is Platonic, one feels that his natural temperament has been overpowered by the teaching to which he has been subjected. He is not passionate, or in any profound sense religious. The errors of his predecessors were the glorious errors of youth attempting the impossible; his errors are those of age which cannot free itself of habitual prejudices. He is best in detail and in criticism; he fails in large construction, for lack of fundamental clarity and Titanic fire.

It is difficult to decide at what point to begin an account of Aristotle's metaphysics, but perhaps the best place is his criticism of the theory of ideas, and his own alternative doctrine of universals. He advances against the theory of ideas a number of very good arguments, most of which are already to be found in Plato's *Parmenides*. The strongest argument is that of the 'third man': if a man is a man because he resembles the ideal man, there must be a still more ideal man to whom both ordinary men and the ideal man are similar. Again, Socrates is both a man and an animal, and the question arises whether the ideal man is an ideal animal; if he is, there must be as many ideal animals as there are species of animals. It is needless to pursue the matter; Aristotle makes it obvious that, when a number of individuals share a predicate, this cannot be because of relation to something of the same kind as themselves, but more ideal. This much may be taken as proved, but Aristotle's own doctrine is far from clear. It was this lack of clarity that made possible the medieval controversy between nominalists and realists.

Aristotle's metaphysics, roughly speaking, may be described as Plato diluted by common sense. He is difficult because Plato and common sense do not mix easily. When one tries to understand him, one thinks part of the time that he is expressing the ordinary views of a person innocent of philosophy, and the rest of the time that he is setting forth Platonism with a new vocabulary. It does not do to lay too much stress on any single passage, because there is liable to be a correction or modification of it in some later passage. On the whole, the easiest way to understand both his theory of universals and his theory of matter and form is to set forth first the common-sense doctrine which is half of his view, and then to consider the Platonic modifications to which he subjects it.

Up to a certain point, the theory of universals is quite simple. In language, there are proper names, and there are adjectives. The proper names apply to 'things' or 'persons', each of which is the only thing or person to which the name in question applies. The sun, the moon, France, Napoleon, are unique; there are not a number of instances of things to which these names apply. On the other hand, words like 'cat', 'dog', 'man' apply to many different things. The problem of universals is concerned with the meanings of such words, and also of adjectives, such as 'white', 'hard', 'round', and so on. He says:[1] 'By the term "universal" I mean that which is of such a nature as to be predicated of many subjects, by "individual" that which is not thus predicated.'

What is signified by a proper name is a 'substance', while what is signified by an adjective or class-name, such as 'human' or 'man', is called a 'universal'. A substance is a 'this', but a universal is a 'such'—it indicates the *sort* of thing, not the actual particular thing. A universal is not a substance, because it is not a 'this'. (Plato's heavenly bed would be a 'this' to those who could perceive it; this is a matter as to which Aristotle disagrees with Plato.) 'It seems impossible,' Aristotle says, 'that any universal term should be the name of a substance. For . . . the substance of each thing is that which is peculiar to it, which does not belong to anything else; but the universal is common, since that is called universal which is such as to belong to more than one thing.' The gist of the matter, so far, is that a universal cannot exist by itself, but only *in* particular things.

Superficially, Aristotle's doctrine is plain enough. Suppose I say 'there is such a thing as the game of football,' most people would regard the remark as a truism. But if I were to infer that football could exist without football-players, I should be rightly held to be talking nonsense. Similarly, it would be held, there is such a thing as parenthood, but only because there are parents; there is such a thing as sweetness, but only because there are sweet things; and there is redness, but only because there are red things. And this dependence is thought to be not reciprocal: the men who play football would still exist even if they never played football; things which are usually sweet may turn sour; and my face, which is usually red, may turn pale without ceasing to be my face. In this way we are led to conclude that what is meant by an adjective is dependent for its being on what is meant by a proper name, but not vice versa. This is, I think, what Aristotle means. His doctrine on this point, as on many others, is a common-sense prejudice pedantically expressed.

But it is not easy to give precision to the theory. Granted that football could not exist without football-players, it could perfectly well exist without this or that football-player. And granted that a person can exist without playing football, he nevertheless cannot exist without doing *something*. The quality *redness* cannot exist without *some* subject, but it can exist without this or that subject; similarly a subject cannot exist without *some* quality, but can exist

[1] *On interpretation*, 17ᵃ.

without this or that quality. The supposed ground for the distinction between things and qualities thus seems to be illusory.

The true ground of the distinction is, in fact, linguistic; it is derived from syntax. There are proper names, adjectives, and relation-words; we may say 'John is wise, James is foolish, John is taller than James.' Here 'John' and 'James' are proper names, 'wise' and 'foolish' are adjectives, and 'taller' is a relation-word. Metaphysicians, ever since Aristotle, have interpreted these syntactical differences metaphysically: John and James are substances, wisdom and folly are universals. (Relation-words were ignored or misinterpreted.) It may be that, given sufficient care, metaphysical differences can be found that have some relation to these syntactical differences, but, if so, it will be only by means of a long process, involving, incidentally, the creation of an artificial philosophical language. And this language will contain no such names as 'John' and 'James', and no such adjectives as 'wise' and 'foolish'; all the words of ordinary languages will have yielded to analysis, and been replaced by words having a less complex significance. Until this labour has been performed, the question of particulars and universals cannot be adequately discussed. And when we reach the point at which we can at last discuss it, we shall find that the question we are discussing is quite different from what we supposed it to be at the outset.

If, therefore, I have failed to make Aristotle's theory of universals clear, that is (I maintain) because it is not clear. But it is certainly an advance on the theory of ideas, and is certainly concerned with a genuine and very important problem.

There is another term which is important in Aristotle and in his scholastic followers, and that is the term 'essence'. This is by no means synonymous with 'universal'. Your 'essence' is 'what you are by your very nature'. It is, one may say, those of your properties which you cannot lose without ceasing to be yourself, not only an individual thing, but a species, has an essence. The definition of a species should consist in mentioning its essence. I shall return to the conception of 'essence' in connection with Aristotle's logic. For the present I will merely observe that it seems to me a muddle-headed notion, incapable of precision.

The next point in Aristotle's metaphysics is the distinction of 'form' and 'matter'. (It must be understood that 'matter', in the sense in which it is opposed to 'form', is different from 'matter' as opposed to 'mind'.)

Here, again, there is a common-sense basis for Aristotle's theory, but here, more than in the case of universals, the Platonic modifications are very important. We may start with a marble statue:

here marble is the matter, while the shape conferred by the sculptor is the form. Or, to take Aristotle's examples, if a man makes a bronze sphere, bronze is the matter, and sphericity is the form; while in the case of a calm sea, water is the matter and smoothness is the form. So far, all is simple.

He goes on to say that it is in virtue of the form that the matter is some one definite thing, and this is the substance of the thing. What Aristotle means seems to be plain common sense: a 'thing' must be bounded, and the boundary constitutes its form. Take, say, a volume of water: any part of it *can* be marked off from the rest by being enclosed in a vessel, and then this part becomes a 'thing', but so long as the part is in no way marked out from the rest of the homogeneous mass it is not a 'thing'. A statue is a 'thing', and the marble of which it is composed is, in a sense, unchanged from what it was as part of a lump or as part of the contents of a quarry. *We* should not naturally say that it is the form that confers substantiality, but that is because the atomic hypothesis is ingrained in our imagination. Each atom, however, if it is a 'thing', is so in virtue of its being delimited from other atoms, and so having, in some sense, a 'form'.

We now come to a new statement, which at first sight seems difficult. The soul, we are told, is the form of the body. Here it is clear that 'form' does not mean 'shape'. I shall return later to the sense in which the soul is the form of the body; for the present, I will only observe that, in Aristotle's system, the soul is what makes the body *one* thing, having unity of purpose, and the characteristics that we associate with the word 'organism'. The purpose of an eye is to see, but it cannot see when parted from its body. In fact, it is the soul that sees.

It would seem, then, that 'form' is what gives unity to a portion of matter, and that this unity is usually, if not always, teleological. But 'form' turns out to be much more than this, and the more is very difficult.

The form of a thing, we are told, is its essence and primary substance. Forms are substantial, although universals are not. When a man makes a brazen sphere, both the matter and the form already existed, and all that he does is to bring them together; the man does not make the form, any more than he makes the brass. Not everything has matter; there are eternal things, and these have no matter, except those of them that are movable in space. Things increase in actuality by acquiring form; matter without form is only a potentiality.

The view that forms are substances, which exist independently of the matter in which they are exemplified, seems to expose

Aristotle to his own arguments against Platonic ideas. A form is intended by him to be something quite different from a universal, but it has many of the same characteristics. Form is, we are told, more real than matter; this is reminiscent of the sole reality of the ideas. The change that Aristotle makes in Plato's metaphysic is, it would seem, less than he represents it as being. This view is taken by Zeller, who, on the question of matter and form says:[1]

'The final explanation of Aristotle's want of clearness on this subject is, however, to be found in the fact that he *had* only half emancipated himself, as we shall see, from Plato's tendency to hypostatize ideas. The "Forms" had for him, as the "Ideas" had for Plato, a metaphysical existence of their own, as conditioning all individual things. And keenly as he followed the growth of ideas out of experience, it is none the less true that these ideas, especially at the point where they are farthest removed from experience and immediate perception, are metamorphosed in the end from a logical product of human thought into an immediate presentment of a supersensible world, and the object, in that sense, of an intellectual intuition.'

I do not see how Aristotle could have found a reply to this criticism.

The only answer that I can imagine would be one that maintained that no two things could have the *same* form. If a man makes two brass spheres (we should have to say), each has its own special sphericity, which is substantial and particular, an instance of the universal 'sphericity', but not identical with it. I do not think the language of the passages I quoted would readily support this interpretation. And it would be open to the objection that the particular sphericity would, on Aristotle's view, be unknowable, whereas it is of the essence of his metaphysics that, as there comes to be more of form and less of matter, things become gradually more knowable. This is not consistent with the rest of his views unless the form can be embodied in many particular things. If he were to say that there are as many forms that are instances of sphericity as there are spherical things, he would have to make very radical alterations in his philosophy. For instance, his view that a form is identical with its essence is incompatible with the above suggested escape.

The doctrine of matter and form in Aristotle is connected with the distinction of potentiality and actuality. Bare matter is conceived as a potentiality of form; all change is what we should call 'evolution', in the sense that after the change the thing in question has more form than before. That which has more form is considered to be more 'actual'. God is pure form and pure actuality; in Him, therefore, there can be no change. It will be seen that this doctrine is optimistic and teleological: the universe and everything in it is developing towards something continually better than what went before.

The concept of potentiality is convenient in some connections, provided it is so used that we can translate our statements into a form in which the concept is absent. 'A block of marble is a potential statue' means 'from a block of marble, by suitable acts, a statue is produced.' But when potentiality is used as a fundamental and irreducible concept, it always conceals confusion of thought. Aristotle's use of it is one of the bad points in his system.

Aristotle's theology is interesting, and closely connected with the rest of his metaphysics—indeed, 'theology' is one of his names for what we call 'metaphysics'. (The book which we know under that name was not so called by him.)

There are, he says, three kinds of substances: those that are sensible and perishable, those that are sensible but not perishable, and those that are neither sensible nor perishable. The first class includes plants and animals, the second includes the heavenly bodies (which Aristotle believed to undergo no change except motion), the third includes the rational soul in man, and also God.

The main argument for God is the First Cause: there must be something which originates motion, and this something must itself be unmoved, and must be eternal, substance, and actuality. The object of desire and the object of thought, Aristotle says, cause movement in this way, without themselves being in motion. So God produces motion by being loved, whereas every other cause of motion works by being itself in motion (like a billiard ball). God is pure thought; for thought is what is best. 'Life also belongs to God; for the actuality of thought is life, and God is that actuality; and God's self-dependent actuality is life most good and eternal. We say therefore that God is a living being, eternal, most good, so that life and duration continuous and eternal belong to God; for this *is* God' (1072^b).

'It is clear then from what has been said that there is a substance which is eternal and unmovable and separate from sensible things. It has been shown that this substance cannot have any magnitude, but is without parts and indivisible. . . . But it has also been shown that it is impassive and unalterable; for all the other changes are posterior to change of place' (1073^a).

God does not have the attributes of a Christian Providence, for it would derogate from His perfection to think about anything except what is perfect, i.e. Himself. 'It must be of itself that the divine thought thinks (since it is the most excellent of things), and its thinking is a thinking on thinking.' (1074^b). We must infer that God does not know of the existence of our sublunary world. Aristotle, like Spinoza, holds that, while men must love God, it is impossible that God should love men.

God is not *definable* as 'the unmoved mover'. On the contrary, astronomical considerations lead to the conclusion that there are either forty-seven or fifty-five unmoved movers (1074^a). The relation of these to God is not made clear; indeed the natural interpretation would be that there are forty-seven or fifty-five gods. For after one of the above passages on God Aristotle proceeds: 'We must not ignore the question whether we are to suppose one such substance or more than one,' and at once embarks upon the argument that leads to the forty-seven or fifty-five unmoved movers.

The conception of an unmoved mover is a difficult one. To a modern mind, it would seem that the cause of a change must be a previous change, and that, if the universe were ever wholly static, it would remain so eternally. To understand what Aristotle means, we must take account of what he says about causes. There are, according to him, four kinds of causes, which were called, respectively, material, formal, efficient, and final. Let us take again the man who is making a statue. The material cause of the statue is the marble, the formal cause is the essence of the statue to be produced, the efficient cause is the contact of the chisel with the marble, and the final cause is the end that the sculptor has in view. In modern terminology, the word 'cause' would be confined to the efficient cause. The unmoved mover may be regarded as a final cause: it supplies a purpose for change, which is essentially an evolution towards likeness with God.

I said that Aristotle was not by temperament deeply religious, but this is only partly true. One could, perhaps, interpret one aspect of his religion, somewhat freely, as follows:

God exists eternally, as pure thought, happiness, complete self-fulfilment, without any unrealized purposes. The sensible world, on the contrary, is imperfect, but it has life, desire, thought of an imperfect kind, and aspiration. All living things are in a greater or less degree aware of God, and are moved to action by admiration and love of God. Thus God is the final cause of all activity. Change consists in giving form to matter, but, where sensible things are concerned, a substratum of matter always remains. Only God consists of form without matter. The world is continually evolving towards a greater degree of form, and thus becoming progressively more like God. But the process cannot be completed, because matter cannot be wholly eliminated. This is a religion of progress and evolution, for God's static perfection moves the world only through the love that finite beings feel for Him. Plato was mathematical, Aristotle was biological; this accounts for the differences in their religions.

This would, however, be a one-sided view of Aristotle's religion; he has also the Greek love of static perfection and preference for contemplation rather than action. His doctrine of the soul illustrates this aspect of his philosophy.

Whether Aristotle taught immortality in any form, or not, was a vexed question among commentators. Averroes, who held that he did not, had followers in Christian countries, of whom the more extreme were called Epicureans, and whom Dante found in hell. In fact, Aristotle's doctrine is complex, and easily lends itself to mis-understandings. In his book *On the Soul*, he regards the soul as bound up with the body, and ridicules the Pythagorean doctrine of transmigration (407^b). The soul, it seems, perishes with the body: 'it indubitably follows that the soul is inseparable from its body' (413^a); but he immediately adds: 'or at any rate certain parts of it are'. Body and soul are related as matter and form: 'the soul must be a substance in the sense of the form of a material body having life potentially within it. But substance is actuality, and thus soul is the actuality of a body as above characterized' (412^a). Soul 'is substance in the sense which corresponds to the definitive formula of a thing's essence. That means that it is the "essential whatness" of a body of the character just assigned' (i.e. having life) (412^b). The soul is the first grade of actuality of a natural body having life potentially in it. The body so described is a body which is organized (412^a). To ask whether soul and body are one is as meaningless as to ask whether the wax and the shape given it by the stamp are one (412^b). Self-nutrition is the only psychic power possessed by plants (413^a). The soul is the final cause of the body (414^a).

In this book, he distinguishes between 'soul' and 'mind', making mind higher than soul, and less bound to the body. After speaking of the relation of soul and body, he says: 'The case of mind is different; it seems to be an independent substance implanted within the soul and to be incapable of being destroyed' (408^b). Again: 'We have no evidence as yet about mind or the power to think; it seems to be a widely different kind of soul, differing as what is eternal from what is perishable; it alone is capable of existence in isolation from all other psychic powers. All the other parts of soul, it is evident from what we have said, are, in spite of certain statements to the contrary, incapable of separate existence' (413^b). The mind is the part of us that understands mathematics and philosophy; its objects are timeless, and therefore it is regarded as itself timeless. The soul is what moves the body and perceives sensible objects; it is characterized by self-nutrition, sensation, feeling, and motivity (413^b); but the mind has the higher function of thinking, which has no relation to the body or to the senses. Hence the mind can be immortal, though the rest of the soul cannot.

To understand Aristotle's doctrine of the soul, we must remember that the soul is the 'form' of the body, and that spatial shape is one kind of 'form'. What is there in common between soul and shape? I think what is in common is the conferring of unity upon a certain amount of matter. The part of a block of marble which afterwards becomes a statute is, as yet, not separated from the rest of the marble; it is not yet a 'thing', and has not yet any unity. After the sculptor has made the statue, it has unity, which it derives from its shape. Now the essential feature of the soul, in virtue of which it is the 'form' of the body, is that it makes the body an organic whole, having purposes as a unit. A single organ has purposes lying outside itself; the eye, in isolation, cannot see. Thus many things can be said in which an animal or plant as a whole is the subject, which cannot be said about any part of it. It is in this sense that organization, or form, confers substantiality. That which confers substantiality upon a plant or animal is what Aristotle calls its 'soul'. But 'mind' is something different, less intimately bound up with the body; perhaps it is a part of the soul, but it is possessed by only a small minority of living beings (415^a). Mind as speculation cannot be the cause of movement, for it never thinks about what is practicable, and never says what is to be avoided or what pursued (432^b).

A similar doctrine, though with a slight change of terminology, is set forth in the *Nicomachean Ethics*. There is in the soul one element that is rational, and one that is irrational. The irrational part is two-fold: the vegetative, which is found in everything living, even in plants, and the appetitive, which exists in all animals (1102^b). The life of the rational soul consists in contemplation, which is the complete happiness of man though not fully attainable. 'Such a life would be too high for man; for it is not in so far as he is man that he will live so, but in so far as something divine is present in him; and by so much as this is superior to our composite nature is its activity superior to that which is the exercise of the other kind of virtue (the practical kind). If reason is divine, then, in comparison with man, the life in accordance with it is divine in comparison with human life. But we must not follow those who advise us, being men, to think of human things, and being mortal, of mortal things, but must, so far as we can, make ourselves immortal, and strain every nerve to live in accordance with the best thing in us; for even if it be small in bulk, much more does it in power and worth surpass everything' (1177^b).

It seems, from these passages, that individuality—what distinguishes one man from another—is connected with the body and the irrational soul, while the rational soul or mind is divine and impersonal. One man likes oysters, and another likes pineapples; this distinguishes between them. But when they think about the multiplication table, provided they think correctly, there is no difference between them. The irrational separates us, the rational unites us. Thus the immortality of mind or reason is not a personal immortality of separate men, but a share in God's immortality. It does not appear that Aristotle believed in *personal* immortality, in the sense in which it was taught by Plato and afterwards by Christianity. He believed only that, in so far as men are rational, they partake of the divine, which is immortal. It is open to man to increase the element of the divine in his nature, and to do so is the highest virtue. But if he succeeded completely, he would have ceased to exist as a separate person. This is perhaps not the only possible interpretation of Aristotle's words, but I think it is the most natural.

Chapter XX

ARISTOTLE'S ETHICS

In the corpus of Aristotle's works, three treatises on ethics have a place, but two of these are now generally held to be by disciples. The third, the *Nicomachean Ethics*, remains for the most part unquestioned as to authenticity, but even in this book there is a portion (Books V, VI, and VII) which is held by many to have been incorporated from one of the works of disciples. I shall, however, ignore this controversial question, and treat the book as a whole and as Aristotle's.

The views of Aristotle on ethics represents, in the main, the prevailing opinions of educated and experienced men of his day. They are not, like Plato's, impregnated with mystical religion; nor do they countenance such unorthodox theories as are to be found in the *Republic* concerning property and the family. Those who neither fall below nor rise above the level of decent, well-behaved citizens will find in the *Ethics* a systematic account of the principles by which they hold that their conduct should be regulated. Those who demand anything more will be disappointed. The book appeals to the respectable middle-aged, and has been used by them, especially since the seventeenth century, to repress the ardours and enthusiasms of the young. But to a man with any depth of feeling it is likely to be repulsive.

The good, we are told, is *happiness*, which is an activity of the soul. Aristotle says that Plato was right in dividing the soul into two parts, one rational, the other irrational. The irrational part itself he divides into the vegetative (which is found even in plants) and the appetitive (which is found in all animals). The appetitive part may be in some degree rational, when the goods that it seeks are such as reason approves of. This is essential to the account of virtue, for reason alone, in Aristotle, is purely contemplative, and does not, without the help of appetite, lead to any practical activity.

There are two kinds of virtues, *intellectual* and *moral*, corresponding to the two parts of the soul. Intellectual virtues result from teaching, moral virtues from habit. It is the business of the legislator to make the citizens good by forming good habits. We become just by performing just acts, and similarly as regards other virtues. By being compelled to acquire good habits, we shall in time, Aristotle thinks, come to find pleasure in performing good actions. One is reminded of Hamlet's speech to his mother:

> Assume a virtue if you have it not.
> That monster, custom, who all sense doth eat,
> Of habits devil, is angel, yet in this
> That to the use of actions fair and good
> He likewise gives a frock or livery
> That aptly is put on.

We now come to the famous doctrine of the golden mean. Every virtue is a mean between two extremes, each of which is a vice. This is proved by an examination of the various virtues. Courage is a mean between cowardice and rashness; liberality, between prodigality and meanness; proper pride, between vanity and humility; ready wit, between buffoonery and boorishness; modesty, between bashfulness and shamelessness. Some virtues do not seem to fit into this scheme; for instance, truthfulness. Aristotle says that this is a mean between boastfulness and mock-modesty (1108^a), but this only applies to truthfulness about oneself. I do not see how truthfulness in any wider sense can be fitted into the scheme. There was once a mayor who had adopted Aristotle's doctrine; at the end of his term of office he made a speech saying that he had endeavoured to steer the narrow line between partiality on the one hand and impartiality on the other. The view of truthfulness as a mean seems scarcely less absurd.

Aristotle's opinions on moral questions are always such as were conventional in his day. On some points they differ from those of our time, chiefly where some form of aristocracy comes in. We think that human beings, at least in ethical theory, all have equal rights, and that justice involves equality; Aristotle thinks that justice involves, not equality, but right proportion, which is only *sometimes* equality (1131^b).

The justice of a master or a father is a different thing from that of a citizen, for a son or slave is property, and there can be no injustice to one's own property (1134^b). As regards slaves, however, there is a slight modification of this doctrine in connection with the question whether it is possible for a man to be a friend of his slave: 'There is nothing in common between the two parties; the slave is a living tool. . . . *Qua* slave, then, one cannot be friends with him. But *qua* man one can; for there seems to be some justice between any man and any other who can share in a system of law or be a party to an agreement; therefore there can also be friendship with him in so far as he is a man' (1161^b).

A father can repudiate his son if he is wicked, but a son cannot repudiate his father, because he owes him more than he can possibly repay, especially existence (1163^b). In unequal relations, it is right, since everybody should be loved in proportion to his worth, that the inferior should love the superior more than the superior loves the inferior: wives, children, subjects, should have more love for husbands, parents, and monarchs than the latter have for them. In a good marriage, 'the man rules in accordance with his worth, and in those matters in which a man should rule, but the matters that befit a woman he hands over to her' (1160^b). He should not rule in her province; still less should she rule in his, as sometimes happens when she is an heiress.

The best individual, as conceived by Aristotle, is a very different person from the Christian saint. He should have proper pride, and not underestimate his own merits. He should despise whoever deserves to be despised (1124^b). The description of the proud or magnanimous man[1] is very interesting as showing the difference between pagan and Christian ethics, and the sense in which Nietzsche was justified in regarding Christianity as a slave-morality.

The magnanimous man, since he deserves most, must be good, in the highest degree; for the better man always deserves more, and the best man most. Therefore the truly magnanimous man must be good. And greatness in every virtue would seem to be characteristic of the magnanimous man. And it would be most unbecoming for the magnanimous man to fly from danger, swinging his arms by his sides, or to wrong another; for to what end should he do disgraceful acts, he to whom nothing is great? . . . magnanimity, then, seems to be a sort of crown of the virtues; for it makes them greater, and it is not found without them. Therefore it is hard to be truly magnanimous; for it is impossible without nobility and goodness of character. It is chiefly with honours and dishonours, then, that the magnanimous man is concerned; and at honours that are great and conferred by good men he will be moderately pleased, thinking that he is coming by his own or even less than his own; for there can be no honour that is worthy of perfect virtue, yet he will at any rate accept it since they have nothing greater to bestow on him; but honour from casual people and on trifling grounds he will utterly despise, since it is not this that he deserves, and dishonour too, since in his case it cannot be just. . . . Power and wealth are desirable for the sake of honour; and to him for whom even honour is a little thing the others must be so too. Hence magnanimous men are thought to be disdainful. . . . The magnanimous man does not

[1] The Greek word means, literally, 'great-souled', and is usually translated 'magnanimous', but the Oxford translation renders it 'proud'. Neither word, in its modern usage, quite expresses Aristotle's meaning, but I prefer 'magnanimous', and have therefore substituted it for 'proud' in the above quotation from the Oxford translation.

run into trifling dangers, . . . but he will face great dangers, and when he is in danger he is unsparing of his life, knowing that there are conditions on which life is not worth having. And he is the sort of man to confer benefits, but he is ashamed of receiving them; for the one is the mark of a superior, the other of an inferior. And he is apt to confer greater benefits in return; for thus the original bene-factor besides being repaid will incur a debt to him. . . . It is the mark of the magnanimous man to ask for nothing or scarcely any-thing, but to give help readily, and to be dignified towards people who enjoy a high position but unassuming towards those of the middle class; for it is a difficult and lofty thing to be superior to the former, but easy to be so to the latter, and a lofty bearing over the former is no mark of ill-breeding, but among humble people it is as vulgar as a display of strength against the weak. . . . He must also be open in his hate and in his love, for to conceal one's feelings, i.e. to care less for truth than for what people think, is a coward's part. . . . He is free of speech because he is contemptuous, and he is given to telling the truth, except when he speaks in irony to the vulgar. . . . Nor is he given to admiration, for to him nothing is great. . . . Nor is he a gossip; for he will speak neither about himself nor about another, since he cares not to be praised nor for others to be blamed. . . . He is one who will possess beautiful and profitless things rather than profitable and useful ones. . . . Further, a slow step is thought proper to the magnanimous man, a deep voice, and a level utterance. . . . Such, then, is the mag-nanimous man; the man who falls short of him is unduly humble, and the man who goes beyond him is vain' (1123^b—1125^a).

One shudders to think what a vain man would be like.

Whatever may be thought of the magnanimous man, one thing is clear: there cannot be very many of him in a community. I do not mean merely in the general sense in which there are not likely to be many virtuous men, on the ground that virtue is difficult; what I mean is that the virtues of the magnanimous man largely depend upon his having an exceptional social position. Aristotle con-siders ethics a branch of politics, and it is not surprising, after his praise of pride, to find that he considers monarchy the best form of government, and aristocracy the next best. Monarchs and aristo-crats can be 'magnanimous', but ordinary citizens would be laugh-able if they attempted to live up to such a pattern.

This brings up a question which is half ethical, half political. Can we regard as morally satisfactory a community which, by its essential constitution, confines the best things to a few, and requires the majority to be content with the second-best? Plato and Aristotle say yes, and Nietzsche agrees with them. Stoics, Christians, and democrats say no. But there are great differences in their ways of saying no. Stoics and early Christians consider that the greatest good is virtue, and that external circumstances cannot prevent a man from being virtuous; there is therefore no need to seek a just social system, since social injustice affects only unimportant matters. The democrat, on the contrary, usually holds that, at least so far as politics are concerned, the most important goods are power and property; he cannot, therefore, acquiesce in a social system which is unjust in these respects.

The Stoic-Christian view requires a conception of virtue very different from Aristotle's, since it must hold that virtue is as possible for the slave as for his master. Christian ethics disapproves of pride, which Aristotle thinks a virtue, and praises humility, which he thinks a vice. The intellectual virtues, which Plato and Aristotle value above all others, have to be thrust out of the list altogether, in order that the poor and humble may be able to be as virtuous as any one else. Pope Gregory the Great solemnly reproved a bishop for teaching grammar.

The Aristotelian view, that the highest virtue is for the few, is logically connected with the subordination of ethics to politics. If the aim is the good community rather than the good individual, it is possible that the good community may be one in which there is subordination. In an orchestra, the first violin is more important than the oboe, though both are necessary for the excellence of the whole. It is impossible to organize an orchestra on the principle of giving to each man what would be best for him as an isolated individual. The same sort of thing applies to the government of a large modern State, however democratic. A modern democracy —unlike those of antiquity—confers great power upon certain chosen individuals, Presidents or Prime Ministers, and must expect of them such kinds of merit which are not expected of the ordinary citizen. When people are not thinking in terms of religion or political controversy, they are likely to hold that a good President is more to be honoured than a good bricklayer. In a democracy a President is not expected to be quite like Aristotle's magnanimous man, but still he is expected to be rather different from the average citizen, and to have certain merits connected with his station. These peculiar merits would perhaps not be considered 'ethical', but that is because we use this adjective in a narrower sense than that in which it is used by Aristotle.

As a result of Christian dogma, the distinction between moral and other merits has become much sharper than it was in Greek times. It is a merit in a man to be a great poet or composer or painter, but not a *moral* merit; we do not consider him the more virtuous for possessing such aptitudes, or the more likely to go to heaven. *Moral* merit is concerned solely with acts of will, i.e. with choosing rightly among *possible* courses of action.[1] I am not to blame for not composing an opera, because I don't know how to do it. The orthodox view is that, wherever two courses of action are possible, conscience tells me which is right, and to choose the other is sin. Virtue consists mainly in the avoidance of sin, rather than in anything positive. There is no reason to expect an educated man to be *morally* better than an uneducated man, or a clever man than a stupid man. In this way, a number of merits of great social importance are shut out from the realm of ethics. The adjective 'unethical', in modern usage, has a much narrower range than the adjective 'undesirable'. It is undesirable to be feeble-minded, but not unethical.

Many modern philosophers, however, have not accepted this view of ethics. They have thought that one should first define the good, and then say that our actions ought to be such as tend to realize the good. This point of view is more like that of Aristotle, who holds that happiness is the good. The highest happiness, it is true, is only open to the philosopher, but to Aristotle that is no objection to the theory.

Ethical theories may be divided into two classes, according as they regard virtue as an end or a means. Aristotle, on the whole, takes the view that virtues are means to an end, namely happiness. 'The end, then, being what we wish for, the means what we deliberate about and choose, actions concerning means must be according to choice and voluntary. Now the exercise of the virtues is concerned with means' (1113^b). But there is another sense of virtue in which it is included in the ends of action: 'Human good is activity of soul in accordance with virtue in a complete life' (1098^a). I think he would say that the intellectual virtues are ends, but the practical virtues are only means. Christian moralists hold that, while the consequences of virtuous actions are in general good, they are not *as* good as the virtuous actions themselves, which are to be valued on their own account, and not on account of their effects. On the other hand, those who consider pleasure the good regard virtues solely as means. Any other definition of the good, except the definition as virtue, will have the same consequence, that virtues are means to goods other than themselves. On this question, Aristotle, as already said, agrees mainly, though not wholly, with those who think the first business of ethics is to define the good, and that virtue is to be defined as action tending to produce the good.

The relation of ethics to politics raises another ethical question

[1] It is true that Aristotle also says this (1105^a), but as he means it the consequences are not so far-reaching as in the Christian interpretation.

of considerable importance. Granted that the good at which right action should aim is the good of the whole community, or, ultimately, of the whole human race, is this social good a sum of goods enjoyed by individuals, or is it something belonging essentially to the whole, not to the parts? We may illustrate the problem by the analogy of the human body. Pleasures are largely associated with different parts of the body, but we consider them as belonging to a person as a whole; we may enjoy a pleasant smell, but we know that the nose alone could not enjoy it. Some contend that, in a closely organized community, there are, analogously, excellences belonging to the whole, but not to any part. If they are metaphysicians, they may hold, like Hegel, that whatever quality is good is an attribute of the universe as a whole; but they will generally add that it is less mistaken to attribute good to a State than to an individual. Logically, the view may be put as follows. We can attribute to a State various predicates that cannot be attributed to its separate members—that it is populous, extensive, powerful, etc. The view we are considering puts ethical predicates in this class, and says that they only derivatively belong to individuals. A man may belong to a populous State, or to a good State; but he, they say, is no more good than he is populous. This view, which has been widely held by German philosophers, is not Aristotle's, except possibly, in some degree, in his conception of justice.

A considerable part of the *Ethics* is occupied with the discussion of friendship, including all relations that involve affection. Perfect friendship is only possible between the good, and it is impossible to be friends with many people. One should not be friends with a person of higher station than one's own, unless he is also of higher virtue, which will justify the respect shown to him. We have seen that, in unequal relations, such as those of man and wife or father and son, the superior should be the more loved. It is impossible to be friends with God, because He cannot love us. Aristotle discusses whether a man can be a friend to himself, and decides that this is only possible if he is a good man; wicked men, he asserts, often hate themselves. The good man should love himself, but nobly (1169[a]). Friends are a comfort in misfortune, but one should not make them unhappy by seeking their sympathy, as is done by women and womanish men (1171[b]). It is not only in misfortune that friends are desirable, for the happy man needs friends with whom to share his happiness. 'No one would choose the whole world on condition of being alone, since man is a political creature and one whose nature is to live with others' (1169[b]). All that is said about friendship is sensible, but there is not a word that rises above common sense.

Aristotle again shows his good sense in the discussion of *pleasure*, which Plato had regarded somewhat ascetically. Pleasure, as Aristotle uses the word, is distinct from happiness, though there can be no happiness without pleasure. There are, he says, three views of pleasure: (1) that it is never good; (2) that some pleasure is good, but most is bad; (3) that pleasure is good, but not the best. He rejects the first of these on the ground that pain is certainly bad, and therefore pleasure must be good. He says, very justly, that it is nonsense to say a man can be happy on the rack: some degree of external good fortune is necessary for happiness. He also disposes of the view that all pleasures are bodily; all things have something divine, and therefore some capacity for higher pleasures. Good men have pleasure unless they are unfortunate, and God always enjoys a single and simple pleasure (1152-1154).

There is another discussion of pleasure, in a later part of the book, which is not wholly consistent with the above. Here it is argued that there are bad pleasures, which, however, are not pleasures to good people (1173^b); that perhaps pleasures differ in kind (*ibid.*); and that pleasures are good or bad according as they are connected with good or bad activities (1175^b). There are things that are valued more than pleasure; no one would be content to go through life with a child's intellect, even if it were pleasant to do so. Each animal has its proper pleasure, and the proper pleasure of man is connected with reason.

This leads on to the only doctrine in the book which is not mere common sense. Happiness lies in virtuous activity, and perfect happiness lies in the best activity, which is contemplative. Contemplation is preferable to war or politics or any other practical career, because it allows leisure, and leisure is essential to happiness. Practical virtue brings only a secondary kind of happiness; the supreme happiness is in the exercise of reason, for reason, more than anything else, *is* man. Man cannot be *wholly* contemplative, but in so far as he is so he shares in the divine life. 'The activity of God, which surpasses all others in blessedness, must be contemplative.' Of all human beings, the philosopher is the most godlike in his activity, and therefore the happiest and best:

He who exercises his reason and cultivates it seems to be both in the best state of mind and most dear to the gods. For if the gods have any care for human affairs, as they are thought to have, it would be reasonable both that they should delight in that which was best and most akin to them (i.e. reason) and that they should reward those who love and honour this most, as caring for the things that are dear to them and acting both rightly and nobly. And that all these attributes belong most of all to the philosopher is manifest. He, therefore, is the dearest to the gods. And he who is that will presumably be also the happiest; so that in this way too the philosopher will more than any other be happy (1179ᵃ).

This passage is virtually the peroration of the *Ethics*; the few paragraphs that follow are concerned with the transition to politics.

Let us now try to decide what we are to think of the merits and demerits of the *Ethics*. Unlike many other subjects treated by Greek philosophers, ethics has not made any definite advances, in the sense of ascertained discoveries; nothing in ethics is *known* in a scientific sense. There is therefore no reason why an ancient treatise on it should be in any respect inferior to a modern one. When Aristotle talks about astronomy, we can say definitely that he is wrong; but when he talks about ethics we cannot say, in the same sense, either that he is wrong or that he is right. Broadly speaking, there are three questions that we can ask about the ethics of Aristotle, or of any other philosopher: (1) Is it internally self-consistent? (2) Is it consistent with the remainder of the author's views? (3) Does it give answers to ethical problems that are consonant to our own ethical feelings? If the answer to either the first or second question is in the negative, the philosopher in question has been guilty of some intellectual error. But if the answer to the third question is in the negative, we have no right to say that he is mistaken; we have only the right to say that we do not like him.

Let us examine these three questions in turn, as regards the ethical theory set forth in the *Nicomachean Ethics*.

(1) On the whole, the book is self-consistent, except in a few not very important respects. The doctrine that the good is happiness, and that happiness consists in successful activity, is well worked out. The doctrine that every virtue is a mean between two extremes, though very ingeniously developed, is less successful, since it does not apply to intellectual contemplation, which, we are told, is the best of all activities. It can, however, be maintained that the doctrine of the mean is only intended to apply to the practical virtues, not to those of the intellect. Perhaps, to take another point, the position of the legislator is somewhat ambiguous. He is to cause children and young people to acquire the habit of performing good actions, which will, in the end, lead them to find pleasure in virtue, and to act virtuously without the need of legal compulsion. It is obvious that the legislator might equally well cause the young to acquire *bad* habits; if this is to be avoided, he must have all the wisdom of a Platonic guardian; and if it is not avoided, the argument that a virtuous life is pleasant will fail. This problem, how-

ever, belongs perhaps more to politics than to ethics.

(2) Aristotle's ethics is, at all points, consistent with his metaphysics. Indeed, his metaphysical theories are themselves the expression of an ethical optimism. He believes in the scientific importance of final causes, and this implies the belief that purpose governs the course of development in the universe. He thinks that changes are, in the main, such as embody an increase of organization or 'form', and at bottom virtuous actions are those that favour this tendency. It is true that a great deal of his practical ethics is not particularly philosophical, but merely the result of observation of human affairs; but this part of his doctrine, though it may be independent of his metaphysics, is not inconsistent with it.

(3) When we come to compare Aristotle's ethical tastes with our own, we find, in the first place, as already noted, an acceptance of inequality which is repugnant to much modern sentiment. Not only is there no objection to slavery, or to the superiority of husbands and fathers over wives and children, but it is held that what is best is essentially only for the few—magnanimous men and philosophers. Most men, it would seem to follow, are mainly means for the production of a few rulers and sages. Kant maintained that every human being is an end in himself, and this may be taken as an expression of the view introduced by Christianity. There is, however, a logical difficulty in Kant's view, since it gives no means of reaching a decision when two men's interests clash. If each is an end in himself, how are we to arrive at a principle for determining which shall give way? Such a principle must have to do with the community rather than with the individual. In the broadest sense of the word, it will have to be a principle of 'justice'. Bentham and the utilitarians interpret 'justice' as 'equality': when two men's interests clash, the right course is that which produces the greatest total of happiness, regardless of which of the two enjoys it, or how it is shared among them. If more is given to the better man than to the worse, that is because, in the long run, the general happiness is increased by rewarding virtue and punishing vice, not because of an ultimate ethical doctrine that the good deserve more than the bad. 'Justice', in this view, consists in considering only the amount of happiness involved, without favour to one individual·or class as against another. Greek philosophers, including Plato and Aristotle, had a different conception of justice, and it is one which is still widely prevalent. They thought—originally on grounds derived from religion—that each thing or person had its or his proper sphere, to overstep which is 'unjust'. Some men, in virtue of their character and aptitudes, have a wider sphere than others, and there is no injustice if they enjoy a greater share of happiness. This view

is taken for granted in Aristotle, but its basis in primitive religion, which is evident in the earliest philosophers, is no longer apparent in his writings.

There is in Aristotle an almost complete absence of what may be called benevolence or philanthropy. The sufferings of mankind, in so far as he is aware of them, do not move him emotionally; he holds them, intellectually, to be an evil, but there is no evidence that they cause him unhappiness except when the sufferers happen to be his friends.

More generally, there is an emotional poverty in the *Ethics*, which is not found in the earlier philosophers. There is something unduly smug and comfortable about Aristotle's speculations on human affairs; everything that makes men feel a passionate interest in each other seems to be forgotten. Even his account of friendship is tepid. He shows no sign of having had any of those experiences which make it difficult to preserve sanity; all the more profound aspects of the moral life are apparently unknown to him. He leaves out, one may say, the whole sphere of human experience with which religion is concerned. What he has to say is what will be useful to comfortable men of weak passions; but he has nothing to say to those who are possessed by a god or a devil, or whom outward misfortune drives to despair. For these reasons, in my judgment, his *Ethics*, in spite of its fame, is lacking in intrinsic importance.

Chapter XXI

ARISTOTLE'S POLITICS

ARISTOTLE'S *Politics* is both interesting and important—interesting, as showing the common prejudices of educated Greeks in his time, and important as a source of many principles which remained influential until the end of the Middle Ages. I do not think there is much in it that could be of any practical use to a statesman of the present day, but there is a great deal that throws light on the conflicts of parties in different parts of the Hellenic world. There is not very much awareness of methods of government in non-Hellenic States. There are, it is true, allusions to Egypt, Babylon, Persia, and Carthage, but except in the case of Carthage they are somewhat perfunctory. There is no mention of Alexander, and not even the faintest awareness of the complete transformation that he was effecting in the world. The whole discussion is concerned with City States, and there is no prevision of their obsolescence. Greece, owing to its division into independent cities, was a laboratory of political experiment; but nothing to which these experiments were relevant existed from Aristotle's time until the rise of the Italian cities in the Middle Ages. In many ways, the experience to which Aristotle appeals is more relevant to the comparatively modern world than to any that existed for fifteen hundred years after the book was written.

There are many pleasant incidental remarks, some of which may be noted before we embark upon political theory. We are told that Euripides, when he was staying at the court of Archelaus, King of Macedon, was accused of halitosis by a certain Decamnichus. To soothe his fury, the king gave him permission to scourge Decamnichus, which he did. Decamnichus, after waiting many years, joined in a successful plot to kill the king; but by this time Euripides was dead. We are told that children should be conceived in winter, when the wind is in the north; that there must be a careful avoidance of indecency, because 'shameful words lead to shameful acts', and that obscenity is never to be tolerated except in temples, where the law permits even ribaldry. People should not marry too young, because, if they do, the children will be weak and female, the wives will become wanton, and the husbands stunted in their growth. The right age for marriage is thirty-seven in men, eighteen in women.

We learn how Thales, being taunted with his poverty, bought up all the olive-presses on the instalment plan, and was then able to charge monopoly rates for their use. This he did to show that philosophers *can* make money, and, if they remain poor, it is because they have something more important than wealth to think about. All this, however, is by the way; it is time to come to more serious matters.

The book begins by pointing out the importance of the State; it is the highest kind of community, and aims at the highest good. In order of time, the family comes first; it is built on the two fundamental relations of man and woman, master and slave, both of which are natural. Several families combined make a village; several villages, a State, provided the combination is nearly large enough to be self-sufficing. The State, though later in time than the family, is prior to it, and even to the individual, by nature; for 'what each thing is when fully developed we call its nature', and human society, fully developed, is a State, and the whole is prior to the part. The conception involved here is that of *organism*: a hand, when the body is destroyed, is, we are told, no longer a hand. The implication is that a hand is to be defined by its purpose—that of grasping—which it can only perform when joined to a living body. In like manner an individual cannot fulfil his purpose unless he is part of a State. He who founded the State, Aristotle says, was the greatest of benefactors; for without *law* man is the worst of animals, and law depends for its existence on the State. The State is not a mere society for exchange and the prevention of crime: 'The end of the State is the good life. . . . And the State is the union of families and villages in a perfect and self-sufficing life, by which we mean a happy and honourable life' (1280b). 'A political society exists for the sake of noble actions, not of mere companionship' (1281a).

A State being composed of households, each of which consists of one family, the discussion of politics should begin with the family. The bulk of this discussion is concerned with slavery—for in antiquity the slaves were always reckoned as part of the family. Slavery is expedient and right, but the slave should be *naturally* inferior to the master. From birth, some are marked out for subjection, others for rule; the man who is by nature not his own but another man's is by nature a slave. Slaves should not be Greeks, but of an inferior race with less spirit (1255a and 1330a). Tame animals are better off when ruled by man, and so are those who are naturally inferior when ruled by their superiors. It may be questioned whether the practice of making slaves out of prisoners of war is justified; power, such as leads to victory in war, seems to imply superior virtue, but this is not always the case. War, however, is just when waged against men who, though intended by nature to be governed, will not submit (1256[b]); and in this case, it is implied, it would be right to make slaves of the conquered. This would seem enough to justify any conqueror who ever lived; for no nation will admit that it is intended by nature to be governed, and the only evidence as to nature's intentions must be derived from the outcome of war. In every war, therefore, the victors are in the right and the vanquished in the wrong. Very satisfactory!

Next comes a discussion of trade, which profoundly influenced scholastic casuistry. There are two uses of a thing, one proper, the other improper; a shoe, for instance, may be worn, which is its proper use, or exchanged, which is its improper use. It follows that there is something degraded about a shoemaker, who must exchange his shoes in order to live. Retail trade, we are told, is not a natural part of the art of getting wealth (1257[a]). The natural way to get wealth is by skilful management of house and land. To the wealth that can be made in this way there is a limit, but to what can be made by trade there is none. Trade has to do with *money*, but wealth is not the acquisition of coin. Wealth derived from trade is justly hated, because it is unnatural. 'The most hated sort, and with the greatest reason is usury, which makes a gain out of money itself, and not from the natural object of it. For money was intended to be used in exchange, but not to increase at interest. . . . Of all modes of getting wealth this is the most unnatural' (1258).

What came of this dictum you may read in Tawney's *Religion and the Rise of Capitalism*. But while his history is reliable, his comment has a bias in favour of what is pre-capitalistic.

'Usury' means *all* lending money at interest, not only, as now, lending at an exorbitant rate. From Greek times to the present day, mankind, or at least the economically more developed portion of them, have been divided into debtors and creditors; debtors have disapproved of interest, and creditors have approved of it. At most times, landowners have been debtors, while men engaged in commerce have been creditors. The views of philosophers, with few exceptions, have coincided with the pecuniary interests of their class. Greek philosophers belonged to, or were employed by, the landowning class; they therefore disapproved of interest. Medieval philosophers were churchmen, and the property of the Church was mainly in land; they therefore saw no reason to revise Aristotle's opinion. Their objection to usury was reinforced by anti-Semitism, for most fluid capital was Jewish. Ecclesiastics and barons had their quarrels, sometimes very bitter; but they could combine against the wicked Jew who had tided them over a bad harvest by means of a loan, and considered that he deserved some reward for his thrift.

With the Reformation, the situation changed. Many of the most earnest Protestants were business men, to whom lending money at interest was essential. Consequently first Calvin, and then other Protestant divines, sanctioned interest. At last the Catholic Church was compelled to follow suit, because the old prohibitions did not suit the modern world. Philosophers, whose incomes are derived from the investments of universities, have favoured interest ever since they ceased to be ecclesiastics and therefore connected with landowning. At every stage, there has been a wealth of theoretical argument to support the economically convenient opinion.

Plato's Utopia is criticized by Aristotle on various grounds. There is first the very interesting comment that it gives too much unity to the State, and would make it into an individual. Next comes the kind of argument against the proposed abolition of the family that naturally occurs to every reader. Plato thinks that, by merely giving the title of 'son' to all who are of an age that makes their sonship possible, a man will acquire towards the whole multitude the sentiments that men have at present towards their actual sons, and correlatively as regards the title 'father'. Aristotle, on the contrary, says that what is common to the greatest number receives the least care, and that if 'sons' are common to many 'fathers' they will be neglected in common; it is better to be a cousin in reality than a 'son' in Plato's sense; Plato's plan would make love watery. Then there is a curious argument that, since abstinence from adultery is a virtue, it would be a pity to have a social system which abolishes this virtue and the correlative vice (1263^b). Then we are asked: if women are common, who will manage the house? I wrote an essay once, called 'Architecture and the Social System', in which I pointed out that all who combine communism with abolition of the family also advocate communal houses for large numbers, with communal kitchens, dining-rooms, and nurseries. This system may be described as monasteries without celibacy. It is essential to the carrying out of Plato's plans, but it is certainly not more impossible than many other things that he recommends.

Plato's communism annoys Aristotle. It would lead, he says, to anger against lazy people, and to the sort of quarrels that are common between fellow-travellers. It is better if each minds his own business. Property should be private, but people should be so trained in benevolence as to allow the use of it to be largely common. Benevolence and generosity are virtues, and without private property they are impossible. Finally we are told that, if Plato's plans were good, someone would have thought of them sooner.[1] I do not agree with Plato, but if anything could make me do so, it would be Aristotle's arguments against him.

As we have seen in connection with slavery, Aristotle is no believer in equality. Granted, however, the subjection of slaves and women, it still remains a question whether all *citizens* should be politically equal. Some men, he says, think this desirable, on the ground that all revolutions turn on the regulation of property. He rejects this argument, maintaining that the greatest crimes are due to excess rather than want; no man becomes a tyrant in order to avoid feeling the cold.

A government is good when it aims at the good of the whole community, bad when it cares only for itself. There are three kinds of government that are good: monarchy, aristocracy, and constitutional government (or polity); there are three that are bad: tyranny, oligarchy, and democracy. There are also many mixed intermediate forms. It will be observed that the good and bad governments are defined by the ethical qualities of the holders of power, not by the form of the constitution. This, however, is only partly true. An aristocracy is a rule of men of virtue, an oligarchy is a rule of the rich, and Aristotle does not consider virtue and wealth strictly synonymous. What he holds, in accordance with the doctrine of the golden mean, is that a moderate competence is most likely to be associated with virtue: 'Mankind do not acquire or preserve virtue by the help of external goods, but external goods by the help of virtue and happiness, whether consisting in pleasure or virtue, or both, is more often found with those who are most highly cultivated in their mind and in their character, and have only a moderate share of external goods, than among those who possess external goods to a useless extent but are deficient in higher qualities' (1323^a and ^{b}). There is therefore a difference between the rule of the best (aristocracy) and of the richest (oligarchy), since the best are likely to have only moderate fortunes. There is also a difference between democracy and polity, in addition to the ethical difference in the government, for what Aristotle calls 'polity' retains some oligarchic elements (1293^b). But between monarchy and tyranny the only difference is ethical.

He is emphatic in distinguishing oligarchy and democracy by the economic status of the governing party: there is oligarchy when the rich govern without consideration for the poor, democracy when power is in the hands of the needy and they disregard the interest of the rich.

[1] Cf. The Noodle's Oration in Sydney Smith; 'If the proposal be sound, would the Saxon have passed it by? Would the Dane have ignored it? Would it have escaped the wisdom of the Norman?' (I quote from memory.)

Monarchy is better than aristocracy, aristocracy is better than polity. But the corruption of the best is worst; therefore tyranny is worse than oligarchy, and oligarchy than democracy. In this way Aristotle arrives at a qualified defence of democracy; for most actual governments are bad, and therefore, among actual governments, democracies tend to be best.

The Greek conception of democracy was in many ways more extreme than ours; for instance, Aristotle says that to elect magistrates is oligarchic, while it is democratic to appoint them by lot. In extreme democracies, the assembly of the citizens was above the law, and decided each question independently. The Athenian law-courts were composed of a large number of citizens chosen by lot, unaided by any jurist; they were, of course, liable to be swayed by eloquence or party passion. When democracy is criticized, it must be understood that this sort of thing is meant.

There is a long discussion of causes of revolution. In Greece, revolutions were as frequent as formerly in Latin America, and therefore Aristotle had a copious experience from which to draw inferences. The main cause was the conflict of oligarchs and democrats. Democracy, Aristotle says, arises from the belief that men who are equally free should be equal in all respects; oligarchy, from the fact that men who are superior in some respect claim too much. Both have a kind of justice, but not the best kind. 'Therefore both parties, whenever their share in the government does not accord with their preconceived ideas, stir up revolution' (1301ª). Democratic governments are less liable to revolutions than oligarchies, because oligarchs may fall out with each other. The oligarchs seem to have been vigorous fellows. In some cities, we are told, they swore an oath: 'I will be an enemy to the people, and will devise all the harm against them which I can.' Nowadays reactionaries are not so frank.

The three things needed to prevent revolution are government propaganda in education, respect for law, even in small things, and justice in law and administration, i.e. 'equality according to proportion, and for every man to enjoy his own' (1307ª, 1307ᵇ, 1310ª). Aristotle never seems to have realized the difficulty of 'equality according to proportion'. If this is to be true justice, the proportion must be of *virtue*. Now virtue is difficult to measure, and is a matter of party controversy. In political practice, therefore, virtue tends to be measured by income; the distinction between aristocracy and oligarchy, which Aristotle attempts to make, is only possible where there is a very well-established hereditary nobility. Even then, as soon as there exists a large class of rich men who are not noble, they have to be admitted to power for fear of their making a revolution. Hereditary aristocracies cannot long retain their power except where land is almost the only source of wealth. All social inequality, in the long run, is inequality of income. That is part of the argument for democracy: that the attempt to have a 'proportionate justice' based on any merit other than wealth is sure to break down. Defenders of oligarchy pretend that income is proportional to virtue; the psalmist said he had never seen a righteous man begging his bread, and Aristotle thinks that good men acquire just about his own income, neither very large nor very small. But such views are absurd. Every kind of 'justice' other than absolute equality will, in practice, reward some quality quite other than virtue, and is therefore to be condemned.

There is an interesting section on tyranny. A tyrant desires riches, whereas a king desires honour. The tyrant has guards who are mercenaries, whereas the king has guards who are citizens. Tyrants are mostly demagogues, who acquire power by promising to protect the people against the notables. In an ironically Machiavellian tone, Aristotle explains what a tyrant must do to retain power. He must prevent the rise of any person of exceptional merit, by execution or assassination if necessary. He must prohibit common meals, clubs, and any education likely to produce hostile sentiment. There must be no literary assemblies or discussions. He must prevent people from knowing each other well, and compel them to live in public at his gates. He should employ spies, like the female detectives at Syracuse. He must sow quarrels, and impoverish his subjects. He should keep them occupied in great works, as the king of Egypt did in getting the pyramids built. He should give power to women and slaves, to make them informers. He should make war, in order that his subjects may have something to do and be always in want of a leader (1313ᵃ and ᵇ).

It is a melancholy reflection that this passage is, of the whole book, the one most appropriate to the present day. Aristotle concludes that there is no wickedness too great for a tyrant. There is, however, he says, another method of preserving a tyranny, namely by moderation and by seeming religious. There is no decision as to which method is likely to prove the more successful.

There is a long argument to prove that foreign conquest is not the end of the State, showing that many people took the imperialist view. There is, it is true, an exception: conquest of 'natural slaves' is right and just. This would, in Aristotle's view, justify wars against barbarians, but not against Greeks, for no Greeks are 'natural slaves'. In general, war is only a means, not an end; a city in an isolated situation, where conquest is not possible, may be happy; States that live in isolation need not be inactive. God and the universe are active, though foreign conquest is impossible for them. The happiness that a State should seek, therefore, though war may sometimes be a necessary means to it, should not *be* war, but the activities of peace.

This leads to the question: how large should a State be? Large cities, we are told, are never well governed, because a great multitude cannot be orderly. A State ought to be large enough to be more or less self-sufficing, but not too large for constitutional government. It ought to be small enough for the citizens to know each other's characters, otherwise right will not be done in elections and law-suits. The territory should be small enough to be surveyed in its entirety from a hill-top. We are told both that it should be self-sufficient (1326ᵇ) and that it should have an export and import trade (1327ᵃ), which seems an inconsistency.

Men who work for their living should not be admitted to citizenship. 'Citizens should not lead the life of mechanics or tradesmen, for such a life is ignoble and inimical to virtue.' Nor should they be husbandmen, because they need leisure. The citizens should own the property, but the husbandmen should be slaves of a different race (1330ᵃ). Northern races, we are told, are spirited; southern races, intelligent; therefore slaves should be of southern races, since it is inconvenient if they are spirited. The Greeks alone are both spirited and intelligent; they are better governed than barbarians, and if united could rule the world (1327ᵇ). One might have expected at this point some allusion to Alexander but there is none.

With regard to the size of States, Aristotle makes, on a different scale, the same mistake that is made by many modern liberals. A State must be able to defend itself in war, and even, if any liberal culture is to survive, to defend itself without very great difficulty. How large this requires a State to be, depends upon the technique of war and industry. In Aristotle's day, the City State was obsolete because it could not defend itself against Macedonia. In our day, Greece as a whole, including Macedonia, is obsolete in this sense, as has been recently proved.[1] To advocate complete independence for Greece, or any other small country, is now as futile as to advocate complete independence for a single city, whose territory can be seen entire from an eminence. There can be no true independence except for a State or alliance strong enough, by its own efforts, to repel all attempts at foreign conquest. Nothing smaller than America and the British Empire combined will satisfy this requirement; and perhaps even this would be too small a unit.

The book, which, in the form in which we have it, appears to be unfinished, ends with a discussion of education. Education, of

[1] This was written in May, 1941.

course, is only for children who are going to be citizens; slaves may be taught useful arts, such as cooking, but these are no part of education. The citizen should be moulded to the form of government under which he lives, and there should therefore be differences according as the city in question is oligarchic or democratic. In the discussion, however, Aristotle assumes that the citizens will all have a share of political power. Children should learn what is useful to them, but not vulgarizing; for instance, they should not be taught any skill that deforms the body, or that would enable them to earn money. They should practise athletics in moderation, but not to the point of acquiring professional skill; the boys who train for the Olympic games suffer in health, as is shown by the fact that those who have been victors as boys are hardly ever victors as men. Children should learn drawing, in order to appreciate the beauty of the human form; and they should be taught to appreciate such painting and sculpture as expresses moral ideas. They may learn to sing and to play musical instruments enough to be able to enjoy music critically, but not enough to be skilled performers; for no freeman would play or sing unless drunk. They must of course, learn to read and write, in spite of the usefulness of these arts. But the purpose of education is 'virtue', not usefulness. What Aristotle means by 'virtue' he has told us in the *Ethics*, to which this book frequently refers.

Aristotle's fundamental assumptions, in his *Politics*, are very different from those of any modern writer. The aim of the State, in his view, is to produce cultured gentlemen—men who combine the aristocratic mentality with love of learning and the arts. This combination existed, in its highest perfection, in the Athens of Pericles, not in the population at large, but among the well-to-do. It began to break down in the last years of Pericles. The populace, who had no culture, turned against the friends of Pericles who were driven to defend the privileges of the rich, by treachery, assassination, illegal despotism, and other such not very gentlemanly methods. After the death of Socrates, the bigotry of the Athenian democracy diminished, and Athens remained the centre of ancient culture, but political power went elsewhere. Throughout later antiquity, power and culture were usually separate: power was in the hands of rough soldiers, culture belonged to powerless Greeks, often slaves. This is only partially true of Rome in its great days, but it is emphatically true before Cicero and after Marcus Aurelius. After the barbarian invasion, the 'gentlemen' were northern barbarians, the men of culture subtle southern ecclesiastics. This state of affairs continued, more or less, until the Renaissance, when the laity began to acquire culture. From the Renais sance onwards, the Greek conception of government by cultured gentlemen gradually prevailed more and more, reaching its acme in the eighteenth century.

Various forces have put an end to this state of affairs. First, democracy, as embodied in the French Revolution and its aftermath. The cultured gentlemen, as after the age of Pericles, had to defend their privileges against the populace, and in the process ceased to be either gentlemen or cultured. A second cause was the rise of industrialism, with a scientific technique very different from traditional culture. A third cause was popular education, which conferred the power to read and write, but did not confer culture; this enabled a new type of demagogue to practise a new type of propaganda, as seen in the dictatorships.

Both for good and evil, therefore, the day of the cultured gentleman is past.

Chapter XXII

ARISTOTLE'S LOGIC

A RISTOTLE'S influence, which was very great in many different fields, was greatest of all in logic. In late antiquity, when Plato was still supreme in metaphysics, Aristotle was the recognized authority in logic, and he retained this position throughout the Middle Ages. It was not till the thirteenth century that Christian philosophers accorded him supremacy in the field of metaphysics. This supremacy was largely lost after the Renaissance, but his supremacy in logic survived. Even at the present day, all Catholic teachers of philosophy and many others still obstinately reject the discoveries of modern logic, and adhere with a strange tenacity to a system which is as definitely antiquated as Ptolemaic astronomy. This makes it difficult to do historical justice to Aristotle. His present-day influence is so inimical to clear thinking that it is hard to remember how great an advance he made upon all his predecessors (including Plato), or how admirable his logical work would still seem if it had been a stage in a continual progress, instead of being (as in fact it was) a dead end, followed by over two thousand years of stagnation. In dealing with the predecessors of Aristotle, it is not necessary to remind the reader that they are not verbally inspired; one can therefore praise them for their ability without being supposed to subscribe to all their doctrines. Aristotle, on the contrary, is still, especially in logic, a battle-ground, and cannot be treated in a purely historical spirit.

Aristotle's most important work in logic is the doctrine of the syllogism. A syllogism is an argument consisting of three parts, a major premiss, a minor premiss, and a conclusion. Syllogisms are of a number of different kinds, each of which has a name, given by the scholastics. The most familiar is the kind called 'Barbara':

All men are mortal (Major premiss).
Socrates is a man (Minor premiss).
Therefore: Socrates is mortal (Conclusion).
Or: all men are mortal.
All Greeks are men.
Therefore: All Greeks are mortal.

(Aristotle does not distinguish between these two forms; this, as we shall see later, is a mistake.)

Other forms are: No fishes are rational, all sharks are fishes, therefore no sharks are rational. (This is called 'Celarent'.)

All men are rational, some animals are men, therefore some animals are rational. (This is called 'Darii'.)

No Greeks are black, some men are Greeks, therefore some men are not black. (This is called 'Ferio'.)

These four make up the 'first figure'; Aristotle adds a second and third figure, and the schoolmen added a fourth. It is shown that the three later figures can be reduced to the first by various devices.

There are some inferences that can be made from a single premiss. From 'some men are mortal' we can infer that 'some mortals are men'. According to Aristotle, this can be also inferred from 'all men are mortal'. From 'no gods are mortal' we can infer 'no mortals are gods', but from 'some men are not Greeks' it does not follow that 'some Greeks are not men'.

Apart from such inferences as the above, Aristotle and his followers thought that all deductive inference, when strictly stated, is syllogistic. By setting forth all tne valid kinds of syllogism, and setting out any suggested argument in syllogistic form, it should therefore be possible to avoid all fallacies.

This system was the beginning of formal logic, and, as such, was both important and admirable. But considered as the end, not the beginning, of formal logic, it is open to three kinds of criticism:

(1) Formal defects within the system itself.

(2) Over-estimation of the syllogism, as compared to other forms of deductive argument.

(3) Over-estimation of deduction as a form of argument.

On each of these three, something must be said.

(1) *Formal defects*. Let us begin with the two statements 'Socrates is a man' and 'all Greeks are men'. It is necessary to make a sharp distinction between these two, which is not done in Aristotelian logic. The statement 'all Greeks are men' is commonly interpreted as implying that there are Greeks; without this implication, some of Aristotle's syllogisms are not valid. Take for instance:

'All Greeks are men, All Greeks are white, therefore some men are white.' This is valid if there are Greeks, but not otherwise. If I were to say:

'All golden mountains are mountains, all golden mountains are golden, therefore some mountains are golden,' my conclusion would be false, though in some sense my premisses would be true. If we are to be explicit, we must therefore divide the one statement 'all Greeks are men' into two, one saying 'there are Greeks', and the other saying 'if anything is a Greek it is a man'. The latter statement is purely hypothetical, and does not imply that there are Greeks.

The statement 'all Greeks are men' is thus much more complex in form than the statement 'Socrates is a man'. 'Socrates is a man' has 'Socrates' for its subject, but 'all Greeks are men' does not have 'all Greeks' for its subject, for there is nothing about 'all Greeks' either in the statement 'there are Greeks', or in the statement 'if anything is a Greek it is a man'.

This purely formal error was a source of errors in metaphysics and theory of knowledge. Consider the state of our knowledge in regard to the two propositions 'Socrates is mortal' and 'all men are mortal'. In order to know the truth of 'Socrates is mortal', most of us are content to rely upon testimony; but if testimony is to be reliable, it must lead us back to some one who knew Socrates and saw him dead. The one perceived fact—the dead body of Socrates—together with the knowledge that this was called 'Socrates', was enough to assure us of the mortality of Socrates. But when it comes to 'all men are mortal', the matter is different. The question of our knowledge of such general propositions is a very difficult one. Sometimes they are merely verbal: 'all Greeks are men' is known because nothing is called 'a Greek' unless it is a man. Such general statements can be ascertained from the dictionary; they tell us nothing about the world except how words are used. But 'all men are mortal' is not of this sort; there is nothing logically self-contradictory about an immortal man. We believe the proposition on the basis of induction, because there is no well-authenticated case of a man living more than (say) 150 years; but this only makes the proposition probable, not certain. It cannot be certain so long as living men exist.

Metaphysical errors arose through supposing that 'all men' is the subject of 'all men are mortal' in the same sense as that in which 'Socrates' is the subject of 'Socrates is mortal'. It made it possible to hold that, in some sense, 'all men' denotes an entity of the same sort as that denoted by 'Socrates'. This led Aristotle to say that in a sense a species is a substance. He is careful to qualify this statement, but his followers, especially Porphyry, showed less caution.

Another error into which Aristotle falls through this mistake is to think that a predicate of a predicate can be a predicate of the original subject. If I say 'Socrates is Greek, all Greeks are human', Aristotle thinks that 'human' is a predicate of 'Greek', while 'Greek' is a predicate of 'Socrates', and obviously 'human' is a predicate of 'Socrates'. But in fact 'human' is not a predicate of 'Greek'. The distinction between names and predicates, or in metaphysical language, between particulars and universals, is thus blurred, with disastrous consequences to philosophy. One of the resulting confusions was to suppose that a class with only one member is identical with that one member. This made it impossible to have a correct theory of the number *one*, and led to endless bad metaphysics about unity.

(2) *Over-estimation of the syllogism*. The syllogism is only one kind of deductive argument. In mathematics, which is wholly deductive, syllogisms hardly ever occur. Of course, it would be possible to re-write mathematical arguments in syllogistic form, but this would be very artificial and would not make them any more cogent. Take arithmetic, for example. If I buy goods worth 16s. 3d., and tender a £1 note in payment, how much change is due to me? To put this simple sum in the form of a syllogism would be absurd, and would tend to conceal the real nature of the argument. Again, within logic there are non-syllogistic inferences such as: 'A horse is an animal, therefore a horse's head is an animal's head.' Valid syllogisms, in fact, are only some among valid deductions, and have no logical priority over others. The attempt to give pre-eminence to the syllogism in deduction misled philosophers as to the nature of mathematical reasoning. Kant, who perceived that mathematics is not syllogistic, inferred that it uses extra-logical principles, which, however, he supposed to be as certain as those of logic. He, like his predecessors, though in a different way, was misled by respect for Aristotle.

(3) *Over-estimation of deduction*. The Greeks in general attached more importance to deduction as a source of knowledge than modern philosophers do. In this respect, Aristotle was less at fault than Plato; he repeatedly admitted the importance of induction, and he devoted considerable attention to the question: how do we know the first premisses from which deduction must start? Nevertheless, he, like other Greeks, gave undue prominence to deduction in his theory of knowledge. We shall agree that Mr Smith (say) is mortal, and we may, loosely, say that we know this because we know that all men are mortal. But what we really know is not 'all men are mortal'; we know rather something like 'all men born more than one hundred and fifty years ago are mortal, and so are almost all men born more than one hundred years ago'. This is our reason for thinking that Mr Smith will die. But this argument is an induction, not a deduction. It has less cogency than a deduction, and yields only a probability, not a certainty; but on the other hand it gives *new* knowledge, which deduction does not. All the important inferences outside logic and pure mathematics are induc-

tive, not deductive; the only exceptions are law and theology, each of which derives its first principles from an unquestionable text, viz. the statute books or the scriptures.

Apart from *The Prior Analytics*, which deals with the syllogism, there are other logical writings of Aristotle which have considerable importance in the history of philosophy. One of these is the short work on *The Categories*. Porphyry the Neoplatonist wrote a commentary on this book, which had a very notable influence on medieval philosophy; but for the present let us ignore Porphyry and confine ourselves to Aristotle.

What, exactly is meant by the word 'category', whether in Aristotle or in Kant and Hegel, I must confess that I have never been able to understand. I do not myself believe that the term 'category' is in any way useful in philosophy, as representing any clear idea. There are, in Aristotle, ten categories: substance, quantity, quality, relation, place, time, position, state, action, and affection. The only definition offered of the term 'category' is: 'expressions which are in no way composite signify'—and then follows the above list. This seems to mean that every word of which the meaning is not compounded of the meanings of other words signifies a substance or a quantity or etc. There is no suggestion of any principle on which the list of ten categories has been compiled.

'Substance' is primarily what is not predicable of a subject nor present in a subject. A thing is said to be 'present in a subject' when, though not a part of the subject, it cannot exist without the subject. The instances given are a piece of grammatical knowledge which is present in a mind, and a certain whiteness which may be present in a body. A substance in the above primary sense is an individual thing or person or animal. But in a secondary sense a species or a genus—e.g. 'man' or 'animal'—may be called a substance. This secondary sense seems indefensible, and opened the door, in later writers, to much bad metaphysics.

The Posterior Analytics is a work largely concerned with a question which must trouble any deductive theory, namely: How are first premisses obtained? Since deduction must start from somewhere, we must begin with something unproved, which must be known otherwise than by demonstration. I shall not give Aristotle's theory in detail, since it depends upon the notion of *essence*. A definition, he says, is a statement of a thing's essential nature. The notion of essence is an intimate part of every philosophy subsequent to Aristotle, until we come to modern times. It is, in my opinion, a hopelessly muddle-headed notion, but its historical importance requires us to say something about it.

The 'essence' of a thing appears to have meant 'those of its properties which it cannot change without losing its identity'. Socrates may be sometimes happy, sometimes sad; sometimes well, sometimes ill. Since he can change these properties without ceasing to be Socrates, they are no part of his essence. But it is supposed to be of the essence of Socrates that he is a man, though a Pythagorean, who believes in transmigration, will not admit this. In fact, the question of 'essence' is one as to the use of words. We apply the same name, on different occasions, to somewhat different occurrences, which we regard as manifestations of a single 'thing' or 'person'. In fact, however, this is only a verbal convenience. The 'essence' of Socrates thus consists of those properties in the absence of which we should not use the name 'Socrates'. The question is purely linguistic : a *word* may have an essence, but a *thing* cannot.

The conception of 'substance', like that of 'essence', is a transference to metaphysics of what is only a linguistic convenience. We find it convenient, in describing the world, to describe a certain number of occurrences as events in the life of 'Socrates', and a certain number of others as events in the life of 'Mr Smith'. This leads us to think of 'Socrates' or 'Mr Smith' as denoting something that persists through a certain number of years, and as in some way more 'solid' and 'real' than the events that happen to him. If Socrates is ill, we think that Socrates, at other times, is well, and therefore the being of Socrates is independent of his illness; illness, on the other hand, requires somebody to be ill. But although Socrates need not be ill, *something* must be occurring to him if he is to be considered to exist. He is not, therefore, really any more 'solid' than the things that happen to him.

'Substance', when taken seriously, is a concept impossible to free from difficulties. A substance is supposed to be the subject of properties, and to be something distinct from all its properties. But when we take away the properties, and try to imagine the substance by itself, we find that there is nothing left. To put the matter in another way : What distinguishes one substance from another? Not difference of properties, for, according to the logic of substance, difference of properties presupposes numerical diversity between the substances concerned. Two substances, therefore, must be *just* two, without being, in themselves, in any way distinguishable. How, then, are we ever to find out that they *are* two?

'Substance', in fact is merely a convenient way of collecting events into bundles. What can we know about Mr Smith? When we look at him, we see a pattern of colours; when we listen to him talking, we hear a series of sounds. We believe that, like us, he has thoughts and feelings. But what is Mr Smith apart from all these occurrences? A mere imaginary hook, from which the occurrences are supposed to hang. They have in fact no need of a hook, any more than the earth needs an elephant to rest upon. Any one can see, in the analogous case of a geographical region, that such a word as 'France' (say) is only a linguistic convenience, and that there is not a *thing* called 'France' over and above its various parts. The same holds of 'Mr Smith'; it is a collective name for a number of occurrences. If we take it as anything more, it denotes something completely unknowable, and therefore not needed for the expression of what we know.

'Substance', in a word, is a metaphysical mistake, due to transference to the world-structure of the structure of sentences composed of a subject and a predicate.

I conclude that the Aristotelian doctrines with which we have been concerned in this chapter are wholly false, with the exception of the formal theory of the syllogism, which is unimportant. Any person in the present day who wishes to learn logic will be wasting his time if he reads Aristotle or any of his disciples. None the less, Aristotle's logical writings show great ability, and would have been useful to mankind if they had appeared at a time when intellectual originality was still active. Unfortunately, they appeared at the very end of the creative period of Greek thought, and therefore came to be accepted as authoritative. By the time that logical originality revived, a reign of two thousand years had made Aristotle very difficult to dethrone. Throughout modern times, practically every advance in science, in logic, or in philosophy has had to be made in the teeth of opposition from Aristotle's disciples.

Chapter XXIII

ARISTOTLE'S PHYSICS

I N this chapter I propose to consider two of Aristotle's books, the one called *Physics* and the one called *On the Heavens*. These two books are closely connected; the second takes up the argument at the point at which the first has left it. Both were extremely influential, and dominated science until the time of Galileo. Words such as 'quintessence' and 'sublunary' are derived from the theories expressed in these books. The historian of philosophy, accordingly, must study them, in spite of the fact that hardly a sentence in either can be accepted in the light of modern science.

To understand the views of Aristotle, as of most Greeks, on physics, it is necessary to apprehend their imaginative background. Every philosopher, in addition to the formal system which he offers to the world, has another, much simpler, of which he may be quite unaware. If he is aware of it, he probably realizes that it won't quite do; he therefore conceals it, and sets forth something more sophisticated, which he believes because it is like his crude system, but which he asks others to accept because he thinks he has made it such as cannot be disproved. The sophistication comes in by way of refutation of refutations, but this alone will never give a positive result: it shows, at best, that a theory *may* be true, not that it *must* be. The positive result, however little the philosopher may realize it, is due to his imaginative preconceptions, or to what Santayana calls 'animal faith'.

In relation to physics, Aristotle's imaginative background was very different from that of a modern student. Nowadays, a boy begins with mechanics, which, by its very name, suggests machines. He is accustomed to motor-cars and aeroplanes; he does not, even in the dimmest recesses of his subconscious imagination, think that a motor-car contains some sort of horse in its inside, or that an aeroplane flies because its wings are those of a bird possessing magical powers. Animals have lost their importance in our imaginative pictures of the world, in which man stands comparatively alone as master of a mainly lifeless and largely subservient material environment.

To the Greek, attempting to give a scientific account of motion, the purely mechanical view hardly suggested itself, except in the case of a few men of genius such as Democritus and Archimedes.

Two sets of phenomena seemed important: the movements of animals, and the movements of the heavenly bodies. To the modern man of science, the body of an animal is a very elaborate machine, with an enormously complex physico-chemical structure; every new discovery consists in diminishing the apparent gulf between animals and machines. To the Greek, it seemed more natural to assimilate apparently lifeless motions to those of animals. A child still distinguishes live animals from other things by the fact that they can move of themselves; to many Greeks, and especially to Aristotle, this peculiarity suggested itself as the basis of a general theory of physics.

But how about the heavenly bodies? They differ from animals by the regularity of their movements, but this may be only due to their superior perfection. Every Greek philosopher, whatever he may have come to think in adult life, had been taught in childhood to regard the sun and moon as gods; Anaxagoras was prosecuted for impiety because he thought that they were not alive. It was natural that a philosopher who could no longer regard the heavenly bodies themselves as divine should think of them as moved by the will of a Divine Being who had a Hellenic love of order and geometrical simplicity. Thus the ultimate source of all movement is Will: on earth the capricious Will of human beings and animals, but in heaven the unchanging Will of the Supreme Artificer.

I do not suggest that this applies to every detail of what Aristotle has to say. What I do suggest is that it gives his imaginative background, and represents the sort of thing which, in embarking on his investigations, he would expect to find true.

After these preliminaries, let us examine what it is that he actually says.

Physics, in Aristotle, is the science of what the Greeks called 'phusis' (or 'physis'), a word which is translated 'nature', but has not exactly the meaning which we attach to that word. We still speak of 'natural science' and 'natural history', but 'nature' by itself, though it is a very ambiguous word, seldom means just what 'phusis' meant. 'Phusis' had to do with growth; one might say it is the 'nature of an acorn to grow into an oak, and in that case one would be using the word in the Aristotelian sense. The 'nature' of a thing, Aristotle says, is its end, that for the sake of which it exists. Thus the word has a teleological implication. Some things exist by nature, some from other causes. Animals, plants, and simple bodies (elements) exist by nature; they have an internal principle of motion (the word translated 'motion' or 'movement' has a wider meaning than 'locomotion'; in addition to locomotion it includes change of quality or of size). Nature is a source of being moved or at rest.

Things 'have a nature' if they have an internal principle of this kind. The phrase 'according to nature' applies to these things and their essential attributes. (It was through this point of view that 'unnatural' came to express blame.) Nature is in form rather than in matter; what is potentially flesh or bone has not yet acquired its own nature, and a thing is more what it is when it has attained to fulfilment. This whole point of view seems to be suggested by biology: the acorn is 'potentially' an oak.

Nature belongs to the class of causes which operate for the sake of something. This leads to a discussion of the view that nature works of necessity, without purpose, in connection with which Aristotle discusses the survival of the fittest, in the form taught by Empedocles. This cannot be right, he says, because things happen in fixed ways, and when a series has a completion, all preceding steps are for its sake. Those things are 'natural' which 'by a continuous movement, originated from an internal principle, arrive at some completion' (199ᵇ).

This whole conception of 'nature', though it might well seem admirably suited to explain the growth of animals and plants, became, in the event, a great obstacle to the progress of science, and a source of much that was bad in ethics. In the latter respect, it is still harmful.

Motion, we are told, is the fulfilling of what exists potentially. This view, apart from other defects, is incompatible with the relativity of locomotion. When A moves relatively to B, B moves relatively to A, and there is no sense in saying that one of the two is in motion while the other is at rest. When a dog seizes a bone, it seems to common sense that the dog moves while the bone remains at rest (until seized), and that the motion has a purpose, namely to fulfil the dog's 'nature'. But it has turned out that this point of view cannot be applied to dead matter, and that, for the purposes of scientific physics, no conception of an 'end' is useful, nor can any motion, in scientific strictness, be treated as other than relative.

Aristotle rejects the void, as maintained by Leucippus and Democritus. He then passes on to a rather curious discussion of time. It might, he says, be maintained that time does not exist, since it is composed of past and future, of which one no longer exists while the other does not yet exist. This view, however, he rejects. Time, he says, is motion that admits of numeration. (It is not clear why he thinks numeration essential.) We may fairly ask, he continues, whether time could exist without the soul, since there cannot be anything to count unless there is someone to count, and time involves numeration. It seems that he thinks of time as so many hours or days or years. Some things, he adds, are eternal, in the sense of not being in time; presumably he is thinking of such things as numbers.

There always has been motion, and there always will be; for there cannot be time without motion, and all are agreed that time is uncreated, except Plato. On this point, Christian followers of Aristotle were obliged to dissent from him, since the Bible tells us that the universe had a beginning.

The *Physics* ends with the argument for an unmoved mover, which we considered in connection with the *Metaphysics*. There is one unmoved mover, which directly causes a circular motion. Circular motion is the primary kind, and the only kind which can be continuous and infinite. The first mover has no parts or magnitude and is at the circumference of the world.

Having reached this conclusion, we pass on to the heavens.

The treatise *On the Heavens* sets forth a pleasant and simple theory. Things below the moon are subject to generation and decay; from the moon upwards, everything is ungenerated and indestructible. The earth, which is spherical, is at the centre of the universe. In the sublunary sphere, everything is composed of the four elements, earth, water, air, and fire; but there is a fifth element, of which the heavenly bodies are composed. The natural movement of the terrestrial elements is rectilinear, but that of the fifth element is circular. The heavens are perfectly spherical, and the upper regions are more divine than the lower. The stars and planets are not composed of fire, but of the fifth element; their motion is due to that of spheres to which they are attached. (All this appears in poetical form in Dante's *Paradiso*.)

The four terrestrial elements are not eternal, but are generated out of each other—fire is absolutely light, in the sense that its natural motion is upward; earth is absolutely heavy. Air is relatively light, and water is relatively heavy.

This theory provided many difficulties for later ages. Comets, which were recognized as destructible, had to be assigned to the sublunary sphere, but in the seventeenth century it was found that they describe orbits round the sun, and are very seldom as near as the moon. Since the natural motion of terrestrial bodies is rectilinear, it was held that a projectile fired horizontally will move horizontally for a time, and then suddenly begin to fall vertically. Galileo's discovery that a projectile moves in a parabola shocked his Aristotelian colleagues. Copernicus, Kepler, and Galileo had to combat Aristotle as well as the Bible in establishing the view that the earth is not the centre of the universe, but rotates once a day and goes round the sun once a year.

To come to a more general matter: Aristotelian physics is incompatible with Newton's 'First Law of Motion', originally enunciated by Galileo. This law states that every body, left to itself, will, if already in motion, continue to move in a straight line with uniform velocity. Thus outside causes are required, not to account for motion, but to account for *change* of motion, either in velocity or in direction. Circular motion, which Aristotle thought 'natural' for the heavenly bodies, involves a continual change in the direction of motion, and therefore requires a force directed towards the centre of the circle, as in Newton's law of gravitation.

Finally: The view that the heavenly bodies are eternal and incorruptible has had to be abandoned. The sun and stars have long lives, but do not live for ever. They are born from a nebula, and in the end they either explode or die of cold. Nothing in the visible world is exempt from change and decay; the Aristotelian belief to the contrary, though accepted by medieval Christians, is a product of the pagan worship of sun and moon and planets.

Chapter XXIV

EARLY GREEK MATHEMATICS AND ASTRONOMY

I AM concerned in this chapter with mathematics, not on its own account, but as it was related to Greek philosophy—a relation which, especially in Plato, was very close. The pre-eminence of the Greeks appears more clearly in mathematics and astronomy than in anything else. What they did in art, in literature, and in philosophy, may be judged better or worse according to taste, but what they accomplished in geometry is wholly beyond question. They derived something from Egypt, and rather less from Babylonia; but what they obtained from these sources was, in mathematics, mainly simple rules, and in astronomy records of observations extended over very long periods. The art of mathematical demonstration was, almost wholly, Greek in origin.

There are many pleasant stories, probably unhistorical, showing what practical problems stimulated mathematical investigations. The earliest and simplest relates to Thales, who, when in Egypt was asked by the king to find out the height of a pyramid. He waited for the time of day when his shadow was as long as he was tall; he then measured the shadow of the pyramid, which was of course equal to its height. It is said that the laws of perspective were first studied by the geometer Agatharcus, in order to paint scenery for the plays of Aeschylus. The problem of finding the distance of a ship at sea, which was said to have been studied by Thales, was correctly solved at an early stage. One of the great problems that occupied Greek geometers, that of the duplication of the cube, originated, we are told, with the priests of a certain temple, who were informed by the oracle that the god wanted a statue twice as large as the one they had. At first they thought simply of doubling all the dimensions of the statue, but then they realized that the result would be eight times as large as the original, which would involve more expense than the god had demanded. So they sent a deputation to Plato to ask whether anybody in the Academy could solve their problem. The geometers took it up, and worked at it for centuries, producing, incidentally, much admirable work. The problem is, of course, that of determining the cube root of 2.

The square root of 2, which was the first irrational to be discovered, was known to the early Pythagoreans, and ingenious methods of approximating to its value were discovered. The best was as follows: Form two columns of numbers, which we will call the a's and the b's; each starts with 1. The next a, at each stage, is formed by adding the last a and b already obtained; the next b is formed by adding twice the previous a to the previous b. The first 6 pairs so obtained are (1, 1), (2, 3), (5, 7), (12, 17), (29, 41), (70, 99).

In each pair, $2a^2 - b^2$ is 1 or $- 1$. Thus $\dfrac{b}{a}$ is nearly the square root of two, and at each fresh step it gets nearer. For instance, the reader may satisfy himself that the square of 99/70 is very nearly equal to 2.

Pythagoras—always a rather misty figure—is described by Proclus as the first who made geometry a liberal education. Many authorities, including Sir Thomas Heath,[1] believe that he probably discovered the theorem that bears his name, to the effect that, in a right-angled triangle, the square on the side opposite the right angle is equal to the sum of the squares on the other two sides. In any case, this theorem was known to the Pythagoreans at a very early date. They knew also that the sum of the angles of a triangle is two right angles.

Irrationals other than the square root of two were studied, in particular cases by Theodorus, a contemporary of Socrates, and in a more general way by Theaetetus, who was roughly contemporary with Plato, but somewhat older. Democritus wrote a treatise on irrationals, but very little is known as to its contents. Plato was profoundly interested in the subject; he mentions the work of Theodorus and Theaetetus in the dialogue called after the latter. In the *Laws* (819-820), he says that the general ignorance on this subject is disgraceful, and implies that he himself began to know about it rather late in life. It had of course an important bearing on the Pythagorean philosophy.

One of the most important consequences of the discovery of irrationals was the invention of the geometrical theory of proportion by Eudoxus (*ca.* 408—*ca.* 355 B.C.). Before him, there was only the arithmetical theory of proportion. According to this theory, the ratio of a to b is equal to the ratio of c to d if a times d is equal to b times c. This definition, in the absence of an arithmetical theory of irrationals, is only applicable to rationals. Eudoxus, however, gave a new definition not subject to this restriction, framed in a manner which suggests the methods of modern analysis. The theory is developed in Euclid, and has great logical beauty.

Eudoxus also either invented or perfected the 'method of exhaustion', which was subsequently used with great success by Archi-

[1] *Greek Mathematics*, Vol. I, p. 145.

medes. This method is an anticipation of the integral calculus. Take, for example, the question of the area of a circle. You can inscribe in a circle a regular hexagon, or a regular dodecagon, or a regular polygon of a thousand or a million sides. The area of such a polygon, however many sides it has, is proportional to the square on the diameter of the circle. The more sides the polygon has, the more nearly it becomes equal to the circle. You can prove that, if you give the polygon enough sides, its area can be got to differ from that of the circle by less than any previously assigned area, however small. For this purpose, the 'axiom of Archimedes' is used. This states (when somewhat simplified) that if the greater of two quantities is halved, and then the half is halved, and so on, a quantity will be reached, at last, which is less than the smaller of the original two quantities. In other words, if a is greater than b, there is some whole number n such that 2^n times b is greater than a.

The method of exhaustion sometimes leads to an exact result, as in squaring the parabola, which was done by Archimedes; sometimes, as in the attempt to square the circle, it can only lead to successive approximations. The problem of squaring the circle is the problem of determining the ratio of the circumference of a circle to the diameter, which is called π Archimedes used the approximation $\frac{22}{7}$ in calculations; by inscribing and circumscribing a regular polygon of 96 sides, he proved that π is less than $3\frac{1}{7}$ and greater than $3\frac{10}{71}$. The method could be carried to any required degree of approximation, and that is all that any method can do in this problem. The use of inscribed and circumscribed polygons for approximations to π goes back to Antiphon, who was a contemporary of Socrates.

Euclid, who was still, when I was young, the sole acknowledged text-book of geometry for boys, lived in Alexandria, about 300 B.C., a few years after the death of Alexander and Aristotle. Most of his *Elements* was not original, but the order of propositions, and the logical structure, were largely his. The more one studies geometry, the more admirable these are seen to be. The treatment of parallels by means of the famous postulate of parallels has the twofold merit of rigour in deduction and of not concealing the dubiousness of the initial assumption. The theory of proportion, which follows Eudoxus, avoids all the difficulties connected with irrationals, by methods essentially similar to those introduced by Weierstrass into nineteenth-century analysis. Euclid then passes on to a kind of geometrical algebra, and deals, in Book X, with the subject of irrationals. After this he proceeds to solid geometry, ending with the construction of the regular solids, which had been perfected by Theaetetus and assumed in Plato's *Timaeus*.

Euclid's *Elements* is certainly one of the greatest books ever written, and one of the most perfect monuments of the Greek intellect. It has, of course, the typical Greek limitations: the method is purely deductive, and there is no way, within it, of testing the initial assumptions. These assumptions were supposed to be unquestionable, but in the nineteenth century non-Euclidean geometry showed that they *might* be in part mistaken, and that only observation could decide whether they were so.

There is in Euclid the contempt for practical utility which had been inculcated by Plato. It is said that a pupil, after listening to a demonstration, asked what he would gain by learning geometry, whereupon Euclid called a slave and said 'Give the young man threepence, since he must needs make a gain out of what he learns.' The contempt for practice was, however, pragmatically justified. No one, in Greek times, supposed that conic sections had any utility; at last, in the seventeenth century, Galileo discovered that projectiles move in parabolas, and Kepler discovered that planets move in ellipses. Suddenly the work that the Greeks had done from pure love of theory became the key to warfare and astronomy.

The Romans were too practical-minded to appreciate Euclid; the first of them to mention him is Cicero, in whose time there was probably no Latin translation; indeed there is no *record* of any Latin translation before Boethius (*ca.* A.D. 480). The Arabs were more appreciative: a copy was given to the caliph by the Byzantine emperor about A.D. 760, and a translation into Arabic was made under Harun al Rashid, about A.D. 800. The first still extant Latin translation was made from the Arabic by Adelard of Bath in A.D. 1120. From that time on, the study of geometry gradually revived in the West; but it was not until the late Renaissance that important advances were made.

I come now to astronomy, where Greek achievements were as remarkable as in geometry. Before their time, among the Babylonians and Egyptians, many centuries of observation had laid a foundation. The apparent motions of the planets had been recorded, but it was not known that the morning and evening star were the same. A cycle of eclipses had been discovered, certainly in Babylonia and probably in Egypt, which made the prediction of lunar eclipses fairly reliable, but not of solar eclipses, since those were not always visible at a given spot. We owe to the Babylonians the division of the right angle into ninety degrees, and of the degree into sixty minutes; they had a liking for the number sixty, and even a system of numeration based upon it. The Greeks were fond of attributing the wisdom of their pioneers to travels in Egypt, but what had really been achieved before the Greeks was very little.

The prediction of an eclipse by Thales was, however, an example of foreign influence; there is no reason to suppose that he added anything to what he learnt from Egyptian or Babylonian sources, and it was a stroke of luck that his prediction was verified.

Let us begin with some of the earliest discoveries and correct hypotheses. Anaximander thought that the earth floats freely, and is not supported on anything. Aristotle,[1] who often rejected the best hypotheses of his time, objected to the theory of Anaximander, that the earth, being at the centre, remained immovable because there was no reason for moving in one direction rather than another. If this were valid, he said, a man placed at the centre of a circle with food at various points of the circumference would starve to death for lack of reason to choose one portion of food rather than another This argument reappears in scholastic philosophy, not in connection with astronomy, but with free will. It reappears in the form of 'Buridan's ass', which was unable to choose between two bundles of hay placed at equal distances to right and left, and therefore died of hunger.

Pythagoras, in all probability, was the first to think the earth spherical, but his reasons were (one must suppose) aesthetic rather than scientific. Scientific reasons, however, were soon found. Anaxagoras discovered that the moon shines by reflected light, and gave the right theory of eclipses. He himself still thought the earth flat, but the shape of the earth's shadow in lunar eclipses gave the Pythagoreans conclusive arguments in favour of its being spherical. They went further, and regarded the earth as one of the planets. They knew—from Pythagoras himself, it is said—that the morning star and the evening star are identical, and they thought that all the planets, including the earth, move in circles, not round the sun, but round the 'central fire'. They had discovered that the moon always turns the same face to the earth, and they thought that the earth always turns the same face to the 'central fire'. The Mediterranean regions were on the side turned away from the central fire, which was therefore always invisible. The central fire was called 'the house of Zeus', or 'the Mother of the gods'. The sun was supposed to shine by light reflected from the central fire. In addition to the earth, there was another body, the counter-earth, at the same distance from the central fire. For this, they had two reasons, one scientific, one derived from their arithmetical mysticism. The scientific reason was the correct observation that an eclipse of the moon sometimes occurs when both sun and moon are above the horizon. Refraction, which is the cause of this phenomenon, was unknown to them, and they thought that, in such cases, the eclipse must be due to the

[1] *De Caelo*, 295^b

shadow of a body other than the earth. The other reason was that the sun and moon, the five planets, the earth and counter-earth, and the central fire, made *ten* heavenly bodies, and ten was the mystic number of the Pythagoreans.

This Pythagorean theory is attributed to Philolaus, a Theban, who lived at the end of the fifth century B.C. Although it is fanciful and in part quite unscientific, it is very important, since it involves the greater part of the imaginative effort required for conceiving the Copernican hypothesis. To conceive of the earth, not as the centre of the universe, but as one among the planets, not as eternally fixed, but as wandering through space, showed an extra-ordinary emancipation from anthropocentric thinking. When once this jolt had been given to men's natural picture of the universe, it was not so very difficult to be led by scientific arguments to a more accurate theory.

To this various observations contributed. Oenopides, who was slightly later than Anaxagoras, discovered the obliquity of the ecliptic. It soon became clear that the sun must be much larger than the earth, which fact supported those who denied that the earth is the centre of the universe. The central fire and the counter-earth were dropped by the Pythagoreans soon after the time of Plato. Heraclides of Pontus (whose dates are about 388 to 315 B.C., contemporary with Aristotle) discovered that Venus and Mercury revolve about the sun, and adopted the view that the earth rotates on its own axis once every twenty-four hours. This last was a very important step, which no predecessor had taken. Heraclides was of Plato's school, and must have been a great man, but was not as much respected as one would expect; he is described as a fat dandy.

Aristarchus of Samos, who lived approximately from 310 to 230 B.C., and was thus about twenty-five years older than Archimedes, is the most interesting of all ancient astronomers, because he advanced the complete Copernican hypothesis, that all the planets, including the earth, revolve in circles round the sun, and that the earth, rotates on its axis once in twenty-four hours. It is a little disappointing to find that the only extant work of Aristarchus, *On the Sizes and Distances of the Sun and the Moon*, adheres to the geocentric view. It is true that, for the problems with which this book deals, it makes no difference which theory is adopted, and he may therefore have thought it unwise to burden his calculations with an unnecessary opposition to the general opinion of astron-omers; or he may have only arrived at the Copernican hypothesis after writing this book. Sir Thomas Heath, in his work on Aristarchus,[1] which contains the text of this book with a translation, inclines to the latter view. The evidence that Aristarchus suggested the Copernican view is, in any case, quite conclusive.

The first and best evidence is that of Archimedes, who, as we have seen, was a younger contemporary of Aristarchus. Writing to Gelon, King of Syracuse, he says that Aristarchus brought out 'a book consisting of certain hypotheses', and continues: 'His hypotheses are that the fixed stars and the sun remain unmoved, that the earth revolves about the sun in the circumference of a circle, the sun lying in the middle of the orbit.' There is a passage in Plutarch saying that Cleanthes 'thought it was the duty of the Greeks to indict Aristarchus of Samos on the charge of impiety for putting in motion the Hearth of the Universe (i.e. the earth), this being the effect of his attempt to save the phenomena by supposing the heaven to remain at rest and the earth to revolve in an oblique circle, while it rotates, at the same time, about its own axis'. Cleanthes was a contemporary of Aristarchus, and died about 232 B.C. In another passage, Plutarch says that Aristarchus advanced this view only as a hypothesis, but that his successor Seleucus maintained it as a definite opinion. (Seleucus flourished about 150 B.C.) Aëtius and Sextus Empiricus also assert that Aristarchus advanced the heliocentric hypothesis, but do not say that it was set forth by him *only* as a hypothesis. Even if he did so, it seems not unlikely that he, like Galileo two thousand years later, was influenced by the fear of offending religious prejudices, a fear which the attitude of Cleanthes (mentioned above) shows to have been well grounded.

The Copernican hypothesis, after being advanced, whether positively or tentatively, by Aristarchus, was definitely adopted by Seleucus, but by no other ancient astronomer. This general rejection was mainly due to Hipparchus, who flourished from 161 to 126 B.C. He is described by Heath as 'the greatest astronomer of antiquity'.[2] He was the first to write systematically on trigonometry; he discovered the precession of the equinoxes; he estimated the length of the lunar month with an error of less than one second; he improved Aristarchus's estimates of the sizes and distances of the sun and moon; he made a catalogue of eight hundred and fifty fixed stars, giving their latitude and longitude. As against the heliocentric hypothesis of Aristarchus, he adopted and improved the theory of epicycles which had been invented by Apollonius, who flourished about 220 B.C.; it was a development of this theory that came to be

---

[1] *Aristarchus of Samos, the Ancient Copernicus.* By Sir Thomas Heath, Oxford, 1913. What follows is based on this book.
[2] *Greek Mathematics*, Vol. II, p. 253.

known, later, as the Ptolemaic system, after the astronomer Ptolemy, who flourished in the middle of the second century A.D.

Copernicus perhaps came to know something, though not much, of the almost forgotten hypothesis of Aristarchus, and was encouraged by finding ancient authority for his innovation. Otherwise, the effect of this hypothesis on subsequent astronomy was practically *nil*.

Ancient astronomers, in estimating the sizes of the earth, moon, and sun, and the distances of the moon and sun, used methods which were theoretically valid, but they were hampered by the lack of instruments of precision. Many of their results, in view of this lack, were surprisingly good. Eratosthenes estimated the earth's diameter at 7,850 miles, which is only about fifty miles short of the truth. Ptolemy estimated the mean distance of the moon at 29½ times the earth's diameter; the correct figure is about 30.2. None of them got anywhere near the size and distance of the sun, which all under-estimated. Their estimates, in terms of the earth's diameter, were:

Aristarchus, 180;
Hipparchus, 1,245;
Posidonius, 6,545.

The correct figure is 11,726. It will be seen that these estimates continually improved (that of Ptolemy, however, showed a retrogression); that of Posidonius[1] is about half the correct figure. On the whole, their picture of the solar system was not so very far from the truth.

Greek astronomy was geometrical, not dynamic. The ancients thought of the motions of the heavenly bodies as uniform and circular, or compounded of circular motions. They had not the conception of *force*. There were spheres which moved as a whole, and on which the various heavenly bodies were fixed. With Newton and gravitation a new point of view, less geometrical, was introduced. It is curious to observe that there is a reversion to the geometrical point of view in Einstein's General Theory of Relativity, from which the conception of force, in the Newtonian sense, has been banished.

The problem for the astronomer is this: given the apparent motions of the heavenly bodies on the celestial sphere, to introduce, by hypothesis, a third co-ordinate, depth, in such a way as to make the description of the phenomena as simple as possible. The merit of the Copernican hypothesis is not *truth*, but simplicity; in view of the relativity of motion, no question of truth is involved. The

[1] Posidonius was Cicero's teacher. He flourished in the latter half of the second century B.C.

Greeks, in their search for hypotheses which would 'save the phenomena', were in effect, though not altogether in intention, tackling the problem in the scientifically correct way. A comparison with their predecessors, and with their successors until Copernicus, must convince every student of their truly astonishing genius.

Two very great men, Archimedes and Apollonius, in the third century B.C., complete the list of first-class Greek mathematicians. Archimedes was a friend, probably a cousin, of the king of Syracuse, and was killed when that city was captured by the Romans in 212 B.C. Apollonius, from his youth, lived at Alexandria. Archimedes was not only a mathematician, but also a physicist and student of hydrostatics. Apollonius is chiefly noted for his work on conic sections. I shall say no more about them, as they came too late to influence philosophy.

After these two men, though respectable work continued to be done in Alexandria, the great age was ended. Under the Roman domination, the Greeks lost the self-confidence that belongs to political liberty, and in losing it acquired a paralysing respect for their predecessors. The Roman soldier who killed Archimedes was a symbol of the death of original thought that Rome caused throughout the Hellenic world.

PART III

ANCIENT PHILOSOPHY AFTER ARISTOTLE

Chapter XXV

THE HELLENISTIC WORLD

THE history of the Greek-speaking world in antiquity may be divided into three periods: that of the free City States, which was brought to an end by Philip and Alexander; that of the Macedonian domination, of which the last remnant was extinguished by the Roman annexation of Egypt after the death of Cleopatra; and finally that of the Roman Empire. Of these three periods, the first is characterized by freedom and disorder, and the second by subjection and disorder, the third by subjection and order.

The second of these periods is known as the Hellenistic age. In science and mathematics, the work done during this period is the best ever achieved by the Greeks. In philosophy, it includes the foundation of the Epicurean and Stoic schools, and also of scepticism as a definitely formulated doctrine; it is therefore still important philosophically, though less so than the period of Plato and Aristotle. After the third century B.C., there is nothing really new in Greek philosophy until the Neoplatonists in the third century A.D. But meanwhile the Roman world was being prepared for the victory of Christianity.

The brief career of Alexander suddenly transformed the Greek world. In the ten years from 334 to 324 B.C., he conquered Asia Minor, Syria, Egypt, Babylonia, Persia, Samarcand, Bactria, and the Punjab. The Persian Empire, the greatest that the world had known, was destroyed by three battles. The ancient lore of the Babylonians, along with their ancient superstitions, became familiar to Greek curiosity; so did the Zoroastrian dualism and (in a lesser degree) the religions of India, where Buddhism was moving towards supremacy. Wherever Alexander penetrated, even in the mountains of Afghanistan, on the banks of the Jaxartes, and on the tributaries of the Indus, he founded Greek cities, in which he tried to reproduce Greek institutions, with a measure of self-government. Although his army was composed mainly of Macedonians, and although most European Greeks submitted to him unwillingly, he considered himself, at first, as the apostle of Hellenism. Gradually, however, as his conquests extended, he adopted the policy of promoting a friendly fusion between Greek and barbarian.

For this he had various motives. On the one hand, it was obvious that his armies, which were not very large, could not permanently hold so vast an empire by force, but must, in the long run, depend upon conciliation of the conquered populations. On the other hand, the East was unaccustomed to any form of government except that of a divine king, a role which Alexander felt himself well fitted to perform. Whether he believed himself a god, or only took on the attributes of divinity from motives of policy, is a question for the psychologist, since the historical evidence is indecisive. In any case, he clearly enjoyed the adulation which he received in Egypt as successor of the Pharaohs, and in Persia as the Great King. His Macedonian captains—the 'Companions', as they were called—had towards him the attitude of western nobles to their constitutional sovereign: they refused to prostrate themselves before him, they gave evidence and criticism even at the risk of their lives, and at a crucial moment they controlled his actions, when they compelled him to turn homewards from the Indus instead of marching on to the conquest of the Ganges. Orientals were more accommodating, providing their religious prejudices were respected. This offered no difficulty to Alexander; it was only necessary to identify Ammon or Bel with Zeus, and to declare himself the son of the god. Psychologists observe that Alexander hated Philip, and was probably privy to his murder; he would have liked to believe that his mother Olympias, like some lady of Greek mythology, had been beloved of a god. Alexander's career was so miraculous that he may well have thought a miraculous origin the best explanation of his prodigious success.

The Greeks had a very strong feeling of superiority to the barbarians; Aristotle no doubt expresses the general view when he says that northern races are spirited, southern races civilized, but the Greeks alone are both spirited and civilized. Plato and Aristotle thought it wrong to make slaves of Greeks, but not of barbarians. Alexander, who was not quite a Greek, tried to break down this attitude of superiority. He himself married two barbarian princesses, and he compelled his leading Macedonians to marry Persian women of noble birth. His innumerable Greek cities, one would suppose, must have contained many more male than female colonists, and their men must therefore have followed his example in intermarrying with the women of the locality. The result of this policy was to bring into the minds of thoughtful men the conception of mankind as a whole; the old loyalty to the City State and (in a lesser degree) to the Greek race seemed no longer adequate. In philosophy, this cosmopolitan point of view begins with the Stoics, but in practice it begins earlier, with Alexander. It had the result that the interaction of Greek and barbarian was reciprocal: the barbarians learnt something of Greek science, while the Greeks learnt much of barbarian superstition. Greek civilization, in covering a wider area, became less purely Greek.

Greek civilization was essentially urban. There were, of course, many Greeks engaged in agriculture, but they contributed little to what was distinctive in Hellenic culture. From the Milesian school onwards, the Greeks who were eminent in science and philosophy and literature were associated with rich commercial cities, often surrounded by barbarian populations. This type of civilization was inaugurated, not by the Greeks, but by the Phoenicians; Tyre and Sidon and Carthage depended on slaves for manual labour at home, and on hired mercenaries in the conduct of their wars. They did not depend, as modern capital cities do, upon large rural populations of the same blood and with equal political rights. The nearest modern analogue is to be seen in the Far East during the latter half of the nineteenth century. Singapore and Hong Kong, Shainghai and the other treaty ports of China, were little European islands, where the white men formed a commercial aristocracy living on coolie labour. In North America, north of the Mason-Dixon line, since such labour was not available, white men were compelled to practise agriculture. For this reason, the hold of the white man on North America is secure, while his hold on the Far East has already been greatly diminished, and may easily cease altogether. Much of his type of culture, especially industrialism, will, however, survive. This analogue will help us to understand the position of the Greeks in the eastern parts of Alexander's empire.

The effect of Alexander on the imagination of Asia was great and lasting. The *First Book of the Maccabees*, written centuries after his death, opens with an account of his career:

'And it happened, after that Alexander, son of Philip, the Macedonian, who came out of the land of Chettiim, had smitten Darius, king of the Persians and Medes, that he reigned in his stead, the first over Greece, and made many wars, and won many strong holds, and slew the kings of the earth, and went through to the ends of the earth, and took spoil of many nations, insomuch that the earth was quiet before him; whereupon he was exalted, and his heart was lifted up. And he gathered a mighty strong host, and ruled over countries, and nations, and kings, who became tributaries unto him. And after these things he fell sick, and perceived that he should die. Wherefore he called his servants, such as were honorable, and had been brought up with him from his youth, and parted his kingdom among them, while he was yet alive.[1] So Alexander reigned twelve years, and then died.'

[1] This is not historically true.

He survived as a legendary hero in the Mohammedan religion, and to this day petty chieftains in the Himalayas claim to be descended from him.[1] No other fully historical hero has ever furnished such a perfect opportunity for the mythopoeic faculty.

At Alexander's death, there was an attempt to preserve the unity of his empire. But of his two sons, one was an infant and the other was not yet born. Each had supporters, but in the resultant civil war both were thrust aside. In the end, his empire was divided between the families of three generals, of whom, roughly speaking, one obtained the European, one the African, and one the Asiatic parts of Alexander's possessions. The European part fell ultimately to Antigonus's descendants; Ptolemy, who obtained Egypt, made Alexandria his capital; Seleucus, who obtained Asia after many wars, was too busy with campaigns to have a fixed capital, but in later times Antioch was the chief city of his dynasty.

Both the Ptolemies and the Seleucids (as the dynasty of Seleucus was called) abandoned Alexander's attempts to produce a fusion of Greek and barbarian, and established military tyrannies based, at first, upon their part of the Macedonian army strengthened with Greek mercenaries. The Ptolemies held Egypt fairly securely, but in Asia two centuries of confused dynastic wars were only ended by the Roman conquest. During these centuries, Persia was conquered by the Parthians, and the Bactrian Greeks were increasingly isolated.

In the second century B.C. (after which they rapidly declined) they had a king, Menander, whose Indian Empire was very extensive. A couple of dialogues between him and a Buddhist sage have survived in Pali, and, in part, in a Chinese translation. Dr Tarn suggests that the first of these is based on a Greek original; the second, which ends with Menander abdicating and becoming a Buddhist saint, is certainly not.

Buddhism, at this time, was a vigorous proselytizing religion. Asoka (264-228), the saintly Buddhist king, records, in a still extant inscription, that he sent missionaries to all the Macedonian kings: 'And this is the chiefest conquest in His Majesty's opinion—the conquest by the Law; this also is that effected by His Majesty both in his own dominions and in all the neighbouring realms as far as six hundred leagues—even to where the Greek king Antiochus dwells, and beyond that Antiochus to where dwell the four kings severally named Ptolemy, Antigonus, Magas, and Alexander . . . and likewise here, in the king's dominions, among the Yonas'[2] (i.e. the Greeks of the Punjab). Unfortunately no western account of

---

[1] Perhaps this is no longer true, as the sons of those who held this belief have been educated at Eton.

[2] Quoted in Bevan, *House of Seleucus*, Vol. I, p..298n.

these missionaries has survived.

Babylonia was much more profoundly influenced by Hellenism. As we have seen, the only ancient who followed Aristarchus of Samos in maintaining the Copernican system was Seleucus of Seleucia on the Tigris, who flourished about 150 B.C. Tacitus tells us that in the first century A.D. Seleucia had not 'lapsed into the barbarous usages of the Parthians, but still retained the institutions of Seleucus,[1] its Greek founder. Three hundred citizens, chosen for their wealth or wisdom, compose as it were a Senate; the populace too have their share of power.'[2] Throughout Mesopotamia, as further West, Greek became the language of literature and culture, and remained so until the Mohammedan conquest.

Syria (excluding Judea) became completely Hellenized in the cities, in so far as language and literature were concerned. But the rural populations, which were more conservative, retained the religions and the languages to which they were accustomed.[3] In Asia Minor, the Greek cities of the coast had, for centuries, had an influence on their barbarian neighbours. This was intensified by the Macedonian conquest. The first conflict of Hellenism with the Jews is related in the *Books of the Maccabees.* It is a profoundly interesting story, unlike anything else in the Macedonian Empire. I shall deal with it at a later stage, when I come to the origin and growth of Christianity. Elsewhere, Greek influence encountered no such stubborn opposition.

From the point of view of Hellenistic culture, the most brilliant success of the third century B.C. was the city of Alexandria. Egypt was less exposed to war than the European and Asiatic parts of the Macedonian domain, and Alexandria was in an extraordinarily favoured position for commerce. The Ptolemies were patrons of learning, and attracted to their capital many of the best men of the age. Mathematics became, and remained until the fall of Rome, mainly Alexandrian. Archimedes, it is true, was a Sicilian, and belonged to the one part of the world where the Greek City States (until the moment of his death in 212 B.C.) retained their independence; but he too had studied in Alexandria. Eratosthenes was chief librarian of the famous library of Alexandria. The mathematicians and men of science connected, more or less closely, with Alexandria in the third century before Christ were as able as any of the Greeks of the previous centuries, and did work of equal importance. But they were not, like their predecessors, men who took all learning for their province, and propounded universal philosophies; they

---

[1] The king, not the astronomer.
[2] *Annals,* Book VI, chap. 42.
[3] See *Cambridge Ancient History,* Vol. VII, pp. 194-5.

were specialists in the modern sense. Euclid, Aristarchus, Archimedes, and Apollonius, were content to be mathematicians; in philosophy they did not aspire to originality.

Specialization characterized the age in all departments, not only in the world of learning. In the self-governing Greek cities of the fifth and fourth centuries, a capable man was assumed to be capable of everything. He would be, as occasion arose, a soldier, a politician, a lawgiver, or a philosopher. Socrates, though he disliked politics, could not avoid being mixed up with political disputes. In his youth he was a soldier, and (in spite of his disclaimer in the *Apology*) a student of physical science. Protagoras, when he could spare time from teaching scepticism to aristocratic youths in search of the latest thing, was drawing up a code of laws for Thurii. Plato dabbled in politics, though unsuccessfully. Xenophon, when he was neither writing about Socrates nor being a country gentleman, spent his spare time as a general. Pythagorean mathematicians attempted to acquire the government of cities. Everybody had to serve on juries and perform various other public duties. In the third century all this was changed. There continued, it is true, to be politics in the old City States, but they had become parochial and unimportant, since Greece was at the mercy of Macedonian armies. The serious struggles for power were between Macedonian soldiers; they involved no question of principle, but merely the distribution of territory between rival adventurers. On administrative and technical matters, these more or less uneducated soldiers employed Greeks as experts; in Egypt, for example, excellent work was done in irrigation and drainage. There were soldiers, administrators, physicians, mathematicians, philosophers, but there was no one who was all these at once.

The age was one in which a man who had money and no desire for power could enjoy a very pleasant life—always assuming that no marauding army happened to come his way. Learned men who found favour with some prince could enjoy a high degree of luxury, provided they were adroit flatterers and did not mind being the butt of ignorant royal witticisms. But there was no such thing as security. A palace revolution might displace the sycophantic sage's patron; the Galatians might destroy the rich man's villa; one's city might be sacked as an incident in a dynastic war. In such circumstances it is no wonder that people took to worshipping the goddess Fortune, or Luck. There seemed nothing rational in the ordering of human affairs. Those who obstinately insisted upon finding rationality somewhere withdrew into themselves, and decided, like Milton's Satan, that

> The mind is its own place, and in itself
> Can make a heaven of hell, a hell of heaven.

Except for adventurous self-seekers, there was no longer any incentive to take an interest in public affairs. After the brilliant episode of Alexander's conquests, the Hellenistic world was sinking into chaos, for lack of a despot strong enough to achieve stable supremacy, or a principle powerful enough to produce social cohesion. Greek intelligence, confronted with new political problems, showed complete incompetence. The Romans, no doubt, were stupid and brutal compared to the Greeks, but at least they created order. The old disorder of the days of freedom had been tolerable, because every citizen had a share in it; but the new Macedonian disorder, imposed upon subjects by incompetent rulers, was utterly intolerable—far more so than the subsequent subjection to Rome.

There was widespread social discontent and fear of revolution. The wages of free labour fell, presumably owing to the competition of eastern slave labour; and meantime the prices of necessaries rose. One finds Alexander, at the outset of his enterprise, having time to make treaties designed to keep the poor in their place. 'In the treaties made in 335 between Alexander and the States of the League of Corinth it was provided that the Council of the League and Alexander's representative were to see to it that in no city of the League should there be either confiscation of personal property, or division of land, or cancellation of debt, or liberation of slaves for the purpose of revolution.'[1] The temples, in the Hellenistic world, were the bankers; they owned the gold reserve, and controlled credit. In the early third century, the temple of Apollo at Delos made loans at ten per cent; formerly, the rate of interest had been higher.[2]

Free labourers who found wages insufficient even for bare necessities must, if young and vigorous, have been able to obtain employment as mercenaries. The life of a mercenary, no doubt, was filled with hardships and dangers, but it also had great possibilities. There might be the loot of some rich eastern city; there might be a chance of lucrative mutiny. It must have been dangerous for a commander to attempt to disband his army, and this must have been one of the reasons why wars were almost continuous.

The old civic spirit more or less survived in the old Greek cities, but not in the new cities founded by Alexander—not excepting

[1] 'The Social Question in the Third Century', by W. T. Tarn, in *The Hellenistic Age* by various authors. Cambridge, 1923. This essay is exceedingly interesting, and contains many facts not elsewhere readily accessible.
[2] *Ibid.*

Alexandria. In earlier times, a new city was always a colony composed of emigrants from some one older city, and it remained connected with its parent by a bond of sentiment. This kind of sentiment had great longevity, as is shown, for example, by the diplomatic activities of Lampsacus on the Hellespont in the year 196 B.C. This city was threatened with subjugation by the Seleucid King Antiochus III, and decided to appeal to Rome for protection. An embassy was sent, but it did not go direct to Rome; it went first, in spite of the immense distance, to Marseilles, which, like Lampsacus, was a colony of Phocaea, and was, moreover, viewed with friendly eyes by the Romans. The citizens of Marseilles, having listened to an oration by the envoy, at once decided to send a diplomatic mission of their own to Rome to support their sister city. The Gauls who lived inland from Marseilles joined in with a letter to their kinsmen of Asia Minor, the Galatians, recommending Lampsacus to their friendship. Rome, naturally, was glad of a pretext for meddling in the affairs of Asia Minor, and by Rome's intervention Lampsacus preserved its freedom—until it became inconvenient to the Romans.[1]

In general, the rulers of Asia called themselves 'Phil-Hellene', and befriended the old Greek cities as far as policy and military necessity allowed. The cities desired, and (when they could) claimed as a right, democratic self-government, absence of tribute, and freedom from a royal garrison. It was worth while to conciliate them, because they were rich, they could supply mercenaries, and many of them had important harbours. But if they took the wrong side in a civil war, they exposed themselves to sheer conquest. On the whole, the Seleucids, and the other dynasties which gradually grew up, dealt tolerably with them, but there were exceptions.

The new cities, though they had a measure of self-government, had not the same traditions as the older ones. Their citizens were not of homogeneous origin, but were from all parts of Greece. They were in the main adventurers like the *conquistadores* or the settlers in Johannesburg, not pious pilgrims like the earlier Greek colonists or the New England pioneers. Consequently no one of Alexander's cities formed a strong political unit. This was convenient from the standpoint of the king's government, but a weakness from the standpoint of the spread of Hellenism.

The influence of non-Greek religion and superstition in the Hellenistic world was mainly, but not wholly, bad. This might not have been the case. Jews, Persians, and Buddhists all had religions that were very definitely superior to the popular Greek polytheism, and could even have been studied with profit by the best philo-

[1] Bevan, *House of Seleucus*, Vol. II, pp. 45-6.

sophers. Unfortunately it was the Babylonians, or Chaldeans, who most impressed the imagination of the Greeks. There was, first of all, their fabulous antiquity; the priestly records went back for thousands of years, and professed to go back for thousands more. Then there was some genuine wisdom: the Babylonians could more or less predict eclipses long before the Greeks could. But these were merely the causes of receptiveness; what was received was mainly astrology and magic. 'Astrology,' says Professor Gilbert Murray, 'fell upon the Hellenistic mind as a new disease falls upon some remote island people. The tomb of Ozymandias, as described by Diodorus, was covered with astrological symbols, and that of Antiochus I, which has been discovered in Commagene, is of the same character. It was natural for monarchs to believe that the stars watched over them. But every one was ready to receive the germ.'[1] It appears that astrology was first taught to the Greeks in the time of Alexander, by a Chaldean named Berosus, who taught in Cos, and, according to Seneca, 'interpreted Bel'. 'This,' says Professor Murray, 'must mean that he translated into Greek the "Eye of Bel", a treatise in seventy tablets found in the library of Assurbani-pal (686-626 B.C.) but composed for Sargon I in the third millennium B.C.' (ibid., p. 176).

As we shall see, the majority even of the best philosophers fell in with the belief in astrology. It involved, since it thought the future predictable, a belief in necessity or fate, which could be set against the prevalent belief in fortune. No doubt most men believed in both, and never noticed the inconsistency.

The general confusion was bound to bring moral decay, even more than intellectual enfeeblement. Ages of prolonged uncertainty, while they are compatible with the highest degree of saintliness in a few, are inimical to the prosaic every-day virtues of respectable citizens. There seems no use in thrift, when tomorrow all your savings may be dissipated; no advantage in honesty, when the man towards whom you practise it is pretty sure to swindle you; no point in steadfast adherence to a cause, when no cause is important or has a chance of stable victory; no argument in favour of truthfulness, when only supple tergiversation makes the preservation of life and fortune possible. The man whose virtue has no source except a purely terrestrial prudence will, in such a world, become an adventurer if he has the courage, and, if not, will seek obscurity as a timid time-server.

Menander, who belongs to this age, says:

So many cases I have known

[1] *Five Stages of Greek Religion*, pp. 177-8.

Of men who, though not naturally rogues,
Became so, through misfortune, by constraint.

This sums up the moral character of the third century B.C., except for a few exceptional men. Even among these few, fear took the place of hope; the purpose of life was rather to escape misfortune than to achieve any positive good. 'Metaphysics sink into the background, and ethics, now individual, become of the first importance. Philosophy is no longer the pillar of fire going before a few intrepid seekers after truth: it is rather an ambulance following in the wake of the struggle for existence and picking up the weak and wounded.'[1]

[1] C. F. Angus in *Cambridge Ancient History*, Vol. VII, p. 231. The above quotation from Menander is taken from the same chapter.

Chapter XXVI

CYNICS AND SCEPTICS

THE relation of intellectually eminent men to contemporary society has been very different in different ages. In some fortunate epochs they have been on the whole in harmony with their surroundings—suggesting, no doubt, such reforms as seemed to them necessary, but fairly confident that their suggestions would be welcomed, and not disliking the world in which they found themselves even if it remained unreformed. At other times they have been revolutionary, considering that radical alterations were called for, but expecting that, partly as a result of their advocacy, these alterations would be brought about in the near future. At yet other times they have despaired of the world, and felt that, though they themselves knew what was needed, there was no hope of its being brought about. This mood sinks easily into the deeper despair which regards life on earth as essentially bad, and hopes for good only in a future life or in some mystical transfiguration.

In some ages, all these attitudes have been adopted by different men living at the same time. Consider, for example, the early nineteenth century. Goethe is comfortable, Bentham is a reformer, Shelley is a revolutionary, and Leopardi is a pessimist. But in most periods there has been a prevailing tone among great writers. In England they were comfortable under Elizabeth and in the eighteenth century; in France, they became revolutionary about 1750; in Germany, they have been nationalistic since 1813.

During the period of ecclesiastical domination, from the fifth century to the fifteenth, there was a certain conflict between what was theoretically believed and what was actually felt. Theoretically, the world was a vale of tears, a preparation, amid tribulation, for the world to come. But in practice the writers of books, being almost all clerics, could not help feeling exhilarated by the power of the Church; they found opportunity for abundant activity of a sort that they believed to be useful. They had therefore the mentality of a governing class, not of men who feel themselves exiles in an alien world. This is part of the curious dualism that runs through the Middle Ages, owing to the fact that the Church, though based on other-worldly beliefs, was the most important institution in the every-day world.

The psychological preparation for the other-worldliness of Christianity begins in the Hellenistic period, and is connected with the eclipse of the City State. Down to Aristotle, Greek philosophers, though they might complain of this or that, were, in the main, not cosmically despairing, nor did they feel themselves politically impotent. They might, at times, belong to a beaten party, but, if so, their defeat was due to the chances of conflict, not to any inevitable powerlessness of the wise. Even those who, like Pythagoras, and Plato in certain moods, condemned the world of appearance and sought escape in mysticism, had practical plans for turning the governing classes into saints and sages. When political power passed into the hands of the Macedonians, Greek philosophers, as was natural, turned aside from politics and devoted themselves more to the problem of individual virtue or salvation. They no longer asked: how can men create a good State? They asked instead: how can men be virtuous in a wicked world, or happy in a world of suffering? The change, it is true, is only one of degree; such questions had been asked before, and the later Stoics, for a time, again concerned themselves with politics—the politics of Rome, not of Greece. But the change was none the less real. Except to a limited extent during the Roman period in Stoicism, the outlook of those who thought and felt seriously became increasingly subjective and individualistic, until, at last, Christianity evolved a gospel of individual salvation which inspired missionary zeal and created the Church. Until that happened, there was no institution to which the philosopher could give whole-hearted adherence, and therefore there was no adequate outlet for his legitimate love of power. For this reason, the philosophers of the Hellenistic period are more limited as human beings than the men who lived while the City State could still inspire allegiance. They still think, because they cannot help thinking; but they scarcely hope that their thought will bear fruit in the world of affairs.

Four schools of philosophy were founded about the time of Alexander. The two most famous, the Stoics and Epicureans, will be the subjects of later chapters; in the present chapter we shall be concerned with the Cynics and Sceptics.

The first of these schools is derived, through its founder Diogenes, from Antisthenes, a disciple of Socrates, about twenty years older than Plato. Antisthenes was a remarkable character, in some ways rather like Tolstoy. Until after the death of Socrates, he lived in the aristocratic circle of his fellow disciples, and showed no sign of unorthodoxy. But something—whether the defeat of Athens, or the death of Socrates, or a distaste for philosophic quibbling—caused him, when no longer young, to despise the things that he had formerly valued. He would have nothing but simple goodness. He associated with working men, and dressed as one of them. He took to open-air preaching, in a style that the uneducated could understand. All refined philosophy he held to be worthless; what could be known, could be known by the plain man. He believed in the 'return to nature', and carried this belief very far. There was to be no government, no private property, no marriage, no established religion. His followers, if not he himself, condemned slavery. He was not exactly ascetic, but he despised luxury and all pursuit of artificial pleasures of the senses. 'I had rather be mad than delighted,' he said.[1]

The fame of Antisthenes was surpassed by that of his disciple Diogenes, 'a young man from Sinope, on the Euxine, whom he [Antisthenes] did not take to at first sight; the son of a disreputable money-changer who had been sent to prison for defacing the coinage. Antisthenes ordered the lad away, but he paid no attention; he beat him with his stick, but he never moved. He wanted "wisdom", and saw that Antisthenes had it to give. His aim in life was to do as his father had done, to "deface the coinage", but on a much larger scale. He would deface all the coinage current in the world. Every conventional stamp was false. The men stamped as generals and kings; the things stamped as honour and wisdom and happiness and riches; all were base metal with lying superscription.'[2]

He decided to live like a dog, and was therefore called a 'cynic', which means 'canine'. He rejected all conventions—whether of religion, of manners, of dress, of housing, of food, or of decency. One is told that he lived in a tub, but Gilbert Murray assures us that this is a mistake: it was a large pitcher, of the sort used in primitive times for burials.[3] He lived, like an Indian fakir, by begging. He proclaimed his brotherhood, not only with the whole human race, but also with animals. He was a man about whom stories gathered, even in his lifetime. Everyone knows how Alexander visited him, and asked if he desired any favour; 'only to stand out of my light,' he replied.

The teaching of Diogenes was by no means what we now call 'cynical'—quite the contrary. He had an ardent passion for 'virtue', in comparison with which he held worldly goods of no account. He sought virtue and moral freedom in liberation from desire: be indifferent to the goods that fortune has to bestow, and you will be emancipated from fear. In this respect, his doctrine, as we shall see, was taken up by the Stoics, but they did not follow him in rejecting the amenities of civilization. He considered that Prome-

---

' Benn, Vol. II, pp. 4, 5: Murray, *Five Stages*, pp. 113-14.
- *Ibid.*, p. 117.   [3] *Ibid.*, p. 119

theus was justly punished for bringing to man the arts that have produced the complication and artificiality of modern life. In this he resembled the Taoists and Rousseau and Tolstoy, but was more consistent than they were.

His doctrine, though he was a contemporary of Aristotle, belongs in its temper to the Hellenistic age. Aristotle is the last Greek philosopher who faces the world cheerfully; after him, all have, in one form or another, a philosophy of retreat. The world is bad; let us learn to be independent of it. External goods are precarious; they are the gift of fortune, not the reward of our own efforts. Only subjective goods—virtue, or contentment through resignation—are secure, and these alone, therefore, will be valued by the wise man. Diogenes personally was a man full of vigour, but his doctrine, like all those of the Hellenistic age, was one to appeal to weary men, in whom disappointment had destroyed natural zest. And it was certainly not a doctrine calculated to promote art or science or statesmanship, or any useful activity except one of protest against powerful evil.

It is interesting to observe what the Cynic teaching became when it was popularized. In the early part of the third century B.C., the cynics were the fashion, especially in Alexandria. They published little sermons pointing out how easy it is to do without material possessions, how happy one can be on simple food, how warm one can keep in winter without expensive clothes (which might be true in Egypt!), how silly it is to feel affection for one's native country, or to mourn when one's children or friends die. 'Because my son or wife is dead,' says Teles, who was one of these popularizing Cynics, 'is that any reason for my neglecting myself, who am still alive, and ceasing to look after my property.'[1] At this point, it becomes difficult to feel any sympathy with the simple life, which has grown altogether too simple. One wonders who enjoyed these sermons. Was it the rich, who wished to think the sufferings of the poor imaginary? Or was it the new poor, who were trying to despise the successful business man? Or was it sycophants who persuaded themselves that the charity they accepted was unimportant? Teles says to a rich man: 'You give liberally and I take valiantly from you, neither grovelling nor demeaning myself basely nor grumbling.'[2] A very convenient doctrine. Popular Cynicism did not teach abstinence from the good things of this world, but only a certain indifference to them. In the case of a borrower, this might take the form of minimizing the obligation to the lender. One can see how the word 'cynic' acquired its everyday meaning.

What was best in the Cynic doctrine passed over into Stoicism,

[1] *The Hellenistic Age* (Cambridge, 1923), p. 84 ff. [2] *Ibid.*, p. 86.

which was an altogether more complete and rounded philosophy.

Scepticism, as a doctrine of the schools, was first proclaimed by Pyrrho, who was in Alexander's army, and campaigned with it as far as India. It seems that this gave him a sufficient taste of travel, and that he spent the rest of his life in his native city, Elis, where he died in 275 B.C. There was not much that was new in his doctrine, beyond a certain systematizing and formalizing of older doubts. Scepticism with regard to the senses had troubled Greek philosophers from a very early stage; the only exceptions were those who, like Parmenides and Plato, denied the cognitive value of perception, and made their denial into an opportunity for an intellectual dogmatism. The Sophists, notably Protagoras and Gorgias, had been led by the ambiguities and apparent contradictions of sense-perception to a subjectivism not unlike Hume's. Pyrrho seems (for he very wisely wrote no books) to have added moral and logical scepticism to scepticism as to the senses. He is said to have maintained that there could never be any rational ground for preferring one course of action to another. In practice, this meant that one conformed to the customs of whatever country one inhabited. A modern disciple would go to church on Sundays and perform the correct genuflexions, but without any of the religious beliefs that are supposed to inspire these actions. Ancient Sceptics went through the whole pagan ritual, and were even sometimes priests; their Scepticism assured them that this behaviour could not be proved wrong, and their common sense (which survived their philosophy) assured them that it was convenient.

Scepticism naturally made an appeal to many unphilosophic minds. People observed the diversity of schools and the acerbity of their disputes, and decided that all alike were pretending to knowledge which was in fact unattainable. Scepticism was a lazy man's consolation, since it showed the ignorant to be as wise as the reputed men of learning. To men who, by temperament, required a gospel, it might seem unsatisfying, but like every doctrine of the Hellenistic period it recommended itself as an antidote to worry. Why trouble about the future? It is wholly uncertain. You may as well enjoy the present; 'what's to come is still unsure.' For these reasons, Scepticism enjoyed a considerable popular success.

It should be observed that Scepticism as a philosophy is not merely doubt, but what may be called dogmatic doubt. The man of science says 'I think it is so-and-so, but I am not sure.' The man of intellectual curiosity says 'I don't know how it is, but I hope to find out.' The philosophical Sceptic says 'nobody knows, and nobody ever can know.' It is this element of dogmatism that makes the system vulnerable. Sceptics, of course, deny that they assert the possibility of knowledge dogmatically, but their denials are not ry convincing.

Pyrrho's disciple Timon, however, advanced some intellectual arguments which, from the standpoint of Greek logic, were very hard to answer. The only logic admitted by the Greeks was deductive, and all deduction had to start, like Euclid, from general principles regarded as self-evident. Timon denied the possibility of finding such principles. Everything, therefore, will have to be proved by means of something else, and all argument will be either circular or an endless chain hanging from nothing. In either case nothing can be proved. This argument, as we can see, cut at the root of the Aristotelian philosophy which dominated the Middle Ages.

Some forms of Scepticism which, in our own day, are advocated by men who are by no means wholly sceptical, had not occurred to the Sceptics of antiquity. They did not doubt phenomena, or question propositions which, in their opinion, only expressed what we know directly concerning phenomena. Most of Timon's work is lost, but two surviving fragments will illustrate this point. One says 'The phenomenon is always valid.' The other says: 'That honey *is* sweet I refuse to assert; that it appears sweet, I fully grant.'[1] A modern Sceptic would point out that the phenomenon merely *occurs*, and is not either valid or invalid; what is valid or invalid must be a statement, and no statement can be so closely linked to the phenomenon as to be incapable of falsehood. For the same reason, he would say that the statement 'honey appears sweet' is only highly probable, not absolutely certain.

In some respects, the doctrine of Timon was very similar to that of Hume. He maintained that something which had never been observed—atoms, for instance—could not be validly inferred; but when two *phenomena* had been frequently observed together, one could be inferred from the other.

Timon lived at Athens throughout the later years of his long life, and died there in 235 B.C. With his death, the school of Pyrrho, as a school, came to an end, but his doctrines, somewhat modified, were taken up, strange as it may seem, by the Academy, which represented the Platonic tradition.

The man who effected this surprising philosophic revolution was Arcesilaus, a contemporary of Timon, who died as an old man about 240 B.C. What most men have taken from Plato is belief in a supersensible intellectual world and in the superiority of the immortal soul to the mortal body. But Plato was many-sided, and in some respects could be regarded as teaching scepticism. The Platonic Socrates professes to know nothing; we naturally treat this as irony,

[1] Quoted by Edwyn Bevan, *Stoics and Sceptics*, p. 126.

but it could be taken seriously. Many of the dialogues reach no positive conclusion, and aim at leaving the reader in a state of doubt. Some—the latter half of the *Parmenides*, for instance—might seem to have no purpose except to show that either side of any question can be maintained with equal plausibility. The Platonic dialectic could be treated as an end, rather than a means, and if so treated it lent itself admirably to the advocacy of Scepticism. This seems to have been the way in which Arcesilaus interpreted the man whom he still professed to follow. He had decapitated Plato, but at any rate the torso that remained was genuine.

The manner in which Arcesilaus taught would have had much to commend it, if the young men who learnt from him had been able to avoid being paralysed by it. He maintained no thesis, but would refute any thesis set up by a pupil. Sometimes he would himself advance two contradictory propositions on successive occasions, showing how to argue convincingly in favour of either. A pupil sufficiently vigorous to rebel might have learnt dexterity and the avoidance of fallacies; in fact, none seem to have learnt anything except cleverness and indifference to truth. So great was the influence of Arcesilaus that the Academy remained sceptical for about two hundred years.

In the middle of this sceptical period, an amusing incident occurred. Carneades, a worthy successor of Arcesilaus as head of the Academy, was one of three philosophers sent by Athens on a diplomatic mission to Rome in the year 156 B.C. He saw no reason why his ambassadorial dignity should interfere with the main chance, so he announced a course of lectures in Rome. The young men, who, at that time, were anxious to ape Greek manners and acquire Greek culture, flocked to hear him. His first lecture expounded the views of Aristotle and Plato on justice, and was thoroughly edifying. His second, however, was concerned in refuting all that he had said in his first, not with a view to establishing opposite conclusions, but merely to show that every conclusion is unwarranted. Plato's Socrates had argued that to inflict injustice was a greater evil to the perpetrator than to suffer it. Carneades, in his second lecture, treated this contention with scorn. Great States, he pointed out, had become great by unjust aggressions against their weaker neighbours; in Rome, this could not well be denied. In a shipwreck, you may save your life at the expense of some one weaker, and you are a fool if you do not. 'Women and children first', he seems to think, is not a maxim that leads to personal survival. What would you do if you were flying from a victorious enemy, you had lost your horse, but you found a wounded comrade on a horse? If you were sensible, you would drag him off and seize his horse, whatever justice might ordain. All this not very edifying argumentation is surprising in a nominal follower of Plato, but it seems to have pleased the modern-minded Roman youths.

There was one man whom it did not please, and that was the elder Cato, who represented the stern, stiff, stupid, and brutal moral code by means of which Rome had defeated Carthage. From youth to old age, he lived simply, rose early, practised severe manual labour, ate only coarse food, and never wore a gown that cost over a hundred pence. Towards the State he was scrupulously honest, avoiding all bribery and plunder. He exacted of other Romans all the virtues that he practised himself, and asserted that to accuse and pursue the wicked was the best thing an honest man could do. He enforced, as far as he could, the old Roman severity of manners:

'Cato put out of the Senate also, one Manilius, who was in great towardness to have been made Consul the next year following, only because he kissed his wife too lovingly in the day time, and before his daughter: and reproving him for it, he told him, his wife never kissed him, but when it thundered.'[1]

When he was in power, he put down luxury and feasting. He made his wife suckle not only her own children, but also those of his slaves, in order that, having been nourished by the same milk, they might love his children. When his slaves were too old to work, he sold them remorselessly. He insisted that his slaves should always be either working or sleeping. He encouraged his slaves to quarrel with each other, for 'he could not abide that they should be friends'. When a slave had committed a grave fault, he would call in his other slaves, and induce them to condemn the delinquent to death; he would then carry out the sentence with his own hands in the presence of the survivors.

The contrast between Cato and Carneades was very complete: the one brutal through a morality that was too strict and too traditional, the other ignoble through a morality that was too lax and too much infected with the social dissolution of the Hellenistic world.

'Marcus Cato, even from the beginning that young men began to study the Greek tongue, and that it grew in estimation in Rome, did dislike of it: fearing lest the youth of Rome that were desirous of learning and eloquence, would utterly give over the honour and glory of arms. . . . So he openly found fault one day in the Senate, that the Ambassadors were long there, and had no dispatch: considering also they were cunning men, and could easily persuade what they would. And if there were no other respect, this only might persuade them to determine some answers for them, and to send them home again to their schools, to teach their children of

[1] North's Plutarch, *Lives*, Marcus Cato.

Greece, and to let alone the children of Rome, that they might learn to obey the laws and the Senate, as they had done before. Now he spake thus to the Senate, not of any private ill will or malice he bare to Carneades, as some men thought: but because he generally hated philosophy.'[1]

The Athenians, in Cato's view, were a lesser breed without the law; it did not matter if *they* were degraded by the shallow sophistries of intellectuals, but the Roman youth must be kept puritanical, imperialistic, ruthless, and stupid. He failed, however; later Romans, while retaining many of his vices, adopted those of Carneades also.

The next head of the Academy, after Carneades (*ca.* 180 to *ca.* 110 B.C.), was a Carthaginian whose real name was Hasdrubal, but who, in his dealings with Greeks, preferred to call himself Clitomachus. Unlike Carneades, who confined himself to lecturing, Clitomachus wrote over four hundred books, some of them in the Phoenician language. His principles appear to have been the same as those of Carneades. In some respects, they were useful. These two Sceptics set themselves against the belief in divination, magic, and astrology, which was becoming more and more widespread. They also developed a constructive doctrine, concerning degrees of probability: although we can never be justified in feeling certainty, some things are more likely to be true than others. Probability should be our guide in practice, since it is reasonable to act on the most probable of possible hypotheses. This view is one with which most modern philosophers would agree. Unfortunately, the books setting it forth are lost, and it is difficult to reconstruct the doctrine from the hints that remain.

After Clitomachus, the Academy ceased to be sceptical, and from the time of Antiochus (who died in 69 B.C.) its doctrines became, for centuries, practically indistinguishable from those of the Stoics.

Scepticism, however, did not disappear. It was revived by the Cretan Aenesidemus, who came from Knossos, where, for aught we know, there may have been Sceptics two thousand years earlier, entertaining dissolute courtiers with doubts as to the divinity of the mistress of animals. The date of Aenesidemus is uncertain. He threw over the doctrines on probability advocated by Carneades, and reverted to the earliest forms of Scepticism. His influence was considerable; he was followed by the satirist Lucian in the second century A.D., and also, slightly later, by Sextus Empiricus, the only Sceptic philosopher of antiquity whose works survive. There is, for example, a short treatise, 'Arguments Against Belief in a God', translated by Edwyn Bevan in his *Later Greek Religion*, pp. 52-56, and

[1] North's Plutarch, *Lives*, Marcus Cato.

said by him to be probably taken by Sextus Empiricus from Carneades, as reported by Clitomachus.

This treatise begins by explaining that, in *behaviour*, the Sceptics are orthodox: 'We sceptics follow in practice the way of the world, but without holding any opinion about it. We speak of the Gods as existing and offer worship to the Gods and say that they exercise providence, but in saying this we express no belief, and avoid the rashness of the dogmatizers.'

He then argues that people differ as to the nature of God; for instance, some think Him corporeal, some incorporeal. Since we have no experience of Him, we cannot know His attributes. The existence of God is not self-evident, and therefore needs proof. There is a somewhat confused argument to show that no such proof is possible. He next takes up the problem of evil, and concludes with the words:

'Those who affirm positively that God exists cannot avoid falling into an impiety. For if they say that God controls everything, they make Him the author of evil things; if, on the other hand, they say that He controls some things only, or that He controls nothing, they are compelled to make God either grudging or impotent, and to do that is quite obviously an impiety.'

Scepticism, while it continued to appeal to some cultivated individuals until somewhere in the third century A.D., was contrary to the temper of the age, which was turning more and more to dogmatic religion and doctrines of salvation. Scepticism had enough force to make educated men dissastisfied with the State religions, but it had nothing positive, even in the purely intellectual sphere, to offer in their place. From the Renaissance onwards, theological scepticism has been supplemented, in most of its advocates, by an enthusiastic belief in science, but in antiquity there was no such supplement to doubt. Without answering the arguments of the Sceptics, the ancient world turned aside from them. The Olympians being discredited, the way was left clear for an invasion of oriental religions, which competed for the favour of the superstitious until the triumph of Christianity.

Chapter XXVII

THE EPICUREANS

THE two great new schools of the Hellenistic period, the Stoics and Epicureans, were contemporaneous in their foundation. Their founders, Zeno and Epicurus, were born at about the same time, and settled in Athens as heads of their respective sects within a few years of each other It is therefore a matter of taste which to consider first. I shall begin with the Epicureans, because their doctrines were fixed once for all by their founder, whereas Stoicism had a long development, extending as far as the Emperor Marcus Aurelius, who died in A.D. 180.

The main authority for the life of Epicurus is Diogenes Laertius, who lived in the third century A.D. There are, however, two difficulties: first, Diogenes Laertius is himself ready to accept legends of little or no historical value; second, part of his *Life* consists in reporting the scandalous accusations brought against Epicurus by the Stoics, and it is not always clear whether he is asserting something himself or merely mentioning a libel. The scandals invented by the Stoics are facts about them, to be remembered when their lofty morality is praised; but they are not facts about Epicurus. For instance, there was a legend that his mother was a quack priestess, as to which Diogenes says:

'They (apparently the Stoics) say that he used to go round from house to house with his mother reading out the purification prayers, and assisted his father in elementary teaching for a miserable pittance.'

On this Bailey comments:[1] 'If there is any truth in the story that he went about with his mother as an acolyte, reciting the formulae of her incantations, he may well have been inspired in quite early years with the hatred of superstition, which was afterwards so prominent a feature in his teaching.' This theory is attractive, but, in view of the extreme unscrupulousness of later antiquity in inventing a scandal, I do not think it can be accepted as having any foundation.[2] There is against it the fact that he had an unusually

[1] *The Greek Atomists and Epicurus*, by Cyril Bailey, Oxford, 1928, p. 221. Mr. Bailey has made a specialty of Epicurus, and his book is invaluable to the student.

[2] The Stoics were very unjust to Epicurus. Epictetus, for example, addressing him, says; 'This is the life of which you pronounce yourself worthy: eating, drinking, copulation, evacuation and snoring.' Book II, chap. xx, *Discourses* of Epictetus.

strong affection for his mother.[1]

The main facts of the life of Epicurus seem, however, fairly certain. His father was a poor Athenian colonist in Samos; Epicurus was born in 342-1 B.C., but whether in Samos or in Attica is not known. In any case, his boyhood was passed in Samos. He states that he took to the study of philosophy at the age of fourteen. At the age of eighteen, about the time of Alexander's death, he went to Athens, apparently to establish his citizenship, but while he was there the Athenian colonists were turned out of Samos (322 B.C.). The family of Epicurus became refugees in Asia Minor, where he rejoined them. At Taos, either at this time, or perhaps earlier, he was taught philosophy by a certain Nausiphanes, apparently a follower of Democritus. Although his mature philosophy owes more to Democritus than to any other philosopher, he never expressed anything but contempt for Nausiphanes, whom he alluded to as 'The Mollusc'.

In the year 311 he founded his school, which was first in Mitylene, then in Lampsacus, and, from 307 onwards, in Athens where he died in 270-1 B.C.

After the hard years of his youth, his life in Athens was placid, and was only troubled by his ill health. He had a house and a garden (apparently separate from the house), and it was in the garden that he taught. His three brothers, and some others had been members of his school from the first, but in Athens his community was increased, not only by philosophic disciples, but by friends and their children, slaves and *hetaerae*. These last were made an occasion of scandal by his enemies, but apparently quite unjustly. He had a very exceptional capacity for purely human friendship, and wrote pleasant letters to the young children of members of the community. He did not practise that dignity and reserve in the expression of the emotions that was expected of ancient philosophers; his letters are amazingly natural and unaffected.

The life of the community was very simple, partly on principle, and partly (no doubt) for lack of money. Their food and drink was mainly bread and water, which Epicurus found quite satisfying. 'I am thrilled with pleasure in the body,' he says, 'when I live on bread and water, and I spit on luxurious pleasures, not for their own sake, but because of the inconveniences that follow them.' The community depended financially, at least in part, on voluntary contributions. 'Send me some preserved cheese,' he writes, 'that when I like, I may have a feast.' To another friend: 'Send us offerings for the sustenance of our holy body on behalf of yourself and your children.' And again: 'The only contribution I require is that

[1] Gilbert Murray, *Five Stages*, p. 130.

which —— ordered the disciples to send me, even if they be among the Hyperboreans. I wish to receive from each of you two hundred and twenty drachmae[1] a year and no more.'

Epicurus suffered all his life from bad health, but learnt to endure it with great fortitude. It was he, not a Stoic, who first maintained that a man could be happy on the rack. Two letters written, one a few days before his death, the other on the day of his death, show that he had some right to this opinion. The first says: 'Seven days before writing this the stoppage became complete and I suffered pains such as bring men to their last day. If anything happens to me, do you look after the children of Metrodorus for four or five years, but do not spend any more on them than you now spend on me.' The second says: 'On this truly happy day of my life, as I am at the point of death, I write this to you. The diseases in my bladder and stomach are pursuing their course, lacking nothing of their usual severity: but against all this is the joy in my heart at the recollection of my conversations with you. Do you, as I might expect from your devotion from boyhood to me and to philosophy, take good care of the children of Metrodorus.' Metrodorus, who had been one of his first disciples, was dead; Epicurus provided for his children in his will.

Although Epicurus was gentle and kindly towards most people, a different side of his character appeared in his relations to philosophers, especially those to whom he might be considered indebted. 'I suppose,' he says, 'that these grumblers will believe me to be a disciple of The Mollusc (Nausiphanes) and to have listened to his teaching in company with a few bibulous youths. For indeed the fellow was a bad man and his habits such as could never lead to wisdom.'[2] He never acknowledged the extent of his indebtedness to Democritus, and as for Leucippus, he asserted that there was no such philosopher—meaning, no doubt, not that there was no such man, but that the man was not a philosopher. Diogenes Laertius gives a whole list of abusive epithets that he is supposed to have applied to the most eminent of his predecessors. With this lack of generosity towards other philosophers goes another grave fault, that of dictatorial dogmatism. His followers had to learn a kind of creed embodying his doctrines, which they were not allowed to question. To the end, none of them added or modified anything. When Lucretius, two hundred years later, turned the philosophy of Epicurus into poetry, he added, so far as can be judged, nothing theoretical to the master's teaching. Wherever comparison is possible, Lucre-

[1] About five pounds.
[2] *The Stoic and Epicurean Philosophers*, by W. J. Oates, p. 47. Where possible, I have availed myself of Mr Oates's translations.

tius is found to agree closely with the original, and it is generally held that, elsewhere, he may be used to fill in the gaps in our knowledge caused by the loss of all of Epicurus's three hundred books. Of his writings, nothing remains except a few letters, some fragments, and a statement of 'Principal Doctrines'.

The philosophy of Epicurus, like all those of his age (with the partial exception of Scepticism), was primarily designed to secure tranquillity. He considered pleasure to be the good, and adhered, with remarkable consistency, to all the consequences of this view. 'Pleasure,' he said, 'is the beginning and end of the blessed life.' Diogenes Laertius quotes him as saying, in a book on *The End of Life*, 'I know not how I can conceive the good, if I withdraw the pleasures of taste and withdraw the pleasures of love and those of hearing and sight.' Again: 'The beginning and the root of all good is the pleasure of the stomach; even wisdom and culture must be referred to this.' The pleasure of the mind, we are told, is the contemplation of pleasures of the body. Its only advantage over bodily pleasures is that we can learn to contemplate pleasure rather than pain, and thus have more control over mental than over physical pleasures. 'Virtue', unless it means 'prudence in the pursuit of pleasure', is an empty name. Justice, for example, consists in so acting as not to have occasion to fear other men's resentment—a view which leads to a doctrine of the origin of society not unlike the theory of the Social Contract.

Epicurus disagrees with some of his hedonist predecessors in distinguishing between *active* and *passive* pleasures, or *dynamic* and *static* pleasures. Dynamic pleasures consist in the attainment of a desired end, the previous desire having been accompanied by pain. Static pleasures consist in a state of equilibrium, which results from the existence of the kind of state of affairs that would be desired if it were absent. I think one may say that the satisfying of hunger, while it is in progress, is a dynamic pleasure, but the state of quiescence which supervenes when hunger is completely satisfied is a static pleasure. Of these two kinds, Epicurus holds it more prudent to pursue the second, since it is unalloyed, and does not depend upon the existence of pain as a stimulus to desire. When the body is in a state of equilibrium, there is no pain, we should, therefore, aim at equilibrium and the quiet pleasures rather than at more violent joys. Epicurus, it seems, would wish, if it were possible, to be always in the state of having eaten moderately, never in that of voracious desire to eat.

He is thus led, in practice, to regarding absence of pain, rather than presence of pleasure, as the wise man's goal.[1] The stomach may be at the root of things, but the pains of stomach-ache outweigh the pleasures of gluttony; accordingly Epicurus lived on bread, with a little cheese on feast days. Such desires as those for wealth and honour are futile, because they make a man restless when he might be contented. 'The greatest good of all is prudence; it is a more precious thing even than philosophy.' Philosophy, as he understood it, was a practical system designed to secure a happy life; it required only common sense, not logic or mathematics or any of the elaborate training prescribed by Plato. He urges his young disciple and friend Pythocles to 'flee from every form of culture'. It was a natural consequence of his principles that he advised abstinence from public life, for in proportion as a man achieves power he increases the number of those who envy him and therefore wish to do him injury. Even if he escapes outward misfortune, peace of mind is impossible in such a situation. The wise man will try to live unnoticed, so as to have no enemies.

Sexual love, as one of the most 'dynamic' of pleasures, naturally comes under the ban. 'Sexual intercourse,' the philosopher declares, 'has never done a man good and he is lucky if it has not harmed him.' He was fond of children (other people's), but for the gratification of this taste he seems to have relied upon other people not to follow his advice. He seems, in fact, to have liked children against his better judgment; for he considered marriage and children a distraction from more serious pursuits. Lucretius, who follows him in denouncing love, sees no harm in sexual intercourse provided it is divorced from passion.

The safest of social pleasures, in the opinion of Epicurus, is friendship. Epicurus, like Bentham, is a man who considers that all men, at all times, pursue only their own pleasure, sometimes wisely, sometimes unwisely; but, again like Bentham, he is constantly seduced by his own kindly and affectionate nature into admirable behaviour from which, on his own theories, he ought to have refrained. He obviously liked his friends without regard to what he got out of them, but he persuaded himself that he was as selfish as his philosophy held all men to be. According to Cicero, he held that 'friendship cannot be divorced from pleasure, and for that reason must be cultivated, because without it neither can we live in safety and without fear, nor even pleasantly'. Occasionally, however, he forgets his theories more or less: 'all friendship is desirable in itself,' he says, adding 'though it starts from the need of help.'[2]

[1] (For Epicurus) 'Absence of pain is in itself pleasure, indeed in his ultimate analysis the truest pleasure.' Bailey, *op. cit.*, p. 249.

[2] On the subject of friendship and Epicurus's amiable inconsistency, see Bailey, *op. cit.*, pp. 517-20.

Epicurus, though his ethic seemed to others swinish and lacking in moral exaltation, was very much in earnest. As we have seen, he speaks of the community in the garden as 'our holy body'; he wrote a book *On Holiness*; he had all the fervour of a religious reformer. He must have had a strong emotion of pity for the sufferings of mankind, and an unshakeable conviction that they would be greatly lessened if men would adopt his philosophy. It was a valetudinarian's philosophy, designed to suit a world in which adventurous happiness had become scarcely possible. Eat little, for fear of indigestion: drink little, for fear of next morning; eschew politics and love and all violently passionate activities; do not give hostages to fortune by marrying and having children; in your mental life, teach yourself to contemplate pleasures rather than pains. Physical pain is certainly a great evil, but if severe, it is brief, and if prolonged, it can be endured by means of mental discipline and the habit of thinking of happy things in spite of it. Above all, live so as to avoid fear.

It was through the problem of avoiding fear that Epicurus was led into theoretical philosophy. He held that two of the greatest sources of fear were religion and the dread of death, which were connected, since religion encouraged the view that the dead are unhappy. He therefore sought a metaphysic which would prove that the gods do not interfere in human affairs, and that the soul perishes with the body. Most modern people think of religion as a consolation, but to Epicurus it was the opposite. Supernatural interference with the course of nature seemed to him a source of terror, and immortality fatal to the hope of release from pain. Accordingly he constructed an elaborate doctrine designed to cure men of the beliefs that inspire fear.

Epicurus was a materialist, but not a determinist. He followed Democritus in believing that the world consists of atoms and the void; but he did not believe, as Democritus did, that the atoms are at all times completely controlled by natural laws. The conception of necessity in Greece was, as we have seen, religious in origin, and perhaps he was right in considering that an attack on religion would be incomplete if it allowed necessity to survive. His atoms had weight, and were continually falling; not towards the centre of the earth, but downwards in some absolute sense. Every now and then, however, an atom, actuated by something like free will, would swerve slightly from the direct downward path,[1] and so would come into collision with some other atom. From this point onwards, the development of vortices, etc., proceeded in much the same way

[1] An analogous view is urged in our day by Eddington, in his interpretation of the principle of indeterminacy.

as in Democritus. The soul is material, and is composed of particles like those of breath and heat. (Epicurus thought breath and wind different in substance from air; they were not merely air in motion.) Soul-atoms are distributed throughout the body. Sensation is due to thin films thrown off by bodies and travelling on until they touch soul-atoms. These films may still exist when the bodies from which they originally proceeded have been dissolved; this accounts for dreams. At death, the soul is dispersed, and its atoms, which of course survive, are no longer capable of sensation, because they are no longer connected with the body. It follows, in the words of Epicurus, that 'Death is nothing to us; for that which is dissolved, is without sensation, and that which lacks sensation is nothing to us.'

As for the gods, Epicurus firmly believes in their existence, since he cannot otherwise account for the widespread existence of the idea of gods. But he is persuaded that they do not trouble themselves with the affairs of our human world. They are rational hedonists, who follow his precepts, and abstain from public life; government would be an unnecessary labour, to which, in their life of complete blessedness, they feel no temptation. Of course, divination and augury and all such practices are purely superstitious, and so is the belief in Providence.

There is therefore no ground for the fear that we may incur the anger of the gods, or that we may suffer in Hades after death. Though subject to the powers of nature, which can be studied scientifically, we yet have free will, and are, within limits, the masters of our fate. We cannot escape death, but death, rightly understood, is no evil. If we live prudently, according to the maxims of Epicurus, we shall probably achieve a measure of freedom from pain. This is a moderate gospel, but to a man impressed with human misery it sufficed to inspire enthusiasm.

Epicurus has no interest in science on its own account; he values it solely as providing naturalistic explanations of phenomena which superstition attributes to the agency of the gods. When there are several possible naturalistic explanations, he holds that there is no point in trying to decide between them. The phases of the moon, for example, have been explained in many different ways; any one of these, so long as it does not bring in the gods, is as good as any other, and it would be idle curiosity to attempt to determine which of them is true. It is no wonder that the Epicureans contributed practically nothing to natural knowledge. They served a useful purpose by their protest against the increasing devotion of the later pagans to magic, astrology, and divination; but they remained, like their founder, dogmatic, limited, and without genuine interest in anything outside individual happiness. They learnt by heart the creed of Epicurus, and added nothing to it throughout the centuries during which the school survived.

The only eminent disciple of Epicurus is the poet Lucretius (99-55 B.C.), who was a contemporary of Julius Caesar. In the last days of the Roman Republic, free thought was the fashion, and the doctrines of Epicurus were popular among educated people. The Emperor Augustus introduced an archaistic revival of ancient virtue and ancient religion, which caused the poem of Lucretius *On the Nature of Things* to become unpopular, and it remained so until the Renaissance. Only one manuscript of it survived the Middle Ages, and that narrowly escaped destruction by bigots. Hardly any great poet has had to wait so long for recognition, but in modern times his merits have been almost universally acknowledged. For example, he and Benjamin Franklin were Shelley's favourite authors.

His poem sets forth in verse the philosophy of Epicurus. Although the two men have the same doctrine, their temperaments are very different. Lucretius was passionate, and much more in need of exhortations to prudence than Epicurus was. He committed suicide, and appears to have suffered from periodic insanity—brought on, so some averred, by the pains of love or the unintended effects of a love philtre. He feels towards Epicurus as towards a saviour, and applies language of religious intensity to the man whom he regards as the destroyer of religion:[1]

> When prostrate upon earth lay human life
> Visibly trampled down and foully crushed
> Beneath Religion's cruelty, who meanwhile
> Out of the regions of the heavens above
> Showed forth her face, lowering on mortal men
> With horrible aspect, first did a man of Greece
> Dare to lift up his mortal eyes against her;
> The first was he to stand up and defy her.
> Him neither stories of the gods, nor lightnings,
> Nor heaven with muttering menaces could quell,
> But all the more did they arouse his soul's
> Keen valour, till he longed to be the first
> To break through the fast-bolted doors of Nature.
> Therefore his fervent energy of mind
> Prevailed, and he passed onward, voyaging far
> Beyond the flaming ramparts of the world,
> Ranging in mind and spirit far and wide
> Throughout the unmeasured universe; and thence
> A conqueror he returns to us, bringing back
> Knowledge both of what can and what cannot
> Rise into being, teaching us in fine

[1] I quote the translation of Mr R. C. Trevelyan, Book I, 60-79.

Upon what principle each thing has its powers
Limited, and its deep-set boundary stone.
Therefore now has Religion been cast down
Beneath men's feet, and trampled on in turn:
Ourselves heaven-high his victory exalts

The hatred of religion expressed by Epicurus and Lucretius is not altogether easy to understand, if one accepts the conventional accounts of the cheerfulness of Greek religion and ritual. Keats's *Ode on a Grecian Urn*, for instance, celebrates a religious ceremony, but not one which could fill men's minds with dark and gloomy terrors. I think popular beliefs were very largely not of this cheerful kind. The worship of the Olympians had less of superstitious cruelty than the other forms of Greek religion, but even the Olympian gods had demanded occasional human sacrifice until the seventh or sixth century B.C., and this practice was recorded in myth and drama.[1] Throughout the barbarian world, human sacrifice was still recognized in the time of Epicurus; until the Roman conquest, it was practised in times of crisis, such as the Punic Wars, by even the most civilized of barbarian populations.

As was shown most convincingly by Jane Harrison, the Greeks had, in addition to the official cults of Zeus and his family, other more primitive beliefs associated with more or less barbarous rites. These were to some extent incorporated in Orphism, which became the prevalent belief among men of religious temperament. It is sometimes supposed that Hell was a Christian invention, but this is a mistake. What Christianity did in this respect was only to systematize earlier popular beliefs. From the beginning of Plato's *Republic* it is clear that the fear of punishment after death was common in fifth-century Athens, and it is not likely that it grew less in the interval between Socrates and Epicurus. (I am thinking not of the educated minority, but of the general population.) Certainly, also, it was common to attribute plagues, earthquakes, defeats in war, and such calamities, to divine displeasure or to failure to respect the omens. I think that Greek literature and art are probably very misleading as regards popular beliefs. What should we know of Methodism in the late eighteenth century if no record of the period survived except its aristocratic books and paintings? The influence of Methodism, like that of religiosity in the Hellenistic age, rose from below; it was already powerful in the time of Boswell and Sir Joshua Reynolds, although from their allusions to it the strength of its influence is not apparent. We must not, therefore, judge of popular religion in Greece by the pictures on 'Grecian Urns' or by

[1] Lucretius instances the sacrifice of Iphigenia as an example of the harm wrought by religion. Book I, 85-100.

the works of poets and aristocratic philosophers. Epicurus was not aristocratic, either by birth or through his associates; perhaps this explains his exceptional hostility to religion.

It is through the poem of Lucretius that the philosophy of Epicurus has chiefly become known to readers since the Renaissance. What has most impressed them, when they were not professional philosophers, is the contrast with Christian belief in such matters as materialism, denial of Providence, and rejection of immortality. What is especially striking to a modern reader is to have these views—which, nowadays, are generally regarded as gloomy and depressing—presented as a gospel of liberation from the burden of fear. Lucretius is as firmly persuaded as any Christian of the importance of true belief in matters of religion. After describing how men seek escape from themselves when they are the victims of an inner conflict, and vainly seek relief in change of place, he says:[1]

> Each man flies from his own self;
> Yet from that self in fact he has no power
> To escape: he clings to it in his own despite,
> And loathes it too, because, though he is sick,
> He perceives not the cause of his disease.
> Which if he could but comprehend aright,
> Each would put all things else aside and first
> Study to learn the nature of the world,
> Since 'tis our state during eternal time,
> Not for one hour merely, that is in doubt,
> That state wherein mortals will have to pass.
> The whole time that awaits them after death.

The age of Epicurus was a weary age, and extinction could appear as a welcome rest from travail of spirit. The last age of the Republic, on the contrary, was not, to most Romans, a time of disillusionment: men of titanic energy were creating out of chaos a new order, which the Macedonians had failed to do. But to the Roman aristocrat who stood aside from politics, and cared nothing for the scramble for power and plunder, the course of events must have been profoundly discouraging. When to this was added the affliction of recurrent insanity, it is not to be wondered at that Lucretius accepted the hope of non-existence as a deliverance.

But the fear of death is so deeply rooted in instinct that the gospel of Epicurus could not, at any time, make a wide popular appeal; it remained always the creed of a cultivated minority. Even among philosophers, after the time of Augustus, it was, as a rule, rejected in favour of Stoicism. It survived, it is true, though with diminishing

[1] Book III, 1068-76. I again quote Mr. R. C Trevelyan's translation.

vigour, for six hundred years after the death of Epicurus; but as men became increasingly oppressed by the miseries of our terrestrial existence, they demanded continually stronger medicine from philosophy or religion. The philosophers took refuge, with few exceptions, in Neoplatonism; the uneducated turned to various Eastern superstitions, and then, in continually increasing numbers, to Christianity, which, in its early form, placed all good in the life beyond the grave, thus offering men a gospel which was the exact opposite of that of Epicurus. Doctrines very similar to his, however, were revived by the French *philosophes* at the end of the eighteenth century, and brought to England by Bentham and his followers; this was done in conscious opposition to Christianity, which these men regarded as hostilely as Epicurus regarded the religions of his day.

Chapter XXVIII

STOICISM

STOICISM, while in origin contemporaneous with Epicureanism, had a longer history and less constancy in doctrine. The teaching of its founder Zeno, in the early part of the third century B.C., was by no means identical with that of Marcus Aurelius in the latter half of the second century A.D. Zeno was a materialist, whose doctrines were, in the main, a combination of Cynicism and Heraclitus; but gradually, through an admixture of Platonism, the Stoics abandoned materialism, until, in the end, little trace of it remained. Their ethical doctrine, it is true, changed very little, and was what most of them regarded as of the chief importance. Even in this respect, however, there is some change of emphasis. As time goes on, continually less is said about the other aspects of Stoicism, and continually more exclusive stress is laid upon ethics and those parts of theology that are most relevant to ethics. With regard to all the earlier Stoics, we are hampered by the fact that their works survive only in a few fragments. Seneca, Epictetus, and Marcus Aurelius, who belong to the first and second centuries A.D., alone survive in complete books.

Stoicism is less Greek than any school of philosophy with which we have been hitherto concerned. The early Stoics were mostly Syrian, the later ones mostly Roman. Tarn (*Hellenistic Civilization*, p. 287) suspects Chaldean influences in Stoicism. Ueberweg justly observes that, in Hellenizing the barbarian world, the Greeks dropped what only suited themselves. Stoicism, unlike the earlier purely Greek philosophies, is emotionally narrow, and in a certain sense fanatical; but it also contains religious elements of which the world felt the need, and which the Greeks seemed unable to supply. In particular, it appealed to rulers: 'nearly all the successors of Alexander—we may say all the principal kings in existence in the generations following Zeno—professed themselves Stoics,' says Professor Gilbert Murray.

Zeno was a Phoenician, born at Citium, in Cyprus, at some time during the latter half of the fourth century B.C. It seems probable that his family were engaged in commerce, and that business interests were what first took him to Athens. When there, however, he became anxious to study philosophy. The views of the Cynics were more congenial to him than those of any other school, but he was something of an eclectic. The followers of Plato accused him of plagiarizing the Academy. Socrates was the chief saint of the Stoics throughout their history; his attitude at the time of his trial, his refusal to escape, his calmness in the face of death, and his contention that the perpetrator of injustice injures himself more than his victim, all fitted in perfectly with Stoic teaching. So did his indifference to heat and cold, his plainness in matters of food and dress, and his complete independence of all bodily comforts. But the Stoics never took over Plato's doctrine of ideas, and most of them rejected his arguments for immortality. Only the later Stoics followed him in regarding the soul as immaterial; the earlier Stoics agreed with Heraclitus in the view that the soul is composed of material fire. Verbally, this doctrine is also to be found in Epictetus and Marcus Aurelius, but it seems that in them the fire is not to be taken literally as one of the four elements of which physical things are composed.

Zeno had no patience with metaphysical subtleties. Virtue was what he thought important, and he only valued physics and metaphysics in so far as they contributed to virtue. He attempted to combat the metaphysical tendencies of the age by means of common sense, which, in Greece, meant materialism. Doubts as to the trustworthiness of the senses annoyed him, and he pushed the opposite doctrine to extremes.

Zeno began by asserting the existence of the real world. "What do you mean by real?" asked the Sceptic. "I mean solid and material. I mean that this table is solid matter." "And God," asked the Sceptic, "and the Soul?" "Perfectly solid," said Zeno, "more solid if anything, than the table." "And virtue or justice or the Rule of Three; also solid matter?" "Of course," said Zeno, "quite solid." "[1]

It is evident that, at this point, Zeno, like many others, was hurried by anti-metaphysical zeal into a metaphysic of his own.

The main doctrines to which the school remained constant throughout are concerned with cosmic determinism and human freedom. Zeno believed that there is no such thing as chance, and that the course of nature is rigidly determined by natural laws. Originally there was only fire; then the other elements—air, water, earth, in that order—gradually emerged. But sooner or later there will be a cosmic conflagration, and all will again become fire. This, according to most Stoics, is not a final consummation, like the end of the world in Christian doctrine, but only the conclusion of a cycle; the whole process will be repeated endlessly. Everything that happens has happened before, and will happen again, not once, but countless times.

[1] Gilbert Murray, *The Stoic Philosophy* (1915), p. 25.

So far, the doctrine might seem cheerless, and in no respect more comforting than ordinary materialism such as that of Democritus. But this was only one aspect of it. The course of nature, in Stoicism as in eighteenth-century theology, was ordained by a Lawgiver who was also a beneficent Providence. Down to the smallest detail, the whole was designed to secure certain ends by natural means. These ends, except in so far as they concern gods and daemons, are to be found in the life of man. Everything has a purpose connected with human beings. Some animals are good to eat, some afford tests of courage; even bed bugs are useful, since they help us to wake in the morning and not lie in bed too long. The supreme Power is called sometimes God, sometimes Zeus. Seneca distinguished this Zeus from the object of popular belief, who was also real, but subordinate.

God is not separate from the world; He is the soul of the world, and each of us contains a part of the Divine Fire. All things are parts of one single system, which is called Nature; the individual life is good when it is in harmony with Nature. In one sense, *every* life is in harmony with Nature, since it is such as Nature's laws have caused it to be; but in another sense a human life is only in harmony with Nature when the individual will is directed to ends which are among those of Nature. *Virtue* consists in a *will* which is in agreement with Nature. The wicked, though perforce they obey God's law, do so involuntarily; in the simile of Cleanthes, they are like a dog tied to a cart, and compelled to go wherever it goes.

In the life of an individual man, virtue is the sole good; such things as health, happiness, possessions, are of no account. Since virtue resides in the will, everything really good or bad in a man's life depends only upon himself. He may become poor, but what of it? He can still be virtuous. A tyrant may put him in prison, but he can still persevere in living in harmony with Nature. He may be sentenced to death, but he can die nobly, like Socrates. Other men have power only over externals; virtue, which alone is truly good, rests entirely with the individual. Therefore every man has perfect freedom, provided he emancipates himself from mundane desires. It is only through false judgments that such desires prevail; the sage whose judgments are true is master of his fate in all that he values, since no outside force can deprive him of virtue.

There are obvious logical difficulties about this doctrine. If virtue is really the sole good, a beneficent Providence must be solely concerned to cause virtue, yet the laws of Nature have produced abundance of sinners. If virtue is the sole good, there can be no reason against cruelty and injustice, since, as the Stoics are never tired of pointing out, cruelty and injustice afford thè sufferer the

best opportunities for the exercise of virtue. If the world is completely deterministic, natural laws will decide whether I shall be
virtuous or not. If I am wicked, Nature compels me to be wicked,
and the freedom which virtue is supposed to give is not possible
for me.

To a modern mind, it is difficult to feel enthusiastic about a
virtuous life if nothing is going to be achieved by it. We admire a
medical man who risks his life in an epidemic of plague, because
we think illness is an evil, and we hope to diminish its frequency.
But if illness is no evil, the medical man might as well stay comfortably at home. To the Stoic, his virtue is an end in itself, not
something that does good. And when we take a longer view, what
is the ultimate outcome? A destruction of the present world by
fire, and then a repetition of the whole process. Could anything be
more devastatingly futile? There may be progress here and there,
for a time, but in the long run there is only recurrence. When we
see something unbearably painful, we hope that in time such things
will cease to happen; but the Stoic assures us that what is happening
now will happen over and over again. Providence, which sees the
whole, must, one would think, ultimately grow weary through
despair.

There goes with this a certain coldness in the Stoic conception of
virtue. Not only bad passions are condemned, but all passions. The
sage does not feel sympathy; when his wife or his children die, he
reflects that this event is no obstacle to his own virtue, and therefore he does not suffer deeply. Friendship, so highly prized by
Epicurus, is all very well, but it must not be carried to the point
where your friend's misfortunes can destroy your holy calm. As for
public life, it may be your duty to engage in it, since it gives opportunities for justice, fortitude, and so on; but you must not be
actuated by a desire to benefit mankind, since the benefits you can
confer—such as peace, or a more adequate supply of food—are no
true benefits, and, in any case, nothing matters to you except your
own virtue. The Stoic is not virtuous in order to do good, but does
good in order to be virtuous. It has not occurred to him to love his
neighbour as himself; love, except in a superficial sense, is absent
from his conception of virtue.

When I say this, I am thinking of love as an emotion, not as a principle. As a principle, the Stoics preached universal love; this principle
is found in Seneca and his successors, and probably was taken by
them from earlier Stoics. The logic of the school led to doctrines
which were softened by the humanity of its adherents, who were
much better men than they would have been if they had been consistent. Kant—who resembles them—says that you must be kind to

your brother, not because you are fond of him, but because the moral law enjoins kindness; I doubt, however, whether, in private life, he lived down to this precept.

Leaving these generalities, let us come to the history of Stoicism. Of Zeno,[1] only some fragments remain. From these it appears that he defined God as the fiery mind of the world, that he said God was a bodily substance, and that the whole universe formed the substance of God; Tertullian says that, according to Zeno, God runs through the material world as honey runs through the honeycomb. According to Diogenes Laertius, Zeno held that the General Law, which is Right Reason, pervading everything, is the same as Zeus, the Supreme Head of the government of the universe: God, Mind, Destiny, Zeus, are one thing. Destiny is a power which moves matter; 'Providence' and 'Nature' are other names for it. Zeno does not believe that there should be temples to the gods: 'To build temples there will be no need: for a temple must not be held a thing of great worth or anything holy. Nothing can be of great worth or holy which is the work of builders and mechanics.' He seems, like the later Stoics, to have believed in astrology and divination. Cicero says that he attributed a divine potency to the stars. Diogenes Laertius says: 'All kinds of divination the Stoics leave valid. There must be divination, they say, if there is such a thing as Providence. They prove the reality of the art of divination by a number of cases in which predictions have come true, as Zeno asserts.' Chrysippus is explicit on this subject.

The Stoic doctrine as to virtue does not appear in the surviving fragments of Zeno, but seems to have been held by him.

Cleanthes of Assos, the immediate successor of Zeno, is chiefly notable for two things. First: as we have already seen, he held that Aristarchus of Samos should be prosecuted for impiety because he made the sun, instead of the earth, the centre of the universe. The second thing is his *Hymn to Zeus*, much of which might have been written by Pope, or any educated Christian in the century after Newton. Even more Christian is the short prayer of Cleanthes:

> Lead me, O Zeus, and thou, O Destiny,
> Lead thou me on.
> To whatsoever task thou sendest me,
> Lead thou me on.
> I follow fearless, or, if in mistrust
> I lag and will not, follow still I must.

Chrysippus (280-207 B.C.), who succeeded Cleanthes, was a

[1] For the sources of what follows, see Bevan, *Later Greek Religion*, p. 1 ff

voluminous author, and is said to have written seven hundred and five books. He made Stoicism systematic and pedantic. He held that only Zeus, the Supreme Fire, is immortal; the other gods, including the sun and moon, are born and die. He is said to have considered that God has no share in the causation of evil, but it is not clear how he reconciled this with determinism. Elsewhere he deals with evil after the manner of Heraclitus, maintaining that opposites imply one another, and good without evil is logically impossible: 'There can be nothing more inept than the people who suppose that good could have existed without the existence of evil. Good and evil being antithetical, both must needs subsist in opposition.' In support of this doctrine he appeals to Plato, not to Heraclitus.

Chrysippus maintained that the good man is always happy and the bad man unhappy, and that the good man's happiness differs in no way from God's. On the question whether the soul survives death, there were conflicting opinions. Cleanthes maintained that all souls survive until the next universal conflagration (when everything is absorbed into God); but Chrysippus maintained that this is only true of the souls of the wise. He was less exclusively ethical in his interests than the later Stoics; in fact, he made logic fundamental. The hypothetical and disjunctive syllogism, as well as the word 'disjunction', are due to the Stoics; so is the study of grammar and the inventions of 'cases' in declension.[1] Chrysippus, or other Stoics inspired by his work, had an elaborate theory of knowledge, in the main empirical and based on perception, though they allowed certain ideas and principles, which were held to be established by *consensus gentium*, the agreement of mankind. But Zeno, as well as the Roman Stoics, regarded all theoretical studies as subordinate to ethics: he says that philosophy is like an orchard, in which logic is the walls, physics the trees, and ethics the fruit; or like an egg, in which logic is the shell, physics the white, and ethics the yolk.[2] Chrysippus, it would seem, allowed more independent value to theoretical studies. Perhaps his influence accounts for the fact that among the Stoics there were many men who made advances in mathematics and other sciences.

Stoicism, after Chrysippus, was considerably modified by two important men, Panaetius and Posidonius. Panaetius introduced a considerable element of Platonism, and abandoned materialism. He was a friend of the younger Scipio, and had an influence on Cicero, through whom, mainly, Stoicism became known to the Romans. Posidonius, under whom Cicero studied in Rhodes, influenced him even more. Posidonius was taught by Panaetius, who died about 110 B.C.

[1] See Barth, *Die Stoa*, 4th edition, Stuttgart, 1922. [2] *Ibid.*

Posidonius (*ca.* 135-*ca.* 51 B.C.) was a Syrian Greek, and was a child when the Seleucid empire came to an end. Perhaps it was his experience of anarchy in Syria that caused him to travel westward, first to Athens, where he imbibed the Stoic philosophy, and then further afield, to the western parts of the Roman Empire. 'He saw with his own eyes the sunset in the Atlantic beyond the verge of the known world, and the African coast over against Spain, where the trees were full of apes, and the villages of barbarous people inland from Marseilles, where human heads hanging at the house-doors for trophies were an every-day sight.'[1] He became a volum-inous writer on scientific subjects; indeed, one of the reasons for his travels was a wish to study the tides, which could not be done in the Mediterranean. He did excellent work in astronomy; as we saw in Chapter XXIV his estimate of the distance of the sun was the best in antiquity.[2] He was also a historian of note—he continued Polybius. But it was chiefly as an eclectic philosopher that he was known: he combined with Stoicism much of Plato's teaching, which the Academy, in its sceptical phase, appeared to have forgotten.

This affinity to Plato is shown in his teaching about the soul and the life after death. Panaetius had said, as most Stoics did, that the soul perishes with the body. Posidonius, on the contrary, says that it continues to live in the air, where, in most cases, it remains unchanged until the next world-conflagration. There is no hell, but the wicked, after death, are not so fortunate as the good, for sin makes the vapours of the soul muddy, and prevents it from rising as far as the good soul rises. The *very* wicked stay near the earth and are reincarnated; the truly virtuous rise to the stellar sphere and spend their time watching the stars go round. They can help other souls; this explains (he thinks) the truth of astrology. Bevan suggests that, by this revival of Orphic notions and incorporation of Neo-Pythagorean beliefs, Posidonius may have paved the way for Gnosticism. He adds, very truly, that what was fatal to such philosophies as his was not Christianity but the Copernican theory.[3] Cleanthes was right in regarding Aristarchus of Samos as a dangerous enemy.

Much more important historically (though not philosophically) than the earlier Stoics were the three who were connected with

---

[1] Bevan, *Stoics and Sceptics*, p. 88.
[2] He estimated that by sailing westward from Cadiz, India could be reached after 70,000 stades. 'This remark was the ultimate foundation of Columbus's confidence.' Tarn, *Hellenistic Civilization*, p. 249.
[3] The above account of Posidonius is mainly based on Chapter III of Edwyn Bevan's *Stoics and Sceptics*.

Rome: Seneca, Epictetus, and Marcus Aurelius—a minister, a slave, and an emperor, respectively.

Seneca (*ca.* 3 B.C. to A.D. 65) was a Spaniard, whose father was a cultivated man living in Rome. Seneca adopted a political career, and was being moderately successful when he was banished to Corsica (A.D. 41) by the Emperor Claudius, because he had incurred the enmity of the Empress Messalina. Claudius's second wife Agrippina recalled Seneca from exile in A.D. 48, and appointed him tutor to her son, aged eleven. Seneca was less fortunate than Aristotle in his pupil, who was the Emperor Nero. Although, as a Stoic, Seneca officially despised riches, he amassed a huge fortune, amounting, it was said, to three hundred million sesterces (about three million pounds). Much of this he acquired by lending money in Britain; according to Dio, the excessive rates of interest that he exacted were among the causes of revolt in that country. The heroic Queen Boadicea, if this is true, was heading a rebellion against capitalism as represented by the philosophic apostle of austerity.

Gradually, as Nero's excesses grew more unbridled, Seneca fell increasingly out of favour. At length he was accused, justly or unjustly, of complicity in a widespread conspiracy to murder Nero and place a new emperor—some said, Seneca himself—upon the throne. In view of his former services, he was graciously permitted to commit suicide (A.D. 65).

His end was edifying. At first, on being informed of the Emperor's decision, he set about making a will. When told that there was no time allowed for such a lengthy business, he turned to his sorrowing family and said: 'Never mind, I leave you what is of far more value than earthly riches, the example of a virtuous life'—or words to that effect. He then opened his veins, and summoned his secretaries to take down his dying words; according to Tacitus, his eloquence continued to flow during his last moments. His nephew Lucan, the poet, suffered a similar death at the same time, and expired reciting his own verses. Seneca was judged, in future ages, rather by his admirable precepts than by his somewhat dubious practice. Several of the Fathers claimed him as a Christian, and a supposed correspondence between him and Saint Paul was accepted as genuine by such men as Saint Jerome.

Epictetus (born about A.D. 60, died about A.D. 100) is a very different type of man, though closely akin as a philosopher. He was a Greek, originally a slave of Epaphroditus, a freedman of Nero and then his minister. He was lame—as a result, it was said of a cruel punishment in his days of slavery. He lived and taught at Rome until A.D. 90, when the Emperor Domitian, who had no use for intellectuals, banished all philosophers. Epictetus thereupon retired to Nicopolis in Epirus, where, after some years spent in writing and teaching, he died.

Marcus Aurelius (A.D. 121-180) was at the other end of the social scale. He was the adopted son of the good Emperor Antoninus Pius, who was his uncle and his father-in-law, whom he succeeded in A.D. 161, and whose memory he revered. As Emperor, he devoted himself to Stoic virtue. He had much need of fortitude, for his reign was beset by calamities—earthquakes, pestilences, long and difficult wars, military insurrections. His *Meditations*, which are addressed to himself, and apparently not intended for publication, show that he felt his public duties burdensome, and that he suffered from a great weariness. His only son Commodus, who succeeded him, turned out to be one of the worst of the many bad emperors, but successfully concealed his vicious propensities so long as his father lived. The philosopher's wife Faustina was accused, perhaps unjustly, of gross immorality, but he never suspected her, and after her death took trouble about her deification. He persecuted the Christians, because they rejected the State religion, which he considered politically necessary. In all his actions he was conscientious, but in most he was unsuccessful. He is a pathetic figure: in a list of mundane desires to be resisted, the one that he finds most seductive is the wish to retire to a quiet country life. For this, the opportunity never came. Some of his *Meditations* are dated from the camp, on distant campaigns, the hardships of which eventually caused his death.

It is remarkable that Epictetus and Marcus Aurelius are completely at one on all philosophical questions. This suggests that although social circumstances affect the philosophy of an age, individual circumstances have less influence than is sometimes thought upon the philosophy of an individual. Philosophers are usually men with a certain breadth of mind, who can largely discount the accidents of their private lives; but even they cannot rise above the larger good or evil of their time. In bad times they invent consolations; in good times their interests are more purely intellectual.

Gibbon, whose detailed history begins with the vices of Commodus, agrees with most eighteenth-century writers in regarding the period of the Antonines as a golden age. 'If a man were called upon,' he says, 'to fix the period in the history of the world, during which the condition of the human race was most happy and prosperous, he would, without hesitation, name that which elapsed from the death of Domitian to the accession of Commodus.' It is impossible to agree altogether with this judgment. The evil of slavery involved immense suffering, and was sapping the vigour of the ancient world. There were gladiatorial shows and fights with wild beasts, which were intolerably cruel and must have debased the populations that enjoyed the spectacle. Marcus Aurelius, it is true, decreed that gladiators should fight with blunted swords; but this reform was short-lived, and he did nothing about fights with wild beasts. The economic system was very bad; Italy was going out of cultivation, and the population of Rome depended upon the free distribution of grain from the provinces. All initiative was concentrated in the Emperor and his ministers; throughout the vast extent of the Empire, no one, except an occasional rebellious general, could do anything but submit. Men looked to the past for what was best; the future, they felt, would be at best a weariness, and at worst a horror. When we compare the tone of Marcus Aurelius with that of Bacon, or Locke, or Condorcet, we see the difference between a tired and a hopeful age. In a hopeful age, great present evils can be endured, because it is thought that they will pass; but in a tired age even real goods lose their savour. The Stoic ethic suited the times of Epictetus and Marcus Aurelius, because its gospel was one of endurance rather than hope.

Undoubtedly the age of the Antonines was much better than any later age until the Renaissance, from the point of view of the general happiness. But careful study shows that it was not so prosperous as its architectural remains would lead one to suppose. Graeco-Roman civilization had made very little impression on the agricultural regions; it was practically limited to the cities. Even in the cities, there was a proletariat which suffered very great poverty, and there was a large slave class. Rostovtseff sums up a discussion of social and economic conditions in the cities as follows:[1]

'This picture of their social conditions is not so attractive as the picture of their external appearance. The impression conveyed by our sources is that the splendour of the cities was created by, and existed for, a rather small minority of their populations, that the welfare even of this small minority was based on comparatively weak foundations; that the large masses of the city population had either a very moderate income or lived in extreme poverty. In a word, we must not exaggerate the wealth of the cities: their external aspect is misleading.'

On earth, says Epictetus, we are prisoners, and in an earthly body. According to Marcus Aurelius, he used to say 'Thou art a little soul bearing about a corpse.' Zeus could not make the body free, but he gave us a portion of his divinity. God is the father of men, and we are all brothers. We should not say 'I am an Athenian' or 'I am a

[1] Rostovtseff, *The Social and Economic History of the Roman Empire*, p. 179.

Roman,' but 'I am a citizen of the universe.' If you were a kinsman of Caesar, you would feel safe; how much more should you feel safe in being a kinsman of God? If we understand that virtue is the only true good, we shall see that no real evil can befall us.

I must die. But must I die groaning? I must be imprisoned. But must I whine as well? I must suffer exile. Can any one then hinder me from going with a smile, and a good courage, and at peace? 'Tell the secret.' I refuse to tell, for this is in my power. 'But I will chain you.' What say you, fellow? Chain me? My leg you will chain—yes, but my will—no, not even Zeus can conquer that. 'I will imprison you.' My bit of a body, you mean. 'I will behead you.' Why? When did I ever tell you that I was the only man in the world that could not be beheaded?

These are the thoughts that those who pursue philosophy should ponder, these are the lessons they should write down day by day, in these they should exercise themselves.[1]

Slaves are the equals of other men, because all alike are sons of God.

We must submit to God as a good citizen submits to the law. 'The soldier swears to respect no man above Caesar, but we to respect ourselves first of all.'[2] 'When you appear before the mighty of the earth, remember that Another looks from above on what is happening, and that you must please Him rather than this man.'[3]

Who then is a Stoic?

Show me a man moulded to the pattern of the judgments that he utters, in the same way as we call a statue Phidian that is moulded according to the art of Phidias. Show me one who is sick and yet happy, in peril and yet happy, dying and yet happy, in exile and happy, in disgrace and happy. Show him me. By the gods I would fain see a Stoic. Nay you cannot show me a finished Stoic; then show me one in the moulding, one who has set his feet on the path. Do me this kindness, do not grudge an old man like me a sight I never saw till now. What! You think you are going to show me the Zeus of Phidias or his Athena, that work of ivory and gold? It is a soul I want; let one of you show me the soul of a man who wishes to be one with God, and to blame God or man no longer, to fail in nothing, to feel no misfortune, to be free from anger, envy, and jealousy—one who (why wrap up my meaning?) desires to change his manhood for godhead, and who in this poor body of his has his purpose set upon communion with God. Show him to me. Nay, you cannot.

Epictetus is never weary of showing how we should deal with

[1] Quoted from Oates, *op. cit.* pp. 225-6.
[2] *Ibid.*, p. 251.
[3] *Ibid.*, p. 280.

what are considered misfortunes, which he does often by means of homely dialogues.

Like the Christians, he holds that we should love our enemies. In general, in common with other Stoics, he despises pleasure, but there is a kind of happiness that is not to be despised. 'Athens is beautiful. Yes, but happiness is far more beautiful—freedom from passion and disturbance, the sense that your affairs depend on no one' (p. 428). Every man is an actor in a play, in which God has assigned the parts; it is our duty to perform our part worthily, whatever it may be.

There is great sincerity and simplicity in the writings which record the teaching of Epictetus. (They are written down from notes by his pupil Arrian.) His morality is lofty and unworldly; in a situation in which a man's main duty is to resist tyrannical power, it would be difficult to find anything more helpful. In some respects, for instance in recognizing the brotherhood of man and in teaching the equality of slaves, it is superior to anything to be found in Plato or Aristotle or any philosopher whose thought is inspired by the City State. The actual world, in the time of Epictetus, was very inferior to the Athens of Pericles; but the evil in what existed liberated his aspirations, and his ideal world is as superior to that of Plato as his actual world is inferior to the Athens of the fifth century.

The *Meditations* of Marcus Aurelius begin by acknowledging his indebtedness to his grandfather, father, adopted father, various teachers, and the gods. Some of the obligations he enumerates are curious. He learned (he says) from Diognetus not to listen to miracle-workers; from Rusticus not to write poetry; from Sextus to prac- tise gravity without affectation; from Alexander the grammarian, not to correct bad grammar in others, but to use the right expres- sion shortly afterwards; from Alexander the Platonist, not to excuse tardiness in answering a letter by the plea of press of business; from his adopted father, not to fall in love with boys. He owes it to the gods (he continues) that he was not brought up too long with his grandfather's concubine, and did not make proof of his virility too soon; that his children are neither stupid nor deformed in body; that his wife is obedient, affectionate, and simple; and that when he took to philosophy he did not waste time on history, syllogism, or astronomy.

What is impersonal in the *Meditations* agrees closely with Epic- tetus. Marcus Aurelius is doubtful about immortality, but says, as a Christian might: 'Since it is possible that thou mayst depart from life this very moment, regulate every act and thought accordingly.' Life in harmony with the universe is what is good; and harmony with the universe is the same thing as obedience to the will of God.

'Everything harmonizes with me which is harmonious to thee, O Universe. Nothing for me is too early or too late, which is in due time for thee. Everything is fruit to me which thy seasons bring, O Nature: from thee are all things, in thee are all things, to thee all things return. The poet says, Dear city of Cecrops; and wilt not thou say, Dear city of Zeus?'

One sees that Saint Augustine's City of God was in part taken over from the pagan Emperor.

Marcus Aurelius is persuaded that God gives every man a special daemon as his guide—a belief which reappears in the Christian guardian angel. He finds comfort in the thought of the universe as a closely-knit whole; it is, he says, one living being, having one substance and one soul. One of his maxims is: 'Frequently consider the connection of all things in the universe.' 'Whatever may happen to thee, it was prepared for thee from all eternity; and the implication of causes was from eternity spinning the thread of thy being.' There goes with this, in spite of his position in the Roman State, the Stoic belief in the human race as one community: 'My city and country, so far as I am Antoninus, is Rome, but so far as I am a man, it is the world.' There is the difficulty that one finds in all Stoics, of reconciling determinism with the freedom of the will. 'Men exist for the sake of one another,' he says, when he is thinking of his duty as ruler. 'The wickedness of one man does no harm to another,' he says on the same page, when he is thinking of the doctrine that the virtuous will alone is good. He never inferred that the goodness of one man does no good to another, and that he would do no harm to anybody but himself if he were as bad an Emperor as Nero; and yet this conclusion seems to follow.

'It is peculiar to man,' he says, 'to love even those who do wrong. And this happens if, when they do wrong, it occurs to thee that they are kinsmen, and that they do wrong through ignorance and unintentionally, and that soon both of you will die; and above all, that the wrong-doer has done thee no harm, for he has not made thy ruling faculty worse than it was before.'

And again: 'Love mankind, Follow God. . . . And it is enough to remember that Law rules all.'

These passages bring out very clearly the inherent contradictions in Stoic ethics and theology. On the one hand, the universe is a rigidly deterministic single whole, in which all that happens is the result of previous causes. On the other hand, the individual will is completely autonomous, and no man can be forced to sin by outside causes. This is one contradiction, and there is a second closely connected with it. Since the will is autonomous, and the virtuous will alone is good, one man cannot do either good or harm to another; therefore benevolence is an illusion. Something must be said about each of these contradictions.

The contradiction between free will and determinism is one of those that run through philosophy from early times to our own day, taking different forms at different times. At present it is the Stoic form that concerns us.

I think that a Stoic, if we could make him submit to a Socratic interrogation, would defend his view more or less as follows: The universe is a single animate Being, having a soul which may also be called God or Reason. As a whole, this Being is free. God decided, from the first, that He would act according to fixed general laws, but He chose such laws as would have the best results. Sometimes, in particular cases, the results are not wholly desirable, but this inconvenience is worth enduring, as in human codes of law, for the sake of the advantage of legislative fixity. A human being is partly fire, partly of lower clay; in so far as he is fire (at any rate when it is of the best quality), he is part of God. When the divine part of a man exercises will virtuously, this will is part of God's, which is free; therefore in these circumstances the human will also is free.

This is a good answer up to a point, but it breaks down when we consider the causes of our volitions. We all know, as a matter of empirical fact, that dyspepsia, for example, has a bad effect on a man's virtue, and that, by suitable drugs forcibly administered, will-power can be destroyed. Take Epictetus's favourite case, the man unjustly imprisoned by a tyrant, of which there have been more examples in recent years than at any other period in human history. Some of these men have acted with Stoic heroism; some, rather mysteriously, have not. It has become clear, not only that sufficient torture will break down almost any man's fortitude, but also that morphia or cocaine can reduce a man to docility. The will, in fact, is only independent of the tyrant so long as the tyrant is unscientific. This is an extreme example; but the same arguments that exist in favour of determinism in the inanimate world exist also in the sphere of human volitions in general. I do not say—I do not think—that these arguments are conclusive; I say only that they are of equal strength in both cases, and that there can be no good reason for accepting them in one region and rejecting them in another. The Stoic, when he is engaged in urging a tolerant attitude to sinners, will himself urge that the sinful will is a result of previous causes; it is only the virtuous will that seems to him free. This, however, is inconsistent. Marcus Aurelius explains his own virtue as due to the good influence of parents, grandparents, and teachers; the good will is just as much a result of previous causes as the bad will. The Stoic may say truly that his philosophy is a cause of virtue in those who adopt it, but it seems that it will not have this desirable effect unless there is a certain admixture of intellectual error. The realization that virtue and sin alike are the inevitable result of previous causes (as the Stoics should have held) is likely to have a somewhat paralysing effect on moral effort.

I come now to the second contradiction, that the Stoic, while he preached benevolence, held, in theory, that no man can do either good or harm to another, since the virtuous will alone is good, and the virtuous will is independent of outside causes. This contradiction is more patent than the other, and more peculiar to the Stoics (including certain Christian moralists). The explanation of their not noticing it is that, like many other people, they had two systems of ethics, a superfine one for themselves, and an inferior one for 'the lesser breeds without the law'. When the Stoic philosopher is thinking of himself, he holds that happiness and all other worldly so-called goods are worthless; he even says that to desire happiness is contrary to nature, meaning that it involves lack of resignation to the will of God. But as a practical man administering the Roman Empire, Marcus Aurelius knows perfectly well that this sort of thing won't do. It is his duty to see that the grain-ships from Africa duly reach Rome, that measures are taken to relieve the sufferings caused by pestilence, and that barbarian enemies are not allowed to cross the frontier. That is to say, in dealing with those of his subjects whom he does not regard as Stoic philosophers, actual or potential, he accepts ordinary mundane standards of what is good or bad. It is by applying these standards that he arrives at his duty as an administrator. What is odd is that this duty, itself, is in the higher sphere of what the Stoic sage should do, although it is deduced from an ethic which the Stoic sage regards as fundamentally mistaken.

The only reply that I can imagine to this difficulty is one which is perhaps logically unassailable, but is not very plausible. It would, I think, be given by Kant, whose ethical system is very similar to that of the Stoics. True, he might say, there is nothing good but the good will, but the will is good when it is directed to certain ends, that, in themselves, are indifferent. It does not matter whether Mr A is happy or unhappy, but I, if I am virtuous, shall act in a way which I believe will make him happy, because that is what the moral law enjoins. I cannot make Mr A virtuous, because his virtue depends only upon himself; but I can do something towards making him happy, or rich, or learned, or healthy. The Stoic ethic may therefore be stated as follows: Certain things are vulgarly considered goods, but this is a mistake; what *is* good is a will directed towards securing these false goods for other people. This doctrine involves no logical contradiction, but it loses all plausibility if we genuinely believe that what are commonly considered goods are worthless, for in that case the virtuous will might just as well be directed to quite other ends.

There is, in fact, an element of sour grapes in Stoicism. We can't be happy, but we can be good; let us therefore pretend that, so long as we are good, it doesn't matter being unhappy. This doctrine is heroic, and, in a bad world, useful; but it is neither quite true nor, in a fundamental sense, quite sincere.

Although the main importance of the Stoics was ethical, there were two respects in which their teaching bore fruit in other fields. One of these is theory of knowledge; the other is the doctrine of natural law and natural rights.

In theory of knowledge, in spite of Plato, they accepted perception; the deceptiveness of the senses, they held, was really false judgment, and could be avoided by a little care. A Stoic philosopher, Sphaerus, an immediate disciple of Zeno, was once invited to dinner by King Ptolemy, who, having heard of this doctrine, offered him a pomegranate made of wax. The philosopher proceeded to try to eat it, whereupon the king laughed at him. He replied that he had felt no *certainty* of its being a real pomegranate, but had thought it unlikely that anything inedible would be supplied at the royal table.[1] In this answer he appealed to a Stoic distinction, between those things which can be known with certainty on the basis of perception, and those which, on this basis, are only probable. On the whole, this doctrine was sane and scientific.

Another doctrine of theirs in theory of knowledge was more influential, though more questionable. This was their belief in innate ideas and principles. Greek logic was wholly deductive, and this raised the question of first premises. First premises had to be, at least in part, general, and no method existed of proving them. The Stoics held that there are certain principles which are luminously obvious, and are admitted by all men; these could be made, as in Euclid's *Elements*, the basis of deduction. Innate ideas, similarly, could be used as the starting-point of definitions. This point of view was accepted throughout the Middle Ages, and even by Descartes.

The doctrine of *natural right*, as it appears in the sixteenth, seventeenth, and eighteenth centuries, is a revival of a Stoic doctrine, though with important modifications. It was the Stoics who distinguished *jus naturale* from *jus gentium*. Natural law was derived from first principles of the kind held to underlie all general know-

[1] *Diogenes Laertius*, Vol. VII. 177.

ledge. By nature, the Stoics held, all human beings are equal. Marcus Aurelius, in his *Meditations*, favours 'a polity in which there is the same law for all, a polity administered with regard to equal rights and equal freedom of speech, and kingly government which respects most of all the freedom of the governed'. This was an ideal which could not be consistently realized in the Roman Empire, but it influenced legislation, particularly in improving the status of women and slaves. Christianity took over this part of Stoic teaching along with much of the rest. And when at last, in the seventeenth century, the opportunity came to combat despotism effectually, the Stoic doctrines of natural law and natural equality, in their Christian dress, acquired a practical force which, in antiquity, not even an emperor could give to them.

Chapter XXIX

THE ROMAN EMPIRE IN RELATION
TO CULTURE

THE Roman Empire affected the history of culture in various more or less separate ways.

First: there is the direct effect of Rome on Hellenistic thought. This is not very important or profound.

Second: the effect of Greece and the East on the western half of the empire. This was profound and lasting, since it included the Christian religion.

Third: the importance of the long Roman peace in diffusing culture and in accustoming men to the idea of a single civilization associated with a single government.

Fourth: the transmission of Hellenistic civilization to the Mohammedans, and thence ultimately to western Europe.

Before considering these influences of Rome, a very brief synopsis of the political history will be useful.

Alexander's conquests had left the western Mediterranean untouched; it was dominated, at the beginning of the third century B.C., by two powerful City States, Carthage and Syracuse. In the first and second Punic Wars (264-241 and 218-201), Rome conquered Syracuse and reduced Carthage to insignificance. During the second century, Rome conquered the Macedonian monarchies—Egypt, it is true, lingered on as a vassal state until the death of Cleopatra (30 B.C.). Spain was conquered as an incident in the war with Hannibal; France was conquered by Caesar in the middle of the first century B.C., and England was conquered about a hundred years later. The frontiers of the Empire, in its great days, were the Rhine and Danube in Europe, the Euphrates in Asia, and the desert in North Africa.

Roman imperialism was, perhaps, at its best in North Africa (important in Christian history as the home of Saint Cyprian and Saint Augustine), where large areas, uncultivated before and after Roman times, were rendered fertile and supported populous cities. The Roman Empire was on the whole stable and peaceful for over two hundred years, from the accession of Augustus (30 B.C.) until the disasters of the third century.

Meanwhile the constitution of the Roman State had undergone important developments. Originally Rome was a small City State, not very unlike those of Greece, especially such as, like Sparta, did not depend upon foreign commerce. Kings, like those of Homeric Greece, had been succeeded by an aristocratic republic. Gradually, while the aristocratic element, embodied in the Senate, remained powerful, democratic elements were added; the resulting compromise was regarded by Panaetius the Stoic (whose views are reproduced by Polybius and Cicero) as an ideal combination of monarchical, aristocratic, and democratic elements. But conquest upset the precarious balance; it brought immense new wealth to the senatorial class, and, in a slightly lesser degree, to the 'knights', as the upper middle class were called. Italian agriculture, which had been in the hands of small farmers growing grain by their own labour and that of their families, came to be a matter of huge estates belonging to the Roman aristocracy, where vines and olives were cultivated by slave labour. The result was the virtual omnipotence of the Senate, which was used shamelessly for the enrichment of individuals, without regard for the interests of the State or the welfare of its subjects.

A democratic movement, inaugurated by the Gracchi in the latter half of the second century B.C., led to a series of civil wars, and finally—as so often in Greece—to the establishment of a 'tyranny'. It is curious to see the repetition, on such a vast scale, of developments which, in Greece, had been confined to minute areas. Augustus, the heir and adopted son of Julius Caesar, who reigned from 30 B.C. to A.D. 14, put an end to civil strife, and (with few exceptions) to external wars of conquest. For the first time since the beginnings of Greek civilization, the ancient world enjoyed peace and security.

Two things had ruined the Greek political system: first, the claim of each city to absolute sovereignty; second, the bitter and bloody strife between rich and poor within most cities. After the conquest of Carthage and the Hellenistic kingdoms, the first of these causes no longer afflicted the world, since no effective resistance to Rome was possible. But the second cause remained. In the civil wars, one general would proclaim himself the champion of the Senate, the other of the people. Victory went to the one who offered the highest rewards to the soldiers. The soldiers wanted not only pay and plunder, but grants of land; therefore each civil war ended in the formally legal expulsion of many existing landholders, who were nominally tenants of the State, to make room for the legionaries of the victor. The expenses of the war, while in progress, were defrayed by executing rich men and confiscating their property. This system, disastrous as it was, could not easily be ended; at last, to every one's surprise, Augustus was so completely victorious that no competitor remained to challenge his claim to power.

To the Roman world, the discovery that the period of civil war was ended came as a surprise, which was a cause of rejoicing to all except a small senatorial party. To every one else, it was a profound relief when Rome, under Augustus, at last achieved the stability and order which Greeks and Macedonians had sought in vain, and which Rome, before Augustus, had also failed to produce. In Greece, according to Rostovtseff, republican Rome had 'introduced nothing new, except pauperization, bankruptcy, and a stoppage of all independent political activity'.[1]

The reign of Augustus was a period of happiness for the Roman Empire. The administration of the provinces was at last organized with some regard to the welfare of the population, and not on a purely predatory system. Augustus was not only officially deified after his death, but was spontaneously regarded as a god in various provincial cities. Poets praised him, the commercial classes found the universal peace convenient, and even the Senate, which he treated with all the outward forms of respect, lost no opportunity of heaping honours and offices on his head.

But although the world was happy, some savour had gone out of life, since safety had been preferred to adventure. In early times, every free Greek had had the opportunity of adventure; Philip and Alexander put an end to this state of affairs, and in the Hellenistic world only Macedonian dynasts enjoyed anarchic freedom. The Greek world lost its youth, and became either cynical or religious. The hope of embodying ideals in earthly institutions faded, and with it the best men lost their zest. Heaven, for Socrates, was a place where he could go on arguing; for philosophers after Alexander, it was something more different from their existence here below.

In Rome, a similar development came later, and in a less painful form. Rome was not conquered, as Greece was, but had, on the contrary, the stimulus of successful imperialism. Throughout the period of the civil wars, it was Romans who were responsible for the disorders. The Greeks had not secured peace and order by submitting to the Macedonians, whereas both Greeks and Romans secured both by submitting to Augustus. Augustus was a Roman, to whom most Romans submitted willingly, not *only* on account of his superior power; moreover he took pains to disguise the military origin of his government, and to base it upon decrees of the Senate. The adulation expressed by the Senate was, no doubt, largely insincere, but outside the senatorial class no one felt humiliated.

[1] *History of the Ancient World*, Vol. II, p. 255

The mood of the Romans was like that of a *jeune homme rangé* in nineteenth-century France, who, after a life of amatory adventure, settles down to a marriage of reason. This mood, though contented, is not creative. The great poets of the Augustan age had been formed in more troubled times; Horace fled at Philippi, and both he and Virgil lost their farms in confiscations for the benefit of victorious soldiers. Augustus, for the sake of stability, set to work, somewhat insincerely, to restore ancient piety, and was therefore necessarily rather hostile to free inquiry. The Roman world began to become stereotyped, and the process continued under later emperors.

The immediate successors of Augustus indulged in appalling cruelties towards Senators and towards possible competitors for the purple. To some extent, the misgovernment of this period extended to the provinces; but in the main the administrative machine created by Augustus continued to function fairly well.

A better period began with the accession of Trajan in A.D. 98, and continued until the death of Marcus Aurelius in A.D. 180. During this time, the government of the Empire was as good as any despotic government can be. The third century, on the contrary, was one of appalling disaster. The army realized its power, made and unmade emperors in return for cash and the promise of a life without warfare, and ceased, in consequence, to be an effective fighting force. The barbarians, from north and east, invaded and plundered Roman territory. The army, preoccupied with private gain and civil discord, was incompetent in defence. The whole fiscal system broke down, since there was an immense diminution of resources and, at the same time, a vast increase of expenditure in unsuccessful war and in bribery of the army. Pestilence, in addition to war, greatly diminished the population. It seemed as if the Empire was about to fall.

This result was averted by two energetic men, Diocletian (A.D. 286-305) and Constantine, whose undisputed reign lasted from A.D. 312 to 337. By them the Empire was divided into an eastern and western half, corresponding, approximately, to the division between Greek and Latin languages. By Constantine the capital of the eastern half was established at Byzantium, to which he gave the new name of Constantinople. Diocletian curbed the army, for a while, by altering its character; from his time onwards, the most effective fighting forces were composed of barbarians, chiefly German, to whom all the highest commands were open. This was obviously a dangerous expedient, and early in the fifth century it bore its natural fruit. The barbarians decided that it was more profitable to fight for themselves than for a Roman master. Nevertheless it served its purpose for over a century. Diocletian's administrative reforms were equally successful for a time, and equally disastrous in the long run. The Roman system was to allow local self-government to the towns, and to leave their officials to collect the taxes, of which only the total amount due from any one town was fixed by the central authorities. This system had worked well enough in prosperous times, but now, in the exhausted state of the empire, the revenue demanded was more than could be borne without excessive hardship. The municipal authorities were personally responsible for the taxes, and fled to escape payment. Diocletian compelled well-to-do citizens to accept municipal office, and made flight illegal. From similar motives he turned the rural population into serfs, tied to the soil and forbidden to migrate. This system was kept on by later emperors.

Constantine's most important innovation was the adoption of Christianity as the State religion, apparently because a large proportion of the soldiers were Christian.[1] The result of this was that when, during the fifth century, the Germans destroyed the Western Empire, its prestige caused them to adopt the Christian religion, thereby preserving for western Europe so much of ancient civilizations as had been absorbed by the Church.

The development of the territory assigned to the eastern half of the Empire was different. The Eastern Empire, though continually diminishing in extent (except for the transient conquests of Justinian in the sixth century), survived until 1453, when Constantinople was conquered by the Turks. But most of what had been Roman provinces in the east, including also Africa and Spain in the west, became Mohammedan. The Arabs, unlike the Germans, rejected the religion, but adopted the civilization, of those whom they had conquered. The Eastern Empire was Greek, not Latin, in its civilization; accordingly, from the seventh to the eleventh centuries, it was it and the Arabs who preserved Greek literature and whatever survived of Greek, as opposed to Latin, civilization. From the eleventh century onward, at first through Moorish influences, the west gradually recovered what it had lost of the Grecian heritage.

I come now to the four ways in which the Roman Empire affected the history of culture.

I. *The direct effect of Rome on Greek thought.* This begins in the second century B.C., with two men, the historian Polybius, and the Stoic philosopher Panaetius. The natural attitude of the Greek to the Roman was one of contempt mingled with fear; the Greek felt himself more civilized, but politically less powerful. If the Romans

[1] See Rostovtseff, *History of the Ancient World*, Vol. II, p. 332.

were more successful in politics, that only showed that politics is an ignoble pursuit. The average Greek of the second century B.C. was pleasure-loving, quick-witted, clever in business, and unscrupulous in all things. There were, however, still men of philosophic capacity. Some of these—notably the sceptics, such as Carneades—had allowed cleverness to destroy seriousness. Some, like the Epicureans and a section of the Stoics, had withdrawn wholly into a quiet private life. But a few, with more insight than had been shown by Aristotle in relation to Alexander, realized that the greatness of Rome was due to certain merits which were lacking among the Greeks.

The historian Polybius, born in Arcadia about 200 B.C., was sent to Rome as a prisoner, and there had the good fortune to become the friend of the younger Scipio, whom he accompanied on many of his campaigns. It was uncommon for a Greek to know Latin, though most educated Romans knew Greek; the circumstances of Polybius, however, led him to a thorough familiarity with Latin. He wrote, for the benefit of the Greeks, the history of the later Punic Wars, which enabled Rome to conquer the world. His admiration of the Roman constitution was becoming out of date while he wrote, but until his time it had compared very favourably, in stability and efficiency, with the continually changing constitutions of most Greek cities. The Romans naturally read his history with pleasure; whether the Greeks did so is more doubtful.

Panaetius the Stoic has been already considered in the preceding chapter. He was a friend of Polybius, and, like him, a protégé of the younger Scipio. While Scipio lived, he was frequently in Rome, but after Scipio's death in 129 B.C. he stayed in Athens as head of the Stoic school. Rome still had, what Greece had lost, the hopefulness connected with the opportunity for political activity. Accordingly the doctrines of Panaetius were more political, and less akin to those of the Cynics, than were those of earlier Stoics. Probably the admiration of Plato felt by cultivated Romans influenced him in abandoning the dogmatic narrowness of his Stoic predecessors. In the broader form given to it by him and by his successor Posidonius, Stoicism strongly appealed to the more serious among the Romans.

At a later date, Epictetus, though a Greek, lived most of his life in Rome. Rome supplied him with most of his illustrations; he is always exhorting the wise man not to tremble in the presence of the Emperor. We know the influence of Epictetus on Marcus Aurelius, but his influence on the Greeks is hard to trace.

Plutarch (ca. A.D. 46-120), in his *Lives of the Noble Grecians and Romans*, traced a parallelism between the most eminent men of the two countries. He spent a considerable time in Rome, and was honoured by the Emperors Hadrian and Trajan. In addition to his *Lives*, he wrote numerous works on philosophy, religion, natural history, and morals. His *Lives* are obviously concerned to reconcile Greece and Rome in men's thoughts.

On the whole, apart from such exceptional men, Rome acted as a blight on the Greek-speaking part of the Empire. Thought and art alike declined. Until the end of the second century A.D., life, for the well-to-do, was pleasant and easy-going; there was no incentive to strenuousness, and little opportunity for great achievement. The recognized schools of philosophy—the Academy, the Peripatetics, the Epicureans, and the Stoics—continued to exist until they were closed by Justinian. None of these, however, showed any vitality throughout the time after Marcus Aurelius, except the Neo-platonists in the third century A.D., whom we shall consider in the next chapter; and these men were hardly at all influenced by Rome. The Latin and Greek halves of the Empire became more and more divergent; the knowledge of Greek became rare in the west, and after Constantine Latin, in the east, survived only in law and in the army.

II. *The influence of Greece and the East on Rome.* There are here two very different things to consider : first, the influence of Hellenic art and literature and philosophy on the most cultivated Romans; second, the spread of non-Hellenic religions and superstitions throughout the Western world.

(1) When the Romans first came in contact with Greeks, they became aware of themselves as comparatively barbarous and un-couth. The Greeks were immeasurably their superiors in many ways : in manufacture and in the technique of agriculture; in the kinds of knowledge that are necessary for a good official; in conversation and the art of enjoying life; in art and literature and philosophy. The only things in which the Romans were superior were military tactics and social cohesion. The relation of the Romans to the Greeks was something like that of the Prussians to the French in 1814 and 1815; but this latter was temporary, whereas the other lasted a long time. After the Punic Wars, young Romans conceived an admiration for the Greeks. They learnt the Greek language, they copied Greek architecture, they employed Greek sculptors. The Roman gods were identified with the gods of Greece. The Trojan origin of the Romans was invented to make a connection with the Homeric myths. Latin poets adopted Greek metres, Latin philosophers took over Greek theories. To the end, Rome was culturally parasitic on Greece. The Romans invented no art forms,

constructed no original system of philosophy, and made no scientific discoveries. They made good roads, systematic legal codes, and efficient armies; for the rest they looked to Greece.

The Hellenizing of Rome brought with it a certain softening of manners, abhorrent to the elder Cato. Until the Punic Wars, the Romans had been a bucolic people, with the virtues and vices of farmers: austere, industrious, brutal, obstinate, and stupid. Their family life had been stable and solidly built on the *patria potestas*; women and young people were completely subordinated. All this changed with the influx of sudden wealth. The small farms disappeared, and were gradually replaced by huge estates on which slave labour was employed to carry out new scientific kinds of agriculture. A great class of traders grew up, and a large number of men enriched by plunder, like the nabobs in eighteenth-century England. Women, who had been virtuous slaves, became free and dissolute; divorce became common; the rich ceased to have children. The Greeks, who had gone through a similar development centuries ago, encouraged, by their example, what historians call the decay of morals. Even in the most dissolute times of the Empire, the average Roman still thought of Rome as the upholder of a purer ethical standard against the decadent corruption of Greece.

The cultural influence of Greece on the Western Empire diminished rapidly from the third century A.D. onwards, chiefly because culture in general decayed. For this there were many causes, but one in particular must be mentioned. In the last times of the Western Empire, the government was more undisguisedly a military tyranny than it had been, and the army usually selected a successful general as emperor; but the army, even in its highest ranks, was no longer composed of cultivated Romans, but of semi-barbarians from the frontier. These rough soldiers had no use for culture, and regarded the civilized citizens solely as sources of revenue. Private persons were too impoverished to support much in the way of education, and the State considered education unnecessary. Consequently, in the West, only a few men of exceptional learning continued to read Greek.

(2) Non-Hellenic religion and superstition, on the contrary, acquired, as time went on, a firmer and firmer hold on the West. We have already seen how Alexander's conquests introduced the Greek world to the beliefs of Babylonians, Persians, and Egyptians. Similarly the Roman conquests made the Western world familiar with these doctrines, and also with those of Jews and Christians. I shall consider what concerns the Jews and Christians at a later stage; for the present, I shall confine myself as far as possible to

pagan superstitions.[1]

In Rome every sect and every prophet was represented, and sometimes won favour in the highest government circles. Lucian, who stood for sane scepticism in spite of the credulity of his age, tells an amusing story, generally accepted as broadly true, about a prophet and miracle-worker called Alexander the Paphlagonian. This man healed the sick and foretold the future, with excursions into blackmail. His fame reached the ears of Marcus Aurelius, then fighting the Marcomanni on the Danube. The Emperor consulted him as to how to win the war, and was told that if he threw two lions into the Danube a great victory would result. He followed the advice of the seer, but it was the Marcomanni who won the great victory. In spite of this mishap, Alexander's fame continued to grow. A prominent Roman of consular rank, Rutilianus, after consulting him on many points, at last sought his advice as to the choice of a wife. Alexander, like Endymion, had enjoyed the favours of the moon, and by her had a daughter, whom the oracle recommended to Rutilianus. 'Rutilianus, who was at the time sixty years old, at once complied with the divine injunction, and celebrated his marriage by sacrificing whole hecatombs to his celestial mother-in-law.'[2]

More important than the career of Alexander the Paphlagonian was the reign of the Emperor Elagabalus or Heliogabalus (A.D. 218-22), who was, until his elevation by the choice of the army, a Syrian priest of the sun. In his slow progress from Syria to Rome, he was preceded by his portrait, sent as a present to the Senate. 'He was drawn in his sacerdotal robes of silk and gold, after the loose flowing fashion of the Medes and Phoenicians; his head was covered with a lofty tiara, his numerous collars and bracelets were adorned with gems of inestimable value. His eyebrows were tinged with black, and his cheeks painted with an artificial red and white. The grave senators confessed with a sigh, that, after having long experienced the stern tyranny of their own countrymen, Rome was at length humbled beneath the effeminate luxury of Oriental despotism.'[3] Supported by a large section in the army, he proceeded, with fanatical zeal, to introduce in Rome the religious practices of the East; his name was that of the sun-god worshipped at Emesa, where he had been chief priest. His mother, or grandmother, who was the real ruler, perceived that he had gone too far, and deposed him in favour of her nephew Alexander (222-35), whose Oriental proclivities were more moderate. The mixture of creeds that was possible in his day was illustrated in his private chapel, in which he

---

[1] See Cumont, *Oriental Religions in Roman Paganism*.
[2] Benn, *The Greek Philosophers*, Vol. II, p. 226.
[3] Gibbon, chap. vi.

placed the statues of Abraham, Orpheus, Apollonius of Tyana, and Christ.

The religion of Mithras, which was of Persian origin, was a close competitor of Christianity, especially during the latter half of the third century A.D. The emperors, who were making desperate attempts to control the army, felt that religion might give a much needed stability; but it would have to be one of the new religions, since it was these that the soldiers favoured. The cult was introduced at Rome, and had much to commend it to the military mind. Mithras was a sun-god, but not so effeminate as his Syrian colleague; he was a god concerned with war, the great war between good and evil which had been part of the Persian creed since Zoroaster. Rostovtseff[1] reproduces a bas-relief representing his worship, which was found in a subterranean sanctuary at Heddernheim in Germany, and shows that his disciples must have been numerous among the soldiers, not only in the East, but in the West also.

Constantine's adoption of Christianity was politically successful, whereas earlier attempts to introduce a new religion failed; but the earlier attempts were, from a governmental point of view, very similar to his. All alike derived their possibility of success from the misfortunes and weariness of the Roman world. The traditional religions of Greece and Rome were suited to men interested in the terrestrial world, and hopeful of happiness on earth. Asia, with a longer experience of despair, had evolved more successful antidotes in the form of other-worldly hopes; of all these, Christianity was the most effective in bringing consolation. But Christianity, by the time it became the State religion, had absorbed much from Greece, and transmitted this, along with the Judaic element, to succeeding ages in the West.

III. *The unification of government and culture.* We owe it first to Alexander and then to Rome that the achievements of the great age of Greece were not lost to the world, like those of the Minoan age. In the fifth century B.C., a Jenghiz Khan, if one had happened to arise, could have wiped out all that was important in the Hellenic world; Xerxes, with a little more competence, might have made Greek civilization very greatly inferior to what it became after he was repulsed. Consider the period from Aeschylus to Plato: all that was done in this time was done by a minority of the population of a few commercial cities. These cities, as the future showed, had no great capacity for withstanding foreign conquest, but by an extraordinary stroke of good fortune their conquerors, Macedonian and Roman, were Philhellenes, and did not destroy what they con-

[1] *History of the Ancient World*, Vol. II, p. 343.

quered, as Xerxes or Carthage would have done. The fact that we are acquainted with what was done by the Greeks in art and literature and philosophy and science is due to the stability introduced by Western conquerors who had the good sense to admire the civilization which they governed but did their utmost to preserve.

In certain respects, political and ethical, Alexander and the Romans were the causes of a better philosophy than any that was professed by Greeks in their days of freedom. The Stoics, as we have seen, believed in the brotherhood of man, and did not confine their sympathies to the Greeks. The long dominion of Rome accustomed men to the idea of a single civilization under a single government. We are aware that there were important parts of the world which were not subject to Rome—India and China, more especially. But to the Roman it seemed that outside the Empire there were only more or less barbarian tribes, who might be conquered whenever it should be worth while to make the effort. Essentially and in idea, the empire, in the minds of the Romans, was world-wide. This conception descended to the Church, which was 'Catholic' in spite of Buddhists, Confucians, and (later) Mohammedans. *Securus judicat orbis terrarum* is a maxim of St Augustine's embodying the doctrine of the later Stoics; it owes its appeal to the apparent universality of the Roman Empire. Throughout the Middle Ages, after the time of Charlemagne, the Church and the Holy Roman Empire were world-wide in idea, although everybody knew that they were not so in fact. The conception of one human family, one Catholic religion, one universal culture, and one world-wide State, has haunted men's thoughts ever since its approximate realization by Rome.

The part played by Rome in enlarging the area of civilization was of immense importance. Northern Italy, Spain, France, and parts of western Germany, were civilized as a result of forcible conquest by the Roman legions. All these regions proved themselves just as capable of a high level of culture as Rome itself. In the last days of the Western Empire, Gaul produced men who were at least the equals of their contemporaries in regions of older civilization. It was owing to the diffusion of culture by Rome that the barbarians produced only a temporary eclipse, not a permanent darkness. It may be argued that the *quality* of civilization was never again as good as in the Athens of Pericles; but in a world of war and destruction, quantity is, in the long run, almost as important as quality, and quantity was due to Rome.

IV. *The Mohammedans as vehicles of Hellenism.* In the seventh century, the disciples of the Prophet conquered Syria, Egypt, and

North Africa; in the following century, they conquered Spain. Their victories were easy, and the fighting was slight. Except possibly during the first few years, they were not fanatical; Christians and Jews were unmolested so long as they paid the tribute. Very soon the Arabs acquired the civilization of the Eastern Empire, but with the hopefulness of a rising polity instead of the weariness of decline. Their learned men read Greek authors in translation, and wrote commentaries. Aristotle's reputation is mainly due to them; in antiquity, he was not regarded as on a level with Plato.

It is instructive to consider some of the words that we derive from Arabic, such as: algebra, alcohol, alchemy, alembic, alkali, azimuth, zenith. With the exception of 'alcohol'—which meant, not a drink, but a substance used in chemistry—these words would give a good picture of some of the things we owe to the Arabs. Algebra had been invented by the Alexandrian Greeks, but was carried further by the Mohammedans. 'Alchemy', 'alembic', 'alkali' are words connected with the attempt to turn base metals into gold, which the Arabs took over from the Greeks, and in pursuit of which they appealed to Greek philosophy.[1] 'Azimuth' and 'zenith' are astronomical terms, chiefly useful to the Arabs in connection with astrology.

The etymological method conceals what we owe to the Arabs as regards knowledge of Greek philosophy, because, when it was again studied in Europe, the technical terms required were taken from Greek or Latin. In philosophy, the Arabs were better as commentators than as original thinkers. Their importance, for us, is that they, and not the Christians, were the immediate inheritors of those parts of the Greek tradition which only the Eastern Empire had kept alive. Contact with the Mohammedans, in Spain, and to a lesser extent in Sicily, made the West aware of Aristotle; also of Arabic numerals, algebra, and chemistry. It was this contact that began the revival of learning in the eleventh century, leading to the Scholastic philosophy. It was later, from the thirteenth century onward, that the study of Greek enabled men to go direct to the works of Plato and Aristotle and other Greek writers of antiquity. But if the Arabs had not preserved the tradition, the men of the Renaissance might not have suspected how much was to be gained by the revival of classical learning.

[1] See *Alchemy, Child of Greek Philosophy*, by Arthur John Hopkins, Columbia, 1934.

Chapter XXX

PLOTINUS

PLOTINUS (A.D. 204-70), the founder of Neoplatonism, is the last of the great philosophers of antiquity. His life is almost co-extensive with one of the most disastrous periods in Roman history. Shortly before his birth, the army had become conscious of its power, and had adopted the practice of choosing emperors in return for monetary rewards, and assassinating them afterwards to give occasion for a renewed sale of the empire. These preoccupations unfitted the soldiers for the defence of the frontier, and permitted vigorous incursions of Germans from the north and Persians from the East. War and pestilence diminished the population of the empire by about a third, while increased taxation and diminished resources caused financial ruin in even those provinces to which no hostile forces penetrated. The cities, which had been the bearers of culture, were especially hard hit; substantial citizens, in large numbers, fled to escape the tax-collector. It was not till after the death of Plotinus that order was re-established and the empire temporarily saved by the vigorous measures of Diocletian and Constantine.

Of all this there is no mention in the works of Plotinus. He turned aside from the spectacle of ruin and misery in the actual world, to contemplate an eternal world of goodness and beauty. In this he was in harmony with all the most serious men of his age. To all of them, Christians and pagans alike, the world of practical affairs seemed to offer no hope, and only the Other World seemed worthy of allegiance. To the Christian, the Other World was the Kingdom of Heaven, to be enjoyed after death; to the Platonist, it was the eternal world of ideas, the real world as opposed to that of illusory appearance. Christian theologians combined these points of view, and embodied much of the philosophy of Plotinus. Dean Inge, in his invaluable book on Plotinus, rightly emphasizes what Christianity owes to him. 'Platonism,' he says, 'is part of the vital structure of Christian theology, with which no other philosophy, I venture to say, can work without friction.' There is, he says, an 'utter impossibility of excising Platonism from Christianity without tearing Christianity to pieces'. He points out that Saint Augustine speaks of Plato's system as 'the most pure and bright in all philosophy', and of Plotinus as a man in whom 'Plato lived again', and

289

who, if he had lived a little later, would have 'changed a few words and phrases and become Christian'. Saint Thomas Aquinas, according to Dean Inge, 'is nearer to Plotinus than to the *real* Aristotle'.

Plotinus, accordingly, is historically important as an influence in moulding the Christianity of the Middle Ages and of Catholic theology. The historian, in speaking of Christianity, has to be careful to recognize the very great changes that it has undergone, and the variety of forms that it may assume even at one epoch. The Christianity of the Synoptic Gospels is almost innocent of metaphysics. The Christianity of modern America, in this respect, is like primitive Christianity; Platonism is alien in popular thought and feeling in the United States, and most American Christians are much more concerned with duties here on earth, and with social progress in the everyday world, than with the transcendental hopes that consoled men when everything terrestrial inspired despair. I am not speaking of any change of dogma, but of a difference of emphasis and interest. A modern Christian, unless he realizes how great this difference is, will fail to understand the Christianity of the past. We, since our study is historical, are concerned with the effective beliefs of past centuries, and as to these it is impossible to disagree with what Dean Inge says on the influence of Plato and Plotinus.

Plotinus, however, is not *only* historically important. He represents, better than any other philosopher, an important type of theory. A philosophical system may be judged important for various different kinds of reasons. The first and most obvious is that we think it may be true. Not many students of philosophy at the present time would feel this about Plotinus; Dean Inge is, in this respect, a rare exception. But truth is not the only merit that a metaphysic can possess. It may have beauty, and this is certainly to be found in Plotinus; there are passages that remind one of the later cantos of Dante's *Paradiso*, and of almost nothing else in literature. Now and again, his descriptions of the eternal world of glory

> To our high-wrought fantasy present
> That undisturbed song of pure concent
> Aye sung before the sapphire-coloured throne
> To Him that sits thereon.

Again, a philosophy may be important because it expresses well what men are prone to believe in certain moods or in certain circumstances. Uncomplicated joy and sorrow is not matter for philosophy, but rather for the simpler kinds of poetry and music. Only joy and sorrow accompanied by reflection on the universe generate metaphysical theories. A man may be a cheerful pessimist or a melancholy optimist. Perhaps Samuel Butler may serve as an example of the first; Plotinus is an admirable example of the second. In an age such as that in which he lived, unhappiness is immediate and pressing, whereas happiness, if attainable at all, must be sought by reflection upon things that are remote from the impressions of sense. Such happiness has in it always an element of strain; it is very unlike the simple happiness of a child. And since it is not derived from the everyday world, but from thought and imagination, it demands a power of ignoring or despising the life of the senses. It is, therefore, not those who enjoy instinctive happiness who invent the kinds of metaphysical optimism that depend upon belief in the reality of a super-sensible world. Among the men who have been unhappy in a mundane sense, but resolutely determined to find a higher happiness in the world of theory, Plotinus holds a very high place.

Nor are his purely intellectual merits by any means to be despised. He has, in many respects, clarified Plato's teaching; he has developed, with as much consistency as possible, the type of theory advocated by him in common with many others. His arguments against materialism are good, and his whole conception of the relation of soul and body is clearer than that of Plato or Aristotle.

Like Spinoza, he has a certain kind of moral purity and loftiness, which is very impressive. He is always sincere, never shrill or censorious, invariably concerned to tell the reader, as simply as he can, what he believes to be important. Whatever one may think of him as a theoretical philosopher, it is impossible not to love him as a man.

The life of Plotinus is known, so far as it is known, through the biography written by his friend and disciple Porphyry, a Semite whose real name was Malchus. There are, however, miraculous elements in this account, which make it difficult to place a complete reliance upon its more credible portions.

Plotinus considered his spatio-temporal appearance unimportant, and was loath to talk about the accidents of his historical existence. He stated, however, that he was born in Egypt, and it is known that as a young man he studied in Alexandria, where he lived until the age of thirty-nine, and where his teacher was Ammonius Saccas, often regarded as the founder of Neoplatonism. He then joined the expedition of the Emperor Gordian III against the Persians, with the intention, it is said, of studying the religions of the East. The Emperor was still a youth, and was murdered by the army, as was at that time the custom. This occurred during his campaign in Mesopotamia in A.D. 244. Plotinus thereupon abandoned his oriental projects and settled in Rome, where he soon began to teach. Among his hearers were many influential men, and he was favoured by the Emperor Gallienus.[1] At one time he formed a project of founding Plato's Republic in Campania, and building for the purpose a new city to be called Platonopolis. The Emperor, at first, was favourable, but ultimately withdrew his permission. It may seem strange that there should be room for a new city so near Rome, but probably by that time the region was malarial, as it is now, but had not been earlier. He wrote nothing until the age of forty-nine; after that, he wrote much. His works were edited and arranged by Porphyry, who was more Pythagorean than Plotinus, and caused the Neoplatonist school to become more supernaturalist than it would have been if it had followed Plotinus more faithfully.

The respect of Plotinus for Plato is very great; Plato is usually alluded to as 'He'. In general, the 'blessed ancients' are treated with reverence, but this reverence does not extend to the atomists. The Stoics and Epicureans, being still active, are controverted, the Stoics only for their materialism, the Epicureans for every part of their philosophy. Aristotle plays a larger part than appears, as borrowings from him are often unacknowledged. One feels the influence of Parmenides at many points.

The Plato of Plotinus is not so full-blooded as the real Plato. The theory of ideas, the mystical doctrines of the *Phaedo* and of Book VI of the *Republic*, and the discussion of love in the *Symposium*, make up almost the whole of Plato as he appears in the *Enneads* (as the books of Plotinus are called). The political interests, the search for definitions of separate virtues, the pleasure in mathematics, the dramatic and affectionate appreciation of individuals, and above all the playfulness of Plato, are wholly absent from Plotinus. Plato, as Carlyle said is 'very much at his ease in Zion'; Plotinus, on the contrary, is always on his best behaviour.

The metaphysics of Plotinus begins with a Holy Trinity: The One, Spirit and Soul. These three are not equal, like the Persons of the Christian Trinity; the One is supreme, Spirit comes next, and Soul last.[2]

---

[1] Concerning Gallienus, Gibbon remarks: 'He was a master of several curious but useless sciences, a ready orator and an elegant poet, a skilful gardener, an excellent cook, and most contemptible prince. When the great emergencies of the State required his presence and attention, he was engaged in conversation with the philosopher Plotinus, wasting his time in trifling or licentious pleasures, preparing his initiation to the Grecian mysteries, or soliciting a place in the Areopagus of Athens' (chap. x).

[2] Origen, who was a contemporary of Plotinus and had the same teacher in philosophy, taught that the First Person was superior to the Second, and the Second to the Third, agreeing in this with Plotinus. But Origen's view was subsequently declared heretical.

The One is somewhat shadowy. It is sometimes called God, some-times the Good; it transcends Being, which is the first sequent upon the One. We must not attribute predicates to it, but only say 'It is.' (This is reminiscent of Parmenides.) It would be a mistake to speak of God as 'the All', because God transcends the All. God is present through all things. The One can be present without any coming: 'while it is nowhere, nowhere is it not'. Although the One is some-times spoken of as the Good, we are also told that it precedes both the Good and the Beautiful.[1] Sometimes, the One appears to re-semble Aristotle's God; we are told that God has no need of His derivatives, and ignores the created world. The One is indefinable, and in regard to it there is more truth in silence than in any words whatever.

We now come to the Second Person, whom Plotinus calls *nous*. It is always difficult to find an English word to represent *nous*. The standard dictionary translation is 'mind', but this does not have the correct connotations, particularly when the word is used in a religious philosophy. If we were to say that Plotinus put mind above soul, we should give a completely wrong impression. McKenna, the translator of Plotinus, uses 'Intellectual-Principle', but this is awk-ward, and does not suggest an object suitable for religious venera-tion. Dean Inge uses 'Spirit', which is perhaps the best word avail-able. But it leaves out the intellectual element which was important in all Greek religious philosophy after Pythagoras. Mathematics, the world of ideas, and all thought about what is not sensible, have, for Pythagoras, Plato, and Plotinus, something divine; they con-stitute the activity of *nous*, or at least the nearest approach to its activity that we can conceive. It was this intellectual element in Plato's religion that led Christians—notably the author of Saint John's Gospel—to identify Christ with the *Logos*. *Logos* should be translated 'reason' in this connection; this prevents us from using 'reason' as the translation of *nous*. I shall follow Dean Inge in using 'Spirit', but with the proviso that *nous* has an intellectual connota-tion which is absent from 'Spirit' as usually understood. But often I shall use the word *nous* untranslated.

Nous, we are told, is the image of the One; it is engendered because the One, in its self-quest, has vision; this seeing is *nous*. This is a difficult conception. A Being without parts, Plotinus says, may know itself; in this case, the seer and the seen are one. In God, who is conceived, as by Plato, on the analogy of the sun, the light-giver and what is lit are the same. Pursuing the analogy, *nous* may be considered as the light by which the One sees itself. It is possible for us to know the Divine Mind, which we forget through self-will.

[1] *Fifth Ennead*, Fifth Tractate, chap. 12.

To know the Divine Mind, we must study our own soul when it is most god-like: we must put aside the body, and the part of the soul that moulded the body, and 'sense with desires and impulses and every such futility'; what is then left is an image of the Divine Intellect.

'Those divinely possessed and inspired have at least the knowledge that they hold some greater thing within them, though they cannot tell what it is; from the movements that stir them and the utterances that come from them they perceive the power, not themselves, that moves them: in the same way, it must be, we stand towards the Supreme when we hold *nous* pure; we know the Divine Mind within, that which gives Being and all else of that order: but we know, too, that other, know that it is none of these, but a nobler principle than anything we know as Being; fuller and greater; above reason, mind, and feeling; conferring these powers, not to be confounded with them.'[1]

Thus when we are 'divinely possessed and inspired' we see not only *nous*, but also the One. When we are thus in contact with the Divine, we cannot reason or express the vision in words; this comes later. 'At the moment of touch there is no power whatever to make any affirmation; there is no leisure; reasoning upon the vision is for afterwards. We may know we have had the vision when the Soul has suddenly taken light. This light is from the Supreme and is the Supreme; we may believe in the Presence when, like that other God on the call of a certain man, He comes bringing light; the light is the proof of the advent. Thus, the Soul unlit remains without that vision; lit, it possesses what it sought. And this is the true end set before the Soul, to take that light, to see the Supreme by the Supreme and not by the light of any other principle—to see the Supreme which is also the means to the vision; for that which illumines the Soul is that which it is to see just as it is by the sun's own light that we see the sun.

But how is this to be accomplished?
Cut away everything.[2]

The experience of 'ecstasy' (standing outside one's own body) happened frequently to Plotinus:

Many times it has happened: Lifted out of the body into myself; becoming external to all other things and self-encentred; beholding a marvellous beauty; then, more than ever, assured of community with the loftiest order; enacting the noblest life, acquiring

[1] *Enneads*, V, 3, 14. McKenna's translation.
[2] *Enneads*, V, 3, 17.

identity with the divine; stationing within It by having attained that activity; poised above whatsoever in the Intellectual is less than the Supreme: yet, there comes the moment of descent from intellection to reasoning, and after that sojourn in the divine, I ask myself how it happens that I can now be descending, and how did the Soul ever enter into my body, the Soul which even within the body, is the high thing it has shown itself to be.[1]

This brings us to Soul, the third and lowest member of the Trinity. Soul, though inferior to *nous*, is the author of all living things; it made the sun and moon and stars, and the whole visible world. It is the offspring of the Divine Intellect. It is double: there is an inner soul, intent on *nous*, and another, which faces the external. The latter is associated with a downward movement, in which the Soul generates its image, which is Nature and the world of sense. The Stoics had identified Nature with God, but Plotinus regards it as the lowest sphere, something emanating from the Soul when it forgets to look upward towards *nous*. This might suggest the Gnostic view that the visible world is evil, but Plotinus does not take this view. The visible world is beautiful, and is the abode of blessed spirits; it is only less good than the intellectual world. In a very interesting controversial discussion of the Gnostic view, that the cosmos and its Creator are evil, he admits that some parts of Gnostic doctrine, such as the hatred of matter, may be due to Plato, but holds that the other parts, which do not come from Plato, are untrue.

His objections to Gnosticism are of two sorts. On the one hand, he says that Soul, when it creates the material world, does so from memory of the divine, and not because it is fallen; the world of sense, he thinks, is as good as a sensible world can be. He feels strongly the beauty of things perceived by the senses:

Who that truly perceives the harmony of the Intellectual Realm could fail, if he has any bent towards music, to answer to the harmony in sensible sounds? What geometrician or arithmetician could fail to take pleasure in the symmetries, correspondences and principles of order observed in visible things? Consider, even, the case of pictures: those seeing by the bodily sense the productions of the art of painting do not see the one thing in the one only way; they are deeply stirred by recognizing in the objects depicted to the eyes the presentation of what lies in the idea, and so are called to recollection of the truth—the very experience out of which Love rises. Now, if the sight of Beauty excellently reproduced upon a face hurries the mind to that other Sphere, surely no one seeing the loveliness lavish in the world of sense—this vast orderliness, the

[1] IV, 8, 1.

295

form which the stars even in their remoteness display, no one could be so dull-witted, so immoveable, as not to be carried by all this to recollection, and gripped by reverent awe in the thought of all this, so great, sprung from that greatness. Not to answer thus could only be to have neither fathomed this world nor had any vision of that other (II, 9 16).

There is another reason for rejecting the Gnostic view. The Gnostics think that nothing divine is associated with the sun, moon, and stars; they were created by an evil spirit. Only the soul of man, among things perceived, has any goodness. But Plotinus is firmly persuaded that the heavenly bodies are the bodies of god-like beings, immeasurably superior to man. According to the Gnostics, 'their own soul, the soul of the least of mankind, they declare deathless, divine; but the entire heavens and the stars within the heavens have had no communion with the Immortal Principle, though these are far purer and lovelier than their own souls' (II, 9, 5). For the view of Plotinus there is authority in the *Timaeus*, and it was adopted by some Christian Fathers, for instance, Origen. It is imaginatively attractive; it expresses feelings that the heavenly bodies naturally inspire, and makes man less lonely in the physical universe.

There is in the mysticism of Plotinus nothing morose or hostile to beauty. But he is the last religious teacher, for many centuries, of whom this can be said. Beauty, and all the pleasures associated with it, came to be thought to be of the Devil; pagans, as well as Christians, came to glorify ugliness and dirt. Julian the Apostate, like contemporary orthodox saints, boasted of the populousness of his beard. Of all this, there is nothing in Plotinus.

Matter is created by Soul, and has no independent reality. Every Soul has it hour; when that strikes, it descends, and enters the body suitable to it. The motive is not reason, but something more analogous to sexual desire. When the soul leaves the body, it must enter another body if it has been sinful, for justice requires that it should be punished. If, in this life, you have murdered your mother, you will, in the next life, be a woman, and be murdered by your son (III, 2, 13). Sin must be punished; but the punishment happens naturally, through the restless driving of the sinner's errors.

Do we remember this life after we are dead? The answer is perfectly logical, but not what most modern theologians would say. Memory is concerned with our life in time, whereas our best and truest life is in eternity. Therefore, as the soul grows towards eternal life, it will remember less and less; friends, children, wife, will be gradually forgotten; ultimately, we shall know nothing of the things of this world, but only contemplate the intellectual realm. There will be no memory of personality, which, in contemplative vision, is unaware of itself. The soul will become one with *nous*, but not to its own destruction: *nous* and the individual soul will be simultaneously two *and* one (IV, 4, 2).

In the *Fourth Ennead*, which is on the Soul, one section, the Seventh Tractate, is devoted to the discussion of immortality.

The body, being compound, is clearly not immortal; if, then, it is part of us, we are not wholly immortal. But what is the relation of the soul to the body? Aristotle (who is not mentioned explicitly) said the soul was the form of the body, but Plotinus rejects this view, on the ground that the intellectual act would be impossible if the soul were any form of body. The Stoics think that the soul is material, but the unity of the soul proves that this is impossible. Moreover, since matter is passive, it cannot have created itself; matter could not exist if soul had not created it, and, if soul did not exist, matter would disappear in a twinkling. The soul is neither matter nor the form of a material body, but Essence, and Essence is eternal. This view is implicit in Plato's argument that the soul is immortal because ideas are eternal; but it is only with Plotinus that it becomes explicit.

How does the soul enter the body from the aloofness of the intellectual world? The answer is, through appetite. But appetite though sometimes ignoble, may be comparatively noble. At best, the soul 'has the desire of elaborating order on the model of what it has seen in the Intellectual-Principle (*nous*)'. That is to say, soul contemplates the inward realm of essence, and wishes to produce something, as like it as possible, that can be seen by looking without instead of looking within—like (we might say) a composer who first imagines his music, and then wishes to hear it performed by an orchestra.

But this desire of the soul to create has unfortunate results. So long as the soul lives in the pure world of essence, it is not separated from other souls living in the same world; but as soon as it becomes joined to a body, it has the task of governing what is lower than itself, and by this task it becomes separate from other souls, which have other bodies. Except in a few men at a few moments, the soul becomes chained to the body. 'The body obscures the truth, but there[1] all stands out clear and separate' (IV, 9, 5).

This doctrine, like Plato's, has difficulty in avoiding the view that the creation was a mistake. The soul at its best is content with *nous*, the world of essence; if it were always at its best, it would not create, but only contemplate. It seems that the act of creation is to

[1] Plotinus habitually uses 'There' as a Christian might—as it is used, for instance, in

The life that knows no ending,
The tearless life is There.

be excused on the ground that the created world, in its main lines, is the best that is logically possible; but this is a copy of the eternal world, and as such has the beauty that is possible to a copy. The most definite statement is in the Tractate on the Gnostics (II, 9, 8):

To ask why the Soul has created the Kosmos, is to ask why there is a Soul and why a Creator creates. The question, also, implies a beginning in the eternal and, further, represents creation as the act of a changeful Being who turns from this to that.

Those that think so must be instructed—if they would but bear with correction—in the nature of the Supernals, and brought to desist from that blasphemy of majestic powers which comes so easily to them, where all should be reverent scruple.

Even in the administration of the Universe there is no ground for such attack, for it affords manifest proof of the greatness of the Intellectual Kind.

This All that has emerged into life is no amorphous structure—like those lesser forms within it which are born night and day out of the lavishness of its vitality—the Universe is a life organised, effective, complex, all-comprehensive, displaying an unfathomable wisdom. How, then, can anyone deny that it is a clear image, beautifully formed, of the Intellectual Divinities? No doubt it is a copy, not original; but that is its very nature; it cannot be at once symbol and reality. But to say that it is an inadequate copy is false; nothing has been left out which a beautiful representation within the physical order could include.

Such a reproduction there must necessarily be—thought not by deliberation and contrivance—for the Intellectual could not be the last of things, but must have a double Act, one within itself, and one outgoing; there must, then, be something later than the Divine; for only the thing with which all power ends fails to pass downwards something of itself.

This is perhaps the best answer to the Gnostics that the principles of Plotinus make possible. The problem, in slightly different language, was inherited by Christian theologians; they, also, have found it difficult to account for the creation without allowing the blasphemous conclusion that, before it, something was lacking to the Creator. Indeed, their difficulty is greater than that of Plotinus, for he may say that the nature of Mind made creation inevitable, whereas, for the Christian, the world resulted from the untrammelled exercise of God's free will.

Plotinus has a very vivid sense of a certain kind of abstract beauty. In describing the position of Intellect as intermediate between the One and Soul, he suddenly bursts out into a passage of rare eloquence:

The Supreme in its progress could never be borne forward upon some soulless vehicle nor even directly upon the Soul: it will be heralded by some ineffable beauty: before the Great King in his progress there comes first the minor train, then rank by rank the greater and more exalted, closer to the King the kinglier; next his own honoured company until, last among all these grandeurs, suddenly appears the Supreme Monarch himself, and all—unless indeed for those who have contented themselves with the spectacle before his coming and gone away—prostrate themselves and hail him (V, 5, 3).

There is a Tractate on Intellectual Beauty, which shows the same kind of feeling (V, 8):

Assuredly all the gods are august and beautiful in a beauty beyond our speech. And what makes them so? Intellect; and especially Intellect operating within them (the divine sun and stars) to visibility. . . .

To 'live at ease' is There; and to these divine beings verity is mother and nurse, existence and sustenance; all that is not of process but of authentic being they see, and themselves in all; for all is transparent, nothing dark, nothing resistant; every being is lucid to every other, in breadth and depth; light runs through light. And each of them contains all within itself, and at the same time sees all in every other, so that everywhere there is all, and all is all and each all, and infinite the glory. Each of them is great; the small is great; the sun, There, is all the stars; and every star, again, is all the stars and sun. While some manner of being is dominant in each, all are mirrored in every other.

In addition to the imperfection which the world inevitably possesses because it is a copy, there is, for Plotinus as for the Christians, the more positive evil that results from sin. Sin is a consequence of free will, which Plotinus upholds as against the determinists, and, more particularly, the astrologers. He does not venture to deny the validity of astrology altogether, but he attempts to set bounds to it, so as to make what remains compatible with free will. He does the same as regards magic; the sage, he says, is exempt from the power of the magician. Porphyry relates that a rival philosopher tried to put evil spells on Plotinus, but that, because of his holiness and wisdom, the spells recoiled on the rival. Porphyry, and all the followers of Plotinus, are much more superstitious than he is. Superstition, in him, is as slight as was possible in that age.

Let us now endeavour to sum up the merits and defects of the doctrine taught by Plotinus, and in the main accepted by Christian theology so long as it remained systematic and intellectual.

There is, first and foremost, the construction of what Plotinus believed to be a secure refuge for ideals and hopes, and one, more-over, which involved both moral and intellectual effort. In the third century, and in the centuries after the barbarian invasion, western civilization came near to total destruction. It was fortunate that, while theology was almost the sole surviving mental activity, the system that was accepted was not purely superstitious, but pre-served, though sometimes deeply buried, doctrines which embodied much of the work of Greek intellect and much of the moral devo-tion that is common to the Stoics and the Neoplatonists. This made possible the rise of the scholastic philosophy, and later, with the Renaissance, the stimulus derived from the renewed study of Plato, and thence of the other ancients.

On the other hand, the philosophy of Plotinus has the defect of encouraging men to look within rather than to look without: when we look within we see *nous*, which is divine, while when we look without we see the imperfections of the sensible world. This kind of subjectivity was a gradual growth; it is to be found in the doc-trines of Protagoras, Socrates, and Plato, as well as in the Stoics and Epicureans. But at first it was only doctrinal, not temperamental; for a long time it failed to kill scientific curiosity. We saw how Posidonius, about 100 B.C., travelled to Spain and the Atlantic coast of Africa to study the tides. Gradually, however, subjectivism invaded men's feelings as well as their doctrines. Science was no longer cultivated, and only virtue was thought important. Virtue, as conceived by Plato, involved all that was then possible in the way of mental achievement; but in later centuries it came to be thought of, increasingly, as involving only the virtuous will, and not a desire to understand the physical world or improve the world of human institutions. Christianity, in its ethical doctrines, was not free from this defect, although in practice belief in the importance of spreading the Christian faith gave a practicable object for moral activity, which was no longer confined to the perfecting of self.

Plotinus is both an end and a beginning—an end as regards the Greeks, a beginning as regards Christendom. To the ancient world, weary with centuries of disappointment, exhausted by despair, his doctrine might be acceptable, but could not be stimulating. To the cruder barbarian world, where superabundant energy needed to be restrained and regulated rather than stimulated, what could penetrate in his teaching was beneficial, since the evil to be com-bated was not languor but brutality. The work of transmitting what could survive of his philosophy was performed by the Christian philosophers of the last age of Rome.

BOOK TWO

CATHOLIC PHILOSOPHY

———————————

INTRODUCTION

CATHOLIC philosophy, in the sense in which I shall use the term, is that which dominated European thought from Augustine to the Renaissance. There have been philosophers, before and after this period of ten centuries, who belonged to the same general school. Before Augustine there were the early Fathers, especially Origen; after the Renaissance there are many, including, at the present day, all orthodox Catholic teachers of philosophy, who adhere to some medieval system, especially that of Thomas Aquinas. But it is only from Augustine to the Renaissance that the greatest philosophers of the age are concerned in building up or perfecting the Catholic synthesis. In the Christian centuries before Augustine, Stoics and Neoplatonists outshine the Fathers in philosophic ability; after the Renaissance, none of the outstanding philosophers, even among those who were orthodox Catholics, were concerned to carry on the Scholastic or the Augustinian tradition.

The period with which we shall be concerned in this book differs from earlier and later times not only in philosophy, but in many other ways. The most notable of these is the power of the Church. The Church brought philosophic beliefs into a closer relation to social and political circumstances than they have ever had before or since the medieval period, which we may reckon from about A.D. 400 to about A.D. 1400. The Church is a social institution built upon a creed, partly philosophic, partly concerned with sacred history. It achieved power and wealth by means of its creed. The lay rulers, who were in frequent conflict with it, were defeated because the great majority of the population, including most of the lay rulers themselves, were profoundly convinced of the truth of the Catholic faith. There were traditions, Roman and Germanic, against which the Church had to fight. The Roman tradition was strongest in Italy, especially among lawyers; the German tradition was strongest in the feudal aristocracy that arose out of the barbarian conquest. But for many centuries neither of these traditions proved strong enough to generate a successful opposition to the Church; and this was largely due to the fact that they were not embodied in any adequate philosophy.

A history of thought, such as that upon which we are engaged, is unavoidably one-sided in dealing with the Middle Ages. With very few exceptions, all the men of this period who contributed to the intellectual life of their time were churchmen. The laity in the Middle Ages slowly built up a vigorous political and economic system, but their activities were in a sense blind. There was in the later Middle Ages an important lay literature, very different from that of the Church; in a general history, this literature would demand more consideration than is called for in a history of philosophic thought. It is not until we come to Dante that we find a layman writing with full knowledge of the ecclesiastical philosophy of his time. Until the fourteenth century, ecclesiastics have a virtual monopoly of philosophy, and philosophy, accordingly, is written from the standpoint of the Church. For this reason, medieval thought cannot be made intelligible without a fairly extensive account of the growth of ecclesiastical institutions, and especially of the papacy.

The medieval world, as contrasted with the world of antiquity, is characterized by various forms of dualism. There is the dualism of clergy and laity, the dualism of Latin and Teuton, the dualism of the kingdom of God and the kingdoms of this world, the dualism of the spirit and the flesh. All these are exemplified in the dualism of Pope and Emperor. The dualism of Latin and Teuton is an outcome of the barbarian invasion, but the others have older sources. The relations of clergy and laity, for the Middle Ages, were to be modelled on the relations of Samuel and Saul; the demand for the supremacy of the clergy arose out of the period of Arian or semi-Arian emperors and kings. The dualism of the kingdom of God and the kingdoms of this world is found in the New Testament, but was systematized in Saint Augustine's *City of God*. The dualism of the spirit and the flesh is to be found in Plato, and was emphasized by the Neoplatonists; it is important in the teaching of St Paul; and it dominated the Christian asceticism of the fourth and fifth centuries.

Catholic philosophy is divided into two periods by the dark ages, during which, in Western Europe, intellectual activity was almost non-existent. From the conversion of Constantine to the death of Boethius, the thoughts of Christian philosophers are still dominated by the Roman Empire, either as an actuality or as a recent memory. The barbarians, in this period, are regarded merely as a nuisance, not as an independent part of Christendom. There is still a civilized community, in which all well-to-do people can read and write, and a philosopher has to appeal to the laity as well as to the clergy. Between this period and the dark ages, at the end of the sixth century, stands Gregory the Great, who regards himself as a subject of the Byzantine emperor, but is lordly in his attitude to barbarian kings. After his time, throughout Western Christendom, the separation of clergy and laity becomes more and more marked. The lay aristocracy creates the feudal system, which slightly tempers the prevailing turbulent anarchy; Christian humility is preached by the clergy, but practised only by the lower classes; pagan pride is embodied in the duel, trial by battle, tournaments, and private revenge, all of which the Church dislikes but cannot prevent. With great difficulty, beginning in the eleventh century, the Church succeeds in emancipating itself from the feudal aristocracy, and this emancipation is one of the causes of the emergence of Europe from the dark ages.

The first great period of Catholic philosophy was dominated by St Augustine, and by Plato among the pagans. The second period culminates in St Thomas Aquinas, for whom, and for his successors, Aristotle far outweighs Plato. The dualism of *The City of God*, however, survives in full force. The Church represents the City of God, and politically philosophers stand for the interests of the Church. Philosophy was concerned to defend the faith, and invoked reason to enable it to argue with those who, like the Mohammedans, did not accept the validity of the Christian revelation. By this invocation of reason the philosophers challenged criticism, not merely as theologians, but as inventors of systems designed to appeal to men of no matter what creed. In the long run, the appeal to reason was perhaps a mistake, but in the thirteenth century it seemed highly successful.

The thirteenth-century synthesis, which had an air of completeness and finality, was destroyed by a variety of causes. Perhaps the most important of these was the growth of a rich commercial class, first in Italy, and then elsewhere. The feudal aristocracy, in the main, had been ignorant, stupid, and barbaric; the common people had sided with the Church as superior to the nobles in intelligence, in morality, and in capacity to combat anarchy. But the new commercial class were as intelligent as the clergy, as well-informed in mundane matters, more capable of coping with the nobles, and more acceptable to the urban lower classes as champions of civic liberty. Democratic tendencies came to the fore, and after helping the Pope to defeat the Emperor, set to work to emancipate economic life from ecclesiastical control.

Another cause of the end of the Middle Ages was the rise of strong national monarchies in France, England, and Spain. Having suppressed internal anarchy, and allied themselves with the rich merchants against the aristocracy, the kings, after the middle of the fifteenth century, were strong enough to fight the Pope in the national interest.

The papacy, meanwhile, had lost the moral prestige which it had enjoyed, and on the whole deserved, in the eleventh, twelfth, and thirteenth centuries. First by subservience to France during the period when the popes lived at Avignon, then by the Great Schism, they had unintentionally persuaded the Western world that an unchecked papal autocracy was neither possible nor desirable. In the fifteenth century, their position as rulers of Christendom became subordinate, in practice, to their position as Italian princes, involved in the complex and unscrupulous game of Italian power politics.

And so the Renaissance and the Reformation disrupted the medieval synthesis, which has not yet been succeeded by anything so tidy and so apparently complete. The growth and decay of this synthesis is the subject of Book II.

The mood of thoughtful men, throughout the whole period, was one of deep unhappiness in regard to the affairs of this world, only rendered endurable by the hope of a better world hereafter. This unhappiness was a reflection of what was happening throughout Western Europe. The third century was a period of disaster, when the general level of well-being was sharply lowered. After a lull during the fourth century, the fifth brought the extinction of the Western Empire and the establishment of barbarians throughout its former territory. The cultivated urban rich, upon whom late Roman civilization depended, were largely reduced to the condition of destitute refugees; the remainder took to living on their rural estates. Fresh shocks continued until about A.D. 1000, without any sufficient breathing space to allow of recovery. The wars of Byzantines and Lombards destroyed most of what remained of the civilization of Italy. The Arabs conquered most of the territory of the Eastern Empire, established themselves in Africa and Spain, threatened France, and even, on one occasion, sacked Rome. The Danes and Normans caused havoc in France and England, in Sicily and Southern Italy. Life, throughout these centuries, was precarious and full of hardship. Bad as it was in reality, gloomy superstitions made it even worse. It was thought that the great majority even of Christians would go to hell. At every moment, men felt themselves encompassed by evil spirits, and exposed to the machinations of sorcerers and witches. No joy of life was possible, except, in fortunate moments, to those who retained the thoughtlessness of children. The general misery heightened the intensity of religious feeling. The life of the good here below was a pilgrimage to the heavenly city; nothing of value was possible in the sublunary world except the steadfast virtue that would lead, in the end, to eternal bliss. The Greeks, in their great days, had found joy and beauty in the everyday world. Empedocles, apostrophizing his fellow-citizens, says: 'Friends, that inhabit the great city looking down on the yellow rock of Acragas, up by the citadel, busy in goodly works, harbour of honour for the stranger, men unskilled in meanness, all hail.' In later times, until the Renaissance, men had no such simple happiness in the visible world, but turned their hopes to the unseen. Acragas is replaced in their love by Jerusalem the Golden. When earthly happiness at last returned, the intensity of longing for the other world grew gradually less. Men used the same words, but with a less profound sincerity.

In the attempt to make the genesis and significance of Catholic philosophy intelligible, I have found it necessary to devote more space to general history than is demanded in connection with either ancient or modern philosophy. Catholic philosophy is essentially the philosophy of an institution, namely the Catholic Church; modern philosophy, even when it is far from orthodox, is largely concerned with problems, especially in ethics and political theory, which are derived from Christian views of the moral law and from Catholic doctrines as to the relations of Church and State. In Graeco-Roman paganism there is no such dual loyalty as the Christian, from the very beginning, has owed to God and Caesar, or, in political terms, to Church and State.

The problems raised by this dual loyalty were, for the most part, worked out in practice before the philosophers supplied the necessary theory. In this process there were two very distinct stages: one before the fall of the Western Empire, and one after it. The practice of a long line of bishops, culminating in St Ambrose, supplied the basis for St Augustine's political philosophy. Then came the barbarian invasion, followed by a long time of confusion and increasing ignorance. Between Boethius and St Anselm, a period of over five centuries, there is only one eminent philosopher, John the Scot, and he, as an Irishman, had largely escaped the various processes that were moulding the rest of the Western world. But this period, in spite of the absence of philosophers, was not one during which there was no intellectual development. Chaos raised urgent practical problems, which were dealt with by means of institutions and modes of thought that dominated scholastic philosophy, and are, to a great extent, still important at the present day. These institutions and modes of thought were not introduced to the world by theorists but by practical men in the stress of conflict. The moral reform of the Church in the eleventh century, which was the immediate prelude to the scholastic philosophy, was a reaction against the increasing absorption of the Church into the feudal system. To understand the scholastics we must understand Hildebrand, and to understand Hildebrand we must know something of the evils against which he contended. Nor can we ignore the foundation of the Holy Roman Empire and its effect upon European thought.

For these reasons, the reader will find in the following pages much ecclesiastical and political history of which the relevance to the development of philosophic thought may not be immediately evident. It is the more necessary to relate something of this history as the period concerned is obscure, and is unfamiliar to many who are at home with both ancient and modern history. Few technical philosophers have had as much influence on philosophic thought as St Ambrose, Charlemagne, and Hildebrand. To relate what is essential concerning these men and their times is therefore indispensable in any adequate treatment of our subject.

PART I

THE FATHERS

Chapter I

THE RELIGIOUS DEVELOPMENT
OF THE JEWS

THE Christian religion, as it was handed over by the late Roman
Empire to the barbarians, consisted of three elements: first,
certain philosophical beliefs, derived mainly from Plato and
the Neoplatonists, but also in part from the Stoics; second, a conception of morals and history derived from the Jews; and third,
certain theories, more especially as to salvation, which were on the
whole new in Christianity, though in part traceable to Orphism,
and to kindred cults of the Near East.

The most important Jewish elements in Christianity appear to
me to be the following:

1. A sacred history, beginning with the Creation, leading to a
consummation in the future, and justifying the ways of God to
man.

2. The existence of a small section of mankind whom God
specially loves. For Jews, this section was the Chosen People; for
Christians, the elect.

3. A new conception of 'righteousness'. The virtue of almsgiving,
for example, was taken over by Christianity from later Judaism.
The importance attached to baptism might be derived from Orphism
or from oriental pagan mystery religions, but practical philanthropy, as an element in the Christian conception of virtue, seems
to have come from the Jews.

4. The Law. Christians kept part of the Hebrew Law, for instance
the Decalogue, while they rejected its ceremonial and ritual parts.
But in practice they attached to the Creed much the same feelings
that the Jews attached to the Law. This involved the doctrine that
correct belief is at least as important as virtuous action, a doctrine
which is essentially Hellenic. What is Jewish in origin is the
exclusiveness of the elect.

5. The Messiah. The Jews believed that the Messiah would bring
them temporal prosperity, and victory over their enemies here on
earth; moreover, he remained in the future. For Christians, the
Messiah was the historical Jesus, who was also identified with the
Logos of Greek philosophy; and it was not on earth, but in heaven,
that the Messiah was to enable his followers to triumph over their
enemies.

6. The Kingdom of Heaven. Other-worldliness is a conception which Jews and Christians, in a sense, share with later Platonism, but it takes, with them, a much more concrete form than with Greek philosophers. The Greek doctrine—which is to be found in much Christian philosophy, but not in popular Christianity—was that the sensible world, in space and time, is an illusion, and that, by intellectual and moral discipline, a man can learn to live in the eternal world, which alone is real. The Jewish and Christian doctrine, on the other hand, conceived the Other World as not *metaphysically* different from this world, but as in the future, when the virtuous would enjoy everlasting bliss and the wicked would suffer everlasting torment. This belief embodied revenge psychology, and was intelligible to all and sundry, as the doctrines of Greek philosophers were not.

To understand the origin of these beliefs, we must take account of certain facts in Jewish history, to which we will now turn our attention.

The early history of the Israelites cannot be confirmed from any source outside the Old Testament, and it is impossible to know at what point it ceases to be purely legendary. David and Solomon may be accepted as kings who probably had a real existence, but at the earliest points at which we come to something certainly historical there are already two kingdoms of Israel and Judah. The first person mentioned in the Old Testament of whom there is an independent record is Ahab, King of Israel, who is spoken of in an Assyrian letter of 853 B.C. The Assyrians finally conquered the Northern kingdom in 722 B.C., and removed a great part of the population. After this time, the kingdom of Judah alone preserved the Israelite religion and tradition. The kingdom of Judah just survived the Assyrians, whose power came to an end with the capture of Nineveh by the Babylonians and Medes in 606 B.C. But in 586 B.C. Nebuchadrezzar captured Jerusalem, destroyed the Temple, and removed a large part of the population to Babylon. The Babylonian kingdom fell in 538 B.C., when Babylon was taken by Cyrus, king of the Medes and Persians. Cyrus, in 537 B.C. issued an edict allowing the Jews to return to Palestine. Many of them did so, under the leadership of Nehemiah and Ezra; the Temple was rebuilt, and Jewish orthodoxy began to be crystallized.

In the period of the captivity, and for some time before and after this period, Jewish religion went through a very important development. Originally, there appears to have been not very much difference, from a religious point of view, between the Israelites and surrounding tribes. Yahweh was, at first, only a tribal god who favoured the children of Israel, but it was not denied that there were other gods, and their worship was habitual. When the first Commandment says 'Thou shalt have none other gods but me,' it is saying something which was an innovation in the time immediately preceding the captivity. This is made evident by various texts in the earlier prophets. It was the prophets at this time who first taught that the worship of heathen gods was sin. To win the victory in the constant wars of that time, they proclaimed, the favour of Yahweh was essential; and Yahweh would withdraw his favour if other gods were also honoured. Jeremiah and Ezekiel, especially, seem to have invented the idea that all religions except one are false, and that the Lord punishes idolatry.

Some quotations will illustrate their teachings, and the prevalence of the heathen practices against which they protested. 'Seest Thou not what they do in the cities of Judah and in the streets of Jeru-salem? The children gather wood, and the fathers kindle the fire, and the women knead their dough, to make cakes to the queen of heaven [Ishtar], and pour out drink offerings unto other gods, that they may provoke me to anger.'[1] The Lord is angry about it. 'And they have built the high places of Tophet, which is in the valley of the son of Hinnom, to burn their sons and their daughters in the fire; which I commanded them not, neither came it into my heart.'[2]

There is a very interesting passage in Jeremiah in which he denounces the Jews in Egypt for their idolatry. He himself had lived among them for a time. The prophet tells the Jewish refugees in Egypt that Yahweh will destroy them all because their wives have burnt incense to other gods. But they refuse to listen to him, saying: 'We will certainly do whatsoever thing goeth forth out of our own mouth, to burn incense unto the queen of heaven, and to pour out drink offerings unto her, as we have done, we and our fathers, our kings and our princes, in the cities of Judah, and in the streets of Jerusalem; for then had we plenty of victuals, and were well, and saw no evil.' But Jeremiah assures them that Yahweh noticed these idolatrous practices, and that misfortune has come because of them. 'Behold, I have sworn by my great name, saith the Lord, that my name shall no more be named in the mouth of any man of Judah in all the land of Egypt. . . . I will watch over them for evil, and not for good; and all the men of Judah that are in the land of Egypt shall be consumed by the sword and by the famine, until there be an end of them.'[3]

Ezekiel is equally shocked by the idolatrous practices of the Jews. The Lord in a vision shows him women at the north gate of the temple weeping for Tammuz (a Babylonian deity); then He shows him 'greater abominations', five and twenty men at the door of the

[1] Jeremiah vii, 17-18. [2] *Ibid.*, vii, 31. [3] Jeremiah xliv, 11-end.

temple worshipping the sun. The Lord declares: 'Therefore will I also deal in fury: mine eye shall not spare, neither will I have pity: and though they cry in mine ears with a loud voice, yet will I not hear them.'[1]

The idea that all religions but one are wicked, and that the Lord punishes idolatry, was apparently invented by these prophets. The prophets, on the whole, were fiercely nationalistic, and looked forward to the day when the Lord would utterly destroy the gentiles.

The captivity was taken to justify the denunciations of the prophets. If Yahweh was all-powerful, and the Jews were his Chosen People, their sufferings could only be explained by their wickedness. The psychology is that of paternal correction: the Jews are to be purified by punishment. Under the influence of this belief, they developed, in exile, an orthodoxy much more rigid and much more nationally exclusive than that which had prevailed while they were independent. The Jews who remained behind and were not transplanted to Babylon did not undergo this development to anything like the same extent. When Ezra and Nehemiah came back to Jerusalem after the captivity, they were shocked to find that mixed marriages had been common, and they dissolved all such marriages.[2]

The Jews were distinguished from the other nations of antiquity by their stubborn national pride. All the others, when conquered, acquiesced inwardly as well as outwardly; the Jews alone retained the belief in their own pre-eminence, and the conviction that their misfortunes were due to God's anger, because they had failed to preserve the purity of their faith and ritual. The historical books of the Old Testament, which were mostly compiled after the captivity, give a misleading impression, since they suggest that the idolatrous practices against which the prophets protested were a falling-off from earlier strictness, whereas in fact the earlier strictness had never existed. The prophets were innovators to a much greater extent than appears in the Bible when read unhistorically.

Some things which were afterwards characteristic of Jewish religion were developed, though in part from previously existing sources, during the captivity. Owing to the destruction of the Temple, where alone sacrifices could be offered, the Jewish ritual perforce became non-sacrificial. Synagogues began at this time, with readings from such portions of the Scriptures as already existed. The importance of the Sabbath was first emphasized at this time, and so was circumcision as the mark of the Jew. As we have already seen, it was only during the exile that marriage with gentiles came

[1] Ezekiel vii, 11-end. [2] Ezra ix-x, 5.

314

to be forbidden. There was a growth of every form of exclusiveness, 'I am the Lord your God, which have separated you from other people.'[1] 'Ye shall be holy, for I the Lord your God am holy.'[2] The Law is a product of this period. It was one of the chief forces in preserving national unity.

What we have as the Book of Isaiah is the work of two different prophets, one before the exile and one after. The second of these, who is called by Biblical students Deutero-Isaiah, is the most remarkable of the prophets. He is the first who reports the Lord as saying 'There is no God but I.' He believes in the resurrection of the body, perhaps as a result of Persian influence. His prophecies of the Messiah were, later, the chief Old Testament texts used to show that the prophets foresaw the coming of Christ.

In Christian arguments with both pagans and Jews, these texts from Deutero-Isaiah played a very important part, and for this reason I shall quote the most noteworthy of them. All nations are to be converted in the end: 'They shall beat their swords into ploughshares, and their spears into pruning-hooks: nation shall not lift up sword against nation, neither shall they learn war any more' (Is. ii, 4): 'Behold a virgin shall conceive and bear a son, and shall call his name Immanuel.'[3] (As to this text there was a controversy between Jews and Christians; the Jews said that the correct translation is 'a young woman shall conceive', but the Christians thought the Jews were lying.) 'The people that walked in darkness have seen a great light; they that dwell in the land of the shadow of death, upon them hath the light shined. . . . For unto us a child is born, unto us a son is given: and the government shall be upon his shoulder: and his name shall be called Wonderful, Counsellor, the mighty God, the everlasting Father, the Prince of Peace.'[4] The most apparently prophetic of these passages is the fifty-third chapter, which contains the familiar texts: 'He is despised and rejected of men; a man of sorrows and acquainted with grief. . . . Surely he hath borne our griefs, and carried our sorrows. . . . But he was wounded for our transgressions, he was bruised for our iniquities: the chastisement of our peace was upon him; and with his stripes we are healed. . . . He was oppressed, and he was afflicted, yet he opened not his mouth: he is brought as a lamb to the slaughter, and as a sheep before her shearers is dumb, so he openeth not his mouth.' The inclusion of the gentiles in the ultimate salvation is explicit: 'And the gentiles shall come to thy light, and kings to the brightness of thy rising.'[5]

After Ezra and Nehemiah, the Jews for a while disappear from

---

[1] Leviticus xx, 24. [2] *Ibid.*, xix, 2. [3] Isaiah vii, 14.
[4] *Ibid.*, x, 2, 6. [5] *Ibid*, lx, 3.

history. The Jewish State survived as a theocracy, but its territory was very small—only the region of ten to fifteen miles around Jerusalem, according to E. Bevan.[1] After Alexander, it became a disputed territory between the Ptolemies and Seleucids. This, however, seldom involved fighting in actual Jewish territory, and left the Jews, for a long time, to the free exercise of their religion.

Their moral maxims, at this time, are set forth in Ecclesiasticus, probably written about 200 B.C. Until recently, this book was only known in a Greek version; this is the reason for its being banished to the Apocrypha. But a Hebrew manuscript has lately been discovered, in some respects different from the Greek text translated in our version of the Apocrypha. The morality taught is very mundane. Reputation among neighbours is highly prized. Honesty is the best policy, because it is useful to have Yahweh on your side. Almsgiving is recommended. The only sign of Greek influence is in the praise of medicine.

Slaves must not be treated too kindly. 'Fodder, a wand, and burdens, are for the ass: and bread, correction, and work, for a servant. . . . Set him to work, as is fit for him: if he be not obedient, put on more heavy fetters' (xxiii, 24, 28). At the same time, remember that you have paid a price for him, and that if he runs away you will lose your money; this sets a limit to profitable severity (*ibid*, 30, 31). Daughters are a great source of anxiety; apparently in the writer's day they were much addicted to immorality (xlii, 9-11). He has a low opinion of women: 'From garments cometh a moth, and from women wickedness' (*ibid*., 13). It is a mistake to be cheerful with your children; the right course is to 'bow down their neck from their youth' (vii. 23, 24).

Altogether, like the elder Cato, he represents the morality of the virtuous business man in a very unattractive light.

This tranquil existence of comfortable self-righteousness was rudely interrupted by the Seleucid king Antiochus IV, who was determined to hellenize all his dominions. In 175 B.C. he established a gymnasium in Jerusalem, and taught young men to wear Greek hats and practise athletics. In this he was helped by a hellenizing Jew named Jason, whom he made high priest. The priestly aristocracy had become lax, and had felt the attraction of Greek civilization; but they were vehemently opposed by a party called the 'Hasidim' (meaning 'Holy'), who were strong among the rural population.[2] When, in 170 B.C., Antiochus became involved in war

---

[1] *Jerusalem under the High Priests*, p. 12.
[2] From them, probably, developed the sect of the Essenes, whose doctrines seem to have influenced primitive Christianity. See Oesterley and Robinson, *History of Israel*, Vol. II, p. 323 ff. The Pharisees also descended from them.

with Egypt, the Jews rebelled. Thereupon Antiochus took the holy vessels from the Temple, and placed in it the image of the God. He identified Yahweh with Zeus, following a practice which had been successful everywhere else.[1] He resolves to extirpate the Jewish religion, and to stop circumcision and the observance of the laws relating to food. To all this Jerusalem submitted, but outside Jerusalem the Jews resisted with the utmost stubbornness.

The history of this period is told in the first Book of Maccabees. The first chapter tells how Antiochus decreed that all the inhabitants of his kingdom should be one people, and abandon their separate laws. All the heathen obeyed, and many of the Israelites, although the king commanded that they should profane the sabbath, sacrifice swine's flesh, and leave their children uncircumcised. All who disobeyed were to suffer death. Many, nevertheless, resisted. 'They put to death certain women, that had caused their children to be circumcised. And they hanged the infants about their necks, and rifled their houses, and slew them that had circumcised them. Howbeit many in Israel were fully resolved and confirmed in themselves not to eat any unclean thing. Wherefore they chose rather to die, that they might not be defiled with meats, and that they mighty not profane the holy covenant: so then they died.'[2]

It was at this time that the doctrine of immortality came to be widely believed among the Jews. It had been thought that virtue would be rewarded here on earth; but persecution, which fell upon the most virtuous, made it evident that this was not the case. In order to safeguard divine justice, therefore, it was necessary to believe in rewards and punishments hereafter. This doctrine was not universally accepted among the Jews; in the time of Christ, the Sadducees still rejected it. But by that time they were a small party, and in later times all Jews believed in immortality.

The revolt against Antiochus was led by Judas Maccabæus, an able military commander, who first recaptured Jerusalem (164 B.C.), and then embarked upon aggression. Sometimes he killed all the males, sometimes he circumcised them by force. His brother Jonathan was made high priest, was allowed to occupy Jerusalem with a garrison, and conquered part of Samaria, acquiring Joppa and Akra. He negotiated with Rome, and was successful in securing complete autonomy. His family were high priests until Herod, and are known as the Hasmonean dynasts.

In enduring and resisting persecution the Jews of this time showed immense heroism, although in defence of things that do

[1] Some Alexandrian Jews did not object to this identification. See *Letter of Aristeas*, 15, 16.
[2] I Maccabees i, 60-3.

not strike us as important, such as circumcision and the wickedness of eating pork.

The time of the persecution by Antiochus IV was crucial in Jewish history. The Jews of the Dispersion were, at this time, becoming more and more hellenized; the Jews of Judea were few; and even among them the rich and powerful were inclined to acquiesce in Greek innovations. But for the heroic resistance of the Hasidim, the Jewish religion might easily have died out. If this had happened, neither Christianity nor Islam could have existed in anything like the form they actually took. Townsend, in his Introduction to the translation of the Fourth Book of Maccabees, says:

'It has been finely said that if Judaism as a religion had perished under Antiochus, the seed-bed of Christianity would have been lacking; and thus the blood of the Maccabean martyrs, who saved Judaism, ultimately became the seed of the Church. Therefore as not only Christendom but also Islam derive their monotheism from a Jewish source, it may well be that the world to-day owes the very existence of monotheism both in the East and in the West to the Maccabees.'[1]

The Maccabees themselves, however, were not admired by later Jews, because their family, as high priests, adopted, after their successes, a worldly and temporizing policy. Admiration was for the martyrs. The Fourth Book of Maccabees, written probably in Alexandria about the time of Christ, illustrates this as well as some other interesting points. In spite of its title, it nowhere mentions the Maccabees, but relates the amazing fortitude, first of an old man, and then of seven young brothers, all of whom were first tortured and then burnt by Antiochus, while their mother, who was present, exhorted them to stand firm. The king, at first, tried to win them by friendliness, telling them that, if they would only consent to eat pork, he would take them into his favour, and secure successful careers for them. When they refused, he showed them the instruments of torture. But they remained unshakable, telling him that he would suffer eternal torment after death, while they would inherit everlasting bliss. One by one, in each other's presence, and in that of their mother, they were first exhorted to eat pork, then, when they refused, tortured and killed. At the end, the king turned round to his soldiers and told them he hoped they would profit by such an example of courage. The account is of course embellished by legend, but it is historically true that the persecution was severe and was endured heroically; also that the main points at issue were circumcision and eating pork.

[1] *The Apocrypha and Pseudepigrapha of the Old Testament in English.* Edited by R. H. Charles, Vol. II, p. 659.

This book is interesting in another respect. Although the writer is obviously an orthodox Jew, he uses the language of the Stoic philosophy, and is concerned to prove that the Jews live most completely in accordance with its precepts. The book opens with the sentence:

'Philosophical in the highest degree is the question I propose to discuss, namely whether the Inspired Reason is supreme ruler over the passions; and to the philosophy of it I would seriously entreat your earnest attention.'

Alexandrian Jews were willing, in philosophy, to learn from the Greeks, but they adhered with extraordinary tenacity to the Law, especially circumcision, observance of the Sabbath, and abstinence from pork and other unclean meats. From the time of Nehemiah till after the fall of Jerusalem in A.D. 70, the importance that they attached to the Law steadily increased. They no longer tolerated prophets who had anything new to say. Those among them who felt impelled to write in the style of the prophets pretended that they had discovered an old book, by Daniel or Solomon or some other ancient of impeccable respectability. Their ritual peculiarities held them together as a nation, but emphasis on the Law gradually destroyed originality and made them intensely conservative. This rigidity makes the revolt of St Paul against the domination of the Law very remarkable.

The New Testament, however, is not such a completely new beginning as it is apt to seem to those who know nothing of Jewish literature in the times just before the birth of Christ. Prophetic fervour was by no means dead, though it had to adopt the device of pseudonymity, in order to obtain a hearing. Of the greatest interest, in this respect, is the Book of Enoch,[1] a composite work, due to various authors, the earliest being slightly before the time of the Maccabees, and the latest about 64 B.C. Most of it professes to relate apocalyptic visions of the patriarch Enoch. It is very important for the side of Judaism which turned to Christianity. The New Testament writers are familiar with it; St Jude considers it to be actually by Enoch. Early Christian Fathers, for instance Clement of Alexandria and Tertullian, treated it as canonical, but Jerome and Augustine rejected it. It fell, consequently, into oblivion, and was lost until, early in the nineteenth century, three manuscripts of it, in Ethiopic, were found in Abyssinia. Since then, manuscripts of parts of it have been found in Greek and Latin versions. It appears to have been originally written partly in Hebrew, partly in Aramaic. Its authors were members of the Hasidim, and their suc-

[1] For the text of this book, in English, see Charles, *op. cit.*, whose introduction also is valuable.

cessors the Pharisees. It denounces kings and princes, meaning the Hasmonean dynasty and the Sadducees. It influenced New Testament doctrine, particularly as regards the Messiah, Sheol (hell), and demonology.

The book consists mainly of 'parables', which are more cosmic than those of the New Testament. There are visions of heaven and hell, of the Last Judgment, and so on; one is reminded of the first two Books of *Paradise Lost* where the literary quality is good, and of Blake's Prophetic Books where it is inferior.

There is an expansion of Genesis vi. 2, 4, which is curious and Promethean. The angels taught men metallurgy, and were punished for revealing 'eternal secrets'. They were also cannibals. The angels that had sinned became pagan gods, and their women became sirens; but at the last, they were punished with everlasting torments.

There are descriptions of heaven and hell which have considerable literary merit. The Last Judgment is performed by 'the Son of Man, who hath righteousness' and who sits on the throne of His glory. Some of the gentiles, at the last, will repent and be forgiven; but most gentiles, and all hellenizing Jews, will suffer eternal damnation, for the righteous will pray for vengeance, and their prayer will be granted.

There is a section on astronomy, where we learn that the sun and moon have chariots driven by the wind, that the year consists of 364 days, that human sin causes the heavenly bodies to depart from their courses, and that only the virtuous can know astronomy. Falling stars are falling angels, and are punished by the seven archangels.

Next comes sacred history. Up to the Maccabees, this pursues the course known from the Bible in its earlier portions, and from history in the later parts. Then the author goes on into the future: the New Jerusalem, the conversion of the remnant of the gentiles the resurrection of the righteous, and the Messiah.

There is a great deal about the punishment of sinners and the reward of the righteous, who never display an attitude of Christian forgiveness towards sinners. 'What will ye do, ye sinners, and whither will ye flee on that day of judgment, when ye hear the voice of the prayer of the righteous?' 'Sin has not been sent upon the earth, but man of himself has created it.' Sins are recorded in heaven. 'Ye sinners shall be cursed for ever, and ye shall have no peace.' Sinners may be happy all their lives, and even in dying, but their souls descend into Sheol, where they shall suffer 'darkness and chains and a burning flame'. But as for the righteous, 'I and my Son will be united with them for ever.'

The last words of the book are: 'To the faithful he will give faithfulness in the habitation of upright paths. And they shall see those who were born in darkness led into darkness, while the righteous shall be resplendent. And the sinners shall cry aloud and see them resplendent, and they indeed will go where days and seasons are prescribed for them.'

Jews, like Christians, thought much about sin, but few of them thought of *themselves* as sinners. This was, in the main, a Christian innovation, introduced by the parable of the Pharisee and the publican, and taught as a virtue in Christ's denunciations of the Scribes and Pharisees. The Christians endeavoured to practise Christian humility; the Jews, in general, did not.

There are, however, important exceptions among orthodox Jews just before the time of Christ. Take, for instance, 'The Testaments of the Twelve Patriarchs,' written between 109 and 107 B.C. by a Pharisee who admired John Hyrcanus, a high priest of the Hasmonean dynasty. This book, in the form in which we have it, contains Christian interpolations, but these are all concerned with dogma. When they are excised, the ethical teaching remains closely similar to that of the Gospels. As the Rev. Dr R. H. Charles says: 'The Sermon on the Mount reflects in several instances the spirit and even reproduces the very phrases of our text: many passages in the Gospels exhibit traces of the same, and St Paul seems to have used the book as a vade mecum' (*op. cit.*, pp. 291-2). We find in this book such precepts as the following:

'Love ye one another from the heart; and if a man sin against thee, speak peaceably to him, and in thy soul hold not guile; and if he repent and confess, forgive him. But if he deny it, do not get into a passion with him, lest catching the poison from thee he take to swearing, and so then sin doubly. . . . And if he be shameless and persist in wrong-doing, even so forgive him from the heart, and leave to God the avenging.'

Dr Charles is of opinion that Christ must have been acquainted with this passage. Again we find:

'Love the Lord and your neighbour.'

'Love the Lord through all your life, and one another with a true heart.'

'I love the Lord; likewise also every man with all my heart.' These are to be compared with Matthew xxii, 37-39. There is a reprobation of all hatred in 'The Testaments of the Twelve Patriarchs'; for instance:

'Anger is blindness, and does not suffer one to see the face of any man with truth.'

'Hatred, therefore, is evil; for it constantly mateth with lying.' The author of this book, as might be expected, holds that not only

321

the Jews, but all the gentiles, will be saved.

Christians have learnt from the Gospels to think ill of Pharisees, yet the author of this book was a Pharisee, and he taught, as we have seen, those very ethical maxims which we think of as most distinctive of Christ's preaching. The explanation, however, is not difficult. In the first place, he must have been, even in his own day, an exceptional Pharisee; the more usual doctrine was, no doubt, that of the Book of Enoch. In the second place, we know that all movements tend to ossify; who could infer the principles of Jefferson from those of the Daughters of the American Revolution? In the third place, we know, as regards the Pharisees in particular, that their devotion to the Law, as the absolute and final truth, soon put an end to all fresh and living thought and feeling among them. As Dr Charles says:

'When Pharisaism, breaking with the ancient ideals of its party, committed itself to political interests and movements, and concurrently therewith surrendered itself more and more wholly to the study of the letter of the Law, it soon ceased to offer scope for the development of such a lofty system of ethics as the Testaments [of the Patriarchs] attest, and so the true successors of the early Hasids and their teaching quitted Judaism and found their natural home in the bosom of primitive Christianity.'

After a period of rule by the High Priests, Mark Antony made his friend Herod King of the Jews. Herod was a gay adventurer, often on the verge of bankruptcy, accustomed to Roman society, and very far removed from Jewish piety. His wife was of the family of the high priests, but he was an Idumæan, which alone would suffice to make him an object of suspicion to the Jews. He was a skilful time-server, and deserted Antony promptly when it became evident that Octavius was going to be victorious. However, he made strenuous attempts to reconcile the Jews to his rule. He rebuilt the Temple, though in a hellenistic style, with rows of Corinthian pillars; but he placed over the main gate a large golden eagle, thereby infringing the second Commandment. When it was rumoured that he was dying, the Pharisees pulled down the eagle, but he, in revenge, caused a number of them to be put to death. He died in 4 B.C., and soon after his death the Romans abolished the kingship, putting Judea under a procurator. Pontius Pilate, who became procurator in A.D. 26, was tactless, and was soon retired.

In A.D. 66, the Jews, led by the party of the Zealots, rebelled against Rome. They were defeated, and Jerusalem was captured in A.D. 70. The Temple was destroyed, and few Jews were left in Judea.

The Jews of the Dispersion had become important centuries before this time. The Jews had been originally an almost wholly agricultural people, but they learnt trading from the Babylonians during the captivity. Many of them remained in Babylon after the time of Ezra and Nehemiah, and among these some were very rich. After the foundation of Alexandria, great numbers of Jews settled in that city; they had a special quarter assigned to them, not as a ghetto, but to keep them from danger of pollution by contact with gentiles. The Alexandrian Jews became much more hellenized than those of Judea, and forgot Hebrew. For this reason it became necessary to translate the Old Testament into Greek; the result was the Septuagint. The Pentateuch was translated in the middle of the third century B.C.; the other parts somewhat later.

Legends arose about the Septuagint, so called because it was the work of seventy translators. It was said that each of the seventy translated the whole independently, and that when the versions were compared they were found to be identical down to the smallest detail, having all been divinely inspired. Nevertheless, later scholarship showed that the Septuagint was gravely defective. The Jews, after the rise of Christianity, made little use of it, but reverted to reading the Old Testament in Hebrew. The early Christians, on the contrary, few of whom knew Hebrew, depended upon the Septuagint, or upon translations from it into Latin. A better text was produced by the labours of Origen in the third century, but those who only knew Latin had very defective versions until Jerome, in the fifth century, produced the Vulgate. This was, at first, received with much criticism, because he had been helped by Jews in establishing the text, and many Christians thought that Jews had deliberately falsified the prophets in order that they should not seem to foretell Christ. Gradually, however, the work of St Jerome was accepted, and it remains to this day authoritative in the Catholic Church.

The philosopher Philo, who was a contemporary of Christ, is the best illustration of Greek influence on the Jews in the sphere of thought. While orthodox in religion, Philo is, in philosophy primarily a Platonist; other important influences are those of the Stoics and Neo-pythagoreans. While his influence among the Jews ceased after the fall of Jerusalem, the Christian Fathers found that he had shown the way to reconcile Greek philosophy with acceptance of the Hebrew Scriptures.

In every important city of antiquity there came to be considerable colonies of Jews, who shared with the representatives of other Eastern religions an influence upon those who were not content either with scepticism or with the official religions of Greece and Rome. Many converts were made to Judaism, not only in the Empire, but also in South Russia. It was probably to Jewish and semi-Jewish circles that Christianity first appealed. Orthodox Judaism, however, became more orthodox and more narrow after the fall of Jerusalem, just as it had done after the earlier fall due to Nebuchadrezzar. After the first century, Christianity also crystallized, and the relations of Judaism and Christianity were wholly hostile and external; as we shall see, Christianity powerfully stimulated anti-Semitism. Throughout the Middle Ages, Jews had no part in the culture of Christian countries, and were too severely persecuted to be able to make contributions to civilization, beyond supplying capital for the building of cathedrals and such enterprises. It was only among the Mohammedans, at that period, that Jews were treated humanely, and were able to pursue philosophy and enlightened speculation.

Throughout the Middle Ages, the Mohammedans were more civilized and more humane than the Christians. Christians persecuted Jews, especially at times of religious excitement; the Crusades were associated with appalling pogroms. In Mohammedan countries, on the contrary, Jews at most times were not in any way ill treated. Especially in Moorish Spain, they contributed to learning; Maimonides (1135-1204), who was born at Cordova, is regarded by some as the source of much of Spinoza's philosophy. When the Christians reconquered Spain, it was largely the Jews who transmitted to them the learning of the Moors. Learned Jews, who knew Hebrew, Greek, and Arabic, and were acquainted with the philosophy of Aristotle, imparted their knowledge to less learned schoolmen. They transmitted also less desirable things, such as alchemy and astrology.

After the Middle Ages, the Jews still contributed largely to civilization as individuals, but no longer as a race.

Chapter II

CHRISTIANITY DURING THE FIRST FOUR CENTURIES

CHRISTIANITY, at first, was preached by Jews to Jews, as a reformed Judaism. St James, and to a lesser extent St Peter, wished it to remain no more than this, and they might have prevailed but for St Paul, who was determined to admit gentiles without demanding circumcision or submission to the Mosaic Law. The contention between the two factions is related in the Acts of the Apostles, from a Pauline point of view. The communities of Christians that St Paul established in many places, were, no doubt, composed partly of converts from among the Jews, partly of gentiles seeking a new religion. The certainties of Judaism made it attractive in that age of dissolving faiths, but circumcision was an obstacle to the conversion of men. The ritual laws in regard to food were also inconvenient. These two obstacles, even if there had been no others, would have made it almost impossible for the Hebrew religion to become universal. Christianity, owing to St Paul, retained what was attractive in the doctrines of the Jews, without the features that gentiles found hardest to assimilate.

The view that the Jews were the Chosen People remained, however, obnoxious to Greek pride. This view was radically rejected by the Gnostics. They, or at least some of them, held that the sensible world had been created by an inferior deity named Ialdabaoth, the rebellious son of Sophia (heavenly wisdom). He, they said, is the Yahweh of the Old Testament, while the serpent, so far from being wicked, was engaged in warning Eve against his deceptions. For a long time, the supreme deity allowed Ialdabaoth free play; at last He sent His Son to inhabit temporarily the body of the man Jesus, and to liberate the world from the false teaching of Moses. Those who held this view, or something like it, combined it, as a rule, with a Platonic philosophy; Plotinus, as we saw, found some difficulty in refuting it. Gnosticism afforded a half-way house between philosophic paganism and Christianity, for, while it honoured Christ, it thought ill of the Jews. The same was true, later, of Manichæism, through which St Augustine came to the Catholic Faith. Manichæism combined Christian and Zoroastrian elements, teaching that evil is a positive prinicple, embodied in matter, while the good principle is embodied in spirit. It condemned meat-eating, and all sex, even in marriage. Such intermediate doctrines helped much in the gradual conversion of cultivated men of Greek speech; but the New Testament warns true believers against them: 'O Timothy, keep that which is committed to thy trust, avoiding profane and vain babblings, and oppositions of science [Gnosis] falsely so called: which some professing have erred concerning the faith.'[1]

Gnostics and Manichæans continued to flourish until the government became Christian. After that time they were led to conceal their beliefs, but they still had a subterranean influence. One of the doctrines of a certain sect of Gnostics was adopted by Mohammed. They taught that Jesus was a mere man, and that the Son of God descended upon him at the baptism, and abandoned him at the time of the Passion. In support of this view they appealed to the text: 'My God, my God, why hast thou forsaken me?'[2]—a text which, it must be confessed, Christians have always found difficult. The Gnostics considered it unworthy of the Son of God to be born, to be an infant, and, above all, to die on the cross; they said that these things had befallen the man Jesus, but not the divine Son of God. Mohammed, who recognized Jesus as a prophet, though not as divine, had a strong class feeling that prophets ought not to come to a bad end. He therefore adopted the view of the Docetics (a Gnostic sect), according to which it was a mere phantom that hung upon the cross, upon which, impotently and ignorantly, Jews and Romans wreaked their ineffectual vengeance. In this way, something of Gnosticism passed over into the orthodox doctrine of Islam.

The attitude of Christians to contemporary Jews early became hostile. The received view was that God had spoken to the patriarchs and prophets, who were holy men, and had foretold the coming of Christ; but when Christ came, the Jews failed to recognize Him, and were thenceforth to be accounted wicked. Moreover Christ had abrogated the Mosaic Law, substituting the two commandments to love God and our neighbour; this, also, the Jews perversely failed to recognize. As soon as the State became Christian, anti-Semitism, in its medieval form, began, nominally as a manifestation of Christian zeal. How far the economic motives, by which it was inflamed in later times, operated in the Christian Empire, it seems impossible to ascertain.

In proportion as Christianity became hellenized, it became theological. Jewish theology was always simple. Yahweh developed from a tribal deity into the sole omnipotent God who created heaven and earth; divine justice, when it was seen not to confer earthly prosperity upon the virtuous, was transferred to heaven, which

[1] I Timothy vi, 20, 21.
[2] Mark xxv, 34.

entailed belief in immortality. But throughout its evolution the Jewish creed involved nothing complicated and metaphysical; it had no mysteries, and every Jew could understand it.

This Jewish simplicity, on the whole, still characterizes the synoptic Gospels (Matthew, Mark, and Luke), but has already disappeared in St John, where Christ is identified with the Platonic-Stoic Logos. It is less Christ the Man than Christ the theological figure that interests the fourth evangelist. This is still more true of the Fathers; you will find, in their writings, many more allusions to St John than to the other three gospels put together. The Pauline epistles also contain much theology, especially as regards salvation; at the same time they show a considerable acquaintance with Greek culture—a quotation from Menander, an allusion to Epimenides the Cretan who said that all Cretans are liars, and so on. Nevertheless St Paul[1] says: 'Beware lest any man spoil you through philosophy and vain deceit.'

The synthesis of Greek philosophy and Hebrew scriptures remained more or less haphazard and fragmentary until the time of Origen (A.D. 185-254). Origen, like Philo, lived in Alexandria, which, owing to commerce and the university, was, from its foundation to its fall, the chief centre of learned syncretism. Like his contemporary Plotinus, he was a pupil of Ammonius Saccas, whom many regard as the founder of Neoplatonism. His doctrines, as set forth in his work *De Principiis*, have much affinity to those of Plotinus—more, in fact, than is compatible with orthodoxy.

There is, Origen says, nothing wholly incorporeal except God—Father, Son, and Holy Ghost. The stars are living rational beings, to whom God has given souls that were already in existence. The sun, he thinks, can sin. The souls of men, as Plato taught, come to them at birth from elsewhere, having existed even since the Creation. *Nous* and soul are distinguished more or less as in Plotinus. When *Nous* falls away, it becomes soul; soul, when virtuous, becomes *Nous*. Ultimately all spirits will become wholly submissive to Christ, and will then be bodiless. Even the devil will be saved at the last.

Origen, in spite of being recognized as one of the Fathers, was, in later times, condemned as having maintained four heresies:

1. The pre-existence of souls, as taught by Plato.

2. That the human nature of Christ, and not only His divine nature, existed before the Incarnation.

3. That, at the resurrection, our bodies will be transformed into absolutely ethereal bodies.

4. That all men, and even devils, shall be saved at the last.

[1] Or rather the author of an Epistle attributed to St Paul—Colossians ii, 8.

St Jerome, who had expressed a somewhat unguarded admiration of Origen for his work in establishing the text of the Old Testament, found it prudent, subsequently, to expend much time and vehemence in repudiating his theological errors.

Origen's aberrations were not only theological; in his youth he was guilty of an irreparable error through a too literal interpretation of the text: 'There be eunuchs, which have made themselves eunuchs for the kingdom of heaven's sake.'[1] This method of escaping the temptations of the flesh, which Origen rashly adopted, had been condemned by the Church; moreover it made him ineligible for holy orders, although some ecclesiastics seem to have thought otherwise, thereby giving rise to unedifying controversies.

Origen's longest work is a book entitled *Against Celsus*. Celsus was the author of a book (now lost) against Christianity, and Origen set to work to answer him point by point. Celsus begins by objecting to Christians because they belong to illegal associations; this Origen does not deny, but claims to be a virtue, like tyrannicide. He then comes to what is no doubt the real basis for the dislike of Christianity: Christianity, says Celsus, comes from the Jews, who are barbarians; and only Greeks can extract sense out of the teachings of barbarians. Origen replies that anyone coming from Greek philosophy to the Gospels would conclude that they are true, and supply a demonstration satisfying to the Greek intellect. But further, 'The Gospel has a demonstration of its own, more divine than any established by Grecian dialectics. And this diviner method is called by the apostle the "manifestation of the Spirit and of power"; of "the Spirit", on account of the prophecies, which are sufficient to produce faith in any one who reads them, especially in those things which relate to Christ; and of "power", because of the signs and wonders which we must believe to have been performed, both on many other grounds, and on this, that traces of them are still preserved among those who regulate their lives by the precepts of the Gospel.'[2]

This passage is interesting, as showing already the twofold argument for belief which is characteristic of Christian philosophy. On the one hand, pure reason, rightly exercised, suffices to establish the essentials of the Christian faith, more especially God, immortality, and free will. But on the other hand the Scriptures prove not only these bare essentials, but much more; and the divine inspiration of the Scriptures is proved by the fact that the prophets foretold the coming of the Messiah, by the miracles, and by the beneficent effects of belief on the lives of the faithful. Some of these arguments

---

[1] Matthew xix, 12.
[2] Origen, *Contra Celsum*, Book I, chap. ii.

are now considered out of date, but the last of them was still employed by William James. All of them, until the Renaissance, were accepted by every Christian philosopher.

Some of Origen's arguments are curious. He says that magicians invoke the 'God of Abraham', often without knowing who He is; but apparently this invocation is specially potent. Names are essential in magic; it is not indifferent whether God is called by His Jewish, Egyptian, Babylonian, Greek, or Brahman name. Magic formulae lose their efficacy when translated. One is led to suppose that the magicians of the time used formulae from all known religions, but if Origen is right, those derived from Hebrew sources were the most effective. The argument is the more curious as he points out that Moses forbade sorcery.[1]

Christians, we are told, should not take part in the government of the State, but only of the 'divine nation', i.e., the Church.[2] This doctrine, of course, was somewhat modified after the time of Constantine, but something of it survived. It is implicit in St Augustine's *City of God*. It led churchmen, at the time of the fall of the Western Empire, to look on passively at secular disasters, while they exercised their very great talents in Church discipline, theological controversy, and the spread of monasticism. Some trace of it still exists: most people regard politics as 'worldly' and unworthy of any really holy man.

Church government developed slowly during the first three centuries, and rapidly after the conversion of Constantine. Bishops were popularly elected; gradually they acquired considerable power over Christians in their own dioceses, but before Constantine there was hardly any form of central government over the whole Church. The power of bishops in great cities was enhanced by the practice of almsgiving: the offerings of the faithful were administered by the bishop, who could give or withhold charity to the poor. There came thus to be a mob of the destitute, ready to do the bishop's will. When the State became Christian, the bishops were given judicial and administrative functions. There came also to be a central government, at least in matters of doctrine. Constantine was annoyed by the quarrel between Catholics and Arians; having thrown in his lot with the Christians, he wanted them to be a united party. For the purpose of healing dissensions, he caused the convening of the oecumenical Council of Nicæa, which drew up the Nicene Creed,[3] and, so far as the Arian controversy was concerned, determined for all time the standard of orthodoxy. Other

[1] *Ibid.*, Book I, chap. xxvi.
[2] *Ibid.*, Book VIII, chap. lxxv.
[3] Not exactly in its present form, which was decided upon in 362.

later controversies were similarly decided by oecumenical councils, until the division between East and West and the Eastern refusal to admit the authority of the Pope made them impossible.

The Pope, though officially the most important individual in the Church, had no authority over the Church as a whole until a much later period. The gradual growth of the papal power is a very interesting subject, which I shall deal with in later chapters.

The growth of Christianity before Constantine, as well as the motives of his conversion, has been variously explained by various authors. Gibbon[1] assigns five causes:

'I. The inflexible, and, if we may use the expression, the intolerant zeal of the Christians, derived, it is true, from the Jewish religion, but purified from the narrow and unsocial spirit which, instead of inviting, had deterred the Gentiles from embracing the law of Moses.

'II. The doctrine of a future life, improved by every additional circumstance which could give weight and efficacy to that important truth.

'III. The miraculous powers ascribed to the primitive Church.

'IV. The pure and austere morals of the Christians.

'V. The union and discipline of the Christian republic, which gradually formed an independent and increasing State in the heart of the Roman empire.'

Broadly speaking, this analysis may be accepted, but with some comments. The first cause—the inflexibility and intolerance derived from the Jews—may be wholly accepted. We have seen in our own day the advantages of intolerance in propaganda. The Christians, for the most part, believed that they alone would go to heaven, and that the most awful punishments would, in the next world, fall upon the heathen. The other religions which competed for favour during the third century had not this threatening character. The worshippers of the Great Mother, for example, while they had a ceremony—the Taurobolium—which was analogous to baptism, did teach that those who omitted it would go to hell. It may be remarked, incidentally, that the Taurobolium was expensive: a bull had to be killed, and its blood allowed to trickle over the convert. A rite of this sort is aristocratic, and cannot be the basis of a religion which is to embrace the great bulk of the population, rich and poor, free and slave. In such respects, Christianity had an advantage over all its rivals.

As regards the doctrine of a future life, in the West it was first

[1] *The Decline and Fall of the Roman Empire*, chap. xv.

taught by the Orphics and thence adopted by Greek philosophers. The Hebrew prophets, some of them, taught the resurrection of the body, but it seems to have been from the Greeks that the Jews learnt to believe in the resurrection of the spirit.[1] The doctrine of immortality, in Greece, had a popular form in Orphism and a learned form in Platonism. The latter, being based upon difficult arguments, could not become widely popular; the Orphic form, however, probably had a great influence on the general opinions of later antiquity, not only among pagans, but also among Jews and Christians. Elements of mystery religions, both Orphic and Asiatic, enter largely into Christian theology; in all of them, the central myth is that of the dying god who rises again.[2] I think, therefore, that the doctrine of immortality must have had less to do with the spread of Christianity than Gibbon thought.

Miracles certainly played a very large part in Christian propaganda. But miracles, in later antiquity, were very common, and were not the prerogative of any one religion. It is not altogether easy to see why, in this competition, the Christian miracles came to be more widely believed than those of other sects. I think Gibbon omits one very important matter, namely the possession of a Sacred Book. The miracles to which Christians appealed had begun in a remote antiquity, among a nation which the ancients felt to be mysterious; there was a consistent history, from the Creation onwards, according to which Providence had always worked wonders, first for the Jews, then for the Christians. To a modern historical student it is obvious that the early history of the Israelites is in the main legendary, but not so to the ancients. They believed in the Homeric account of the siege of Troy, in Romulus and Remus, and so on; why, asks Origen, should you accept these traditions and reject those of the Jews? To this argument there was no logical answer. It was therefore natural to accept Old Testament miracles, and, when they had been admitted, those of more recent date became credible, especially in view of the Christian interpretation of the prophets.

The morals of the Christians, before Constantine, were undoubtedly very superior to those of average pagans. The Christians were persecuted at times, and were almost always at a disadvantage in competition with pagans. They believed firmly that virtue would be rewarded in heaven and sin punished in hell. Their sexual ethics had a strictness that was rare in antiquity. Pliny, whose official duty it was to persecute them, testifies to their high moral character. After the conversion of Constantine, there were, of course, time-

[1] See Oesterley and Robinson, *Hebrew Religion.*
[2] See Angus, *The Mystery Religions and Christianity.*

servers among Christians; but prominent ecclesiastics, with some exceptions, continued to be men of inflexible moral principles. I think Gibbon is right in attributing great importance to this high moral level as one of the causes of the spread of Christianity.

Gibbon puts last 'the union and discipline of the Christian republic'. I think that, from a political point of view, this was the most important of his five causes. In the modern world, we are accustomed to political organization; every politician has to reckon with the Catholic vote, but it is balanced by the vote of other organized groups. A Catholic candidate for the American Presidency is at a disadvantage, because of Protestant prejudice. But, if there were no such thing as Protestant prejudice, a Catholic candidate would stand a better chance than any other. This seems to have been Constantine's calculation. The support of the Christians, as a single organized bloc, was to be obtained by favouring them. Whatever dislike of the Christians existed was unorganized and politically ineffective. Probably Rostovtseff is right in holding that a large part of the army was Christian, and that this was what most influenced Constantine. However that may be, the Christians, while still a minority, had a kind of organization which was then new, though now common, and which gave them all the political influence of a pressure group to which no other pressure groups are opposed. This was the natural consequence of their virtual monopoly of zeal, and their zeal was an inheritance from the Jews.

Unfortunately, as soon as the Christians acquired political power, they turned their zeal against each other. There had been heresies, not a few, before Constantine, but the orthodox had had no means of punishing them. When the State became Christian, great prizes, in the shape of power and wealth, became open to ecclesiastics; there were disputed elections, and theological quarrels were also quarrels for worldly advantages. Constantine himself preserved a certain degree of neutrality in the disputes of theologians, but after his death (337) his successors (except for Julian the Apostate) were, in a greater or less degree, favourable to the Arians, until the accession of Theodosius in 379.

The hero of this period is Athanasius (ca. 297-373), who was throughout his long life the most intrepid champion of Nicene orthodoxy.

The period from Constantine to the Council of Chalcedon (451) is peculiar owing to the political importance of theology. Two questions successively agitated the Christian world: first, the nature of the Trinity, and then the doctrine of the Incarnation. Only the first of these was to the fore in the time of Athanasius. Arius, a cultivated Alexandrian priest, maintained that the Son is not the equal of the Father, but created by Him. At an earlier period, this view might not have aroused much antagonism, but in the fourth century most theologians rejected it. The view which finally prevailed was that the Father and the Son were equal, and of the same substance; they were, however, distinct Persons. The view that they were not distinct, but only different aspects of one Being, was the Sabellian heresy, called after its founder Sabellius. Orthodoxy thus had to tread a narrow line: those who unduly emphasized the distinctness of the Father and the Son were in danger of Arianism, and those who unduly emphasized their oneness were in danger of Sabellianism.

The doctrines of Arius were condemned by the Council of Nicæa (325) by an overwhelming majority. But various modifications were suggested by various theologians, and favoured by Emperors Athanasius, who was Bishop of Alexandria from 328 till his death, was constantly in exile because of his zeal for Nicene orthodoxy. He had immense popularity in Egypt, which, throughout the controversy, followed him unwaveringly. It is curious that, in the course of theological controversy, national (or at least regional) feeling, which had seemed extinct since the Roman conquest, revived. Constantinople and Asia inclined to Arianism; Egypt was fanatically Athanasian; the West steadfastly adhered to the decrees of the Council of Nicæa. After the Arian controversy was ended, new controversies, of a more or less kindred sort, arose, in which Egypt became heretical in one direction and Syria in another. These heresies, which were persecuted by the orthodox, impaired the unity of the Eastern Empire, and facilitated the Mohammedan conquest. The separatist movements, in themselves, are not surprising, but it is curious that they should have been associated with very subtle and abtruse theological questions.

The Emperors, from 335 to 378, favoured more or less Arian opinions as far as they dared, except for Julian the Apostate (361-363), who, as a pagan, was neutral as regards the internal disputes of the Christians. At last, in 379, the Emperor Theodosius gave his full support to the Catholics, and their victory throughout the Empire was complete. St Ambrose, St Jerome, and St Augustine, whom we shall consider in the next chapter, lived most of their lives during this period of Catholic triumph. It was succeeded, however, in the West, by another Arian domination, that of the Goths and Vandals, who, between them, conquered most of the Western Empire. Their power lasted for about a century, at the end of which it was destroyed by Justinian, the Lombards, and the Franks, of whom Justinian and the Franks, and ultimately the Lombards also, were orthodox. Thus at last the Catholic faith achieved definitive success.

Chapter III

THREE DOCTORS OF THE CHURCH

FOUR men are called the Doctors of the Western Church: St Ambrose, St Jerome, St Augustine, and Pope Gregory the Great. Of these the first three were contemporaries, while the fourth belonged to a later date. I shall, in this chapter, give some account of the life and times of the first three, reserving for a later chapter an account of the doctrines of St Augustine, who is, for us, the most important of the three.

Ambrose, Jerome, and Augustine all flourished during the brief period between the victory of the Catholic Church in the Roman Empire and the barbarian invasion. All three were young during the reign of Julian the Apostate; Jerome lived ten years after the sack of Rome by the Goths under Alaric; Augustine lived till the irruption of the Vandals into Africa, and died while they were besieging Hippo, of which he was bishop. Immediately after their time, the masters of Italy, Spain, and Africa were not only barbarians, but Arian heretics. Civilization declined for centuries, and it was not until nearly a thousand years later that Christendom again produced men who were their equals in learning and culture. Throughout the dark ages and the medieval period, their authority was revered; they, more than any other men, fixed the mould into which the Church was shaped. Speaking broadly, St Ambrose determined the ecclesiastical conception of the relation of Church and State; St Jerome gave the Western Church its Latin Bible and a great part of the impetus to monasticism; while St Augustine fixed the theology of the Church until the Reformation, and, later, a great part of the doctrines of Luther and Calvin. Few men have surpassed these three in influence on the course of history. The independence of the Church in relation to the secular State, as successfully maintained by St Ambrose, was a new and revolutionary doctrine, which prevailed until the Reformation; when Hobbes combated it in the seventeenth century, it was against St Ambrose that he chiefly argued. St Augustine was in the forefront of theological controversy during the sixteenth and seventeenth centuries, Protestants and Jansenists being for him, and orthodox Catholics against him.

The capital of the Western Empire, at the end of the fourth century, was Milan, of which Ambrose was bishop. His duties brought him constantly into relations with the emperors, to whom he spoke habitually as an equal, sometimes as a superior. His dealings with the imperial court illustrate a general contrast characteristic of the times: while the State was feeble, incompetent, governed by unprincipled self-seekers, and totally without any policy beyond that of momentary expedients, the Church was vigorous, able, guided by men prepared to sacrifice everything personal in its interests, and with a policy so far-sighted that it brought victory for the next thousand years. It is true that these merits were offset by fanaticism and superstition, but without these no reforming movement could, at that time, have succeeded.

St Ambrose had every opportunity to seek success in the service of the State. His father, also named Ambrose, was a high official —prefect of the Gauls. The Saint was born, probably, at Treves, a frontier garrison town, where the Roman legions were stationed to keep the Germans at bay. At the age of thirteen he was taken to Rome, where he had a good education, including a thorough grounding in Greek. When he grew up he took to the law, in which he was very successful; and at the age of thirty he was made governor of Liguria and Æmilia. Nevertheless, four years later he turned his back on secular government, and by popular acclaim became bishop of Milan, in opposition to an Arian candidate. He gave all his worldly goods to the poor, and devoted the whole of the rest of his life to the service of the Church, sometimes at great personal risk. This choice was certainly not dictated by worldly motives, but, if it had been, it would have been wise. In the State, even if he had become Emperor. he could at that time have found no such scope for his administrative statesmanship as he found in the discharge of his episcopal duties.

During the first nine years of Ambrose's episcopate, the Emperor of the West was Gratian, who was Catholic, virtuous, and careless. He was so devoted to the chase that he neglected the government, and in the end was assassinated. He was succeeded, throughout most of the Western Empire, by a usurper named Maximus; but in Italy the succession passed to Gratian's younger brother Valentinian II, who was still a boy. At first, the imperial power was exercised by his mother, Justina, widow of the Emperor Valentinian I; but as she was an Arian, conflicts between her and St Ambrose were inevitable.

All the three Saints with whom we are concerned in this chapter wrote innumerable letters, of which many are preserved; the consequence is that we know more about them than about any of the pagan philosophers, and more than about all but a few of the ecclesiastics of the Middle Ages. St Augustine wrote letters to all and sundry, mostly on doctrine or Church discipline; St Jerome's letters are mainly addressed to ladies, giving advice on how to preserve virginity; but St Ambrose's most important and interesting letters are to Emperors, telling them in what respects they have fallen short of their duty, or, on occasion, congratulating them on having performed it.

The first public question with which Ambrose had to deal was that of the altar and statue of Victory in Rome. Paganism lingered longer among the senatorial families of the capital than it did elsewhere; the official religion was in the hands of an aristocratic priesthood, and was bound up with the imperial pride of the conquerors of the world. The statue of Victory in the Senate House had been removed by Constantius, the son of Constantine, and restored by Julian the Apostate. The Emperor Gratian again removed the statue, whereupon a deputation of the Senate, headed by Symmachus, prefect of the City, asked for its renewed restoration.

Symmachus, who also played a part in the life of Augustine, was a distinguished member of a distinguished family—rich, aristocratic, cultivated, and pagan. He was banished from Rome by Gratian in 382 for his protest against the removal of the statue of Victory, but not for long, as he was prefect of the City in 384. He was the grandfather of the Symmachus who was the father-in-law of Boethius, and who was prominent in the reign of Theodoric.

The Christian senators objected, and by the help of Ambrose and the Pope (Damasus) their view was made to prevail with the Emperor. After the death of Gratian, Symmachus and the pagan senators petitioned the new Emperor, Valentinian II, in A.D. 384. In rebuttal of this renewed attempt, Ambrose wrote to the Emperor, setting forth the thesis that, as all Romans owed military service to their sovereign, so he (the Emperor) owed service to Almighty God.[1] 'Let no one,' he says, 'take advantage of your youth; if he be a heathen who demands this, it is not right that he should bind your mind with the bonds of his own superstition; but by his zeal he ought to teach and admonish you how to be zealous for the true faith, since he defends vain things with all the passion of truth.' To be compelled to swear at the altar of an idol, he says, is, to a Christian, persecution. 'If it were a civil cause the right of reply would be reserved for the opposing party; it is a religious cause, and I the bishop make a claim. . . . Certainly if anything else is decreed, we bishops cannot constantly suffer it and take no notice; you indeed may come to the Church, but will find either no priest there, or one who will resist you.'[2]

The next epistle points out that the endowments of the Church

---

[1] This thesis seems to anticipate the outlook of feudalism.
[2] Epistle xvii.

serve purposes never served by the wealth of heathen temples. 'The possessions of the Church are the maintenance of the poor. Let them count up how many captives the temples have ransomed, what food they have contributed for the poor, to what exiles they have supplied the means of living.' This was a telling argument, and one which was quite justified by Christian practice.

St Ambrose won his point, but a subsequent usurper, Eugenius, who favoured the heathen, restored the altar and statue. It was only after the defeat of Eugenius by Theodosius in 394 that the question was finally decided in favour of the Christians.

The bishop was, at first, on very friendly terms with the imperial court, and was employed on a diplomatic mission to the usurper Maximus, who, it was feared, might invade Italy. But before long a grave matter of controversy arose. The Empress Justina, as an Arian, requested that one church in Milan might be ceded to the Arians, but Ambrose refused. The people sided with him, and thronged the basilica in great crowds. Gothic soldiers, who were Arians, were sent to take possession, but fraternized with the people. 'The Counts and Tribunes,' he says in a spirited letter to his sister,[1] 'came and urged me to cause the basilica to be quickly surrendered, saying that the Emperor was exercising his rights since everything was under his power. I answered that if he asked of me what was mine, that is, my land, my money, or whatever of this kind was my own, I would not refuse it, although all that I have belonged to the poor, but that those things which are God's are not subject to the imperial power. "If my patrimony is required, enter upon it; if my body, I will go at once. Do you wish to cast me into chains, or to give me to death? It will be a pleasure to me. I will not defend myself with throngs of people, nor will I cling to the altars and entreat for my life, but will more gladly be slain myself for the altars." I was indeed struck with horror when I learnt that armed men had been sent to take possession of the basilica, lest while the people were defending the basilica, there might be some slaughter which would tend to the injury of the whole city. I prayed that I might not survive the destruction of so great a city, or it might be of the whole of Italy.'

These fears were not exaggerated, as the Gothic soldiery were liable to break out into savagery, as they did twenty-five years later in the sack of Rome.

Ambrose's strength lay in the support of the people. He was accused of inciting them, but replied that 'it was in my power not to excite them, but in God's hands to quiet them'. None of the Arians, he says, dared to go forth, as there was not one Arian among the citizens. He was formally commanded to surrender the basilica,

[1] *Ibid.* xx.

and the soldiers were ordered to use violence if necessary. But in the end they refused to use violence, and the Emperor was compelled to give way. A great battle had been won in the contest for ecclesiastical independence; Ambrose had demonstrated that there were matters in which the State must yield to the Church, and had thereby established a new principle which retains its importance to the present day.

His next conflict was with the Emperor Theodosius. A synagogue had been burnt, and the Count of the East reported that this had been done at the instigation of the local bishop. The Emperor ordered that the actual incendiaries should be punished, and that the guilty bishop should rebuild the synagogue. St Ambrose neither admits nor denies the bishop's complicity, but is indignant that the Emperor should seem to side with Jews against Christians. Suppose the bishop refuses to obey? He will then have to become a martyr if he persists, or an apostate if he gives way. Suppose the Count decides to rebuild the synagogue himself at the expense of the Christians? In that case the Emperor will have an apostate Count, and Christian money will be taken to support unbelief. 'Shall, then, a place be made for the unbelief of the Jews out of the spoils of the Church, and shall the patrimony, which by the favour of Christ has been gained for Christians, be transferred to the treasuries of unbelievers?' He continues: 'But perhaps the cause of discipline moves you, O Emperor. Which, then, is of greater importance, the show of discipline or the cause of religion? It is needful that judgment should yield to religion. Have you not heard, O Emperor, how, when Julian commanded that the Temple of Jerusalem should be restored, those who were clearing the rubbish were consumed by fire?'

It is clear that, in the Saint's opinion, the destruction of synagogues should not be punished in any way. This is an example of the manner in which, as soon as it acquired power, the Church began to stimulate anti-Semitism.

The next conflict between Emperor and Saint was more honourable to the latter. In A.D. 390, when Theodosius was in Milan, a mob in Thessalonica murdered the captain of the garrison. Theodosius, on receiving the news, was seized with ungovernable fury, and ordered an abominable revenge. When the people were assembled in the circus, the soldiers fell upon them, and massacred at least seven thousand of them in an indiscriminate slaughter. Hereupon Ambrose, who had endeavoured in advance to restrain the Emperor, but in vain, wrote him a letter full of splendid courage, on a purely moral issue, involving, for once, no question of theology or the power of the Church:

'There was that done in the city of the Thessalonians of which no similar record exists, which I was not able to prevent happening; which, indeed, I had before said would be most atrocious when I so often petitioned against it.'

David repeatedly sinned, and confessed his sin with penitence.[1] Will Theodosius do likewise? Ambrose decides that 'I dare not offer the sacrifice if you intend to be present. Is that which is not allowed after shedding the blood of one innocent person, allowed after shedding the blood of many? I do not think so.'

The Emperor repented, and, divested of the purple, did public penance in the cathedral of Milan. From that time until his death in 395, he had no friction with Ambrose.

Ambrose, while he was eminent as a statesman, was, in other respects, merely typical of his age. He wrote, like other ecclesiastical authors, a treatise in praise of virginity, and another deprecating the remarriage of widows. When he had decided on the site for his new cathedral, two skeletons (revealed in a vision, it was said) were conveniently discovered on the spot, were found to work miracles, and were declared by him to be those of two martyrs. Other miracles are related in his letters, with all the credulity characteristic of his times. He was inferior to Jerome as a scholar, and to Augustine as a philosopher. But as a statesman, who skilfully and courageously consolidated the power of the Church, he stands out as a man of the first rank.

Jerome is chiefly notable as the translator who produced the Vulgate, which remains to this day the official Catholic version of the Bible. Until his day the Western Church relied, as regards the Old Testament, chiefly on translations from the Septuagint, which, in important ways, differed from the Hebrew original. Christians, as we have seen, were given to maintaining that the Jews, since the rise of Christianity, had falsified the Hebrew text where it seemed to predict the Messiah. This was a view which sound scholarship showed to be untenable, and which Jerome firmly rejected. He accepted the help of rabbis, given secretly for fear of the Jews. In defending himself against Christian criticism he said: 'Let him who would challenge aught in this translation ask the Jews.' Because of his acceptance of the Hebrew text in the form which the Jews regarded as correct, his version had, at first, a largely hostile reception; but it won its way, partly because St Augustine on the whole supported it. It was a great achievement, involving considerable textual criticism.

[1] This allusion to the Books of Samuel begins a line of biblical argument against kings which persisted throughout the Middle Ages, and even in the conflict of the Puritans with the Stuarts. It appears for instance in Milton.

Jerome was born in 345—five years after Ambrose—not far from Aquileia, at a town called Stridon, which was destroyed by the Goths in 377. His family were well-to-do, but not rich. In 363 he went to Rome, where he studied rhetoric and sinned. After travelling in Gaul, he settled in Aquileia, and become an ascetic. The next five years he spent as a hermit in the Syrian wilderness. 'His life while in the desert was one of rigorous penance, of tears and groans alternating with spiritual ecstasy, and of temptations from haunting memories of Roman life; he lived in a cell or cavern; he earned his daily bread, and was clad in sackcloth.'[1] After this period, he travelled to Constantinople, and lived in Rome for three years, where he became the friend and adviser of Pope Damasus, with whose encouragement he undertook his translation of the Bible.

St Jerome was a man of many quarrels. He quarrelled with St Augustine about the somewhat questionable behaviour of St Peter as related by St Paul in Galatians ii; he broke with his friend Rufinus over Origen; and he was so vehement against Pelagius that his monastery was attacked by a Pelagian mob. After the death of Damasus, he seems to have quarrelled with the new Pope; he had, while in Rome, become acquainted with various ladies who were both aristocratic and pious, some of whom he persuaded to adopt the ascetic life. The new Pope, in common with many other people in Rome, disliked this. For this reason among others, Jerome left Rome for Bethlehem, where he remained from 386 till his death in 420.

Among his distinguished female converts, two were especially notable: the widow Paula and her daughter Eustochium. Both these ladies accompanied him on his circuitous journey to Bethlehem. They were of the highest nobility, and one cannot but feel a flavour of snobbery in the Saint's attitude to them. When Paula died and was buried at Bethlehem, Jerome composed an epitaph for her tomb:

> Within this tomb a child of Scipio lies,
> A daughter of the far-famed Pauline house,
> A scion of the Gracchi, of the stock
> Of Agamemnon's self, illustrious:
> Here rests the lady Paula, well-beloved
> Of both her parents, with Eustochium
> For daughter; she the first of Roman dames
> Who hardship chose and Bethlehem for Christ.[2]

Some of Jerome's letters to Eustochium are curious. He gives her advice on the preservation of virginity, very detailed and frank;

[1] Select Library of Nicene and Post-Nicene Fathers, Vol. VI, p. 17.
[2] Select Library of Nicene and Post-Nicene Fathers, Vol. VI, p. 212.

he explains the exact anatomical meaning of certain euphemisms in the Old Testament; and he employs a kind of erotic mysticism in praising the joys of conventual life. A nun is the Bride of Christ; this marriage is celebrated in the Song of Solomon. In a long letter written at the time when she took the vows, he gives a remarkable message to her mother: 'Are you angry with her because she chooses to be a king's [Christ's] wife and not a soldier's? She has conferred on you a high privilege; you are now the mother-in-law of God.'[1]

To Eustochium herself, in the same letter (xxii), he says:

'Ever let the privacy of your chamber guard you; ever let the Bridegroom sport with you within. Do you pray? You speak to the Bridegroom. Do you read? He speaks to you. When sleep overtakes you He will come behind and put His hand through the hole of the door, and your heart shall be moved for Him; and you will awake and rise up and say: "I am sick of love." Then He will reply: "A garden enclosed is my sister, my spouse; a spring shut up, a fountain sealed." '

In the same letter he relates how, after cutting himself off from relations and friends, 'and—harder still—from the dainty food to which I had been accustomed', he still could not bear to be parted from his library, and took it with him to the desert. 'And so, miserable man that I was, I would fast only that I might afterwards read Cicero.' After days and nights of remorse, he would fall again, and read Plautus. After such indulgence, the style of the prophets seemed 'rude and repellent'. At last, during a fever, he dreamed that, at the Last Judgment, Christ asked him who he was, and he replied that he was a Christian. The answer came: 'Thou liest, thou art a follower of Cicero and not of Christ.' Thereupon he was ordered to be scourged. At length Jerome, in his dream, cried out: 'Lord, if ever again I possess worldly books, or if ever again I read such, I have denied Thee.' This, he adds, 'was no sleep or idle dream'.[2]

After this, for some years, his letters contain few classical quotations. But after a certain time he lapses again into verses from Virgil, Horace, and even Ovid. They seem, however, to be from memory, particularly as some of them are repeated over and over again.

Jerome's letters express the feelings produced by the fall of the Roman Empire more vividly than any others known to me. In 396 he writes:[3]

[1] *Ibid.*, p. 30.
[2] This hostility to pagan literature persisted in the Church until the eleventh century, except in Ireland, where the Olympian gods had never been worshipped, and were therefore not feared by the Church.
[3] Letter lx.

'I shudder when I think of the catastrophes of our time. For twenty years and more the blood of Romans has been shed daily between Constantinople and the Julian Alps. Scythia, Thrace, Macedonia, Dacia, Thessaly, Achaia, Epirus, Dalmatia, the Pannonias—each and all of these have been sacked and pillaged and plundered by Goths and Sarmatians, Quadi and Alans, Huns and Vandals and Marchmen. . . . The Roman world is falling: yet we hold up our heads instead of bowing them. What courage, think you, have the Corinthians now, or the Athenians or the Lacedaemonians or the Arcadians, or any of the Greeks over whom the barbarians bear sway? I have mentioned only a few cities, but these once the capitals of no mean States.'

He goes on to relate the ravages of the Huns in the East, and ends with the reflection: 'To treat such themes as they deserve, Thucydides and Sallust would be as good as dumb.'

Seventeen years later, three years after the sack of Rome, he writes:[1]

'The world sinks into ruin: yes! but shameful to say our sins still live and flourish. The renowned city, the capital of the Roman Empire, is swallowed up in one tremendous fire; and there is no part of the earth where Romans are not in exile. Churches once held sacred are now but heaps of dust and ashes; and yet we have our minds set on the desire of gain. We live as though we were going to die to-morrow; yet we build as though we were going to live always in this world. Our walls shine with gold, our ceilings also and the capitals of our pillars; yet Christ dies before our doors naked and hungry in the person of His poor.'

This passage occurs incidentally in a letter to a friend who has decided to devote his daughter to perpetual virginity, and most of it is concerned with the rules to be observed in the education of girls so dedicated. It is strange that, with all Jerome's deep feeling about the fall of the ancient world, he thinks the preservation of virginity more important than victory over the Huns and Vandals and Goths. Never once do his thoughts turn to any possible measure of practical statesmanship; never once does he point out the evils of the fiscal system, or of reliance on an army composed of barbarians. The same is true of Ambrose and of Augustine; Ambrose, it is true, was a statesman, but only on behalf of the Church. It is no wonder that the Empire fell into ruin when all the best and most vigorous minds of the age were so completely remote from secular concerns. On the other hand, if ruin was inevitable, the Christian outlook was admirably fitted to give men fortitude, and to enable them to preserve their religious hopes when earthly hopes seemed

[1] Letter cxxviii.

vain. The expression of this point of view, in *The City of God*, was the supreme merit of St Augustine.

Of St Augustine I shall speak, in this chapter, only as a man; as a theologian and philosopher, I shall consider him in the next chapter.

He was born in 354, nine years after Jerome, and fourteen years after Ambrose; he was a native of Africa, where he passed much the greater part of his life. His mother was a Christian, but his father was not. After a period as a Manichæan, he became a Catholic, and was baptized by Ambrose in Milan. He became bishop of Hippo, not far from Carthage, about the year 396. There he remained until his death in 430.

Of his early life we know much more than in the case of most ecclesiastics, because he has told of it in his *Confessions*. This book has had famous imitators, particularly Rousseau and Tolstoy, but I do not think it had any comparable predecessors. St Augustine is in some ways similar to Tolstoy, to whom, however, he is superior in intellect. He was a passionate man, in youth very far from a pattern of virtue, but driven by an inner impulse to search for truth and righteousness. Like Tolstoy, he was obsessed, in his later years, by a sense of sin, which made his life stern and his philosophy inhuman. He combated heresies vigorously, but some of his views, when repeated by Jansenius in the seventeenth century, were pronounced heretical. Until the Protestants took up his opinions, however, the Catholic Church had never impugned their orthodoxy.

One of the first incidents of his life related in the *Confessions* occurred in his boyhood, and did not, in itself, greatly distinguish him from other boys. It appears that, with some companions of his own age, he despoiled a neighbour's pear tree, although he was not hungry, and his parents had better pears at home. He continued throughout his life to consider this an act of almost incredible wickedness. It would not have been so bad if he had been hungry, or had had no other means of getting pears; but, as it was, the act was one of pure mischief, inspired by the love of wickedness for its own sake. It is this that makes it so unspeakably black. He beseeches God to forgive him:

'Behold my heart, O God, behold my heart, which Thou hadst pity upon in the bottom of the abyss. Now, behold, let my heart tell Thee, what it sought there, that I should be gratuitously wicked, having no temptation to that evil deed, but the evil deed itself. It was foul, and I loved it; I loved to perish, I loved mine own fault, not that for the sake of which I committed the fault, but my fault itself I loved. Foul soul, falling from the firmament to expulsion from Thy presence; not seeking aught through the shame, but the shame itself!'[1]

He goes on like this for seven chapters, and all about some pears plucked from a tree in a boyish prank. To a modern mind, this seems morbid;[2] but in his own age it seemed right and a mark of holiness. The sense of sin, which was very strong in his day, came to the Jews as a way of reconciling self-importance with outward defeat. Yahweh was omnipotent, and Yahweh was specially interested in the Jews; why, then, did they not prosper? Because they were wicked: they were idolators, they married gentiles, they failed to observe the Law. God's purposes were centred on the Jews, but, since righteousness is the greatest of goods, and is achieved through tribulation, they must first be chastised, and must recognize their chastisement as a mark of God's paternal love.

Christians put the Church in place of the Chosen People, but except in one respect this made little difference to the psychology of sin. The Church, like the Jews, suffered tribulation; the Church was troubled by heresies; individual Christians fell into apostasy under the stress of persecution. There was, however, one important development, already made, to a great extent, by the Jews, and that was the substitution of individual for communal sin. Originally, it was the Jewish nation that sinned, and that was collectively punished; but later sin became more personal, thus losing its political character. When the Church was substituted for the Jewish nation, this change became essential, since the Church, as a spiritual entity, could not sin, but the individual sinner could cease to be in communion with the Church. Sin, as we said just now, is connected with self-importance. Originally the importance was that of the Jewish nation, but subsequently it was that of the individual—not of the Church, because the Church never sinned. It thus came about that Christian theology had two parts, one concerned with the Church, and one with the individual soul. In later times, the first of these was most emphasized by Catholics, and the second by Protestants, but in St Augustine both exist equally, without his having any sense of disharmony. Those who are saved are those whom God has predestined to salvation; this is a direct relation of the soul to God. But no one will be saved unless he has been baptized, and thereby become a member of the Church; this makes the Church an intermediary between the soul and God.

Sin is what is essential to the direct relation, since it explains how a beneficent Deity can cause men to suffer, and how, in spite of this, individual souls can be what is of most importance in the

[1] *Confessions*, Book II, chap. iv.
[2] I must except Mahatma Gandhi, whose autobiography contains passages closely similar to the above.

created world. It is therefore not surprising that the theology upon which the Reformation relied should be due to a man whose sense of sin was abnormal.

So much for the pears. Let us now see what the *Confessions* have to say on some other subjects.

Augustine relates how he learnt Latin, painlessly, at his mother's knee, but hated Greek, which they tried to teach him at school, because he was 'urged vehemently with cruel threats and punishments'. To the end of his life, his knowledge of Greek remained slight. One might have supposed that he would go on, from this contrast, to draw a moral in favour of gentle methods in education. What he says, however, is:

'It is quite clear, then, that a free curiosity has more power to make us learn these things than a terrifying obligation. Only this obligation restrains the waverings of that freedom by Thy laws, O my God, Thy laws, from the master's rod to the martyr's trials, for Thy laws have the effect of mingling for us certain wholesome bitters, which recall us to Thee away from that pernicious blithesomeness, by means of which we depart from Thee.'

The schoolmaster's blows, though they failed to make him know Greek, cured him of being perniciously blithesome, and were, on this ground, a desirable part of education. For those who make sin the most important of all human concerns, this view is logical. He goes on to point out that he sinned, not only as a school-boy, when he told lies and stole food, but even earlier; indeed he devotes a whole chapter (Book I, chap. vii) to proving that even infants at the breast are full of sin—gluttony, jealousy, and other horrible vices.

When he reached adolescence, the lusts of the flesh overcame him. 'Where was I, and how far was I exiled from the delights of Thy house, in that sixteenth year of the age of my flesh, when the madness of lust which hath licence through man's viciousness, though forbidden by Thy laws, took the rule over me, and I resigned myself wholly to it?'[1]

His father took no pains to prevent this evil, but confined himself to giving help in Augustine's studies. His mother, St Monica, on the contrary, exhorted him to chastity, but in vain. And even she did not, at that time, suggest marriage, 'lest my prospects might be embarrassed by the clog of a wife'.

At the age of sixteen he went to Carthage, 'where there seethed all around me a cauldron of lawless loves. I loved not yet, yet I loved to love, and out of a deep-seated want, I hated myself for wanting not. I sought what I might love, in love with loving, and I

[1] *Confessions*, Book II, chap. ii.

346

hated safety. . . . To love then, and to be beloved, was sweet to me; but more, when I obtained to enjoy the person I loved. I defiled, therefore, the spring of friendship with the filth of concupiscence, and I beclouded its brightness with the hell of lustfulness.'[1] These words describe his relation to a mistress whom he loved faithfully for many years,[2] and by whom he had a son, whom he also loved, and to whom, after his conversion, he gave much care in religious education.

The time came when he and his mother thought he ought to begin to think of marrying. He became engaged to a girl of whom she approved, and it was held necessary that he should break with his mistress. 'My mistress,' he says, 'being torn from my side as a hindrance to my marriage, my heart which clave unto her was torn and wounded and bleeding. And she returned to Africa [Augustine was at this time in Milan], vowing unto Thee never to know any other man, leaving with me my son by her.'[3] As, however, the marriage could not take place for two years, owing to the girl's youth, he took meanwhile another mistress, less official and less acknowledged. His conscience increasingly troubled him, and he used to pray: 'Give me chastity and continence, only not yet.'[4] At last, before the time had come for his marriage, religion won a complete victory, and he dedicated the rest of his life to celibacy.

To return to an earlier time: in his nineteenth year, having achieved proficiency in rhetoric, he was recalled to philosophy by Cicero. He tried reading the Bible, but found it lacking in Ciceronian dignity. It was at this time that he became a Manichæan, which grieved his mother. By profession he was a teacher of rhetoric. He was addicted to astrology, to which, in later life, he was averse, because it teaches that 'the inevitable cause of thy sin is in the sky'.[5] He read philosophy, so far as it could be read in Latin; he mentions particularly Aristotle's *Ten Categories*, which, he says, he understood without the help of a teacher. 'And what did it profit me, that I, the vilest slave of evil passions, read by myself all the books of so-called "liberal" arts, and understood whatever I could read? . . . For I had my back to the light, and my face to the things enlightened; whence my face . . . itself was not enlightened.'[6] At this time he believed that God was a vast and bright body, and he himself a part of that body. One could wish that he had told in detail the tenets of the Manichæans, instead of merely saying they were erroneous.

It is interesting that St Augustine's first reasons for rejecting the

[1] *Ibid.*, Book III, chap. i. [2] *Ibid.*, Book IV, chap. ii.
[3] *Ibid.*, Book VI, chap. xv. [4] *Ibid.*, Book VIII, chap. vii.
[5] *Confessions*, Book IV, chap. iii. [6] *Ibid.*, Book IV, chap. xvi.

doctrines of Manichæus were scientific. He remembered—so he tells us[1]—what he had learned of astronomy from the writings of the best astronomers, 'and I compared them with the sayings of Manichæus, who in his crazy folly has written much and copiously upon these subjects; but none of his reasoning of the solstices, nor equinoxes, nor eclipses, nor whatever of this kind I had learned in books of secular philosophy, was satisfactory to me. But I was commanded to believe; and yet it corresponded not with reasonings obtained by calculations, and by my own observations, but was quite contrary.' He is careful to point out that scientific mistakes are not in themselves a sign of errors as to the faith, but only become so when delivered with an air of authority as known through divine inspiration. One wonders what he would have thought if he had lived in the time of Galileo.

In the hope of resolving his doubts, a Manichæan bishop named Faustus, reputed the most learned member of the sect, met him and reasoned with him. But 'I found him first utterly ignorant of liberal sciences, save grammar, and that but in an ordinary way. But because he had read some of Tully's Orations, a very few books of Seneca, some things of the poets, and such few volumes of his own sect, as were written in Latin and in logical order, and was daily practised in speaking, he acquired a certain eloquence, which proved the more pleasing and seductive, because under the control of his good sense, and with a certain natural grace.'[2]

He found Faustus quite unable to solve his astronomical difficulties. The books of the Manichæans, he tells us, 'are full of lengthy fables, of the heaven, and stars, sun, and moon', which do not agree with what has been discovered by astronomers; but when he questioned Faustus on these matters, Faustus frankly confessed his ignorance. 'Even for this I liked him the better. For the modesty of a candid mind is even more attractive than the knowledge of those things which I desired; and such I found him, in all the more difficult and subtle questions.'[3]

This sentiment is surprisingly liberal; one would not have expected it in that age. Nor is it quite in harmony with St Augustine's later attitude towards heretics.

At this time he decided to go to Rome, not, he says, because there the income of a teacher was higher than at Carthage, but because he had heard that classes were more orderly. At Carthage, the disorders perpetrated by students were such that teaching was almost impossible; but at Rome, while there was less disorder, students fraudulently evaded payment.

[1] *Ibid.*, Book V, chap. iii.   [2] *Confessions*, Book V, chap. vi.
[3] *Ibid.*, Book II, chap. vii.

In Rome, he still associated with the Manichæans, but with less conviction of their rightness. He began to think that the Academics were right in holding that men ought to doubt everything.[1] He still, however, agreed with the Manichæans in thinking 'that it is not we ourselves that sin, but that some other nature (what, I know not) sins in us', and he believed Evil to be some kind of substance. This makes it clear that, before as after his conversion, the question of sin pre-occupied him.

After about a year in Rome, he was sent to Milan by the Prefect Symmachus, in response to a request from that city for a teacher of rhetoric. At Milan he became acquainted with Ambrose, 'known to the whole world as among the best of men'. He came to love Ambrose for his kindness, and to prefer the Catholic doctrine to that of the Manichæans; but for a while he was held back by the scepticism he had learnt from the Academics, 'to which philosophers notwithstanding, because they were without the saving name of Christ, I utterly refused to commit the care of my sick soul'.[2]

In Milan he was joined by his mother, who had a powerful influence in hastening the last steps of his conversion. She was a very earnest Catholic, and he writes of her always in a tone of reverence. She was the more important to him at this time, because Ambrose was too busy to converse with him privately.

There is a very interesting chapter[3] in which he compares the Platonic philosophy with Christian doctrine. The Lord, he says, at this time provided him with 'certain books of the Platonists, translated from Greek into Latin. And therein I read, not indeed in these words, but to the same purpose, enforced by many and diverse reasons, that "In the beginning was the Word, and the Word was with God, and the Word was God: the same was in the beginning with God; all things were made by Him, and without Him was nothing made: that which was made by Him is life, and the life was the light of men, and the light shineth in the darkness, and the darkness comprehended it not. And that the soul of man, though it "bears witness to the light", yet itself "is not that light", but God, the Word of God, "is that true light that lighteth every man that cometh into the world". And that "He was in the world, and the world was made by Him, and the world knew Him not." But that "He came unto His own, and His own received him not; but as many as received Him, to them gave He power to become the sons of God, even to them that believe on His Name": this I read not

---

[1] *Ibid.*, Book V, chap. x.
[2] *Confessions*, Book V, chap. xiv.
[3] *Ibid.*, Book VII, chap. ix.

there.' He also did not read there that 'the Word was made flesh, and dwelt among us'; nor that 'He humbled Himself, and became obedient unto death, even the death of the Cross'; nor that 'at the name of Jesus every knee should bow'.

Broadly speaking, he found in the Platonists the metaphysical doctrine of the Logos, but not the doctrine of the Incarnation and the consequent doctrine of human salvation. Something not unlike these doctrines existed in Orphism and the other mystery religions; but of this St Augustine appears to have been ignorant. In any case, none of these were connected with a comparatively recent historical event, as Christianity was.

As against the Manichæans, who were dualists, Augustine came to believe that evil originates not from some substance, but from perverseness of will.

He found especial comfort in the writings of St Paul.[1]

At length, after passionate inward struggles, he was converted (386); he gave up his professorship, his mistress, and his bride, and, after a brief period of meditation in retirement, was baptized by St Ambrose. His mother rejoiced, but died not long afterwards. In 388 he returned to Africa, where he remained for the rest of his life, fully occupied with his episcopal duties and with controversial writings against various heresies, Donatist, Manichæan, and Pelagian.

[1] *Confessions*, Book VII, chap. xxi.

Chapter IV

ST AUGUSTINE'S PHILOSOPHY AND THEOLOGY

ST AUGUSTINE was a very voluminous writer, mainly on theological subjects. Some of his controversial writing was topical, and lost interest through its very success; but some of it, especially what is concerned with the Pelagians, remained practically influential down to modern times. I do not propose to treat his works exhaustively, but only to discuss what seems to me important, either intrinsically or historically. I shall consider:

First: his pure philosophy, particularly his theory of time;
Second: his philosophy of history, as developed in *The City of God*;
Third: his theory of salvation, as propounded against the Pelagians.

I. PURE PHILOSOPHY

St Augustine, at most times, does not occupy himself with pure philosophy, but when he does he shows very great ability. He is the first of a long line whose purely speculative views are influenced by the necessity of agreeing with Scripture. This cannot be said of earlier Christian philosophers, e.g. Origen; in Origen, Christianity and Platonism lie side by side, and do not interpenetrate. In St Augustine, on the other hand, original thinking in pure philosophy is stimulated by the fact that Platonism, in certain respects, is not in harmony with Genesis.

The best purely philosophical work in St Augustine's writings is the eleventh book of the *Confessions*. Popular editions of the *Confessions* end with Book X, on the ground that what follows is uninteresting; it is uninteresting because it is good philosophy, not biography. Book XI is concerned with the problem: Creation having occurred as the first chapter of Genesis asserts, and as Augustine maintains against the Manichæans, it should have occurred as soon as possible. So he imagines an objector arguing.

The first point to realize, if his answer is to be understood, is that creation out of nothing, which was taught in the Old Testament, was an idea wholly foreign to Greek philosophy. When Plato speaks of creation, he imagines a primitive matter to which God gives form; and the same is true of Aristotle. Their God is an artificer or architect, rather than a Creator. Substance is thought of as eternal and uncreated; only form is due to the will of God. As against this view, St Augustine maintains, as every orthodox Christian must, that the world was created not from any certain matter, but from nothing. God created substance, not only order and arrangement.

The Greek view, that creation out of nothing is impossible, has recurred at intervals in Christian times, and has led to pantheism. Pantheism holds that God and the world are not distinct, and that everything in the world is part of God. This view is developed most fully in Spinoza, but is one to which almost all mystics are attracted. It has thus happened, throughout the Christian centuries, that mystics have had difficulty in remaining orthodox, since they find it hard to believe that the world is outside God. Augustine, however, feels no difficulty on this point; Genesis is explicit, and that is enough for him. His view on this matter is essential to his theory of time.

Why was the world not created sooner? Because there was no 'sooner'. Time was created when the world was created. God is eternal, in the sense of being timeless; in God there is no before and after, but only an eternal present. God's eternity is exempt from the relation of time; all time is present to Him at once. He did not *precede* His own creation of time, for that would imply that He was in time, whereas He stands eternally outside the stream of time. This leads St Augustine to a very admirable relativistic theory of time.

'What, then, is time?' he asks. 'If no one asks of me, I know; if I wish to explain to him who asks, I know not.' Various difficulties perplex him. Neither past nor future, he says, but only the present, really *is*; the present is only a moment, and time can only be measured while it is passing. Nevertheless, there really is time past and future. We seem here to be led into contradictions. The only way Augustine can find to avoid these contradictions is to say that past and future can only be thought of as present: 'past' must be identified with memory, and 'future' with expectation, memory and expectation being both present facts. There are, he says, three times: 'a present of things past, a present of things present, and a present of things future'. 'The present of things past is memory,' the present of things present is sight; and the present of things future is expectation.'[1] To say that there are three times, past, present, and future, is a loose way of speaking.

[1] *Confessions*, Book XI, chap. xx.

He realizes that he has not really solved all difficulties by this theory. 'My soul yearns to know this most entangled enigma,' he says, and he prays to God to enlighten him, assuring Him that his interest in the problem does not arise from vain curiosity. 'I confess to Thee, O Lord, that I am as yet ignorant what time is.' But the gist of the solution he suggests is that time is subjective: time is in the human mind, which expects, considers, and remembers.[1] It follows that there can be no time without a created being,[2] and that to speak of time before the Creation is meaningless.

I do not myself agree with this theory, in so far as it makes time something mental. But it is clearly a very able theory, deserving to be seriously considered. I should go further, and say that it is a great advance on anything to be found on the subject in Greek philosophy. It contains a better and clearer statement than Kant's of the subjective theory of time—a theory which, since Kant, has been widely accepted among philosophers.

The theory that time is only an aspect of our thoughts is one of the most extreme forms of that subjectivism which, as we have seen, gradually increased in antiquity from the time of Protagoras and Socrates onwards. Its emotional aspect is obsession with sin, which came later than its intellectual aspects. St Augustine exhibits both kinds of subjectivism. Subjectivism led him to anticipate not only Kant's theory of time, but Descartes' *cogito*. In his *Soliloquia* he says: 'You, who wish to know, do you know you are? I know it. Whence are you? I know not. Do you feel yourself single or multiple? I know not. Do you feel yourself moved? I know not. Do you know that you think? I do.' This contains not only Descarte's *cogito*, but his reply to Gassendi's *ambulo ergo sum*. As a philosopher, therefore, Augustine deserves a high place.

II. THE CITY OF GOD

When, in 410, Rome was sacked by the Goths, the pagans, not unnaturally, attributed the disaster to the abandonment of the ancient gods. So long as Jupiter was worshipped, they said, Rome remained powerful; now that the Emperors have turned away from him, he no longer protects his Romans. This pagan argument called for an answer. *The City of God*, written gradually between 412 and 427, was St Augustine's answer; but it took, as it proceeded, a far wider flight, and developed a complete Christian scheme of history, past, present, and future. It was an immensely influential book throughout the Middle Ages, especially in the struggles of the

[1] *Ibid.*, chap. xxviii.   [2] *Ibid.*, chap. xxx.

Church with secular princes.

Like some other very great books, it composes itself, in the memory of those who have read it, into something better than at first appears on re-reading. It contains a great deal that hardly anyone at the present day can accept, and its central thesis is somewhat obscured by excrescences belonging to his age. But the broad conception of a contrast between the City of this world and the City of God has remained an inspiration to many, and even now can be restated in non-theological terms.

To omit detail in an account of the book, and concentrate on the central idea, would give an unduly favourable view; on the other hand, to concentrate on the detail would be to omit what is best and most important. I shall endeavour to avoid both errors by first giving some account of the detail and then passing on to the general idea as it appeared in historical development.

The book begins with considerations arising out of the sack of Rome, and designed to show that even worse things happened in pre-Christian times. Among the pagans who attribute the disaster to Christianity, there are many, the Saint says, who, during the sack, sought sanctuary in the churches, which the Goths, because they were Christians, respected. In the sack of Troy, on the contrary, Juno's temple afforded no protection, nor did the gods preserve the city from destruction. The Romans never spared temples in conquered cities; in this respect, the sack of Rome was milder than most, and the mitigation was a result of Christianity.

Christians who suffered the sack have no right to complain, for several reasons. Some wicked Goths may have prospered at their expense, but they will suffer hereafter: if all sin were punished on earth, there would be no need of the Last Judgment. What Christians endured would, if they were virtuous, turn to their edification, for saints, in the loss of things temporal, lose nothing of any value. It does not matter if their bodies lie unburied, because ravenous beasts cannot interfere with the resurrection of the body.

Next comes the question of pious virgins who were raped during the sack. There were apparently some who held that these ladies, by no fault of their own, had lost the crown of virginity. This view the Saint very sensibly opposes. 'Tush, another's lust cannot pollute thee.' Chastity is a virtue of the mind, and is not lost by rape, but is lost by the intention of sin, even if unperformed. It is suggested that God permitted rapes because the victims had been too proud of their continence. It is wicked to commit suicide in order to avoid being raped; this leads to a long discussion of Lucretia, who ought not to have killed herself, because suicide is always a sin.

There is one proviso to the exculpation of virtuous women who are raped: they must not enjoy it. If they do, they are sinful.

He comes next to the wickedness of the heathen gods. For example: 'Your stage-plays, those spectacles of uncleanness, those licentious vanities, were not first brought up at Rome by the corruptions of men, but by the direct command of your gods.'[1] It would be better to worship a virtuous man, such as Scipio, than these immoral gods. But as for the sack of Rome, it need not trouble Christians, who have a sanctuary in the 'pilgrim city of God'.

In this world, the two cities—the earthly and the heavenly—are commingled; but hereafter the predestinate and the reprobate will be separated. In this life, we cannot know who, even among our seeming enemies, are to be found ultimately among the elect.

The most difficult part of the work, we are told, will consist in the refutation of the philosophers, with the best of whom Christians are to a large extent in agreement—for instance as to immortality and the creation of the world by God.[2]

The philosophers did not throw over the worship of the heathen gods, and their moral instructions were weak because the gods were wicked. It is not suggested that the gods are mere fables; they are held by St Augustine to exist, but to be devils. They liked to have filthy stories told of them, because they wanted to injure men. Jupiter's deeds count more, with most pagans, than Plato's doctrines or Cato's opinions. 'Plato, who would not allow poets to dwell in a well-governed city, showed that his sole worth was better than those gods, that desire to be honoured with stage-plays.'[3]

Rome was always wicked, from the rape of the Sabine women onwards. Many chapters are devoted to the sinfulness of Roman imperialism. Nor is it true that Rome did not suffer before the State became Christian; from the Gauls and the civil wars it suffered as much as from the Goths, and more.

Astrology is not only wicked, but false; this may be proved from the different fortunes of twins, who have the same horoscope.[4] The Stoic conception of Fate (which was connected with astrology) is mistaken, since angels and men have free will. It is true that God has foreknowledge of our sins, but we do not sin *because* of His foreknowledge. It is a mistake to suppose that virtue brings unhappiness, even in this world: Christian emperors, if virtuous, have been happy even if not fortunate, and Constantine and Theodosius were fortunate as well; again, the Jewish kingdom lasted as long as the Jews adhered to the truth of religion.

There is a very sympathetic account of Plato, whom he places

[1] *The City of God*, I, 31.   [2] *Ibid.*, I, 35.   [3] *The City of God*, II, 14.
[4] This argument is not original: it is derived from the academic sceptic Carneades. Cf. Cumont, *Oriental Religions in Roman Paganism*, p. 166.

above all other philosophers. All others are to give place to him: 'Let Thales depart with his water, Anaximenes with the air, the Stoics with their fire, Epicurus with his atoms.'[1] All these were materialists; Plato was not. Plato saw that God is not any bodily thing, but that all things have their being from God, and from something immutable. He was right, also, in saying that perception is not the source of truth. Platonists are the best in logic and ethics, and nearest to Christianity. 'It is said that Plotinus, that lived but lately, understood Plato the best of any.' As for Aristotle, he was Plato's inferior, but far above the rest. Both, however, said that all gods are good, and to be worshipped.

As against the Stoics, who condemned all passion, St Augustine holds that the passions of Christians may be causes of virtue; anger, or pity, is not to be condemned *per se*, but we must inquire into its cause.

Platonists are right about God, wrong about gods. They are also wrong in not acknowledging the Incarnation.

There is a long discussion of angels and demons, which is connected with the Neoplatonists. Angels may be good or bad, but demons are always bad. To angels, knowledge of temporal things (though they have it) is vile. St Augustine holds with Plato that the sensible world is inferior to the eternal.

Book XI begins the account of the nature of the City of God. The City of God is the society of the elect. Knowledge of God is obtained only through Christ. There are things that can be discovered by reason (as in the philosophers), but for all further religious knowledge we must rely on the Scriptures. We ought not to seek to understand time and space before the world was made: there was no time before the Creation, and there is no place where the world is not.

Everything blessed is eternal, but not everything eternal is blessed —e.g. hell and Satan. God foreknew the sins of devils, but also their use in improving the universe as a whole, which is analogous to antithesis in rhetoric.

Origen errs in thinking that souls were given bodies as a punishment. If this were so, bad souls would have bad bodies; but devils, even the worst of them, have airy bodies, which are better than ours.

The reason the world was created in six days is that six is a perfect number (i.e. equal to the sum of its factors).

There are good and bad angels, but even the bad angels do not have an essence which is contrary to God. God's enemies are not so by nature, but by will. The vicious will has no *efficient* cause, but only a *deficient* one; it is not an *effect*, but a *defect*.

[1] *The City of God*, VIII, 5.

The world is less than six thousand years old. History is not cyclic, as some philosophers suppose: 'Christ died *once* for our sins.'[1]

If our first parents had not sinned, they would not have died, but, because they sinned, all their posterity die. Eating the apple brought not only natural death, but eternal death, i.e. damnation.

Porphyry is wrong in refusing bodies to saints in heaven. They will have better bodies than Adam's before the fall; their bodies will be spiritual, but not spirits, and will not have weight. Men will have male bodies, and women female bodies, and those who have died in infancy will rise again with adult bodies.

Adam's sin would have brought all mankind to eternal death (i.e. damnation), but that God's grace has freed many from it. Sin came from the soul, not from the flesh. Platonists and Manichæans both err in ascribing sin to the nature of the flesh, though Platonists are not so bad as Manichæans. The punishment of all mankind for Adam's sin was just; for, as a result of this sin, man, that might have been spiritual in body, became carnal in mind.[2]

This leads to a long and minute discussion of sexual lust, to which we are subject as part of our punishment for Adam's sin. This discussion is very important as revealing the psychology of asceticism; we must therefore go into it, although the Saint confesses that the theme is immodest. The theory advanced is as follows.

It must be admitted that sexual intercourse in marriage is not sinful, provided the intention is to beget offspring. Yet even in marriage a virtuous man will wish that he could manage without lust. Even in marriage, as the desire for privacy shows, people are ashamed of sexual intercourse, because 'this lawful act of nature is (from our first parents) accompanied with our penal shame'. The cynics thought that one should be without shame, and Diogenes would have none of it, wishing to be in all things like a dog; yet even he, after one attempt, abandoned, in practice, this extreme of shamelessness. What is shameful about lust is its independence of the will. Adam and Eve, before the fall, could have had sexual intercourse without lust, though in fact they did not. Handicraftsmen, in the pursuit of their trade, move their hands without lust; similarly Adam, if only he had kept away from the apple-tree, could have performed the business of sex without the emotions that it now demands. The sexual members, like the rest of the body, would have obeyed the will. The need of lust in sexual intercourse is a punishment for Adam's sin, but for which sex might have been divorced from pleasure. Omitting some physiological details which

[1] Romans vi, 10; Hebrews vii, 27.
[2] *The City of God*, XIV, 15.

the translator has very properly left in the decent obscurity of the original Latin, the above is St Augustine's theory as regards sex.

It is evident from the above that what makes the ascetic dislike sex is its independence of the will. Virtue, it is held, demands a complete control of the will over the body, but such control does not suffice to make the sexual act possible. The sexual act, therefore, seems inconsistent with a perfectly virtuous life.

Ever since the Fall, the world has been divided into two cities, of which one shall reign eternally with God, the other shall be in eternal torment with Satan. Cain belongs to the city of the Devil, Abel to the City of God. Abel, by grace, and in virtue of predestination, was a pilgrim on earth and a citizen of heaven. The patriarchs belonged to the City of God. Discussion of the death of Methuselah brings St Augustine to the vexed question of the comparison of the Septuagint with the Vulgate. The data, as given in the Septuagint, lead to the conclusion that Methuselah survived the flood by fourteen years, which is impossible, since he was not in the Ark. The Vulgate, following the Hebrew manuscripts, gives data from which it follows that he died in the year of the flood. On this point, St Augustine holds that St Jerome and the Hebrew manuscripts must be right. Some people maintained that the Jews had deliberately falsified the Hebrew manuscripts, out of malice towards the Christians; this hypothesis is rejected. On the other hand, the Septuagint must have been divinely inspired. The only conclusion is that Ptolemy's copyists made mistakes in transcribing the Septuagint. Speaking of the translations of the Old Testament, he says: 'The Church has received that of the Seventy, as if there were no other, as many of the Greek Christians, using this wholly, know not whether there be or no. Our Latin translation is from this also. Although one Jerome, a learned priest, and a great linguist, has translated the same Scriptures from the Hebrew into Latin. But although the Jews affirm his learned labour to be all truth, and avouch the Seventy to have oftentimes erred, yet the Churches of Christ hold no one man to be preferred before so many, especially being selected by the high priest, for this work.' He accepts the story of the miraculous agreement of the seventy independent translations, and considers this a proof that the Septuagint is divinely inspired. The Hebrew, however, is equally inspired. This conclusion leaves undecided the question as to the authority of Jerome's translation. Perhaps he might have been more decidedly on Jerome's side if the two Saints had not had a quarrel about St Peter's time-serving propensities.[1]

He gives a synchronism of sacred and profane history. We learn

[1] Galatians ii, 11-14.

that Æneas came to Italy when Abdon[1] was judge in Israel, and that the last persecution will be under Antichrist, but its date is unknown.

After an admirable chapter against judicial torture, St Augustine proceeds to combat the new Academicians, who hold all things to be doubtful. 'The Church of Christ detests these doubts as madness, having a most certain knowledge of the things it apprehends.' We should believe in the truth of the Scriptures. He goes on to explain that there is no true virtue apart from true religion. Pagan virtue is 'prostituted with the influence of obscene and filthy devils'. What would be virtues in a Christian are vices in a pagan. 'Those things which she [the soul] seems to account virtues, and thereby to sway her affections, if they be not all referred unto God, are indeed vices rather than virtues.' They that are not of this society (the Church) shall suffer eternal misery. 'In our conflicts here on earth, either the pain is victor, and so death expels the sense of it, or nature conquers, and expels the pain. But there, pain shall afflict eternally, and nature shall suffer eternally, both enduring to the continuance of the inflicted punishment.'

There are two resurrections, that of the soul at death, and that of the body at the Last Judgment. After a discussion of various difficulties concerning the millennium, and the subsequent doings of Gog and Magog, he comes to a text in II Thessalonians (ii, 11, 12): 'God shall send them strong delusion, that they should believe a lie, that they all might be damned who believed not the truth, but had pleasure in unrighteousness.' Some people might think it unjust that the Omnipotent should first deceive them, and then punish them for being deceived; but to St Augustine this seems quite in order. 'Being condemned, they are seduced, and, being seduced, condemned. But their seducement is by the secret judgment of God, justly secret, and secretly just; even His that hath judged continually, ever since the world began.' St Augustine holds that God divided mankind into the elect and the reprobate, not because of their merits or demerits, but arbitrarily, All alike deserve damnation, and therefore the reprobate have no ground of complaint. From the above passage of St Paul, it appears that they are wicked because they are reprobate, not reprobate because they are wicked.

After the resurrection of the body, the bodies of the damned will burn eternally without being consumed. In this there is nothing strange; it happens to the salamander and Mount Etna. Devils, though incorporeal, can be burnt by corporeal fire. Hell's torments are not purifying, and will not be lessened by the intercessions of

Of Abdon we know only that he had forty sons and thirty nephews, and that all these seventy rode donkeys (Judges xii, 14).

saints. Origen erred in thinking hell not eternal. Heretics, and sinful Catholics, will be damned.

The book ends with a description of the Saints' vision of God in heaven, and of the eternal felicity of the City of God.

From the above summary, the importance of the work may not be clear. What was influential was the separation of Church and State, with the clear implication that the State could only be part of the City of God by being submissive towards the Church in all religious matters. This has been the doctrine of the Church ever since. All through the Middle Ages, during the gradual rise of the papal power, and throughout the conflict between Pope and Emperor, St Augustine supplied the Western Church with the theoretical justification of its policy. The Jewish State, in the legendary time of the Judges, and in the historical period after the return from the Babylonian captivity, had been a theocracy; the Christian State should imitate it in this respect. The weakness of the emperors, and of most Western medieval monarchs, enabled the Church, to a great extent, to realize the ideal of the City of God. In the East, where the emperor was strong, this development never took place, and the Church remained much more subject to the State than it became in the West.

The Reformation, which revived St Augustine's doctrine of salvation, threw over his theocratic teaching, and became Erastian,[1] largely owing to the practical exigencies of the fight with Catholicism. But Protestant Erastianism was half-hearted, and the most religious among Protestants were still influenced by St Augustine. Anabaptists, Fifth Monarchy Men, and Quakers took over a part of his doctrine, but laid less stress on the Church. He held to predestination, and also to the need of baptism for salvation; these two doctrines do not harmonize well, and the extreme Protestants threw over the latter. But their eschatology remained Augustinian.

The City of God contains little that is fundamentally original. The eschatology is Jewish in origin, and came into Christianity mainly through the Book of Revelation. The doctrine of predestination and election is Pauline, though St Augustine gave it a much fuller and more logical development than is to be found in the Epistles. The distinction between sacred and profane history is quite clearly set forth in the Old Testament. What St Augustine did was to bring these elements together, and to relate them to the history of his own time, in such a way that the fall of the Western Empire, and the subsequent period of confusion, could be assimilated by Christians without any unduly severe trial of their faith.

[1] Erastianism is the doctrine that the Church should be subject to the State.

The Jewish pattern of history, past and future, is such as to make a powerful appeal to the oppressed and unfortunate at all times. St Augustine adapted this pattern to Christianity, Marx to Socialism. To understand Marx psychologically, one should use the following dictionary:

> Yahweh = Dialectical Materialism
> The Messiah = Marx
> The Elect = The Proletariat
> The Church = The Communist Party
> The Second Coming = The Revolution
> Hell = Punishment of the Capitalists
> The Millennium = The Communist Commonwealth

The terms on the left give the emotional content of the terms on the right, and it is this emotional content, familiar to those who have had a Christian or a Jewish upbringing, that makes Marx's eschatology credible. A similar dictionary could be made for the Nazis, but their conceptions are more purely Old Testament and less Christian than those of Marx, and their Messiah is more analogous to the Maccabees than to Christ.

III. THE PELAGIAN CONTROVERSY

Much of the most influential part of St Augustine's theology was concerned in combating the Pelagian heresy. Pelagius was a Welshman, whose real name was Morgan, which means 'man of the sea', as 'Pelagius' does in Greek. He was a cultivated and agreeable ecclesiastic, less fanatical than many of his contemporaries. He believed in free will, questioned the doctrine of original sin, and thought that, when men act virtuously, it is by reason of their own moral effort. If they act rightly, and are orthodox, they go to heaven as a reward of their virtues.

These views, though they may now seem commonplace, caused, at the time, a great commotion, and were, largely through St Augustine's efforts, declared heretical. They had, however, a considerable temporary success. Augustine had to write to the patriarch of Jerusalem to warn him against the wily heresiarch, who had persuaded many Eastern theologians to adopt his views. Even after his condemnation, other people, called semi-Pelagians, advocated weakened forms of his doctrines. It was a long time before the purer teaching of the Saint was completely victorious, especially in France, where the final condemnation of the semi-Pelagian heresy took place at the Council of Orange in 529.

St Augustine taught that Adam, before the Fall, had had free will, and could have abstained from sin. But as he and Eve ate the apple, corruption entered into them, and descended to all their posterity, none of whom can, of their own power, abstain from sin. Only God's grace enables men to be virtuous. Since we all inherit Adam's sin, we all deserve eternal damnation. All who die unbaptized, even infants, will go to hell and suffer unending torment. We have no reason to complain of this, since we are all wicked. (In the *Confessions*, the Saint enumerates the crimes of which he was guilty in the cradle.) But by God's free grace certain people, among those who have been baptized, are chosen to go to heaven; these are the elect. They do not go to heaven because they are good; we are all totally depraved, except in so far as God's grace, which is only bestowed on the elect, enables us to be otherwise. No reason can be given why some are saved and the rest damned; this is due to God's unmotived choice. Damnation proves God's justice; salvation, His mercy. Both equally display His goodness.

The arguments in favour of this ferocious doctrine—which was revived by Calvin, and has since then not been held by the Catholic Church—are to be found in the writings of St Paul, particularly the Epistle to the Romans. These are treated by Augustine as a lawyer treats the law : the interpretation is able, and the texts are made to yield their utmost meaning. One is persuaded, at the end, not that St Paul believed what Augustine deduces, but that, taking certain texts in isolation, they do imply just what he says they do. It may seem odd that the damnation of unbaptized infants should not have been thought shocking, but should have been attributed to a good God. The conviction of sin, however, so dominated him that he really believed new-born children to be limbs of Satan. A great deal of what is most ferocious in the medieval Church is traceable to his gloomy sense of universal guilt.

There is only one intellectual difficulty that really troubles St Augustine. This is not that it seems a pity to have created Man, since the immense majority of the human race are predestined to eternal torment. What troubles him is that, if original sin is inherited from Adam, as St Paul teaches, the soul, as well as the body, must be propagated by the parents, for sin is of the soul, not the body. He sees difficulties in this doctrine, but says that, since Scripture is silent, it cannot be necessary to salvation to arrive at a just view on the matter. He therefore leaves it undecided.

It is strange that the last men of intellectual eminence before the dark ages were concerned, not with saving civilization or expelling the barbarians or reforming the abuses of the administration, but with preaching the merit of virginity and the damnation of unbaptized infants. Seeing that these were the preoccupations that the Church handed on to the converted barbarians, it is no wonder that the succeeding age surpassed almost all other fully historical periods in cruelty and superstition.

Chapter V

THE FIFTH AND SIXTH CENTURIES

THE fifth century was that of the barbarian invasion and the the fall of the Western Empire. After the death of Augustine in 430, there was little philosophy; it was a century of destructive action, which, however, largely determined the lines upon which Europe was to be developed. It was in this century that the English invaded Britain, causing it to become England; it was also in this century that the Frankish invasion turned Gaul into France, and that the Vandals invaded Spain, giving their name to Andalusia. St Patrick, during the middle years of the century, converted the Irish to Christianity. Throughout the Western World, rough Germanic kingdoms succeeded the centralized bureaucracy of the Empire. The imperial post ceased, the great roads fell into decay, war put an end to large-scale commerce, and life again became local both politically and economically. Centralized authority was preserved only in the Church, and there with much difficulty.

Of the Germanic tribes that invaded the Empire in the fifth century, the most important were the Goths. They were pushed westwards by the Huns, who attacked them from the East. At first they tried to conquer the Eastern Empire, but were defeated; then they turned upon Italy. Since Diocletian, they had been employed as Roman mercenaries; this had taught them more of the art of war than barbarians would otherwise have known. Alaric, king of the Goths, sacked Rome in 410, but died the same year. Odovaker, king of the Ostrogoths, put an end to the Western Empire in 476, and reigned until 493, when he was treacherously murdered by another Ostrogoth, Theodoric, who was king of Italy until 526. Of him I shall have more to say shortly. He was important both in history and legend; in the Niebelungenlied he appears as 'Dietrich von Bern' ('Bern' being Verona).

Meanwhile the Vandals established themselves in Africa, the Visigoths in the south of France, and the Franks in the north.

In the middle of the Germanic invasion came the inroads of the Huns under Attila. The Huns were of Mongul race, and yet they were often allied with the Goths. At the crucial moment, however, when they invaded Gaul in 451, they had quarrelled with the Goths; the Goths and Romans together defeated them in that year at Chalons. Attila then turned against Italy, and thought of marching on Rome, but Pope Leo dissuaded him, pointing out that Alaric had died after sacking Rome. His forbearance, however, did him no service, for he died in the following year. After his death the power of the Huns collapsed.

During this period of confusion the Church was troubled by a complicated controversy on the Incarnation. The protagonists in the debates were two ecclesiastics, Cyril and Nestorius, of whom, more or less by accident, the former was proclaimed a saint and the latter a heretic. St Cyril was patriarch of Alexandria from about 412 till his death in 444; Nestorius was patriarch of Constantinople. The question at issue was the relation of Christ's divinity to His humanity. Were there two Persons, one human and one divine? This was the view held by Nestorius. If not, was there only one nature, or were there two natures in one person, a human nature and a divine nature? These questions roused, in the fifth century, an almost incredible degree of passion and fury. 'A secret and incurable discord was cherished between those who were most apprehensive of confounding, and those who were most fearful of separating, the divinity and the humanity of Christ.'[1]

St Cyril, the advocate of unity, was a man of fanatical zeal. He used his position as patriarch to incite pogroms against the very large Jewish colony in Alexandria. His chief claim to fame is the lynching of Hypatia, a distinguished lady who, in an age of bigotry, adhered to the Neoplatonic philosophy and devoted her talents to mathematics. She was 'torn from her chariot, stripped naked, dragged to the church, and inhumanly butchered by the hands of Peter the Reader and a troop of savage and merciless fanatics: her flesh was scraped from her bones with sharp oyster-shells and her quivering limbs were delivered to the flames. The just progress of inquiry and punishment was stopped by seasonable gifts.'[2] After this, Alexandria was no longer troubled by philosophers.

St Cyril was pained to learn that Constantinople was being led astray by the teaching of its patriarch Nestorius, who maintained that there were two Persons in Christ, one human and one divine. On this ground Nestorius objected to the new practice of calling the Virgin 'Mother of God'; she was, he said, only the mother of the human Person, while the divine Person, who was God, had no mother. On this question the Church was divided: roughly speaking, bishops east of Suez favoured Nestorius, while those west of Suez favoured St Cyril. A council was summoned to meet at Ephesus in 431 to decide the question. The Western bishops arrived first, and proceeded to lock the doors against latecomers and decide in hot haste for St Cyril, who presided. 'This episcopal tumult, at the

---

[1] Gibbon, *op. cit.*, chap. xlvii.   [2] *Ibid.*

distance of thirteen centuries, assumes the venerable aspect of the third oecumenical Council.'[1]

As a result of this council, Nestorius was condemned as a heretic. He did not recant, but was the founder of the Nestorian sect, which had a large following in Syria and throughout the East. Some centuries later, Nestorianism was so strong in China that it seemed to have a chance of becoming the established religion. Nestorians were found in India by the Spanish and Portuguese missionaries in the sixteenth century. The persecution of Nestorianism by the Catholic government of Constantinople caused disaffection which helped the Mohammedans in their conquest of Syria.

The tongue of Nestorius, which by its eloquence had seduced so many, was eaten by worms—so at least we are assured.

Ephesus had learnt to substitute the Virgin for Artemis, but had still the same intemperate zeal for its goddess as in the time of St Paul. It was said that the Virgin was buried there. In 449, after the death of St Cyril, a synod at Ephesus tried to carry the triumph further, and thereby fell into the heresy opposite to that of Nestorius; this is called the Monophysite heresy, and maintains that Christ has only one nature. If St Cyril had still been alive, he would certainly have supported this view, and have become heretical. The Emperor supported the synod, but the Pope repudiated it. At last Pope Leo—the same Pope who turned Attila from attacking Rome—in the year of the battle of Chalons secured the summoning of an oecumenical council at Chalcedon in 451, which condemned the Monophysites and finally decided the orthodox doctrine of the Incarnation. The Council of Ephesus had decided that there is only one *Person* of Christ, but the Council of Chalcedon decided that He exists in two *natures*, one human and one divine. The influence of the Pope was paramount in securing this decision.

The Monophysites, like the Nestorians, refused to submit. Egypt, almost to a man, adopted their heresy, which spread up the Nile and as far as Abyssinia. The heresy of the Abyssinians was given by Mussolini as one of his reasons for conquering them. The heresy of Egypt, like the opposite heresy of Syria, facilitated the Arab conquest.

During the sixth century, there were four men of great importance in the history of culture: Boethius, Justinian, Benedict, and Gregory the Great. They will be my chief concern in the remainder of this chapter and in the next.

The Gothic conquest of Italy did not put an end to Roman civilization. Under Theodoric, king of Italy and of the Goths, the civil administration of Italy was entirely Roman; Italy enjoyed peace

[1] Gibbon, *op. cit.*, chap. xlvii.

and religious toleration (till near the end); the king was both wise and vigorous. He appointed consuls, preserved Roman law, and kept up the Senate: when in Rome, his first visit was to the Senate House.

Though an Arian, Theodoric was on good terms with the Church until his last years. In 523, the Emperor Justin proscribed Arianism, and this annoyed Theodoric. He had reason for fear, since Italy was Catholic, and was led by theological sympathy to side with the Emperor. He believed, rightly or wrongly, that there was a plot involving men in his own government. This led him to imprison and execute his minister, the senator Boethius, whose *Consolations of Philosophy* was written while he was in prison.

Boethius is a singular figure. Throughout the Middle Ages he was read and admired, regarded always as a devout Christian and treated almost as if he had been one of the Fathers. Yet his *Consolations of Philosophy*, written in 524 while he was awaiting execution, is purely Platonic; it does not prove that he was not a Christian, but it does show that pagan philosophy had a much stronger hold on him than Christian theology. Some theological works, especially one on the Trinity, which are attributed to him, are by many authorities considered to be spurious; but it was probably owing to them that the Middle Ages were able to regard him as orthodox, and to imbibe from him much Platonism which would otherwise have been viewed with suspicion.

The work is an alternation of verse and prose: Boethius, in his own person, speaks in prose, while Philosophy answers in verse. There is a certain resemblance to Dante, who was no doubt influenced by him in the *Vita Nuova*.

The *Consolations*, which Gibbon rightly calls a 'golden volume', begins by the statement that Socrates, Plato, and Aristotle are the true philosophers; Stoics, Epicureans, and the rest are usurpers whom the profane multitude mistook for the friends of philosophy. Boethius says he obeyed the Pythagorean command to 'follow God' (not the *Christian* command). Happiness, which is the same thing as blessedness, is the good, not pleasure. Friendship is a 'most sacred thing'. There is much morality that agrees closely with Stoic doctrine, and is in fact largely taken from Seneca. There is a summary, in verse, of the beginning of the *Timaeus*. This is followed by a great deal of purely Platonic metaphysics. Imperfection, we are told, is a lack, implying the existence of a perfect pattern. He adopted the privative theory of evil. He then passes on to a pantheism which should have shocked Christians, but for some reason did not. Blessedness and God, he says, are both the chiefest good, and are therefore identical. 'Men are made happy by the obtaining of divinity.' 'They who obtain divinity become gods. Wherefore every one that is happy is a god, but by nature there is only one God, but there may be many by participation.' 'The sum, origin, and cause of all that is sought after is rightly thought to be goodness.' 'The substance of God consisteth in nothing else but in goodness.' Can God do evil? No. Therefore evil is nothing, since God can do everything. Virtuous men are always powerful, and bad men always weak; for both desire the good, but only the virtuous get it. The wicked are more unfortunate if they escape punishment than if they suffer it. 'In wise men there is no place for hatred.'

The tone of the book is more like that of Plato than that of Plotinus. There is no trace of the superstition or morbidness of the age, no obsession with sin, no excessive straining after the unattainable. There is perfect philosophic calm—so much that, if the book had been written in prosperity, it might almost have been called smug. Written when it was, in prison under sentence of death, it is as admirable as the last moments of the Platonic Socrates.

One does not find a similar outlook until after Newton. I will quote *in extenso* one poem from the book, which, in its philosophy, is not unlike Pope's *Essay on Man*.

If Thou wouldst see
God's laws with purest mind,
Thy sight on heaven fixed must be,
Whose settled course the stars in peace doth bind,
The sun's bright fire
Stops not his sister's team,
Nor doth the northern bear desire
Within the ocean's wave to hide her beam.
Though she behold
The other stars there crouching,
Yet she incessantly is rolled
About high heaven, the ocean never touching.
The evening light
With certain course doth show
The coming of the shady night,
And Lucifer before the day doth go.
This mutual love
Courses eternal makes,
And from the starry spheres above
All cause of war and dangerous discord takes.
This sweet consent
In equal bands doth tie
The nature of each element
So that the moist things yield unto the dry.
The piercing cold

With flames doth friendship heap
The trembling fire the highest place doth hold,
And the gross earth sinks down into the deep.
The flowery year
Breathes odours in the spring,
The scorching summer corn doth bear,
The autumn fruit from laden trees doth bring.
The falling rain
Doth winter's moisture give.
These rules thus nourish and maintain
All creatures which we see on earth to live.
And when they die,
These bring them to their end,
While their Creator sits on high,
Whose hand the reins of the whole world doth bend.
He as their king
Rules them with lordly might.
From Him they rise, flourish, and spring,
He as their law and judge decides their right.
Those things whose course
Most swiftly glides away
His might doth often backward force,
And suddenly their wandering motion stay.
Unless his strength
Their violence should bound,
And them which else would run at length,
Should bring within the compass of a round,
That firm decree
Which now doth all adorn
Would soon destroyed and broken be,
Things being far from their beginning borne.
This powerful love
Is common unto all,
Which for desire of good do move
Back to the springs from when they first did fall.
No worldly thing
Can a continuance have
Unless love back again it bring
Unto the cause which first the essence gave.

Boethius was, until the end, a friend of Theodoric. His father
was consul, he was consul, and so were his two sons. His father-
in-law Symmachus (probably grandson of the one who had a
controversy with Ambrose about the statue of Victory) was an important man in the court of the Gothic king. Theodoric employed
Boethius to reform the coinage, and to astonish less sophisticated
barbarian kings with such devices as sun-dials and water-clocks. It
may be that his freedom from superstition was not so exceptional

in Roman aristocratic families as elsewhere; but its combination with great learning and zeal for the public good was unique in that age. During the two centuries before his time and the ten centuries after it, I cannot think of any European man of learning so free from superstition and fanaticism. Nor are his merits merely negative; his survey is lofty, disinterested, and sublime. He would have been remarkable in any age; in the age in which he lived, he is utterly amazing.

The medieval reputation of Boethius was partly due to his being regarded as a martyr to Arian persecution—a view which began two or three hundred years after his death. In Pavia, he was *regarded* as a saint, but in fact he was not canonized. Though Cyril was a saint. Boethius was not.

Two years after the execution of Boethius, Theodoric died. In the next year, Justinian became Emperor. He reigned until 565, and in this long time managed to do much harm and some good. He is of course chiefly famous for his *Digest*, but I shall not venture on this topic, which is one for the lawyers. He was a man of deep piety, which he signalized, two years after his accession, by closing the schools of philosophy in Athens, where paganism still reigned. The dispossessed philosophers betook themselves to Persia, where the king received them kindly. But they were shocked—more so, says Gibbon, than became philosophers—by the Persian practices of polygamy and incest, so they returned home again, and faded into obscurity. Three years after this exploit (532), Justinian embarked upon another, more worthy of praise—the building of St Sophia. I have never seen St Sophia, but I have seen the beautiful contemporary mosaics at Ravenna, including portraits of Justinian and his empress Theodora. Both were very pious, though Theodora was a lady of easy virtue whom he had picked up in the circus. What is even worse, she was inclined to be a Monophysite.

But enough of scandal. The Emperor himself, I am happy to say, was of impeccable orthodoxy, even in the matter of the 'Three Chapters'. This was a vexatious controversy. The Council of Chalcedon had pronounced orthodox three Fathers suspected of Nestorianism; Theodora, along with many others, accepted all the other decrees of the Council, but not this one. The Western Church stood for everything decided by the Council, and the empress was driven to persecute the Pope. Justinian adored her, and after her death in 548, she became to him what the dead Prince Consort was to Queen Victoria. So in the end he lapsed into heresy, that of Aphthartodocetism. A contemporary historian (Evagrius) writes: 'Having since the end of his life received the wages of his misdeeds,

370

he has gone to seek the justice which was his due before the judgment-seat of hell.'

Justinian aspired to reconquer as much as possible of the Western Empire. In 535 he invaded Italy, and at first had quick success against the Goths. The Catholic population welcomed him, and he came as representing Rome against the barbarians. But the Goths rallied, and the war lasted eighteen years, during which Rome, and Italy generally, suffered far more than in the barbarian invasion.

Rome was five times captured, thrice by Byzantines, twice by Goths, and sank to a small town. The same sort of thing happened in Africa, which Justinian also more or less reconquered. At first his armies were welcomed; then it was found that Byzantine administration was corrupt and Byzantine taxes were ruinous. In the end, many people wished the Goths and Vandals back. The Church, however, until his last years, was steadily on the side of the Emperor, because of his orthodoxy. He did not attempt the reconquest of Gaul, partly because of distance, but partly also because the Franks were orthodox.

In 568, three years after Justinian's death, Italy was invaded by a new and fierce German tribe, the Lombards. Wars between them and the Byzantines continued intermittently for two hundred years, until nearly the time of Charlemagne. The Byzantines held gradually less and less of Italy; in the South, they had also to face the Saracens. Rome remained nominally subject to them, and the popes treated the Eastern emperors with deference. But in most parts of Italy the emperors, after the coming of the Lombards, had very little authority or even none at all. It was this period that ruined Italian civilization. It was refugees from the Lombards who founded Venice, not, as tradition avers, fugitives from Attila.

Chapter VI

ST BENEDICT AND GREGORY THE GREAT

IN the general decay of civilization that came about during the incessant wars of the sixth and succeeding centuries, it was above all the Church that preserved whatever survived of the culture of ancient Rome. The Church performed this work very imperfectly, because fanaticism and superstition prevailed among even the greatest ecclesiastics of the time, and secular learning was thought wicked. Nevertheless, ecclesiastical institutions created a solid framework, within which, in later times, a revival of learning and civilized arts became possible.

In the period with which we are concerned, three of the activities of the Church call for special notice: first, the monastic movement; second, the influence of the papacy, especially under Gregory the Great; third, the conversion of the heathen barbarians by means of missions. I will say something about each of these in succession.

The monastic movement began simultaneously in Egypt and Syria about the beginning of the fourth century. It had two forms, that of solitary hermits, and that of monasteries. St Anthony, the first of the hermits, was born in Egypt about 250, and withdrew from the world about 270. For fifteen years he lived alone in a hut near his home; then, for twenty years, in remote solitude in the desert. But his fame spread, and multitudes longed to hear him preach. Accordingly, about 305, he came forth to teach, and to encourage the hermit's life. He practised extreme austerities, reducing food, drink, and sleep to the minimum required to support life. The devil constantly assailed him with lustful visions, but he manfully withstood the malign diligence of Satan. By the end of his life, the Thebaid[1] was full of hermits who had been inspired by his example and his precepts.

A few years later—about 315 or 320—another Egyptian, Pachomius, founded the first monastery. Here the monks had a common life, without private poverty, with communal meals and communal religious observances. It was in this form, rather than in that of St Anthony, that monasticism conquered the Christian world. In the monasteries derived from Pachomius, the monks did much work, chiefly agricultural, instead of spending the whole of their time in resisting the temptations of the flesh.

[1] The desert near Egyptian Thebes.

At about the same time, monasticism sprang up in Syria and Mesopotamia. Here asceticism was carried to even greater lengths than in Egypt. St Simeon Stylites and the other pillar hermits were Syrian. It was from the East that monasticism came to Greek-speaking countries, chiefly owing to St Basil (about 360). His monasteries were less ascetic; they had orphanages, and schools for boys (not only for such as intended to become monks).

At first, monasticism was a spontaneous movement, quite outside Church organization. It was St Athanasius who reconciled ecclesiastics to it. Partly as a result of his influence, it came to be the rule that monks should be priests. It was he also, while he was in Rome in 339, who introduced the movement into the West. St Jerome did much to promote it, and St Augustine introduced it into Africa. St Martin of Tours inaugurated monasteries in Gaul, St Patrick in Ireland. The monastery of Iona was founded by St Columba in 566. In early days, before monks had been fitted into the the the ecclesiastical organization, they had been a source of disorder. To begin with, there was no way of discriminating between genuine ascetics and men who, being destitute, found monastic establishments comparatively luxurious. Then again there was the difficulty that the monks gave a turbulent support to their favourite bishop, causing synods (and almost causing Councils) to fall into heresy. The synod (not the Council) of Ephesus, which decided for the Monophysites, was under a monkish reign of terror. But for the resistance of the Pope, the victory of the Monophysites might have been permanent. In later times, such disorders no longer occurred.

There seem to have been nuns before there were monks—as early as the middle of the third century.

Cleanliness was viewed with abhorrence. Lice were called 'pearls of God', and were a mark of saintliness. Saints, male and female, would boast that water had never touched their feet except when they had to cross rivers. In later centuries, monks served many useful purposes; they were skilled agriculturists, and some of them kept alive or revived learning. But in the beginning, especially in the eremitic section, there was none of this. Most monks did no work, never read anything except what religion prescribed, and conceived virtue in an entirely negative manner, as abstention from sin, especially the sins of the flesh. St Jerome, it is true, took his library with him into the desert, but he came to think that this had been a sin.

In Western monasticism, the most important name is that of St Benedict, the founder of the Benedictine Order. He was born about 480, near Spoleto, of a noble Umbrian family; at the age of twenty, he fled from the luxuries and pleasures of Rome to the solitude of a cave, where he lived for three years. After this period, his life was less solitary, and about the year 520 he founded the famous monastery of Monte Cassino, for which he drew up the 'Benedictine rule'. This was adapted to Western climates, and demanded less austerity than had been common among Egyptian and Syrian monks. There had been an unedifying competition in ascetic extravagance, the most extreme practitioner being considered the most holy. To this St Benedict put an end, decreeing that austerities going beyond the rule could only be practised by permission of the abbot. The abbot was given great power; he was elected for life, and had (within the Rule and the limits of orthodoxy) an almost despotic control over his monks, who were no longer allowed, as previously, to leave their monastery for another if they felt so inclined. In later times, Benedictines have been remarkable for learning, but at first all their reading was devotional.

Organizations have a life of their own, independent of the intentions of their founders. Of this fact, the most striking example is the Catholic Church, which would astonish Jesus, and even Paul. The Benedictine Order is a lesser example. The monks take a vow of poverty, obedience, and chastity. As to this, Gibbon remarks: 'I have somewhere heard or read the frank confession of a Benedictine abbot: "My vow of poverty has given me an hundred thousand crowns a year; my vow of obedience has raised me to the rank of a sovereign prince." I forget the consequences of his vow of chastity.'[1] The departures of the Order from the founder's intentions were, however, by no means all regrettable. This is true, in particular, of learning. The library of Monte Cassino was famous, and in various ways the world is much indebted to the scholarly tastes of later Benedictines.

St Benedict lived at Monte Cassino from its foundation until his death in 543. The monastery was sacked by the Lombards, shortly before Gregory the Great, himself a Benedictine, became Pope. The monks fled to Rome; but when the fury of the Lombards had abated, they returned to Monte Cassino.

From the dialogues of Pope Gregory the Great, written in 593, we learn much about St Benedict. He was 'brought up at Rome in the study of humanity. But forasmuch as he saw many by the reason of such learning to fall to dissolute and lewd life, he drew back his foot, which he had as it were now set forth into the world, lest, entering too far in acquaintance therewith, he likewise might have fallen into that dangerous and godless gulf: wherefore, giving over his book, and forsaking his father's house and wealth, with a resolute mind only to serve God, he sought for some place, where

[1] *Op. cit.*, xxxvii, note 57.

he might attain to the desire of his holy purpose: and in this sort he departed, instructed with learned ignorance, and furnished with unlearned wisdom.'

He immediately acquired the power to work miracles. The first of these was the mending of a broken sieve by means of prayer. The townsmen hung the sieve over the church door, and it 'continued there many years after, even to these very troubles of the Lombards'. Abandoning the sieve, he went to his cave, unknown to all but one friend, who secretly supplied him with food let down by a rope, to which a bell was tied to let the saint know when his dinner had come. But Satan threw a stone at the rope, breaking both it and the bell. Nevertheless, the enemy of mankind was foiled in his hope of disrupting the Saint's food-supply.

When Benedict had been as long in the cave as God's purposes required, our Lord appeared on Easter Sunday to a certain priest, revealed the hermit's whereabouts, and bade him share his Easter feast with the Saint. About the same time certain shepherds found him. 'At the first, when they espied him through the bushes, and saw his apparel made of skins, they verily thought that it had been some beast: but after they were acquainted with the servant of God, many of them were by his means converted from their beastly life to grace, piety, and devotion.'

Like other hermits, Benedict suffered from the temptations of the flesh. 'A certain woman there was which some time he had seen, the memory of which the wicked spirit put into his mind, and by the memory of her did so mightily inflame with concupiscence the soul of God's servant, which did so increase that, almost overcome with pleasure, he was of mind to have forsaken the wilderness. But suddenly, assisted with God's grace, he came to himself; and seeing many thick briers and nettle bushes to grow hard by, off he cast his apparel, and threw himself into the midst of them, and there wallowed so long that, when he rose up, all his flesh was pitifully torn: and so by the wounds of his body, he cured the wounds of his soul.'

His fame being spread abroad, the monks of a certain monastery, whose abbot had lately died, besought him to accept the succession. He did so, and insisted upon observance of strict virtue, so that the monks, in a rage, decided to poison him with a glass of poisoned wine. He, however, made the sign of the cross over the glass, whereupon it broke in pieces. So he returned to the wilderness.

The miracle of the sieve was not the only practically useful one performed by St Benedict. One day, a virtuous Goth was using a bill-hook to clear away briers, when the head of it flew off the handle and fell into deep water. The Saint, being informed, held the handle in the water, whereupon the iron head rose up and joined itself again to the handle.

A neighbouring priest, envious of the holy man's reputation, sent him a poisoned loaf. But Benedict miraculously knew it was poisoned. He had the habit of giving bread to a certain crow, and when the crow came on the day in question, the Saint said to it: 'In the name of Jesus Christ our Lord, take up that loaf and leave it in some place where no man may find it.' The crow obeyed, and on its return was given its usual dinner. The wicked priest, seeing he could not kill Benedict's body, decided to kill his soul, and sent seven naked young women into the monastery. The saint feared lest some of the younger monks might be moved to sin, and therefore departed himself, that the priest might no longer have a motive for such acts. But the priest was killed by the ceiling of his room falling on him. A monk pursued Benedict with the news, rejoicing, and bidding him return. Benedict mourned over the death of the sinner, and imposed a penance on the monk for rejoicing.

Gregory does not only relate miracles, but deigns, now and then, to tell facts in the career of St Benedict. After founding twelve monasteries, he finally came to Monte Cassino, where there was a 'chapel' to Apollo, still used by the country people for heathen worship. 'Even to that very time, the mad multitude of infidels did offer most wicked sacrifice.' Benedict destroyed the altar, substituted a church, and converted the neighbouring pagans. Satan was annoyed:

'The old enemy of mankind, not taking this in good part, did not now privily or in a dream, but in open sight present himself to the eyes of that holy father, and with great outcries complained that he had offered him violence. The noise which he made, the monks did hear; but, as the venerable father told them, he appeared visibly unto him most fell and cruel, and as though, with his fiery mouth and flaming eyes, he would have torn him in pieces: what the devil said unto him, all the monks did hear; for first he would call him by his name, and because the man of God vouchsafed him not any answer, then would he fall a reviling and railing at him: for when he cried out, calling him "Blessed Bennet", and yet found that he gave him no answer, straightways he would turn his tune and say: "Cursed Bennet, and not blessed: what hast thou to do with me? and why dost thou thus persecute me?" ' Here the story ends; one gathers that Satan gave up in despair.

I have quoted at some length from these dialogues, because they have a threefold importance. First, they are the principal source for our knowledge of the life of St Benedict, whose Rule became the model for all Western monasteries except those of Ireland or founded by Irishmen. Secondly, they give a vivid picture of the mental atmosphere among the most civilized people living at the end of the sixth century. Thirdly, they are written by Pope Gregory the Great, fourth and last of the Doctors of the Western Church, and politically one of the most eminent of the popes. To him we must now turn our attention.

The Venerable W. H. Hutton, Archdeacon of Northampton,[1] claims that Gregory was the greatest man of the sixth century; the only rival claimants, he says, would be Justinian and St Benedict. All three, certainly, had a profound effect on future ages; Justinian by his Laws (not by his conquests, which were ephemeral); Benedict by his monastic order; and Gregory by the increase of papal power which he brought about. In the dialogues that I have been quoting he appears childish and credulous, but as a statesman he is astute, masterful, and very well aware of what can be achieved in the complex and changing world in which he has to operate. The contrast is surprising; but the most effective men of action are often intellectually second-rate.

Gregory the Great, the first Pope of that name, was born in Rome, about 540, of a rich and noble family. It seems his grandfather had been Pope after he became a widower. He himself, as a young man, had a palace and immense wealth. He had what was considered a good education, though it did not include a knowledge of Greek, which he never acquired, although he lived for six years in Constantinople. In 573 he was prefect of the City of Rome. But religion claimed him: he resigned his office, gave his wealth to the founding of monasteries and to charity, and turned his own palace into a house for monks, himself becoming a Benedictine. He devoted himself to meditation, and to austerities which permanently injured his health. But Pope Pelagius II had become aware of his political abilities, and sent him as his envoy to Constantinople, to which, since Justinian's time, Rome was nominally subject. Gregory lived in Constantinople from 579 to 585, representing papal interests at the Emperor's court, and papal theology in discussions with Eastern ecclesiastics, who were always more prone to heresy than those of the West. The patriarch of Constantinople, at this time, held the erroneous opinion that our resurrection bodies will be impalpable, but Gregory saved the Emperor from falling into this departure from the true faith. He was unable, however, to persuade the Emperor to undertake a campaign against the Lombards, which was the principal object of his mission.

The five years 585-90 Gregory spent as head of his monastery.

[1] *Cambridge Medieval History*, II, chap. viii.

Then the Pope died, and Gregory succeeded him. The times were difficult, but by their very confusion offered great opportunities to an able statesman. The Lombards were ravaging Italy; Spain and Africa were in a state of anarchy due to the weakness of the Byzantines and the decadence of Visigoths and the depredations of Moors. In France there were wars between North and South. Britain, which had been Christian under the Romans, had reverted to paganism since the Saxon invasion. There were still remnants of Arianism, and the heresy of the Three Chapters was by no means extinct. The turbulent time infected even bishops, many of whom led far from exemplary lives. Simony was rife, and remained a crying evil until the latter half of the eleventh century.

All these sources of trouble Gregory combated with energy and sagacity. Before his pontificate, the bishop of Rome, though acknowledged to be the greatest man in the hierarchy, was not regarded as having any jurisdiction outside his own diocese. St Ambrose, for example, who was on the best of terms with the Pope of his day, obviously never regarded himself as in any degree subject to his authority. Gregory, owing partly to his personal qualities and partly to the prevailing anarchy, was able to assert successfully an authority which was admitted by ecclesiastics throughout the West, and even, to a lesser degree, in the East. He exerted this authority chiefly by means of letters to bishops and secular rulers in all parts of the Roman world, but also in other ways. His *Book of Pastoral Rule*, containing advice to bishops, had a great influence throughout the earlier Middle Ages. It was intended as a guide to the duties of bishops, and was accepted as such. He wrote it in the first instance for the bishop of Ravenna, and sent it also to the bishop of Seville. Under Charlemagne, it was given to bishops at consecration. Alfred the Great translated in into Anglo-Saxon. In the East it was circulated in Greek. It gives sound, if not surprising, advice to bishops, such as not to neglect business. It tells them also that rulers should not be criticized, but should be kept alive to the danger of hell-fire if they fail to follow the advice of the Church.

Gregory's letters are extraordinarily interesting, not only as showing his character, but as giving a picture of his age. His tone, except to the Emperor and the ladies of the Byzantine court, is that of a head master—sometimes commending, often reproving, never showing the faintest hesitation as to his right to give orders.

Let us take as a sample his letters during one year (599). The first is a letter to the bishop of Cagliari in Sardinia, who, though old, was bad. It says, in part: 'It has been told me that on the Lord's day, before celebrating the solemnities of mass, thou wentest forth to plough up the crop of the bearer of these presents. . . . Also, after the solemnities of mass thou didst not fear to root up the landmarks of that possession. . . . Seeing that we still spare thy grey hairs, bethink thee at length, old man, and restrain thyself from such levity of behaviour, and perversity of deeds.' He writes at the same time to the secular authorities of Sardinia on the same subject. The bishop in question next has to be reproved because he makes a charge for conducting funerals; and then again because, with his sanction, a converted Jew placed the Cross and an image of the Virgin in a synagogue. Moreover, he and other Sardinian bishops have been known to travel without permission of their metropolitan; this must cease. Then follows a very severe letter to the proconsul of Dalmatia, saying, among other things: 'We see not of what sort your satisfaction is either to God or men'; and again: 'With regard to your seeking to be in favour with us, it is fitting that with your whole heart and soul, and with tears, as becomes you, you should satisfy your Redeemer for such things as these.' I am ignorant as to what the wretch had done.

Next comes a letter to Callincus, exarch of Italy, congratulating him on a victory over the Slavs, and telling him how to act towards the heretics of Istria, who erred as to the Three Chapters. He writes also on this subject to the bishop of Ravenna. Once, by way of exception, we find a letter to the bishop of Syracuse, in which Gregory defends himself instead of finding fault with others. The question at issue is a weighty one, namely whether 'Alleluia' should be said at a certain point in the mass. Gregory's usage, he says, is not adopted from subservience to the Byzantines, as the bishop of Syracuse suggests, but is derived from St James via the blessed Jerome. Those who thought he was being unduly subservient to Greek usage were therefore in error. (A similar question was one of the causes of the schism of the Old Believers in Russia.)

There are a number of letters to barbarian sovereigns, male and female. Brunichild, queen of the Franks, wanted the pallium conferred on a certain French bishop, and Gregory was willing to grant her request; but unfortunately the emissary she sent was a schismatic. To Agilulph king of the Lombards he writes congratulating him on having made peace. 'For, if unhappily peace had not been made, what else could have ensued but, with sin and danger on both sides, the shedding of the blood of miserable peasants whose labour profits both?' At the same time he writes to Agilulph's wife, Queen Theodelinda, telling her to influence her husband to persist in good courses. He writes again to Brunichild to find fault with two things in her kingdom: that laymen are promoted at once to be bishops, without a probationary time as ordinary priests; and that Jews are allowed to have Christian slaves. To Theodoric and Theodebert, kings of the Franks, he writes saying that, owing to the exemplary piety of the Franks, he would like to utter only pleasant things, but he cannot refrain from pointing out the prevalence of simony in their kingdom. He writes again about a wrong done to the Bishop of Turin. One letter to a barbarian sovereign is wholly complimentary; it is to Richard, king of the Visigoths, who had been an Arian, but became a Catholic in 587. For this the Pope rewards him by sending him 'a small key from the most sacred body of the blessed apostle Peter to convey his blessing, containing iron from his chains, that what had bound his neck for martyrdom may loose yours from all sins.' I hope His Majesty was pleased with this present.

The Bishop of Antioch is instructed as to the heretical synod of Ephesus, and informed that 'it has come to our ears that in the Churches of the East no one attains to a sacred order except by giving bribes'—a matter which the bishop is to rectify wherever it is in his power to do so. The Bishop of Marseilles is reproached for breaking certain images which were being adored: it is true that adoration of images is wrong, but images, nevertheless, are useful and should be treated with respect. Two bishops of Gaul are reproached because a lady who had become a nun was afterwards forced to marry. 'If this be so, . . . you shall have the office of hirelings, and not the merit of shepherds.'

The above are a few of the letters of a single year. It is no wonder that he found no time for contemplation, as he laments in one of the letters of this year (cxxi).

Gregory was no friend to secular learning. To Desiderius, Bishop of Vienne in France, he writes:

'It came to our ears, what we cannot mention without shame, that thy Fraternity is [i.e. thou art] in the habit of expounding grammar to certain persons. This thing we took so much amiss, and so strongly disapproved it, that we changed what had been said before into groaning and sadness, since the praises of Christ cannot find room in one mouth with the praises of Jupiter . . . . In proportion as it is execrable for such a thing to be related of a priest, it ought to be ascertained by strict and veracious evidence whether or not it be so.'

This hostility to pagan learning survived in the Church for at least four centuries, till the time of Gerbert (Sylvester II). It was only from the eleventh century onward that the Church became friendly to learning.

Gregory's attitude to the emperor is much more deferential than his attitude to barbarian kings. Writing to a correspondent in Constantinople he says: 'What pleases the most pious emperor, whatever he commands to be done, is in his power. As he determines, so let him provide. Only let him not cause us to be mixed up in the deposition [of an orthodox bishop]. Still, what he does, if it is canonical, we will follow. But, if it is not canonical, we will bear it, so far as we can without sin of our own." When the Emperor Maurice was dethroned by a mutiny, of which the leader was an obscure centurion named Phocas, this upstart acquired the throne, and proceeded to massacre the five sons of Maurice in their father's presence, after which he put to death the aged Emperor himself. Phocas was of course crowned by the patriarch of Constantinople, who had no alternative but death. What is more surprising is that Gregory, from the comparatively safe distance of Rome, wrote letters of fulsome adulation to the usurper and his wife. 'There is this difference,' he writes, 'between the kings of the nations and the emperors of the republic, that the kings of the nations are lords of slaves, but the emperors of the republic lords of freemen. . . . May Almighty God in every thought and deed keep the heart of your Piety [i.e. you] in the hand of His grace; and whatsoever things should be done justly, whatsoever things with clemency. may the Holy Spirit who dwells in your breast direct.' And to the wife of Phocas, the Empress Leontia, he writes: 'What tongue may suffice to speak, what mind to think, what great thanks we owe to Almighty God for the serenity of your empire, in that such hard burdens of long duration have been removed from our necks, and the gentle yoke of imperial supremacy has returned.' One might suppose Maurice to have been a monster; in fact, he was a good old man. Apologists excuse Gregory on the plea that he did not know what atrocities had been committed by Phocas; but he certainly knew the customary behaviour of Byzantine usurpers, and he did not wait to ascertain whether Phocas was an exception.

The conversion of the heathen was an important part of the increasing influence of the Church. The Goths had been converted before the end of the fourth century by Ulphilas, or Ulfila—unfortunately to Arianism, which was also the creed of the Vandals. After the death of Theodoric, however, the Goths became gradually Catholic: the king of the Visigoths, as we have seen, adopted the orthodox faith in the time of Gregory. The Franks were Catholic from the time of Clovis. The Irish were converted before the fall of the Western Empire by St Patrick, a Somersetshire country gentleman[1] who lived among them from 432 till his death in 461. The Irish in turn did much to evangelize Scotland and the North of England. In this work the greatest missionary was St Columba; another was St Columban, who wrote long letters to Gregory on

[1] So at least Bury says in his Life of the Saint.

the date of Easter and other important questions. The conversion of England, apart from Northumbria, was Gregory's special care. Every one knows how, before he was Pope, he saw two fair-haired blue-eyed boys in the slave market in Rome, and on being told they were Angles replied, 'No, angels.' When he became Pope he sent St Augustine to Kent to convert the Angles. There are many letters in his correspondence to St Augustine, to Edilbert, king of the Angeli, and to others, about the mission. Gregory decrees that heathen temples in England are not to be destroyed, but the idols are to be destroyed and the temples then consecrated as churches. St Augustine puts a number of queries to the Pope, such as whether cousins may marry, whether spouses who have had intercourse the previous night may come to church (yes, if they have washed, says Gregory), and so on. The mission, as we know, prospered, and that is why we are all Christians at this day.

The period we have been considering is peculiar in the fact that, though its great men are inferior to those of many other epochs, their influence on future ages has been greater. Roman law, monasticism, and the papacy owe their long and profound influence very largely to Justinian, Benedict, and Gregory. The men of the sixth century, though less civilized than their predecessors, were much more civilized than the men of the next four centuries, and they succeeded in framing institutions that ultimately tamed the barbarians. It is noteworthy that, of the above three men, two were aristocratic natives of Rome, and the third was Roman Emperor. Gregory is in a very real sense the last of the Romans. His tone of command, while justified by his office, has its instinctive basis in Roman aristocratic pride. After him, for many ages, the city of Rome ceased to produce great men. But in its downfall it succeeded in fettering the souls of its conquerors: the reverence which they felt for the Chair of Peter was an outcome of the awe which they felt for the throne of the Caesars.

In the East, the course of history was different. Mohammed was born when Gregory was about thirty years old.

PART 2

THE SCHOOLMEN

Chapter VII

THE PAPACY IN THE DARK AGES

DURING the four centuries from Gregory the Great to Sylvester II, the papacy underwent astonishing vicissitudes. It was subject, at times, to the Greek Emperor, at other times to the Western Emperor, and at yet other times to the local Roman aristocracy; nevertheless, vigorous popes in the eighth and ninth centuries, seizing propitious moments, built up the tradition of papal power. The period from A.D. 600 to 1000 is of vital importance for the understanding of the medieval Church and its relation to the State.

The popes achieved independence of the Greek emperors, not so much by their own efforts, as by the arms of the Lombards, to whom, however, they felt no gratitude whatever. The Greek Church remained always, in a great measure, subservient to the Emperor, who considered himself competent to decide on matters of faith, as well as to appoint and depose bishops, even patriarchs. The monks strove for independence of the Emperor, and for that reason sided, at times, with the Pope. But the patriarchs of Constantinople, though willing to submit to the Emperor, refused to regard themselves as in any degree subject to papal authority. At times, when the Emperor needed the Pope's help against barbarians in Italy, he was more friendly to the Pope than the patriarch of Constantinople was. The main cause of the ultimate separation of the Eastern and the Western Churches was the refusal of the former to submit to papal jurisdiction.

After the defeat of the Byzantines by the Lombards, the popes had reason to fear that they also would be conquered by these vigorous barbarians. They saved themselves by an alliance with the Franks, who, under Charlemagne, conquered Italy and Germany. This alliance produced the Holy Roman Empire, which had a constitution that assumed harmony between Pope and Emperor. The power of the Carolingian dynasty, however, decayed rapidly. At first, the Pope reaped the advantage of this decay, and in the latter half of the ninth century Nicholas I raised the papal power to hitherto unexampled heights. The general anarchy, however, led to the practical independence of the Roman aristocracy, which, in the tenth century, controlled the papacy, with disastrous results. The way in which, by a great movement of reform, the papacy, and the

Church generally, was saved from subordination to the feudal aristocracy, will be the subject of a later chapter.

In the seventh century, Rome was still subject to the military power of the emperors, and popes had to obey or suffer. Some, e.g. Honorius, obeyed, even to the point of heresy; others, e.g. Martin I, resisted, and were imprisoned by the Emperor. From 685 to 752, most of the popes were Syrians or Greeks. Gradually, however, as the Lombards acquired more and more of Italy, Byzantine power declined. The Emperor Leo the Isaurian in 726, issued his iconoclast decree, which was regarded as heretical, not only throughout the West, but by a large party in the East. This the popes resisted vigorously and successfully; at last, in 787 under the Empress Irene (at first as regent), the East abandoned the iconoclast heresy. Meanwhile, however, events in the West had put an end forever to the control of Byzantium over the papacy.

In about the year 751, the Lombards captured Ravenna, the capital of Byzantine Italy. This event, while it exposed the popes to great danger from the Lombards, freed them from all dependence on the Greek emperors. The popes had preferred the Greeks to the Lombards for several reasons. First, the authority of the emperors was legitimate, whereas barbarian kings, unless recognized by the emperors, were regarded as usurpers. Second, the Greeks were civilized. Third, the Lombards were nationalists, whereas the Church retained Roman internationalism. Fourth, the Lombards had been Arians, and some odium still clung to them after their conversion.

The Lombards, under King Liutprand, attempted to conquer Rome in 739, and were hotly opposed by Pope Gregory III, who turned to the Franks for aid. The Merovingian kings, the descendants of Clovis, had lost all real power in the Frankish kingdom, which was governed by the 'Mayors of the Palace'. At this time the Mayor of the Palace was an exceptionally vigorous and able man, Charles Martel, like William the Conqueror a bastard. In 732 he had won the decisive battle of Tours against the Moors thereby saving France for Christendom. This should have won him the gratitude of the Church, but financial necessity led him to seize some Church lands, which much diminished ecclesiastical appreciation of his merits. However, he and Gregory III both died in 741, and his successor Pepin was wholly satisfactory to the Church. Pope Stephen III, in 754, to escape the Lombards crossed the Alps and visited Pepin, when a bargain was struck which proved highly advantageous to both parties. The Pope needed military protection, but Pepin needed something that only the Pope could bestow: the legitimization of his title as king in place of the last of the Merovingians. In return for this, Pepin bestowed on the Pope Ravenna and all the territory of the former Exarchate in Italy. Since it could not be expected that Constantinople would recognize such a gift, this involved a political severance from the Eastern Empire.

If the popes had remained subject to the Greek emperors, the development of the Catholic Church would have been very different. In the Eastern Church, the patriarch of Constantinople never acquired either that independence of secular authority or that superiority to other ecclesiastics that was achieved by the Pope. Originally all bishops were considered equal, and to a considerable extent this view persisted in the East. Moreover, there were other Eastern patriarchs, at Alexandria, Antioch, and Jerusalem, whereas the Pope was the only patriarch in the West. (This fact, however, lost its importance after the Mohammedan conquest.) In the West, but not in the East, the laity were mostly illiterate for many centuries, and this gave the Church an advantage in the West which it did not possess in the East. The prestige of Rome surpassed that of any Eastern city, for it combined the imperial tradition with legends of the martyrdom of Peter and Paul, and of Peter as first Pope. The Emperor's prestige might have sufficed to cope with that of the Pope, but no Western monarch's could. The Holy Roman emperors were often destitute of real power; moreover they only became emperors when the Pope crowned them. For all these reasons, the emancipation of the Pope from Byzantine domination was essential both to the independence of the Church in relation to secular monarchs, and to the ultimate establishment of the papal monarchy in the government of the Western Church.

Certain documents of great importance, the 'Donation of Constantine' and the False Decretals, belong to this period. The False Decretals need not concern us, but something must be said of the Donation of Constantine. In order to give an air of antique legality to Pepin's gift, churchmen forged a document, purporting to be a decree issued by the Emperor Constantine, by which, when he founded the New Rome, he bestowed upon the Pope the old Rome and all its Western territories. This bequest, which was the basis of the Pope's temporal power, was accepted as genuine by the whole of the subsequent Middle Ages. It was first rejected as a forgery, in the time of the Renaissance, by Lorenzo Valla in 1439. He had written a book 'on the elegancies of the Latin language', which, naturally, were absent in a production of the eighth century. Oddly enough, after he had published his book against the Donation of Constantine, as well as a treatise in praise of Epicurus, he was made apostolic secretary by Pope Nicholas V who cared more for latinity than for the Church. Nicholas V did not, however, propose to give up the States of the Church, though the Pope's title to them had been based upon the supposed Donation.

The contents of this remarkable document are summarized by C. Delisle Burns as follows:[1]

After a summary of the Nicene creed, the fall of Adam, and the birth of Christ, Constantine says he was suffering from leprosy, that doctors were useless, and that he therefore approached 'the priests of the Capitol'. They proposed that he should slaughter several infants and be washed in their blood, but owing to their mothers' tears he restored them. That night Peter and Paul appeared to him and said that Pope Sylvester was hiding in a cave on Soracte and would cure him. He went to Soracte, where the 'universal Pope' told him Peter and Paul were apostles, not gods, showed him portraits which he recognized from his vision, and admitted it before all his 'satraps'. Pope Sylvester thereupon assigned him a period of penance in a hair shirt; then he baptized him, when he saw a hand from heaven touching him. He was cured of leprosy, and gave up worshipping idols. Then 'with all his satraps, the Senate, his nobles and the whole Roman people he thought it good to grant supreme power to the See of Peter', and superiority over Antioch, Alexandria, Jerusalem, and Constantinople. He then built a church in his palace of the Lateran. On the Pope he conferred his crown, tiara, and imperial garments. He placed a tiara on the Pope's head and held the reins of his horse. He left to 'Sylvester and his successors Rome and all the provinces, districts and cities of Italy and the West to be subject to the Roman Church forever'; he then moved East 'because, where the princedom of bishops and the head of the Christian religion has been established by the heavenly Emperor it is not just that an earthly Emperor should have power.'

The Lombards did not tamely submit to Pepin and the Pope, but in repeated wars with the Franks they were worsted. At last, in 774, Pepin's son Charlemagne marched into Italy, completely defeated the Lombards, had himself recognized as their king, and then occupied Rome, where he confirmed Pepin's donation. The Popes of his day, Hadrian and Leo III, found it to their advantage to further his schemes in every way. He conquered most of Germany, converted the Saxons by vigorous persecution, and finally, in his own person, revived the Western Empire, being crowned Emperor by the Pope in Rome on Christmas Day, A.D. 800.

The foundation of the Holy Roman Empire marks an epoch in medieval theory, though much less in medieval practice. The Middle Ages were peculiarly addicted to legal fictions, and until this time the fiction had persisted that the Western provinces of

---

[1] I am quoting a still unpublished book, *The First Europe*.

the former Roman Empire were still subject, *de jure*, to the Emperor in Constantinople, who was regarded as the sole source of *legal* authority. Charlemagne, an adept in legal fictions, maintained that the throne of the Empire was vacant, because the reigning Eastern sovereign Irene (who called herself emperor, not empress) was a usurper, since no woman could be emperor. Charles derived his claim to legitimacy from the Pope. There was thus, from the first, a curious interdependence of pope and emperor. No one could be emperor unless crowned by the Pope in Rome; on the other hand, for some centuries, every strong emperor claimed the right to appoint or depose popes. The medieval theory of legitimate power depended upon both emperor and pope: their mutual dependence was galling to both, but for centuries inescapable. There was constant friction, with advantage now to one side, now to the other. At last, in the thirteenth century, the conflict became irreconcilable. The Pope was victorious, but lost moral authority shortly afterwards. The Pope and the Holy Roman Emperor both survived, the Pope to the present day, the Emperor to the time of Napoleon. But the elaborate medieval theory that had been built up concerning their respective powers ceased to be effective during the fifteenth century. The unity of Christendom, which it maintained, was destroyed by the power of the French, Spanish, and English monarchies in the secular sphere, and by the Reformation in the sphere of religion.

The character of·Charles the Great and his entourage is thus summed up by Dr Gerhard Seeliger:[1]

Vigorous life was developed at Charles's court. We see there magnificence and genius, but immorality also. For Charles was not particular about the people he drew round him. He himself was no model, and he suffered the greatest licence in those whom he liked and found useful. As 'Holy Emperor' he was addressed, though his life exhibited little holiness. He is so addressed by Alcuin, who also praises the Emperor's beautiful daughter Rotrud as distinguished for her virtues in spite of her having borne a son to Count Roderic of Maine, though not his wife. Charles would not be separated from his daughters, he would not allow their marriage, and he was therefore obliged to accept the consequences. The other daughter, Bertha, also had two sons by the pious Abbot Angilbert of St Riquier. In fact the court of Charles was a centre of very loose life.

Charlemagne was a vigorous barbarian, politically in alliance with the Church, but not unduly burdened with personal piety. He could not read or write, but he inaugurated a literary renaissance.

[1] In *Cambridge Medieval History*, II, 663.

He was dissolute in his life, and unduly fond of his daughters, but he did all in his power to promote holy living among his subjects. He, like his father Pepin, made skilful use of the zeal of missionaries to promote his influence in Germany, but he saw to it that Popes obeyed his orders. They did this the more willingly, because Rome had become a barbarous city, in which the person of the Pope was not safe without external protection, and papal elections had degenerated into disorderly faction fights. In 799, local enemies seized the Pope, imprisoned him, and threatened to blind him. During Charles's lifetime, it seemed as if a new order would be inaugurated; but after his death little survived except a theory.

The gains of the Church, and more particularly of the papacy, were more solid than those of the Western Empire. England had been converted by a monastic mission under the orders of Gregory the Great, and remained much more subject to Rome than were the countries with bishops accustomed to local autonomy. The conversion of Germany was largely the work of St Boniface (680-754), an English missionary, who was a friend of Charles Martel and Pepin, and completely faithful to the Pope. Boniface founded many monasteries in Germany; his friend St Gall founded the Swiss monastery which bears his name. According to some authorities, Boniface appointed Pepin as king with a ritual taken from the First Book of Kings.

St Boniface was a native of Devonshire, educated at Exeter and Winchester. He went to Frisia in 716, but soon had to return. In 717 he went to Rome, and in 719 Pope Gregory II sent him to Germany to convert the Germans and to combat the influence of the Irish missionaries (who, it will be remembered, erred as to the date of Easter and the shape of the tonsure). After considerable successes, he returned to Rome in 722, where he was made bishop by Gregory II, to whom he took an oath of obedience. The Pope gave him a letter to Charles Martel, and charged him to suppress heresy in addition to converting the heathen. In 732 he became archbishop; in 738 he visited Rome a third time. In 741 Pope Zacharias made him legate, and charged him to reform the Frankish Church. He founded the abbey of Fulda, to which he gave a rule stricter than the Benedictine. Then he had a controversy with an Irish bishop of Salzburg, named Virgil, who maintained that there are other worlds than ours, but was, nevertheless, canonized. In 754, after returning to Frisia, Boniface and his companions were massacred by the heathen. It was owing to him that German Christianity was papal, not Irish.

English monasteries, particularly those of Yorkshire, were of great importance at this time. Such civilization as had existed in

Roman Britain had disappeared, and the new civilization introduced by Christian missionaries centred entirely round the Benedictine abbeys, which owed everything directly to Rome. The Venerable Bede was a monk at Jarrow. His pupil Ecgbert, first archbishop of York, founded a cathedral school, where Alcuin was educated.

Alcuin is an important figure in the culture of the time. He went to Rome in 780, and in the course of his journey met Charlemagne at Parma. The Emperor employed him to teach Latin to the Franks and to educate the royal family. He spent a considerable part of his life at the court of Charlemagne, engaged in teaching and in founding schools. At the end of his life he was abbot of St Martin's at Tours. He wrote a number of books, including a verse history of the church at York. The emperor, though uneducated, had a considerable belief in the value of culture, and for a brief period diminished the darkness of the dark ages. But his work in this direction was ephemeral. The culture of Yorkshire was for a time destroyed by the Danes, that of France was damaged by the Normans. The Saracens raided Southern Italy, conquered Sicily, and in 846 even attacked Rome. On the whole, the tenth century was, in Western Christendom, about the darkest epoch; for the ninth is redeemed by the English ecclesiastics and by the astonishing figure of Johannes Scotus, as to whom I shall have more to say presently.

The decay of Carolingian power after the death of Charlemagne and the division of his empire redounded, at first, to the advantage of the papacy. Pope Nicholas I (858-67) raised papal power to a far greater height than it had ever attained before. He quarrelled with the Emperors of the East and West, with King Charles the Bald of France and King Lothar II of Lorraine, and with the episcopate of nearly every Christian country; but in almost all his quarrels he was successful. The clergy in many regions had become dependent on the local princes, and he set to work to remedy this state of affairs. His two greatest controversies concerned the divorce of Lothar II and the uncanonical deposition of Ignatius, patriarch of Constantinople. The power of the Church throughout the Middle Ages, had a great deal to do with royal divorces. Kings were men of headstrong passions, who felt that the indissolubility of marriage was a doctrine for subjects only. The Church, however, could alone solemnize a marriage, and if the Church declared a marriage invalid, a disputed succession and a dynastic war were very likely to result. The Church, therefore, was in a very strong position in opposing royal divorces and irregular marriages. In England, it lost this position under Henry VIII, but recovered it under Edward VIII.

When Lothar II demanded a divorce, the clergy of his kingdom agreed. Pope Nicholas, however, deposed the bishops who had acquiesced, and totally refused to admit the King's plea for divorce. Lothar's brother, the Emperor Louis II, thereupon marched on Rome with the intention of overawing the Pope; but superstitious terrors prevailed, and he retired. In the end, the Pope's will prevailed.

The business of the Patriarch Ignatius was interesting, as showing that the Pope could still assert himself in the East. Ignatius, who was obnoxious to the Regent Bardas, was deposed, and Photius, hitherto a layman, was elevated to his place. The Byzantine government asked the Pope to sanction this proceeding. He sent two legates to inquire into the matter; when they arrived in Constantinople, they were terrorized, and gave their assent. For some time, the facts were concealed from the Pope, but when he came to know them, he took a high line. He summoned a council in Rome to consider the question; he deposed one of the legates from his bishopric, and also the archbishop of Syracuse, who had consecrated Photius; he anathematized Photius, deposed all whom he had ordained, and restored all who had been deposed for opposing him. The Emperor Michael III was furious, and wrote the Pope an angry letter, but the Pope replied: 'The day of king-priests and emperor-pontiffs is past, Christianity has separated the two functions, and Christian emperors have need of the Pope in view of the life eternal, whereas popes have no need of emperors except as regards temporal things.' Photius and the Emperor retorted by summoning a council, which excommunicated the Pope and declared the Roman Church heretical. Soon after this, however, Michael III was murdered, and his successor Basil restored Ignatius, explicitly recognizing papal jurisdiction in the matter. This triumph happened just after the death of Nicholas, and was attributable almost entirely to the accidents of palace revolutions. After the death of Ignatius, Photius again became patriarch, and the split between the Eastern and the Western Churches was widened. Thus it cannot be said that Nicholas's policy in this matter was victorious in the long run.

Nicholas had almost more difficulty in imposing his will upon the episcopate than upon kings. Archbishops had come to consider themselves very great men, and they were reluctant to submit tamely to an ecclesiastical monarch. He maintained, however, that bishops owe their existence to the Pope, and while he lived he succeeded, on the whole, in making this view prevail. There was, throughout these centuries, great doubt as to how bishops should be appointed. Originally they were elected by the acclamation of the faithful in their cathedral city; then, frequently, by a synod of neighbouring bishops; then, sometimes by the King, and sometimes by the Pope. Bishops could be deposed for grave causes, but it was not clear whether they should be tried by the Pope or by a provincial synod. All these uncertainties made the powers of an office dependent upon the energy and astuteness of its holders. Nicholas stretched papal power to the utmost limits of which it was then capable; under his successors, it sank again to a very low ebb.

During the tenth century, the papacy was completely under the control of the local Roman aristocracy. There was, as yet, no fixed rule as to the election of Popes; sometimes they owed their elevation to popular acclaim, sometimes to emperors or kings, and sometimes, as in the tenth century, to the holders of local urban power in Rome. Rome was, at this time, not a civilized city, as it had still been in the time of Gregory the Great. At times there were faction fights; at other times some rich family acquired control by a combination of violence and corruption. The disorder and weakness of Western Europe was so great at this period that Christendom might have seemed in danger of complete destruction. The Emperor and the King of France were powerless to curb the anarchy produced in their realms by feudal potentates who were nominally their vassals. The Hungarians made raids on Northern Italy. The Normans raided the French coast, until, in 911, they were given Normandy and in return became Christians. But the greatest danger in Italy and Southern France came from the Saracens, who could not be converted, and had no reverence for the Church. They completed the conquest of Sicily about the end of the ninth century; they were established on the River Garigliano, near Naples; they destroyed Monte Cassino and other great monasteries; they had a settlement on the coast of Provence, whence they raided Italy and the Alpine valleys, interrupting traffic between Rome and the North.

The conquest of Italy by the Saracens was prevented by the Eastern Empire, which overcame the Saracens of the Garigliano in 915. But it was not strong enough to govern Rome, as it had done after Justinian's conquest, and the papacy became, for about a hundred years, a perquisite of the Roman aristocracy or of the counts of Tusculum. The most powerful Romans, at the beginning of the tenth century, were the 'Senator' Theophylact and his daughter Marozia, in whose family the papacy nearly became hereditary. Marozia had several husbands in succession, and an unknown number of lovers. One of the latter she elevated to the papacy, under the title of Sergius II (904-11). His and her son was Pope John XI (931-36); her grandson was John XII (955-64), who became Pope at the age of sixteen and 'completed the debasement of the papacy by his debauched life and the orgies of which the

Lateran palace soon became the scene'.[1] Marozia is presumably the basis for the legend of a female 'Pope Joan'.

The popes of this period naturally lost whatever influence their predecessors had retained in the East. They lost also the power, which Nicholas I had successfully exercised, over bishops north of the Alps. Provincial councils asserted their complete independence of the Pope, but they failed to maintain independence of sovereigns and feudal lords. Bishops, more and more, became assimilated to lay feudal magnates. 'The Church itself thus appears as the victim of the same anarchy in which lay society is weltering; all evil appetites range unchecked, and, more than ever, such of the clergy as still retain some concern for religion and for the salvation of the souls committed to their charge mourn over the universal decadence and direct the eyes of the faithful towards the spectre of the end of the world and of the Last Judgment.'[2]

It is a mistake, however, to suppose that a special dread of the end of the world in the year 1000 prevailed at this time, as used to be thought. Christians, from St Paul onward, believed the end of the world to be at hand, but they went on with their ordinary business none the less.

The year 1000 may be conveniently taken as marking the end of the lowest depth to which the civilization of Western Europe sank. From this point the upward movement began which continued till 1914. In the beginning, progress was mainly due to monastic reform. Outside the monastic orders, the clergy had become, for the most part, violent, immoral, and worldly; they were corrupted by the wealth and power that they owed to the benefactions of the pious. The same thing happened, over and over again, even to the monastic orders; but reformers, with new zeal, revived their moral force as often as it had decayed.

Another reason which makes the year 1000 a turning-point is the cessation, at about this time, of conquest by both Mohammedans and northern barbarians, so far at least as Western Europe is concerned. Goths, Lombards, Hungarians, and Normans came in successive waves; each horde in turn was christianized, but each in turn weakened the civilized tradition. The Western Empire broke up into many barbarian kingdoms; the kings lost authority over their vassals; there was universal anarchy, with perpetual violence both on a large and on a small scale. At last all the races of vigorous northern conquerors had been converted to Christianity, and had acquired settled habitations. The Normans, who were the last comers, proved peculiarly capable of civilization. They reconquered Sicily from the Saracens, and made Italy safe from the Moham-

[1] *Cambridge Medieval History,* III, 455. [2] *Ibid.*

medans. They brought England back into the Roman world, from which the Danes had largely excluded it. Once settled in Normandy, they allowed France to revive, and helped materially in the process.

Our use of the phrase 'the Dark Ages' to cover the period from 600 to 1000 marks our undue concentration on Western Europe. In China, this period includes the time of the Tang dynasty, the greatest age of Chinese poetry, and in many other ways a most remarkable epoch. From India to Spain, the brilliant civilization of Islam flourished. What was lost to Christendom at this time was not lost to civilization, but quite the contrary. No one could have guessed that Western Europe would later become dominant both in power and in culture. To us, it seems that West-European civilization *is* civilization, but this is a narrow view. Most of the cultural content of our civilization comes to us from the Eastern Mediterranean, from Greeks and Jews. As for power: Western Europe was dominant from the Punic Wars to the fall of Rome—say, roughly, during the six centuries from 200 B.C. to A.D. 400. After that time, no State in Western Europe could compare in power with China, Japan, or the Caliphate.

Our superiority since the Renaissance is due partly to science and scientific technique, partly to political institutions slowly built up during the Middle Ages. There is no reason, in the nature of things, why this superiority should continue. In the present war, great military strength has been shown by Russia, China, and Japan. All these combine Western technique with Eastern ideology—Byzantine, Confucian, or Shinto. India, if liberated, will contribute another Oriental element. It seems not unlikely that, during the next few centuries, civilization, if it survives, will have greater diversity than it has had since the Renaissance. There is an imperialism of culture which is harder to overcome than the imperialism of power. Long after the Western Empire fell—indeed until the Reformation—all European culture retained a tincture of Roman imperialism. It now has, for us, a West-European imperialistic flavour. I think that, if we are to feel at home in the world after the present war, we shall have to admit Asia to equality in our thoughts, not only politically, but culturally. What changes this will bring about, I do not know, but I am convinced that they will be profound and of the greatest importance.

Chapter VIII

JOHN THE SCOT

JOHN THE Scot, or Johannes Scotus, to which is sometimes added Eriugena or Erigena,[1] is the most astonishing person of the ninth century; he would have been less surprising if he had lived in the fifth or the fifteenth century. He was an Irishman, a Neoplatonist, an accomplished Greek scholar, a Pelagian, a pantheist. He spent much of his life under the patronage of Charles the Bald, king of France, and though he was certainly far from orthodox, yet, so far as we know, he escaped persecution. He set reason above faith, and cared nothing for the authority of ecclesiastics; yet his arbitrament was invoked to settle their controversies.

To understand the occurrence of such a man, we must turn our attention first to Irish culture in the centuries following St Patrick. Apart from the extremely painful fact that St Patrick was an Englishman, there are two other scarcely less painful circumstances: first, that there were Christians in Ireland before he went there, second, that, whatever he may have done for Irish Christianity, it was not to him that Irish culture was due. At the time of the invasion of Gaul (says a Gaulish author), first by Attila, then by the Goths, Vandals, and Alaric, 'all the learned men on their side the sea fled, and in the countries beyond sea, namely Ireland, and wherever else they betook themselves, brought to the inhabitants of those regions an enormous advance in learning'.[2] If any of these men sought refuge in England, the Angles and Saxons and Jutes must have mopped them up; but those who went to Ireland succeeded, in combination with the missionaries, in transplanting a great deal of the knowledge and civilization that was disappearing from the Continent. There is good reason to believe that, throughout the sixth, seventh, and eighth centuries, a knowledge of Greek, as well as a considerable familiarity with Latin classics, survived among the Irish.[3] Greek was known in England from the time of Theodore, archbishop of Canterbury (669-90), who was himself a Greek, educated at Athens; it may also have become known, in the North, through Irish missionaries. 'During the latter part of the

---

[1] This addition is redundant; it would make his name 'Irish John from Ireland'. In the ninth century 'Scotus' means 'Irishman'.
[2] *Cambridge Medieval History*, III, 501.
[3] This question is discussed carefully in the *Cambridge Medieval History*, III, chap. xix, and the conclusion is in favour of Irish knowledge of Greek.

seventh century,' says Montague James, 'it was in Ireland that the thirst for knowledge was keenest, and the work of teaching was most actively carried on. There the Latin language (and in a less degree the Greek) was studied from a scholar's point of view. . . . It was when, impelled in the first instance by missionary zeal, and later by troubled conditions at home, they passed over in large numbers to the Continent, that they became instrumental in rescuing fragments of the literature which they had already learnt to value.'[1] Heiric of Auxerre, about 876, describes this influx of Irish scholars: 'Ireland, despising the dangers of the sea, is migrating almost *en masse* with her crowd of philosophers to our shores, and all the most learned doom themselves to voluntary exile to attend the bidding of Solomon the wise'—i.e. King Charles the Bald.[2]

The lives of learned men have at many times been perforce nomadic. At the beginning of Greek philosophy, many of the philosophers were refugees from the Persians; at the end of it, in the time of Justinian, they became refugees *to* the Persians. In the fifth century, as we have just seen, men of learning fled from Gaul to the Western Isles to escape the Germans; in the ninth century, they fled back from England and Ireland to escape the Scandinavians. In our own day, German philosophers have to fly even further West to escape their compatriots. I wonder whether it will be equally long before a return flight takes place.

Too little is known of the Irish in the days when they were preserving for Europe the tradition of classical culture. This learning was connected with monasteries, and was full of piety, as their penitentials show; but it does not seem to have been much concerned with theological niceties. Being monastic rather than episcopal, it had not the administrative outlook that characterized Continental ecclesiastics from Gregory the Great onwards. And being in the main cut off from effective contact with Rome, it still regarded the Pope as he was regarded in the time of St Ambrose, not as he came to be regarded later. Pelagius, though probably a Briton, is thought by some to have been an Irishman. It is likely that his heresy survived in Ireland, where authority could not stamp it out, as it did, with difficulty, in Gaul. These circumstances do something to account for the extraordinary freedom and freshness of John the Scot's speculations.

The beginning and the end of John the Scot's life are unknown; we know only the middle period, during which he was employed by the king of France. He is supposed to have been born about 800, and to have died about 877, but both dates are guesswork. He was in France during the papacy of Pope Nicholas I, and we meet again.

[1] *Loc. cit.,* pp. 507-8.   [2] *Loc. cit.,* p. 524.

in his life, the characters who appear in connection with that Pope, such as Charles the Bald and the Emperor Michael and the Pope himself.

John was invited to France by Charles the Bald about the year 843, and was by him placed at the head of the court school. A dispute as to predestination and free will had arisen between Gottschalk, a monk, and the important ecclesiastic Hincmar, Archbishop of Rheims. The monk was predestinarian, the archbishop libertarian. John supported the archbishop in a treatise *On Divine Predestination*, but his support went too far for prudence. The subject was a thorny one; Augustine had dealt with it in his writings against Pelagius, but it was dangerous to agree with Augustine and still more dangerous to disagree with him explicitly. John supported free will, and this might have passed uncensored; but what roused indignation was the purely philosophic character of his argument. Not that he professed to controvert anything accepted in theology, but that he maintained the equal, or even superior, authority of a philosophy independent of revelation. He contended that reason and revelation are both sources of truth, and therefore cannot conflict; but if they ever *seem* to conflict, reason is to be preferred. True religion, he said, is true philosophy; but, conversely, true philosophy is true religion. His work was condemned by two councils, in 855 and 859; the first of these described it as 'Scots porridge'.

He escaped punishment, however, owing to the support of the king, with whom he seems to have been on familiar terms. If William of Malmesbury is to be believed, the king, when John was dining with him, asked: 'What separates a Scot from a sot?' and John replied, 'Only the dinner table.' The king died in 877, and after this date nothing is known as to John. Some think that he also died in that year. There are legends that he was invited to England by Alfred the Great, that he became abbot of Malmesbury or Athelney, and was murdered by the monks. This misfortune, however, seems to have befallen some other John.

John's next work was a translation from the Greek of the pseudo-Dionysius. This was a work which had great fame in the early Middle Ages. When St Paul preached in Athens, 'certain men clave unto him, and believed: among the which was Dionysius the Areopagite' (Acts xvii. 34). Nothing more is now known about this man, but in the Middle Ages a great deal more was known. He had travelled to France, and founded the abbey of St Denis; so at least it was said by Hilduin, who was abbot just before John's arrival in France. Moreover, he was the reputed author of an important work reconciling Neoplatonism with Christianity. The date of this work is unknown; it was certainly before 500 and after Plotinus. It was widely known and admired in the East, but in the West it was not generally known until the Greek Emperor Michael, in 827, sent a copy to Louis the Pious, who gave it to the above-mentioned Abbot Hilduin. He, believing it to have been written by St Paul's disciple, the reputed founder of his abbey, would have liked to know what its contents were; but nobody could translate the Greek until John appeared. He accomplished the translation, which he must have done with pleasure, as his own opinions were in close accord with those of the pseudo-Dionysius, who, from that time onward, had a great influence on Catholic philosophy in the West.

John's translation was sent to Pope Nicholas in 860. The Pope was offended because his permission had not been sought before the work was published, and he ordered Charles to send John to Rome —an order which was ignored. But as to the substance, and more especially the scholarship shown in the translation, he had no fault to find. His librarian Anastasius, an excellent Grecian, to whom he submitted it for an opinion, was astonished that a man from a remote and barbarous country could have possessed such a profound knowledge of Greek.

John's greatest work was called (in Greek) *On the Division of Nature*. This book was what, in scholastic times, would have been termed 'realist'; that is to say, it maintained, with Plato, that universals are anterior to particulars. He includes in 'Nature' not only what is, but also what is not. The whole of Nature is divided into four classes: (1) what creates and is not created, (2) what creates and is created, (3) what is created but does not create, (4) what neither creates nor is created. The first, obviously, is God. The second is the (Platonic) ideas, which subsist in God. The third is things in space and time. The fourth, surprisingly, is again God, not as Creator, but as the End and Purpose of all things. Everything that emanates from God strives to return to Him; thus the end of all such things is the same as their beginning. The bridge between the One and the many is the Logos.

In the realm of not-being he includes various things, for example, physical objects, which do not belong to the intelligible world, and sin, since it means loss of the divine pattern. That which creates and is not created alone has essential subsistence; it is the essence of all things. God is the beginning, middle, and end of things. God's essence is unknowable to men, and even to angels. Even to Himself He is, in a sense, unknowable: 'God does not know himself, what He is, because He is not a *what*; in a certain respect He is incomprehensible to Himself and to every intellect.'[1] In the being of things

---

[1] Cf. Bradley on the inadequacy of all cognition. He holds that no truth is quite true, but the best available truth is not *intellectually* corrigible.

God's being can be seen; in their order, His wisdom; in their movement, His life. His being is the Father, His wisdom the Son, His life
the Holy Ghost. But Dionysius is right in saying that no name can
be truly asserted of God. There is an affirmative theology, in which
He is said to be truth, goodness, essence, etc., but such affirmations
are only symbolically true, for all such predicates have an opposite,
but God has no opposite.

The class of things that both create and are created embraces the
whole of the prime causes or prototypes, or Platonic ideas. The
total of these prime causes is the Logos. The world of ideas is
eternal, and yet created. Under the influence of the Holy Ghost,
these prime causes give rise to the world of particular things, the
materiality of which is illusory. When it is said that God created
things out of 'nothing', this 'nothing' is to be understood as God
Himself, in the sense in which He transcends all knowledge.

Creation is an eternal process: the substance of all finite things
is God. The creature is not a being distinct from God. The creature
subsists in God, and God manifests Himself in the creature in an
ineffable manner. 'The Holy Trinity loves Itself in us and in Itself;[1]
It sees and moves Itself.'

Sin has its source in freedom: it arose because man turned
towards himself instead of towards God. Evil does not have its
ground in God, for in God there is no idea of evil. Evil is not-being
and has no ground, for if it had a ground it would be necessary.
Evil is a privation of good.

The Logos is the principle that brings the many back to the One,
and man back to God; it is thus the Saviour of the world. By union
with God, the part of man that effects union becomes divine.

John disagrees with the Aristotelians in refusing substantiality to
particular things. He calls Plato the summit of philosophers.
But the first three of his kinds of being are derived indirectly from
Aristotle's moving-not-moved, moving-and-moved, moved-but-not-
moving. The fourth kind of being in John's system, that which
neither creates nor is created, is derived from the doctrine of
Dionysius, that all things return into God.

The unorthodoxy of John the Scot is evident from the above
summary. His pantheism, which refuses substantial reality to
creatures, is contrary to Christian doctrine. His interpretation of
the creation out of 'nothing' is not such as any prudent theologian
could accept. His Trinity, which closely resembles that of Plotinus,
fails to preserve the equality of the Three Persons, although he
tries to safeguard himself on this point. His independence of mind
is shown by these heresies, and is astonishing in the ninth century.

[1] Cf. Spinoza.

His Neoplatonic outlook may perhaps have been common in
Ireland, as it was among the Greek Fathers of the fourth and fifth
centuries. It may be that, if we knew more about Irish Christianity
from the fifth to the ninth century, we should find him less surprising. On the other hand, it may be that most of what is heretical in
him is to be attributed to the influence of the pseudo-Dionysius,
who, because of his supposed connection with St Paul, was mistakenly believed to be orthodox.

His view of creation as timeless is, of course, also heretical and
compels him to say that the account in Genesis is allegorical. Paradise
and the fall are not to be taken literally. Like all pantheists, he
has difficulties about sin. He holds that man was originally without
sin, and when he was without sin he was without distinction of sex.
This, of course, contradicts the statement 'male and female created
he them'. According to John, it was only as the result of sin that
human beings were divided into male and female. Woman embodies
man's sensuous and fallen nature. In the end, distinction of sex will
again disappear, and we shall have a purely spiritual body.[1] Sin
consists in misdirected will, in falsely supposing something good
which is not so. Its punishment is natural; it consists in discovering
the vanity of sinful desires. But punishment is not eternal. Like
Origen, John holds that even the devils will be saved at last, though
later than other people.

John's translation of the pseudo-Dionysius had a great influence
on medieval thought, but his *magnum opus* on the division of
Nature had very little. It was repeatedly condemned as heretical,
and at last, in 1225, Pope Honorius III ordered all copies of it to be
burnt. Fortunately this order was not efficiently carried out.

[1] Contrast St Augustine.

Chapter IX

ECCLESIASTICAL REFORM IN THE
ELEVENTH CENTURY

For the first time since the fall of the Western Empire, Europe, during the eleventh century, made rapid progress not subsequently lost. There had been progress of a sort during the Carolingian renaissance, but it proved to be not solid. In the eleventh century, the improvement was lasting and many-sided. It began with monastic reform; it then extended to the papacy and Church government; towards the end of the century it produced the first scholastic philosophers. The Saracens were expelled from Sicily by the Normans; the Hungarians, having become Christians, ceased to be marauders; the conquests of the Normans in France and England saved those countries from further Scandinavian incursions. Architecture, which had been barbaric except where Byzantine influence prevailed, attained sudden sublimity. The level of education rose enormously among the clergy, and considerably in the lay aristocracy.

The reform movement, in its earlier stages, was, in the minds of its promoters, actuated exclusively by moral motives. The clergy, both regular and secular, had fallen into bad ways, and earnest men set to work to make them live more in accordance with their principles. But behind this purely moral motive there was another, at first perhaps unconscious, but gradually becoming more and more open. This motive was to complete the separation between clergy and laity, and, in so doing, to increase the power of the former. It was therefore natural that the victory of reform in the Church should lead straight on to a violent conflict between Emperor and Pope.

Priests had formed a separate and powerful caste in Egypt, Babylonia, and Persia, but not in Greece or Rome. In the primitive Christian Church, the distinction between clergy and laity arose gradually; when we read of 'bishops' in the New Testament, the word does not mean what it has come to mean to us. The separation of the clergy from the rest of the population had two aspects, one doctrinal, the other political; the political aspect depended upon the doctrinal. The clergy possessed certain miraculous powers, especially in connection with the sacraments—except baptism, which could be performed by laymen. Without the help of the clergy, marriage, absolution, and extreme unction were impossible. Even more important, in the Middle Ages, was transubstantiation: only a priest could perform the miracle of the mass. It was not until the eleventh century, in 1079, that the doctrine of transubstantiation became an article of faith, though it had been generally believed for a long time.

Owing to their miraculous powers, priests could determine whether a man should spend eternity in heaven or in hell. If he died while excommunicate, he went to hell; if he died after a priest had performed all the proper ceremonies, he would ultimately go to heaven provided he had duly repented and confessed. Before going to heaven, however, he would have to spend some time—perhaps a very long time—suffering the pains of purgatory. Priests could shorten this time by saying masses for his soul, which they were willing to do for a suitable money payment.

All this, it must be understood, was genuinely and firmly believed both by priests and by laity; it was not merely a creed officially professed. Over and over again, the miraculous powers of the clergy gave them the victory over powerful princes at the head of their armies. This power, however, was limited on two ways: by reckless outbreaks of passion on the part of furious laymen, and by divisions among the clergy. The inhabitants of Rome, until the time of Gregory VII, showed little respect for the person of the Pope. They would kidnap him, imprison him, poison him, or fight against him, whenever their turbulent factional strife tempted them to such action. How is this compatible with their beliefs? Partly, no doubt, the explanation lies in mere lack of self-control; partly, however, in the thought that one could repent on one's deathbed. Another reason, which operated less in Rome than elsewhere, was that kings could bend to their will the bishops in their kingdoms, and thus secure enough priestly magic to save themselves from damnation. Church discipline and a unified ecclesiastical government were therefore essential to the power of the clergy. These ends were secured during the eleventh century, as part and parcel of a moral reformation of the clergy.

The power of the clergy as a whole could only be secured by very considerable sacrifices on the part of individual ecclesiastics. The two great evils against which all clerical reformers directed their energies were simony and concubinage. Something must be said about each of these.

Owing to the benefactions of the pious, the Church had become rich. Many bishops had huge estates, and even parish priests had, as a rule, what for those times was a comfortable living. The appointment of bishops was usually, in practice, in the hands of the king, but sometimes in those of some subordinate feudal noble. It was customary for the king to sell bishoprics; this, in fact, provided a substantial part of his income. The bishop, in turn, sold such ecclesiastical preferment as was in his power. There was no secret about this. Gerbert (Sylvester II) represented bishops as saying: 'I gave gold and I received the episcopate; but yet I do not fear to receive it back if I behave as I should. I ordain a priest and I receive gold; I make a deacon and I receive a heap of silver. Behold the gold which I gave I have once more unlessened in my purse.'[1] Peter Damian in Milan, in 1059, found that every cleric in the city, from the archbishop downwards, had been guilty of simony. And this state of affairs was in no way exceptional.

Simony, of course, was a sin, but that was not the only objection to it. It caused ecclesiastical preferment to go by wealth, not merit; it confirmed lay authority in the appointment of bishops, and episcopal subservience to secular rulers; and it tended to make the episcopate part of the feudal system. Moreover, when a man had purchased preferment, he was naturally anxious to recoup himself, so that worldly rather than spiritual concerns were likely to preoccupy him. For these reasons, the campaign against simony was a necessary part of the ecclesiastical struggle for power.

Very similar considerations applied to clerical celibacy. The reformers of the eleventh century often spoke of 'concubinage' when it would have been more accurate to speak of 'marriage'. Monks, of course, were precluded from marriage by their vow of chastity, but there had been no clear prohibition of marriage for the secular clergy. In the Eastern Church, to this day, parish priests are allowed to be married. In the West, in the eleventh century, most parish priests were married. Bishops, for their part, appealed to St Paul's pronouncement: 'A bishop then must be blameless, the husband of one wife.'[2] There was not the same clear moral issue as in the matter of simony, but in the insistence on clerical celibacy there were political motives very similar to those in the campaign against simony.[3]

When priests were married, they naturally tried to pass on Church property to their sons. They could do this legally if their sons became priests; therefore one of the first steps of the reform party, when it acquired power, was to forbid the ordination of priests' sons.[4] But in the confusion of the times there was still danger that, if priests had sons, they would find means of illegally

[1] *Cambridge Medieval History*, V, chap. 10.
[2] I Timothy iii. 2.
[3] See Henry C. Lea, *The History of Sacerdotal Celibacy*.
[4] In 1046, it was decreed that a clerk's son cannot be a bishop. Later, it was decreed he could not be in holy orders.

alienating parts of the Church lands. In addition to this economic consideration, there was also the fact that, if a priest was a family man like his neighbours, he seemed to them less removed from themselves. There was, from at least the fifth century onwards, an intense admiration for celibacy, and if the clergy were to command the reverence on which their powers depended, it was highly advantageous that they should be obviously separated from other men by abstinence from marriage. The reformers themselves, no doubt, sincerely believed that the married state, though not actually sinful, is lower than the state of celibacy, and is only conceded to the weakness of the flesh. St Paul says 'if they cannot contain, let them marry'[1]; but a really holy man ought to be able to 'contain'. Therefore clerical celibacy is essential to the moral authority of the Church.

After these general preliminaries, let us come to the actual history of the reform movement in the eleventh-century Church.

The beginning goes back to the foundation of the abbey of Cluny in 910 by William the Pious, Duke of Aquitaine. This abbey was, from the first, independent of all external authority except that of the Pope; moreover, its abbot was given authority over other monasteries that owed their origin to it. Most monasteries, at this time, were rich and lax; Cluny, though avoiding extreme asceticism, was careful to preserve decency and decorum. The second abbot, Odo, went to Italy, and was given control of several Roman monasteries. He was not always successful: 'Farfa, divided by a schism between two rival abbots who had murdered their predecessor, resisted the introduction of Cluniac monks by Odo and got rid by poison of the abbot whom Alberic installed by armed force.'[2] (Alberic was the ruler of Rome who had invited Odo.) In the twelfth century Cluny's reforming zeal grew cold. St Bernard objected to its fine architecture; like all the most earnest men of his time, he considered splendid ecclesiastical edifices a sign of sinful pride.

During the eleventh century, various other orders were founded by reformers. Romuald, an ascetic hermit, founded the Camaldolese Order in 1012; Peter Damian, of whom we shall speak shortly, was a follower of his. The Carthusians, who never ceased to be austere, were founded by Bruno of Cologne in 1084. In 1098 the Cictercian Order was founded, and in 1113 it was joined by St Bernard. It adhered strictly to the Benedictine Rule. It forbade stained-glass windows. For labour, it employed *conversi*, or lay brethren. These men took the vows, but were forbidden to learn reading and

[1] I Corinthians vii. 9.
[2] *Cambridge Medieval History*, V, 662.

writing; they were employed mainly in agriculture, but also in other work, such as architecture. Fountains Abbey, in Yorkshire, is Cistercian—a remarkable work for men who thought all beauty of the Devil.

As will be seen from the case of Farfa, which was by no means unique, monastic reformers required great courage and energy. Where they succeeded, they were supported by the secular authorities. It was these men and their followers who made possible the reformation, first of the papacy and then of the Church as a whole.

The reform of the papacy, however, was, at first, mainly the work of the Emperor. The last dynastic Pope was Benedict IX, elected in 1032, and said to have been only twelve years old at the time. He was the son of Alberic of Tusculum, whom we have already met in connection with Abbot Odo. As he grew older, he grew more and more debauched, and shocked even the Romans. At last his wickedness reached such a pitch that he decided to resign the papacy in order to marry. He sold it to his godfather, who became Gregory VI. This man, though he acquired the papacy simoniacally, was a reformer; he was a friend of Hildebrand (Gregory VII). The manner of his acquiring the papacy, however, was too scandalous to be passed over. The young Emperor Henry III (1039-56) was a pious reformer, who had abandoned simony at great cost to his revenue, while retaining the right to appoint bishops. He came to Italy in 1046, at the age of twenty-two, and deposed Gregory VI on the charge of simony.

Henry III retained throughout his reign the power of making and unmaking popes, which, however, he exercised wisely in the interests of reform. After getting rid of Gregory VI, he appointed a German bishop, Suidger of Bamberg; the Romans resigned the election rights which they had claimed and often exercised, almost always badly. The new Pope died next year, and the Emperor's next nominee also died almost immediately—of poison, it was said. Henry III then chose a relation of his own, Bruno of Toul, who became Leo IX (1049-54). He was an earnest reformer, who travelled much and held many councils; he wished to fight the Normans in Southern Italy, but in this he was unsuccessful. Hildebrand was his friend, and might almost be called his pupil. At his death the Emperor appointed one more Pope, Gebhard of Eichstadt, who became Victor II, in 1055. But the Emperor died the next year, and the Pope the year after. From this point onwards, the relations of Emperor and Pope became less friendly. The Pope, having acquired moral authority by the help of Henry III, claimed first independence of the Emperor, and then superiority to him. Thus began the great conflict which lasted two hundred years and ended in the defeat of the Emperor. In the long run, therefore, Henry III's policy of reforming the papacy was perhaps short-sighted.

The next Emperor, Henry IV, reigned for fifty years (1056-1106). At first he was a minor, and the regency was exercised by his mother the Empress Agnes. Stephen IX was Pope for one year, and at his death the cardinals chose one Pope while the Romans, re-asserting the rights they had surrendered, chose another. The Empress sided with the cardinals, whose nominee took the name of Nicholas II. Although his reign only lasted three years, it was important. He made peace with the Normans, thereby making the papacy less dependent on the Emperor. In his time the manner in which popes were to be elected was determined by a decree, accord-ing to which the choice was to be made first by the cardinal bishops, then by the other cardinals, and last by the clergy and people of Rome, whose participation, one gathers, was to be purely formal. In effect, the cardinal bishops were to select the Pope. The election was to take place in Rome if possible, but might take place else-where if circumstances made election in Rome difficult or undesir-able. No part in the election was allotted to the Emperor. This decree, which was accepted only after a struggle, was an essential step in the emancipation of the papacy from lay control.

Nicholas II secured a decree that, for the future, ordinations by men guilty of simony were not to be valid. The decree was not made retroactive, because to do so would have invalidated the great majority of ordinations of existing priests.

During the pontificate of Nicholas II an interesting struggle began in Milan. The Archbishop, following the Ambrosian tradition, claimed a certain independence of the Pope. He and his clergy were in alliance with the aristocracy, and were strongly opposed to reform. The mercantile and lower classes, on the other hand, wished the clergy to be pious; there were riots in support of clerical celibacy, and a powerful reform movement, called 'Patarine', against the archbishop and his supporters. In 1059 the Pope, in support of reform, sent to Milan as his legate the eminent St Peter Damian. Damian was the author of a treatise *On Divine Omni-potence*, which maintained that God can do things contrary to the law of contradiction, and can undo the past. (This view was rejected by St Thomas, and has, since his time, been unorthodox.) He opposed dialectic, and spoke of philosophy as the handmaid of theology. He was, as we have seen, a follower of the hermit Romuald, and engaged with great reluctance in the conduct of affairs. His holiness, however, was such an asset to the papacy that very strong persuasion was brought to bear on him to help in the reform campaign, and he yielded to the Pope's representations. At

Milan in 1059 he made a speech against simony to the assembled clerics. At first they were so enraged that his life was in danger, but at last his eloquence won them over, and with tears they one and all confessed themselves guilty. Moreover, they promised obedience to Rome. Under the next Pope, there was a dispute with the Emperor about the see of Milan, in which, with the help of the Patarines, the Pope was ultimately victorious.

At the death of Nicholas II in 1061, Henry IV being now of age, there was a dispute between him and the cardinals as to the succession to the papacy. The Emperor had not accepted the election decree, and was not prepared to forgo his rights in the election of the Pope. The dispute lasted for three years, but in the end the cardinals' choice prevailed, without a definite trial of strength between Emperor and curia. What turned the scale was the obvious merit of the cardinals' Pope, who was a man combining virtue with experience, and a former pupil of Lanfranc (afterwards Archbishop of Canterbury). The death of this Pope, Alexander II, in 1073, was followed by the election of Hildebrand (Gregory VII).

Gregory VII (1073-85) is one of the most eminent of the Popes. He had long been prominent, and had great influence on papal policy. It was owing to him that Pope Alexander II blessed William the Conqueror's English enterprise; he favoured the Normans both in Italy and in the North. He had been a protégé of Gregory VI, who bought the papacy in order to combat simony; after the deposition of this Pope, Hildebrand passed two years in exile. Most of the rest of his life was spent in Rome. He was not a learned man, but was inspired largely by St Augustine, whose doctrines he learnt at second-hand from his hero Gregory the Great. After he became Pope, he believed himself the mouthpiece of St Peter. This gave him a degree of self-confidence which, on a mundane calculation, was not justified. He admitted that the Emperor's authority was also of divine origin : at first, he compared Pope and Emperor to two eyes; later, when quarrelling with the Emperor, to the sun and moon— the Pope, of course being the sun. The Pope must be supreme in morals, and must therefore have the right to depose the Emperor if the Emperor was immoral. And nothing could be more immoral than resisting the Pope. All this he genuinely and profoundly believed.

Gregory VII did more than any previous Pope to enforce clerical celibacy. In Germany the clergy objected, and on this ground as well as others were inclined to side with the Emperor. The laity, however, everywhere preferred their priests celibate. Gregory stirred up riots of the laity against married priests and their wives, in which both often suffered brutal ill-treatment. He called on the laity not to attend mass when celebrated by a recalcitrant priest. He decreed that the sacraments of married clergy were invalid, and that such clergy must not enter churches. All this roused clerical opposition and lay support; even in Rome, where Popes had usually gone in danger of their lives, he was popular with the people.

In Gregory's time began the great dispute concerning 'investitures'. When a bishop was consecrated, he was invested with a ring and staff as symbols of his office. These had been given by Emperor or king (according to the locality), as the bishop's feudal overlord. Gregory insisted that they should be given by the Pope. The dispute was part of the work of detaching the ecclesiastical from the feudal hierarchy. It lasted a long time, but in the end the papacy was completely victorious.

The quarrel which led to Canossa began over the archbishopric of Milan. In 1075 the Emperor, with the concurrence of the suffragans, appointed an archbishop; the Pope considered this an infringement of his prerogative, and threatened the Emperor with excommunication and deposition. The Emperor retaliated by summoning a council of bishops at Worms, where the bishops renounced their allegiance to the Pope. They wrote him a letter accusing him of adultery and perjury, and (worse than either) ill-treatment of bishops. The Emperor also wrote him a letter, claiming to be above all earthly judgment. The Emperor and his bishops pronounced Gregory deposed; Gregory excommunicated the Emperor and his bishops, and pronounced *them* deposed. Thus the stage was set.

In the first act, victory went to the Pope. The Saxons, who had before rebelled against Henry IV and then made peace with him, rebelled again; the German bishops made their peace with Gregory. The world at large was shocked by the Emperor's treatment of the Pope. Accordingly in the following year (1077) Henry decided to seek absolution from the Pope. In the depth of winter, with his wife and infant son and a few attendants, he crossed the Mont Cenis pass, and presented himself as a suppliant before the castle of Canossa, where the Pope was. For three days the Pope kept him waiting, bare-foot and in penitential garb. At last he was admitted. Having expressed penitence and sworn, in future, to follow the Pope's directions in dealing with his German opponents, he was pardoned and received back into communion.

The Pope's victory, however, was illusory. He had been caught out by the rules of his own theology, one of which enjoined absolution for penitents. Strange to say, he was taken in by Henry, and supposed his repentance sincere. He soon discovered his mistake. He could no longer support Henry's German enemies, who felt that he had betrayed them. From this moment, things began to go against him.

Henry's German enemies elected a rival Emperor, named Rudolf. The Pope, at first, while maintaining that it was for him to decide between Henry and Rudolf, refused to come to a decision. At last, in 1080, having experienced the insincerity of Henry's repentance, he pronounced for Rudolf. By this time, however, Henry had got the better of most of his opponents in Germany. He had an antipope elected by his clerical supporters, and with him, in 1084, he entered Rome. His antipope duly crowned him, but both had to retreat quickly before the Normans, who advanced to the relief of Gregory. The Normans brutally sacked Rome, and took Gregory away with them. He remained virtually their prisoner until his death the next year.

Thus his policies appeared to have ended in disaster. But in fact they were pursued with more moderation, by his successors. A compromise favourable to the papacy was patched up for the moment, but the conflict was essentially irreconcilable. Its later stages will be dealt with in subsequent chapters.

It remains to say something of the intellectual revival in the eleventh century. The tenth century was destitute of philosophers, except for Gerbert (Pope Sylvester II, 999-1003), and even he was more a mathematician than a philosopher. But as the eleventh century advanced, men of real philosophical eminence began to appear. Of these, the most important were Anselm and Roscelin, but some others deserve mention. All were monks connected with the reform movement.

Peter Damian, the oldest of them, has already been mentioned. Berengar of Tours (d. 1088) is interesting as being something of a rationalist. He maintained that reason is superior to authority, in support of which view he appealed to John the Scot, who was therefore posthumously condemned. Berengar denied transubstantiation, and was twice compelled to recant. His heresies were combated by Lanfranc in his book *De corpore et sanguine Domini*. Lanfranc was born at Pavia, studied law at Bologna, and became a first-rate dialectician. But he abandoned dialectic for theology, and entered the monastery of Bec, in Normandy, where he conducted a school. William the Conqueror made him Archbishop of Canterbury in 1070.

St Anselm was, like Lanfranc, an Italian, a monk at Bec, and Archbishop of Canterbury (1093-1109), in which capacity he followed the principles of Gregory VII and quarrelled with the king. He is chiefly known to fame as the inventor of the 'ontological argument' for the existence of God. As he put it, the argument is as follows: We define 'God' as the greatest possible object of thought. Now if an object of thought does not exist, another, exactly like it, which does exist, is greater. Therefore the greatest of all objects of thought must exist, since, otherwise, another, still greater, would be possible. Therefore God exists.

This argument has never been accepted, by theologians. It was adversely criticized at the time; then it was forgotten till the latter half of the thirteenth century. Thomas Aquinas rejected it, and among theologians his authority has prevailed ever since. But among philosophers it has had a better fate. Descartes revived it in a somewhat amended form; Leibniz thought that it could be made valid by the addition of a supplement to prove that God is *possible*. Kant considered that he had demolished it once for all. Nevertheless, in some sense, it underlies the system of Hegel and his followers, and reappears in Bradley's principle: 'What may be and must be, is.'

Clearly an argument with such a distinguished history is to be treated with respect, whether valid or not. The real question is: Is there anything we can think of which, by the mere fact that we can think of it, is shown to exist outside our thought? Every philosopher would *like* to say yes, because a philosopher's job is to find out things about the world by thinking rather than observing. If yes is the right answer, there is a bridge from pure thought to things, if not, not. In this generalized form, Plato uses a kind of ontological argument to prove the objective reality of ideas. But no one before Anselm had stated the argument in its naked logical purity. In gaining purity, it loses plausibility; but this also is to Anselm's credit.

For the rest, Anselm's philosophy is mainly derived from St Augustine, from whom it acquires many Platonic elements. He believes in Platonic ideas, from which he derives another proof of the existence of God. By Neoplatonic arguments he professes to prove not only God, but the Trinity. (It will be remembered that Plotinus has a Trinity, though not one that a Christian can accept as orthodox.) Anselm considers reason subordinate to faith. 'I believe in order to understand,' he says; following Augustine, he holds that without belief it is impossible to understand. God, he says, is not *just*, but *justice*. It will be remembered that John the Scot says similar things. The common origin is in Plato.

St Anselm, like his predecessors in Christian philosophy, is in the Platonic rather than the Aristotelian tradition. For this reason, he has not the distinctive characteristics of the philosophy which is called 'scholastic', which culminated in Thomas Aquinas. This kind of philosophy may be reckoned as beginning with Roscelin, who was Anselm's contemporary, being seventeen years younger than

Anselm. Roscelin marks a new beginning, and will be considered in a later chapter.

When it is said that medieval philosophy, until the thirteenth century, was mainly Platonic, it must be remembered that Plato, except for a fragment of the *Timaeus*, was known only at second or third hand. John the Scot, for example, could not have held the views which he did hold but for Plato, but most of what is Platonic in him comes from the pseudo-Dionysius. The date of this author is uncertain, but it seems probable that he was a disciple of Proclus the Neoplatonist. It is probable, also, that John the Scot had never heard of Proclus or read a line of Plotinus. Apart from the pseudo-Dionysius, the other source of Platonism in the Middle Ages was Boethius. This Platonism was in many ways different from that which a modern student derives from Plato's own writings. It omitted almost everything that had no obvious bearing on religion, and in religious philosophy it enlarged and emphasized certain aspects at the expense of others. This change in the conception of Plato had already been effected by Plotinus. The knowledge of Aristotle was also fragmentary, but in an opposite direction: all that was known of him until the twelfth century was Boethius's translation of the *Categories* and *De Emendatione*. Thus Aristotle was conceived as a mere dialectician, and Plato as only a religious philosopher and the author of the theory of ideas. During the course of the later Middle Ages, both these partial conceptions were gradually emended, especially the conception of Aristotle. But the process, as regards Plato, was not completed until the Renaissance.

Chapter X

MOHAMMEDAN CULTURE AND PHILOSOPHY

THE attacks upon the Eastern Empire, Africa, and Spain, differed from those of Northern barbarians on the West in two respects: first, the Eastern Empire survived till 1453, nearly a thousand years longer than the Western; second, the main attacks upon the Eastern Empire were made by Mohammedans, who did not become Christians after conquest, but developed an important civilization of their own.

The Hegira,[1] with which the Mohammedan era begins, took place in A.D. 622; Mohammed died ten years later. Immediately after his death the Arab conquests began, and they proceeded with extraordinary rapidity. In the East, Syria was invaded in 634, and completely subdued within two years. In 637 Persia was invaded; in 650 its conquest was completed. India was invaded in 664; Constantinople was besieged in 669 (and again in 716-17). The westward movement was not quite so sudden. Egypt was conquered in 642, Carthage not till 697. Spain, except for a small corner in the northwest, was acquired in 711-12. Westward expansion (except in Sicily and Southern Italy) was brought to a standstill by the defeat of the Mohammedans at the battle of Tours in 732, just one hundred years after the death of the prophet. (The Ottoman Turks, who finally conquered Constantinople, belong to a later period than that with which we are now concerned.)

Various circumstances facilitated this expansion. Persia and the Eastern Empire were exhausted by their long wars. The Syrians, who were largely Nestorian, suffered persecution at the hands of the Catholics, whereas Mohammedans tolerated all sects of Christians in return for the payment of tribute. Similarly in Egypt the Monophysites, who were the bulk of the population, welcomed the invaders. In Africa, the Arabs allied themselves with the Berbers, whom the Romans had never thoroughly subdued. Arabs and Berbers together invaded Spain, where they were helped by the Jews, whom the Visigoths had severely persecuted.

The religion of the Prophet was a simple monotheism, uncomplicated by the elaborate theology of the Trinity and the Incarnation. The Prophet made no claim to be divine, nor did his followers make such a claim on his behalf. He revived the Jewish prohibition

---

[1] The Hegira was Mohammed's flight from Mecca to Medina.

of graven images, and forbade the use of wine. It was the duty of the faithful to conquer as much of the world as possible for Islam, but there was to be no persecution of Christians, Jews, or Zoroastrians—the 'people of the Book', as the Koran calls them, i.e. those who followed the teaching of a Scripture.

Arabia was largely desert, and was growing less and less capable of supporting its population. The first conquests of the Arabs began as mere raids for plunder, and only turned into permanent occupation after experience had shown the weakness of the enemy. Suddenly, in the course of some twenty years, men accustomed to all the hardships of a meagre existence on the fringe of the desert found themselves masters of some of the richest regions of the world, able to enjoy every luxury and to acquire all the refinements of an ancient civilization. They withstood the temptations of this transformation better than most of the Northern barbarians had done. As they had acquired their empire without much severe fighting, there had been little destruction, and the civil administration was kept on almost unchanged. Both in Persia and in the Byzantine Empire, the civil government had been highly organized. The Arab tribesmen, at first, understood nothing of its complications, and perforce accepted the services of the trained men whom they found in charge. These men, for the most part, showed no reluctance to serve under their new masters. Indeed, the change made their work easier, since taxation was lightened very considerably. The populations, moreover, in order to escape the tribute, very largely abandoned Christianity for Islam.

The Arab Empire was an absolute monarchy, under the caliph, who was the successor of the Prophet, and inherited much of his holiness. The caliphate was nominally elective, but soon became hereditary. The first dynasty, that of the Umayyads, who lasted till 750, was founded by men whose acceptance of Mohammed was purely political, and it remained always opposed to the more fanatical among the faithful. The Arabs, although they conquered a great part of the world in the name of a new religion, were not a very religious race; the motive of their conquests was plunder and wealth rather than religion. It was only in virtue of their lack of fanaticism that a handful of warriors were able to govern, without much difficulty, vast populations of higher civilization and alien religion.

The Persians, on the contrary, have been, from the earliest times, deeply religious and highly speculative. After their conversion, they made out of Islam something much more interesting, more religious, and more philosophical, than had been imagined by the Prophet and his kinsmen. Ever since the death of Mohammed's son-in-law

Ali in 661, Mohammedans have been divided into two sects, the Sunni and the Shiah. The former is the larger; the latter follows Ali, and considers the Umayyad dynasty to have been usurpers. The Persians have long belonged to the Shiah sect. Largely by Persian influence, the Umayyads were at last overthrown, and succeeded by the Abbasids, who represented Persian interests. The change was marked by the removal of the capital from Damascus to Baghdad.

The Abbasids were, politically, more in favour of the fanatics than the Umayyads had been. They did not, however, acquire the whole of the empire. One member of the Umayyad family escaped the general massacre, fled to Spain, and was there acknowledged as the legitimate ruler. From that time on, Spain was independent of the rest of the Mohammedan world.

Under the early Abbasids the caliphate attained its greatest splendour. The best known of them is Harun-al-Rashid (d. 809), who was a contemporary of Charlemagne and the Empress Irene, and is known to every one in legendary form through the *Arabian Nights*. His court was a brilliant centre of luxury, poetry, and learning; his revenue was enormous; his empire stretched from the Straits of Gibraltar to the Indus. His will was absolute; he was habitually accompanied by the executioner, who performed his office at a nod from the caliph. This splendour, however, was short-lived. His successor made the mistake of composing his army mainly of Turks, who were insubordinate, and soon reduced the caliph to a cipher to be blinded or murdered whenever the soldiery grew tired of him. Nevertheless, the caliphate lingered on; the last caliph of the Abbasid dynasty was put to death by the Mongols in 1256, along with 800,000 of the inhabitants of Baghdad.

The political and social system of the Arabs had defects similar to those of the Roman Empire, together with some others. Absolute monarchy combined with polygamy led, as it usually does, to dynastic wars whenever a ruler died, ending with the victory of one of the ruler's sons and the death of all the rest. There were immense numbers of slaves, largely as a result of successful wars; at times there were dangerous servile insurrections. Commerce was greatly developed, the more so as the caliphate occupied a central position between East and West. 'Not only did the possession of enormous wealth create a demand for costly articles, such as silks from China, and furs from Northern Europe, but trade was promoted by certain special conditions, such as the vast extent of the Muslim Empire, the spread of Arabic as a world-language, and the exalted status assigned to the merchant in the Muslim system of ethics; it was remembered that the Prophet himself had been a merchant and had commended trading during the pilgrimage to

415

Mecca.'[1] This commerce, like military cohesion, depended on the great roads which the Arabs inherited from the Romans and Persians, and which they, unlike the Northern conquerors, did not allow to fall into disrepair. Gradually, however, the empire broke up into fractions—Spain, Persia, North Africa, and Egypt successively split off and acquired complete or almost complete independence.

One of the best features of the Arab economy was agriculture, particularly the skilful use of irrigation, which they learnt from living where water is scarce. To this day Spanish agriculture profits by Arab irrigation works.

The distinctive culture of the Muslim world, though it began in Syria, soon came to flourish most in the Eastern and Western extremities, Persia and Spain. The Syrians, at the time of the conquest, were admirers of Aristotle, whom Nestorians preferred to Plato, the philosopher favoured by Catholics. The Arabs first acquired their knowledge of Greek philosophy from the Syrians, and thus, from the beginning, they thought Aristotle more important than Plato. Nevertheless, their Aristotle wore a Neoplatonic dress. Kindi (d. *ca.* 873), the first to write philosophy in Arabic, and the only philosopher of note who was himself an Arab, translated parts of the *Enneads* of Plotinus, and published his translation under the title *The Theology of Aristotle*. This introduced great confusion into Arabic ideas of Aristotle, from which it took centuries to recover.

Meanwhile, in Persia, Muslims came in contact with India. It was from Sanskrit writings that they acquired, during the eighth century, their first knowledge of astronomy. About 830, Muhammad ibn Musa al-Khwarazmi, a translator of mathematical and astronomical books from the Sanskrit, published a book which was translated into Latin in the twelfth century, under the title *Algoritmi de numero Indrum*. It was from this book that the West first learnt of what we call 'Arabic' numerals, which ought to be called 'Indian'. The same author wrote a book on algebra which was used in the West as a text-book until the sixteenth century.

Persian civilization remained both intellectually and artistically admirable, though it was seriously damaged by the invasion of the Mongols in the thirteenth century. Omar Khayyám, the only man known to me who was both a poet and a mathematician, reformed the calendar in 1079. His best friend, oddly enough, was the founder of the sect of the Assassins, the 'Old Man of the Mountain', of legendary fame. The Persians were great poets: Firdousi (*ca.* 941), author of the *Shahnama*, is said by those who have read him to be

[1] *Cambridge Medieval History*, IV, 286.

comparable to Homer. They were also remarkable as mystics, which other Mohammedans were not. The Sufi sect, which still exists, allowed itself great latitude in the mystical and allegorical interpretation of orthodox dogma; it was more or less Neoplatonic.

The Nestorians, through whom, at first, Greek influences came into the Muslim world, were by no means purely Greek in their outlook. Their school at Edessa had been closed by the Emperor Zeno in 481; its learned men thereupon migrated to Persia, where they continued their work, but not without suffering Persian influences. The Nestorians valued Aristotle only for his logic, and it was above all his logic that the Arabic philosophers thought important at first. Later, however, they studied also his *Metaphysics* and his *De Anima*. Arabic philosophers, in general, are encyclopedic : they are interested in alchemy, astrology, astronomy, and zoology, as much as in what we should call philosophy. They were looked upon with suspicion by the populace, which was fanatical and bigoted; they owed their safety (when they were safe) to the protection of comparatively free-thinking princes.

Two Mohammedan philosophers, one of Persia, one of Spain, demand special notice; they are Avicenna and Averroes. Of these the former is the more famous among Mohammedans, the latter among Christians.

Avicenna (Ibn Sina) (980-1037) spent his life in the sort of places that one used to think only exist in poetry. He was born in the province of Bokhara; at the age of twenty-four he went to Khiva —'lone Khiva in the waste'—then to Khorassan—'the lone Chorasmian shore'. For a while he taught medicine and philosophy at Ispahan; then he settled at Teheran. He was even more famous in medicine than in philosophy, though he added little to Galen. From the twelfth to the seventeenth century, he was used in Europe as a guide to medicine. He was not a saintly character, in fact he had a passion for wine and women. He was suspect to the orthodox, but was befriended by princes on account of his medical skill. At times he got into trouble owing to the hostility of Turkish mercenaries; sometimes he was in hiding, sometimes in prison. He was the author of an encyclopedia, almost unknown to the East because of the hostility of theologians, but influential in the West through Latin translations. His psychology has an empirical tendency.

His philosophy is nearer to Aristotle, and less Neoplatonic, than that of his Muslim predecessors. Like the Christian scholastics later, he is occupied with the problem of universals. Plato said they were anterior to things. Aristotle has two views, one when he is thinking, the other when he is combating Plato. This makes him ideal material for the commentator.

Avicenna invented a formula, which was repeated by Averroes and Albertus Magnus: 'Thought brings about the generality in forms.' From this it might be supposed that he did not believe in universals apart from thought. This, however, would be an unduly simple view. Genera—that is, universals—are, he says, at once before things, in things, and after things. He explains this as follows. They are *before* things in God's understanding. (God decides, for instance, to create cats. This requires that He should have the idea 'cat', which is thus, in this respect, anterior to particular cats.) Genera are *in* things in natural objects. (When cats have been created, felinity is in each of them.) Genera are *after* things in our thought. (When we have seen many cats, we notice their likeness to each other, and arrive at the general idea 'cat'.) This view is obviously intended to reconcile different theories.

Averroes (Ibn Rushd) (1126-98) lived at the opposite end of the Muslim world from Avicenna. He was born at Cordova, where his father and grandfather had been cadis; he himself was a cadi, first in Seville, then in Cordova. He studied, first, theology and juris-prudence, then medicine, mathematics, and philosophy. He was recommended to the 'Caliph' Abu Yaqub Yusuf as a man capable of making an analysis of the works of Aristotle. (It seems, however, that he did not know Greek.) This ruler took him into favour; in 1184 he made him his physician, but unfortunately the patient died two years later. His successor, Yaqub Al-Mansur, for eleven years continued his father's patronage; then, alarmed by the opposition of the orthodox to the philosopher, he deprived him of his position, and exiled him, first to a small place near Cordova, and then to Morocco. He was accused of cultivating the philosophy of the ancients at the expense of the true faith. Al-Mansur published an edict to the effect that God had decreed hell-fire for those who thought that truth could be found by the unaided reason. All the books that could be found on logic and metaphysics were given to the flames.[1]

Shortly after this time the Moorish territory in Spain was greatly diminished by Christian conquests. Muslim philosophy in Spain ended with Averroes; and in the rest of the Mohammedan world a rigid orthodoxy put an end to speculation.

Ueberweg, rather amusingly, undertakes to defend Averroes against the charge of unorthodoxy—a matter, one would say, for Muslims to decide. Ueberweg points out that, according to the mystics, every text of the Koran had 7 or 70 or 700 layers of inter-pretation, the literal meaning being only for the ignorant vulgar.

[1] It is said that Averroes was taken back into favour shortly before his death.

It would seem to follow that a philosopher's teaching could not possibly conflict with the Koran; for among 700 interpretations there would surely be at least one that would fit what the philosopher had to say. In the Mohammedan world, however, the ignorant seem to have objected to all learning that went beyond a knowledge of the Holy Book; it was dangerous, even if no specific heresy could be demonstrated. The view of the mystics, that the populace should take the Koran literally but wise people need not do so, was hardly likely to win wide popular acceptance.

Averroes was concerned to improve the Arabic interpretation of Aristotle, which had been unduly influenced by Neoplatonism. He gave to Aristotle the sort of reverence that is given to the founder of a religion—much more than was given even by Avicenna. He holds that the existence of God can be proved by reason independently of revelation, a view also held by Thomas Aquinas. As regards immortality, he seems to have adhered closely to Aristotle, maintaining that the soul is not immortal, but intellect (nous) is. This, however, does not secure personal immortality, since intellect is one and the same when manifested in different persons. This view, naturally, was combated by Christian philosophers.

Averroes, like most of the later Mohammedan philosophers, though a believer, was not rigidly orthodox. There was a sect of completely orthodox theologians, who objected to all philosophy as deleterious to the faith. One of these, named Algazel, wrote a book called Destruction of the Philosophers, pointing out that, since all necessary truth is in the Koran, there is no need of speculation independent of revelation. Averroes replied by a book called Destruction of the Destruction. The religious dogmas that Algazel specially upheld against the philosophers were the creation of the world in time out of nothing, the reality of the divine attributes, and the resurrection of the body. Averroes regards religion as containing philosophic truth in allegorical form. This applies in particular to creation, which he, in his philosophic capacity, interprets in an Aristotelian fashion.

Averroes is more important in Christian than in Mohammedan philosophy. In the latter he was a dead end; in the former, a beginning. He was translated into Latin early in the thirteenth century by Michael Scott; as his works belong to the latter half of the twelfth century, this is surprising. His influence in Europe was very great, not only on the scholastics, but also on a large body of unprofessional free-thinkers, who denied immortality and were called Averroists. Among professional philosophers, his admirers were at first especially among the Franciscans and at the University of Paris. But this is a topic which will be dealt with in a later chapter.

Arabic philosophy is not important as original thought. Men like Avicenna and Averroes are essentially commentators. Speaking generally, the views of the more scientific philosophers come from Aristotle and the Neoplatonists in logic and metaphysics, from Galen in medicine, from Greek and Indian sources in mathematics and astronomy, and among mystics religious philosophy has also an admixture of old Persian beliefs. Writers in Arabic showed some originality in mathematics and in chemistry—in the latter case, as an incidental result of alchemical researches. Mohammedan civilization in its great days was admirable in the arts and in many technical ways, but it showed no capacity for independent speculation in theoretical matters. Its importance, which must not be underrated, is as a transmitter. Between ancient and modern European civilization, the dark ages intervened. The Mohammedans and the Byzantines, while lacking the intellectual energy required for innovation, preserved the apparatus of civilization—education, books, and learned leisure. Both stimulated the West when it emerged from barbarism—the Mohammedans chiefly in the thirteenth century, the Byzantines chiefly in the fifteenth. In each case the stimulus produced new thought better than any produced by the transmitters —in the one case scholasticism, in the other the Renaissance (which however had other causes also).

Between the Spanish Moors and the Christians, the Jews formed a useful link. There were many Jews in Spain, who remained when the country was reconquered by the Christians. Since they knew Arabic, and perforce acquired the language of the Christians, they were able to supply translations. Another means of transfusion arose through Mohammedan persecution of Aristotelians in the thirteenth century, which led Moorish philosophers to take refuge with Jews, especially in Provence.

The Spanish Jews produced one philosopher of importance, Maimonides. He was born in Cordova in 1135, but went to Cairo at the age of thirty, and stayed there for the rest of his life. He wrote in Arabic, but was immediately translated into Hebrew. A few decades after his death, he was translated into Latin, probably at the request of the Emperor Frederick II. He wrote a book called *Guide to Wanderers*, addressed to philosophers who have lost their faith. Its purpose is to reconcile Aristotle with Jewish theology. Aristotle is the authority on the sublunary world, revelation on the heavenly. But philosophy and revelation come together in the knowledge of God. The pursuit of truth is a religious duty. Astrology is rejected. The Pentateuch is not always to be taken literally; when the literal sense conflicts with reason, we must seek an allegorical interpretation. As against Aristotle, he maintains that God created not only form, but matter, out of nothing. He gives a summary of the *Timaeus* (which he knew in Arabic), preferring it on some points to Aristotle. The essence of God is unknowable, being above all predicated perfections. The Jews considered him heretical, and went so far as to invoke the Christian ecclesiastical authorities against him. Some think that he influenced Spinoza, but this is very questionable.

Chapter XI

THE TWELFTH CENTURY

Four aspects of the twelfth century are especially interesting to us:

(1) The continued conflict of empire and papacy;
(2) The rise of the Lombard cities;
(3) The Crusades; and
(4) The growth of scholasticism.

All these four continued into the following century. The Crusades gradually came to an inglorious end; but, as regards the other three movements, the thirteenth century marks the culmination of what, in the twelfth, is in a transitional stage. In the thirteenth century, the Pope definitely triumphed over the Emperor, the Lombard cities acquired secure independence and scholasticism reached its highest point. All this, however, was an outcome of what the twelfth century had prepared.

Not only the first of these four movements, but the other three also, are intimately bound up with the increase of papal and ecclesiastical power. The Pope was in alliance with the Lombard cities against the Emperor; Pope Urban II inaugurated the first Crusade, and subsequent popes were the main promoters of the later ones; the scholastic philosophers were all clerics, and Church councils took care to keep them within the bounds of orthodoxy, or discipline them if they strayed. Undoubtedly, their sense of the political triumph of the Church, in which they felt themselves participants, stimulated their intellectual initiative.

One of the curious things about the Middle Ages is that they were original and creative without knowing it. All parties justified their policies by antiquarian and archaistic arguments. The Emperor appealed, in Germany, to the feudal principles of the time of Charlemagne; in Italy, to Roman law and the power of ancient Emperors. The Lombard cities went still further back, to the institutions of republican Rome. The papal party based its claims partly on the forged Donation of Constantine, partly on the relations of Saul and Samuel as told in the Old Testament. The scholastics appealed either to the Scriptures or at first to Plato and then to Aristotle; when they were original, they tried to conceal the fact. The Crusades were an endeavour to restore the state of affairs that had existed before the rise of Islam.

We must not be deceived by this literary archaism. Only in the case of the Emperor did it correspond with the facts. Feudalism was in decay, especially in Italy; the Roman Empire was a mere memory. Accordingly, the Emperor was defeated. The cities of North Italy, while, in their later development, they showed much similarity to the cities of ancient Greece, repeated the pattern, not from imitation, but from similarity of circumstances: that of small, rich, highly civilized republican commercial communities surrounded by monarchies at a lower level of culture. The scholastics, however they might revere Aristotle, showed more originality than any of the Arabs—more, indeed, than any one since Plotinus, or at any rate since Augustine. In politics as in thought, there was the same distinguished originality.

CONFLICT OF EMPIRE AND PAPACY

From the time of Gregory VII to the middle of the thirteenth century, European history centres round the struggle for power between the Church and the lay monarchs—primarily the Emperor, but also, on occasion, the kings of France and England. Gregory's pontificate had ended in apparent disaster, but his policies were resumed, though with more moderation, by Urban II (1088-99), who repeated the decrees against lay investiture, and desired episcopal elections to be made freely by clergy and people. (The share of the people was, no doubt, to be purely formal.) In practice, however, he did not quarrel with lay appointments if they were good.

At first, Urban was safe only in Norman territory. But in 1093 Henry IV's son Conrad rebelled against his father, and, in alliance with the Pope, conquered North Italy, where the Lombard League, an alliance of cities with Milan at its head, favoured the Pope. In 1094, Urban made a triumphal procession through North Italy and France. He triumphed over Philip, King of France, who desired a divorce, and was therefore excommunicated by the Pope, but submitted. At the Council of Clermont, in 1095, Urban proclaimed the first Crusade, which produced a wave of religious enthusiasm leading to increase of papal power—also to atrocious pogroms of Jews. The last year of Urban's life he spent in safety in Rome, where popes were seldom safe.

The next Pope, Paschal II, like Urban, came from Cluny. He continued the struggle on investitures, and was successful in France and England. But after the death of Henry IV in 1106, the next Emperor, Henry V, got the better of the Pope, who was an unworldly man and allowed his saintliness to outweigh his political sense. The Pope proposed that the Emperor should renounce investitures, but in return bishops and abbots should renounce temporal possessions. The Emperor professed to agree; but when the suggested compromise was made public, the ecclesiastics rebelled furiously against the Pope. The Emperor, who was in Rome, took the opportunity to seize the Pope, who yielded to threats, gave way on investitures, and crowned Henry V. Eleven years later, however, by the Concordat of Worms in 1122, Pope Calixtus II compelled Henry V to give way on investitures, and to surrender control over episcopal elections in Burgundy and Italy.

So far, the net result of the struggle was that the Pope, who had been subject to Henry III, had become the equal of the Emperor. At the same time, he had become more completely sovereign in the Church, which he governed by means of legates. This increase of papal power had diminished the relative importance of bishops. Papal elections were now free from lay control, and ecclesiastics generally were more virtuous than they had been before the reform movement.

RISE OF THE LOMBARD CITIES

The next stage was connected with the Emperor Frederick Barbarossa (1152-90), an able and energetic man, who would have succeeded in any enterprise in which success was possible. He was a man of education, who read Latin with pleasure, though he spoke it with difficulty. His classical learning was considerable, and he was an admirer of Roman law. He thought of himself as the heir of the Roman Emperors, and hoped to acquire their power. But as a German he was unpopular in Italy. The Lombard cities, while willing to acknowledge his formal overlordship, objected when he interfered in their affairs—except those which feared Milan, against which city some of them invoked his protection. The Patarine movement in Milan continued, and was associated with a more or less democratic tendency; most, but by no means all, of the North Italian cities sympathized with Milan, and made common cause against the Emperor.

Hadrian IV, a vigorous Englishman who had been a missionary in Norway, became Pope two years after the accession of Barbarossa, and was, at first, on good terms with him. They were reconciled by a common enmity. The city of Rome claimed independence from both alike, and, as a help in the struggle, had invited a saintly heretic, Arnold of Brescia.[1] His heresy was very grave : he maintained that 'clerks who have estates, bishops who hold fiefs, monks who possess property, cannot be saved'. He held this view because he thought that the clergy ought to devote themselves entirely to spiritual matters. No one questioned his sincere austerity, although he was accounted wicked on account of his heresy. St Bernard, who vehemently opposed him, said, 'He neither eats nor drinks, but only, like the Devil, hungers and thirsts for the blood of souls.' Hadrian's predecessor in the papacy had written to Barbarossa to complain that Arnold supported the popular faction, which wished to elect one hundred senators and two consuls, and to have an Emperor of their own. Frederick, who was setting out for Italy, was naturally scandalized. The Roman demand for communal liberty, which was encouraged by Arnold, led to a riot in which a cardinal was killed. The newly-elected Pope Hadrian thereupon placed Rome under an interdict. It was Holy Week, and superstition got the better of the Romans; they submitted, and promised to banish Arnold. He hid, but was captured by the Emperor's troops. He was burnt, and his ashes were thrown into the Tiber, for fear of their being preserved as holy relics. After a delay caused by Frederick's unwillingness to hold the Pope's bridle and stirrup while he dismounted, the Pope crowned the Emperor in 1155 amid the resistance of the populace, which was quelled with great slaughter.

The honest man being disposed of, the practical politicians were free to resume their quarrel.

The Pope, having made peace with the Normans, ventured in 1157 to break with the Emperor. For twenty years there was almost continuous war between the Emperor on the one side, and the Pope with the Lombard cities on the other. The Normans mostly supported the Pope. The bulk of the fighting against the Emperor was done by the Lombard League, which spoke of 'liberty' and was inspired by intense popular feeling. The Emperor besieged various cities, and in 1162 even captured Milan, which he razed to the ground, compelling its citizens to live elsewhere. But five years later the League rebuilt Milan and the former inhabitants returned. In this same year, the Emperor, duly provided with an antipope,[2] marched on Rome with a great army. The Pope fled, and his cause

---

[1] He was said to be a pupil of Abélard, but this is doubtful.

[2] There was an antipope throughout most of this time. At the death of Hadrian IV, the two claimants, Alexander III and Victor IV, had a tug-of-war for the papal mantle. Victor IV (who was the antipope), having failed to snatch the mantle, obtained from his partisans a substitute which he had prepared, but in his haste he put it on inside-out.

seemed desperate, but pestilence destroyed Frederick's army, and he returned to Germany a solitary fugitive. Although not only Sicily, but the Greek Emperor, now sided with the Lombard League, Barbarossa made another attempt, ending in his defeat at the battle of Legnano in 1176. After this he was compelled to make peace, leaving to the cities all the substance of liberty. In the conflict between Empire and papacy, however, the terms of peace gave neither party complete victory.

Barbarossa's end was seemly. In 1189 he went on the third Crusade, and in the following year he died.

The rise of free cities is what proved of most ultimate importance in this long strife. The power of the Emperor was associated with the decaying feudal system; the power of the Pope, though still growing, was largely dependent upon the world's need of him as an antagonist to the Emperor, and therefore decayed when the Empire ceased to be a menace; but the power of the cities was new, a result of economic progress, and a source of new political forms. Although this does not appear in the twelfth century, the Italian cities, before long, developed a non-clerical culture which reached the very highest levels in literature, in art, and in science. All this was rendered possible by their successful resistance to Barbarossa.

All the great cities of Northern Italy lived by trade, and in the twelfth century the more settled conditions made traders more prosperous than before. The maritime cities, Venice, Genoa, and Pisa, never had to fight for their liberty, and were therefore less hostile to the Emperor than the cities at the foot of the Alps, which were important to him as the gateways to Italy. It is for this reason that Milan is the most interesting and important of Italian cities at this time.

Until the time of Henry III, the Milanese had usually been content to follow their archbishop. But the Patarine movement, mentioned in an earlier chapter, changed this: the archbishop sided with the nobility, while a powerful popular movement opposed him and them. Some beginnings of democracy resulted, and a constitution arose under which the rulers of the city were elected by the citizens. In various northern cities, but especially in Bologna, there was a learned class of lay lawyers, well versed in Roman law; moreover the rich laity, from the twelfth century onwards, were much better educated than the feudal nobility north of the Alps. Although they sided with the Pope against the Emperor, the rich commercial cities were not ecclesiastical in their outlook. In the twelfth and thirteenth centuries, many of them adopted heresies of a Puritan sort, like the merchants of England and Holland after the Reformation. Later, they tended to be free-thinkers, paying lip-service to the

Church, but destitute of all real piety. Dante is the last of the old type, Boccaccio the first of the new.

THE CRUSADES

The Crusades need not concern us as wars, but they have a certain importance in relation to culture. It was natural for the papacy to take the lead in the initiating of a Crusade, since the object was (at least ostensibly) religious; thus the power of the popes was increased by the war propaganda and by the religious zeal that was excited. Another important effect was the massacre of large numbers of Jews; those who were not massacred were often despoiled of their property and forcibly baptized. There were large-scale murders of Jews in Germany at the time of the first Crusade, and in England, at the time of the third Crusade, on the accession of Richard Cœur de Lion. York, where the first Christian Emperor had begun his reign, was the scene of one of the most appalling mass-atrocities against Jews. The Jews, before the Crusades, had almost a monopoly of the trade in Eastern goods throughout Europe; after the Crusades, as a result of the persecution of Jews, this trade was largely in Christian hands.

Another and very different effect of the Crusades was to stimulate literary intercourse with Constantinople. During the twelfth and early thirteenth centuries, many translations from Greek into Latin were made as a result of this intercourse. There had always been much trade with Constantinople, especially by Venetians; but Italian traders did not trouble themselves with Greek classics, any more than English or American traders in Shanghai troubled themselves with the classics of China. (European knowledge of Chinese classics was derived mainly from missionaries.)

THE GROWTH OF SCHOLASTICISM

Scholasticism, in its narrower sense, begins early in the twelfth century. As a philosophic school, it has certain definite characteristics. First, it is confined within the limits of what appears to the writer to be orthodoxy; if his views are condemned by a council, he is usually willing to retract. This is not to be attributed entirely to cowardice, it is analogous to the submission of a judge to the decision of a Court of Appeal. Second, within the limits of orthodoxy, Aristotle, who gradually became more fully known during the twelfth and thirteenth centuries, is increasingly accepted as the supreme authority; Plato no longer holds the first place. Third, there is a great belief in 'dialectic' and in syllogistic reasoning; the general temper of the scholastics is minute and disputatious rather than mystical. Fourth, the question of universals is brought to the fore by the discovery that Aristotle and Plato do not agree about it; it would be a mistake to suppose, however, that universals are the main concern of the philosophers of this period.

The twelfth century, in this as in other matters, prepares the way for the thirteenth, to which the greatest names belong. The earlier men have, however, the interest of pioneers. There is a new intellectual confidence, and, in spite of the respect for Aristotle, a free and vigorous exercise of reason wherever dogma has not made speculation too dangerous. The defects of the scholastic method are those that inevitably result from laying stress on 'dialectic'. These defects are: indifference to facts and science, belief in reasoning in matters which only observation can decide, and an undue emphasis on verbal distinctions and subtleties. These defects we had occasion to mention in connection with Plato, but in the scholastics they exist in a much more extreme form.

The first philosopher who can be regarded as strictly a scholastic is Roscelin. Not very much is known about him. He was born at Compiègne about 1050, and taught at Loches, in Brittany, where Abélard was his pupil. He was accused of heresy at a council at Rheims in 1092, and recanted for fear of being stoned to death by ecclesiastics with a taste for lynching. He fled to England, but there he was rash enough to attack St Anselm. This time he fled to Rome, where he was reconciled to the Church. He disappears from history about 1120; the date of his death is purely conjectural.

Nothing remains of Roscelin's writings except a letter to Abélard on the Trinity. In this letter be belittles Abélard and makes merry over his castration. Ueberweg, who seldom displays emotion, is led to observe that he can't have been a very nice man. Apart from this letter, Roscelin's views are chiefly known through the controversial writings of Anselm and Abélard. According to Anselm, he said that universals are mere *flatus vocis*, 'breath of the voice'. If this is to be taken literally, it means that a universal is a physical occurrence, that, namely, which takes place when we pronounce a word. It is hardly to be supposed, however, that Roscelin maintained anything so foolish. Anselm says that, according to Roscelin, *man* is not a unity, but only a common name; this view Anselm, like a good Platonist, attributes to Roscelin's only conceding reality to what is sensible. He seems to have held, generally, that a whole which has parts has no reality of its own, but is a mere word; the reality is in the parts. This view should have led him, and perhaps did lead him, to an extreme atomism. In any case, it led him into trouble about the Trinity. He considered that the Three Persons are three distinct substances, and that only usage stands in the way of our saying that there are Three Gods. The alternative, which he does not accept, is, according to him, to say that not only the Son, but the Father and the Holy Ghost, were incarnate. All this speculation, in so far as it was heretical, he recanted at Rheims in 1092. It is impossible to know exactly what he thought about universals, but at any rate it is plain that he was some sort of nominalist.

His pupil Abélard (or Abailard) was much abler and much more distinguished. He was born near Nantes in 1079, was a pupil of William of Champeaux (a realist) in Paris, and then a teacher in the Paris cathedral school, where he combated William's views and compelled him to modify them. After a period devoted to the study of theology under Anselm of Laon (not the archbishop), he returned to Paris in 1113, and acquired extraordinary popularity as a teacher. It was at this time that he became the lover of Héloïse, niece of Canon Fulbert. The canon had him castrated, and he and Héloïse had to retire from the world, he into a monastery at St Denis, she into a nunnery at Argenteuil. Their famous correspondence is said, by a learned German named Schmeidler, to have been entirely composed by Abélard as a literary fiction. I am not competent to judge as to the correctness of this theory, but nothing in Abélard's character makes it impossible. He was always vain, disputatious, and contemptuous; after his misfortune he was also angry and humiliated. Héloïse's letters are much more devoted than his, and one can imagine him composing them as a balm to his wounded pride.

Even in his retirement, he still had great success as a teacher; the young liked his cleverness, his dialectical skill, and his irreverence towards their older teachers. Older men felt the correlative dislike of him, and in 1121 he was condemned at Soissons for an unorthodox book on the Trinity. Having made due submission, he became abbot of St Gildas in Brittany, where he found the monks savage boors. After four miserable years in this exile, he returned to comparative civilization. His further history is obscure, except that he continued to teach with great success, according to the testimony of John of Salisbury. In 1141, at the instance of St Bernard, he was again condemned, this time at Sens. He retired to Cluny, and died the next year.

Abélard's most famous book, composed in 1121-22, is *Sic et Non*, 'Yes and No'. Here he gives dialectical arguments for and against a great variety of theses, often without attempting to arrive at a conclusion; clearly he likes the disputation itself, and considers it useful as sharpening the wits. The book had a considerable effect in waking people from their dogmatic slumbers. Abélard's view, that (apart from Scripture) dialectic is the sole road to truth, while no empiricist can accept it, had, at the time, a valuable effect as a solvent of prejudices and an encouragement to the fearless use of the intellect. Nothing outside the Scriptures, he said, is infallible; even Apostles and Fathers may err.

His valuation of logic was, from a modern point of view excessive. He considered it pre-eminently *the* Christian science' and made play with its derivation from 'Logos'. 'In the beginning was the Logos', says St John's Gospel, and this, he thought, proves the dignity of Logic.

His chief importance is in logic and theory of knowledge. His philosophy is a critical analysis, largely linguistic. As for universals, i.e. what can be predicated of many different things, he holds that we do not predicate a *thing*, but a *word*. In this sense he is a nominalist. But as against Roscelin he points out that a *'flatus vocis'* *is* a thing; it is not the word as a physical occurrence that we predicate, but the word as *meaning*. Here he appeals to Aristotle. Things, he says, resemble each other, and these resemblances give rise to universals. But the point of resemblance between two similar things is not itself a thing; this is the mistake of realism. He says some things that are even more hostile to realism, for example, that general concepts are not based in the nature of things, but are confused images of many things. Nevertheless he does not wholly refuse a place to Platonic ideas: they exist in the divine mind as patterns for creation; they are, in fact, God's concepts.

All this, whether right or wrong, is certainly very able. The most modern discussions of the problem of universals have not got much further.

St Bernard, whose saintliness did not suffice to make him intelligent,[1] failed to understand Abélard, and brought unjust accusations against him. He asserted that Abélard treats the Trinity like an Arian, grace like a Pelagian, and the Person of Christ like a Nestorian; that he proves himself a heathen in sweating to prove Plato a Christian; and further, that he destroys the merit of the Christian faith by maintaining that God can be completely understood by human reason. In fact Abélard never maintained this last, and always left a large province to faith, although, like St Anselm, he thought that the Trinity could be rationally demonstrated without the help of revelation. It is true that, at one time, he identified the Holy Ghost with the Platonic Soul of the World, but he abandoned

[1] 'The greatness of St Bernard lay not in the qualities of his intellect, but of his character.'—*Encyclopaedia Britannica*.

this view as soon as its heretical character was pointed out to him. Probably it was more his combativeness than his doctrines that caused him to be accused of heresy, for his habit of criticizing pundits made him violently unpopular with all influential persons.

Most of the learned men of the time were less devoted to dialectic than Abélard was. There was, especially in the School of Chartres, a humanistic movement, which admired antiquity, and followed Plato and Boethius. There was a renewed interest in mathematics: Adelard of Bath went to Spain early in the twelfth century, and in consequence translated Euclid.

As opposed to the dry scholastic method, there was a strong mystical movement, of which St Bernard was the leader. His father was a knight who died in the first Crusade. He himself was a Cistercian monk, and in 1115 became abbot of the newly-founded abbey of Clairvaux. He was very influential in ecclesiastical politics— turning the scales against antipopes, combating heresy in Northern Italy and Southern France, bringing the weight of orthodoxy to bear on adventurous philosophers, and preaching the second Crusade. In attacking philosophers he was usually successful; but after the collapse of his Crusade he failed to secure the conviction of Gilbert de la Porrée, who agreed with Boethius more than seemed right to the saintly heresy-hunter. Although a politician and a bigot, he was a man of genuinely religious temperament, and his Latin hymns have great beauty.[1] Among those influenced by him, mysticism became increasingly dominant, till it passed into something like heresy in Joachim of Flora (d. 1202). The influence of this man, however, belongs to a later time. St Bernard and his followers sought religious truth, not in reasoning, but in subjective experience and contemplation. Abélard and Bernard are perhaps equally one-sided

Bernard, as a religious mystic, deplored the absorption of the papacy in worldly concerns, and disliked the temporal power. Although he preached the Crusade, he did not seem to understand that a war requires organization, and cannot be conducted by religious enthusiasm alone. He complains that 'the law of Justinian, not the law of the Lord' absorbs men's attention. He is shocked when the Pope defends his domain by military force. The function of the Pope is spiritual, and he should not attempt actual government. This point of view, however, is combined with unbounded reverence for the Pope, whom he calls 'prince of bishops, heir of the apostles, of the primacy of Abel, the governance of Noah, the patriarchate of Abraham, the order of Melchizedek, the dignity

[1] Medieval Latin hymns, rhymed and accentual, give expression, sometimes sublime, sometimes gentle and pathetic, to the best side of the religious feeling of the times.

of Aaron, the authority of Moses, in judgeship Samuel, in power Peter, in unction Christ'. The net result of St Bernard's activities was, of course, a great increase of the power of the Pope in secular affairs.

John of Salisbury, though not an important thinker, is valuable for our knowledge of his times, of which he wrote a gossipy account. He was secretary to three Archbishops of Canterbury, one of whom was Becket; he was a friend of Hadrian IV; at the end of his life he was bishop of Chartres, where he died in 1180. In matters outside the faith, he was a man of sceptical temper; he called himself an Academic (in the sense in which St Augustine uses this term). His respect for kings was limited: 'an illiterate king is a crowned ass'. He revered St Bernard, but was well aware that his attempt to reconcile Plato and Aristotle must be a failure. He admired Abélard, but laughed at his theory of universals, and at Roscelin's equally. He thought logic a good introduction to learning, but in itself bloodless and sterile. Aristotle, he says, can be improved on, even in logic; respect for ancient authors should not hamper the critical exercise of reason. Plato is still to him the 'prince of all philosophers'. He knows personally most of the learned men of his time, and takes a friendly part in scholastic debates. On revisiting one school of philosophy after thirty years, he smiles to find them still discussing the same problems. The atmosphere of the society that he frequents is very like that of Oxford Common Rooms thirty years ago. Towards the end of his life, the cathedral schools gave place to universities, and universities, at least in England, have had a remarkable continuity from that day to this.

During the twelfth century, translators gradually increased the number of Greek books available to Western students. There were three main sources of such translations: Constantinople, Palermo, and Toledo. Of these Toledo was the most important, but the translations coming from there were often from the Arabic, not direct from the Greek. In the second quarter of the twelfth century, Archbishop Raymond of Toledo instituted a college of translators, whose work was very fruitful. In 1128, James of Venice translated Aristotle's *Analytics*, *Topics*, and *Sophistici Elenchi*; the *Posterior Analytics* were found difficult by Western philosophers. Henry Aristippus of Catania (d. 1162) translated the *Phaedo* and *Meno*, but his translations had no immediate effect. Partial as was the knowledge of Greek philosophy in the twelfth century, learned men were aware that much of it remained to be discovered by the West, and a certain eagerness arose to acquire a fuller knowledge of antiquity. The yoke of orthodoxy was not so severe as is sometimes supposed; a man could always write his book, and then, if necessary, withdraw its heretical portions after full public discussion. Most of the philosophers of the time were French, and France was important to the Church as a make-weight against the Empire. Whatever theological heresies might occur among them, learned clerics were almost all politically orthodox; this made the peculiar wickedness of Arnold of Brescia, who was an exception to the rule. The whole of early scholasticism may be viewed, politically, as an offshoot of the Church's struggle for power.

Chapter XII

THE THIRTEENTH CENTURY

In the thirteenth century the Middle Ages reached a culmination. The synthesis which had been gradually built up since the fall of Rome became as complete as it was capable of being. The fourteenth century brought a dissolution of institutions and philosophies the fifteenth brought the beginning of those that we still regard as modern. The great men of the thirteenth century were very great: Innocent III, St Francis, Frederick II, and Thomas Aquinas are, in their different ways, supreme representatives of their respective types. There were also great achievements not so definitely associated with great names: the Gothic cathedrals of France, the romantic literature of Charlemagne, Arthur, and the Niebelungen, the beginnings of constitutional government in Magna Carta and the House of Commons. The matter that concerns us most directly is the scholastic philosophy, especially as set forth by Aquinas; but I shall leave this for the next chapter, and attempt, first, to give an outline of the events that did most to form the mental atmosphere of the age.

The central figure at the beginning of the century is Pope Innocent III (1198-1216), a shrewd politician, a man of infinite vigour, a firm believer in the most extreme claims of the papacy, but not endowed with Christian humility. At his consecration, he preached from the text: 'See, I have this day set thee over the nations and over the kingdoms, to pluck up and to break down, to destroy and to overthrow, to build and to plant.' He called himself 'king of kings, lord of lords, a priest for ever and ever according to the order of Melchizedek'. In enforcing this view of himself, he took advantage of ever favourable circumstance. In Sicily, which had been conquered by the Emperor Henry VI (d. 1197), who had married Constance, heiress of the Norman kings, the new king was Frederick, only three years old at the time of Innocent's accession. The kingdom was turbulent, and Constance needed the Pope's help. She made him guardian of the infant Frederick, and secured his recognition of her son's rights in Sicily by acknowledging papal superiority. Portugal and Aragon made similar acknowledgments. In England, King John, after vehement resistance, was compelled to yield his kingdom to Innocent and receive it back as a papal fief.

To some degree, the Venetians got the better of him in the matter of the fourth Crusade. The soldiers of the Cross were to embark at Venice, but there were difficulties in procuring enough ships. No one had enough except the Venetians, and they maintained (for purely commercial reasons) that it would be much better to conquer Constantinople than Jerusalem—in any case, it would be a useful stepping-stone, and the Eastern Empire had never been very friendly to Crusaders. It was found necessary to give way to Venice; Constantinople was captured, and a Latin Emperor established. At first Innocent was annoyed; but he reflected that it might now be possible to re-unite the Eastern and Western Churches. (This hope proved vain.) Except in this instance, I do not know of anybody who ever in any degree got the better of Innocent III. He ordered the great Crusade against the Albigenses, which rooted out heresy, happiness, prosperity, and culture from southern France. He deposed Raymond, Count of Toulouse, for lukewarmness about the Crusade, and secured most of the region of the Albigenses for its leader, Simon de Montfort, father of the father of Parliament. He quarrelled with the Emperor Otto, and called upon the Germans to depose him. They did so, and at his suggestion elected Frederick II, now just of age, in his stead. But for his support of Frederick he exacted a terrific price in promises—which, however, Frederick was determined to break as soon as possible.

Innocent III was the first *great* Pope in whom there was no element of sanctity. The reform of the Church made the hierarchy feel secure as to its moral prestige, and therefore convinced that it need no longer trouble to be holy. The power motive, from his time on, more and more exclusively dominated the papacy, and produced opposition from some religious men even in his day. He codified the canon law so as to increase the power of the Curia; Walther von der Vogelweide called this code 'the blackest book that hell ever gave'. Although the papacy still had resounding victories to win, the manner of its subsequent decline might already have been foreseen.

Frederick II, who had been the ward of Innocent III, went to Germany in 1212, and by the Pope's help was elected to replace Otto. Innocent did not live to see what a formidable antagonist he had raised up against the papacy.

Frederick—one of the most remarkable rulers known to history—had passed his childhood and youth in difficult and adverse circumstances. His father Henry VI (son of Barbarossa) had defeated the Normans of Sicily, and married Constance, heiress to the kingdom. He established a German garrison, which was hated by the Sicilians; but he died in 1197, when Frederick was two years old. Constance thereupon turned against the Germans, and tried to govern without them by the help of the Pope. The Germans were resentful, and Otto tried to conquer Sicily; this was the cause of his quarrel with the Pope. Palermo, where Frederick passed his childhood, was subject to other troubles. There were Muslim revolts; the Pisans and Genoese fought each other and everyone else for possession of the island; the important people in Sicily were constantly changing sides, according as one party or the other offered the higher price for treachery. Culturally, however, Sicily had great advantages. Muslim, Byzantine, Italian, and German civilization met and mingled there as nowhere else. Greek and Arabic were still living languages in Sicily. Frederick learnt to speak six languages fluently, and in all six he was witty. He was at home in Arabian philosophy, and had friendly relations with Mohammedans, which scandalized pious Christians. He was a Hohenstaufen, and in Germany could count as a German. But in culture and sentiment he was Italian, with a tincture of Byzantine and Arab. His contemporaries gazed upon him with astonishment gradually turning into horror; they called him 'wonder of the world and marvellous innovator'. While still alive, he was the subject of myths. He was said to be the author of a book *De Tribus Impostoribus*—the three impostors were Moses, Christ, and Mohammed. This book, which never existed, was attributed, successively, to many enemies of the Church, the last of whom was Spinoza.

The words 'Guelf' and 'Ghibelline' began to be used at the time of Frederick's contest with the Emperor Otto. They are corruptions of 'Welf' and 'Waiblingen', the family names of the two contestants. (Otto's nephew was an ancestor of the British royal family.)

Innocent III died in 1216; Otto, whom Frederick had defeated died in 1218. The new Pope, Honorius III, was at first on good terms with Frederick, but difficulties soon arose. First, Frederick refused to go on crusade; then he had trouble with the Lombard cities, which in 1226 contracted an offensive and defensive alliance for twenty-five years. They hated the Germans; one of their poets wrote fiery verses against them. 'Love not the folk of Germany; far, far from you be these mad dogs.' This seems to have expressed the general feeling in Lombardy. Frederick wanted to remain in Italy to deal with the cities, but in 1227 Honorius died, and was succeeded by Gregory IX, a fiery ascetic who loved St Francis and was beloved by him. (He canonized St Francis two years after his death.) Gregory thought nothing else so important as the Crusade, and excommunicated Frederick for not undertaking it. Frederick, who had married the daughter and heiress of the King of Jerusalem, was willing enough to go when he could, and called himself King of Jerusalem. In 1228, while still excommunicate, he went; this made Gregory even more angry than his previously not going, for how could the crusading host be led by a man whom the Pope had banned? Arrived in Palestine, Frederick made friends with the Mohammedans, explained to them that the Christians attached importance to Jerusalem although it was of little strategic value, and succeeded in inducing them peaceably to restore the city to him. This made the Pope still more furious—one should fight the infidel, not negotiate with him. However, Frederick was duly crowned in Jerusalem, and no one could deny that he had been successful. Peace between Pope and Emperor was restored in 1230.

During the few years of peace that followed, the Emperor devoted himself to the affairs of the kingdom of Sicily. By the help of his prime minister, Pietro della Vigna, he promulgated a new legal code, derived from Roman law, and showing a high level of civilization in his southern dominion; the code was at once translated into Greek, for the benefit of the Greek-speaking inhabitants. He founded an important university at Naples. He minted gold coins, called 'augustals', the first gold coins in the West for many centuries. He established freer trade, and abolished all internal customs. He even summoned elected representatives of the cities to his council, which, however, had only consultative powers.

This period of peace ended when Frederick again came into conflict with the Lombard League in 1237; the Pope threw in his lot with them, and again excommunicated the Emperor. From this time until Frederick's death in 1250, the war was practically continuous, growing, on both sides, gradually more bitter, cruel and treacherous. There were great fluctuations of fortune, and the issue was still undecided when the Emperor died. But those who attempted to be his successors had not his power, and were gradually defeated, leaving Italy divided and the Pope victorious.

Deaths of popes made little difference in the struggle; each new Pope took up his predecessor's policy practically unchanged. Gregory IX died in 1241; in 1243 Innocent IV, a bitter enemy of Frederick, was elected. Louis IX, in spite of his impeccable orthodoxy, tried to moderate the fury of Gregory and Innocent IV, but in vain, Innocent, especially, rejected all overtures from the Emperor, and used all manner of unscrupulous expedients against him. He pronounced him deposed, declared a crusade against him, and excommunicated all who supported him. The friars preached against him, the Muslims rose, there were plots among his prominent nominal supporters. All this made Frederick increasingly cruel; plotters were ferociously punished, and prisoners were deprived of the right eye and the right hand.

At one time during this titanic struggle, Frederick thought of founding a new religion, in which he was to be the Messiah, and his minister Pietro della Vigna was to take the place of St Peter.[1] He did not get so far as to make this project public, but wrote about it to della Vigna. Suddenly, however, he became convinced, rightly or wrongly, that Pietro was plotting against him; he blinded him, and exhibited him publicly in a cage; Pietro, however, avoided further suffering by suicide.

Frederick, in spite of his abilities, could not have succeeded, because the antipapal forces that existed in his time were pious and democratic, whereas his aim was something like a restoration of the pagan Roman Empire. In culture he was enlightened, but politically he was retrograde. His court was oriental; he had a harem with eunuchs. But it was in this court that Italian poetry began; he himself had some merit as a poet. In his conflict with the papacy, he published controversial statements as to the dangers of ecclesiastical absolutism, which would have been applauded in the sixteenth century, but fell flat in his own day. The heretics, who should have been his allies, appeared to him simply rebels, and to please the Pope he persecuted them. The free cities, but for the Emperor, might have opposed the Pope; but so long as Frederick demanded their submission they welcomed the Pope as an ally. Thus, although he was free from the superstitions of his age, and in culture far above other contemporary rulers, his position as Emperor compelled him to oppose all that was politically liberal. He failed inevitably, but of all the failures in history he remains one of the most interesting.

The heretics, against whom Innocent III crusaded, and whom all rulers (including Frederick) persecuted, deserve study, both in themselves and as giving a glimpse of popular feeling, of which, otherwise, hardly a hint appears in the writings of the time.

The most interesting, and also the largest, of the heretical sects were the Cathari, who, in the South of France, are better known as Albigenses. Their doctrines came from Asia by way of the Balkans; they were widely held in Northern Italy, and in the South of France they were held by the great majority, including nobles, who liked the excuse to seize Church lands. The cause of this wide diffusion of heresy was partly disappointment at the failure of the Crusades, but mainly moral disgust at the wealth and wickedness of the clergy. There was a widespread feeling, analogous to later puritanism, in favour of personal holiness; this was associated with a cult of poverty. The Church was rich and largely worldly; very many priests were grossly immoral. The friars brought accusations against the older orders and the parish priests, asserting abuse of

[1] See the life of Frederick II, by Hermann Kantorowicz

the confessional for purposes of seduction; and the enemies of the friars retorted the accusation. There can be no doubt that such charges were largely justified. The more the Church claimed supremacy on religious grounds, the more plain people were shocked by the contrast between profession and performance. The same motives which ultimately led to the Reformation were operative in the thirteenth century. The main difference was that secular rulers were not ready to throw in their lot with the heretics; and this was largely because no existing philosophy could reconcile heresy with the claims of kings to dominion.

The tenets of the Cathari cannot be known with certainty, as we are entirely dependent on the testimony of their enemies. Moreover ecclesiastics, being well versed in the history of heresy, tended to apply some familiar label, and to attribute to existing sects all the tenets of former ones, often on the basis of some not very close resemblance. Nevertheless, there is a good deal that is almost beyond question. It seems that the Cathari were dualists and that, like the Gnostics, they considered the Old Testament Jehovah a wicked demiurge, the true God being only revealed in the New Testament. They regarded matter as essentially evil, and believed that for the virtuous there is no resurrection of the body. The wicked, however, will suffer transmigration into the bodies of animals. On this ground they were vegetarians, abstaining even from eggs, cheese, and milk. They ate fish, however, because they believed that fishes are not sexually generated. All sex was abhorrent to them; marriage, some said, is even worse than adultery, because it is continuous and complacent. On the other hand, they saw no objection to suicide. They accepted the New Testament more literally than did the orthodox; they abstained from oaths, and turned the other cheek. The persecutors record a case of a man accused of heresy, who defended himself by saying that he ate meat, lied, swore, and was a good Catholic.

The stricter precepts of the sect were only to be observed by certain exceptionally holy people called the 'perfected'; the others might eat meat and even marry.

It is interesting to trace the genealogy of these doctrines. They came to Italy and France, by way of the Crusaders, from a sect called the Bogomiles in Bulgaria; in 1167, when the Cathari held a council near Toulouse, Bulgarian delegates attended. The Bogomiles, in turn, were the result of a fusion of Manichæans and Paulicians. The Paulicians were an Armenian sect who rejected infant baptism, purgatory, the invocation of saints, and the Trinity; they spread gradually into Thrace, and thence into Bulgaria. The Paulicians were followers of Marcion (*ca* A.D. 150), who considered himself to be following St Paul in rejecting the Jewish elements in Christianity, and who had some affinity with the Gnostics without being one of them.

The only other popular heresy that I shall consider is that of the Waldenses. These were the followers of Peter Waldo, an enthusiast who, in 1170, started a 'crusade' for observance of the law of Christ. He gave all his goods to the poor, and founded a society called the 'Poor men of Lyons', who practised poverty and a strictly virtuous life. At first they had papal approval, but they inveighed somewhat too forcibly against the immorality of the clergy, and were condemned by the Council of Verona in 1184. Thereupon they decided that every good man is competent to preach and expound the Scriptures; they appointed their own ministers, and dispensed with the services of the Catholic priesthood. They spread to Lombardy, and to Bohemia, where they paved the way for the Hussites. In the Albigensian persecution, which affected them also, many fled to Piedmont; it was their persecution in Piedmont in Milton's time that occasioned his sonnet 'Avenge, O Lord, thy slaughtered saints.' They survive to this day in remote Alpine valleys and in the United States.

All this heresy alarmed the Church, and vigorous measures were taken to suppress it. Innocent III considered that heretics deserved death, being guilty of treason to Christ. He called upon the king of France to embark upon a crusade against the Albigenses, which was done in 1209. It was conducted with incredible ferocity; after the taking of Carcassonne, especially, there was an appalling massacre. The ferreting out of heresy had been the business of the bishops, but it became too onerous to be performed by men who had other duties, and in 1233 Gregory IX founded the Inquisition, to take over this part of the work of the episcopate. After 1254, those accused by the Inquisition were not allowed counsel. If condemned, their property was confiscated—in France, to the crown. When an accused person was found guilty, he was handed over to the secular arm with a prayer that his life might be spared; but if the secular authorities failed to burn him, they were liable to be themselves brought before the Inquisition. It dealt not only with heresy in the ordinary sense, but with sorcery and witchcraft. In Spain, it was chiefly directed against the crypto-Jews. Its work was performed mainly by Dominicans and Franciscans. It never penetrated to Scandinavia or England, but the English were quite ready to make use of it against Joan of Arc. On the whole, it was very successful; at the outset, it completely stamped out the Albigensian heresy.

The Church, in the early thirteenth century, was in danger of a revolt scarcely less formidable than that of the sixteenth. From this it was saved, very largely, by the rise of the mendicant orders; St Francis and St Dominic did much more for orthodoxy than was done by even the most vigorous popes.

St Francis of Assisi (1181 or 1182-1226) was one of the most lovable men known to history. He was of a well-to-do family, and in his youth was not averse from ordinary gaieties. But one day, as he was riding by a leper, a sudden impulse of pity led him to dismount and kiss the man. Soon afterwards, he decided to forgo all worldly goods, and devote his life to preaching and good works. His father, a respectable business man, was furious, but could not deter him. He soon gathered a band of followers, all vowed to complete poverty. At first, the Church viewed the movement with some suspicion; it seemed too like the 'Poor Men of Lyons'. The first missionaries whom St Francis sent to distant places were taken for heretics, because they practised poverty instead of (like the monks) only taking a vow which no one regarded as serious. But Innocent III was shrewd enough to see the value of the movement, if it could be kept within the bounds of orthodoxy, and in 1209 or 1210 he gave recognition to the new order. Gregory IX, who was a personal friend of St Francis, continued to favour him, while imposing certain rules which were irksome to the Saint's enthusiastic and anarchic impulses. Francis wished to interpret the vow of poverty in the strictest possible way; he objected to houses or churches for his followers. They were to beg their bread, and to have no lodging but what chance hospitality provided. In 1219, he travelled to the East and preached before the Sultan, who received him courteously but remained a Mohammedan. On his return, he found that the Franciscans had built themselves a house; he was deeply pained, but the Pope induced or compelled him to give way. After his death, Gregory canonized him but softened his rule in the article of poverty.

In the matter of saintliness, Francis has had equals; what makes him unique among saints is his spontaneous happiness, his universal love, and his gifts as a poet. His goodness appears always devoid of effort, as though it had no dross to overcome. He loved all living things, not only as a Christian or a benevolent man, but as a poet. His hymn to the sun, written shortly before his death, might *almost* have been written by Ikhnaton the sun-worshipper, but not quite —Christianity informs it, though not very obviously. He felt a duty to lepers, for their sake, not for his; unlike most Christian saints, he was more interested in the happiness of others than in his own salvation. He never showed any feeling of superiority, even to the humblest or most wicked. Thomas of Celano said of him that he was more than a saint among saints; among sinners he was one of themselves.

If Satan existed, the future of the order founded by St Francis would afford him the most exquisite gratification. The saint's immediate successor as head of the order, Brother Elias, wallowed in luxury, and allowed a complete abandonment of poverty. The chief work of the Franciscans in the years immediately following the death of their founder was as recruiting sergeants in the bitter and bloody wars of Guelfs and Ghibellines. The Inquisition, founded seven years after his death, was, in several countries, chiefly conducted by Franciscans. A small minority, called the Spirituals, remained true to his teaching; many of these were burnt by the Inquisition for heresy. These men held that Christ and the Apostles owned no property, not even the clothes they wore; this opinion was condemned as heretical in 1323 by John XXII. The net result of St Francis's life was to create yet one more wealthy and corrupt order, to strengthen the hierarchy, and to facilitate the persecution of all who excelled in moral earnestness or freedom of thought. In view of his own aims and character, it is impossible to imagine any more bitterly ironical outcome.

St Dominic (1170-1221) is much less interesting than St Francis. He was a Castilian, and had, like Loyola, a fanatical devotion to orthodoxy. His main purpose was to combat heresy, and he adopted poverty as a means to this end. He was present throughout the Albigensian war, though he is said to have deplored some of its more extreme atrocities. The Dominican Order was founded in 1215 by Innocent III, and won quick success. The only human trait known to me in St Dominic is his confession to Jordan of Saxony that he liked talking to young women better than to old ones. In 1242, the Order solemnly decreed that this passage should be deleted from Jordan's life of the founder.

The Dominicans were even more active than the Franciscans in the work of the Inquisition. They performed, however, a valuable service to mankind by their devotion to learning. This was no part of St Dominic's intention; he had decreed that his friars were 'not to learn secular sciences or liberal arts except by dispensation'. This rule was abrogated in 1259, after which date everything was done to make a studious life easy for Dominicans. Manual labour was no part of their duties, and the hours of devotion were shortened to give them more time for study. They devoted themselves to reconciling Aristotle and Christ; Albertus Magnus and Thomas Aquinas, both Dominicans, accomplished this task as well as it is capable of being accomplished. The authority of Thomas Aquinas was so overwhelming that subsequent Dominicans did not achieve much in philosophy; though Francis, even more than Dominic, had disliked learning, the greatest names in the immediately following period are Franciscan: Roger Bacon, Duns Scotus, and William of Occam were all Franciscans. What the friars accomplished for philosophy will be the subject of the following chapters.

Chapter XIII

ST THOMAS AQUINAS

THOMAS AQUINAS (b. 1225 or 1226, d. 1274) is regarded as the greatest of scholastic philosophers. In all Catholic educational institutions that teach philosophy his system has to be taught as the only right one; this has been the rule since a rescript of 1879 by Leo XIII. St Thomas, therefore, is not only of historical interest, but is a living influence, like Plato, Aristotle, Kant, and Hegel—more, in fact, than the latter two. In most respects, he follows Aristotle so closely that the Stagyrite has, among Catholics, almost the authority of one of the Fathers; to criticize him in matters of pure philosophy has come to be thought almost impious.[1] This was not always the case. In the time of Aquinas, the battle for Aristotle, as against Plato, still had to be fought. The influence of Aquinas secured the victory until the Renaissance; then Plato, who became better known than in the Middle Ages, again acquired supremacy in the opinion of most philosophers. In the seventeenth century, it was possible to be orthodox and a Cartesian; Malebranche, though a priest, was never censured. But in our day such freedoms are a thing of the past; Catholic ecclesiastics must accept St Thomas if they concern themselves with philosophy.

St Thomas was the son of the Count of Aquino, whose castle, in the kingdom of Naples, was close to Monte Cassino, where the education of the 'angelic doctor' began. He was for six years at Frederick II's university of Naples; then he became a Dominican and went to Cologne, to study under Albertus Magnus, who was the leading Aristotelian among the philosophers of the time. After a period in Cologne and Paris, he returned to Italy in 1259, where he spent the rest of his life except for the three years 1269-72. During these three years he was in Paris, where the Dominicans, on account of their Aristotelianism, were in trouble with the university authorities, and were suspected of heretical sympathy with the Averroists, who had a powerful party in the university. The Averroists held, on the basis of their interpretation of Aristotle, that the soul, in so far as it is individual, is not immortal; immortality belongs only to the intellect, which is impersonal, and identical in different intellectual beings. When it was forcibly brought to their

[1] When I did so in a broadcast, very many protests from Catholics resulted.

notice that this doctrine is contrary to the Catholic faith, they took refuge in the subterfuge of 'double truth'; one sort, based on reason, in philosophy, and another, based on revelation, in theology. All this brought Aristotle into bad odour, and St Thomas, in Paris, was concerned to undo the harm done by too close adherence to Arabian doctrines. In this he was singularly successful.

Aquinas, unlike his predecessors, had a really competent knowledge of Aristotle. His friend William of Moerbeke provided him with translations from the Greek, and he himself wrote commentaries. Until his time, men's notions of Aristotle had been obscured by Neoplatonic accretions. He, however, followed the genuine Aristotle, and disliked Platonism, even as it appears in St Augustine. He succeeded in persuading the Church that Aristotle's system was to be preferred to Plato's as the basis of Christian philosophy, and that Mohammedans and Christian Averroists had misinterpreted Aristotle. For my part, I should say that the *De Anima* leads much more naturally to the view of Averroes than to that of Aquinas; however, the Church, since St Thomas, has thought otherwise. I should say, further, that Aristotle's views on most questions of logic and philosophy were not final, and have since been proved to be largely erroneous; this opinion, also, is not allowed to be professed by any Catholic philosopher or teacher of philosophy.

St Thomas's most important work, the *Summa contra Gentiles*, was written during the years 1259-64. It is concerned to establish the truth of the Christian religion by arguments addressed to a reader supposed to be not already a Christian; one gathers that the imaginary reader is usually thought of as a man versed in the philosophy of the Arabs. He wrote another book, *Summa Theologiae*, of almost equal importance, but of somewhat less interest to us because less designed to use arguments not assuming in advance the truth of Christianity.

What follows is an abstract of the *Summa contra Gentiles*.

Let us first consider what is meant by 'wisdom'. A man may be wise in some particular pursuit, such as making houses; this implies that he knows the means to some particular end. But all particular ends are subordinate to the end of the universe, and wisdom *per se* is concerned with the end of the universe. Now the end of the universe is the good of the intellect, i.e. *truth*. The pursuit of wisdom in this sense is the most perfect, sublime, profitable, and delightful of pursuits. All this is proved by appeal to the authority of the 'The Philosopher', i.e. Aristotle.

My purpose (he says) is to declare the truth which the Catholic Faith professes. But here I must have recourse to natural reason, since the gentiles do not accept the authority of Scripture. Natural reason, however, is deficient in the things of God; it can prove some parts of the faith, but not others. It can prove the existence of God and the immortality of the soul, but not the Trinity, the Incarnation, or the Last Judgment. Whatever is demonstrable is, so far as it goes, in accordance with the Christian faith, and nothing in revelation is *contrary* to reason. But it is important to separate the parts of the faith which can be proved by reason from those which cannot. Accordingly, of the four books into which the *Summa* is divided, the first three make no appeal to revelation, except to show that it is in accordance with conclusions reached by reason; only in the fourth book are matters treated which cannot be known apart from revelation.

The first step is to prove the existence of God. Some think this unnecessary, since the existence of God (they say) is self-evident. If we knew God's essence, this would be true, since (as is proved later) in God, essence and existence are one. But we do not know His essence, except very imperfectly. Wise men know more of His essence than do the ignorant, and angels know more than either; but no creature knows enough of it to be able to deduce God's existence from His essence. On this ground, the ontological argument is rejected.

It is important to remember that religious truths which can be proved can also be known by faith. The proofs are difficult, and can only be understood by the learned; but faith is necessary also to the ignorant, to the young, and to those who, from practical preoccupations, have not the leisure to learn philosophy. For them, revelation suffices.

Some say that God is *only* knowable by faith. They argue that, if the principles of demonstration became known to us through experience derived from the senses, as is said in the *Posterior Analytics*, whatever transcends sense cannot be proved. This, however, is false; and even if it were true, God could be known from His sensible effects.

The existence of God is proved, as in Aristotle, by the argument of the unmoved mover.[1] There are things which are only moved, and other things which both move and are moved. Whatever is moved is moved by something, and, since an endless regress is impossible, we must arrive somewhere at something which moves other things without being moved. This unmoved mover is God. It might be objected that this argument involves the eternity of movement, which Catholics reject. This would be an error: it is valid on the hypothesis of the eternity of movement, but is only

[1] But in Aristotle the argument leads to 47 or 55 Gods.

strengthened by the opposite hypothesis, which involves a beginning, and therefore a First Cause.

In the *Summa Theologiae*, five proofs of God's existence are given. First, the argument of the unmoved mover, as above. Second, the argument of the First Cause, which again depends upon the impossibility of an infinite regress. Third, that there must be an ultimate source of all necessity; this is much the same as the second argument. Fourth, that we find various perfections in the world, and that these must have their source in something completely perfect. Fifth, that we find even lifeless things serving a purpose, which must be that of some being outside them, since only living things can have an internal purpose.

To return to the *Summa contra Gentiles*, having proved the existence of God, we can now say many things about Him, but these are all, in a sense, negative; God's nature is only known to us through what is not. God is eternal, since He is unmoved; He is unchanging, since He contains no passive potentiality. David of Dinant (a materialistic pantheist of the early thirteenth century) 'raved' that God is the same as primary matter; this is absurd, since primary matter is pure passivity, and God is pure activity. In God, there is no composition, therefore He is not a body, because bodies have parts.

God is His own essence, since otherwise He would not be simple, but would be compounded of essence and existence. (This point is important.) In God, essence and existence are identical. There are no accidents in God. He cannot be specified by any substantial difference; He is not in any genus; He cannot be defined. But He lacks not the excellence of any genus. Things are in some ways like God, in others not. It is more fitting to say that things are like God than that God is like things.

God is good, and is His own goodness; He is the good of every good. He is intelligent, and His act of intelligence is His essence. He understands by His essence, and understands Himself perfectly. (John the Scot, it will be remembered, thought otherwise.)

Although there is no composition in the divine intellect, God understands many things. This might seem a difficulty, but the things that He understands have no distinct being in Him. Nor do they exist *per se*, as Plato thought, because forms of natural things cannot exist or be understood apart from matter. Nevertheless, God must understand forms before creating. The solution of this difficulty is as follows: 'The concept of the divine intellect, according as He understands Himself, which concept is His Word, is the likeness not only of God Himself understood, but also of all the things of which the divine essence is the likeness. Accordingly many things

447

can be understood by God, by one intelligible species which is the divine essence, and by one understood intention which is the divine Word.'[1] Every form, so far as it is something positive, is a perfection. God's intellect includes in His essence what is proper to each thing, by understanding where it is like Him and where unlike; for instance life, not knowledge, is the essence of a plant, and knowledge, not intellect, is the essence of an animal. Thus a plant is like God in being alive, but unlike in not having knowledge; an animal is like God in having knowledge, but unlike in not having intellect. It is always by a negation that a creature differs from God.

God understands all things at the same instant. His knowledge is not a habit, and is not discursive or argumentative. God is truth. (This is to be understood literally.)

We come now to a question which had already troubled both Plato and Aristotle. Can God know particular things, or does He only know universals and general truths? A Christian, since he believes in Providence, must hold that God knows particular things; nevertheless, there are weighty arguments against this view. St Thomas enumerates seven such arguments, and then proceeds to refute them. The seven arguments are as follows:

1. Singularity being signate matter, nothing immaterial can know it.

2. Singulars do not always exist, and cannot be known when they do not exist; therefore they cannot be known by an unchanging being.

3. Singulars are contingent, not necessary; therefore there can be no certain knowledge of them except when they exist.

4. Some singulars are due to volitions, which can only be known to the person willing.

5. Singulars are infinite in number, and the infinite as such is unknown.

6. Singulars are too petty for God's attention.

7. In some singulars there is evil, but God cannot know evil.

Aquinas replies that God knows singulars as their cause; that He knows things that do not yet exist, just as an artificer does when he is making something; that He knows future contingents, because He sees each thing in time as if present, He Himself being not in time; that He knows our minds and secret wills, and that He knows an infinity of things, although we cannot do so. He knows trivial things, because nothing is *wholly* trivial, and everything has *some* nobility; otherwise God would know only Himself. Moreover the

[1] *Summa contra Gentiles*, Book I, chap. liii.

order of the universe is very noble, and this cannot be known without knowing even the trivial parts. Finally, God knows evil things, because knowing anything good involves knowing the opposite evil.

In God there is Will; His Will is His essence, and its principal object is the divine essence. In willing Himself, God wills other things also, for God is the end of all things. He wills even things that are not yet, He wills His own being and goodness, but other things, though He wills them, He does not will *necessarily*. There is free will in God; a *reason* can be assigned for His volition, but not a *cause*. He cannot will things impossible in themselves; for example, He cannot make a contradiction true. The Saint's example of something beyond even divine power is not an altogether happy one; he says that God could not make a man be an ass.

In God are delight and joy and love; God hates nothing, and possesses the contemplative and active virtues. He is happy, and is His own happiness.

We come now (in Book II) to the consideration of creatures. This is useful for refuting errors against God. God created the world out of nothing, contrary to the opinions of the ancients. The subject of the things that God cannot do is resumed. He cannot be a body, or change Himself; He cannot fail; He cannot be weary, or forget, or repent, or be angry or sad; He cannot make a man have no soul, or make the sum of the angles of a triangle be not two right angles. He cannot undo the past, commit sins, make another God, or make Himself not exist.

Book II is mainly occupied with the soul in man. All intellectual substances are immaterial and incorruptible; angels have no bodies, but in men the soul is united to a body. It is the form of the body, as in Aristotle. There are not three souls in man, but only one. The whole soul is present entire in every part of the body. The souls of animals, unlike those of men, are not immortal. The intellect is part of each man's soul; there is not, as Averroes maintained, only one intellect, in which various men participate. The soul is not transmitted with the semen, but is created afresh with each man. There is, it is true, a difficulty: when a man is born out of wedlock, this seems to make God an accomplice in adultery. This objection, however, is only specious. (There is a grave objection, which troubled St Augustine, and that is as to the transmission of original sin. It is the soul that sins, and if the soul is not transmitted, but created afresh, how can it inherit the sin of Adam? This is not discussed.)

In connection with the intellect, the problem of universals is discussed. St Thomas's position is that of Aristotle. Universals do not subsist outside the soul, but the intellect, in understanding universals, understands things that are outside the soul.

The Third Book is largely concerned with ethical questions. Evil is unintentional, not an essence, and has an accidental cause which is good. All things tend to be like God who is the end of all things. Human happiness does not consist in carnal pleasures, honour, glory, wealth, worldly power, or goods of the body, and is not seated in the senses. Man's ultimate happiness does not consist in acts of moral virtue, because these are means; it consists in the contemplation of God. But the knowledge of God possessed by the majority does not suffice; nor the knowledge of Him obtained by demonstration; nor even the knowledge obtained by faith. In this life, we cannot see God in His essence, or have ultimate happiness; but hereafter we shall see Him face to face. (Not literally, we are warned, because God has no face.) This will happen, not by our natural power, but by the divine light; and even then, we shall not see all of Him. By this vision we become partakers of eternal life, i.e. of life outside time.

Divine Providence does not exclude evil, contingency, free will, chance or luck. Evil comes through second causes, as in the case of a good artist with bad tools.

Angels are not all equals; there is an order among them. Each angel is the sole specimen of his species, for, since angels have no bodies, they can only be distinct through specific differences, not through position in space.

Astrology is to be rejected, for the usual reasons. In answer to the question 'Is there such a thing as fate?' Aquinas replies that we *might* give the name 'fate' to the order impressed by Providence, but it is wiser not to do so, as 'fate' is a pagan word. This leads to an argument that prayer is useful although Providence is unchangeable. (I have failed to follow this argument.) God sometimes works miracles, but no one else can. Magic, however, is possible with the help of demons; this is not properly miraculous, and is not by the help of the stars.

Divine law directs us to love God; also, in a lesser degree, our neighbour. It forbids fornication, because the father should stay with the mother while the children are being reared. It forbids birth control, as being against nature; it does not, however, on this account forbid life-long celibacy. Matrimony should be indissoluble, because the father is needed in the education of the children, both as more rational than the mother, and as having more physical strength when punishment is required. Not all carnal intercourse is sinful, since it is natural; but to think the married state as good as continence is to fall into the heresy of Jovinian. There must be strict monogamy; polygyny is unfair to women, and polyandry makes paternity certain. Incest is to be forbidden because it would complicate family life. Against brother-sister incest there is a very curious argument: that if the love of husband and wife were combined with that of brother and sister, mutual attraction would be so strong as to cause unduly frequent intercourse.

All these arguments on sexual ethics, it is to be observed, appeal to purely rational considerations, not to divine commands and prohibitions. Here, as throughout the first three books, Aquinas is glad, at the end of a piece of reasoning, to quote texts showing that reason has led him to a conclusion in harmony with the Scriptures, but he does not appeal to authority until his result has been reached.

There is a most lively and interesting discussion of voluntary poverty, which, as one might expect, arrives ultimately at a conclusion in harmony with the principles of the mendicant Orders, but states the objections with a force and realism which shows them to be such as he had actually heard urged by the secular clergy.

He then passes on to sin, predestination, and election, on which his view is broadly that of Augustine. By mortal sin a man forfeits his last end to all eternity, and therefore eternal punishment is his due. No man can be freed from sin except by grace, and yet the sinner is to be blamed if he is not converted. Man needs grace to persevere in good, but no one can *merit* divine assistance. God is not the cause of sinning, but some He leaves in sin, while others He delivers from it. As regards predestination, St Thomas seems to hold, with St Augustine, that no reason can be given why some are elected and go to heaven, while others are left reprobate and go to hell. He holds also that no man can enter heaven unless he has been baptized. This is not one of the truths that can be proved by the unaided reason; it is revealed in John iii. 5.[1]

The fourth book is concerned with the Trinity, the Incarnation, the supremacy of the Pope, the sacraments, and the resurrection of the body. In the main, it is addressed to theologians rather than philosophers, and I shall therefore deal with it briefly.

There are three ways of knowing God: by reason, by revelation, and by intuition of things previously known only by revelation. Of the third way, however, he says almost nothing. A writer inclined to mysticism would have said more of it than of either of the others, but Aquinas's temperament is ratiocinative rather than mystical.

The Greek Church is blamed for denying the double procession of the Holy Ghost and the supremacy of the Pope. We are warned

---

[1] 'Jesus answered, verily, verily, I say unto thee, except a man be born of water and of the Spirit, he cannot enter into the kingdom of God.'

that, although Christ was conceived of the Holy Ghost, we must not suppose that He was the son of the Holy Ghost according to the flesh.

The sacraments are valid even when dispensed by wicked ministers. This was an important point in Church doctrine. Very many priests lived in mortal sin, and pious people feared that such priests could not administer the sacraments. This was awkward; no one could know if he was really married, or if he had received valid absolution. It led to heresy and schism, since the puritanically minded sought to establish a separate priesthood of more impeccable virtue. The Church, in consequence, was obliged to assert with great emphasis that sin in a priest did not incapacitate him for the performance of his functions.

One of the last questions discussed is the resurrection of the body. Here, as elsewhere, Aquinas states very fairly the arguments that have been brought against the orthodox position. One of these, at first sight, offers great difficulties. What is to happen, asks the Saint, to a man who never, throughout his life, ate anything but human flesh, and whose parents did likewise? It would seem unfair to his victims that they should be deprived of their bodies at the last day as a consequence of his greed; yet, if not, what will be left to make up his body? I am happy to say that this difficulty, which might at first sight seem insuperable, is triumphantly met. The identity of the body, St Thomas points out, is not dependent on the persistence of the same material particles; during life, by the processes of eating and digesting, the matter composing the body undergoes perpetual change. The cannibal may, therefore, receive the same body at the resurrection, even if it is not composed of the same matter as was in his body when he died. With this comforting thought we may end our abstract of the *Summa contra Gentiles*.

In its general outlines, the philosophy of Aquinas agrees with that of Aristotle, and will be accepted or rejected by a reader in the measure in which he accepts or rejects the philosophy of the Stagyrite. The originality of Aquinas is shown in his adaptation of Aristotle to Christian dogma, with a minimum of alteration. In his day he was considered a bold innovator; even after his death many of his doctrines were condemned by the universities of Paris and Oxford. He was even more remarkable for systematizing than for originality. Even if every one of his doctrines were mistaken, the *Summa* would remain an imposing intellectual edifice. When he wishes to refute some doctrine, he states it first, often with great force, and almost always with an attempt at fairness. The sharpness and clarity with which he distinguishes arguments derived from reason and arguments derived from revelation are admirable.

He knows Aristotle well, and understands him thoroughly, which cannot be said of any earlier Catholic philosopher.

These merits, however, seem scarcely sufficient to justify his immense reputation. The appeal to reason is, in a sense, insincere, since the conclusion to be reached is fixed in advance. Take, for example, the indissolubility of marriage. This is advocated on the ground that the father is useful in the education of the children, (a) because he is more rational than the mother, (b) because, being stronger, he is better able to inflict physical punishment. A modern educator might retort (a) that there is no reason to suppose men in general more rational than women, (b) that the sort of punishment that requires great physical strength is not desirable in education. He might go on to point out that fathers, in the modern world, have scarcely any part in education. But no follower of St Thomas would, on that account, cease to believe in lifelong monogamy, because the real grounds of belief are not those which are alleged.

Or take again the arguments professing to prove the existence of God. All these, except the one from teleology in lifeless things, depend upon the supposed impossibility of a series having no first term. Every mathematician knows that there is no such impossibility; the series of negative integers ending with minus one is an instance to the contrary. But here again no Catholic is likely to abandon belief in God even if he becomes convinced that St Thomas's arguments are bad; he will invent other arguments, or take refuge in revelation.

The contentions that God's essence and existence are one and the same, that God *is* His own goodness, His own power, and so on, suggest a confusion, found in Plato, but supposed to have been avoided by Aristotle, between the manner of being of particulars and the manner of being of universals. God's essence is, one must suppose, of the nature of universals, while His existence is not. It is difficult to state this difficulty satisfactorily, since it occurs within a logic that can no longer be accepted. But it points clearly to some kind of syntactical confusion, without which much of the argumentation about God would lose its plausibility.

There is little of the true philosophic spirit in Aquinas. He does not, like the Platonic Socrates, set out to follow wherever the argument may lead. He is not engaged in an enquiry, the result of which it is impossible to know in advance. Before he begins to philosophize, he already knows the truth; it is declared in the Catholic faith. If he can find apparently rational arguments for some parts of the faith, so much the better; if he cannot, he need only fall back on revelation. The finding of arguments for a con-

453

clusion given in advance is not philosophy, but special pleading. I cannot, therefore, feel that he deserves to be put on a level with the best philosophers either of Greece or of modern times.

Chapter XIV

FRANCISCAN SCHOOLMEN

FRANCISCANS, on the whole, were less impeccably orthodox than Dominicans. Between the two orders there was keen rivalry, and the Franciscans were not inclined to accept the authority of St Thomas. The three most important of Franciscan philosophers were Roger Bacon, Duns Scotus and William of Occam. St Bonaventura and Matthew of Aquasparta also call for notice.

Roger Bacon (ca. 1214-ca. 1294) was not greatly admired in his own day, but in modern times has been praised far beyond his deserts. He was not so much a philosopher, in the narrow sense, as a man of universal learning with a passion for mathematics and science. Science, in his day, was mixed up with alchemy, and thought to be mixed up with black magic; Bacon was constantly getting into trouble through being suspected of heresy and magic. In 1257, St Bonaventura, the General of the Franciscan order, placed him under surveillance in Paris, and forbade him to publish. Nevertheless, while this prohibition was still in force, the papal legate in England, Guy de Foulques, commanded him, contrary orders notwithstanding, to write out his philosophy for the benefit of the Pope. He therefore produced in a very short time three books, *Opus Majus*, *Opus Minus*, and *Opus Tertium*. These seem to have produced a good impression, and in 1268 he was allowed to return to Oxford, from which he had been removed to a sort of imprisonment in Paris. However, nothing could teach him caution. He made a practice of contemptuous criticism of all the most learned of his contemporaries; in particular, he maintained that the translators from Greek and Arabic were grossly incompetent. In 1271, he wrote a book called *Compendium Studii Philosophiae*, in which he attacked clerical ignorance. This did nothing to add to his popularity among his colleagues, and in 1278 his books were condemned by the General of the Order, and he was put in prison for fourteen years. In 1292 he was liberated, but died not long afterwards.

He was encyclopaedic in his learning, but not systematic. Unlike most philosophers of the time, he valued experiment highly, and illustrated its importance by the theory of the rainbow. He wrote well on geography; Columbus read this part of his work, and was influenced by it. He was a good mathematician; he quotes the sixth and ninth books of Euclid. He treated of perspective, following

Arabic sources. Logic he thought a useless study; alchemy, on the other hand, he valued enough to write on it.

To give an idea of his scope and method, I will summarize some parts of the *Opus Majus*.

There are, he says, four causes of ignorance: First, the example of frail and unsuited authority. (The work being written for the Pope, he is careful to say that this does not include the Church.) Second, the influence of custom. Third, the opinion of the unlearned crowd. (This, one gathers, includes all his contemporaries except himself.) Fourth, the concealment of one's ignorance in a display of apparent wisdom. From these four plagues, of which the fourth is the worst, spring all human evils.

In supporting an opinion, it is a mistake to argue from the wisdom of our ancestors, or from customs, or from common belief. In support of his view he quotes Seneca, Cicero, Avicenna, Averroes, Adelard of Bath, St Jerome, and St Chrysostom. These authorities, he seems to think, suffice to prove that one should not respect authority.

His respect for Aristotle is great, but not unbounded. 'Only Aristotle, together with his followers, has been called philosopher in the judgment of all wise men.' Like almost all his contemporaries, he uses the designation, 'The Philosopher', when he speaks of Aristotle, but even the Stagyrite, we are told, did not come to the limit of human wisdom. After him, Avicenna was 'the prince and leader of philosophy', though he did not fully understand the rainbow, because he did not recognize its final cause, which, according to Genesis, is the dissipation of aqueous vapour. (Nevertheless, when Bacon comes to treat of the rainbow, he quotes Avicenna with great admiration.) Every now and then he says something that has a flavour of orthodoxy, such as that the only perfect wisdom is in the Scriptures, as explained by canon law and philosophy. But he sounds more sincere when he says that there is no objection to getting knowledge from the heathen; in addition to Avicenna and Averroes, he quotes Alfarabi[1] very often, and Albumazar[2] and others from time to time. Albumazar is quoted to prove that mathematics was known before the Flood and by Noah and his sons; this, I suppose, is a sample of what we may learn from infidels. Bacon praises mathematics as the sole (unrevealed) source of certitude, and as needed for astronomy and astrology.

Bacon follows Averroes in holding that the active intellect is a substance separated from the soul in essence. He quotes various eminent divines, among them Grosseteste, Bishop of Lincoln, as also supporting this opinion, which is contrary to that of St

[1] Follower of Kindi: d. 950.　　　　　　　　[2] Astronomer, 805-885.

Thomas. Apparently contrary passages in Aristotle, he says, are due to mistranslation. He does not quote Plato at first hand, but at second hand through Cicero, or at third hand through the Arabs on Porphyry. Not that he has much respect for Porphyry, whose doctrine on universals he calls 'childish'.

In modern times Bacon has been praised because he valued experiment, as a source of knowledge, more than argument. Certainly his interests and his way of dealing with subjects are very different from those of the typical scholastics. His encyclopaedic tendencies are like those of the Arabic writers, who evidently influenced him more profoundly than they did most other Christian philosophers. They, like him, were interested in science, and believed in magic and astrology, whereas Christians thought magic wicked and astrology a delusion. He is astonishing because he differs so widely from other medieval Christian philosophers, but he had little influence in his own time, and was not, to my mind, so scientific as is sometimes thought. English writers used to say that he invented gunpowder, but this, of course, is untrue.

St Bonaventura (1221-1274), who, as General of the Franciscan order, forbade Bacon to publish, was a man of a totally different kind. He belonged to the tradition of St Anselm, whose ontological argument he upheld. He saw in the new Aristotelianism a fundamental opposition to Christianity. He believed in Platonic ideas, which, however, only God knows perfectly. In his writings Augustine is quoted constantly, but one finds no quotations from Arabs, and few from pagan antiquity.

Matthew of Aquasparta (ca. 1235-1302) was a follower of Bonaventura, but less untouched by the new philosophy. He was a Franciscan, and became a cardinal; he opposed St Thomas from an Augustinian point of view. But to him Aristotle has become 'The Philosopher'; he is quoted constantly. Avicenna is frequently mentioned; St Anselm is quoted with respect, as is the pseudo-Dionysius; but the chief authority is St Augustine. We must, he says, find a middle way between Plato and Aristotle. Plato's ideas are 'utterly erroneous'; they establish wisdom, but not knowledge. On the other hand, Aristotle is also wrong; he establishes knowledge, but not wisdom. Our knowledge—so it is concluded—is caused by both lower and higher things, by external objects and ideal reasons.

Duns Scotus (ca. 1270-1308) carried on the Franciscan controversy with Aquinas. He was born in Scotland or Ulster, became a Franciscan at Oxford, and spent his later years at Paris. Against St Thomas, he defended the Immaculate Conception, and in this the University of Paris, and ultimately the whole Catholic Church, agreed with him. He is Augustinian, but in a less extreme form than

Bonaventura, or even Matthew of Aquasparta; his differences from St Thomas, like theirs, come of a larger admixture of Platonism (via Augustine) in his philosophy.

He discusses, for example, the question 'Whether any sure and pure truth can be known naturally by the understanding of the wayfarer without the special illumination of the uncreated light?' And he argues that it cannot. He supports this view, in his opening argument, solely by quotations from St Augustine; the only difficulty he finds in Romans i, 20: 'The invisible things of God, understood by means of those things that have been made, are clearly comprehended from the creation of the world.'

Duns Scotus was a moderate realist. He believed in free will and had leanings towards Pelagianism. He held that *being* is no different from *essence*. He was mainly interested in *evidence*, i.e. the kinds of things that can be known without proof. Of these there are three kinds: (1) principles known by themselves, (2) things known by experience, (3) our own actions. But without divine illumination we can know nothing.

Most Franciscans followed Duns Scotus rather than Aquinas.

Duns Scotus held that, since there is no difference between being and essence, the 'principle of individuation'—i.e. that which makes one thing not identical with another—must be form, not matter. The 'principle of individuation' was one of the important problems of the scholastic philosophy. In various forms, it has remained a problem to the present day. Without reference to any particular author, we may perhaps state the problem as follows.

Among the properties of individual things, some are essential, others accidental; the accidental properties of a thing are those it can lose without losing its identity—such as wearing a hat, if you are a man. The question now arises: given two individual things belonging to the same species, do they always differ in essence, or is it possible for the essence to be exactly the same in both? St Thomas holds the latter view as regards material substances, the former as regards those that are immaterial. Duns Scotus holds that there are *always* differences of essence between two different individual things. The view of St Thomas depends upon the theory that pure matter consists of undifferentiated parts, which are distinguished solely by difference of position in space. Thus a person, consisting of mind and body, may differ *physically* from another person solely by the spatial position of his body. (This might happen with identical twins, theoretically.) Duns Scotus, on the other hand, holds that if things are distinct, they must be distinguished by some qualitative difference. This view, clearly, is nearer to Platonism than is that of St Thomas.

Various stages have to be traversed before we can state this problem in modern terms. The first step, which was taken by Leibniz, was to get rid of the distinction between essential and accidental properties, which, like many that the scholastics took over from Aristotle, turns out to be unreal as soon as we attempt to state it carefully. We thus have, instead of 'essence', 'all the propositions that are true of the thing in question'. (In general, however, spatial and temporal position would still be excluded.) Leibniz contends that it is impossible for two things to be exactly alike in this sense; this is his principle of the 'identity of indiscernibles'. This principle was criticized by physicists, who maintained that two particles of matter might differ solely as regards position in space and time—a view which has been rendered more difficult by relativity, which reduces space and time to relations.

A further step is required in modernizing the problem, and that is, to get rid of the conception of 'substance'. When this is done, a 'thing' has to be a bundle of qualities, since there is no longer any kernel of pure 'thinghood'. It would seem to follow that, if 'substance' is rejected, we must take a view more akin to that of Scotus than to that of Aquinas. This, however, involves much difficulty in connection with space and time. I have treated the question as I see it, under the heading 'Proper Names', in my *Inquiry into Meaning and Truth*.

William of Occam is, after St Thomas, the most important schoolman. The circumstances of his life are very imperfectly known. He was born probably between 1290 and 1300; he died on April 10th, but whether in 1349 or 1350 is uncertain. (The Black Death was raging in 1349, so that this is perhaps the more probable year.) Most people say he was born at Ockham in Surrey, but Delisle Burns prefers Ockham in Yorkshire. He was at Oxford, and then at Paris, where he was first the pupil and afterwards the rival of Duns Scotus. He was involved in the quarrel of the Franciscan order with Pope John XXII on the subject of poverty. The Pope had persecuted the Spirituals, with the support of Michael of Cesena, General of the Order. But there had been an arrangement by which property left to the friars was given by them to the Pope, who allowed them the benefit of it without the sin of ownership. This was ended by John XXII, who said they should accept outright ownership. At this a majority of the Order, headed by Michael of Cesena, rebelled. Occam, who had been summoned to Avignon by the Pope to answer charges of heresy as to transubstantiation, sided with Michael of Cesena, as did another important man, Marsiglio of Padua. All three were excommunicated in 1328, but escaped from Avignon, and took refuge with the Emperor Louis. Louis was one of the two claimants

459

to the Empire; he was the one favoured by Germany, but the other was favoured by the Pope. The Pope excommunicated Louis, who appealed against him to a General Council. The Pope himself was accused of heresy.

It is said that Occam, on meeting the Emperor, said: 'Do you defend me with the sword, and I will defend you with the pen.' At any rate, he and Marsiglio of Padua settled in Munich, under the protection of the Emperor, and there wrote political treatises of considerable importance. What happened to Occam after the Emperor's death in 1338 is uncertain. Some say he was reconciled to the Church, but this seems to be false.

The Empire was no longer what it had been in the Hohenstaufen era; and the papacy, though its pretensions had grown continually greater, did not command the same reverence as formerly. Clement V had moved it to Avignon at the beginning of the fourteenth century, and the Pope had become a political subordinate of the King of France. The Empire had sunk even more; it could no longer claim even the most shadowy kind of universal dominion, because of the strength of France and England; on the other hand, the Pope, by subservience to the King of France, also weakened his claim to universality in temporal matters. Thus the conflict between Pope and Emperor was really a conflict between France and Germany. England, under Edward III, was at war with France, and therefore in alliance with Germany; this caused England, also, to be anti-papal. The Pope's enemies demanded a General Council—the only ecclesiastical authority which could be regarded as superior to the Pope.

The character of the opposition to the Pope changed at this time. Instead of being merely in favour of the Emperor, it acquired a democratic tone, particularly in matters of Church government. This gave it a new strength, which ultimately led to the Reformation.

Dante (1265-1321), though as a poet he was a great innovator, was, as a thinker, somewhat behind the times. His book *De Monarchia* is somewhat Ghibelline in outlook, and would have been more timely a hundred years earlier. He regards Emperor and Pope as independent, and both divinely appointed. In the *Divine Comedy*, his Satan has three mouths, in which he eternally chews Judas Iscariot, Brutus, and Cassius, who are all three equally traitors, the first against Christ, the other two against Caesar. Dante's thought is interesting, not only in itself, but as that of a layman; but it was not influential, and was hopelessly out of date.

Marsiglio of Padua (1270-1342), on the contrary, inaugurated the new form of opposition to the Pope, in which the Emperor has mainly a role of decorative dignity. He was a close friend of William of Occam, whose political opinions he influenced. Politically, he is more important than Occam. He holds that the legislator is the majority of the people, and that the majority has the right to punish princes. He applies popular sovereignty also to the Church, and he includes the laity. There are to be local councils of the people, including the laity, who are to elect representatives to General Councils. The General Council alone should have power to excommunicate, and to give authoritative interpretations of Scripture. Thus all believers will have a voice in deciding doctrine. The Church is to have no secular authority; there is to be no excommunication without civil concurrence; and the Pope is to have no special powers.

Occam did not go quite so far as Marsiglio, but he worked out a completely democratic method of electing the General Council.

The conciliar movement came to a head in the early fifteenth century, when it was needed to heal the Great Schism. But having accomplished this task, it subsided. Its standpoint, as may be seen already in Marsiglio, was different from that afterwards adopted, in theory, by the Protestants. The Protestants claimed the right of private judgment, and were not willing to submit to a General Council. They held that religious belief is not a matter to be decided by any governmental machinery. Marsiglio, on the contrary, still aims at preserving the unity of the Catholic faith, but wishes this to be done by democratic means, not by the papal absolutism. In practice, most Protestants, when they acquired the government, merely substituted the King for the Pope, and thus secured neither liberty of private judgment nor a democratic method of deciding doctrinal questions. But in their opposition to the Pope they found support in the doctrines of the conciliar movement. Of all the schoolmen, Occam was the one whom Luther preferred. It must be said that a considerable section of Protestants held to the doctrine of private judgment even where the State was Protestant. This was the chief point of difference between Independents and Presbyterians in the English Civil War.

Occam's political works[1] are written in the style of philosophic disputations, with arguments for and against various theses, sometimes not reaching any conclusion. We are accustomed to a more forthright kind of political propaganda, but in his day the form he chose was probably effective.

A few samples will illustrate his method and outlook.

There is a long treatise called 'Eight Questions Concerning the

[1] See *Guillelmi de Ockham Opera Politica*, Manchester University Press, 1940.

Power of the Pope. The first question is whether one man can rightfully be supreme both in Church and State. The second: Is secular authority derived immediately from God or not? Third: Has the Pope the right to grant secular jurisdiction to the Emperor and other princes? Fourth: Does election by the electors give full powers to the German king? Fifth and sixth: What rights does the Church acquire through the right of bishops to anoint kings? Seventh: Is a coronation ceremony valid if performed by the wrong archbishop? Eighth: Does election by the electors give the German king the title of Emperor? All these were, at the time, burning questions of practical politics.

Another treatise is on the question whether a prince can obtain the goods of the Church without the Pope's permission. This is concerned to justify Edward III in taxing the clergy for his war with France. It will be remembered that Edward was an ally of the Emperor.

Then comes a 'Consultation on a matrimonial cause', on the question whether the Emperor was justified in marrying his cousin.

It will be seen that Occam did his best to deserve the protection of the Emperor's sword.

It is time now to turn to Occam's purely philosophical doctrines. On this subject there is a very good book, *The Logic of William of Occam*, by Ernest E. Moody. Much of what I shall have to say is based on this book, which takes a somewhat unusual view, but, I think, a correct one. There is a tendency in writers on history of philosophy to interpret men in the light of their successors, but this is generally a mistake. Occam has been regarded as bringing about the breakdown of scholasticism, as a precursor of Descartes or Kant or whoever might be the particular commentator's favourite among modern philosophers. According to Moody, with whom I agree, all this is a mistake. Occam, he holds, was mainly concerned to restore a pure Aristotle, freed from both Augustinian and Arabic influences. This had also been, to a considerable extent, the aim of St Thomas; but the Franciscans, as we have seen, had continued to follow St Augustine much more closely than he did. The interpretation of Occam by modern historians, according to Moody, has been vitiated by the desire to find a *gradual* transition from scholastic to modern philosophy; this has caused people to read modern doctrines into him, when in fact he is only interpreting Aristotle.

Occam is best known for a maxim which is not to be found in his works, but has acquired the name of 'Occam's razor'. This maxim says: 'Entities are not to be multiplied without necessity.' Although he did not say this, he said something which has much the same effect, namely: 'It is vain to do with more what can be

462

done with fewer.' That is to say, if everything in some science can be interpreted without assuming this or that hypothetical entity, there is no ground for assuming it. I have myself found this a most fruitful principle in logical analysis.

In logic, though apparently not in metaphysics, Occam was a nominalist; the nominalists of the fifteenth century[1] looked upon him as the founder of their school. He thought that Aristotle had been misinterpreted by the Scotists, and that this misinterpretation was due partly to the influence of Augustine, partly to Avicenna, but partly to an earlier cause, Porphyry's treatise on Aristotle's *Categories*. Porphyry in this treatise raised three questions: (1) Are genera and species substances? (2) Are they corporeal or incorporeal? (3) If the latter, are they in sensible things or separated from them? He raised these questions as relevant to Aristotle's Categories, and thus led the Middle Ages to interpret the *Organon* too metaphysically. Aquinas had attempted to undo this error, but it had been reintroduced by Duns Scotus. The result had been that logic and theory of knowledge had become dependent on metaphysics and theology. Occam set to work to separate them again.

For Occam, logic is an instrument for the philosophy of nature, which can be independent of metaphysics. Logic is the analysis of discursive science; science is about things, but logic is not. Things are individual, but among terms there are universals; logic treats of universals, while science uses them without discussing them. Logic is concerned with terms or concepts, not as psychical states, but as having meaning. 'Man is a species' is not a proposition of logic, because it requires a knowledge of man. Logic deals with things fabricated by the mind within itself, which cannot exist except through the existence of reason. A concept is a *natural* sign, a word is a *conventional* sign. We must distinguish when we are speaking of the word as a thing, and when we are using it as having meaning, otherwise we may fall into fallacies such as: 'Man is a species, Socrates is a man, therefore Socrates is a species.'

Terms which point at things are called 'terms of first intention'; terms which point at terms are called 'terms of second intention'. The terms in science are of first intention; in logic, of second. *Meta-physical* terms are peculiar in that they signify both things signified by words of first intention and things signified by words of second intention. There are exactly six metaphysical terms: being, thing, something, one, true, good.[2] These terms have the peculiarity that they can all be predicated of each other. But logic can be pursued independently of them.

---

[1] E.g., Swineshead, Heytesbury, Gerson, and d'Ailly.
[2] I do not here pause to criticize the use to which Occam puts these terms.

Understanding is of things, not of forms produced by the mind; these are not *what* is understood, but that *by* which things are understood. Universals, in logic, are only terms or concepts predicable of many other terms or concepts. *Universal, genus, species* are terms of second intention, and therefore cannot mean *things*. But since *one* and *being* are convertible, if a universal existed, it would be one, and an individual thing. A universal is merely a sign of many things. As to this, Occam agrees with Aquinas, as against Averroes, Avicenna, and the Augustinians. Both hold that there are only individual things, individual minds, and acts of understanding. Both Aquinas and Occam, it is true, admit the *universale ante rem*, but only to explain creation; it had to be in the mind of God before He could create. But this belongs to theology, not to the explanation of *human* knowledge, which is only concerned with the *universale post rem*. In explaining human knowledge, Occam never allows universals to be *things*. Socrates is similar to Plato, he says, but not in virtue of a third *thing* called similarity. Similarity is a term of second intention, and is in the mind. (All this is good.)

Propositions about future contingents, according to Occam, are not yet either true or false. He makes no attempt to reconcile this view with divine omniscience. Here, as elsewhere, he keeps logic free from metaphysics and theology.

Some samples of Occam's discussions may be useful.

He asks: 'Whether that which is known by the understanding first according to a primacy of generation is the individual.'

Against: The universal is the first and proper object of the understanding.

For: The object of sense and the object of understanding are the same, but the individual is the first object of sense.

Accordingly, the meaning of the question must be stated. (Presumably, because both arguments seem strong.)

He continues: 'The thing outside the soul which is not a sign is understood first by such knowledge (i.e. by knowledge which is individual), therefore the individual is known first, since everything outside the soul is individual.'

He goes on to say that abstract knowledge always presupposes knowledge which is 'intuitive' (i.e. of perception), and this is caused by individual things.

He then enumerates four doubts which may arise, and proceeds to resolve them.

He concludes with an affirmative answer to his original question, but adds that 'the universal is the first object by primacy of adequation, not by the primacy of generation'.

464

The question involved is whether, or how far, perception is the source of knowledge. It will be remembered that Plato, in the *Theaetetus*, rejects the definition of knowledge as perception. Occam, pretty certainly, did not know the *Theaetetus*, but if he had he would have disagreed with it.

To the question 'whether the sensitive soul and the intellective soul are really distinct in man', he answers that they are, though this is hard to prove. One of his arguments is that we may with our appetites desire something which with our understanding we reject; therefore appetite and understanding belong to different subjects. Another argument is that sensations are subjectively in the sensitive soul, but not subjectively in the intellective soul. Again: the sensitive soul is extended and material, while the intellective soul is neither. Four objections are considered, all theological,[1] but they are answered. The view taken by Occam on this question is not, perhaps, what might be expected. However, he agrees with St Thomas and disagrees with Averroes in thinking that each man's intellect is his own, not something impersonal.

By insisting on the possibility of studying logic and human knowledge without reference to metaphysics and theology, Occam's work encouraged scientific research. The Augustinians, he said, erred in first supposing things unintelligible and men unintelligent, and then adding a light from Infinity by which knowledge became possible. He agreed in this with Aquinas, but differed in emphasis, for Aquinas was primarily a theologian, and Occam was, so far as logic is concerned, primarily a secular philosopher.

His attitude gave confidence to students of particular problems, for instance, his immediate follower Nicholas of Oresme (d. 1382), who investigated planetary theory. This man was, to a certain extent, a precursor of Copernicus; he set forth both the geocentric and the heliocentric theories, and said that each would explain all the facts known in his day, so that there was no way of deciding between them.

After William of Occam there are no more great scholastics. The next time for great philosophers began in the late Renaissance.

[1] For instance: Between Good Friday and Easter, Christ's soul descended into hell, whereas His body remained in the tomb of Joseph of Arimathea. If the sensitive soul is distinct from the intellective soul, did Christ's sensitive soul spend this time in hell or in the tomb?

Chapter XV

THE ECLIPSE OF THE PAPACY

THE thirteenth century had brought to completion a great synthesis, philosophical, theological, political, and social, which had been slowly built up by the combination of many elements. The first element was pure Greek philosophy, especially the philosophies of Pythagoras, Parmenides, Plato and Aristotle. Then came, as a result of Alexander's conquests, a great influx of oriental beliefs.[1] These, taking advantage of Orphism and the Mysteries, transformed the outlook of the Greek-speaking world, and ultimately of the Latin-speaking world also. The dying and resurrected god, the sacramental eating of what purported to be the flesh of the god, the second birth into a new life through some ceremony analogous to baptism, came to be part of the theology of large sections of the pagan Roman world. With these was associated an ethic of liberation from bondage to the flesh, which was, at least theoretically, ascetic. From Syria, Egypt, Babylonia, and Persia came the institution of a priesthood separated from the lay population, possessed of more or less magical powers, and able to exert considerable political influence. Impressive rituals, largely connected with belief in a life after death, came from the same sources. From Persia, in particular, came a dualism which regarded the world as the battleground of two great hosts, one, which was good, led by Ahura Mazda, the other, which was evil, led by Ahriman. *Black magic* was the kind that was worked by the help of Ahriman and his followers in the world of spirits. Satan is a development of Ahriman.

This influx of barbarian ideas and practices was synthesized with certain Hellenic elements in the Neoplatonic philosophy. In Orphism, Pythagoreanism, and some parts of Plato, the Greeks had developed points of view which were easy to combine with those of the Orient, perhaps because they had been borrowed from the East at a much earlier time. With Plotinus and Porphyry the development of pagan philosophy ends.

The thought of these men, however, though deeply religious, was not capable, without much transformation, of inspiring a victorious popular religion. Their philosophy was difficult, and could not be generally understood; their way of salvation was too intellectual

[1] See Cumont, *Oriental Religions in Roman Paganism.*

466

for the masses. Their conservatism led them to uphold the traditional religion of Greece, which, however, they had to interpret allegorically in order to soften its immoral elements and to reconcile it with their philosophical monotheism. The Greek religion had fallen into decay, being unable to compete with Eastern rituals and theologies. The oracles had become silent, and the priesthood had never formed a powerful distinct caste. The attempt to revive Greek religion had therefore an archaistic character which gave it a certain feebleness and pedantry, especially noticeable in the Emperor Julian. Already in the third century, it could have been foreseen that some Asiatic religion would conquer the Roman world, though at that time there were still several competitors which all seemed to have a chance of victory.

Christianity combined elements of strength from various sources. From the Jews it accepted a Sacred Book and the doctrine that all religions but one are false and evil; but it avoided the racial exclusiveness of the Jews and the inconveniences of the Mosaic law. Later Judaism had already learnt to believe in the life after death, but the Christians gave a new definiteness to heaven and hell, and to the ways of reaching the one and escaping the other. Easter combined the Jewish Passover with pagan celebrations of the resurrected God. Persian dualism was absorbed, but with a firmer assurance of the ultimate omnipotence of the good principle, and with the addition that the pagan gods were followers of Satan. At first the Christians were not the equals of their adversaries in philosophy or in ritual, but gradually these deficiencies were made good. At first, philosophy was more advanced among the semi-Christian Gnostics than among the orthodox; but from the time of Origen onwards, the Christians developed an adequate philosophy by modification of Neoplatonism. Ritual among the early Christians is a somewhat obscure subject, but at any rate by the time of St Ambrose it had become extremely impressive. The power and the separateness of the priesthood were taken from the East, but were gradually strengthened by methods of government, in the Church, which owed much to the practice of the Roman Empire. The Old Testament, the mystery religions, Greek philosophy, and Roman methods of administration were all blended in the Catholic Church, and combined to give it a strength which no earlier social organization had equalled.

The Western Church, like ancient Rome, developed, though more slowly, from a republic into a monarchy. We have seen the stages in the growth of papal power, from Gregory the Great through Nicholas I, Gregory VII, and Innocent III, to the final defeat of the Hohenstaufen in the wars of Guelfs and Ghibellines. At the same

time Christian philosophy, which had hitherto been Augustinian
and therefore largely Platonic, was enriched by new elements due
to contact with Constantinople and the Mohammedans. Aristotle,
during the thirteenth century, came to be known fairly completely
in the West, and, by the influence of Albertus Magnus and Thomas
Aquinas, was established in the minds of the learned as the supreme
authority after Scripture and the Church. Down to the present day,
he has retained this position among Catholic philosophers. I cannot
but think that the substitution of Aristotle for Plato and St Augustine was a mistake from the Christian point of view. Plato's
temperament was more religious than Aristotle's, and Christian
theology had been, from almost the first, adapted to Platonism.
Plato had taught that knowledge is not perception, but a kind of
reminiscent vision; Aristotle was much more of an empiricist. St
Thomas, little though he intended it, prepared the way for the
return from Platonic dreaming to scientific observation.

Outward events had more to do than philosophy with the dis-
integration of the Catholic synthesis which began in the fourteenth
century. The Byzantine Empire was conquered by the Latins in
1204, and remained in their hands till 1261. During this time the
religion of its government was Catholic, not Greek; but after 1261
Constantinople was lost to the Pope and never recovered, in spite
of nominal union at Ferrara in 1438. The defeat of the Western
Empire in its conflict with the papacy proved useless to the Church,
owing to the rise of national monarchies in France and England;
throughout most of the fourteenth century the Pope was, politically,
a tool in the hands of the king of France. More important than
these causes was the rise of a rich commercial class and the increase
of knowledge in the laity. Both of these began in Italy, and
remained more advanced in that country than in other parts of the
West until the middle of the sixteenth century. North Italian cities
were much richer, in the fourteenth century, than any of the cities
of the North; and learned laymen, especially in law and medicine,
were becoming increasingly numerous. The cities had a spirit of
independence which, now that the Emperor was no longer a
menace, was apt to turn against the Pope. But the same movements,
though to a lesser degree, existed elsewhere. Flanders prospered;
so did the Hanse towns. In England the wool trade was a source of
wealth. The age was one in which tendencies which may be broadly
called democratic were very strong, and nationalistic tendencies
were even stronger. The papacy, which had become very worldly,
appeared largely as a taxing agency, drawing to itself vast revenues
which most countries wished to retain at home. The popes no
longer had or deserved the moral authority which had given them

power. St Francis had been able to work in harmony with Innocent III and Gregory IX, but the most earnest men of the fourteenth century were driven into conflict with the papacy.

At the beginning of the century, however, these causes of decline in the papacy were not yet apparent. Boniface VIII, in the Bull *Unam Sanctam*, made more extreme claims than had ever been made by any previous Pope. He instituted, in 1300, the year of Jubilee, when plenary indulgence is granted to all Catholics who visit Rome and perform certain ceremonies while there. This brought immense sums of money to the coffers of the Curia and the pockets of the Roman people. There was to be a Jubilee every hundredth year, but the profits were so great that the period was shortened to fifty years, and then to twenty-five, at which it remains to the present day. The first Jubilee, that of 1300, showed the Pope at the summit of his success, and may be conveniently regarded as the date from which the decline began.

Boniface VIII was an Italian, born at Anagni. He had been besieged in the Tower of London when in England, on behalf of the Pope, to support Henry III against the rebellious barons, but he was rescued in 1267 by the King's son, afterwards Edward I. There was already in his day a powerful French party in the Church, and his election was opposed by the French cardinals. He came into violent conflict with the French king Philip IV, on the question whether the King had the right to tax the French clergy. Boniface was addicted to nepotism and avarice; he therefore wished to retain control over as many sources of revenue as possible. He was accused of heresy, probably with justice; it seems that he was an Averroist and did not believe in immortality. His quarrel with the king of France became so bitter that the king sent a force to arrest him, with a view to his being deposed by a General Council. He was caught at Anagni, but escaped to Rome, where he died. After this, for a long time, no pope ventured to oppose the king of France.

After a very brief intermediate reign, the cardinals in 1305 elected the Archbishop of Bordeaux, who took the name of Clement V. He was a Gascon, and consistently represented the French party in the Church. Throughout his pontificate he never went to Italy. He was crowned in Lyons, and in 1309, he settled in Avignon, where the popes remained for about seventy years. Clement V signalized his alliance with the king of France by their joint action against the Templars. Both needed money, the Pope because he was addicted to favouritism and nepotism, Philip for the English war, the Flemish revolt, and the costs of an increasingly energetic government. After he had plundered the bankers of Lombardy, and persecuted the Jews to the limit of 'what the traffic would bear', it occurred to him that the Templars, in addition to being bankers, had immense landed estates in France, which, with the Pope's help, he might acquire. It was therefore arranged that the Church should discover that the Templars had fallen into heresy, and that king and pope should share the spoils. On a given day in 1307, all the leading Templars in France were arrested; a list of leading questions, previously drawn up, was put to them all; under torture, they confessed that they had done homage to Satan and committed various other abominations; at last, in 1313, the Pope suppressed the order, and all its property was confiscated. The best account of this proceeding is in Henry C. Lea's *History of the Inquisition*, where, after full investigation, the conclusion is reached that the charges against the Templars were wholly without foundation.

In the case of the Templars, the financial interests of pope and king coincided. But on most occasions in most parts of Christendom, they conflicted. In the time of Boniface VIII, Philip IV had secured the support of the Estates (even the Estate of the Church) in his disputes with the Pope as to taxation. When the popes became politically subservient to France, the sovereigns hostile to the French king were necessarily hostile to the Pope. This led to the protection of William of Occam and Marsiglio of Padua by the Emperor; at a slightly later date, it led to the protection of Wycliffe by John of Gaunt.

Bishops, in general, were by this time completely in subjection to the Pope; in an increasing proportion, they were actually appointed by him. The monastic Orders and the Dominicans were equally obedient, but the Franciscans still had a certain spirit of independence. This led to their conflict with John XXII, which we have already considered in connection with William of Occam. During this conflict, Marsiglio persuaded the Emperor to march on Rome, where the imperial crown was conferred on him by the populace, and a Franciscan antipope was elected after the populace had declared John XXII deposed. However, nothing came of all this beyond a general diminution of respect for the papacy.

The revolt against papal domination took different forms in different places. Sometimes it was associated with monarchical nationalism, sometimes with a Puritan horror of the corruption and worldliness of the papal court. In Rome itself, the revolt was associated with an archaistic democracy. Under Clement VI (1342-52) Rome, for a time, sought to free itself from the absentee Pope under the leadership of a remarkable man, Cola di Rienzi. Rome suffered not only from the rule of the popes, but also from the local aristocracy, which continued the turbulence that had degraded the papacy in the tenth century. Indeed it was partly to escape from the lawless Roman nobles that the popes had fled to Avignon. At first Rienzi, who was the son of a tavern-keeper, rebelled only against the nobles, and in this he had the support of the Pope. He roused so much popular enthusiasm that the nobles fled (1347). Petrarch, who admired him and wrote an ode to him, urged him to continue his great and noble work. He took the title of tribune, and proclaimed the sovereignty of the Roman people over the Empire. He seems to have conceived this sovereignty democratically, for he called representatives from the Italian cities to a sort of parliament. Success, however, gave him delusions of grandeur. At this time, as at many others, there were rival claimants to the Empire. Rienzi summoned both of them, and the Electors, to come before him to have the issue decided. This naturally turned both imperial candidates against him, and also the Pope, who considered that it was for him to pronounce judgment in such matters. Rienzi was captured by the Pope (1352), and kept in prison for two years, until Clement VI died. Then he was released, and returned to Rome, where he acquired power again for a few months. On this second occasion, however, his popularity was brief, and in the end he was murdered by the mob. Byron, as well at Petrarch, wrote a poem in his praise.

It became evident that, if the papacy was to remain effectively the head of the whole Catholic Church, it must free itself from dependence on France by returning to Rome. Moreover, the Anglo-French war, in which France was suffering severe defeats, made France unsafe. Urban V therefore went to Rome in 1367; but Italian politics were too complicated for him, and he returned to Avignon shortly before his death. The next Pope, Gregory XI, was more resolute. Hostility to the French curia had made many Italian towns, especially Florence, bitterly anti-papal, but by returning to Rome and opposing the French cardinals Gregory did everything in his power to save the situation. However, at his death the French and Roman parties in the College of Cardinals proved irreconcilable. In accordance with the wishes of the Roman party, an Italian, Bartolomeo Prignano, was elected, and took the name of Urban VI. But a number of Cardinals declared his election uncanonical, and proceeded to elect Robert of Geneva, who belonged to the French party. He took the name of Clement VII, and lived in Avignon.

Thus began the Great Schism, which lasted for some forty years. France, of course, recognized the Avignon Pope, and the enemies of France recognized the Roman Pope. Scotland was the enemy of England, and England of France; therefore Scotland recognized the Avignon Pope. Each pope chose cardinals from among his own partisans, and when either died his cardinals quickly elected another. Thus there was no way of healing the schism except by bringing to bear some power superior to both popes. It was clear that one of them must be legitimate, therefore a power superior to a *legitimate* pope had to be found. The only solution lay in a General Council. The University of Paris, led by Gerson, developed a new theory, giving powers of initiative to a Council. The lay sovereigns, to whom the schism was inconvenient, lent their support. At last, in 1409, a Council was summoned, and met at Pisa. It failed, however, in a ridiculous manner. It declared both popes deposed for heresy and schism, and elected a third, who promptly died; but his cardinals elected as his successor an ex-pirate named Baldassare Cossa, who took the name of John XXIII. Thus the net result was that there were three popes instead of two, the conciliar pope being a notorious ruffian. At this stage, the situation seemed more hopeless than ever.

But the supporters of the conciliar movement did not give in. In 1414, a new Council was summoned at Constance, and proceeded to vigorous action. It first decreed that popes cannot dissolve councils, and must submit to them in certain respects; it also decided that future popes must summon a General Council every seven years. It deposed John XXIII, and induced the Roman Pope to resign. The Avignon Pope refused to resign, and after his death the king of Aragon caused a successor to be elected. But France, at this time at the mercy of England, refused to recognize him, and his party dwindled into insignificance and finally ceased to exist. Thus at last there was no opposition to the Pope chosen by the Council, who was elected in 1417, and took the name Martin V.

These proceedings were creditable, but the treatment of Huss, the Bohemian disciple of Wycliffe, was not. He was brought to Constance with the promise of a safe conduct, but when he got there he was condemned and suffered death at the stake. Wycliffe was safely dead, but the Council ordered his bones to be dug up and burnt. The supporters of the conciliar movement were anxious to free themselves from all suspicion of unorthodoxy.

The Council of Constance had healed the schism, but it had hoped to do much more, and to substitute a constitutional monarchy for the papal absolutism. Martin V had made many promises before his election; some he kept, some he broke. He had assented to the decree that a council should be summoned every seven years, and to this decree he remained obedient. The Council of Constance having been dissolved in 1417, a new Council, which proved of no importance, was summoned in 1424; then, in 1431, another was convoked to meet at Basel. Martin V died just at this moment, and his successor Eugenius IV was, throughout his pontificate, in bitter conflict with the reformers who controlled the Council. He dissolved the Council, but it refused to consider itself dissolved; in 1433 he gave way for a time, but in 1437 he dissolved it again. Nevertheless it remained in session till 1448, by which time it was obvious to all that the Pope had won a complete triumph. In 1439 the Council had alienated sympathy by declaring the Pope deposed and electing an antipope (the last in history), who, however, resigned almost immediately. In the same year Eugenius IV won prestige by holding a Council of his own at Ferrara, where the Greek Church, in desperate fear of the Turks, made a nominal submission to Rome. The papacy thus emerged politically triumphant, but with very greatly diminished power of inspiring moral reverence.

Wycliffe (ca. 1320-84) illustrates, by his life and doctrine, the diminished authority of the papacy in the fourteenth century. Unlike the earlier schoolmen, he was a secular priest, not a monk or friar. He had a great reputation in Oxford, where he became a doctor of theology in 1372. For a short time he was Master of Balliol. He was the last of the important Oxford scholastics. As a philosopher, he was not progressive; he was a realist, and a Platonist rather than an Aristotelian. He held that God's decrees are not arbitrary, as some maintained; the actual world is not one among possible worlds, but is the only possible world, since God is bound to choose what is best. All this is not what makes him interesting, nor does it seem to have been what most interested him, for he retired from Oxford to the life of a country clergyman. During the last ten years of his life he was the parish priest of Lutterworth, by crown appointment. He continued, however, to lecture at Oxford.

Wycliffe is remarkable for the extreme slowness of his development. In 1372, when his age was fifty or more, he was still orthodox; it was only after this date, apparently, that he became heretical. He seems to have been driven into heresy entirely by the strength of his moral feelings—his sympathy with the poor, and his horror of rich worldly ecclesiastics. At first his attack on the papacy was only political and moral, not doctrinal; it was only gradually that he was driven into wider revolt.

Wycliffe's departure from orthodoxy began in 1376 with a course of lectures at Oxford 'On Civil Dominion'. He advanced the theory that righteousness alone gives the title to dominion and property; that unrighteous clergy have no such title; and that the decision as to whether an ecclesiastic should retain his property or not ought to be taken by the civil power. He taught, further, that property is the result of sin; Christ and the Apostles had no property, and the clergy ought to have none. These doctrines offended all clerics except the friars. The English government, however, favoured them,

473

for the Pope drew a huge tribute from England, and the doctrine that money should not be sent out of England to the Pope was a convenient one. This was especially the case while the Pope was subservient to France, and England was at war with France. John of Gaunt, who held power during the minority of Richard II, befriended Wycliffe as long as possible. Gregory XI, on the other hand, condemned eighteen theses in Wycliffe's lectures, saying that they were derived from Marsiglio of Padua. Wycliffe was summoned to appear for trial before a tribunal of bishops, but the Queen and the mob protected him, while the University of Oxford refused to admit the Pope's jurisdiction over its teachers. (Even in those days, English universities believed in academic freedom.)

Meanwhile Wycliffe continued, during 1378 and 1379, to write learned treatises, maintaining that the king is God's vicar, and that bishops are subject to him. When the great schism came, he went further than before, branding the Pope as Antichrist, and saying that acceptance of the Donation of Constantine had made all subsequent popes apostates. He translated the Vulgate into English, and established 'poor priests', who were secular. (By this action he at last annoyed the friars.) He employed the 'poor priests' as itinerant preachers, whose mission was especially to the poor. At last, in attacking sacerdotal power, he was led to deny transubstantiation, which he called a deceit and a blasphemous folly. At this point, John of Gaunt ordered him to be silent.

The Peasants' Revolt of 1381, led by Wat Tyler, made matters more difficult for Wycliffe. There is no evidence that he actively encouraged it, but, unlike Luther in similar circumstances, he refrained from condemning it. John Ball, the Socialist unfrocked priest who was one of the leaders, admired Wycliffe, which was embarrassing. But as he had been excommunicated in 1366, when Wycliffe was still orthodox, he must have arrived independently at his opinions. Wycliffe's communistic opinions, though no doubt the 'poor priests' disseminated them, were, by him, only stated in Latin, so that at first hand they were inaccessible to peasants.

It is surprising that Wycliffe did not suffer more than he did for his opinions and his democratic activities. The University of Oxford defended him against the bishops as long as possible. When the House of Lords condemned his itinerant preachers, the House of Commons refused to concur. No doubt trouble would have accumulated if he had lived longer, but when he died in 1384 he had not yet been formally condemned. He was buried at Lutterworth, where he died, and his bones were left in peace until the Council of Constance had them dug up and burnt.

His followers in England, the Lollards, were severely persecuted and practically stamped out. But owing to the fact that Richard II's wife was a Bohemian, his doctrines became known in Bohemia, where Huss was his disciple; and in Bohemia, in spite of persecution, they survived until the Reformation. In England, although driven underground, the revolt against the papacy remained in men's thoughts, and prepared the soil for Protestantism.

During the fifteenth century, various other causes were added to the decline of the papacy to produce a very rapid change, both political and cultural. Gunpowder strengthened central governments at the expense of the feudal nobility. In France and England, Louis XI and Edward IV allied themselves with the rich middle class, who helped them to quell aristocratic anarchy. Italy, until the last years of the century, was fairly free from Northern armies, and advanced rapidly both in wealth and culture. The new culture was essentially pagan, admiring Greece and Rome, and despising the Middle Ages. Archictecture and literary style were adapted to ancient models. When Constantinople, the last survival of antiquity, was captured by the Turks, Greek refugees in Italy were welcomed by humanists. Vasco da Gama and Columbus enlarged the world, and Copernicus enlarged the heavens. The Donation of Constantine was rejected as a fable, and overwhelmed with scholarly derision. By the help of the Byzantines, Plato came to be known, not only in Neoplatonic and Augustinian versions, but at first hand. This sublunary sphere appeared no longer as a vale of tears, a place of painful pilgrimage to another world, but as affording opportunity for pagan delights, for fame and beauty and adventure. The long centuries of asceticism were forgotten in a riot of art and poetry and pleasure. Even in Italy, it is true, the Middle Ages did not die without a struggle; Savonarola and Leonardo were born in the same year. But in the main the old terrors had ceased to be terrifying, and the new liberty of the spirit was found intoxicating. The intoxication could not last, but for the moment it shut out fear. In this moment of joyful liberation the modern world was born.

BOOK THREE
MODERN PHILOSOPHY

———

Chapter I

GENERAL CHARACTERISTICS

THE period of history which is commonly called 'modern' has a mental outlook which differs from that of the medieval period in many ways. Of these, two are the most important: the diminishing authority of the Church, and the increasing authority of science. With these two, others are connected. The culture of modern times is more lay than clerical. States increasingly replace the Church as the governmental authority that controls culture. The government of nations is, at first, mainly in the hands of kings; then, as in ancient Greece, the kings are gradually replaced by democracies or tyrants. The power of the national State, and the functions that it performs, grow steadily throughout the whole period (apart from some minor fluctuations); but at most times the State has less influence on the opinions of philosophers than the Church had in the Middle Ages. The feudal aristocracy, which, north of the Alps, had been able, till the fifteenth century, to hold its own against central governments, loses first its political and then its economic importance. It is replaced by the king in alliance with rich merchants; these two share power in different proportions in different countries. There is a tendency for the rich merchants to become absorbed into the aristocracy. From the time of the American and French Revolutions onwards, democracy, in the modern sense, becomes an important political force. Socialism, as opposed to democracy based on private property, first acquires governmental power in 1917. This form of government, however, if it spreads, must obviously bring with it a new form of culture; the culture with which we shall be concerned is in the main 'liberal', that is to say, of the kind most naturally associated with commerce. To this there are important exceptions, especially in Germany; Fichte and Hegel, to take two examples, have an outlook which is totally unconnected with commerce. But such exceptions are not typical of their age.

The rejection of ecclesiastical authority, which is the negative characteristic of the modern age, begins earlier than the positive characteristic, which is the acceptance of scientific authority. In the Italian renaissance, science played a very small part; the opposition to the Church, in men's thoughts, was connected with antiquity, and looked still to the past, but to a more distant past than that of

479

the early Church and the Middle Ages. The first serious irruption of science was the publication of the Copernican theory in 1543; but this theory did not become influential until it was taken up and improved by Kepler and Galileo in the seventeenth century. Then began the long fight between science and dogma, in which traditionalists fought a losing battle against new knowledge.

The authority of science, which is recognized by most philosophers of the modern epoch, is a very different thing from the authority of the Church, since it is intellectual, not governmental. No penalties fall upon those who reject it; no prudential arguments influence those who accept it. It prevails solely by its intrinsic appeal to reason. It is, moreover, a piecemeal and partial authority; it does not, like the body of Catholic dogma, lay down a complete system, covering human morality, human hopes, and the past and future history of the universe. It pronounces only on whatever, at the time, appears to have been scientifically ascertained, which is a small island in an ocean of nescience. There is yet another difference from ecclesiastical authority, which declares its pronouncements to be absolutely certain and eternally unalterable: the pronouncements of science are made tentatively, on a basis of probability, and are regarded as liable to modification. This produces a temper of mind very different from that of the medieval dogmatist.

So far, I have been speaking of *theoretical* science, which is an attempt to *understand* the world. *Practical* science, which is an attempt to *change* the world, has been important from the first, and has continually increased in importance, until it has almost ousted theoretical science from men's thoughts. The practical importance of science was first recognized in connection with war; Galileo and Leonardo obtained government employment by their claim to improve artillery and the art of fortification. From their time onwards, the part of men of science in war has steadily grown greater. Their part in developing machine production, and accustoming the population to the use, first of steam, then of electricity, came later, and did not begin to have important political effects until near the end of the nineteenth century. The triumph of science has been mainly due to its practical utility, and there has been an attempt to divorce this aspect from that of theory, thus making science more and more a technique, and less and less a doctrine as to the nature of the world. The penetration of this point of view to the philosophers is very recent.

Emancipation from the authority of the Church led to the growth of individualism, even to the point of anarchy. Discipline, intellectual, moral, and political, was associated in the minds of the men of the Renaissance with the scholastic philosophy and ecclesiastical government. The Aristotelian logic of the Schoolmen was narrow, but afforded a training in a certain kind of accuracy. When this school of logic became unfashionable, it was not, at first, succeeded by something better, but only by an eclectic imitation of ancient models. Until the seventeenth century, there was nothing of importance in philosophy. The moral and political anarchy of fifteenth-century Italy was appalling, and gave rise to the doctrines of Machiavelli. At the same time, the freedom from mental shackles led to an astonishing display of genius in art and literature. But such a society is unstable. The Reformation and the Counter-Reformation, combined with the subjection of Italy to Spain, put an end to both the good and the bad of the Italian Renaissance. When the movement spread north of the Alps, it had not the same anarchic character.

Modern philosophy, however, has retained, for the most part, an individualistic and subjective tendency. This is very marked in Descartes, who builds up all knowledge from the certainty of his own existence, and accepts clearness and distinctness (both subjective) as criteria of truth. It is not prominent in Spinoza, but reappears in Leibniz's windowless monads. Locke, whose *temperament* is thoroughly objective, is forced reluctantly into the subjective doctrine that knowledge is of the agreement or disagreement of ideas—a view so repulsive to him that he escapes from it by violent inconsistencies. Berkeley, after abolishing matter, is only saved from complete subjectivism by a use of God which most subsequent philosophers have regarded as illegitimate. In Hume, the empiricist philosophy culminated in a scepticism which none could refute and none could accept. Kant and Fichte were subjective in temperament as well as in doctrine; Hegel saved himself by means of the influence of Spinoza. Rousseau and the romantic movement extended subjectivity from theory of knowledge to ethics and politics, and ended, logically, in complete anarchism such as that of Bakunin. This extreme of subjectivism is a form of madness.

Meanwhile science as technique was building up in practical men a quite different outlook from any that was to be found among theoretical philosophers. Technique conferred a sense of power: man is now much less at the mercy of his environment than he was in former times. But the power conferred by technique is social, no individual; an average individual wrecked on a desert island could have achieved more in the seventeenth century than he could now. Scientific technique requires the co-operation of a large number of individuals organized under a single direction. Its tendency, therefore, is against anarchism and even individualism, since it demands a well-knit social structure. Unlike religion, it is ethically neutral: it assures men that they can perform wonders, but does not tell them what wonders to perform. In this way it is incomplete. In practice, the purposes to which scientific skill will be devoted depend largely on chance. The men at the head of the vast organizations which it necessitates can, within limits, turn it this way or that as they please. The power impulse thus has a scope which it never had before. The philosophies that have been inspired by scientific *technique* are power philosophies, and tend to regard everything non-human as mere raw material. Ends are no longer considered; only the skilfulness of the process is valued. This also is a form of madness. It is, in our day, the most dangerous form, and the one against which a sane philosophy should provide an antidote.

The ancient world found an end to anarchy in the Roman Empire, but the Roman Empire was a brute fact, not an idea. The Catholic world sought an end to anarchy in the Church, which was an idea, but was never adequately embodied in fact. Neither the ancient nor the medieval solution was satisfactory—the one because it could not be idealized, the other because it could not be actualized. The modern world, at present, seems to be moving towards a solution like that of antiquity: a social order imposed by force, representing the will of the powerful rather than the hopes of common men. The problem of a durable and satisfactory social order can only be solved by combining the solidity of the Roman Empire with the idealism of St Augustine's City of God. To achieve this a new philosophy will be needed.

Chapter II

THE ITALIAN RENAISSANCE

THE modern as opposed to the medieval outlook began in Italy with the movement called the Renaissance. At first, only a few individuals, notably Petrarch, had this outlook, but during the fifteenth century it spread to the great majority of cultivated Italians, both lay and clerical. In some respects, Italians of the Renaissance—with the exception of Leonardo and a few others—had not the respect for science which has characterized most important innovators since the seventeenth century; with this lack is associated their very partial emancipation from superstition, especially in the form of astrology. Many of them had still the reverence for authority that medieval philosophers had had, but they substituted the authority of the ancients for that of the Church. This was, of course, a step towards emancipation, since the ancients disagreed with each other, and individual judgment was required to decide which of them to follow. But very few Italians of the fifteenth century would have dared to hold an opinion for which no authority could be found either in antiquity or in the teaching of the Church.

To understand the Renaissance, it is necessary first to review briefly the political condition of Italy. After the death of Frederick II in 1250, Italy was, in the main, free from foreign interference until the French king Charles VIII invaded the country in 1494. There were in Italy five important States: Milan, Venice, Florence, the Papal Domain, and Naples; in addition to these there were a number of small principalities, which varied in their alliance with or subjection to some one of the larger States. Until 1378, Genoa rivalled Venice in commerce and naval power, but after that year Genoa became subject to Milanese suzerainty.

Milan, which led the resistance to feudalism in the twelfth and thirteenth centuries, fell, after the final defeat of the Hohenstaufen, under the dominion of the Visconti, an able family whose power was plutocratic, not feudal. They ruled for 170 years, from 1277 to 1447; then, after three years of restored republican government, a new family, that of the Sforza, connected with the Visconti, acquired the government, and took the title of Dukes of Milan. From 1494 to 1535, Milan was a battle-ground between the French and the Spaniards; the Sforza allied themselves sometimes with one side, sometimes with the other. During this period they were sometimes in exile, sometimes in nominal control. Finally, in 1535, Milan was annexed by the Emperor Charles V.

The Republic of Venice stands somewhat outside Italian politics, especially in the earlier centuries of its greatness. It had never been conquered by the barbarians, and at first regarded itself as subject to the Eastern emperors. This tradition, combined with the fact that its trade was with the East, gave it an independence of Rome, which still persisted down to the time of the Council of Trent (1545), of which the Venetian Paolo Sarpi wrote a very anti-papal history. We have seen how, at the time of the fourth Crusade, Venice insisted upon the conquest of Constantinople. This improved Venetian trade, which, conversely, suffered by the Turkish conquest of Constantinople in 1453. For various reasons, partly connected with food supply, the Venetians found it necessary, during the fourteenth and fifteenth centuries, to acquire considerable territory on the mainland of Italy; this roused enmities, and led finally, in 1509, to the formation of the League of Cambrai, a combination of powerful States by which Venice was defeated. It might have been possible to recover from this misfortune, but not from Vasco da Gama's discovery of the Cape route to India (1497-8). This, added to the power of the Turks, ruined Venice, which, however, lingered on until deprived of independence by Napoleon.

The constitution of Venice, which had originally been democratic, became gradually less so, and was, after 1297, a close oligarchy. The basis of political power was the Great Council, membership of which, after that date, was hereditary, and was confined to the leading families. Executive power belonged to the Council of Ten, which was elected by the Great Council. The Doge, the ceremonial head of the State, was elected for life; his nominal powers were very restricted, but in practice his influence was usually decisive. Venetian diplomacy was considered exceedingly astute, and the reports of Venetian ambassadors were remarkably penetrating. Since Ranke, historians have used them as among the best sources for knowledge of the events with which they deal.

Florence was the most civilized city in the world, and the chief source of the Renaissance. Almost all the great names in literature, and the earlier as well as some of the later of the great names in art, are connected with Florence; but for the present we are concerned with politics rather than culture. In the thirteenth century, there were three conflicting classes in Florence: the nobles, the rich merchants, and the small men. The nobles, in the main, were Ghibelline, the other two classes Guelf. The Ghibellines were finally defeated in 1266, and during the fourteenth century the party of the small men got the better of the rich merchants. The conflict, however, led not to a stable democracy, but to the gradual growth of what the Greeks would have called a 'tyranny'. The Medici family, who ultimately became the rulers of Florence, began as political bosses on the democratic side. Cosimo dei Medici (1389-1464), the first of the family to achieve clear pre-eminence, still had no official position; his power depended upon skill in manipulating elections. He was astute, conciliatory when possible, ruthless when necessary. He was succeeded, after a short interval, by his grandson Lorenzo the Magnificent, who held power from 1469 till his death in 1492. Both these men owed their position to their wealth, which they had acquired mainly in commerce, but also in mining and other industries. They understood how to make Florence rich, as well as themselves, and under them the city prospered.

Lorenzo's son Pietro lacked his father's merits, and was expelled in 1494. Then followed the four years of Savonarola's influence, when a kind of Puritan revival turned men against gaiety and luxury, away from free-thought and towards the piety supposed to have characterized a simpler age. In the end, however, mainly for political reasons, Savonarola's enemies triumphed, he was executed and his body was burnt (1498). The Republic, democratic in intention but plutocratic in fact, survived till 1512, when the Medici were restored. A son of Lorenzo, who had become a cardinal at the age of fourteen, was elected Pope in 1513, and took the title of Leo X. The Medici family, under the title of Grand Dukes of Tuscany, governed Florence until 1737; but Florence meanwhile, like the rest of Italy, had become poor and unimportant.

The temporal power of the Pope, which owned its origin to Pepin and the forged Donation of Constantine, increased greatly during the Renaissance; but the methods employed by the popes to this end robbed the papacy of spiritual authority. The conciliar movement, which came to grief in the conflict between the Council of Basel and Pope Eugenius IV (1431-47), represented the most earnest elements in the Church; what was perhaps even more important, it represented ecclesiastical opinion north of the Alps. The victory of the popes was the victory of Italy, and (in a lesser degree) of Spain. Italian civilization, in the latter half of the fifteenth century, was totally unlike that of northern countries, which remained medieval. The Italians were in earnest about culture, but not about morals and religion; even in the minds of ecclesiastics, elegant latinity would cover a multitude of sins. Nicholas V (1447-55), the first humanist Pope, gave papal offices to scholars whose learning he respected, regardless of other considerations; Lorenzo Valla, an Epicurean, and the man who proved the Donation of

Constantine to be a forgery, who ridiculed the style of the Vulgate and accused St Augustine of heresy, was made apostolic secretary. This policy of encouraging humanism rather than piety or orthodoxy continued until the sack of Rome in 1527.

Encouragement of humanism, though it shocked the earnest North, might, from our point of view, be reckoned a virtue; but the warlike policy and immoral life of some of the popes could not be defended from any point of view except that of naked power politics. Alexander VI (1492-1503) devoted his life as Pope to the aggrandizement of himself and his family. He had two sons, the Duke of Gandia and Caesar Borgia, of whom he greatly preferred the former. The duke, however, was murdered, probably by his brother; the Pope's dynastic ambitions therefore had to be concentrated on Caesar. Together they conquered the Romagna and Ancona, which were intended to form a principality for Caesar; but when the Pope died Caesar was very ill, and therefore could not act promptly. Their conquests consequently reverted to the patrimony of St Peter. The wickedness of these two men soon became legendary, and it is difficult to disentangle truth from falsehood as regards the innumerable murders of which they are accused. There can be no doubt, however, that they carried the arts of perfidy further than they had ever been carried before. Julius II (1503-13), who succeeded Alexander VI, was not remarkable for piety, but gave less occasion for scandal than his predecessor. He continued the process of enlarging the papal domain; as a soldier he had merit, but not as the Head of the Christian Church. The Reformation, which began under his successor Leo X (1513-21), was the natural outcome of the pagan policy of the Renaissance popes.

The southern extremity of Italy was occupied by the Kingdom of Naples, with which, at most times, Sicily was united. Naples and Sicily had been the especial personal kingdom of the Emperor Frederick II; he had introduced an absolute monarchy on the Mohammedan model, enlightened but despotic, and allowing no power to the feudal nobility. After his death in 1250, Naples and Sicily went to his natural son Manfred, who, however, inherited the implacable hostility of the Church, and was ousted by the French in 1266. The French made themselves unpopular, and were massacred in the 'Sicilian Vespers' (1282), after which the kingdom belonged to Peter III of Aragon and his heirs. After various complications, leading to the temporary separation of Naples and Sicily, they were reunited in 1443 under Alphonso the Magnanimous, a distinguished patron of letters. From 1495 onwards, three French kings tried to conquer Naples, but in the end the kingdom was acquired by Ferdinand of Aragon (1502). Charles VIII, Louis XII, and Francis I, kings of France, all had claims (not very good in law) on Milan and Naples; all invaded Italy with temporary success, but all were ultimately defeated by the Spaniards. The victory of Spain and the Counter-Reformation put an end to the Italian Renaissance. Pope Clement VII being an obstacle to the Counter-Reformation, and, as a Medici, a friend of France, Charles V, in 1527, caused Rome to be sacked by a largely Protestant army. After this, the popes became religious, and the Italian Renaissance was at an end.

The game of power politics in Italy was unbelievably complex. The minor princes, mostly self-made tyrants, allied themselves now with one of the larger States, now with another; if they played the game unwisely, they were exterminated. There were constant wars, but until the coming of the French in 1494 they were almost bloodless: the soldiers were mercenaries, who were anxious to minimize their vocational risks. These purely Italian wars did not interfere much with trade, or prevent the country from increasing in wealth. There was much statecraft, but no wise statesmanship; when the French came, the country found itself practically defenceless. French troops shocked the Italians by actually killing people in battle. The wars between French and Spaniards which ensued were serious wars, bringing suffering and impoverishment. But the Italian States went on intriguing against each other, invoking the aid of France of Spain in their internal quarrels, without any feeling for national unity. In the end, all were ruined. It must be said that Italy would inevitably have lost its importance, owing to the discovery of America and the Cape route to the East; but the collapse could have been less catastrophic, and less destructive of the quality of Italian civilization.

The Renaissance was not a period of great achievement in philosophy, but it did certain things which were essential preliminaries to the greatness of the seventeenth century. In the first place, it broke down the rigid scholastic system, which had become an intellectual strait jacket. It revived the study of Plato, and thereby demanded at least so much independent thought as was required for choosing between him and Aristotle. In regard to both, it promoted a genuine and first-hand knowledge, free from the glosses of Neoplatonists and Arabic commentators. More important still, it encouraged the habit of regarding intellectual activity as a delightful social adventure, not a cloistered meditation aiming at the preservation of a predetermined orthodoxy.

The substitution of Plato for the scholastic Aristotle was hastened by contact with Byzantine scholarship. Already at the Council of Ferrara (1438), which nominally reunited the Eastern and Western Churches, there was a debate in which the Byzantines maintained the superiority of Plato to Aristotle. Gemistus Pletho, an ardent Greek Platonist of doubtful orthodoxy, did much to promote Platonism in Italy; so did Bessarion, a Greek who became a cardinal. Cosimo and Lorenzo dei Medici were both addicted to Plato; Cosimo founded and Lorenzo continued the Florentine Academy, which was largely devoted to the study of Plato. Cosimo died listening to one of Plato's dialogues. The humanists of the time, however, were too busy acquiring knowledge of antiquity to be able to produce anything original in philosophy.

The Renaissance was not a popular movement; it was a movement of a small number of scholars and artists, encouraged by liberal patrons, especially the Medici and the humanist popes. But for these patrons, it might have had very much less success. Petrarch and Boccaccio, in the fourteenth century, belong mentally to the Renaissance, but owing to the different political conditions of their time their immediate influence was less than that of the fifteenth-century humanists.

The attitude of Renaissance scholars to the Church is difficult to characterize simply. Some were avowed free-thinkers, though even these usually received extreme unction, making peace with the Church when they felt death approaching. Most of them were impressed by the wickedness of contemporary popes, but were nevertheless glad to be employed by them. Guicciardini the historian wrote in 1529:

'No man is more disgusted than I am with the ambition, the avarice, and the profligacy of the priests, not only because each of these vices is hateful in itself, but because each and all of them are most unbecoming in those who declare themselves to be men in special relations with God, and also because they are vices so opposed to one another, that they can only co-exist in very singular natures. Nevertheless, my position at the Court of several popes forced me to desire their greatness, for the sake of my own interest. But, had it not been for this, I should have loved Martin Luther as myself, not in order to free myself from the laws which Christianity, as generally understood and explained, lays upon us, but in order to see this swarm of scoundrels put back into their proper place, so that they may be forced to live either without vices or without power.'[1]

This is delightfully frank, and shows clearly why the humanists could not inaugurate a reformation. Moreover, most of them saw no half-way house between orthodoxy and free-thought; such a position as Luther's was impossible for them, because they no longer had the medieval feeling for the subtleties of theology.

[1] Quoted from Burckhardt, *Renaissance in Italy*, part iv, chap. ii.

Masuccio, after describing the wickedness of monks and nuns and friars, says: 'The best punishment for them would be for God to abolish purgatory; they would then receive no more alms, and would be forced to go back to their spades.'[1] But it does not occur to him, as to Luther, to deny purgatory, while retaining most of the Catholic faith.

The wealth of Rome depended only in small part upon the revenues obtained from the papal dominions; in the main, it was a tribute, drawn from the whole Catholic world, by means of a theological system which maintained that the popes held the keys of heaven. An Italian who effectively questioned this system risked the impoverishment of Italy, and the loss of the position in the Western world. Consequently Italian unorthodoxy, in the Renaissance, was purely intellectual, and did not lead to schism, or to any attempt to create a popular movement away from the Church. The only exception, and that a very partial one, was Savonarola, who belonged mentally to the Middle Ages.

Most of the humanists retained such superstitious beliefs as had found support in antiquity. Magic and witchcraft might be wicked, but were not thought impossible. Innocent VIII, in 1484, issued a bull against witchcraft, which led to an appalling persecution of witches in Germany and elsewhere. Astrology was prized especially by freethinkers; it acquired a vogue which it had not had since ancient times. The first effect of emancipation from the Church was not to make men think rationally, but to open their minds to every sort of antique nonsense.

Morally, the first effect of emancipation was equally disastrous. The old moral rules ceased to be respected; most of the rulers of States had acquired their position by treachery, and retained it by ruthless cruelty. When cardinals were invited to dine at the coronation of a pope, they brought their own wine and their own cup-bearer, for fear of poison.[2] Except Savonarola, hardly any Italian of the period risked anything for a public object. The evils of papal corruption were obvious, but nothing was done about them. The desirability of Italian unity was evident, but the rulers were incapable of combination. The danger of foreign domination was imminent, yet every Italian ruler was prepared to invoke the aid of any foreign power, even the Turk, in any dispute with any other Italian ruler. I cannot think of any crime, except the destruction of ancient manuscripts, of which the men of the Renaissance were not frequently guilty.

Outside the sphere of morals, the Renaissance had great merits. In architecture, painting, and poetry, it has remained renowned.

[1] *Ibid.*   [2] Burckhardt, *op. cit.*, part vi, chap. i.

It produced very great men, such as Leonardo, Michelangelo, and Machiavelli. It liberated educated men from the narrowness of medieval culture, and, even while still a slave to the worship of antiquity, it made scholars aware that a variety of opinions had been held by reputable authorities on almost every subject. By reviving the knowledge of the Greek world, it created a mental atmosphere in which it was again possible to rival Hellenic achievements, and in which individual genius could flourish with a freedom unknown since the time of Alexander. The political conditions of the Renaissance favoured individual development, but were unstable; the instability and the individualism were closely connected, as in ancient Greece. A stable social system is necessary, but every stable system hitherto devised has hampered the development of exceptional artistic or intellectual merit. How much murder and anarchy are we prepared to endure for the sake of great achievements such as those of the Renaissance? In the past, a great deal; in our own time, much less. No solution of this problem has hitherto been found, although increase of social organization is making it continually more important.

Chapter III

MACHIAVELLI

THE Renaissance, though it produced no important theoretical philosopher, produced one man of supreme eminence in *political* philosophy: Niccolò Machiavelli. It is the custom to be shocked by him, and he certainly is sometimes shocking. But many other men would be equally so if they were equally free from humbug. His political philosophy is scientific and empirical, based upon his own experience of affairs, concerned to set forth the means to assigned ends, regardless of the question whether the ends are to be considered good or bad. When, on occasion, he allows himself to mention the ends that he desires, they are such as we can all applaud. Much of the conventional obloquy that attaches to his name is due to the indignation of hypocrites who hate the frank avowal of evil-doing. There remains, it is true, a good deal that genuinely demands criticism, but in this he is an expression of his age. Such intellectual honesty about political dishonesty would have been hardly possible at any other time or in any other country, except perhaps in Greece among men who owed their theoretical education to the sophists and their practical training to the wars of petty states which, in classical Greece as in Renaissance Italy, were the political accompaniment of individual genius.

Machiavelli (1467-1527) was a Florentine, whose father, a lawyer, was neither rich nor poor. When he was in his twenties, Savonarola dominated Florence; his miserable end evidently made a great impression on Machiavelli, for he remarks that 'all armed prophets have conquered and unarmed ones have failed', proceeding to give Savonarola as an instance of the latter class. On the other side he mentions Moses, Cyrus, Theseus, and Romulus. It is typical of the Renaissance that Christ is not mentioned.

Immediately after Savonarola's execution, Machiavelli obtained a minor post in the Florentine government (1498). He remained in its service, at times on important diplomatic missions, until the restoration of the Medici in 1512; then, having always opposed them, he was arrested, but acquitted, and allowed to live in retirement in the country near Florence. He became an author for want of other occupation. His most famous work, *The Prince*, was written in 1513, and dedicated to Lorenzo the Second, since he hoped (vainly, as it proved) to win the favour of the Medici. Its tone is perhaps partly due to this practical purpose; his longer work, the *Discourses*, which he was writing at the same time, is markedly more republican and more liberal. He says at the beginning of *The Prince* that he will not speak of republics in this book, since he has dealt with them elsewhere. Those who do not read also the *Discourses* are likely to get a very one-sided view of his doctrine.

Having failed to conciliate the Medici, Machiavelli was compelled to go on writing. He lived in retirement until the year of his death, which was that of the sack of Rome by the troops of Charles V. This year may be reckoned also that in which the Italian Renaissance died.

The Prince is concerned to discover, from history and from contemporary events, how principalities are won, how they are held, and how they are lost. Fifteenth-century Italy afforded a multitude of examples, both great and small. Few rulers were legitimate; even the popes, in many cases, secured election by corrupt means. The rules for achieving success were not quite the same as they became when times grew more settled, for no one was shocked by cruelties and treacheries which would have disqualified a man in the eighteenth or the nineteenth century. Perhaps our age, again, can better appreciate Machiavelli, for some of the most notable successes of our time have been achieved by methods as base as any employed in Renaissance Italy. He would have applauded, as an artistic connoisseur in statecraft, Hitler's Reichstag fire, his purge of the party in 1934, and his breach of faith after Munich.

Caesar Borgia, son of Alexander VI, comes in for high praise. His problem was a difficult one: first, by the death of his brother, to become the sole beneficiary of his father's dynastic ambition; second, to conquer by force of arms, in the name of the Pope, territories which should, after Alexander's death, belong to himself and not to the Papal States; third, to manipulate the College of Cardinals so that the next Pope should be his friend. He pursued this difficult end with great skill; from his practice, Machiavelli says, a new prince should derive precepts. Caesar failed, it is true, but only 'by the extraordinary malignity of fortune'. It happened that, when his father died, he also was dangerously ill; by the time he recovered, his enemies had organized their forces, and his bitterest opponent had been elected Pope. On the day of this election, Caesar told Machiavelli that he had provided for everything, 'except that he had never thought that at his father's death he would be dying himself'.

Machiavelli, who was intimately acquainted with his villainies, sums up thus: 'Reviewing thus all the actions of the duke [Caesar],

I find nothing to blame, on the contrary, I feel bound, as I have done, to hold him in as an example to be imitated by all who by fortune and with the arms of others have risen to power.'

There is an interesting chapter 'Of Ecclesiastical Principalities', which, in view of what is said in the *Discourses*, evidently conceals part of Machiavelli's thought. The reason for concealment was, no doubt, that *The Prince* was designed to please the Medici, and that, when it was written, a Medici had just become Pope (Leo X). In regard to ecclesiastical principalities, he says in *The Prince*, the only difficulty is to acquire them, for, when acquired, they are defended by ancient religious customs, which keep their princes in power no matter how they behave. Their princes do not need armies (so he says), because 'they are upheld by higher causes which the human mind cannot attain to'. They are 'exalted and maintained by God', and 'it would be the work of a presumptuous and foolish man to discuss them'. Nevertheless, he continues, it is permissible to inquire by what means Alexander VI so greatly increased the temporal power of the Pope.

The discussion of the papal powers in the *Discourses* is longer and more sincere. Here he begins by placing eminent men in an ethical hierarchy. The best, he says, are the founders of religions; then come the founders of monarchies or republics; then literary men. These are good, but destroyers of religions, subverters of republics or kingdoms, and enemies of virtue or of letters, are bad. Those who establish tyrannies are wicked, including Julius Caesar; on the other hand, Brutus was good. (The contrast between this view and Dante's shows the effect of classical literature.) He holds that religion should have a prominent place in the State, not on the ground of its truth, but as a social cement: the Romans were right to pretend to believe in auguries, and to punish those who disregarded them. His criticisms of the Church in his day are two: that by its evil conduct it has undermined religious belief, and that the temporal power of the popes, with the policy that it inspires, prevents the unification of Italy. These criticisms are expressed with great vigour. 'The nearer people are to the Church of Rome, which is the head of our religion, the less religious are they. . . . Her ruin and chastisement is near at hand. . . . We Italians owe to the Church of Rome and to her priests our having become irreligious and bad; but we owe her a still greater debt, and one that will be the cause of our ruin, namely that the Church has kept and still keeps our country divided.'[1]

In view of such passages, it must be supposed that Machiavelli's admiration of Caesar Borgia was only for his skill, not for his pur-

[1] This remained true until 1870.

493

poses. Admiration of skill, and of the actions that lead to fame, was very great at the time of the Renaissance. This kind of feeling has, of course, always existed; many of Napoleon's enemies enthusiastically admired him as a military strategist. But in the Italy of Machiavelli's time the quasi-artistic admiration of dexterity was much greater than in earlier or later centuries. It would be a mistake to try to reconcile it with the larger political aims which Machiavelli considered important; the two things, love of skill and patriotic desire for Italian unity, existed side by side in his mind, and were not in any degree synthesized. Thus he can praise Caesar Borgia for his cleverness, and blame him for keeping Italy disrupted. The perfect character, one must suppose, would be, in his opinion, a man as clever and unscrupulous as Caesar Borgia where means are concerned, but aiming at a different end. *The Prince* ends with an eloquent appeal to the Medici to liberate Italy from the 'barbarians' (i.e. the French and Spaniards), whose domination 'stinks'. He would not expect such a work to be undertaken from unselfish motives, but from love of power, and still more of fame.

The Prince is very explicit in repudiating received morality where the conduct of rulers is concerned. A ruler will perish if he is always good; he must be as cunning as a fox and as fierce as a lion. There is a chapter (XVIII) entitled: 'In What Way Princes Must Keep Faith.' We learn that they should keep faith when it pays to do so, but not otherwise. A prince must on occasion be faithless.

'But it is necessary to be able to disguise this character well, and to be a great feigner and dissembler; and men are so simple and so ready to obey present necessities, that one who deceives will always find those who allow themselves to be deceived. I will mention only one modern instance. Alexander VI did nothing else but deceive men, he thought of nothing else, and found the occasion for it; no man was ever more able to give assurances, or affirmed things with stronger oaths, and no man observed them less; however, he always succeeded in his deceptions, as he knew well this aspect of things. It is not necessary therefore for a prince to have all the above-named qualities [the conventional virtues], but it is very necessary to seem to have them.'

He goes on to say that, above all, a prince should *seem* to be religious.

The tone of the *Discourses*, which are nominally a commentary on Livy, is very different. There are whole chapters which seem almost as if they had been written by Montesquieu; most of the book could have been read with approval by an eighteenth-century liberal. The doctrine of checks and balances is set forth explicitly. Princes, nobles, and people should all have a part in the Constitution; 'then these three powers will keep each other reciprocally in check'. The constitution of Sparta, as established by Lycurgus, was the best, because it embodied the most perfect balance; that of Solon was too democratic, and therefore led to the tyranny of Peisistratus. The Roman republican constitution was good, owing to the conflict of Senate and people.

The word 'liberty' is used throughout as denoting something precious, though what it denotes is not very clear. This, of course, comes from antiquity, and was passed on to the eighteenth and nineteenth centuries. Tuscany has preserved its liberties, because it contains no castles or gentlemen. ('Gentlemen' is of course a mistranslation, but a pleasing one.) It seems to be recognized that political liberty requires a certain kind of personal virtue in the citizens. In Germany alone, we are told, probity and religion are still common, and therefore in Germany there are many republics. In general, the people are wiser and more constant than princes, although Livy and most other writers maintain the opposite. It is not without good reason that it is said, 'the voice of the people is the voice of God'.

It is interesting to observe how the political thought of the Greeks and Romans, in their republican days, acquired an actuality in the fifteenth century which it had not had in Greece since Alexander or in Rome since Augustus. The Neoplatonists, the Arabs, and the Schoolmen took a passionate interest in the metaphysics of Plato and Aristotle, but none at all in their political writings, because the political systems of the age of City States had completely disappeared. The growth of City States in Italy synchronized with the revival of learning, and made it possible for humanists to profit by the political theories of republican Greeks and Romans. The love of 'liberty', and the theory of checks and balances, came to the Renaissance from antiquity, and to modern times largely from the Renaissance, though also directly from antiquity. This aspect of Machiavelli is at least as important as the more famous 'immoral' doctrines of *The Prince*.

It is to be noted that Machiavelli never bases any political argument on Christian or biblical grounds. Medieval writers had a conception of 'legitimate' power, which was that of the Pope and the Emperor, or derived from them. Northern writers, even so late as Locke, argue as to what happened in the Garden of Eden, and think that they can thence derive proofs that certain kinds of power are 'legitimate'. In Machiavelli there is no such conception. Power is for those who have the skill to seize it in a free competition. His preference for popular government is not derived from any idea of 'rights', but from the observation that popular governments are less cruel, unscrupulous, and inconstant than tyrannies.

Let us try to make a synthesis (which Machiavelli himself did not make) of the 'moral' and 'immoral' parts of his doctrine. In what follows, I am expressing not my own opinions, but opinions which are explicitly or implicitly his.

There are certain political goods, of which three are specially important: national independence, security, and a well-ordered constitution. The best constitution is one which apportions legal rights among prince, nobles, and people in proportion to their real power, for under such a constitution successful revolutions are difficult and therefore stability is possible; but for considerations of stability, it would be wise to give more power to the people. So far as regards ends.

But there is also, in politics, the question of means. It is futile to pursue a political purpose by methods that are bound to fail; if the end is held good, we must choose means adequate to its achievement. The question of means can be treated in a purely scientific manner, without regard to the goodness or badness of the ends. 'Success' means the achievement of your purpose, whatever it may be. If there is a science of success, it can be studied just as well in the successes of the wicked as in those of the good—indeed better, since the examples of successful sinners are more numerous than those of successful saints. But the science, once established, will be just as useful to the saint as to the sinner. For the saint, if he concerns himself with politics, must wish, just as the sinner does, to achieve success.

The question is ultimately one of power. To achieve a political end, power, of one kind or another, is necessary. This plain fact is concealed by slogans, such as 'right will prevail' or 'the triumph of evil is short-lived'. If the side that you think right prevails, that is because it has superior power. It is true that power, often, depends upon opinion, and opinion upon propaganda; it is true, also, that it is an advantage in propaganda to seem more virtuous than your adversary, and that one way of seeming virtuous is to be virtuous. For this reason, it may sometimes happen that victory goes to the side which has the most of what the general public considers to be virtue. We must concede to Machiavelli that this was an important element in the growing power of the Church during the eleventh, twelfth, and thirteenth centuries, as well as in the success of the Reformation in the sixteenth century. But there are important limitations. In the first place, those who have seized power can, by controlling propaganda, cause their party to appear virtuous; no one, for example, could mention the sins of Alexander

VI in a New York or Boston public school. In the second place, there are chaotic periods during which obvious knavery frequently succeeds; the period of Machiavelli was one of them. In such times, there tends to be a rapidly growing cynicism, which makes men forgive anything provided it pays. Even in such times, as Machiavelli himself says, it is desirable to present an appearance of virtue before the ignorant public.

This question can be carried a step further. Machiavelli is of opinion that civilized men are almost certain to be unscrupulous egoists. If a man wished nowadays to establish a republic, he says, he would find it easier with mountaineers than with the men of a large city, since the latter would be already corrupted.[1] If a man is an unscrupulous egoist, his wisest line of conduct will depend upon the population with which he has to operate. The Renaissance Church shocked everybody, but it was only north of the Alps that it shocked people enough to produce the Reformation. At the time when Luther began his revolt, the revenue of the papacy was probably larger than it would have been if Alexander VI and Julius II had been more virtuous, and if this is true, it is so because of the cynicism of Renaissance Italy. It follows that politicians will behave better when they depend upon a virtuous population than when they depend upon one which is indifferent to moral considerations; they will also behave better in a community in which their crimes, if any, can be made widely known, than in one in which there is a strict censorship under their control. A certain amount can, of course, always be achieved by hypocrisy, but the amount can be much diminished by suitable institutions.

Machiavelli's political thinking, like that of most of the ancients, is in one respect somewhat shallow. He is occupied with great law-givers, such as Lycurgus and Solon, who are supposed to create a community all in one piece, with little regard to what has gone before. The conception of a community as an organic growth, which the statesmen can only affect to a limited extent, is in the main modern, and has been greatly strengthened by the theory of evolution. This conception is not to be found in Machiavelli any more than in Plato.

It might, however, be maintained that the evolutionary view of society, though true in the past, is no longer applicable, but must, for the present and the future, be replaced by a much more mechanistic view. In Russia and Germany new societies have been created, in much the same way as the mythical Lycurgus was supposed to have created the Spartan polity. The ancient lawgiver

[1] It is curious to find this anticipation of Rousseau. It would be amusing, and not wholly false, to interpret Machiavelli as a disappointed romantic.

497

was a benevolent myth; the modern lawgiver is a terrifying reality. The world has become more like that of Machiavelli than it was, and the modern man who hopes to refute his philosophy must think more deeply than seemed necessary in the nineteenth century.

Chapter IV

ERASMUS AND MORE

IN northern countries the Renaissance began later than in Italy, and soon became entangled with the Reformation. But there was a brief period, at the beginning of the sixteenth century, during which the new learning was being vigorously disseminated in France, England, and Germany, without having become involved in theological controversy. This northern Renaissance was in many ways very different from that of Italy. It was not anarchic or amoral; on the contrary, it was associated with piety and public virtue. It was much interested in applying standards of scholarship to the Bible, and in obtaining a more accurate text than that of the Vulgate. It was less brilliant and more solid than its Italian progenitor, less concerned with personal display of learning, and more anxious to spread learning as widely as possible.

Two men, Erasmus and Sir Thomas More, will serve as exemplars of the northern Renaissance. They were close friends, and had much in common. Both were learned, though More less so than Erasmus; both despised the scholastic philosophy; both aimed at ecclesiastical reform from within, but deplored the Protestant schism when it came; both were witty, humorous, and highly skilled writers. Before Luther's revolt, they were leaders of thought, but after it the world was too violent, on both sides, for men of their type. More suffered martyrdom, and Erasmus sank into ineffectiveness.

Neither Erasmus nor More was a philosopher in the strict sense of the word. My reason for speaking of them is that they illustrate the temper of a pre-revolutionary age, when there is a widespread demand for moderate reform, and timid men have not yet been frightened into reaction by extremists. They exemplify also the dislike of everything systematic in theology or philosophy which characterized the reactions against scholasticism.

Erasmus (1466-1536) was born at Rotterdam.[1] He was illegitimate and invented a romantically untrue account of the circumstances of his birth. In fact, his father was a priest, a man of some learning, with a knowledge of Greek. His parents died before he was grown up, and his guardians (apparently because they had embezzled his money) cajoled him into becoming a monk at the monastery of

[1] As regards the life of Erasmus, I have mainly followed the excellent biography by Huizinga.

Steyr, a step which he regretted all the rest of his life. One of his guardians was a schoolmaster, but knew less Latin than Erasmus already knew as a schoolboy; in reply to a Latin epistle from the boy, the schoolmaster wrote: 'If you should write again so elegantly, please to add a commentary.'

In 1493, he became secretary to the bishop of Cambrai, who was Chancellor of the Order of the Golden Fleece. This gave him the opportunity to leave the monastery and travel, though not to Italy, as he had hoped. His knowledge of Greek was as yet very slight, but he was a highly accomplished Latinist; he particularly admired Lorenzo Valla, on account of his book on the elegancies of the Latin language. He considered latinity quite compatible with true devotion, and instanced Augustine and Jerome—forgetting, apparently, the dream in which Our Lord denounced the latter for reading Cicero.

He was for a time at the University of Paris, but found nothing there that was of profit to himself. The university had had its great days, from the beginning of scholasticism to Gerson and the conciliar movement, but now the old disputes had become arid. Thomists and Scotists, who jointly were called the Ancients, disputed against Occamists, who were called the Terminists, or Moderns. At last, in 1482, they were reconciled, and made common cause against the humanists, who were making headway in Paris outside university circles. Erasmus hated the scholastics, whom he regarded as superannuated and antiquated. He mentioned in a letter that, as he wanted to obtain the doctor's degree, he tried to say nothing either graceful or witty. He did not really like any philosophy, not even Plato and Aristotle, though they, being ancients, had to be spoken of with respect.

In 1499 he made his first visit to England, where he liked the fashion of kissing girls. In England he made friends with Colet and More, who encouraged him to undertake serious work rather than literary trifles. Colet lectured on the Bible without knowing Greek; Erasmus, feeling that he would like to do work on the Bible, considered that a knowledge of Greek was essential. After leaving England at the beginning of 1500, he set to work to learn Greek, though he was too poor to afford a teacher; by the autumn of 1502 he was proficient, and when in 1506 he went to Italy, he found that the Italians had nothing to teach him. He determined to edit St Jerome, and to bring out a Greek Testament with a new Latin translation; both were achieved in 1516. The discovery of inaccuracies in the Vulgate was subsequently of use to the Protestants in controversy. He tried to learn Hebrew, but gave it up.

The only book by Erasmus that is still read is *The Praise of Folly*.

The conception of this book came to him in 1509, while he was crossing the Alps on the way from Italy to England. He wrote it quickly in London, at the house of Sir Thomas More, to whom it is dedicated, with a playful suggestion of appropriateness since 'moros' means 'fool'. The book is spoken by Folly in her own person; she sings her own praises with great gusto, and her text is enlivened still further with illustrations by Holbein. She covers all parts of human life, and all classes and professions. But for her, the human race would die out, for who can marry without folly? She counsels, as an antidote to wisdom, 'taking a wife, a creature so harmless and silly, and yet so useful and convenient, as might mollify and make pliable the stiffness and morose humour of men'. Who can be happy without flattery or without self-love? Yet such happiness is folly. The happiest men are those who are nearest the brutes and divest themselves of reason. The best happiness is that which is based on delusion, since it costs least: it is easier to imagine oneself a king than to make oneself a king in reality. Erasmus proceeds to make fun of national pride and of professional conceit: almost all professors of the arts and sciences are egregiously conceited, and derive their happiness from their conceit.

There are passages where the satire gives way to invective, and Folly utters the serious opinions of Erasmus; these are concerned with ecclesiastical abuses. Pardons and indulgences, by which priests 'compute the time of each soul's residence in purgatory'; the worship of saints, even of the Virgin, 'whose blind devotees think it manners to place the mother before the Son'; the disputes of theologians as to the Trinity and the Incarnation; the doctrine of transubstantiation; the scholastic sects; popes, cardinals, and bishops —all are fiercely ridiculed. Particularly fierce is the attack on the monastic orders: they are 'brainsick fools', who have very little religion in them, yet are 'highly in love with themselves, and fond admirers of their own happiness'. They behave as if all religion consisted in minute punctilio: 'The precise number of knots to the tying on of their sandals; what distinct colours their respective habits, and what stuff made of; how broad and long their girdles,' and so on. 'It will be pretty to hear their pleas before the great tribunal: one will brag how he mortified his carnal appetite by feeding only upon fish: another will urge that he spent most of his time on earth in the divine exercise of singing psalms: . . . another, that in threescore years he never so much as touched a piece of money, except he fingered it through a thick pair of gloves.' But Christ will interrupt: 'Woe unto you, scribes and pharisees, . . . I left you but one precept, of loving another, which I do not hear any one plead that he has faithfully discharged.' Yet on earth these men are feared, for they know many secrets from the confessional, and often blab them when they are drunk.

Popes are not spared. They should imitate their Master by humility and poverty. 'Their only weapons ought to be those of the Spirit; and of these indeed they are mightily liberal, as of their interdicts, their suspensions, their denunciations, their aggravations, their greater and lesser excommunications, and their roaring bulls, that fight whomever they are thundered against; and these most holy fathers never issue them out more frequently than against those who, at the instigation of the devil, and not having the fear of God before their eyes, do feloniously and maliciously attempt to lessen and impair St Peter's patrimony.'

It might be supposed, from such passages, that Erasmus would have welcomed the Reformation, but it proved otherwise.

The book ends with the serious suggestion that true religion is a form of Folly. There are, throughout, two kinds of Folly, one praised ironically, the other seriously; the kind praised seriously is that which is displayed in Christian simplicity. This praise is of a piece with Erasmus's dislike of scholastic philosophy and of learned doctors whose Latin was unclassical. But it has also a deeper aspect. It is the first appearance in literature, so far as I know, of the view set forth in Rousseau's *Savoyard Vicar*, according to which true religion comes from the heart, not the head, and all elaborate theology is superfluous. This point of view has become increasingly common, and is now pretty generally accepted among Protestants. It is, essentially, a rejection of Hellenic intellectualism by the sentimentalism of the North.

Erasmus, on his second visit to England, remained for five years (1509-14), partly in London, partly at Cambridge. He had a considerable influence in stimulating English humanism. The education at English public schools remained, until recently, almost exactly what he would have wished: a thorough grounding in Greek and Latin, involving not only translation, but verse and prose composition. Science, although intellectually dominant since the seventeenth century, was thought unworthy the attention of a gentleman or a divine; Plato should be studied, but not the subjects which Plato thought worth studying. All this is in line with the influence of Erasmus.

The men of the Renaissance had an immense curiosity; 'these minds', says Huizinga, 'never had their desired share of striking incidents, curious details, rarities and anomalies'. But at first they sought these things, not in the world, but in old books. Erasmus was interested in the world, but could not digest it in the raw: it had to be dished up in Latin or Greek before he could assimilate it.

Travellers' tales were discounted, but any marvel in Pliny was believed. Gradually, however, curiosity became transferred from books to the real world; men became interested in the savages and strange animals that were actually discovered, rather than in those described by classical authors. Caliban comes from Montaigne, and Montaigne's cannibals come from travellers. 'The anthropophagi and men whose heads do grow beneath their shoulders' had been seen by Othello, not derived from antiquity.

And so the curiosity of the Renaissance, from having been literary, gradually became scientific. Such a cataract of new facts overwhelmed men that they could, at first, only be swept along with the current. The old systems were evidently wrong; Aristotle's physics and Ptolemy's astronomy and Galen's medicine could not be stretched to include the discoveries that had been made. Montaigne and Shakespeare are content with confusion: discovery is delightful, and system is its enemy. It was not till the seventeenth century that the system-building faculty caught up with the new knowledge of matters of fact. All this, however, has taken us far from Erasmus, to whom Columbus was less interesting than the Argonauts.

Erasmus was incurably and unashamedly literary. He wrote a book, *Enchiridion militis christiani*, giving advice to illiterate soldiers: they were to read the Bible, but also Plato, Ambrose, Jerome, and Augustine. He made a vast collection of Latin proverbs, to which, in later editions, he added many in Greek; his original purpose was to enable people to write Latin idiomatically. He wrote an immensely successful book of *Colloquies*, to teach people how to talk in Latin about every-day matters, such as a game of bowls. This was, perhaps, more useful than it seems now. Latin was the only international language, and students at the University of Paris came from all over Western Europe. It may have often happened that Latin was the only language in which two students could converse.

After the Reformation, Erasmus lived first in Louvain, which maintained perfect Catholic orthodoxy, then in Basel, which became Protestant. Each side tried to enlist him, but for a long time in vain. He had, as we have seen, expressed himself strongly about ecclesiastical abuses and the wickedness of popes; in 1518, the very year of Luther's revolt, he published a satire, called *Julius exclusus*, describing the failure of Julius II to get to heaven. But Luther's violence repelled him, and he hated war. At last he came down on the Catholic side. In 1524 he wrote a work defending free will, which Luther, following and exaggerating Augustine, rejected. Luther replied savagely, and Erasmus was driven further into reaction. From this time until his death, he became increasingly unimportant. He had always been timid, and the times were no longer suited to timid people. For honest men, the only honourable alternatives were martyrdom or victory. His friend Sir Thomas More was compelled to choose martyrdom, and Erasmus commented: 'Would More had never meddled with that dangerous business, and left the theological cause to the theologians.' Erasmus lived too long, into an age of new virtues and new vices—heroism and intolerance—neither of which he could acquire.

Sir Thomas More (1478-1535) was, as a man, much more admirable than Erasmus, but much less important as an influence. He was a humanist, but also a man of profound piety. At Oxford, he set to work to learn Greek, which was then unusual, and was thought to show a sympathy with Italian infidels. The authorities and his father objected, and he was removed from the university. Thereupon he was attracted to the Carthusians, practised extreme austerities, and contemplated joining the order. He was deterred from doing so, apparently by the influence of Erasmus, whom he first met at this time. His father was a lawyer, and he decided to follow his father's profession. In 1504 he was a Member of Parliament, and led the opposition to Henry VII's demand for new taxes. In this he was successful, but the king was furious; he sent More's father to the Tower, releasing him, however, on payment of £100. On the king's death in 1509, More returned to the practice of the law, and won the favour of Henry VIII. He was knighted in 1514, and employed on various embassies. The king kept inviting him to court, but More would not come; at last the king came uninvited to dine with him at his house in Chelsea. More had no illusions as to Henry VIII; when complimented on the king's favourable disposition, he replied: 'If my head should win him a castle in France it should not fail to go.'

When Wolsey fell, the king appointed More chancellor in his stead. Contrary to the usual practice, he refused all gifts from litigants. He soon fell into disfavour, because the king was determined to divorce Catherine of Aragon in order to marry Anne Boleyn, and More was unalterably opposed to the divorce. He therefore resigned in 1532. His incorruptibility when in office is shown by the fact that after his resignation he had only £100 a year. In spite of his opinions, the king invited him to his wedding with Anne Boleyn, but More refused the invitation. In 1534, the king got Parliament to pass the Act of Supremacy, declaring him, not the Pope, the head of the Church of England. Under this act an Oath of Supremacy was exacted, which More refused to take; this was only misprision of treason, which did not involve the death penalty. It was proved, however, by very dubious testimony, that he had said Parliament *could* not make Henry head of the Church; on this evidence he was convicted of high treason, and beheaded. His property was given to Princess Elizabeth, who kept it to the day of her death.

More is remembered almost solely on account of his *Utopia* (1518). Utopia is an island in the southern hemisphere, where everything is done in the best possible way. It has been visited accidentally by a sailor named Raphael Hythloday, who spent five years there, and only returned to Europe to make its wise institutions known.

In Utopia, as in Plato's Republic, all things are held in common, for the public good cannot flourish where there is private property, and without communism there can be no equality. More, in the dialogue, objects that communism would make men idle, and destroy respect for magistrates; to this Raphael replies that no one would say this who had lived in Utopia.

There are in Utopia fifty-four towns, all on the same plan, except that one is the capital. All the streets are twenty feet broad, and all the private houses are exactly alike, with one door onto the street and one onto the garden. There are no locks on the doors, and everyone may enter any house. The roofs are flat. Every tenth year people change houses—apparently to prevent any feeling of ownership. In the country, there are farms, each containing not fewer than forty persons, including two bondmen; each farm is under the rule of a master and mistress, who are old and wise. The chickens are not hatched by hens, but in incubators (which did not exist in More's time). All are dressed alike, except that there is a difference between the dress of men and women, and of married and unmarried. The fashions never change, and no difference is made between summer and winter clothing. At work, leather or skins are worn; a suit will last seven years. When they stop work, they throw a woollen cloak over their working clothes. All these cloaks are alike, and are the natural colour of wool. Each family makes its own clothes.

Everybody—men and women alike—works six hours a day, three before dinner and three after. All go to bed at eight, and sleep eight hours. In the early morning there are lectures, to which multitudes go, although they are not compulsory. After supper an hour is devoted to play. Six hours' work is enough, because there are no idlers and there is no useless work; with us, it is said, women, priests, rich people, servants, and beggars, mostly do nothing useful, and owing to the existence of the rich much labour is spent in producing unnecessary luxuries; all this is avoided in Utopia. Sometimes it is found that there is a surplus, and the magistrates proclaim a shorter working day for a time.

Some men are elected to become men of learning, and are exempted from other work while they are found satisfactory. All who are concerned with government are chosen from the learned. The government is a representative democracy, with a system of indirect election; at the head is a prince who is elected for life, but can be deposed for tyranny.

Family life is patriarchal; married sons live in their father's house, and are governed by him, unless he is in his dotage. If any family grows too large, the surplus children are moved into another family. If a town grows too large, some of the inhabitants are moved into another town. If all the towns are too large, a new town is built on waste land. Nothing is said as to what is to be done when all the waste land is used up. All killing of beasts for food is done by bondmen, lest free citizens should learn cruelty. There are hospitals for the sick, which are so excellent that people who are ill prefer them. Eating at home is permitted, but most people eat in common halls. Here the 'vile service' is done by bondmen, but the cooking is done by women and the waiting by the older children. Men sit at one bench, women at another; nursing mothers, with children under five, are in a separate parlour. All women nurse their own children. Children over five, if too young to be waiters, 'stand by with marvellous silence', while their elders eat; they have no separate dinner, but must be content with such scraps as are given them from the table.

As for marriage, both men and women are sharply punished if not virgin when they marry; and the householder of any house in which misconduct has occurred is liable to incur infamy for carelessness. Before marriage, bride and groom see each other naked; no one would buy a horse without first taking off the saddle and bridle, and similar considerations should apply in marriage. There is divorce for adultery or 'intolerable waywardness' of either party, but the guilty party cannot remarry. Sometimes divorce is granted solely because both parties desire it. Breakers of wedlock are punished by bondage.

There is foreign trade, chiefly for the purpose of getting iron, of which there is none in the island. Trade is used also for purposes connected with war. The Utopians think nothing of martial glory, though all learn how to fight, women as well as men. They resort to war for three purposes: to defend their own territory when invaded; to deliver the territory of an ally from invaders; and to free an oppressed nation from tyranny. But whenever they can, they get mercenaries to fight their wars for them. They aim at getting other nations into their debt, and letting them work off the debt by supplying mercenaries. For war purposes also they find a store of gold and silver useful, since they can use it to pay foreign mercenaries. For themselves, they have no money, and they teach contempt for gold by using it for chamberpots and the chains of bondmen. Pearls and diamonds are used as ornaments for infants, but never for adults. When they are at war, they offer large rewards to anyone who will kill the prince of the enemy country, and still larger rewards to anyone who will bring him alive, or to himself if he yields himself up. They pity the common people among their enemies, 'knowing that they be driven and enforced to war against their wills by the furious madness of their princes and heads'. Women fight as well as men, but no one is compelled to fight. 'Engines for war they devise and invent wondrous wittily.' It will be seen that their attitude to war is more sensible than heroic, though they display great courage when necessary.

As for ethics, we are told that they are too much inclined to think that felicity consists in pleasure. This view, however, has no bad consequences, because they think that in the next life the good are rewarded and the wicked punished. They are not ascetic, and consider fasting silly. There are many religions among them, all of which are tolerated. Almost all believe in God and immortality; the few who do not are not accounted citizens, and have no part in political life, but are otherwise unmolested. Some holy men eschew meat and matrimony; they are thought holy, but not wise. Women can be priests, if they are old and widowed. The priests are few; they have honour, but no power.

Bondmen are people condemned for heinous offences, or foreigners who have been condemned to death in their own countries, but whom the Utopians have agreed to take as bondmen.

In the case of a painful incurable disease, the patient is advised to commit suicide, but is carefully tended if he refuses to do so.

Raphael Hythloday relates that he preached Christianity to the Utopians, and that many were converted when they learnt that Christ was opposed to private property. The importance of communism is constantly stressed; almost at the end we are told that in all other nations 'I can perceive nothing but a certain conspiracy of rich men procuring their own commodities under the name and title of the common wealth.'

More's *Utopia* was in many ways astonishingly liberal. I am not thinking so much of the preaching of communism, which was in the tradition of many religious movements. I am thinking rather of what is said about war, about religion and religious toleration, against the wanton killing of animals (there is a most eloquent passage against hunting), and in favour of a mild criminal law. (The book opens with an argument against the death penalty for theft.) It must be admitted, however, that life in More's Utopia, as in most others, would be intolerably dull. Diversity is essential to happiness, and in Utopia there is hardly any. This is a defect of all planned social systems, actual as well as imaginary.

Chapter V

THE REFORMATION AND COUNTER-REFORMATION

THE Reformation and Counter-Reformation, alike, represent the rebellion of less civilized nations against the intellectual domination of Italy. In the case of the Reformation, the revolt was also political and theological: the authority of the Pope was rejected, and the tribute which he had obtained from the power of the keys ceased to be paid. In the case of the Counter-Reformation, there was only revolt against the intellectual and moral freedom of Renaissance Italy; the power of the Pope was not diminished, but enhanced, while at the same time it was made clear that his authority was incompatible with the easy-going laxity of the Borgias and Medici. Roughly speaking, the Reformation was German, the Counter-Reformation Spanish; the wars of religion were at the same time wars between Spain and its enemies, coinciding in date with the period when Spanish power was at its height.

The attitude of public opinion in northern nations towards Renaissance Italy is illustrated in the English saying of that time:

> An Englishman Italianate
> Is a devil incarnate.

It will be observed how many of the villains in Shakespeare are Italians. Iago is perhaps the most prominent instance, but an even more illustrative one is Iachimo in *Cymbeline*, who leads astray the virtuous Briton travelling in Italy, and comes to England to practise his wicked wiles upon unsuspecting natives. Moral indignation against Italians had much to do with the Reformation. Unfortunately it involved also intellectual repudiation of what Italy had done for civilization.

The three great men of the Reformation and Counter-Reformation are Luther, Calvin and Loyola. All three, intellectually, are medieval in philosophy, as compared either to the Italians who immediately preceded them, or to such men as Erasmus and More. Philosophically, the century following the beginning of the Reformation is a barren one. Luther and Calvin reverted to St Augustine, retaining, however, only that part of his teaching which deals with the relation of the soul to God, not the part which is concerned with the Church. Their theology was such as to diminish the power of the Church. They abolished purgatory, from which the souls of the dead could be delivered by masses. They rejected the doctrine of Indulgences, upon which a large part of the papal revenue depended. By the doctrine of predestination, the fate of the soul after death was made wholly independent of the actions of priests. These innovations, while they helped in the struggle with the Pope, prevented the Protestant Churches from becoming as powerful in Protestant countries as the Catholic Church was in Catholic countries. Protestant divines were (at least at first) just as bigoted as Catholic theologians, but they had less power, and were therefore less able to do harm.

Almost from the very beginning, there was a division among Protestants as to the power of the State in religious matters. Luther was willing, wherever the prince was Protestant, to recognize him as head of the Church in his own country. In England, Henry VIII and Elizabeth vigorously asserted their claims in this respect, and so did the Protestant princes of Germany, Scandinavia, and (after the revolt from Spain) Holland. This accelerated the already existing tendency to increase in the power of kings.

But those Protestants who took seriously the individualistic aspects of the Reformation were as unwilling to submit to the king as to the Pope. The Anabaptists in Germany were suppressed, but their doctrine spread to Holland and England. The conflict between Cromwell and the Long Parliament had many aspects; in its theological aspect, it was in part a conflict between those who rejected and those who accepted the view that the State should decide in religious matters. Gradually weariness resulting from the wars of religion led to the growth of belief in religious toleration, which was one of the sources of the movement which developed into eighteenth- and nineteenth-century liberalism.

Protestant success, at first amazingly rapid, was checked mainly as a resultant of Loyola's creation of the Jesuit order. Loyola had been a soldier, and his order was founded on military models; there must be unquestioning obedience to the General, and every Jesuit was to consider himself engaged in warfare against heresy. As early as the Council of Trent, the Jesuits began to be influential. They were disciplined, able, completely devoted to the cause, and skilful propagandists. Their theology was the opposite of that of the Protestants; they rejected those elements of St Augustine's teaching which the Protestants emphasized. They believed in free will, and opposed predestination. Salvation was not by faith alone, but by both faith and works. The Jesuits acquired prestige by their missionary zeal, especially in the Far East. They became popular as confessors, because (if Pascal is to be believed) they were more lenient, except towards heresy, than other ecclesiastics. They concentrated on education, and thus acquired a firm hold on the minds of the young. Whenever theology did not interfere, the education they gave was the best obtainable; we shall see that they taught Descartes more mathematics than he would have learnt elsewhere. Politically, they were a single united disciplined body, shrinking from no dangers and no exertions; they urged Catholic princes to practise relentless persecution, and, following in the wake of con- quering Spanish armies, re-established the terror of the Inquisition. even in Italy, which had had nearly a century of free-thought.

The results of the Reformation and Counter-Reformation, in the intellectual sphere, were at first wholly bad, but ultimately bene- ficial. The Thirty Years' War persuaded everybody that neither Protestants nor Catholics could be completely victorious; it became necessary to abandon the medieval hope of doctrinal unity, and this increased men's freedom to think for themselves, even about fundamentals. The diversity of creeds in different countries made it possible to escape persecution by living abroad. Disgust with theological warfare turned the attention of able men increasingly to secular learning, especially mathematics and science. These are among the reasons for the fact that, while the sixteenth century, after the rise of Luther is philosophically barren, the seventeenth contains the greatest names and makes the most notable advance since Greek times. This advance began in science, with which I shall deal in my next chapter.

Chapter VI

THE RISE OF SCIENCE

ALMOST everything that distinguishes the modern world from earlier centuries is attributable to science, which achieved its most spectacular triumphs in the seventeenth century. The Italian Renaissance, though not medieval, is not modern; it is more akin to the best age of Greece. The sixteenth century, with its absorption in theology, is more medieval than the world of Machiavelli. The modern world, so far as mental outlook is concerned, begins in the seventeeth century. No Italian of the Renaissance would have been unintelligible to Plato or Aristotle; Luther would have horrified Thomas Aquinas, but would not have been difficult for him to understand. With the seventeenth century it is different: Plato and Aristotle, Aquinas and Occam, could not have made head or tail of Newton.

The new conceptions that science introduced profoundly influenced modern philosophy. Descartes, who was in a sense the founder of modern philosophy, was himself one of the creators of seventeenth-century science. Something must be said about the methods and results of astronomy and physics before the mental atmosphere of the time in which modern philosophy began can be understood.

Four great men—Copernicus, Kepler, Galileo, and Newton—are pre-eminent in the creation of science. Of these, Copernicus belongs to the sixteenth century, but in his own time he had little influence.

Copernicus (1473-1543) was a Polish ecclesiastic, of unimpeachable orthodoxy. In his youth he travelled in Italy, and absorbed something of the atmosphere of the Renaissance. In 1500 he had a lectureship or professorship of mathematics in Rome, but in 1503 he returned to his native land, where he was a canon of Frauenburg. Much of his time seems to have been spent in combating the Germans and reforming the currency, but his leisure was devoted to astronomy. He came early to believe that the sun is at the centre of the universe, and that the earth has a twofold motion: a diurnal rotation, and an annual revolution about the sun. Fear of ecclesiastical censure led him to delay publication of his views though he allowed them to become known. His chief work, *De Revolutionibus Orbium Cœlestium*, was published in the year of his death (1543), with a preface by his friend Osiander saying that the heliocentric theory was only put forward as a hypothesis. It is uncertain how far Copernicus sanctioned this statement, but the question is not very important, as he himself made similar statements in the body of the book.[1] The book is dedicated to the Pope, and escaped official Catholic condemnation until the time of Galileo. The Church in the lifetime of Copernicus was more liberal than it became after the Council of Trent, the Jesuits, and the revived Inquisition had done their work.

The atmosphere of Copernicus's work is not modern; it might rather be described as Pythagorean. He takes it as axiomatic that all celestial motions must be circular and uniform, and like the Greeks he allows himself to be influenced by æsthetic motives. There are still epicycles in his system, though their centres are at the sun, or, rather, near the sun. The fact that the sun is not exactly in the centre marred the simplicity of his theory. Though he had heard of the Pythagorean doctrines, he does not seem to have known of Aristarchus's heliocentric theory, but there is nothing in his speculations that could not have occurred to a Greek as-tronomer. What was important in his work was the dethronement of the earth from its geometrical pre-eminence. In the long run, this made it difficult to give to man the cosmic importance assigned to him in the Christian theology, but such consequences of his theory would not have been accepted by Copernicus, whose ortho-doxy was sincere, and who protested against the view that his theory contradicted the Bible.

There were genuine difficulties in the Copernican theory. The greatest of these was the absence of stellar parallax. If the earth at any one point of its orbit is 186,000,000 miles from the point at which it will be in six months, this ought to cause a shift in the apparent positions of the stars, just as a ship at sea which is due north from one point of the coast will not be due north from another. No parallax was observed, and Copernicus rightly inferred that the fixed stars must be very much more remote than the sun. It was not till the nineteenth century that the technique of measure-ment became sufficiently precise for stellar parallax to be observed, and then only in the case of a few of the nearest stars.

Another difficulty arose as regards falling bodies. If the earth is continually rotating from west to east, a body dropped from a height ought not to fall to a point vertically below its starting-point, but to a point somewhat further west, since the earth will have slipped away a certain distance during the time of the fall. To this difficulty the answer was found by Galileo's law of inertia, but in

[1] See *Three Copernican Treatises*, translated by Edward Rosen, Chicago, 1939.

the time of Copernicus no answer was forthcoming.

There is an interesting book by E. A. Burtt, called *The Metaphysical Foundations of Modern Physical Science* (1925), which sets forth with much force the many unwarrantable assumptions made by the men who founded modern science. He points out quite truly that there were in the time of Copernicus no known facts which compelled the adoption of his system, and several which militated against it. 'Contemporary empiricists, had they lived in the sixteenth century, would have been the first to scoff out of court the new philosophy of the universe.' The general purpose of the book is to discredit modern science by suggesting that its discoveries were lucky accidents springing by chance from superstitions as gross as those of the Middle Ages. I think this shows a misconception of the scientific attitude: it is not *what* the man of science believes that distinguishes him, but *how* and *why* he believes it. His beliefs are tentative, not dogmatic; they are based on evidence, not on authority or intuition. Copernicus was right to call his theory a hypothesis; his opponents were wrong in thinking new hypotheses undesirable.

The men who founded modern science had two merits which are not necessarily found together: immense patience in observation, and great boldness in framing hypotheses. The second of these merits had belonged to the earliest Greek philosophers; the first existed, to a considerable degree, in the later astronomers of antiquity. But no one among the ancients, except perhaps Aristarchus, possessed both merits, and no one in the Middle Ages possessed either. Copernicus, like his great successors, possessed both. He knew all that could be known, with the instruments existing in his day, about the apparent motions of the heavenly bodies on the celestial sphere, and he perceived that the diurnal rotation of the earth was a more economical hypothesis than the revolution of all the celestial spheres. According to modern views, which regard all motion as relative, simplicity is the only gain resulting from his hypothesis, but this was not his view or that of his contemporaries. As regards the earth's annual revolution, there was again a simplification, but not so notable a one as in the case of the diurnal rotation. Copernicus still needed epicycles, though fewer than were needed in the Ptolemaic system. It was not until Kepler discovered his laws that the new theory acquired its full simplicity.

Apart from the revolutionary effect on cosmic imagination, the great merits of the new astronomy were two: first, the recognition that what had been believed since ancient times might be false; second, that the test of scientific truth is patient collection of facts, combined with bold guessing as to laws binding the facts together.

Neither merit is so fully developed in Copernicus as in his successors, but both are already present in a high degree in his work.

Some of the men to whom Copernicus communicated his theory were German Lutherans, but when Luther came to know of it, he was profoundly shocked. 'People give ear,' he said, 'to an upstart astrologer who strove to show that the earth revolves, not the heavens or the firmament, the sun and the moon. Whoever wishes to appear clever must devise some new system, which of all systems is of course the very best. This fool wishes to reverse the entire science of astronomy; but sacred Scripture tells us that Joshua commanded the sun to stand still, and not the earth.' Calvin similarly, demolished Copernicus with the text: 'The world also is stablished, that it cannot be moved' (Psa. xciii. 1), and exclaimed . 'Who will venture to place the authority of Copernicus above that of the Holy Spirit?' Protestant clergy were at least as bigoted as Catholic ecclesiastics; nevertheless there soon came to be much more liberty of speculation in Protestant than in Catholic countries, because in Protestant countries the clergy had less power. The important aspect of Protestantism was schism, not heresy, for schism led to national Churches, and national Churches were not strong enough to control the lay government. This was wholly a gain, for the Churches, everywhere, opposed as long as they could practically every innovation that made for an increase of happiness or knowledge here on earth.

Copernicus was not in a position to give any conclusive evidence in favour of his hypothesis, and for a long time astronomers rejected it. The next astronomer of importance was Tycho Brahe (1546-1601), who adopted an intermediate position: he held that the sun and moon go round the earth, but the planets go round the sun. As regards theory he was not very original. He gave, however, two good reasons against Aristotle's view that everything above the moon is unchanging. One of these was the appearance of a new star in 1572, which was found to have no daily parallax, and must therefore be more distant than the moon. The other reason was derived from observation of comets, which were also found to be distant. The reader will remember Aristotle's doctrine that change and decay are confined to the sublunary sphere; this, like everything else that Aristotle said on scientific subjects, proved an obstacle to progress.

The importance of Tycho Brahe was not as a theorist, but as an observer, first under the patronage of the king of Denmark, then under the Emperor Rudolf II. He made a star catalogue, and noted the positions of the planets throughout many years. Towards the end of his life Kepler, then a young man, became his assistant. To Kepler his observations were invaluable.

Kepler (1571-1630) is one of the most notable examples of what can be achieved by patience without much in the way of genius. He was the first important astronomer after Copernicus to adopt the heliocentric theory, but Tycho Brahe's data showed that it could not be quite right in the form given to it by Copernicus. He was influenced by Pythagoreanism, and more or less fancifully inclined to sun-worship, though a good Protestant. These motives no doubt gave him a bias in favour of the heliocentric hypothesis. His Pythagoreanism also inclined him to follow Plato's *Timaeus* in supposing that cosmic significance must attach to the five regular solids. He used them to suggest hypotheses to his mind; at last, by good luck, one of these worked.

Kepler's great achievement was the discovery of his three laws of planetary motion. Two of these he published in 1609, and the third in 1619. His first law states: The planets describe elliptic orbits, of which the sun occupies one focus. His second law states: The line joining a planet to the sun sweeps out equal areas in equal times. His third law states: The square of the period of revolution of a planet is proportional to the cube of its average distance from the sun.

Something must be said in explanation of the importance of these laws.

The first two laws, in Kepler's time, could only be *proved* in the case of Mars; as regards the other planets, the observations were compatible with them, but not such as to establish them definitely. It was not long, however, before decisive confirmation was found.

The discovery of the first law, that the planets move in ellipses, required a greater effort of emancipation from tradition than a modern man can easily realize. The one thing upon which all astronomers, without exception, had been agreed, was that all celestial motions are circular, or compounded of circular motions. Where circles were found inadequate to explain planetary motions, epicycles were used. An epicycle is the curve traced by a point on a circle which rolls on another circle. For example: take a big wheel and fasten it flat on the ground; take a smaller wheel (also flat on the ground) which has a nail through it, and roll the smaller wheel round the big wheel, with the point of the nail touching the ground. Then the mark of the nail in the ground will trace out an epicycle. The orbit of the moon, in relation to the sun, is roughly of this kind: approximately, the earth describes a circle round the sun, and the moon meanwhile describes a circle round the earth. But this is only an approximation. As observation grew more exact, it was found that no system of epicycles would exactly fit the facts. Kepler's hypothesis, he found, was far more closely in accord with the recorded positions of Mars than was that of Ptolemy, or even that of Copernicus.

The substitution of ellipses for circles involved the abandonment of the æsthetic bias which had governed astronomy ever since Pythagoras. The circle was a perfect figure, and the celestial orbs were perfect bodies—originally gods, and even in Plato and Aristotle closely related to gods. It seemed obvious that a perfect body must move in a perfect figure. Moreover, since the heavenly bodies move freely, without being pushed or pulled, their motion must be 'natural'. Now it was easy to suppose that there is something 'natural' about a circle, but not about an ellipse. Thus many deep-seated prejudices had to be discarded before Kepler's first law could be accepted. No ancient, not even Aristarchus of Samos, had anticipated such an hypothesis.

The second law deals with the varying velocity of the planet at different points of its orbit. If S is the sun, and P_1, P_2 P_3, P_4 P_5 are successive positions of the planet at equal intervals of time—say at intervals of a month—then Kepler's law states that the areas P_1SP_2, P_2SP_3, P_3SP_4, P_4SP_5 are all equal. The planet therefore moves fastest when it is nearest to the sun, and slowest when it is farthest from it. This, again, was shocking; a planet ought to be too stately to hurry at one time and dawdle at another.

The third law was important because it compared the movements of different planets, whereas the first two laws dealt with the several planets singly. The third law says: If r is the average distance of a planet from the sun, and T is the length of its year, then r^3 divided by T^2 is the same for all the different planets. This law afforded the proof (as far as the solar system is concerned) of Newton's law of the inverse square for gravitation. But of this we shall speak later.

Galileo (1564-1642) is the greatest of the founders of modern science, with the possible exception of Newton. He was born on about the day on which Michelangelo died, and he died in the year in which Newton was born. I commend these facts to those (if any) who still believe in metempsychosis. He is important as an astronomer, but perhaps even more as the founder of dynamics.

Galileo first discovered the importance of *acceleration* in dynamics. 'Acceleration' means change of velocity, whether in magnitude or direction; thus a body moving uniformly in a circle has at all times an acceleration towards the centre of the circle. In the language that had been customary before this time, we might say that he treated uniform motion in a straight line as alone 'natural', whether on earth or in the heavens. It had been thought 'natural' for heavenly bodies to move in circles, and for terrestrial bodies to move in straight lines; but moving terrestrial bodies, it was thought, would gradually cease to move if they were let alone. Galileo held, as against this view, that every body, if left alone, will continue to move in a straight line with uniform velocity; any change, either in the rapidity or the direction of motion, requires to be explained as due to the action of some 'force'. This principle was enunciated by Newton as the 'first law of motion'. It is also called the law of inertia. I shall return to its purport later, but first something must be said as to the detail of Galileo's discoveries.

Galileo was the first to establish the law of falling bodies. This law, given the concept of acceleration', is of the utmost simplicity. It says that, when a body is falling freely, its acceleration is constant, except in so far as the resistance of the air may interfere; further, the acceleration is the same for all bodies, heavy or light, great or small. The complete proof of this law was not possible until the air pump had been invented, which was about 1654. After this, it was possible to observe bodies falling in what was practically a vacuum, and it was found that feathers fell as fast as lead. What Galileo proved was that there is no measurable difference between large and small lumps of the same substance. Until his time it had been supposed that a large lump of lead would fall much quicker than a small one, but Galileo proved by experiment that this is not the case. Measurement, in his day, was not such an accurate business as it has since become; nevertheless he arrived at the true law of falling bodies. If a body is falling freely in a vacuum, its velocity increases at a constant rate. At the end of the first second, its velocity will be 32 feet per second; at the end of another second, 64 feet per second; at the end of the third, 96 feet per second; and so on. The acceleration, i.e. the rate at which the velocity increases, is always the same; in each second, the increase of velocity is (approximately) 32 feet per second.

Galileo also studied projectiles, a subject of importance to his employer, the duke of Tuscany. It had been thought that a projectile fired horizontally will move horizontally for a while, and then suddenly begin to fall vertically. Galileo showed that, apart from the resistance of the air, the horizontal velocity would remain constant, in accordance with the law of inertia, but a vertical velocity would be added, which would grow according to the law of falling bodies. To find out how the projectile will move during some short time, say a second, after it has been in flight for some time, we proceed as follows: First, if it were not falling, it would cover a certain horizontal distance, equal to that which it covered in the first second of its flight. Second, if it were not moving horizontally, but merely falling, it would fall vertically with a velocity proportional to the time since the flight began. In fact, its change of place is what it would be if it first moved horizontally for a second with the initial velocity, and then fell vertically for a second with a velocity proportional to the time during which it has been in flight. A simple calculation shows that its consequent course is a parabola, and this is confirmed by observation except in so far as the resistance of the air interferes.

The above gives a simple instance of a principle which proved immensely fruitful in dynamics, the principle that, when several forces act simultaneously, the effect is as if each acted in turn. This is part of a more general principle called the parallelogram law. Suppose, for example, that you are on the deck of a moving ship, and you walk across the deck. While you are walking the ship has moved on, so that, in relation to the water, you have moved both forward and across the direction of the ship's motion. If you want to know where you will have got to in relation to the water, you may suppose that first you stood still while the ship moved, and then, for an equal time, the ship stood still while you walked across it. The same principle applies to forces. This makes it possible to work out the total effect of a number of forces, and makes it feasible to analyse physical phenomena, discovering the separate laws of the several forces to which moving bodies are subject. It was Galileo who introduced this immensely fruitful method.

In what I have been saying, I have tried to speak, as nearly as possible, in the language of the seventeenth century. Modern language is different in important respects, but to explain what the seventeenth century achieved it is desirable to adopt its modes of expression for the time being.

The law of inertia explained a puzzle which, before Galileo, the Copernican system had been unable to explain. As observed above, if you drop a stone from the top of a tower, it will fall at the foot of the tower, not somewhat to the west of it; yet, if the earth is rotating, it ought to have slipped away a certain distance during the fall of the stone. The reason this does not happen is that the stone retains the velocity of rotation which, before being dropped, it shared with everything else on the earth's surface. In fact, if the tower were high enough, there would be the opposite effect to that expected by the opponents of Copernicus. The top of the tower, being further from the centre of the earth than the bottom, is moving faster, and therefore the stone should fall slightly to the east of the foot of the tower. This effect, however, would be too slight to be measurable.

Galileo ardently adopted the heliocentric system; he corresponded with Kepler, and accepted his discoveries. Having heard that a Dutchman had lately invented a telescope, Galileo made one himself, and very quickly discovered a number of important things. He found that the Milky Way consists of a multitude of separate stars. He observed the phases of Venus, which Copernicus knew to be implied by his theory, but which the naked eye was unable to perceive. He discovered the satellites of Jupiter, which, in honour of his employer, he called 'sidera medicea'. It was found that these satellites obey Kepler's laws. There was, however, a difficulty. There had always been seven heavenly bodies, the five planets and the sun and moon; now seven is a sacred number. Is not the Sabbath the seventh day? Were there not the seven-branched candlesticks and the seven churches of Asia? What, then, could be more appropriate than that there should be seven heavenly bodies? But if we have to add Jupiter's four moons, that makes eleven—a number which has no mystic properties. On this ground the traditionalists denounced the telescope, refused to look through it, and maintained that it revealed only delusions. Galileo wrote to Kepler wishing they could have a good laugh together at the stupidity of 'the mob'; the rest of his letter makes it plain that 'the mob' consisted of the professors of philosophy, who tried to conjure away Jupiter's moons, using 'logic-chopping arguments as though they were magical incantations'.

Galileo, as everyone knows, was condemned by the Inquisition, first privately in 1616, and then publicly in 1633, on which latter occasion he recanted, and promised never again to maintain that the earth rotates or revolves. The Inquisition was successful in putting an end to science in Italy, which did not revive there for centuries. But it failed to prevent men of science from adopting the heliocentric theory, and did considerable damage to the Church by its stupidity. Fortunately there were Protestant countries, where the clergy, however anxious to do harm to science, were unable to gain control of the State.

Newton (1642-1727) achieved the final and complete triumph for which Copernicus, Kepler, and Galileo had prepared the way. Starting from his three laws of motion—of which the first two are due to Galileo—he proved that Kepler's three laws are equivalent to the proposition that every planet, at every moment, has an acceleration towards the sun which varies inversely as the square of the distance from the sun. He showed that acceleration towards the earth and sun, following the same formula, explains the moon's motion, and that the acceleration of falling bodies on the earth's surface is again related to that of the moon according to the inverse square law. He defined 'force' as the cause of change of motion, i.e. of acceleration. He was thus able to enunciate his law of universal gravitation: 'Every body attracts every other with a force directly proportional to the product of their masses and inversely proportional to the square of the distance between them.' From this formula he was able to deduce everything in planetary theory: the motions of the planets and their satellites, the orbits of comets, the tides. It appeared later that even the minute departures from elliptical orbits on the part of the planets were deducible from Newton's law. The triumph was so complete that Newton was in danger of becoming another Aristotle, and imposing an insuperable barrier to progress. In England, it was not till a century after his death that men freed themselves from his authority sufficiently to do important original work in the subjects of which he had treated.

The seventeenth century was remarkable, not only in astronomy and dynamics, but in many other ways connected with science.

Take first the question of scientific instruments.[1] The compound microscope was invented just before the seventeenth century, about 1590. The telescope was invented in 1608, by a Dutchman named Lippershey, though it was Galileo who first made serious use of it for scientific purposes. Galileo also invented the thermometer—at least, this seems most probable. His pupil Torricelli invented the barometer. Guericke (1602-86) invented the air pump. Clocks, though not new, were greatly improved in the seventeenth century, largely by the work of Galileo. Owing to these inventions, scientific observation became immensely more exact and more extensive than it had been at any former time.

Next, there was important work in other sciences than astronomy and dynamics. Gilbert (1540-1603) published his great book on the magnet in 1600. Harvey (1578-1657) discovered the circulation of the blood, and published his discovery in 1628. Leeuwenhoek (1632-1723) discovered spermatozoa, though another man, Stephen Hamm, had discovered them, apparently, a few months earlier; Leeuwenhoek also discovered protozoa or unicellular organisms, and even bacteria. Robert Boyle (1627-91) was, as children were taught when I was young, 'the father of chemistry and son of the Earl of Cork'; he is now chiefly remembered on account of 'Boyle's Law', that in a given quantity of gas at a given temperature, pressure is inversely proportional to volume.

I have hitherto said nothing of the advances in pure mathematics, but these were very great indeed, and were indispensable to much

[1] On this subject, see the chapter 'Scientific Instruments' in *A History of Science, Technology, and Philosophy in the Sixteenth and Seventeenth Centuries*, by A. Wolf.

of the work in the physical sciences. Napier published his invention of logarithms in 1614. Co-ordinate geometry resulted from the work of several seventeenth-century mathematicians, among whom the greatest contribution was made by Descartes. The differential and integral calculus was invented independently by Newton and Leibniz; it is the instrument for almost all higher mathematics. These are only the most outstanding achievements in pure mathematics; there were innumerable others of great importance.

The result of the scientific work we have been considering was that the outlook of educated men was completely transformed. At the beginning of the century, Sir Thomas Browne took part in trials for witchcraft; at the end, such a thing would have been impossible. In Shakespeare's time, comets were still portents; after the publication of Newton's *Principia* in 1687, it was known that he and Halley had calculated the orbits of certain comets, and that they were as obedient as the planets to the law of gravitation. The reign of law had established its hold on men's imaginations, making such things as magic and sorcery incredible. In 1700 the mental outlook of educated men was completely modern; in 1600, except among a very few, it was still largely medieval.

In the remainder of this chapter I shall try to state briefly the philosophical beliefs which appeared to follow from seventeenth-century science, and some of the respects in which modern science differs from that of Newton.

The first thing to note is the removal of almost all traces of animism from the laws of physics. The Greeks, though they did not say so explicitly, evidently considered the power of movement a sign of life. To common-sense observation it seems that animals move themselves, while dead matter only moves when impelled by an external force. The soul of an animal, in Aristotle, has various functions, and one of them is to move the animal's body. The sun and planets, in Greek thinking, are apt to be gods, or at least regulated and moved by gods. Anaxagoras thought otherwise, but was impious. Democritus thought otherwise, but was neglected, except by the Epicureans, in favour of Plato and Aristotle. Aristotle's forty-seven or fifty-five unmoved movers are divine spirits, and are the ultimate source of all the motion in the heavens. Left to itself, any inanimate body would soon become motionless; thus the operation of soul on matter has to be continuous if motion is not to cease.

All this was changed by the first law of motion. Lifeless matter, once set moving, will continue to move for ever unless stopped by some external cause. Moreover the external causes of change of motion turned out to be themselves material, whenever they could be definitely ascertained. The solar system, at any rate, was kept going by its own momentum and its own laws; no outside interference was needed. There might still seem to be need of God to set the mechanism working; the planets, according to Newton, were originally hurled by the hand of God. But when He had done this, and decreed the law of gravitation, everything went on by itself without further need of divine intervention. When Laplace suggested that the same forces which are now operative might have caused the planets to grow out of the sun, God's share in the course of nature was pushed still further back. He might remain as Creator, but even that was doubtful, since it was not clear that the world had a beginning in time. Although most of the men of science were models of piety, the outlook suggested by their work was disturbing to orthodoxy, and the theologians were quite justified in feeling uneasy.

Another thing that resulted from science was a profound change in the conception of man's place in the universe. In the medieval world, the earth was the centre of the heavens, and everything had a purpose concerned with man. In the Newtonian world, the earth was a minor planet of a not specially distinguished star; astronomical distances were so vast that the earth, in comparison, was a mere pin-point. It seemed unlikely that this immense apparatus was all designed for the good of certain small creatures on this pin-point. Moreover purpose, which had since Aristotle formed an intimate part of the conception of science, was now thrust out of scientific procedure. Anyone might still believe that the heavens exist to declare the glory of God, but no one could let this belief intervene in an astronomical calculation. The world might have a purpose, but purposes could no longer enter into scientific explanations.

The Copernican theory should have been humbling to human pride, but in fact the contrary effect was produced, for the triumphs of science revived human pride. The dying ancient world had been obsessed with a sense of sin, and had bequeathed this as an oppression to the Middle Ages. To be humble before God was both right and prudent, for God would punish pride. Pestilences, floods, earthquakes, Turks, Tartars, and comets perplexed the gloomy centuries, and it was felt that only greater and greater humility would avert these real or threatened calamities. But it became impossible to remain humble when men were achieving such triumphs:

> Nature and Nature's laws lay hid in night.
> God said 'Let Newton be', and all was light.

And as for damnation, surely the Creator of so vast a universe had something better to think about than sending men to hell for minute theological errors. Judas Iscariot might be damned, but not Newton, though he were an Arian.

There were of course many other reasons for self-satisfaction. The Tartars had been confined to Asia, and the Turks were ceasing to be a menace. Comets had been humbled by Halley, and as for earthquakes, though they were still formidable, they were so interesting that men of science could hardly regret them. Western Europeans were growing rapidly richer, and were becoming lords of all the world: they had conquered North and South America, they were powerful in Africa and India, respected in China and feared in Japan. When to all this were added the triumphs of science, it is no wonder that the men of the seventeenth century felt themselves to be fine fellows, not the miserable sinners that they still proclaimed themselves on Sundays.

There are some respects in which the concepts of modern theoretical physics differ from those of the Newtonian system. To begin with, the conception of 'force', which is prominent in the seventeenth century, has been found to be superfluous. 'Force', in Newton, is the cause of change of motion, whether in magnitude or direction. The notion of cause is regarded as important, and force is conceived imaginatively as the sort of thing that we experience when we push or pull. For this reason it was considered an objection to gravitation that it acted at a distance, and Newton himself conceded that there must be some medium by which it was transmitted. Gradually it was found that all the equations could be written down without bringing in forces. What was observable was a certain relation between acceleration and configuration; to say that this relation was brought about by the intermediacy of 'force' was to add nothing to our knowledge. Observation shows that planets have at all times an acceleration towards the sun, which varies inversely as the square of their distance from it. To say that this is due to the 'force' of gravitation is merely verbal, like saying that opium makes people sleep because it has a dormitive virtue. The modern physicist, therefore, merely states formulae which determine accelerations, and avoids the word 'force' altogether. 'Force' was the faint ghost of the vitalist view as to the causes of motions, and gradually the ghost has been exorcized.

Until the coming of quantum mechanics, nothing happened to modify in any degree what is the essential purport of the first two laws of motion, namely this: that the laws of dynamics are to be stated in terms of accelerations. In this respect, Copernicus and Kepler are still to be classed with the ancients; they sought laws stating the shapes of the orbits of the heavenly bodies. Newton made it clear that laws stated in this form could never be more than approximate. The planets do not move in *exact* ellipses, because of the perturbations caused by the attractions of other planets. Nor is the orbit of a planet ever exactly repeated, for the same reason. But the law of gravitation, which dealt with accelerations, was very simple, and was thought to be quite exact until two hundred years after Newton's time. When it was amended by Einstein, it still remained a law dealing with accelerations.

It is true that the conservation of energy is a law dealing with velocities, not accelerations. But in calculations which use this law it is still accelerations that have to be employed.

As for the changes introduced by quantum mechanics, they are very profound, but still, to some degree, a matter of controversy and uncertainty.

There is one change from the Newtonian philosophy which must be mentioned now, and that is the abandonment of absolute space and time. The reader will remember a mention of this question in connection with Democritus. Newton believed in a space composed of points, and a time composed of instants, which had an existence independent of the bodies and events that occupied them. As regards space, he had an empirical argument to support his view, namely that physical phenomena enable us to distinguish absolute rotation. If the water in a bucket is rotated, it climbs up the sides and is depressed in the centre; but if the bucket is rotated while the water is not, there is no such effect. Since his day, the experiment of Foucault's pendulum has been devised, giving what has been considered a demonstration of the earth's rotation. Even on the most modern views, the question of absolute rotation presents difficulties. If all motion is relative, the difference between the hypothesis that the earth rotates and the hypothesis that the heavens revolve is purely verbal; it is no more than the difference between 'John is the father of James' and 'James is the son of John'. But if the heavens revolve, the stars move faster than light, which is considered impossible. It cannot be said that the modern answers to this difficulty are completely satisfying, but they are sufficiently satisfying to cause almost all physicists to accept the view that motion and space are purely relative. This, combined with the amalgamation of space and time into space-time, has considerably altered our view of the universe from that which resulted from the work of Galileo and Newton. But of this, as of quantum theory, I will say no more at this time.

Chapter VII

FRANCIS BACON

FRANCIS BACON (1561-1626), although his philosophy is in many ways unsatisfactory, has permanent importance as the founder of modern inductive method and the pioneer in the attempt at logical systematization of scientific procedure.

He was a son of Sir Nicholas Bacon, Lord Keeper of the Great Seal, and his aunt was the wife of Sir William Cecil, afterwards Lord Burghley; he thus grew up in the atmosphere of State affairs. He entered Parliament at the age of twenty-three, and became adviser to Essex. None the less, when Essex fell from favour he helped in his prosecution. For this he has been severely blamed: Lytton Strachey, for example, in his *Elizabeth and Essex*, represents Bacon as a monster of treachery and ingratitude. This is quite unjust. He worked with Essex while Essex was loyal, but abandoned him when continued loyalty to him would have been treasonable; in this there was nothing that even the most rigid moralist of the age could condemn.

In spite of his abandonment of Essex, he was never completely in favour during the lifetime of Queen Elizabeth. With James's accession, however, his prospects improved. In 1617 he acquired his father's office of Keeper of the Great Seal, and in 1618 he became Lord Chancellor. But after he had held this great position for only two years, he was prosecuted for accepting bribes from litigants. He admitted the truth of the accusation, pleading only that presents never influenced his decision. As to that, anyone may form his own opinion, since there can be no evidence as to the decisions that Bacon would have come to in other circumstances. He was condemned to a fine of £40,000, to imprisonment in the Tower during the king's pleasure, to perpetual banishment from Court and inability to hold office. This sentence was only very partially executed. He was not forced to pay the fine, and he was kept to the Tower for only four days. But he was compelled to abandon public life, and to spend the remainder of his days to writing important books.

The ethics of the legal profession, in those days, were somewhat lax. Almost every judge accepted presents, usually from both sides. Nowadays we think it atrocious for a judge to take bribes, but even more atrocious, after taking them, to decide against the givers of them. In those days, presents were a matter of course, and a judge showed his 'virtue' by not being influenced by them. Bacon was condemned as an incident in a party squabble, not because he was exceptionally guilty. He was not a man of outstanding moral eminence, like his forerunner Sir Thomas More, but he was also not exceptionally wicked. Morally, he was an average man, no better and no worse than the bulk of his contemporaries.

After five years spent in retirement, he died of a chill caught while experimenting on refrigeration by stuffing a chicken full of snow.

Bacon's most important book, *The Advancement of Learning*, is in many ways remarkably modern. He is commonly regarded as the originator of the saying 'Knowledge is power', and though he may have had predecessors who said the same thing, he said it with new emphasis. The whole basis of his philosophy was practical: to give mankind mastery over the forces of nature by means of scientific discoveries and inventions. He held that philosophy should be kept separate from theology, not intimately blended with it as in scholasticism. He accepted orthodox religion; he was not the man to quarrel with the government on such a matter. But while he thought that reason could show the existence of God, he regarded everything else in theology as known only by revelation. Indeed he held that the triumph of faith is greatest when to the unaided reason a dogma appears most absurd. Philosophy, however, should depend only upon reason. He was thus an advocate of the doctrine of 'double truth', that of reason and that of revelation. This doctrine had been preached by certain Averroists in the thirteenth century, but had been condemned by the Church. The 'triumph of faith' was, for the orthodox, a dangerous device. Bayle, in the late seventeenth century, made ironical use of it, setting forth at great length all that reason could say against some orthodox belief, and then concluding 'so much the greater is the triumph of faith in nevertheless believing'. How far Bacon's orthodoxy was sincere it is impossible to know.

Bacon was the first of the long line of scientifically minded philosophers who have emphasized the importance of induction as opposed to deduction. Like most of his successors, he tried to find some better kind of induction than what is called 'induction by simple enumeration'. Induction by simple enumeration may be illustrated by a parable. There was once upon a time a census officer who had to record the names of all householders in a certain Welsh village. The first that he questioned was called William Williams; so were the second, third, fourth. . . . At last he said to himself: 'This is tedious; evidently they are all called William Williams. I

527

shall put them down so and take a holiday.' But he was wrong; there was just one whose name was John Jones. This shows that we may go astray if we trust too implicitly to induction by simple enumeration.

Bacon believed that he had a method by which induction could be made something better than this. He wished, for example, to discover the nature of heat, which he supposed (rightly) to consist of rapid irregular motions of the small parts of bodies. His method was to make lists of hot bodies, lists of cold bodies, and lists of bodies of varying degrees of heat. He hoped that these lists would show some characteristic always present in hot bodies and absent in cold bodies, and present in varying degrees in bodies of different degrees of heat. By this method he expected to arrive at general laws, having, in the first instance, the lowest degree of generality. From a number of such laws he hoped to reach laws of the second degree of generality, and so on. A suggested law should be tested by being applied in new circumstances; if it worked in these circumstances it was to that extent confirmed. Some instances are specially valuable because they enable us to decide between two theories, each possible as far as previous observations are concerned; such instances are called 'prerogative' instances.

Bacon not only despised the syllogism, but undervalued mathematics, presumably as insufficiently experimental. He was virulently hostile to Aristotle, but thought very highly of Democritus. Although he did not deny that the course of nature exemplifies a divine purpose, he objected to any admixture of teleological explanation in the actual investigation of phenomena; everything, he held, should be explained as following necessarily from efficient causes.

He valued his method as showing how to arrange the observational data upon which science must be based. We ought, he says, to be neither like spiders, which spin things out of their own insides, nor like ants, which merely collect, but like bees, which both collect and arrange. This is somewhat unfair to the ants, but it illustrates Bacon's meaning.

One of the most famous parts of Bacon's philosophy is his enumeration of what he calls 'idols', by which he means bad habits of mind that cause people to fall into error. Of these he enumerates four kinds. 'Idols of the tribe' are those that are inherent in human nature; he mentions in particular the habit of expecting more order in natural phenomena than is actually to be found. 'Idols of the cave' are personal prejudices, characteristic of the particular investigator. 'Idols of the market-place' are those that have to do with the tyranny of words. 'Idols of the theatre' are those that have to do with received systems of thought; of these, naturally, Aristotle and the scholastics afforded him the most noteworthy instances.

Although science was what interested Bacon, and although his general outlook was scientific, he missed most of what was being done in science in his day. He rejected the Copernican theory, which was excusable so far as Copernicus himself was concerned, since he did not advance any very solid arguments. But Bacon ought to have been convinced by Kepler, whose *New Astronomy* appeared in 1609. Bacon appears not to have known of the work of Vesalius, the pioneer of modern anatomy, though he admired Gilbert, whose work on magnetism brilliantly illustrated inductive method. Surprisingly, he seemed unconscious of the work of Harvey, although Harvey was his medical attendant. It is true that Harvey did not publish his discovery of the circulation of the blood until after Bacon's death, but one would have supposed that Bacon would have been aware of his researches. Harvey had no very high opinion of him, saying 'he writes philosophy like a Lord Chancellor'. No doubt Bacon could have done better if he had been less concerned with worldly success.

Bacon's inductive method is faulty through insufficient emphasis on hypothesis. He hoped that mere orderly arrangement of data would make the right hypothesis obvious, but this is seldom the case. As a rule, the framing of hypotheses is the most difficult part of scientific work, and the part where great ability is indispensable. So far, no method has been found which would make it possible to invent hypotheses by rule. Usually some hypothesis is a necessary preliminary to the collection of facts, since the selection of facts demands some way of determining relevance. Without something of this kind, the mere multiplicity of facts is baffling.

The part played by deduction in science is greater than Bacon supposed. Often, when a hypothesis has to be tested, there is a long deductive journey from the hypothesis to some consequence that can be tested by observation. Usually the deduction is mathematical, and in this respect Bacon underestimated the importance of mathematics in scientific investigation.

The problem of induction by simple enumeration remains unsolved to this day. Bacon was quite right in rejecting simple enumeration where the details of scientific investigation are concerned, for in dealing with details we may assume general laws on the basis of which, so long as they are taken as valid, more or less cogent methods can be built up. John Stuart Mill framed four canons of inductive method, which can be usefully employed so long as the law of causality is assumed; but this law itself, he had to confess, is to be accepted solely on the basis of induction by simple enumeration. The thing that is achieved by the theoretical organization of science is the collection of all subordinate inductions into a few that are very comprehensive—perhaps only one. Such comprehensive inductions are confirmed by so many instances that it is thought legitimate to accept, as regards them, an induction by simple enumeration. This situation is profoundly unsatisfactory, but neither Bacon nor any of his successors have found a way out of it.

Chapter VIII

HOBBES'S LEVIATHAN

Hobbes (1588-1679) is a philosopher whom it is difficult to classify. He was an empiricist, like Locke, Berkeley, and Hume, but unlike them, he was an admirer of mathematical method, not only in pure mathematics, but in its applications. His general outlook was inspired by Galileo rather than Bacon. From Descartes to Kant, Continental philosophy derived much of its conception of the nature of human knowledge from mathematics, but it regarded mathematics as known independently of experience. It was thus led, like Platonism, to minimize the part played by pure thought. English empiricism, on the other hand, was little influenced by mathematics, and tended to have a wrong conception of scientific method. Hobbes had neither of these defects. It is not until our own day that we find any other philosophers who were empiricists and yet laid due stress on mathematics. In this respect, Hobbes's merit is great. He has, however, grave defects, which make it impossible to place him quite in the first rank. He is impatient of subtleties, and too much inclined to cut the Gordian knot. His solutions of problems are logical, but are attained by omitting awkward facts. He is vigorous, but crude; he wields the battle-axe better than the rapier. Nevertheless, his theory of the State deserves to be carefully considered, the more so as it is more modern than any previous theory, even that of Machiavelli.

Hobbes's father was a vicar, who was ill-tempered and uneducated; he lost his job by quarrelling with a neighbouring vicar at the church door. After this, Hobbes was brought up by an uncle. He acquired a good knowledge of the classics, and translated *The Medea* of Euripides into Latin iambics at the age of fourteen. (In later life, he boasted, justifiably, that though he abstained from quoting classical poets and orators, this was not from lack of familiarity with their works.) At fifteen, he went to Oxford, where they taught him scholastic logic and the philosophy of Aristotle. These were his bugbears in later life, and he maintained that he had profited little by his years at the university; indeed universities in general are constantly criticized in his writings. In the year 1610, when he was twenty-two years old, he became tutor to Lord Hardwick (afterwards second Earl of Devonshire), with whom he made the grand tour. It was at this time that he began to know the work of Galileo and Kepler, which profoundly influenced him. His pupil became his patron, and remained so until he died in 1628. Through him, Hobbes met Ben Jonson and Bacon and Lord Herbert of Cherbury, and many other important men. After the death of the Earl of Devonshire, who left a young son, Hobbes lived for a time in Paris, where he began the study of Euclid; then he became tutor to his former pupil's son. With him he travelled to Italy, where he visited Galileo in 1636. In 1637 he came back to England.

The political opinions expressed in the *Leviathan*, which were Royalist in the extreme, had been held by Hobbes for a long time. When the Parliament of 1628 drew up the Petition of Right, he published a translation of Thucydides, with the expressed intention of showing the evils of democracy. When the Long Parliament met in 1640, and Laud and Strafford were sent to the Tower, Hobbes was terrified and fled to France. His book, *De Cive*, written in 1641, though not published till 1647, sets forth essentially the same theory as that of the *Leviathan*. It was not the actual occurrence of the Civil War that caused his opinions, but the prospect of it; naturally, however, his convictions were strengthened when his fears were realized.

In Paris he was welcomed by many of the leading mathematicians and men of science. He was one of those who saw Descartes' *Meditations* before they were published, and wrote objections to them, which were printed by Descartes with his replies. He also soon had a large company of English Royalist refugees with whom to associate. For a time, from 1646 to 1648, he taught mathematics to the future Charles II. When, however, in 1651, he published the *Leviathan*, it pleased no one. Its rationalism offended most of the refugees, and its bitter attacks on the Catholic Church offended the French Government. Hobbes therefore fled secretly to London, where he made submission to Cromwell, and abstained from all political activity.

He was not idle, however, either at this time or at any other during his long life. He had a controversy with Bishop Bramhall on free will; he was himself a rigid determinist. Over-estimating his own capacities as a geometer, he imagined that he had discovered how to square the circle; on this subject he very foolishly embarked on a controversy with Wallis, the professor of geometry at Oxford. Naturally the professor succeeded in making him look silly.

At the Restoration, Hobbes was taken up by the less earnest of the king's friends, and by the king himself, who not only had Hobbes's portrait on his walls, but awarded him a pension of £100 a year—which, however, His Majesty forgot to pay. The Lord Chancellor Clarendon was shocked by the favour shown to a man suspected of atheism, and so was Parliament. After the Plague and the Great Fire, when people's superstitious fears were aroused, the House of Commons appointed a committee to inquire into atheistical writings, specially mentioning those of Hobbes. From this time onwards, he could not obtain leave in England to print anything on controversial subjects. Even his history of the Long Parliament, which he called *Behemoth*, though it set forth the most orthodox doctrine, had to be printed abroad (1668). The collected edition of his works in 1688 appeared in Amsterdam. In his old age, his reputation abroad was much greater than in England. To occupy his leisure, he wrote, at eighty-four, an autobiography in Latin verse, and published, at eighty-seven, a translation of Homer. I cannot discover that he wrote any large books after the age of eighty-seven.

We will now consider the doctrines of the *Leviathan*, upon which the fame of Hobbes mainly rests.

He proclaims, at the very beginning of the book, his thoroughgoing materialism. Life, he says, is nothing but a motion of the limbs, and therefore automata have an artificial life. The commonwealth, which he calls Leviathan, is a creation of art, and is in fact an artificial man. This is intended as more than an analogy, and is worked out in some detail The sovereignty is an artificial soul. The pacts and covenants by which 'Leviathan' is first created take the place of God's fiat when He said 'Let Us make man'.

The first part deals with man as an individual, and with such general philosophy as Hobbes deems necessary. Sensations are caused by the pressure of objects; colours, sounds, etc., are not in the objects. The qualities in objects that correspond to our sensations are motions. The first law of motion is stated, and is immediately applied to psychology: imagination is a decaying sense, both being motions. Imagination when asleep is dreaming; the religions of the gentiles came of not distinguishing dreams from waking life. (The rash reader may apply the same argument to the Christian religion, but Hobbes is much too cautious to do so himself.[1]) Belief that dreams are prophetic is a delusion; so is the belief in witchcraft and in ghosts.

The succession of our thoughts is not arbitrary, but governed by laws—sometimes those of association, sometimes those depending upon a purpose in our thinking. (This is important as an application of determinism to psychology.)

Hobbes, as might be expected, is an out-and-out nominalist. There is, he says, nothing universal but names, and without words

[1] Elsewhere he says that the heathen gods were created by human fear, but that our God is the First Mover.

we could not conceive any general ideas. Without language, there would be no truth or falsehood, for 'true' and 'false' are attributes of speech.

He considers geometry the one genuine science so far created. Reasoning is of the nature of reckoning, and should start from definitions. But it is necessary to avoid self-contradictory notions in definitions, which is not usually done in philosophy. 'Incorporeal substance', for instance, is nonsense. When it is objected that God is an incorporeal substance, Hobbes has two answers: first, that God is not an object of philosophy; second, that many philosophers have thought God corporeal. All error in *general* propositions, he says, comes from absurdity (i.e. self-contradiction); he gives as examples of absurdity the idea of free will, and of cheese having the accidents of bread. (We know that, according to the Catholic faith, the accidents of bread *can* inhere in a substance that is not bread.)

In this passage Hobbes shows an old-fashioned rationalism. Kepler had arrived at a general proposition: 'Planets go round the sun in ellipses'; but other views, such as those of Ptolemy, are not logically absurd. Hobbes has not appreciated the use of induction for arriving at general laws, in spite of his admiration for Kepler and Galileo.

As against Plato, Hobbes holds that reason is not innate, but is developed by industry.

He comes next to a consideration of the passions. 'Endeavour' may be defined as a small beginning of motion; if towards something, it is *desire*, and if away from something it is *aversion*. Love is the same as desire, and hate is the same as aversion. We call a thing 'good' when it is an object of desire, and 'bad' when it is an object of aversion. (It will be observed that these definitions give no objectivity to 'good' and 'bad'; if men differ in their desires, there is no theoretical method of adjusting their differences.) There are definitions of various passions, mostly based on a competitive view of life; for instance, laughter is sudden glory. Fear of invisible power, if publicly allowed, is religion; if not allowed, superstition. Thus the decision as to what is religion and what superstition rests with the legislator. Felicity involves continual progress; it consists in prospering, not in having prospered; there is no such thing as a static happiness—excepting, of course, the joys of heaven, which surpass our comprehension.

Will is nothing but the last appetite or aversion remaining in deliberation. That is to say, will is not something different from desire and aversion, but merely the strongest in a case of conflict. This is connected, obviously, with Hobbes's denial of free will.

Unlike most defenders of despotic government, Hobbes holds that all men are naturally equal. In a state of nature, before there is any government, every man desires to preserve his own liberty, but to acquire dominion over others; both these desires are dictated by the impulse to self-preservation. From their conflict arises a war of all against all, which makes life 'nasty, brutish, and short'. In a state of nature, there is no property, no justice or injustice; there is only war, and 'force and fraud are, in war, the two cardinal virtues'.

The second part tells how men escape from these evils by combining into communities each subject to a central authority. This is represented as happening by means of a social contract. It is supposed that a number of people come together and agree to choose a sovereign, or a sovereign body, which shall exercise authority over them and put an end to the universal war. I do not think this 'covenant' (as Hobbes usually calls it) is thought of as a definite historical event; it is certainly irrelevant to the argument to think of it as such. It is an explanatory myth, used to explain why men submit, and should submit, to the limitations on personal freedom entailed in submission to authority. The purpose of the restraint men put upon themselves, says Hobbes, is self-preservation from the universal war resulting from our love of liberty for ourselves and of dominion over others.

Hobbes considers the question why men cannot co-operate like ants and bees. Bees in the same hive, he says, do not compete; they have no desire for honour; and they do not use reason to criticize the government. Their agreement is natural, but that of men can only be artificial, by covenant. The covenant must confer power on one man or one assembly, since otherwise it cannot be enforced. 'Covenants, without the sword, are but words.' (President Wilson unfortunately forgot this.) The covenant is not, as afterwards in Locke and Rousseau, between the citizens and the ruling power; it is a covenant made by the citizens with each other to obey such ruling power as the majority shall choose. When they have chosen, their political power is at an end. The minority is as much bound as the majority, since the covenant was to obey the government chosen by the majority. When the government has been chosen, the citizens lose all rights except such as the government may find it expedient to grant. There is no right of rebellion, because the ruler is not bound by any contract, whereas the subjects are.

A multitude so united is called a commonwealth. This 'Leviathan' is a mortal God.

Hobbes prefers monarchy, but all his abstract arguments are equally applicable to all forms of government in which there is one supreme authority not limited by the legal rights of other bodies. He could tolerate Parliament alone, but not a system in which governmental power is shared between King and Parliament. This is the exact antithesis to the views of Locke and Montesquieu. The English Civil War occurred, says Hobbes, because power was divided between King, Lords, and Commons.

The supreme power, whether a man or an assembly, is called the Sovereign. The powers of the sovereign, in Hobbes's system, are unlimited. He has the right of censorship over all expression of opinion. It is assumed that his main interest is the preservation of internal peace, and that therefore he will not use the power of censorship to suppress truth, for a doctrine repugnant to peace cannot be true. (A singularly pragmatist view!) The laws of property are to be entirely subject to the sovereign; for in a state of nature there is no property, and therefore property is created by government, which may control its creation as it pleases.

It is admitted that the sovereign may be despotic, but even the worst despotism is better than anarchy. Moreover, in many points the interests of the sovereign are identical with those of his subjects. He is richer if they are richer, safer if they are law-abiding, and so on. Rebellion is wrong, both because it usually fails, and because, if it succeeds, it sets a bad example, and teaches others to rebel. The Aristotelian distinction between tyranny and monarchy is rejected; a 'tyranny', according to Hobbes, is merely a monarchy that the speaker happens to dislike.

Various reasons are given for preferring government by a monarch to government by an assembly. It is admitted that the monarch will usually follow his private interest when it conflicts with that of the public, but so will an assembly. A monarch may have favourites, but so may every member of an assembly; therefore the total number of favourites is likely to be fewer under a monarchy. A monarch can hear advice from anybody secretly; an assembly can only hear advice from its own members, and that publicly. In an assembly, the chance absence of some may cause a different party to obtain the majority, and thus produce a change of policy. Moreover, if the assembly is divided against itself, the result may be civil war. For all these reasons, Hobbes concludes, a monarchy is best.

Throughout the *Leviathan*, Hobbes never considers the possible effect of periodical elections in curbing the tendency of assemblies to sacrifice the public interest to the private interest of their members. He seems, in fact, to be thinking, not of democratically elected Parliaments, but of bodies like the Grand Council in Venice or the House of Lords in England. He conceives democracy, in the manner of antiquity, as involving the direct participation of every citizen in legislation and administration; at least, this seems to be his view.

The part of the people, in Hobbes's system, ends completely with the first choice of a sovereign. The succession is to be determined by the sovereign, as was the practice in the Roman Empire when mutinies did not interfere. It is admitted that the sovereign will usually choose one of his own children, or a near relative if he has no children, but it is held that no law ought to prevent him from choosing otherwise.

There is a chapter on the liberty of subjects, which begins with an admirably precise definition : Liberty is the absence of external impediments to motion. In this sense, liberty is consistent with necessity; for instance, water *necessarily* flows down hill when there are no impediments to its motion, and when, therefore, according to the definition, it is free. A man is free to do what he wills, but necessitated to do what God wills. All our volitions have causes, and are in this sense necessary. As for the liberty of subjects, they are free where the laws do not interfere; this is no limitation of sovereignty, since the laws could interfere if the sovereign so decided. Subjects have no rights as against the sovereign, except what the sovereign voluntarily concedes. When David caused Uriah to be killed, he did no injury to Uriah because Uriah was his subject; but he did an injury to God, because he was God's subject and was disobeying God's law.

The ancient authors, with their praises of liberty, have led men, according to Hobbes, to favour tumults and seditions. He maintains that, when they are rightly interpreted, the liberty they praised was that of sovereigns, i.e. liberty from foreign domination. Internal resistance to sovereigns he condemns even when it might seem most justified. For example, he holds that St Ambrose had no right to excommunicate the Emperor Theodosius after the massacre of Thessalonica. And he vehemently censures Pope Zachary for having helped to depose the last of the Merovingians in favour of Pepin.

He admits, however, one limitation on the duty of submission to sovereigns. The right of self-preservation he regards as absolute, and subjects have the right of self-defence, even against monarchs. This is logical, since he has made self-preservation the motive for instituting government. On this ground he holds (though with limitations) that a man has a right to refuse to fight when called upon by the government to do so. This is a right which no modern government concedes. A curious result of his egoistic ethic is that resistance to the sovereign is only justified in *self*-defence; resistance in defence of another is always culpable.

There is one other quite logical exception: a man has no duty to a sovereign who has not the power to protect him. This justified Hobbes's submission to Cromwell while Charles II was in exile.

There must, of course, be no such bodies, as political parties or what we should now call trade unions. All teachers are to be ministers of the sovereign, and are to teach only what the sovereign thinks useful. The rights of property are only valid as against other subjects, not as against the sovereign. The sovereign has the right to regulate foreign trade. He is not subject to the civil law. His right to punish comes to him, not from any concept of justice, but because he retains the liberty that all men had in the state of nature, when no man could be blamed for inflicting injury on another.

There is an interesting list of the reasons (other than foreign conquest) for the dissolution of commonwealths. These are: giving too little power to the sovereign; allowing private judgment in subjects; the theory that everything that is against conscience is sin; the belief in inspiration; the doctrine that the sovereign is subject to civil laws; the recognition of absolute private property; division of the sovereign power; imitation of the Greeks and Romans; separation of temporal and spiritual powers; refusing the power of taxation to the sovereign; the popularity of potent subjects; and the liberty of disputing with the sovereign. Of all these, there were abundant instances in the then recent history of England and France.

There should not, Hobbes thinks, be much difficulty in teaching people to believe in the rights of the sovereign, for have they not been taught to believe in Christianity, and even in transubstantiation, which is contrary to reason? There should be days set apart for learning the duty of submission. The instruction of the people depends upon right teaching in the universities, which must therefore be carefully supervised. There must be uniformity of worship, the religion being that ordained by the sovereign.

Part II ends with the hope that some sovereign will read the book and make himself absolute—a less chimerical hope than Plato's, that some king would turn philosopher. Monarchs are assured that the book is easy reading and quite interesting.

Part III, 'Of a Christian Commonwealth', explains that there is no universal Church, because the Church must depend upon the civil government. In each country, the king must be head of the Church; the Pope's overlordship and infallibility cannot be admitted. It argues, as might be expected, that a Christian who is a subject of a non-Christian sovereign should yield outwardly, for was not Naaman suffered to bow himself in the house of Rimmon?

Part IV, 'Of the Kingdom of Darkness', is mainly concerned with

538

criticism of the Church of Rome, which Hobbes hates because it puts the spiritual power above the temporal. The rest of this part is an attack on 'vain philosophy', by which Aristotle is usually meant.

Let us now try to decide what we are to think of the *Leviathan*. The question is not easy, because the good and the bad in it are so closely intermingled.

In politics, there are two different questions, one as to the best form of the State, the other as to its powers. The best *form* of State, according to Hobbes, is monarchy, but this is not the important part of his doctrine. The important part is his contention that the *powers* of the State should be absolute. This doctrine, or something like it, had grown up in Western Europe during the Renaissance and the Reformation. First, the feudal nobility were cowed by Louis XI, Edward IV, Ferdinand and Isabella, and their successors. Then the Reformation, in Protestant countries, enabled the lay government to get the better of the Church. Henry VIII wielded a power such as no earlier English king had enjoyed. But in France the Reformation, at first, had the opposite effect; between the Guises and the Huguenots, the kings were nearly powerless. Henry IV and Richelieu, not long before Hobbes wrote, had laid the foundations of the absolute monarchy which lasted in France till the Revolution. In Spain, Charles V had got the better of the Cortes, and Philip II was absolute except in relation to the Church. In England, however, the Puritans had undone the work of Henry VIII; their work suggested to Hobbes that anarchy must result from resistance to the sovereign.

Every community is faced with two dangers, anarchy and despotism. The Puritans, especially the Independents, were most impressed by the danger of despotism. Hobbes, on the contrary having experienced the conflict of rival fanaticisms, was obsessed by the fear of anarchy. The liberal philosophers who arose after the Restoration, and acquired control after 1688, realized both dangers; they disliked both Strafford and the Anabaptists. This led Locke to the doctrine of division of powers, and of checks and balances. In England there was a real division of powers so long as the King had influence; then Parliament became supreme, and ultimately the Cabinet. In America, there are still checks and balances in so far as Congress and the Supreme Court can resist the Administration. In Germany, Italy, Russia, and Japan, the government has had even more power than Hobbes thought desirable. On the whole, therefore, as regards the powers of the State, the world has gone as Hobbes wished, after a long liberal period during which, at least apparently, it was moving in the opposite direction. In spite of the outcome of the present war, it seems evident that the functions of the State must continue to increase, and that resistance to it must grow more and more difficult.

The reason that Hobbes gives for supporting the State, namely that it is the only alternative to anarchy, is in the main a valid one. A State may, however, be so bad that temporary anarchy seems preferable to its continuance, as in France in 1789 and in Russia in 1917. Moreover, the tendency of every government towards tyranny cannot be kept in check unless governments have some fear of rebellion. Governments would be worse than they are if Hobbes's submissive attitude were universally adopted by subjects. This is true in the political sphere, where governments will try, if they can, to make themselves personally irremovable; it is true in the economic sphere, where they will try to enrich themselves and their friends at the public expense; it is true in the intellectual sphere, where they will suppress every new discovery or doctrine that seems to menace their power. These are reasons for not thinking only of the risk of anarchy, but also of the danger of injustice and ossification that is bound up with omnipotence in government.

The merits of Hobbes appear most clearly when he is contrasted with earlier political theorists. He is completely free from superstition; he does not argue from what happened to Adam and Eve at the time of the Fall. He is clear and logical; his ethics, right or wrong, is completely intelligible, and does not involve the use of any dubious concepts. Apart from Machiavelli, who is much more limited, he is the first really modern writer on political theory. Where he is wrong, he is wrong from over-simplification, not because the basis of his thought is unreal and fantastic. For this reason, he is still worth refuting.

Without criticizing Hobbes's metaphysics or ethics, there are two points to make against him. The first is that he always considers the national interest as a whole, and assumes, tacitly, that the major interests of all citizens are the same. He does not realize the importance of the clash between different classes, which Marx makes the chief cause of social change. This is connected with the assumption that the interests of a monarch are roughly identical with those of his subjects. In time of war there is a unification of interests, especially if the war is fierce; but in time of peace the clash may be very great between the interests of one class and those of another. It is not by any means always true that, in such a situation, the best way to avert anarchy is to preach the absolute power of the sovereign. Some concession in the way of sharing power may be the only way to prevent civil war. This should have been obvious to Hobbes from the recent history of England.

Another point in which Hobbes's doctrine is unduly limited is in regard to the relations between different States. There is not a word in *Leviathan* to suggest any relation between them except war and conquest, with occasional interludes. This follows, on his principles, from the absence of an international government, for the relations of States are still in a state of nature, which is that of a war of all against all. So long as there is international anarchy, it is by no means clear that increase of efficiency in the separate States is in the interest of mankind, since it increases the ferocity and destructiveness of war. Every argument that he adduces in favour of government, in so far as it is valid at all, is valid in favour of international government. So long as national States exist and fight each other, only inefficiency can preserve the human race. To improve the fighting quality of separate States without having any means of preventing war is the road to universal destruction.

Chapter IX

DESCARTES

René Descartes (1596-1650) is usually considered the founder of modern philosophy, and, I think, rightly. He is the first man of high philosophic capacity whose outlook is profoundly affected by the new physics and astronomy. While it is true that he retains much of scholasticism, he does not accept foundations laid by predecessors, but endeavours to construct a complete philosophic edifice *de novo*. This had not happened since Aristotle, and is a sign of the new self-confidence that resulted from the progress of science. There is a freshness about his work that is not to be found in any eminent previous philosopher since Plato. All the intermediate philosophers were teachers, with the professional superiority belonging to that avocation. Descartes writes, not as a teacher, but as a discoverer and explorer, anxious to communicate what he has found. His style is easy and unpedantic, addressed to intelligent men of the world rather than to pupils. It is, moreover, an extraordinarily excellent style. It is very fortunate for modern philosophy that the pioneer had such admirable literary sense. His successors, both on the Continent and in England, until Kant, retain his unprofessional character, and several of them retain something of his stylistic merit.

Descartes's father was a councillor of the Parlement of Brittany and possessed a moderate amount of landed property. When Descartes inherited, at his father's death, he sold his estates, and invested the money, obtaining an income of six or seven thousand francs a year. He was educated, from 1604 to 1612, at the Jesuit college of La Flèche, which seems to have given him a much better grounding in modern mathematics than he could have got at most universities at that time. In 1612 he went to Paris, where he found social life boring, and retired to a secluded retreat in the Faubourg St Germain, in which he worked at geometry. Friends nosed him out, however, so, to secure more complete quiet, he enlisted in the Dutch army (1617). As Holland was at peace at the time, he seems to have enjoyed two years of undisturbed meditation. However, the coming of the Thirty Years' War led him to enlist in the Bavarian army (1619). It was in Bavaria, during the winter in 1619-20, that he had the experience he describes in the *Discours de la Méthode*. The weather being cold, he got into a stove[1] in the morning, and stayed there all day meditating; by his own account, his philosophy was half finished when he came out, but this need not be accepted too literally. Socrates used to meditate all day in the snow, but Descartes's mind only worked when he was warm.

In 1621 he gave up fighting; after a visit to Italy, he settled in Paris in 1625. But again friends *would* call on him before he was up (he seldom got up before midday), so in 1628 he joined the army which was besieging La Rochelle, the Huguenot stronghold. When this episode was finished, he decided to live in Holland, probably to escape the risk of persecution. He was a timid man, a practising Catholic, but he shared Galileo's heresies. Some think that he had heard of the first (secret) condemnation of Galileo, which had taken place in 1616. However that may be, he decided not to publish a great book, *Le Monde*, upon which he had been engaged. His reason was that it maintained two heretical doctrines: the earth's rotation and the infinity of the universe. (This book was never published in its entirety, but fragments of it were published after his death.)

He lived in Holland for twenty years (1629-49), except for a few brief visits to France and one to England, all on business. It is impossible to exaggerate the importance of Holland in the seventeenth century, as the one country where there was freedom of speculation. Hobbes had to have his books printed there; Locke took refuge there during the five worst years of reaction in England before 1688; Bayle (of the *Dictionary*) found it necessary to live there; and Spinoza would hardly have been allowed to do his work in any other country.

I said that Descartes was a timid man, but perhaps it would be kinder to say that he wished to be left in peace so as to do his work undisturbed. He always courted ecclesiastics, especially Jesuits—not only while he was in their power, but after his emigration to Holland. His psychology is obscure, but I incline to think that he was a sincere Catholic, and wished to persuade the Church—in its own interests as well as in his—to be less hostile to modern science than it showed itself in the case of Galileo. There are those who think that his orthodoxy was merely politic, but though this is a possible view I do not think it the most probable.

Even in Holland he was subject to vexatious attacks, not by the Roman Church, but by Protestant bigots. It was said that his views led to atheism, and he would have been prosecuted but for the inter-

---

[1] Descartes *says* it was a stove (*poêle*), but most commentators think this impossible. Those who know old-fashioned Bavarian houses, however, assure me that it is entirely credible.

vention of the French ambassador and the Prince of Orange. This attack having failed, another, less direct, was made a few years later by the authorities of the University of Leyden, which forbade all mention of him, whether favourable or unfavourable. Again the Prince of Orange intervened, and told the university not to be silly. This illustrates the gain to Protestant countries from the subordination of the Church to the State, and from the comparative weakness of Churches that were not international.

Unfortunately, through Chanut, the French ambassador at Stockholm, Descartes got into correspondence with Queen Christina of Sweden, a passionate and learned lady who thought that, as a sovereign, she had a right to waste the time of great men. He sent her a treatise on love, a subject which until then he had somewhat neglected. He also sent her a work on the passions of the soul, which he had originally composed for Princess Elizabeth, daughter of the Elector Palatine. These writings led her to request his presence at her court; he at last agreed, and she sent a warship to fetch him (September, 1649). It turned out that she wanted daily lessons from him, but could not spare the time except at five in the morning. This unaccustomed early rising, in the cold of a Scandinavian winter, was not the best thing for a delicate man. Moreover, Chanut became dangerously ill, and Descartes looked after him. The ambassador recovered, but Descartes fell ill and died in February, 1650.

Descartes never married, but he had a natural daughter who died at the age of five; this was, he said, the greatest sorrow of his life. He always was well dressed, and wore a sword. He was not industrious; he worked short hours, and read little. When he went to Holland he took few books with him, but among them were the Bible and Thomas Aquinas. His work seems to have been done with great concentration during short periods; but perhaps, to keep up the appearance of a gentlemanly amateur, he may have pretended to work less than in fact he did, for otherwise his achievements seem scarcely credible.

Descartes was a philosopher, a mathematician, and a man of science. In philosophy and mathematics, his work was of supreme importance; in science, though creditable, it was not so good as that of some of his contemporaries.

His great contribution to geometry was the invention of co-ordinate geometry, though not quite in its final form. He used the analytic method, which supposes a problem solved, and examines the consequences of the supposition; and he applied algebra to geometry. In both of these he had had predecessors—as regards the former, even among the ancients. What was original in him was the use of co-ordinates, i.e. the determination of the position of a point in a plane by its distance from two fixed lines. He did not himself discover all the power of this method, but he did enough to make further progress easy. This was by no means his sole contribution to mathematics, but it was his most important.

The book in which he set forth most of his scientific theories was *Principia Philosophiae*, published in 1644. There were, however, some other books of importance: *Essais philosophiques* (1637) deals with optics as well as geometry, and one of his books is called *De la formation du foetus*. He welcomed Harvey's discovery of the circulation of the blood, and was always hoping (though in vain) to make some discovery of importance in medicine. He regarded the bodies of men and animals as machines; animals he regarded as automata, governed entirely by the laws of physics, and devoid of feeling or consciousness. Men are different: they have a soul, which resides in the pineal gland. There the soul comes in contact with the 'vital spirits', and through this contact there is interaction between soul and body. The total quantity of motion in the universe is constant, and therefore the soul cannot affect it; but it can alter the *direction* of motion of the vital spirits, and hence, indirectly, of other parts of the body.

This part of his theory was abandoned by his school—first by his Dutch disciple Geulincx, and later by Malebranche and Spinoza. The physicists discovered the conservation of momentum, according to which the total quantity of motion in the world in any given *direction* is constant. This showed that the sort of action of mind on matter that Descartes imagined is impossible. Assuming—as was very generally assumed in the Cartesian school—that all physical action is of the nature of impact, dynamical laws suffice to determine the motions of matter, and there is no room for any influence of mind. But this raises a difficulty. My arm moves when I will that it shall move, but my will is a mental phenomenon and the motion of my arm a physical phenomenon. Why then, if mind and matter cannot interact, does my body behave *as if* my mind controlled it? To this Geulincx invented an answer, known as the theory of the 'two clocks'. Suppose you have two clocks which both keep perfect time: whenever one points to the hour, the other will strike, so that if you saw one and heard the other, you would think the one *caused* the other to strike. So it is with mind and body. Each is wound up by God to keep time with the other, so that, on occasion of my volition, purely physical laws cause my arm to move, although my will has not really acted on my body.

There were of course difficulties in this theory. In the first place, it was very odd; in the second place, since the physical series was rigidly determined by natural laws, the mental series, which ran parallel to it, must be equally deterministic. If the theory was valid there should be a sort of possible dictionary, in which each cerebral occurrence would be translated into the corresponding mental occurrence. An ideal calculator could calculate the cerebral occurrence by the laws of dynamics, and infer the concomitant mental occurrence by means of the 'dictionary'. Even without the 'dictionary', the calculator could infer words and actions, since these are bodily movements. This view would be difficult to reconcile with Christian ethics and the punishment of sin.

These consequences, however, were not at once apparent. The theory appeared to have two merits. The first was that it made the soul, in a sense, wholly independent of the body, since it was never acted on by the body. The second was that it allowed the general principle: 'one substance cannot act on another'. There were two substances, mind and matter, and they were so dissimilar that an interaction seemed inconceivable. Geulincx's theory explained the *appearance* of interaction while denying its *reality*.

In mechanics, Descartes accepts the first law of motion, according to which a body left to itself will move with constant velocity in a straight line. But there is no action at a distance, as later in Newton's theory of gravitation. There is no such thing as a vacuum, and there are no atoms; yet all interaction is of the nature of impact. If we knew enough, we should be able to reduce chemistry and biology to mechanics; the process by which a seed develops into an animal or a plant is purely mechanical. There is no need of Aristotle's three souls; only one of them, the rational soul, exists, and that only in man.

With due caution to avoid theological censure, Descartes develops a cosmogony not unlike those of some pre-Platonic philosophers. We know, he says, that the world was created as in Genesis, but it is interesting to see how it *might* have grown naturally. He works out a theory of the formation of vortices: round the sun there is an immense vortex in the plenum, which carries the planets round with it. The theory is ingenious, but cannot explain why planetary orbits are elliptical, not circular. It was generally accepted in France, where it was only gradually ousted by the Newtonian theory. Cotes, the editor of the first English edition of Newton's *Principia*, argues eloquently that the vortex theory leads to atheism, while Newton's requires God to set the planets in motion in a direction not towards the sun. On this ground, he thinks, Newton is to be preferred.

I come now to Descartes's two most important books, so far as pure philosophy is concerned. These are the *Discourse on Method*

(1637) and the *Meditations* (1642). They largely overlap, and it is not necessary to keep them apart.

In these books Descartes begins by explaining the method of 'Cartesian doubt', as it has come to be called. In order to have a firm basis for his philosophy, he resolves to make himself doubt everything that he can manage to doubt. As he foresees that the process may take some time, he resolves, in the meanwhile, to regulate his conduct by commonly received rules; this will leave his mind unhampered by the possible consequences of his doubts in relation to practice.

He begins with scepticism in regard to the senses. Can I doubt, he says, that I am sitting here by the fire in a dressing-gown? Yes, for sometimes I have dreamt that I was here when in fact I was naked in bed. (Pyjamas, and even nightshirts, had not yet been invented.) Moreover madmen sometimes have hallucinations, so it is possible that I may be in like case.

Dreams, however, like painters, present use with copies of real things, at least as regards their elements. (You may dream of a winged horse, but only because you have seen horses and wings.) Therefore corporeal nature in general, involving such matters as extension, magnitude, and number, is less easy to question than beliefs about particular things. Arithmetic and geometry, which are not concerned with particular things, are therefore more certain than physics and astronomy; they are true even of dream objects, which do not differ from real ones as regards number and extension. Even in regard to arithmetic and geometry, however, doubt is possible. It may be that God causes me to make mistakes whenever I try to count the sides of a square or add 2 to 3. Perhaps it is wrong, even in imagination, to attribute such unkindness to God, but there might be an evil demon, no less cunning and deceitful than powerful, employing all his industry in misleading me. If there be such a demon, it may be that all the things I see are only illusions of which he makes use as traps for my credulity.

There remains, however, something that I cannot doubt: no demon, however cunning, could deceive me if I did not exist. I may have no *body*: this might be an illusion. But thought is different. 'While I wanted to think everything false, it must necessarily be that I who thought was something; and remarking that this truth, *I think, therefore I am*, was so solid and so certain that all the most extravagant suppositions of the sceptics were incapable of upsetting it, I judged that I could receive it without scruple as the first principle of the philosophy that I sought.'[1]

[1] The above argument, 'I think, therefore I am' (*cogito ergo sum*), is known as Descartes's *cogito*, and the process by which it is reached is called 'Cartesian doubt'.

This passage is the kernel of Descartes's theory of knowledge, and contains what is most important in his philosophy. Most philosophers since Descartes have attached importance to the theory of knowledge, and their doing so is largely due to him. 'I think, therefore I am' makes mind more certain than matter, and my mind (for me) more certain than the minds of others. There is thus, in all philosophy derived from Descartes, a tendency to subjectivism, and to regarding matter as something only knowable, if at all, by inference from what is known of mind. These two tendencies exist both in Continental idealism and in British empiricism—in the former triumphantly, in the latter regretfully. There has been, in quite recent times, an attempt to escape from this subjectivism by the philosophy known as instrumentalism, but of this I will not speak at present. With this exception, modern philosophy has very largely accepted the formulation of its problems from Descartes, while not accepting his solutions.

The reader will remember that St Augustine advanced an argument closely similar to the *cogito*. He did not, however, give prominence to it, and the problem which it is intended to solve occupied only a small part of his thoughts. Descartes's originality, therefore, should be admitted, though it consists less in inventing the argument than in perceiving its importance.

Having now secured a firm foundation, Descartes sets to work to rebuild the edifice of knowledge. The I that has been proved to exist has been inferred from the fact that I think, therefore I exist while I think, and only then. If I ceased to think, there would be no evidence of my existence. I am a thing that thinks, a substance of which the whole nature or essence consists in thinking, and which needs no place or material thing for its existence. The soul, therefore, is wholly distinct from the body and easier to know than the body; it would be what it is even if there were no body.

Descartes next asks himself: why is the *cogito* so evident? He concludes that it is only because it is clear and distinct. He therefore adopts as a general rule the principle: *All things that we conceive very clearly and very distinctly are true*. He admits, however, that there is sometimes difficulty in knowing which these things are.

'Thinking' is used by Descartes in a very wide sense. A thing that thinks, he says, is one that doubts, understands, conceives, affirms, denies, wills, imagines, and feels—for feeling, as it occurs in dreams, is a form of thinking. Since thought is the essence of mind, the mind must always think, even during deep sleep.

Descartes now resumes the question of our knowledge of bodies. He takes as an example a piece of wax from the honeycomb. Certain things are apparent to the senses: it tastes of honey, it smells of flowers, it has a certain sensible colour, size and shape, it is hard and cold, and if struck it emits a sound. But if you put it near the fire, these qualities change, although the wax persists, therefore what appeared to the senses was not the wax itself. The wax itself is constituted by extension, flexibility, and motion, which are understood by the mind, not by the imagination. The *thing* that is the wax cannot itself be sensible, since it is equally involved in all the appearances of the wax to the various senses. The perception of the wax 'is not a vision or touch or imagination, but an inspection of the mind'. I do not *see* the wax, any more than I see men in the street when I see hats and coats. 'I understand by the sole power of judgment, which resides in my mind, what I thought I saw with my eyes.' Knowledge by the senses is confused, and shared with animals; but now I have stripped the wax of its clothes, and mentally perceive it naked. From my sensibly seeing the wax, my own existence follows with certainty, but not that of the wax. Knowledge of external things must be by the mind, not by the senses.

This leads to a consideration of different kinds of ideas. The commonest of errors, Descartes says, is to think that my ideas are like outside things. (The word 'idea' includes sense-perceptions, as used by Descartes.) Ideas *seem* to be of three sorts: (1) those that are innate, (2) those that are foreign and come from without, (3) those that are invented by me. The second kind of ideas, we naturally suppose, are like outside objects. We suppose this, partly because nature teaches us to think so, partly because such ideas come independently of the will (i.e. through sensation), and it therefore seems reasonable to suppose that a foreign thing imprints its likeness on me. But are these good reasons? When I speak of being 'taught by nature' in this connection, I only mean that I have a certain inclination to believe it, not that I see it by a natural light. What is seen by a natural light cannot be denied, but a mere inclination may be towards what is false. And as for ideas of sense being involuntary, that is no argument, for dreams are involuntary although they come from within. The reasons for supposing that ideas of sense come from without are therefore inconclusive.

Moreover there are sometimes two different ideas of the same external object, e.g. the sun as it appears to the senses and the sun in which the astronomers believe. These cannot both be like the sun, and reason shows that the one which comes directly from experience must be the less like it of the two.

But these considerations have not disposed of the sceptical arguments which threw doubt on the existence of the external world. This can only be done by first proving the existence of God.

Descartes's proofs of the existence of God are not very original; in the main they come from scholastic philosophy. They were better stated by Leibniz, and I will omit consideration of them until we come to him.

When God's existence has been proved, the rest proceeds easily. Since God is good, He will not act like the deceitful demon whom Descartes has imagined as a ground for doubt. Now God has given me such a strong inclination to believe in bodies that He would be deceitful if there were none; therefore bodies exist. He must, more-over, have given me the faculty of correcting errors. I use this faculty when I employ the principle that what is clear and distinct is true. This enables me to know mathematics, and physics also, if I remember that I must know the truth about bodies by the mind alone, not by mind and body jointly.

The constructive part of Descartes's theory of knowledge is much less interesting than the earlier destructive part. It uses all sorts of scholastic maxims, such as that an effect can never have more perfection than its cause, which have somehow escaped the initial critical scrutiny. No reason is given for accepting these maxims, although they are certainly less self-evident than one's own existence, which is *proved* with a flourish of trumpets. Plato, St Augustine, and St Thomas contain most of what is affirmative in the *Meditations*.

The method of critical doubt, though Descartes himself applied it only half-heartedly, was of great philosophic importance. It is clear, as a matter of logic, that it can only yield positive results if scepticism is to stop somewhere. If there is to be both logical and empirical knowledge, there must be two kinds of stopping points: indubitable facts, and indubitable principles of inference. Descartes's indubitable facts are his own thoughts—using 'thought' in the widest possible sense. 'I think' is his ultimate premiss. Here the word 'I' is really illegitimate; he ought to state his ultimate premiss in the form 'there are thoughts'. The word 'I' is grammatically convenient, but does not describe a datum. When he goes on to say 'I am a *thing* which thinks', he is already using uncritically the apparatus of categories handed down by scholasticism. He nowhere proves that thoughts need a thinker, nor is there reason to believe this except in a grammatical sense. The decision, however, to regard thoughts rather than external objects as the prime empirical certainties was very important, and had a profound effect on all subsequent philosophy.

In two other respects the philosophy of Descartes was important. First: it brought to completion, or very nearly to completion, the dualism of mind and matter which began with Plato and was developed, largely for religious reasons, by Christian philosophy. Ignoring the curious transactions in the pineal gland, which were dropped by the followers of Descartes, the Cartesian system presents two parallel but independent worlds, that of mind and that of matter, each of which can be studied without reference to the other. That the mind does not move the body was a new idea, due explicitly to Geulincx but implicitly to Descartes. It had the advantage of making it possible to say that the body does not move the mind. There is a considerable discussion in the *Meditations* as to why the mind feels 'sorrow' when the body is thirsty. The correct Cartesian answer was that the body and the mind were like two clocks, and that when one indicated 'thirst' the other indicated 'sorrow'. From the religious point of view, however, there was a grave drawback to this theory; and this brings me to the second characteristic of Cartesianism that I alluded to above.

In the whole theory of the material world, Cartesianism was rigidly deterministic. Living organisms, just as much as dead matter, were governed by the laws of physics; there was no longer need, as in the Aristotelian philosophy, of an entelechy or soul to explain the growth of organisms and the movements of animals. Descartes himself allowed one small exception: a human soul could, by volition, alter the direction though not the quantity of the motion of the vital spirits. This, however, was contrary to the spirit of the system, and turned out to be contrary to the laws of mechanics; it was therefore dropped. The consequence was that all the movements of matter were determined by physical laws, and, owing to parallelism, mental events must be equally determinate. Consequently Cartesians had difficulty about free will. And for those who paid more attention to Descartes's science than to his theory of knowledge, it was not difficult to extend the theory that animals are automata: why not say the same of men, and simplify the system by making it a consistent materialism? This step was actually taken in the eighteenth century.

There is in Descartes an unresolved dualism between what he learnt from contemporary science and the scholasticism that he had been taught at La Flèche. This led him into inconsistencies, but it also made him more rich in fruitful ideas than any completely logical philosopher could have been. Consistency might have made him merely the founder of a new scholasticism, whereas inconsistency made him the source of two important but divergent schools of philosophy.

Chapter X

SPINOZA

SPINOZA (1632-77) is the noblest and most lovable of the great philosophers. Intellectually, some others have surpassed him, but ethically he is supreme. As a natural consequence, he was considered, during his lifetime and for a century after his death, a man of appalling wickedness. He was born a Jew, but the Jews excommunicated him. Christians abhorred him equally; although his whole philosophy is dominated by the idea of God, the orthodox accused him of atheism. Leibniz, who owed much to him, concealed his debt, and carefully abstained from saying a word in his praise; he even went so far as to lie about the extent of his personal acquaintance with the heretic Jew.

The life of Spinoza was very simple. His family had come to Holland from Spain, or perhaps Portugal, to escape the Inquisition. He himself was educated in Jewish learning, but found it impossible to remain orthodox. He was offered 1000 florins a year to conceal his doubts; when he refused, an attempt was made to assassinate him; when this failed, he was cursed with all the curses in Deuteronomy and with the curse that Elisha pronounced on the children who, in consequence, were torn to pieces by the she-bears. But no she-bears attacked Spinoza. He lived quietly, first at Amsterdam and then at the Hague, making his living by polishing lenses. His wants were few and simple, and he showed throughout his life a rare indifference to money. The few who knew him loved him, even if they disapproved of his principles. The Dutch Government, with its usual liberalism, tolerated his opinions on theological matters, though at one time he was in bad odour politically because he sided with the De Witts against the House of Orange. At the early age of forty-three he died of phthisis.

His chief work, the *Ethics*, was published posthumously. Before considering it, a few words must be said about two of his other books, the *Tractatus Theologico-Politicus* and the *Tractatus Politicus*. The former is a curious combination of biblical criticism and political theory; the latter deals with political theory only. In biblical criticism Spinoza partially anticipates modern views, particularly in assigning much later dates to various books of the Old Testament than those assigned by tradition. He endeavours throughout to show that the Scriptures can be interpreted so as to be compatible with a liberal theology.

Spinoza's political theory is, in the main, derived from Hobbes, in spite of the enormous temperamental difference between the two men. He holds that in a state of nature there is no right or wrong, for wrong consists in disobeying the law. He holds that the sovereign can do no wrong, and agrees with Hobbes that the Church should be entirely subordinate to the State. He is opposed to all rebellion, even against a bad government, and instances the troubles in England as a proof of the harm that comes of forcible resistance to authority. But he disagrees with Hobbes in thinking democracy the 'most natural' form of government. He disagrees also in holding that subjects should not sacrifice *all* their rights to the sovereign. In particular, he holds freedom of opinion important. I do not quite know how he reconciles this with the opinion that religious questions should be decided by the State. I think when he says this he means that they should be decided by the State rather than the Church; in Holland the State was much more tolerant than the Church.

Spinoza's *Ethics* deals with three distinct matters. It begins with metaphysics; it then goes on to the psychology of the passions and the will; and finally it sets forth an ethic based on the preceding metaphysics and psychology. The metaphysic is a modification of Descartes, the psychology is reminiscent of Hobbes, but the ethic is original, and is what is of most value in the book. The relation of Spinoza to Descartes is in some ways not unlike the relation of Plotinus to Plato. Descartes was a many-sided man, full of intellectual curiosity, but not much burdened with moral earnestness. Although he invented 'proofs' intended to support orthodox beliefs, he could have been used by sceptics as Carneades used Plato. Spinoza, although he was not without scientific interests, and even wrote a treatise on the rainbow, was in the main concerned with religion and virtue. He accepted from Descartes and his contemporaries a materialistic and deterministic physics, and sought, within this framework, to find room for reverence and a life devoted to the Good. His attempt was magnificent, and rouses admiration even in those who do not think it successful.

The metaphysical system of Spinoza is of the type inaugurated by Parmenides. There is only one substance, 'God or Nature'; nothing finite is self-subsistent. Descartes admitted three substances, God and mind and matter; it is true that, even for him, God was, in a sense, more substantial than mind and matter, since He had created them, and could, if He chose, annihilate them. But except in relation to God's omnipotence, mind and matter were two independent substances, defined, respectively, by the attributes of thought and extension. Spinoza would have none of this. For him, thought and extension were both attributes of God. God has also an infinite number of other attributes, since He must be in every respect infinite; but these others are unknown to us. Individual souls and separate pieces of matter are, for Spinoza, adjectival; they are not *things*, but merely aspects of the divine Being. There can be no such personal immortality as Christians believe in, but only that impersonal sort that consists in becoming more and more one with God. Finite things are defined by their boundaries, physical or logical, that is to say, by what they are *not*: 'all determination is negation'. There can be only one Being who is wholly positive, and He must be absolutely infinite. Hence Spinoza is led to a complete and undiluted pantheism.

Everything, according to Spinoza, is ruled by an absolute logical necessity. There is no such thing as free will in the mental sphere or chance in the physical world. Everything that happens is a manifestation of God's inscrutable nature, and it is logically impossible that events should be other than they are. This leads to difficulties in regard to sin, which critics were not slow to point out. One of them, observing that, according to Spinoza, everything is decreed by God and is therefore good, asks indignantly: Was it good that Nero should kill his mother? Was it good that Adam ate the apple? Spinoza answers that what was positive in these acts was good, and only what was negative was bad; but negation exists only from the point of view of finite creatures. In God, who alone is completely real, there is no negation, and therefore the evil in what to us seem sins does not exist when they are viewed as parts of the whole. This doctrine, though, in one form or another, it has been held by most mystics, cannot, obviously, be reconciled with the orthodox doctrine of sin and damnation. It is bound up with Spinoza's complete rejection of free will. Although not at all polemical, Spinoza was too honest to conceal his opinions, however shocking to contemporaries; the abhorrence of his teaching is therefore not surprising.

The *Ethics* is set forth in the style of Euclid, with definitions, axioms, and theorems; everything after the axioms is supposed to be rigorously demonstrated by deductive argument. This makes him difficult reading. A modern student, who cannot suppose that there are rigorous 'proofs' of such things as he professes to establish, is bound to grow impatient with the detail of the demonstrations, which is, in fact, not worth mastering. It is enough to read the enunciations of the propositions, and to study the scholia, which contain much of what is best in the *Ethics*. But it would show a lack of understanding to blame Spinoza for his geometrical method.

It was of the essence of his system, ethically as well as metaphysically, to maintain that everything *could* be demonstrated, and it was therefore essential to produce demonstrations. *We* cannot accept his method, but that is because we cannot accept his metaphysic. We cannot believe that the interconnections of the parts of the universe are *logical*, because we hold that scientific laws are to be discovered by observation, not by reasoning alone. But for Spinoza the geometrical method was necessary, and was bound up with the most essential parts of his doctrine.

I come now to Spinoza's theory of the emotions. This comes after a metaphysical discussion of the nature and origin of the mind, which leads up to the astonishing proposition that 'the human mind has an adequate knowledge of the eternal and infinite essence of God'. But the passions, which are discussed in the Third Book of the *Ethics*, distract us and obscure our intellectual vision of the whole. 'Everything,' we are told, 'in so far as it is in itself, endeavours to persevere in its own being.' Hence arise love and hate and strife. The psychology of Book III is entirely egoistic. 'He who conceives that the object of his hate is destroyed will feel pleasure.' 'If we conceive that anyone takes delight in something, which only one person can possess, we shall endeavour to bring it about, that the man in question shall not gain possession thereof.' But even in this Book there are moments when Spinoza abandons the appearance of mathematically demonstrated cynicism, as when he says: 'Hatred is increased by being reciprocated, and can on the other hand be destroyed by love.' Self-preservation is the fundamental motive of the passions, according to Spinoza; but self-preservation alters its character when we realize that what is real and positive in us is what unites us to the whole, and not what preserves the appearance of separateness.

The last two books of the *Ethics*, entitled respectively 'Of human bondage, or the strength of the emotions' and 'Of the power of the understanding, or of human freedom,' are the most interesting. We are in bondage in proportion as what happens to us is determined by outside causes, and we are free in proportion as we are self-determined. Spinoza, like Socrates and Plato, believes that all wrong action is due to intellectual error: the man who adequately understands his own circumstances will act wisely, and will even be happy in the face of what to another would be misfortune. He makes no appeal to unselfishness; he holds that self-seeking, in some sense, and more particularly self-preservation, govern all human behaviour. 'No virtue can be conceived as prior to this endeavour to preserve one's own being.' But his conception of what a wise man will choose as the goal of his self-seeking is different from that of the ordinary egoist: 'The mind's highest good is the know-ledge of God, and the mind's highest virtue is to know God.' Emotions are called 'passions' when they spring from inadequate ideas; passions in different men may conflict, but men who live in obedience to reason will agree together. Pleasure in itself is good, but hope and fear are bad, and so are humility and repentance: 'he who repents of an action is doubly wretched or infirm'. Spinoza regards time as unreal, and therefore all emotions which have to do essentially with an event as future or as past are contrary to reason. 'In so far as the mind conceives a thing under the dictate of reason, it is affected equally, whether the idea be of a thing present, past, or future.'

This is hard saying, but it is of the essence of Spinoza's system, and we shall do well to dwell upon it for a moment. In popular estimation, 'all's well that ends well'; if the universe is gradually improving, we think better of it than if it is gradually deteriorating, even if the sum of good and evil be the same in the two cases. We are more concerned about a disaster in our own time than in the time of Jenghiz Khan. According to Spinoza this is irrational. What-ever happens is part of the eternal timeless world as God sees it; to Him, the date is irrelevant. The wise man, so far as human finitude allows, endeavours to see the world as God sees it, *sub specie æternitatis*, under the aspect of eternity. But, you may retort, we are surely right in being more concerned about future misfortunes, which may possibly be averted, than about past calamities about which we can do nothing. To this argument Spinoza's determinism supplies the answer. Only ignorance makes us think that we can alter the future; what will be will be, and the future is as unalter-ably fixed as the past. That is why hope and fear are condemned: both depend upon viewing the future as uncertain, and therefore spring from lack of wisdom.

When we acquire, in so far as we can, a vision of the world which is analogous to God's, we see everything as part of the whole, and as necessary to the goodness of the whole. Therefore 'the know-ledge of evil is an inadequate knowledge'. God has no knowledge of evil, because there is no evil to be known; the appearance of evil only arises through regarding parts of the universe as if they were self-subsistent.

Spinoza's outlook is intended to liberate men from the tyranny of fear. 'A free man thinks of nothing less than of death; and his wisdom is a meditation not of death, but of life.' Spinoza lived up to this precept very completely. On the last day of his life he was entirely calm, not exalted, like Socrates in the *Phaedo*, but con-versing, as he would on any other day, about matters of interest to his interlocutor. Unlike some other philosophers, he not only believed his own doctrines, but practised them; I do not know of any occasion, in spite of great provocation, in which he was betrayed into the kind of heat or anger that his ethic condemned. In controversy he was courteous and reasonable, never denouncing, but doing his utmost to persuade.

In so far as what happens to us springs from ourselves, it is good; only what comes from without is bad for us. 'As all things whereof a man is the efficient cause are necessarily good, no evil can befall a man except through external causes.' Obviously, therefore, nothing bad can happen to the universe as a whole, since it is not subject to external causes. 'We are a part of universal nature, and we follow her order. If we have a clear and distinct understanding of this, that part of our nature which is defined by intelligence, in other words the better part of ourselves, will assuredly acquiesce in what befalls us, and in such acquiescence will endeavour to persist.' In so far as a man is an unwilling part of a larger whole, he is in bondage; but in so far as, through the understanding, he has grasped the sole reality of the whole, he is free. The implications of this doctrine are developed in the last Book of the *Ethics*.

Spinoza does not, like the Stoics, object to *all* emotions; he objects only to those that are 'passions', i.e. those in which we appear to ourselves to be passive in the power of outside forces. 'An emotion which is a passion ceases to be a passion as soon as we form a clear and distinct idea of it.' Understanding that all things are necessary helps the mind to acquire power over the emotions. 'He who clearly and distinctly understands himself and his emotions, loves God, and so much the more as he more understands himself and his emotions.' This proposition introduces us to the 'intellectual love of God', in which wisdom consists. The intellectual love of God is a union of thought and emotion: it consists, I think one may say, in true thought combined with joy in the apprehension of truth. All joy in true thought is part of the intellectual love of God, for it contains nothing negative, and is therefore truly part of the whole, not only apparently, as are fragmentary things so separated in thought as to appear bad.

I said a moment ago that the intellectual love of God involves joy, but perhaps this was a mistake, for Spinoza says that God is not affected by any emotion of pleasure or pain, and also says that 'the intellectual love of the mind towards God is part of the infinite love wherewith God loves himself'. I think, nevertheless, that there is something in 'intellectual *love*' which is not mere intellect;

557

perhaps the joy involved is considered as something superior to pleasure.

'Love towards God,' we are told, 'must hold the chief place in the mind.' I have omitted Spinoza's demonstrations, but in so doing I have given an incomplete picture of his thought. As the proof of the above proposition is short, I will quote it in full; the reader can then in imagination supply proofs to other propositions. The proof of the above proposition is as follows:

'For this love is associated with all the modifications of the body (V, 14) and is fostered by them all (V, 15); therefore (V, 11) it must hold the chief place in the mind, Q.E.D.'

Of the propositions referred to in the above proof, V, 14 states: 'The mind can bring it about, that all bodily modifications or images of things may be referred to the idea of God'; V. 15, quoted above, states: 'He who clearly and distinctly understands himself and his emotions loves God, and so much the more in proportion as he understands himself and his emotions'; V, 11 states: 'In proportion as a mental image is referred to more objects, so is it more frequent, or more often vivid, and occupies the mind more.'

The 'proof' quoted above might be expressed as follows: Every increase in the understanding of what happens to us consists in referring events to the idea of God, since, in truth, everything is part of God. This understanding of everything as part of God *is* love of God. When *all* objects are referred to God, the idea of God will fully occupy the mind.

Thus the statement that 'love of God must hold the chief place in the mind' is not a primarily moral exhortation, but an account of what must inevitably happen as we acquire understanding.

We are told that no one can hate God, but, on the other hand, 'he who loves God cannot endeavour that God should love him in return'. Goethe, who admired Spinoza without even beginning to understand him, thought this proposition an instance of self-abnegation. It is nothing of the sort, but a logical consequence of Spinoza's metaphysic. He does not say that a man *ought* not to want God to love him; he says that a man who loves God *cannot* want God to love him. This is made plain by the proof, which says: 'For, if a man should so endeavour, he would desire (V, 17, Corol.) that God, whom he loves, should not be God, and consequently he would desire to feel pain (III, 19), which is absurd (III, 28).' V, 17 is the proposition already referred to, which says that God has no passions or pleasures or pains; the corollary referred to above deduces that God loves and hates no one. Here again what is involved is not an ethical precept, but a logical necessity: a man who loved God and wished God to love him would be wishing to feel pain, 'which is absurd'.

The statement that God can love no one should not be considered to contradict the statement that God loves Himself with an infinite intellectual love. He may love Himself, since that is possible without false belief; and in any case intellectual love is a very special kind of love.

At this point Spinoza tells us that he has now given us 'all the remedies against the emotions'. The great remedy is clear and distinct ideas as to the nature of the emotions and their relation to external causes. There is a further advantage in love of God as compared to love of human beings: 'Spiritual unhealthiness and misfortunes can generally be traced to excessive love of something which is subject to many variations.' But clear and distinct knowledge 'begets a love towards a thing immutable and eternal', and such love has not the turbulent and disquieting character of love for an object which is transient and changeable.

Although personal survival after death is an illusion, there is nevertheless something in the human mind that is eternal. The mind can only imagine or remember while the body endures, but there is in God an idea which expresses the essence of this or that human body under the form of eternity, and this idea is the eternal part of the mind. The intellectual love of God, when experienced by an individual, is contained in this eternal part of the mind.

Blessedness, which consists of love towards God, is not the reward of virtue, but virtue itself; we do not rejoice in it because we control our lusts, but we control our lusts because we rejoice in it.

The *Ethics* ends with these words:

'The wise man, in so far as he is regarded as such, is scarcely at all disturbed in spirit, but being conscious of himself, and of God, and of things, by a certain eternal necessity, never ceases to be, but always possesses true aquiescence of his spirit. If the way which I have pointed out as leading to this result seems exceedingly hard, it may nevertheless be discovered. Needs must it be hard, since it is so seldom found. How would it be possible, if salvation were ready to our hand, and could without great labour be found, that it should be by almost all men neglected? But all excellent things are as difficult as they are rare.'

In forming a critical estimate of Spinoza's importance as a philosopher, it is necessary to distinguish his ethics from his metaphysics, and to consider how much of the former can survive the rejection of the latter.

Spinoza's metaphysic is the best example of what may be called 'logical monism'—the doctrine, namely, that the world as a whole is a single substance, none of whose parts are logically capable of existing alone. The ultimate basis for this view is the belief that every proposition has a single subject and a single predicate, which leads us to the conclusion that relations and plurality must be illusory. Spinoza thought that the nature of the world and of human life could be logically deduced from self-evident axioms; we ought to be as resigned to events as to the fact that 2 and 2 are 4, since they are equally the outcome of logical necessity. The whole of this metaphysic is impossible to accept; it is .incompatible with modern logic and with scientific method. *Facts* have to be discovered by observation, not by reasoning; when we successfully infer the future, we do so by means of principles which are not logically necessary, but are suggested by empirical data. And the concept of substance, upon which Spinoza relies, is one which neither science nor philosophy can nowadays accept.

But when we come to Spinoza's ethics, we feel—or at least I feel—that something, though not everything, can be accepted even when the metaphysical foundation has been rejected. Broadly speaking, Spinoza is concerned to show how it is possible to live nobly even when we recognize the limits of human power. He himself, by his doctrine of necessity, makes these limits narrower than they are; but when they indubitably exist, Spinoza's maxims are probably the best possible. Take, for instance, death: nothing that a man can do will make him immortal, and it is therefore futile to spend time in fears and lamentations over the fact that we must die. To be obsessed by the fear of death is a kind of slavery; Spinoza is right in saying that 'the free man thinks of nothing less than of death'. But even in this case, it is only death in general that should be so treated; death of any particular disease should, if possible, be averted by submitting to medical care. What should, even in this case, be avoided, is a certain kind of anxiety or terror; the necessary measures should be taken calmly, and our thoughts should, as far as possible, be then directed to other matters. The same considerations apply to all other purely personal misfortunes.

But how about misfortunes to people whom you love? Let us think of some of the things that are likely to happen in our time to inhabitants of Europe or China. Suppose you are a Jew, and your family has been massacred. Suppose you are an underground worker against the Nazis, and your wife has been shot because you could not be caught. Suppose your husband, for some purely imaginary crime, has been sent to forced labour in the Arctic, and has died of cruelty and starvation. Suppose your daughter has been raped and then killed by enemy soldiers. Ought you, in these circumstances, to preserve a philosophic calm?

If you follow Christ's teaching, you will say 'Father, forgive them, for they know not what they do.' I have known Quakers who could have said this sincerely and profoundly, and whom I admired because they could. But before giving admiration one must be very sure that the misfortune is felt as deeply as it should be. One cannot accept the attitude of some among the Stoics, who said, 'What does it matter to me if my family suffer? I can still be virtuous.' The Christian principle, 'Love your enemies,' is good, but the Stoic principle, 'Be indifferent to your friends,' is bad. And the Christian principle does not inculcate calm, but an ardent love even towards the worst of men. There is nothing to be said against it except that it is too difficult for most of us to practise sincerely.

The primitive reaction to such disasters is revenge. When Macduff learns that his wife and children have been killed by Macbeth, he resolves to kill the tyrant himself. This reaction is still admired by most people, when the injury is great, and such as to arouse moral horror in disinterested people. Nor can it be wholly condemned, for it is one of the forces generating punishment, and punishment is sometimes necessary. Moreover, from the point of view of mental health, the impulse to revenge is likely to be so strong that, if it is allowed no outlet, a man's whole outlook on life may become distorted and more or less insane. This is not true universally, but it is true in a large percentage of cases. But on the other side it must be said that revenge is a very dangerous motive. In so far as society admits it, it allows a man to be the judge in his own case, which is exactly what the law tries to prevent. Moreover it is usually an excessive motive; it seeks to inflict more punishment than is desirable. Torture, for example, should not be punished by torture, but the man maddened by lust for vengeance will think a painless death too good for the object of his hate. Moreover—and it is here that Spinoza is in the right—a life dominated by a single passion is a narrow life, incompatible with every kind of wisdom. Revenge as such is therefore not the best reaction to injury.

Spinoza would say what the Christian says, and also something more. For him, all sin is due to ignorance; he would 'forgive them, for they know not what they do'. But he would have you avoid the limited purview from which, in his opinion, sin springs, and would urge you, even under the greatest misfortunes, to avoid being shut up in the world of your sorrow; he would have you understand it by seeing it in relation to its causes and as a part of the whole order of nature. As we saw, he believes that hatred can be overcome by love: 'Hatred is increased by being reciprocated,

561

and can on the other hand be destroyed by love. Hatred which is completely vanquished by love, passes into love; and love is thereupon greater, than if hatred had not preceded it.' I wish I could believe this, but I cannot, except in exceptional cases where the person hating is completely in the power of the person who refuses to hate in return. In such cases, surprise at being not punished may have a reforming effect. But so long as the wicked have power, it is not much use assuring them that you do not hate them, since they will attribute your words to the wrong motive. And you cannot deprive them of power by non-resistance.

The problem for Spinoza is easier than it is for one who has no belief in the ultimate goodness of the universe. Spinoza thinks that, if you see your misfortunes as they are in reality, as part of the concatenation of causes stretching from the beginning of time to the end, you will see that they are only misfortunes to you, not to the universe, to which they are merely passing discords heightening an ultimate harmony. I cannot accept this; I think that particular events are what they are, and do not become different by absorption into a whole. Each act of cruelty is eternally a part of the universe; nothing that happens later can make that act good rather than bad, or can confer perfection on the whole of which it is a part.

Nevertheless, when it is your lot to have to endure something that is (or seems to you) worse than the ordinary lot of mankind, Spinoza's principle of thinking about the whole, or at any rate about larger matters than your own grief, is a useful one. There are even times when it is comforting to reflect that human life, with all that it contains of evil and suffering, is an infinitesimal part of the life of the universe. Such reflections may not suffice to constitute a religion, but in a painful world they are a help towards sanity and an antidote to the paralysis of utter despair.

Chapter XI

LEIBNIZ

LEIBNIZ (1646-1716) was one of the supreme intellects of all time, but as a human being he was not admirable. He had, it is true, the virtues that one would wish to find mentioned in a testimonial to a prospective employee: he was industrious, frugal, temperate, and financially honest. But he was wholly destitute of those higher philosophic virtues that are so notable in Spinoza. His best thought was not such as would win him popularity, and he left his records of it unpublished in his desk. What he published was designed to win the approbation of princes and princesses. The consequence is that there are two systems of philosophy which may be regarded as representing Leibniz: one, which he proclaimed, was optimistic, orthodox, fantastic, and shallow; the other, which has been slowly unearthed from his manuscripts by fairly recent editors, was profound, coherent, largely Spinozistic, and amazingly logical. It was the popular Leibniz who invented the doctrine that this is the best of all possible worlds (to which F. H. Bradley added the sardonic comment 'and everything in it is a necessary evil'); it was this Leibniz whom Voltaire caricatured as Doctor Pangloss. It would be unhistorical to ignore this Leibniz, but the other is of far greater philosophical importance.

Leibniz was born two years before the end of the Thirty Years' War, at Leipzig, where his father was professor of moral philosophy. At the university he studied law, and in 1666 he obtained a Doctor's degree at Altdorf, where he was offered a professorship, which he refused, saying he had 'very different things in view'. In 1667 he entered the service of the archbishop of Mainz, who, like other West German princes, was oppressed by fear of Louis XIV. With the approval of the archbishop, Leibniz tried to persuade the French king to invade Egypt rather than Germany, but was met with a polite reminder that since the time of St Louis the holy war against the infidel had gone out of fashion. His project remained unknown to the public until it was discovered by Napoleon when he occupied Hanover in 1803, four years after his own abortive Egyptian expedition. In 1672, in connection with this scheme, Leibniz went to Paris, where he spent the greater part of the next four years. His contacts in Paris were of great importance for his intellectual development, for Paris at that time led the world both

563

in philosophy and in mathematics. It was there, in 1675-6, that he invented the infinitesimal calculus, in ignorance of Newton's previous but unpublished work on the same subject. Leibniz's work was first published in 1684, Newton's in 1687. The consequent dispute as to priority was unfortunate, and discreditable to all parties.

Leibniz was somewhat mean about money. When any young lady at the court of Hanover married, he used to give her what he called a 'wedding present', consisting of useful maxims, ending up with the advice not to give up washing now that she had secured a husband. History does not record whether the brides were grateful.

In Germany, Leibniz had been taught a neo-scholastic Aristotelian philosophy, of which he retained something throughout his later life. But in Paris he came to know Cartesianism and the materialism of Gassendi, both of which influenced him; at this time, he said, he abandoned the 'trivial schools', meaning scholasticism. In Paris he came to know Malebranche and Arnauld the Jansenist. The last important influence on his philosophy was that of Spinoza, whom he visited in 1676. He spent a month in frequent discussions with him, and secured part of the *Ethics* in manuscript. In later years he joined in decrying Spinoza, and minimized his contacts with him, saying he had met him once, and Spinoza had told some good anecdotes about politics.

His connection with the House of Hanover, in whose service he remained for the rest of his life, began in 1673. From 1680 onwards he was their librarian at Wolfenbüttel, and was officially employed in writing the history of Brunswick. He had reached the year 1009 when he died. The work was not published till 1843. Some of his time was spent on a project for the reunion of the Churches, but this proved abortive. He travelled to Italy to obtain evidence that the Dukes of Brunswick were connected with the Este family. But in spite of these services he was left behind at Hanover when George I became king of England, the chief reason being that his quarrel with Newton had made England unfriendly to him. However, the Princess of Wales, as he told all his correspondents, sided with him against Newton. In spite of her favour, he died neglected.

Leibniz's popular philosophy may be found in the *Monadology* and the *Principles of Nature and of Grace*, one of which (it is uncertain which) he wrote for Prince Eugene of Savoy, Marlborough's colleague. The basis of his theological optimism is set forth in the *Théodicée*, which he wrote for Queen Charlotte of Prussia. I shall begin with the philosophy set forth in these writings, and then proceed to his more solid work which he left unpublished.

Like Descartes and Spinoza, Leibniz based his philosophy on the notion of substance, but he differed radically from them as regards the relation of mind and matter, and as regards the number of substances. Descartes allowed three substances, God and mind and matter; Spinoza admitted God alone. For Descartes, extension is the essence of matter; for Spinoza, both extension and thought are attributes of God. Leibniz held that extension cannot be an attribute of a substance. His reason was that extension involves plurality, and can therefore only belong to an aggregate of substances; each single substance must be unextended. He believed, consequently, in an infinite number of substances, which he called 'monads'. Each of these would have some of the properties of a physical point, but only when viewed abstractly; in fact, each monad is a soul. This follows naturally from the rejection of extension as an attribute of substance; the only remaining possible essential attribute seemed to be thought. Thus Leibniz was led to deny the reality of matter, and to substitute an infinite family of souls.

The doctrine that substances cannot interact, which had been developed by Descartes' followers, was retained by Leibniz, and led to curious consequences. No two monads, he held, can ever have any causal relation to each other; when it seems as if they had, appearances are deceptive. Monads, as he expressed it, are 'window-less'. This led to two difficulties: one in dynamics, where bodies seem to affect each other, especially in impact; the other in relation to perception, which seems to be an effect of the perceived object upon the percipient. We will ignore the dynamical difficulty for the present, and consider only the question of perception. Leibniz held that every monad mirrors the universe, not because the universe affects it, but because God has given it a nature which spontane-ously produces this result. There is a 'pre-established harmony' between the changes in one monad and those in another, which produces the semblance of interaction. This is obviously an exten-sion of the two clocks, which strike at the same moment because each keeps perfect time. Leibniz has an infinite number of clocks, all arranged by the Creator to strike at the same instant, not because they affect each other, but because each is a perfectly accurate mechanism. To those who thought the pre-established harmony odd, Leibniz pointed out what admirable evidence is afforded of the existence of God.

Monads form a hierarchy, in which some are superior to others in the clearness and distinctness with which they mirror the universe. In all there is some degree of confusion in perception, but the amount of confusion varies according to the dignity of the monad concerned. A human body is entirely composed of monads, each of which is a soul, and each of which is immortal, but there is one dominant monad which is what is called *the* soul of the man of whose body it forms part. This monad is dominant, not only in the sense of having clearer perceptions than the others, but also in another sense. The changes in a human body (in ordinary circumstances) happen for the sake of the dominant monad: when my arm moves, the purpose served by the movement is in the dominant monad, i.e. my mind, not in the monads that compose my arm. This is the truth of what appears to common sense as the control of my will over my arm.

Space, as it appears to the senses, and as it is assumed in physics, is not real, but it has a real counterpart, namely the arrangement of the monads in a three-dimensional order according to the point of view from which they mirror the world. Each monad sees the world in a certain perspective peculiar to itself; in this sense we can speak, somewhat loosely, of the monad as having a spatial position.

Allowing ourselves this way of speaking, we can say that there is no such thing as a vacuum; every possible point of view is filled by one actual monad, and by only one. No two monads are exactly alike; this is Leibniz's principle of the 'identity of indiscernibles'.

In contrasting himself with Spinoza, Leibniz made much of the free will allowed in his system. He had a 'principle of sufficient reason', according to which nothing happens without a reason; but when we are concerned with free agents, the reasons for their actions 'incline without necessitating'. What a human being does always has a motive, but the sufficient reason of his action has no logical necessity. So, at least, Leibniz says when he is writing popularly, but, as we shall see, he had another doctrine which he kept to himself after finding that Arnauld thought it shocking.

God's actions have the same kind of freedom. He always acts for the best, but He is not under any logical compulsion to do so. Leibniz agrees with Thomas Aquinas that God cannot act contrary to the laws of logic, but He can decree whatever is logically possible, and this leaves Him a great latitude of choice.

Leibniz brought into their final form the metaphysical proofs of God's existence. These had a long history; they begin with Aristotle, or even with Plato; they are formalized by the scholastics, and one of them, the ontological argument, was invented by St Anselm. This argument, though rejected by St Thomas, was revived by Descartes. Leibniz, whose logical skill was supreme, stated the arguments better than they had ever been stated before. That is my reason for examining them in connection with him.

Before examining the arguments in detail, it is as well to realize that modern theologians no longer rely upon them. Medieval theology is derivative from the Greek intellect. The God of the Old

Testament is a God of power, the God of the New Testament is also a God of love; but the God of the theologians, from Aristotle to Calvin, is one whose appeal is intellectual: His existence solves certain puzzles which otherwise would create argumentative difficulties in the understanding of the universe. This Deity who appears at the end of a piece of reasoning, like the proof of a proposition in geometry, did not satisfy Rousseau, who reverted to a conception of God more akin to that of the Gospels. In the main, modern theologians, especially such as are Protestant, have followed Rousseau in this respect. The philosophers have been more conservative; in Hegel, Lotze, and Bradley arguments of the metaphysical sort persist, in spite of the fact that Kant professed to have demolished such arguments once for all.

Leibniz's arguments for the existence of God are four in number; they are (1) the ontological argument, (2) the cosmological argument, (3) the argument from eternal truths, (4) the argument from the pre-established harmony, which may be generalized into the argument from design, or the physico-theological argument, as Kant calls it. We will consider these arguments successively.

The ontological argument depends upon the distinction between existence and essence. Any ordinary person or thing, it is held, on the one hand exists, and on the other hand has certain qualities, which make up his or its 'essence'. Hamlet, though he does not exist, has a certain essence; he is melancholy, undecided, witty, etc. When we describe a person, the question whether he is real or imaginary remains open, however minute our description may be. This is expressed in scholastic language by saying that, in the case of any finite substance, its essence does not imply its existence. But in the case of God, defined as the most perfect Being, St Anselm, followed by Descartes, maintains that essence does imply existence, on the ground that a Being who possesses all other perfections is better if He exists than if He does not, from which it follows that if He does not He is not the best possible Being.

Leibniz neither wholly accepts nor wholly rejects this argument; it needs to be supplemented, so he says, by a proof that God, so defined, is possible. He wrote out a proof that the idea of God is possible, which he showed to Spinoza when he saw him at the Hague. This proof defines God as the most perfect Being, i.e. as the subject of all perfections, and a perfection is defined as a 'simple quality which is positive and absolute, and expresses without any limits whatever it does express'. Leibniz easily proves that no two perfections, as above defined, can be incompatible. He concludes: 'There is, therefore, or there can be conceived, a subject of all perfections, or most perfect Being. Whence it follows also that He

567

exists, for existence is among the number of the perfections.'

Kant encountered this argument by maintaining that 'existence' is not a predicate. Another kind of refutation results from my theory of descriptions. The argument does not, to a modern mind, seem very convincing, but it is easier to feel convinced that it must be fallacious than it is to find out precisely where the fallacy lies.

The cosmological argument is more plausible than the ontological argument. It is a form of the First-Cause argument, which is itself derived from Aristotle's argument of the unmoved mover. The First-Cause argument is simple. It points out that everything finite has a cause, which in turn had a cause, and so on. This series of previous causes cannot, it is maintained, be infinite, and the first term in the series must itself be uncaused, since otherwise it would not be the first term. There is therefore an uncaused cause of everything, and this is obviously God.

In Leibniz the argument takes a somewhat different form. He argues that every particular thing in the world is 'contingent', that is to say, it would be logically possible for it not to exist; and this is true, not only of each particular thing, but of the whole universe. Even if we suppose the universe to have always existed, there is nothing within the universe to show why it exists. But everything has to have a sufficient reason, according to Leibniz's philosophy; therefore the universe as a whole must have a sufficient reason, which must be outside the universe. This sufficient reason is God.

This argument is better than the straightforward First-Cause argument, and cannot be so easily refuted. The First-Cause argument rests on the assumption that every series must have a first term, which is false; for example, the series of proper fractions has no first term. But Leibniz's argument does not depend upon the view that the universe must have had a beginning in time. The argument is valid so long as we grant Leibniz's principle of sufficient reason, but if this principle is denied it collapses. What exactly Leibniz meant by the principle of sufficient reason is a controversial question. Couturat maintains that it means that every true proposition is 'analytic', i.e. such that its contradictory is self-contradictory. But this interpretation (which has support in writings that Leibniz did not publish) belongs, if true, to the esoteric doctrine. In his published works he maintains that there is a difference between necessary and contingent propositions, that only the former follow from the laws of logic, and that all propositions asserting existence are contingent, with the sole exception of the existence of God. Though God exists necessarily, He was not compelled by logic to create the world; on the contrary, this was a free choice, motivated, but not necessitated, by His goodness.

It is clear that Kant is right in saying that this argument depends upon the ontological argument. If the existence of the world can only be accounted for by the existence of a necessary Being, then there must be a Being whose essence involves existence, for that is what is meant by a necessary Being. But if it is possible that there should be a Being whose essence involves existence, then reason alone, without experience, can define such a Being, whose existence will follow from the ontological argument; for everything that has to do only with essence can be known independently of experience —such at least is Leibniz's view. The apparent greater plausibility of the cosmological as opposed to the ontological argument is therefore deceptive.

The argument from the eternal truths is a little difficult to state precisely. Roughly, the argument is this: Such a statement as 'it is raining' is sometimes true and sometimes false, but 'two and two are four' is always true. All statements that have only to do with essence, not with existence, are either always true or never true. Those that are always true are called 'eternal truths'. The gist of the argument is that truths are part of the contents of minds, and that an eternal truth must be part of the content of an eternal mind. There is already an argument not unlike this in Plato, where he deduces immortality from the eternity of the ideas. But in Leibniz the argument is more developed. He holds that the ultimate reason for contingent truths must be found in necessary truths. The argument here is as in the cosmological argument: there must be a reason for the whole contingent world, and this reason cannot itself be contingent, but must be sought among eternal truths. But a reason for what exists must itself exist; therefore eternal truths must, in some sense, exist, and they can only exist as thoughts in the mind of God. This argument is really only another form of the cosmological argument. It is, however, open to the further objection that a truth can hardly be said to 'exist' in a mind which apprehends it.

The argument from the pre-established harmony, as Leibniz states it, is only valid for those who accept his windowless monads which all mirror the universe. The argument is that, since all the clocks keep time with each other without any casual interaction, there must have been a single outside Cause that regulated all of them. The difficulty, of course, is the one that besets the whole monadology: if the monads never interact, how does any one of them know that there are any others? What seems like mirroring the universe may be merely a dream. In fact, if Leibniz is right, it *is* merely a dream, but he has ascertained somehow that all the monads have similar dreams at the same time. This, of course, is fantastic, and would never have seemed credible but for the previous history of Cartesianism.

Leibniz's argument, however, can be freed from dependence on his peculiar metaphysic, and transformed into what is called the argument from design. This argument contends that, on a survey of the known world, we find things which cannot plausibly be explained as the product of blind natural forces, but are much more reasonably to be regarded as evidences of a beneficent purpose.

This argument has no formal logical defect; its premises are empirical, and its conclusion professes to be reached in accordance with the usual canons of empirical inference. The question whether it is to be accepted or not turns, therefore, not on general metaphysical questions, but on comparatively detailed considerations. There is one important difference between this argument and the others, namely, that the God whom (if valid) it demonstrates need not have all the usual metaphysical attributes. He need not be omnipotent or omniscient; He may be only vastly wiser and more powerful than we are. The evils in the world may be due to His limited power. Some modern theologians have made use of these possibilities in forming their conception of God. But such speculations are remote from the philosophy of Leibniz, to which we must now return.

One of the most characteristic features of that philosophy is the doctrine of many possible worlds. A world is 'possible' if it does not contradict the laws of logic. There are an infinite number of possible worlds, all of which God contemplated before creating the actual world. Being good, God decided to create the best of the possible worlds, and He considered that one to be the best which had the greatest excess of good over evil. He could have created a world containing no evil, but it would not have been so good as the actual world. That is because some great goods are logically bound up with certain evils. To take a trivial illustration, a drink of cold water when you are very thirsty on a hot day may give you such great pleasure that you think the previous thirst, though painful, was worth enduring, because without it the subsequent enjoyment could not have been so great. For theology, it is not such illustrations that are important, but the connection of sin with free will. Free will is a great good, but it was logically impossible for God to bestow free will and at the same time decree that there should be no sin. God therefore decided to make man free, although he foresaw that Adam would eat the apple, and although sin inevitably brought punishment. The world that resulted, although it contains evil, has a greater surplus of good over evil than any other possible world; it is therefore the best of all possible worlds, and the evil that it contains affords no argument against the goodness of God.

This argument apparently satisfied the Queen of Prussia. Her serfs continued to suffer the evil, while she continued to enjoy the good, and it was comforting to be assured by a great philosopher that this was just and right.

Leibniz's solution of the problem of evil, like most of his other popular doctrines, is logically possible, but not very convincing. A Manichæan might retort that this is the worst of all possible worlds, in which the good things that exist serve only to heighten the evils. The world, he might say, was created by a wicked demiurge, who allowed free will, which is good, in order to make sure of sin, which is bad, and of which the evil outweighs the good of free will. The demiurge, he might continue, created some virtuous men, in order that they might be punished by the wicked; for the punishment of the virtuous is so great an evil that it makes the world worse than if no good men existed. I am not advocating this opinion, which I consider fantastic; I am only saying that it is no more fantastic than Leibniz's theory. People wish to think the universe good, and will be lenient to bad arguments proving that it is so, while bad arguments proving that it is bad are closely scanned. In fact, of course, the world is partly good and partly bad, and no 'problem of evil' arises unless this obvious fact is denied.

I come now to Leibniz's esoteric philosophy, in which we find reasons for much that seems arbitrary or fantastic in his popular expositions, as well as an interpretation of his doctrines which, if it had become generally known, would have made them much less acceptable. It is a remarkable fact that he so imposed upon subsequent students of philosophy that most of the editors who published selections from the immense mass of his manuscripts preferred what supported the received interpretation of his system, and rejected as unimportant essays which prove him to have been a far more profound thinker than he wished to be thought. Most of the texts upon which we must rely for an understanding of his esoteric doctrine were first published in 1901 or 1903, in two works by Louis Couturat. One of these was even headed by Leibniz with the remark: 'Here I have made enormous progress.' But in spite of this, no editor thought it worth printing until Leibniz had been dead for nearly two centuries. It is true that his letters to Arnauld, which contain a part of his more profound philosophy, were published in the nineteenth century; but I was the first to notice their importance. Arnauld's reception of these letters was discouraging. He writes: 'I find in these thoughts so many things which alarm me,

and which almost all men, if I am not mistaken, will find so shocking, that I do not see of what use a writing can be, which
apparently all the world will reject.' This hostile opinion no doubt
led Leibniz, thenceforth, to adopt a policy of secrecy as to his real
thoughts on philosophical subjects.

The conception of substance, which is fundamental in the
philosophies of Descartes, Spinoza, and Leibniz, is derived from the
logical category of subject and predicate. Some words can be either
subjects or predicates; e.g. I can say 'the sky is blue' and 'blue is a
colour'. Other words—of which proper names are the most obvious
instances—can never occur as predicates, but only as subjects, or
as one of the terms of a relation, Such words are held to designate
substances. Substances, in addition to this logical characteristic,
persist through time, unless destroyed by God's omnipotence
(which, one gathers, never happens). Every true proposition is either
general, like 'all men are mortal', in which case it states that one
predicate implies another, or particular, like 'Socrates is mortal', in
which case the predicate is contained in the subject, and the quality
denoted by the predicate is part of the notion of the substance
denoted by the subject. Whatever happens to Socrates can be
asserted in a sentence in which 'Socrates' is the subject and the
words describing the happening in question are the predicate. All
these predicates put together make up the 'notion' of Socrates. All
belong to him necessarily, in this sense, that a substance of which
they could not be truly asserted would not be Socrates, but some
one else.

Leibniz was a firm believer in the importance of logic, not only
in its own sphere, but as the basis of metaphysics. He did work on
mathematical logic which would have been enormously important
if he had published it; he would, in that case, have been the founder
of mathematical logic, which would have become known a century
and a half sooner than it did in fact. He abstained from publishing,
because he kept on finding evidence that Aristotle's doctrine of the
syllogism was wrong on some points; respect for Aristotle made it
impossible for him to believe this, so he mistakenly supposed that
the errors must be his own. Nevertheless he cherished throughout
his life the hope of discovering a kind of generalized mathematics,
which he called *Characteristica Universalis*, by means of which
thinking could be replaced by calculation. 'If we had it,' he says,
'we should be able to reason in metaphysics and morals in much
the same way as in geometry and analysis.' 'If controversies were
to arise, there would be no more need of disputation between two
philosophers than between two accountants. For it would suffice to
take their pencils in their hands, to sit down to their slates, and to

say to each other (with a friend as witness, if they liked): Let us calculate.'

Leibniz based his philosophy upon two logical premises, the law of contradiction and the law of sufficient reason. Both depend upon the notion of an 'analytic' proposition, which is one in which the predicate is contained in the subject—for instance, 'all white men are men'. The law of contradiction states that all analytic propositions are true. The law of sufficient reason (in the esoteric system only) states that all true propositions are analytic. This applies even to what we should regard as empirical statements about matters of fact. If I make a journey, the notion of me must from all eternity have included the notion of this journey, which is a predicate of me. 'We may say that the nature of an individual substance, or complete being, is to have a notion so completed that it suffices to comprehend, and to render deducible from it, all the predicates of the subject to which this notion is attributed. Thus the quality of king, which belongs to Alexander the Great, abstracting from the subject, is not sufficiently determined for an individual, and does not involve other qualities of the same subject, nor all that the notion of this prince contains, whereas God, seeing the individual notion or haecceity of Alexander, sees in it at the same time the foundation and the reason of all the predicates which can be truly attributed to him, as e.g. whether he would conquer Darius and Porus, even to knowing *a priori* (and not by experience) whether he died a natural death or by poison, which we can only know by history.'

One of the most definite statements of the basis of his metaphysic occurs in a letter to Arnauld:

'In consulting the notion which I have of every true proposition, I find that every predicate, necessary or contingent, past, present, or future, is comprised in the notion of the subject, and I ask no more. . . . The proposition in question is of great importance, and deserves to be well established, for it follows that every soul is as a world apart, independent of everything else except God; that it is not only immortal and so to speak impassible, but that it keeps in its substance traces of all that happens to it.'

He goes on to explain that substances do not act on each other, but agree through all mirroring the universe, each from its own point of view. There can be interaction, because all that happens to each subject is part of its own notion, and eternally determined if that substance exists.

This system is evidently just as deterministic as that of Spinoza. Arnauld expresses his horror of the statement (which Leibniz had made): 'That the individual notion of each person involves once for all everything that will ever happen to him.' Such a view is evidently incompatible with the Christian doctrine of sin and free will. Finding it ill received by Arnauld, Leibniz carefully refrained from making it public.

For human beings, it is true, there is a difference between truths known by logic and truths known by experience. This difference arises in two ways. In the first place, although everything that happens to Adam follows from his notion, *if he exists*, we can only ascertain his existence by experience. In the second place, the notion of any individual substance is infinitely complex, and the analysis required to deduce his predicates is only possible for God. These differences, however, are only due to our ignorance and intellectual limitations; for God, they do not exist. God apprehends the notion of Adam in all its infinite complexity, and can therefore see all true propositions about Adam as analytic. God can also ascertain *a priori* whether Adam exists. For God knows His own goodness, from which it follows that He will create the best possible world; and He also knows whether or not Adam forms part of this world. There is therefore no real escape from determinism through our ignorance.

There is, however, a further point, which is very curious. At most times, Leibniz represents the Creation as a free act of God, requiring the exercise of His will. According to this doctrine, the determination of what actually exists is not effected by observation, but must proceed by way of God's goodness. Apart from God's goodness, which leads Him to create the best possible world there is no *a priori* reason why one thing should exist rather than another.

But sometimes, in papers not shown to any human being, there is a quite different theory as to why some things exist and others, equally possible, do not. According to this view, everything that does not exist struggles to exist, but not all possibles can exist, because they are not all 'compossible'. It may be possible that A should exist, and also possible that B should exist, but not possible that both A and B should exist; in that case, A and B are not 'compossible'. Two or more things are only 'compossible' when it is possible for all of them to exist. Leibniz seems to have imagined a sort of war in the Limbo inhabited by essences all trying to exist; in this war, groups of compossibles combine, and the largest group of compossibles wins, like the largest pressure group in a political contest. Leibniz even uses this conception as a way of *defining* existence. He says: 'The existent may be defined as that which is compatible with more things than is anything incompatible with itself'. That is to say, if A is incompatible with B, while A is compatible with C and D and E, but B is only compatible with F and G, then A, but not B, exists *by definition*. 'The existent,' he says, 'is the being which is compatible with the most things.'

In this account, there is no mention of God, and apparently no act of creation. Nor is there need of anything but pure logic for determining what exists. The question whether A and B are compossible is, for Leibniz, a logical question, namely: Does the existence of both A and B involve a contradiction? It follows that, in theory, logic can decide the question what group of compossibles is the largest, and this group consequently will exist.

Perhaps, however, Leibniz did not really mean that the above was a *definition* of existence. If it was merely a criterion, it can be reconciled with his popular views by means of what he calls 'metaphysical perfection'. Metaphysical perfection, as he uses the term, seems to mean quantity of existence. It is, he says, 'nothing but the magnitude of positive reality strictly understood'. He always argues that God created as much as possible; this is one of his reasons for rejecting a vacuum. There is a general belief (which I have never understood) that it is better to exist than not to exist; on this ground children are exhorted to be grateful to their parents. Leibniz evidently held this view, and thought it part of God's goodness to create as full a universe as possible. It would follow that the actual world would consist of the largest group of compossibles. It would still be true that logic alone, given a sufficiently able logician, could decide whether a given possible substance would exist or not.

Leibniz, in his private thinking, is the best example of a philosopher who uses logic as a key to metaphysics. This type of philosophy begins with Parmenides, and is carried further in Plato's use of the theory of ideas to prove various extra-logical propositions. Spinoza belongs to the same type, and so does Hegel. But none of these is so clear cut as Leibniz in drawing inferences from syntax to the real world. This kind of argumentation has fallen into disrepute owing to the growth of empiricism. Whether any valid inferences are possible from language to non-linguistic facts is a question as to which I do not care to dogmatize; but certainly the inferences found in Leibniz and other *a priori* philosophers are not valid, since all are due to a defective logic. The subject-predicate logic, which all such philosophers in the past assumed, either ignores relations altogether, or produces fallacious arguments to prove that relations are unreal. Leibniz is guilty of a special inconsistency in combining the subject-predicate logic with pluralism, for the proposition 'there are many monads' is not of the subject-predicate form. To be consistent, a philosopher who believes all propositions to be of this form should be a monist, like Spinoza. Leibniz rejected monism largely owing to his interest in dynamics, and to his argument that extension involves repetition, and therefore cannot be an attribute of a single substance.

Leibniz is a dull writer, and his effect on German philosophy was to make it pedantic and arid. His disciple Wolf, who dominated the German universities until the publication of Kant's *Critique of Pure Reason*, left out whatever was most interesting in Leibniz, and produced a dry professorial way of thinking. Outside Germany, Leibniz's philosophy had little influence; his contemporary, Locke, governed British philosophy, while in France Descartes continued to reign until he was overthrown by Voltaire, who made English empiricism fashionable.

Nevertheless, Leibniz remains a great man, and his greatness is more apparent now than it was at any earlier time. Apart from his eminence as a mathematician and as the inventor of the infinitesimal calculus, he was a pioneer in mathematical logic, of which he perceived the importance when no one else did so. And his philosophical hypotheses, though fantastic, are very clear, and capable of precise expression. Even his monads can still be useful as suggesting possible ways of viewing perception, though they cannot be regarded as windowless. What I, for my part, think best in his theory of monads is his two kinds of space, one subjective, in the perceptions of each monad, and one objective, consisting of the assemblage of points of view of the various monads. This, I believe, is still useful in relating perception to physics.

Chapter XII

PHILOSOPHICAL LIBERALISM

THE rise of liberalism, in politics and philosophy, provides material for the study of a very general and very important question, namely: What has been the influence of political and social circumstances upon the thoughts of eminent and original thinkers, and, conversely, what has been the influence of these men upon subsequent political and social developments?

Two opposite errors, both common, are to be guarded against. On the one hand, men who are more familiar with books than with affairs are apt to over-estimate the influence of philosophers. When they see some political party proclaiming itself inspired by So-and-So's teaching, they think its actions are attributable to So-and-So, whereas, not infrequently, the philosopher is only acclaimed because he recommends what the party would have done in any case. Writers of books, until recently, almost all exaggerated the effects of their predecessors in the same trade. But conversely, a new error has arisen by reaction against the old one, and this new error consists in regarding theorists as almost passive products of their circumstances, and as having hardly any influence at all upon the course of events. Ideas, according to this view, are the froth on the surface of deep currents, which are determined by material and technical causes: social changes are no more caused by thought than the flow of a river is caused by the bubbles that reveal its direction to an onlooker. For my part, I believe that the truth lies between these two extremes. Between ideas and practical life, as everywhere else, there is reciprocal interaction; to ask which is cause and which effect is as futile as the problem of the hen and the egg. I shall not waste time upon a discussion of this question in the abstract, but shall consider historically one important case of the general question, namely the development of liberalism and its off-shoots from the end of the seventeenth century to the present day.

Early liberalism was a product of England and Holland, and had certain well-marked characteristics. It stood for religious toleration; it was Protestant, but of a latitudinarian rather than of a fanatical kind; it regarded the wars of religion as silly. It valued commerce and industry, and favoured the rising middle class rather than the monarchy and the aristocracy; it had immense respect for the rights of property, especially when accumulated by the labours of the

577

individual possessor. The hereditary principle, though not rejected, was restricted in scope more than it had previously been; in particular, the divine right of kings was rejected in favour of the view that every community has a right, at any rate initially, to choose its own form of government. Implicitly, the tendency of early liberalism was towards democracy tempered by the rights of property. There was a belief—not at first wholly explicit—that all men are born equal, and that their subsequent inequality is a product of circumstances. This led to a great emphasis upon the importance of education as opposed to congenital characteristics. There was a certain bias against government, because governments almost everywhere were in the hands of kings or aristocracies, who seldom either understood or respected the needs of merchants, but this bias was held in check by the hope that the necessary understanding and respect would be won before long.

Early liberalism was optimistic, energetic, and philosophic, because it represented growing forces which appeared likely to become victorious without great difficulty, and to bring by their victory great benefits to mankind. It was opposed to everything medieval, both in philosophy and in politics, because medieval theories had been used to sanction the powers of Church and king, to justify persecution, and to obstruct the rise of science; but it was opposed equally to the then modern fanaticisms of Calvinists and Anabaptists. It wanted an end to political and theological strife, in order to liberate energies for the exciting enterprises of commerce and science, such as the East India Company and the Bank of England, the theory of gravitation and the discovery of the circulation of the blood. Throughout the Western world bigotry was giving place to enlightenment, the fear of Spanish power was ending, all classes were increasing in prosperity, and the highest hopes appeared to be warranted by the most sober judgment. For a hundred years, nothing occurred to dim these hopes; then, at last, they themselves generated the French Revolution, which led directly to Napoleon and thence to the Holy Alliance. After these events, liberalism had to acquire its second wind before the renewed optimism of the nineteenth century became possible.

Before embarking upon any detail, it will be well to consider the general pattern of the liberal movements from the seventeenth to the nineteenth century. This pattern is at first simple, but grows gradually more and more complex. The distinctive character of the whole movement is, in a certain wide sense, individualism; but this is a vague term until further defined. The philosophers of Greece, down to and including Aristotle, were not individualists in the sense in which I wish to use the term. They thought of a man as essentially a member of a community; Plato's *Republic*, for example, is concerned to define the good community, not the good individual. With the loss of political liberty from the time of Alexander onwards, individualism developed, and was represented by the Cynics and Stoics. According to the Stoic philosophy, a man could live a good life in no matter what social circumstances. This was also the view of Christianity, especially before it acquired control of the State. But in the Middle Ages, while mystics kept alive the original individualistic trends in Christian ethics, the outlook of most men, including the majority of philosophers, was dominated by a firm synthesis of dogma, law, and custom, which caused men's theoretical beliefs and practical morality to be controlled by a social institution, namely the Catholic Church: what was true and what was good was to be ascertained, not by solitary thought, but by the collective wisdom of Councils.

The first important breach in this system was made by Protestantism, which asserted that General Councils may err. To determine the truth thus became no longer a social but an individual enterprise. Since different individuals reached different conclusions, the result was strife, and theological decisions were sought, no longer in assemblies of bishops, but on the battle-field. Since neither party was able to extirpate the other, it became evident, in the end, that a method must be found of reconciling intellectual and ethical individualism with ordered social life. This was one of the main problems which early liberalism attempted to solve.

Meanwhile individualism had penetrated into philosophy. Descartes' fundamental certainty, 'I think, therefore I am', made the basis of knowledge different for each person, since for each the starting-point was his own existence, not that of other individuals or of the community. His emphasis upon the reliability of clear and distinct ideas tended in the same direction, since it is by introspection that we think we discover whether our ideas are clear and distinct. Most philosophy since Descartes has had this intellectually individualistic aspect in a greater or less degree.

There are, however, various forms of this general position, which have, in practice, very different consequences. The outlook of the typical scientific discoverer has perhaps the smallest dose of individualism. When he arrives at a new theory, he does so solely because it seems right to him; he does not bow to authority, for, if he did, he would continue to accept the theories of his predecessors. At the same time, his appeal is to generally received canons of truth, and he hopes to persuade other men, not by his authority, but by arguments which are convincing to them as individuals. In science, any clash between the individual and society is in essence transitory, since men of science, broadly speaking, all accept the same intellectual standards, and therefore debate and investigation usually produce agreement in the end. This, however, is a modern development; in the time of Galileo, the authority of Aristotle and the Church was still considered at least as cogent as the evidence of the senses. This shows how the element of individualism in scientific method, though not prominent, is nevertheless essential.

Early liberalism was individualistic in intellectual matters, and also in economics, but was not emotionally or ethically self-assertive. This form of liberalism dominated the English eighteenth century, the founders of the American Constitution, and the French encyclopaedists. During the French Revolution, it was represented by the more moderate parties, including the Girondins, but with their extermination it disappeared for a generation from French politics. In England, after the Napoleonic wars, it again became influential with the rise of the Benthamites and the Manchester School. Its greatest success has been in America, where, unhampered by feudalism and a State Church, it has been dominant from 1776 to the present day, or at any rate to 1933.

A new movement, which has gradually developed into the antithesis of liberalism, begins with Rousseau, and acquires strength from the romantic movement and the principle of nationality. In this movement, individualism is extended from the intellectual sphere to that of the passions, and the anarchic aspects of individualism are made explicit. The cult of the hero, as developed by Carlyle and Nietzsche, is typical of this philosophy. Various elements were combined in it. There was dislike of early industrialism, hatred of the ugliness that it produced, and revulsion against its cruelties. There was a nostalgia for the Middle Ages, which were idealized owing to hatred of the modern world. There was an attempt to combine championship of the fading privileges of Church and aristocracy with defence of wage-earners against the tyranny of manufacturers. There was vehement assertion of the right of rebellion in the name of nationalism, and of the splendour of war in defence of 'liberty'. Byron was the poet of this movement; Fichte, Carlyle, and Nietzsche were its philosophers.

But since we cannot all have the career of heroic leaders, and cannot all make our individual will prevail, this philosophy, like all other forms of anarchism, inevitably leads, when adopted, to the despotic government of the most successful 'hero'. And when his tyranny is established, he will suppress in others the self-assertive ethic by which he has risen to power. This whole theory of life, therefore, is self-refuting, in the sense that its adoption in practice leads to the realization of something utterly different: a dictatorial State in which the individual is severely repressed.

There is yet another philosophy which, in the main, is an off-shoot of liberalism, namely that of Marx. I shall consider him at a later stage, but for the moment he is merely to be borne in mind.

The first comprehensive statement of the liberal philosophy is to be found in Locke, the most influential though by no means the most profound of modern philosophers. In England, his views were so completely in harmony with those of most intelligent men that it is difficult to trace their influence except in theoretical philosophy; in France, on the other hand, where they led to an opposition to the existing regime in practice and to the prevailing Cartesianism in theory, they clearly had a considerable effect in shaping the course of events. This is an example of a general principle: a philosophy developed in a politically and economically advanced country, which is, in its birthplace, little more than a clarification and systemization of prevalent opinion, may become elsewhere a source of revolutionary ardour, and ultimately of actual revolution. It is mainly through theorists that the maxims regulating the policy of advanced countries become known to less advanced countries. In the advanced countries, practice inspires theory; in the others, theory inspires practice. This difference is one of the reasons why transplanted ideas are seldom so successful as they were in their native soil.

Before considering the philosophy of Locke, let us review some of the circumstances in seventeenth-century England that were influential in forming his opinions.

The conflict between King and Parliament in the Civil War gave Englishmen, once for all, a love of compromise and moderation, and a fear of pushing any theory to its logical conclusion, which has dominated them down to the present time. The principles for which the Long Parliament contended had, at first, the support of a large majority. They wished to abolish the king's right to grant trade monopolies, and to make him acknowledge the exclusive right of Parliament to impose taxes. They desired liberty within the Church of England for opinions and practices which were persecuted by Archbishop Laud. They held that Parliament should meet at stated intervals, and should not be convoked only on rare occasions when the king found its collaboration indispensable. They objected to arbitrary arrest and to the subservience of the judges to the royal wishes. But many, while prepared to agitate for these ends, were not prepared to levy war against the king, which appeared to them an act of treason and impiety. As soon as actual war broke out, the division of forces became more nearly equal.

The political development from the outbreak of the Civil War to the establishment of Cromwell as Lord Protector followed the course which has now become familiar but was then unprecedented. The Parliamentary party consisted of two factions, the Presbyterians and the Independents; the Presbyterians desired to preserve a State Church, but to abolish bishops; the Independents agreed with them about bishops, but held that each congregation should be free to choose its own theology, without the interference of any central ecclesiastical government. The Presbyterians, in the main, were of a higher social class than the Independents, and their political opinions were more moderate. They wished to come to terms with the king as soon as defeat had made him conciliatory. Their policy, however, was rendered impossible by two circumstances: first, the king developed a martyr's stubbornness about bishops; second, the defeat of the king proved difficult, and was only achieved by Cromwell's New Model Army, which consisted of Independents. Consequently, when the king's military resistance was broken, he could still not be induced to make a treaty, and the Presbyterians had lost the preponderance of armed force in the Parliamentary armies. The defence of democracy had thrown power into the hands of a minority, and it used its power with a complete disregard for democracy and parliamentary government. When Charles I had attempted to arrest the five members, there had been a universal outcry, and his failure had made him ridiculous. But Cromwell had no such difficulties. By Pride's Purge, he dismissed about a hundred Presbyterian members, and obtained for a time a subservient majority. When, finally, he decided to dismiss Parliament altogether, 'not a dog barked'—war had made only military force seem important, and had produced a contempt for constitutional forms. For the rest of Cromwell's life, the government of England was a military tyranny, hated by an increasing majority of the nation, but impossible to shake off while his partisans alone were armed.

Charles II, after hiding in oak trees and living as a refugee in Holland, determined, at the Restoration, that he would not again set out on his travels. This imposed a certain moderation. He claimed no power to impose taxes not sanctioned by Parliament. He assented to the Habeas Corpus Act, which deprived the Crown of the power of arbitrary arrest. On occasion he could flout the fiscal power of Parliament by means of subsidies from Louis XIV, but in the main he was a constitutional monarch. Most of the limitations of royal power originally desired by the opponents of Charles I were conceded at the Restoration, and were respected by Charles II because it had been shown that kings could be made to suffer at the hands of their subjects.

James II, unlike his brother, was totally destitute of subtlety and finesse. By his bigoted Catholicism he united against himself the Anglicans and Noncomformists, in spite of his attempts to conciliate the latter by granting them toleration in defiance of Parliament. Foreign policy also played a part. The Stuarts, in order to avoid the taxation required in war-time, which would have made them dependent upon Parliament, pursued a policy of subservience, first to Spain and then to France. The growing power of France roused the invariable English hostility to the leading Continental State, and the Revocation of the Edict of Nantes made Protestant feeling bitterly opposed to Louis XIV. In the end, almost everybody in England wished to be rid of James. But almost everybody was equally determined to avoid a return to the days of the Civil War and Cromwell's dictatorship. Since there was no constitutional way of getting rid of James, there must be a revolution, but it must be quickly ended, so as to give no opportunity for disruptive forces. The rights of Parliament must be secured once for all. The king must go, but monarchy must be preserved; it should be, however, not a monarchy of Divine Right, but one dependent upon legislative sanction, and so upon Parliament. By a combination of aristocracy and big business, all this was achieved in a moment, without the necessity of firing a shot. Compromise and moderation had succeeded, after every form of intransigeance had been tried and had failed.

The new king, being Dutch, brought with him the commercial and theological wisdom for which his country was noted. The Bank of England was created; the national debt was made into a secure investment, no longer liable to repudiation at the caprice of the monarch. The Act of Toleration, while leaving Catholics and Nonconformists subject to various disabilities, put an end to actual persecution. Foreign policy became resolutely anti-French, and remained so, with brief intermissions. until the defeat of Napoleon.

Chapter XIII

LOCKE'S THEORY OF KNOWLEDGE

JOHN LOCKE (1632-1704) is the apostle of the Revolution of 1688, the most moderate and the most successful of all revolutions. Its aims were modest, but they were exactly achieved, and no subsequent revolution has hitherto been found necessary in England. Locke faithfully embodies its spirit, and most of his works appeared within a few years of 1688. His chief work in theoretical philosophy, the *Essay Concerning Human Understanding*, was finished in 1687 and published in 1690. His *First Letter on Toleration* was originally published in Latin in 1689, in Holland, to which country Locke had found it prudent to withdraw in 1683. Two further letters on *Toleration* were published in 1690 and 1692. His two *Treatises on Government* were licensed for printing in 1689, and published soon afterwards. His book on *Education* was published in 1693. Although his life was long, all his influential writings are confined to the few years from 1687 to 1693. Successful revolutions are stimulating to those who believe in them.

Locke's father was a Puritan, who fought on the side of Parliament. In the time of Cromwell, when Locke was at Oxford, the university was still scholastic in its philosophy; Locke disliked both scholasticism and the fanaticism of the Independents. He was much influenced by Descartes. He became a physician, and his patron was Lord Shaftesbury, Dryden's 'Achitophel'. When Shaftesbury fell in 1683, Locke fled with him to Holland, and remained there until the Revolution. After the Revolution, except for a few years during which he was employed at the Board of Trade, his life was devoted to literary work and to numerous controversies arising out of his books.

The years before the Revolution of 1688, when Locke could not, without grave risk, take any part, theoretical or practical, in English politics, were spent by him in composing his *Essay Concerning Human Understanding*. This is his most important book, and the one upon which his fame most securely rests; but his influence on the philosophy of politics was so great and so lasting that he must be treated as the founder of philosophical liberalism as much as of empiricism in theory of knowledge.

Locke is the most fortunate of all philosophers. He completed his work in theoretical philosophy just at the moment when the government of his country fell into the hands of men who shared his political opinions. Both in practice and in theory, the views which he advocated were held, for many years to come, by the most vigorous and influential politicians and philosophers. His political doctrines, with the developments due to Montesquieu, are embedded in the American Constitution, and are to be seen at work whenever there is a dispute between President and Congress. The British Constitution was based upon his doctrines until about fifty years ago, and so was that which the French adopted in 1871.

His influence in eighteenth-century France, which was immense, was primarily due to Voltaire, who as a young man spent some time in England, and interpreted English ideas to his compatriots in the *Lettres philosophiques*. The *philosophes* and the moderate reformers followed him; the extreme revolutionaries followed Rousseau. His French followers, rightly or wrongly believed in an intimate connection between his theory of knowledge and his politics.

In England this connection is less evident. Of his two most eminent followers, Berkeley was politically unimportant, and Hume was a Tory who set forth his reactionary views in his *History of England*. But after the time of Kant, when German idealism began to influence English thought, there came to be again a connection between philosophy and politics: in the main, the philosophers who followed the Germans were Conservative, while the Benthamites, who were Radical, were in the tradition of Locke. The correlation, however, is not invariable; T. H. Green, for example, was a Liberal but an idealist.

Not only Locke's valid opinions, but even his errors, were useful in practice. Take, for example, his doctrine as to primary and secondary qualities. The primary qualities are defined as those that are inseparable from body, and are enumerated as solidity, extension, figure, motion or rest, and number. The secondary qualities are all the rest: colours, sounds, smells, etc. The primary qualities, he maintains, are actually in bodies; the secondary qualities, on the contrary, are only in the percipient. Without the eye, there would be no colours; without the ear, no sounds, and so on. For Locke's view as to secondary qualities there are good grounds—jaundice, blue spectacles, etc. But Berkeley pointed out that the same arguments apply to primary qualities. Ever since Berkeley, Locke's dualism on this point has been philosophically out of date. Nevertheless, it dominated practical physics until the rise of quantum theory in our own day. Not only was it assumed, explicitly or tacitly, by physicists, but it proved fruitful as a source of many very important discoveries. The theory that the physical world consists only of matter in motion was the basis of the accepted theories of sound, heat, light, and electricity. Pragmatically, the theory was useful, however mistaken it may have been theoretically. This is typical of Locke's doctrines.

Locke's philosophy, as it appears in the *Essay*, has throughout certain merits and certain demerits. Both alike were useful: the demerits are such only from a *theoretical* standpoint. He is always sensible, and always willing to sacrifice logic rather than become paradoxical. He enunciates general principles which, as the reader can hardly fail to perceive, are capable of leading to strange consequences; but whenever the strange consequences seem about to appear, Locke blandly refrains from drawing them. To a logician this is irritating; to a practical man, it is a proof of a sound judgment. Since the world is what it is, it is clear that valid reasoning from sound principles cannot lead to error; but a principle may be so nearly true as to deserve theoretical respect, and yet may lead to practical consequences which we feel to be absurd. There is therefore a justification for common sense in philosophy, but only as showing that our theoretical principles cannot be quite correct so long as their consequences are condemned by an appeal to common sense which we feel to be irresistible. The theorist may retort that common sense is no more infallible than logic. But this retort, though made by Berkeley and Hume, would have been wholly foreign to Locke's intellectual temper.

A characteristic of Locke, which descended from him to the whole Liberal movement, is lack of dogmatism. Some few certainties he takes over from his predecessors: our own existence, the existence of God, and the truth of mathematics. But wherever his doctrines differ from those of his forerunners, they are to the effect that truth is hard to ascertain, and that a rational man will hold his opinions with some measure of doubt. This temper of mind is obviously connected with religious toleration, with the success of parliamentary democracy, with *laissez-faire*, and with the whole system of liberal maxims. Although he is a deeply religious man, a devout believer in Christianity who accepts revelation as a source of knowledge, he nevertheless hedges round professed revelations with rational safeguards. On one occasion he says: 'The bare testimony of revelation is the highest certainty,' but on another he says: 'Revelation must be judged by reason.' Thus in the end reason remains supreme.

His chapter 'Of Enthusiasm' is instructive in this connection. 'Enthusiasm' had not then the same meaning as it has now; it meant the belief in a personal revelation to a religious leader or to his followers. It was a characteristic of the sects that had been defeated at the Restoration. When there is a multiplicity of such personal revelations, all inconsistent with each other, truth, or what passes as such, becomes purely personal, and loses its social character. Love of truth, which Locke considers essential, is a very different thing from love of some particular doctrine which is proclaimed as the truth. One unerring mark of love of truth, he says, is 'not entertaining any proposition with greater assurance than the proofs it is built upon will warrant'. Forwardness to dictate, he says, shows failure of love of truth. 'Enthusiasm laying by reason, would set up revelation without it; whereby in effect it takes away both reason and revelation, and substitutes in the room of it the ungrounded fancies of a man's own brain.' Men who suffer from melancholy or conceit are likely to have 'persuasions of immediate intercourse with the Deity'. Hence odd actions and opinions acquire Divine sanction, which flatters 'men's laziness, ignorance, and vanity'. He concludes the chapter with the maxim already quoted, that 'revelation must be judged of by reason'.

What Locke means by 'reason' is to be gathered from his whole book. There is, it is true, a chapter called 'Of Reason', but this is mainly concerned to prove that reason does not consist of syllogistic reasoning, and is summed up in the sentence: 'God has not been so sparing to men to make them barely two-legged creatures, and left it to Aristotle to make them rational.' Reason, as Locke uses the term, consists of two parts: first, an inquiry as to what things we know with certainty; second, an investigation of propositions which it is wise to accept in practice, although they have only probability and not certainty in their favour. 'The grounds of probability,' he says, 'are two: conformity with our own experience, or the testimony of others' experience.' The King of Siam, he remarks, ceased to believe what Europeans told him when they mentioned ice.

In his chapter 'Of Degrees of Assent' he says that the degree of assent we give to any proposition should depend upon the grounds of probability in its favour. After pointing out that we must often act upon probabilities that fall short of certainty, he says that the right use of this consideration 'is mutual charity and forbearance. Since therefore it is unavoidable to the greatest part of men, if not all, to have several opinions, without certain and indubitable proofs of their truth; and it carries too great an imputation of ignorance, lightness, or folly, for men to quit and renounce their former tenets presently upon the offer of an argument which they cannot immediately answer and show the insufficiency of; it would, methinks, become all men to maintain peace and the common offices of humanity and friendship in the diversity of opinions, since we cannot reasonably expect that any one should readily and obsequiously quit his own opinion, and embrace ours with a blind resignation to an authority which the understanding of man acknowledges not. For, however it may often mistake, it can own no other guide but reason, nor blindly submit to the will and dictates of another. If he you would bring over to your sentiments be one that examines before he assents, you must give him leave at his leisure to go over the account again, and, recalling what is out of his mind, examine the particulars, to see on which side the advantage lies; and if he will not think over arguments of weight enough to engage him anew in so much pains, it is but what we do often ourselves in the like case; and we should take it amiss if others should prescribe to us what points we should study: and if he be one who wishes to take his opinions upon trust, how can we imagine that he should renounce those tenets which time and custom have so settled in his mind that he thinks them self-evident, and of an unquestionable certainty; or which he takes to be impressions he has received from God himself, or from men sent by him? How can we expect, I say, that opinions thus settled should be given up to the arguments or authority of a stranger or adversary? especially if there be any suspicion of interest or design, as there never fails to be where men find themselves ill-treated. We should do well to commiserate our mutual ignorance, and endeavour to remove it in all the gentle and fair ways of information, and not instantly treat others ill as obstinate and perverse because they will not renounce their own and receive our opinions, or at least those we would force upon them, when it is more than probable that we are no less obstinate in not embracing some of theirs. For where is the man that has uncontestable evidence of the truth of all that he holds, or of the falsehood of all he condemns; or can say, that he has examined to the bottom all his own or other men's opinions? The necessity of believing without knowledge, nay often upon very slight grounds, in this fleeting state of action and blindness we are in, should make us more busy and careful to inform ourselves than to restrain others. . . . There is reason to think, that if men were better instructed themselves, they would be less imposing on others.'[1]

I have dealt hitherto only with the latest chapters of the *Essay*, where Locke is drawing the moral from his earlier theoretical investigation of the nature and limitations of human knowledge. It is time now to examine what he has to say on this more purely philosophical subject.

Locke is, as a rule, contemptuous of metaphysics. *Apropos* of

[1] *Essay Concerning Human Understanding*, Book IV, chap. xvi, sec. 4.

some speculation of Leibniz's, he writes to a friend: 'You and I have had enough of this kind of fiddling.' The conception of substance, which was dominant in the metaphysics of his time, he considers vague and not useful, but he does not venture to reject it wholly. He allows the validity of metaphysical arguments for the existence of God, but he does not dwell on them, and seems somewhat uncomfortable about them. Whenever he is expressing new ideas, and not merely repeating what is traditional, he thinks in terms of concrete detail rather than of large abstractions. His philosophy is piecemeal, like scientific work, not statuesque and all of a piece, like the great Continental systems of the seventeenth century.

Locke may be regarded as the founder of empiricism, which is the doctrine that all our knowledge (with the possible exception of logic and mathematics) is derived from experience. Accordingly the first book of the *Essay* is concerned in arguing, as against Plato, Descartes, and the scholastics, that there are no innate ideas or principles. In the second book he sets to work to show, in detail, how experience gives rise to various kinds of ideas. Having rejected innate ideas, he says:

'Let us then suppose the mind to be, as we say, white paper, void of all characters, without any ideas; how comes it to be furnished? Whence comes it by that vast store, which the busy and boundless fancy of man has painted on it with an almost endless variety? Whence has it all the materials of reason and knowledge? To this I answer in one word, from experience: in that all our knowledge is founded, and from that it ultimately derives itself' (Book II, chap. i, sec. 2).

Our ideas are derived from two sources, (*a*) sensation, and (*b*) perception of the operation of our own mind, which may be called 'internal sense'. Since we can only think by means of ideas, and since all ideas come from experience, it is evident that none of our knowledge can antedate experience.

Perception, he says, is 'the first step and degree towards knowledge, and the inlet of all the materials of it'. This may seem, to a modern, almost a truism, since it has become part of educated commonsense, at least in English-speaking countries. But in his day the mind was supposed to know all sorts of things *a priori*, and the complete dependence of knowledge upon perception, which he proclaimed, was a new and revolutionary doctrine. Plato, in the *Theaetetus*, had set to work to refute the indentification of knowledge with perception, and from his time onwards almost all philosophers, down to and including Descartes and Leibniz, had taught that much of our most valuable knowledge is not derived from experience. Locke's thorough-going empiricism was therefore a bold innovation.

The third book of the *Essay* deals with words, and is concerned, in the main, to show that what metaphysicians present as knowledge about the world is purely verbal. Chapter III, 'Of General Terms', takes up an extreme nominalist position on the subject of universals. All things that exist are particulars, but we can frame general ideas, such as 'man', that are applicable to many particulars, and to these general ideas we can give names. Their generality consists solely in the fact that they are, or may be, applicable to a variety of particular things; in their own being, as ideas in our minds, they are just as particular as everything else that exists.

Chapter VI of Book III, 'Of the Names of Substances', is concerned to refute the scholastic doctrine of essence. Things *may* have a real essence, which will consist of their physical constitution but this is in the main unknown to us, and is not the 'essence' of which scholastics speak. Essence, as we can know it, is purely verbal; it consists merely in the definition of a general term. To argue, for instance, as to whether the essence of body is only extension, or is extension plus solidity, is to argue about words: we may define the word 'body' either way, and no harm can result so long as we adhere to our definition. Distinct species are not a fact of nature, but of language; they are 'distinct complex ideas with distinct names annexed to them'. There are, it is true, differing things in nature, but the differences proceed by continuous gradations: 'the boundaries of the species, whereby men sort them, are made by men'. He proceeds to give instances of monstrosities, concerning which it was doubtful whether they were men or not. This point of view was not generally accepted until Darwin persuaded men to adopt the theory of evolution by gradual changes. Only those who have allowed themselves to be afflicted by the scholastics will realize how much metaphysical lumber it sweeps away.

Empiricism and idealism alike are faced with a problem to which, so far, philosophy has found no satisfactory solution. This is the problem of showing how we have knowledge of other things than ourself and the operations of our own mind. Locke considers this problem, but what he says is very obviously unsatisfactory. In one place[1] we are told: 'Since the mind, in all its thoughts and reasonings, hath no other immediate object but its own ideas, which it alone does or can contemplate, it is evident that our knowledge is only conversant about them.' And again: 'Knowledge is the perception of the agreement or disagreement of two ideas.'

[1] *Op. cit.*, Book IV, chap. i.

From this it would seem to follow immediately that we cannot know of the existence of other people, or of the physical world, for these, if they exist, are not merely ideas in my mind. Each one of us, accordingly, must, so far as knowledge is concerned, be shut up in himself, and cut off from all contact with the outer world.

This, however, is a paradox, and Locke will have nothing to do with paradoxes. Accordingly, in another chapter, he sets forth a different theory, quite inconsistent with the earlier one. We have, he tells us, three kinds of knowledge of real existence. Our knowledge of our own existence is intuitive, our knowledge of God's existence is demonstrative, and our knowledge of things present to sense in sensitive (Book IV, chap. iii).

In the next chapter, he becomes more or less aware of the inconsistency. He suggests that someone might say: 'If knowledge consists in agreement of ideas, the enthusiast and the sober man are on a level.' He replies: 'Not so where ideas agree with things.' He proceeds to argue that all *simple* ideas must agree with things, since 'the mind, as has been showed, can by no means make to itself' any simple ideas, these being all 'the product of things operating on the mind in a natural way'. And as regards complex ideas of substances, 'all our complex ideas of them must be such, and such only, as are made up of such simple ones as have been discovered to coexist in nature'. Again, we can have no knowledge except (1) by intuition, (2) by reason, examining the agreement or disagreement of two ideas, (3) 'by sensation, perceiving the existence of particular things' (Book IV, chap. iii, sec. 2).

In all this, Locke assumes it known that certain mental occurrences, which he calls sensations, have causes outside themselves, and that these causes, at least to some extent and in certain respects, resemble the sensations which are their effects. But how, consistently with the principles of empiricism, is this to be known? We experience the sensations, but not their causes; our experience will be exactly the same if our sensations arise spontaneously. The belief that sensations have causes, and still more the belief that they resemble their causes, is one which, if maintained, must be maintained on grounds wholly independent of experience. The view that 'knowledge is the perception of the agreement or disagreement of two ideas' is the one that Locke is entitled to, and his escape from the paradoxes that it entails is effected by means of an inconsistency so gross that only his resolute adherence to common sense could have made him blind to it.

This difficulty has troubled empiricism down to the present day. Hume got rid of it by dropping the assumption that sensations have external causes, but even he retained this assumption whenever he forgot his own principles, which was very often. His fundamental maxim, 'no idea without an antecedent impression', which he takes over from Locke, is only plausible so long as we think of impressions as having outside causes, which the very word 'impression' irresistibly suggests. And at the moments when Hume achieves some degree of consistency he is wildly paradoxical.

No one has yet succeeded in inventing a philosophy at once credible and self-consistent. Locke aimed at credibility, and achieved it at the expense of consistency. Most of the great philosophers have done the opposite. A philosophy which is not self-consistent cannot be wholly true, but a philosophy which is self-consistent can very well be wholly false. The most fruitful philosophies have contained glaring inconsistencies, but for that very reason have been partially true. There is no reason to suppose that a self-consistent system contains more truth than one which, like Locke's, is obviously more or less wrong.

Locke's ethical doctrines are interesting, partly on their own account, partly as an anticipation of Bentham. When I speak of his ethical doctrines, I do not mean his moral disposition as a practical man, but his general theories as to how men act and how they should act. Like Bentham, Locke was a man filled with kindly feeling, who yet held that everybody (including himself) must always be moved, in action, solely by desire for his own happiness or pleasure. A few quotations will make this clear.

'Things are good or evil only in relation to pleasure or pain. That we call "good" which is apt to cause or increase pleasure, or diminish pain, in us.'

'What is it moves desire? I answer, happiness, and that alone.'

'Happiness, in its full extent, is the utmost pleasure we are capable of.'

'The necessity of pursuing true happiness [is] the foundation of all liberty.'

'The preference of vice to virtue [is] a manifest wrong judgment.'

'The government of our passions [is] the right improvement of liberty.'[1]

The last of these statements depends, it would seem, upon the doctrine of rewards and punishments in the next world. God has laid down certain moral rules; those who follow them go to heaven, and those who break them risk going to hell. The prudent pleasure-seeker will therefore be virtuous. With the decay of the belief that sin leads to hell, it has become more difficult to make a purely self-regarding argument in favour of a virtuous life. Bentham, who was

[1] The above quotations are from Book II, chap. xx.

592

a free-thinker, substituted the human lawgiver in place of God: it was the business of laws and social institutions to make a harmony between public and private interests, so that each man, in pursuing his own happiness, should be compelled to minister to the general happiness. But this is less satisfactory than the reconciliation of public and private interests effected by means of heaven and hell, both because lawgivers are not always wise or virtuous, and because human governments are not omniscient.

Locke has to admit, what is obvious, that men do not always act in the way which, on a rational calculation, is likely to secure them a maximum of pleasure. We value present pleasure more than future pleasure, and pleasure in the near future more than pleasure in the distant future. It may be said—this is not said by Locke—that the rate of interest is a quantitative measure of the general discounting of future pleasures. If the prospect of spending £1,000 a year hence were as delightful as the thought of spending it to-day, I should not need to be paid for postponing my pleasure. Locke admits that devout believers often commit sins which, by their own creed, put them in danger of hell. We all know people who put off going to the dentist longer than they would if they were engaged in the rational pursuit of pleasure. Thus, even if pleasure or the avoidance of pain be our motive, it must be added that pleasures lose their attractiveness and pains their terrors in proportion to their distance in the future.

Since it is only in the long run that, according to Locke, self-interest and the general interest coincide, it becomes important that men should be guided, as far as possible, by their long-run interests. That is to say, men should be prudent. Prudence is the one virtue which remains to be preached, for every lapse from virtue is a failure of prudence. Emphasis on prudence is characteristic of liberalism. It is connected with the rise of capitalism, for the prudent became rich while the imprudent became or remained poor. It is connected also with certain forms of Protestant piety: virtue with a view to heaven is psychologically very analogous to saving with a view to investment.

Belief in the harmony between private and public interests is characteristic of liberalism, and long survived the theological foundation that it had in Locke.

Locke states that liberty depends upon the necessity of pursuing true happiness and upon the government of our passions. This opinion he derives from his doctrine that private and public interests are identical in the long run, though not necessarily over short periods. It follows from this doctrine that, given a community of citizens who are all both pious and prudent, they will all act, given liberty, in a manner to promote the general good. There will be no need of human laws to restrain them, since divine laws will suffice. The hitherto virtuous man who is tempted to become a highwayman will say to himself: 'I might escape the human magistrate, but I could not escape punishment at the hands of the Divine Magistrate.' He will accordingly renounce his nefarious schemes, and live as virtuously as if he were sure of being caught by the police. Legal liberty, therefore, is only completely possible where both prudence and piety are universal; elsewhere, the restraints imposed by the criminal law are indispensable.

Locke states repeatedly that morality is capable of demonstration, but he does not develop this idea so fully as could be wished. The most important passage is:

"*Morality capable of demonstration.* The idea of a Supreme Being, infinite in power, goodness, and wisdom, whose workmanship we are, and on whom we depend; and the idea of ourselves, as understanding, rational beings, being such as are clear in us, would, I suppose, if duly considered and pursued, afford such foundations of our duty and rules of action as might place morality among the sciences capable of demonstration: wherein I doubt not, but from self-evident propositions, by necessary consequences, as incontestable as those in mathematics, the measures of right and wrong might be made out, to any one that will apply himself with the same indifference and attention to the one as he does to the other of these sciences. The relation of other modes may certainly be perceived, as well as those of number and extension: and I cannot see why they should not also be capable of demonstration, if due methods were thought on to examine or pursue their agreement or disagreement. "Where there is no property, there is no justice", is a proposition as certain as any demonstration in Euclid: for the idea of property being a right to anything, and the idea to which the name "injustice" is given being the invasion or violation of that right, it is evident that these ideas being thus established, and these names annexed to them, I can as certainly know this proposition to be true as that a triangle has three angles equal to two right ones. Again: "No government allows absolute liberty": the idea of government being the establishment of society upon certain rules or laws, which require conformity to them; and the idea of absolute liberty being for any one to do whatever he pleases: I am as capable of being certain of the truth of this proposition as of any in the mathematics.'"

This passage is puzzling because, at first, it seems to make moral rules dependent upon God's decrees, while in the instances that are

[1] *Op. cit.*, Book IV, chap. iii, sec. 18.

given it is suggested that moral rules are analytic. I suppose that, in fact, Locke thought some parts of ethics analytic and others dependent upon God's decrees. Another puzzle is that the instances given do not seem to be ethical propositions at all.

There is another difficulty which one could wish to see considered. It is generally held by theologians that God's decrees are not arbitrary, but are inspired by His goodness and wisdom. This requires that there should be some concept of goodness antecedent to God's decrees, which has led Him to make just those decrees rather than any others. What this concept may be, it is impossible to discover from Locke. What he says is that a prudent man will act in such and such ways, since otherwise God will punish him; but he leaves us completely in the dark as to why punishment should be attached to certain acts rather than to their opposites.

Locke's ethical doctrines are, of course, not defensible. Apart from the fact that there is something revolting in a system which regards prudence as the only virtue, there are other, less emotional, objections to his theories.

In the first place, to say that men only desire pleasure is to put the cart before the horse. Whatever I may happen to desire, I shall feel pleasure in obtaining it; but as a rule the pleasure is due to the desire, not the desire to the pleasure. It is possible, as happens with masochists, to desire pain; in that case, there is still pleasure in the gratification of the desire, but it is mixed with its opposite. Even in Locke's own doctrine, it is not pleasure as such that is desired, since a proximate pleasure is more desired than a remote one. If morality is to be deduced from the psychology of desire, as Locke and his disciples attempt to do, there can be no reason for deprecating the discounting of distant pleasures, or for urging prudence as a moral duty. His argument, in a nutshell, is: 'We only desire pleasure. But, in fact, many men desire, not pleasure as such, but proximate pleasure. This contradicts our doctrine that they desire pleasure as such, and is therefore wicked.' Almost all philosophers, in their ethical systems, first lay down a false doctrine, and then argue that wickedness consists in acting in a manner that proves it false, which would be impossible if the doctrine were true. Of this pattern Locke affords an example.

Chapter XIV

LOCKE'S POLITICAL PHILOSOPHY

(A) THE HEREDITARY PRINCIPLE

IN the years 1689 and 1690, just after the Revolution of 1688, Locke wrote his two *Treatises on Government*, of which the second especially is very important in the history of political ideas.

The first of these two treatises is a criticism of the doctrine of hereditary power. It is a reply to Sir Robert Filmer's *Patriarcha : or The Natural Power of Kings*, which was published in 1680, but written under Charles I. Sir Robert Filmer, who was a devout upholder of the divine right of kings, had the misfortune to live till 1653, and must have suffered acutely from the execution of Charles I and the victory of Cromwell. But *Patriarcha* was written before these sad events, though not before the Civil War, so that it naturally shows awareness of the existence of subversive doctrines. Such doctrines, as Filmer points out, were not new in 1640. In fact, both Protestant and Catholic divines, in their contest with Catholic and Protestant monarchs respectively, had vigorously affirmed the right of subjects to resist tyrannical princes, and their writings supplied Sir Robert with abundant material for controversy.

Sir Robert Filmer was knighted by Charles I, and his house is said to have been plundered by the Parliamentarians ten times. He thinks it not unlikely that Noah sailed up the Mediterranean and allotted Africa, Asia, and Europe to Ham, Shem, and Japheth respectively. He held that, by the English Constitution, the Lords only give counsel to the king, and the Commons have even less power; the king, he says, alone makes the laws, which proceed solely from his will. The king, according to Filmer, is perfectly free from all human control, and cannot be bound by the acts of his predecessors, or even by his own, for 'impossible it is in nature that a man should give a law unto himself'.

Filmer, as these opinions show, belonged to the most extreme section of the Divine Right party.

Patriarcha begins by combating the 'common opinion' that 'mankind is naturally endowed and born with freedom from all subjection, and at liberty to choose what form of government it please, and the power which any one man hath over others was first bestowed according to the discretion of the multitude.' 'This tenet,' he says, 'was first hatched in the schools.' The truth, according to him, is quite different; it is, that originally God bestowed the kingly power upon Adam, from whom it descended to his heirs, and ultimately reached the various monarchs of modern times. Kings now, he assures us, 'either are, or are to be reputed, the next heirs to those first progenitors who were at first the natural parents of the whole people'. Our first parent, it seems, did not adequately appreciate his privilege as universal monarch, for 'the desire of liberty was the first cause of the fall of Adam'. The desire of liberty is a sentiment which Sir Robert Filmer regards as impious.

The claims made by Charles I, and by his protagonists on his behalf, were in excess of what earlier times would have conceded to kings. Filmer points out that Parsons, the English Jesuit, and Buchanan, the Scotch Calvinist, who agree in almost nothing else, both maintain that sovereigns can be deposed by the people for misgovernment. Parsons, of course, was thinking of the Protestant Queen Elizabeth, and Buchanan of the Catholic Mary Queen of Scots. The doctrine of Buchanan was sanctioned by success, but that of Parsons was disproved by his colleague Campion's execution.

Even before the Reformation, theologians tended to believe in setting limits to kingly power. This was part of the battle between the Church and the State which raged throughout Europe during most of the Middle Ages. In this battle, the State depended upon armed force, the Church upon cleverness and sanctity. As long as the Church had both these merits, it won; when it came to have cleverness only, it lost. But the things which eminent and holy men had said against the power of kings remained on record. Though intended in the interests of the Pope, they could be used to support the rights of the people to self-government. 'The subtle schoolmen,' says Filmer, 'to be sure to thrust down the king below the Pope, thought it the safest course to advance the people above the king, so that the papal power might take the place of the regal.' He quotes the theologian Bellarmine as saying that secular power is bestowed by men (i.e. not by God), and 'is in the people unless they bestow it on a prince'; thus Bellarmine, according to Filmer, 'makes God the immediate author of a democratical estate'—which sounds to him as shocking as it would to a modern plutocrat to say that God is the immediate author of Bolshevism.

Filmer derives political power, not from any contract, nor yet from any consideration of the public good, but entirely from the authority of a father over his children. His view is: that the source of regal authority is subjection of children to parents; that the patriarchs in Genesis were monarchs; that kings are the heirs of

Adam, or at least are to be regarded as such; that the natural rights of a king are the same as those of a father; and that, by nature, sons are never free of paternal power, even when the son is adult and the parent is in his dotage.

This whole theory seems to a modern mind so fantastic that it is hard to believe it was seriously maintained. We are not accustomed to deriving political rights from the story of Adam and Eve. We hold it obvious that parental power should cease completely when the son or daughter reaches the age of twenty-one, and that before that it should be very strictly limited both by the State and by the right of independent initiative which the young have gradually acquired. We recognize that the mother has rights at least equal to those of the father. But apart from all these considerations, it would not occur to any modern man outside Japan to suppose that political power should be in any way assimilated to that of parents over children. In Japan, it is true, a theory closely similar to Filmer's is held, and must be taught by all professors and school-teachers. The Mikado can trace his descent from the Sun Goddess, whose heir he is; other Japanese are also descended from her, but belong to cadet branches of her family. Therefore the Mikado is divine, and all resistance to him is impious. This theory was, in the main, invented in 1868, but is now alleged in Japan to have been handed down by tradition ever since the creation of the world.

The attempt to impose a similar theory upon Europe—of which attempt Filmer's *Patriarcha* is part—was a failure. Why? The acceptance of such a theory is in no way repugnant to human nature; for example, it was held, apart from Japan, by the ancient Egyptians, and by the Mexicans and Peruvians before the Spanish conquest. At a certain stage of human development it is natural. Stuart England had passed this stage, but modern Japan has not.

The defeat of theories of divine right, in England, was due to two main causes. One was the multiplicity of religions; the other was the conflict for power between the monarchy, the aristocracy, and the higher bourgeoisie. As for religion : the king, since the reign of Henry VIII, was the head of the Church of England, which was opposed both to Rome and to most of the Protestant sects. The Church of England boasted of being a compromise : the Preface to the Authorized Version begins 'It hath been the wisdom of the Church of England, ever since the first compiling of her public liturgy, to keep the mean between two extremes.' On the whole this compromise suited most people. Queen Mary and King James II tried to drag the country over to Rome, and the victors in the Civil War tried to drag it over to Geneva, but these attempts failed, and after 1688 the power of the Church of England was unchallenged.

Nevertheless, its opponents survived. The Nonconformists, especially, were vigorous men, and were numerous among the rich merchants and bankers, whose power was continually increasing.

The theological position of the king was somewhat peculiar, for he was not only head of the Church of England, but also of the Church of Scotland. In England, he had to believe in bishops and reject Calvinism; in Scotland, he had to reject bishops and believe in Calvinism. The Stuarts had genuine religious convictions, which made this ambiguous attitude impossible for them, and caused them even more trouble in Scotland than in England. But after 1688 political convenience led kings to acquiesce in professing two religions at once. This militated against zeal, and made it difficult to regard them as divine persons. In any case, neither Catholics nor Nonconformists could acquiesce in any religious claims on behalf of the monarchy.

The three parties of king, aristocracy, and rich middle class made different combinations at different times. Under Edward IV and Louis XI, king and middle class combined against the aristocracy; under Louis XIV, king and aristocracy combined against the middle class; in England in 1688, aristocracy and middle class combined against the king. When the king had one of the other parties on his side, he was strong; when they combined against him, he was weak.

For these reasons among others, Locke had no difficulty in demolishing Filmer's arguments.

So far as reasoning is concerned, Locke has, of course, an easy task. He points out that, if parental power is what is concerned, the mother's power should be equal to the father's. He lays stress on the injustice of primogeniture, which is unavoidable if inheritance is to be the basis of monarchy. He makes play with the absurdity of supposing that actual monarchs are, in any real sense, the heirs of Adam. Adam can have only one heir, but no one knows who he is. Would Filmer maintain, he asks, that, if the true heir could be discovered, all existing monarchs should lay their crowns at his feet? If Filmer's basis for monarchy were accepted, all kings, except at most one, would be usurpers, and would have no right to demand the obedience of their *de facto* subjects. Moreover paternal power, he says, is temporary, and extends not to life or property.

For such reasons, apart from more fundamental grounds, heredity cannot, according to Locke, be accepted as the basis of legitimate political power. Accordingly, in his Second Treatise on Government he seeks a more defensible basis.

The hereditary principle has almost vanished from politics. During my lifetime, the emperors of Brazil, China, Russia, Germany, and Austria have disappeared, to be replaced by dictators who do not aim at the foundation of a hereditary dynasty. Aristocracy has lost its privileges throughout Europe, except in England, where they have become little more than a historical form. All this, in most countries, is very recent, and has much to do with the rise of dictatorships, since the traditional basis of power has been swept away, and the habits of mind required for the successful practice of democracy have not had time to grow up. There is one great institution that has never had any hereditary element, namely, the Catholic Church. We may expect the dictatorships, if they survive, to develop gradually a form of government analogous to that of the Church. This has already happened in the case of the great corporations in America, which have, or had until Pearl Harbour, powers almost equal to those of the government.

It is curious that the rejection of the hereditary principle in politics has had almost no effect in the economic sphere in democratic countries. (In totalitarian states, economic power has been absorbed by political power.) We still think it natural that a man should leave his property to his children; that is to say, we accept the hereditary principle as regards economic power while rejecting it as regards political power. Political dynasties have disappeared, but economic dynasties survive. I am not at the moment arguing either for or against this different treatment of the two forms of power; I am merely pointing out that it exists, and that most men are unconscious of it. When you consider how natural it seems to us that the power over the lives of others resulting from great wealth should be hereditary, you will understand better how men like Sir Robert Filmer could take the same view as regards the power of kings, and how important was the innovation represented by men who thought as Locke did.

To understand how Filmer's theory could be believed, and how Locke's contrary theory could seem revolutionary, we have only to reflect that a kingdom was regarded then as a landed estate is regarded now. The owner of land has various important legal rights, the chief of which is the power of choosing who shall be on the land. Ownership can be transmitted by inheritance, and we feel that the man who has inherited an estate has a just claim to all the privileges that the law allows him in consequence. Yet at bottom his position is the same as that of the monarchs whose claims Sir Robert Filmer defends. There are at the present day in California a number of huge estates the title to which is derived from actual or alleged grants by the king of Spain. He was only in a position to make such grants (a) because Spain accepted views similar to Filmer's, and (b) because the Spaniards were able to defeat the Indians in battle. Nevertheless we hold the heirs of those to whom he made grants to have a just title. Perhaps in future this will seem as fantastic as Filmer seems now.

B. THE STATE OF NATURE, AND NATURAL LAW

Locke begins his second *Treatise on Government* by saying that, having shown the impossibility of deriving the authority of government from that of a father, he will now set forth what he conceives to be the true origin of government.

He begins by supposing what he calls a 'state of nature', antecedent to all human government. In this state there is a 'law of nature', but the law of nature consists of divine commands, and is not imposed by any human legislator. It is not clear how far the state of nature is, for Locke, a mere illustrative hypothesis, and how far he supposes it to have had a historical existence; but I am afraid that he tended to think of it as a stage that had actually occurred. Men emerged from the state of nature by means of a social contract which instituted civil government. This also he regarded as more or less historical. But for the moment it is the state of nature that concerns us.

What Locke has to say about the state of nature and the law of nature is, in the main, not original, but a repetition of medieval scholastic doctrines. Thus St Thomas Aquinas says:

'Every law framed by man bears the character of a law exactly to that extent to which it is derived from the law of nature. But if on any point it is in conflict with the law of nature, it at once ceases to be a law; it is a mere perversion of law.'[1]

Throughout the Middle Ages, the law of nature was held to condemn 'usury', i.e. lending money at interest. Church property was almost entirely in land, and landowners have always been borrowers rather than lenders. But when Protestantism arose, its support—especially the support of Calvinism—came chiefly from the rich middle class, who were lenders rather than borrowers. Accordingly first Calvin, then other Protestants, and finally the Catholic Church, sanctioned 'usury'. Thus natural law came to be differently conceived, but no one doubted there being such a thing.

Many doctrines which survived the belief in natural law owe their origin to it; for example, *laissez-faire* and the rights of man. These doctrines are connected, and both have their origins in puritanism. Two quotations given by Tawney will illustrate this. A committee of the House of Commons in 1604 stated:

'All free subjects are born inheritable, as to their land, and also

[1] Quoted by Tawney in *Religion and the Rise of Capitalism*.

as to the free exercise of their industry, in those trades whereto they apply themselves and whereby they are to live.'

And in 1656 Joseph Lee writes:

'It is an undeniable maxim that every one by the light of nature and reason will do that which makes for his greatest advantage. . . . The advancement of private persons will be the advantage of the public.'

Except for the words 'by the light of nature and reason', this might have been written in the nineteenth century.

In Locke's theory of government, I repeat, there is little that is original. In this Locke resembles most of the men who have won fame for their ideas. As a rule, the man who first thinks of a new idea is so much ahead of his time that everyone thinks him silly, so that he remains obscure and is soon forgotten. Then, gradually, the world becomes ready for the idea, and the man who proclaims it at the fortunate moment gets all the credit. So it was, for example, with Darwin; poor Lord Monboddo was a laughing-stock.

In regard to the state of nature, Locke was less original than Hobbes, who regarded it as one in which there was war of all against all, and life was nasty, brutish, and short. But Hobbes was reputed an atheist. The view of the state of nature and of natural law which Locke accepted from his predecessors cannot be freed from its theological basis; where it survives without this, as in much modern liberalism, it is destitute of clear logical foundation.

The belief in a happy 'state of nature' in the remote past is derived partly from the biblical narrative of the age of the patriarchs, partly from the classical myth of the golden age. The general belief in the badness of the remote past only came with the doctrine of evolution.

The nearest thing to a definition of the state of nature to be found in Locke is the following:

'Men living together according to reason, without a common superior on earth, with authority to judge between them, is properly the state of nature.'

This is not a description of the life of savages, but of an imagined community of virtuous anarchists, who need no police or law-courts because they always obey 'reason', which is the same as 'natural law', which, in turn, consists of those laws of conduct that are held to have a divine origin. (For example, 'Thou shalt not kill' is part of natural law, but the rule of the roads is not.)

Some further quotations will make Locke's meaning clearer.

'To understand political power right [he says], and derive it from its original, we must consider what state men are naturally in, and that is, a state of perfect freedom to order their actions and dispose of their possessions and persons, as they think fit, within the bounds of the law of nature; without asking leave, or depending upon the will of any other man.

'A state also of equality, wherein all the power and jurisdiction is reciprocal, no one having more than another; there being nothing more evident, than that creatures of the same species and rank, promiscuously born to all the same advantages of nature, and the use of the same faculties, should also be equal one amongst another without subordination or subjection; unless the lord and master of them all should, by any manifest declaration of his will, set one above another, and confer on him, by an evident and clear appointment, an undoubted right to dominion and sovereignty.

'But though this [the state of nature] be a state of liberty, yet it is not a state of licence: though man in that state has an uncontrollable liberty to dispose of his person or possessions, yet he has not liberty to destroy himself, or so much as any creature in his possession, but where some nobler use than its bare preservation calls for it. The state of nature has a law of nature to govern it, which obliges every one; and reason, which is that law, teaches all mankind, who will but consult it, that being all equal and independent, no one ought to harm another in his life, health, liberty, or possessions'[1] (for we are all God's property).[2]

It presently appears, however, that, where most men are in the state of nature, there may nevertheless be some men who do not live according to the law of nature, and that the law of nature provides, up to a point, what may be done to resist such criminals. In a state of nature, we are told, every man can defend himself and what is his. 'Whoso sheddeth man's blood, by man shall his blood be shed' is part of the law of nature. I may even kill a thief while he is engaged in stealing my property, and this right survives the institution of government, although, where there is government, if the thief gets away I must renounce private vengeance and resort to the law.

The great objection to the state of nature is that, while it persists, every man is the judge in his own cause, since he must rely upon himself for the defence of his rights. For this evil, government is the remedy, but this is not a *natural* remedy. The state of nature, according to Locke, was evaded by a compact to create a government. Not any compact ends the state of nature, but only that of making one body politic. The various governments of independent States are now in a state of nature towards each other.

[1] Cf. the Declaration of Independence.
[2] 'They are his property, whose workmanship they are, made to last during his, not another's pleasure.'

The state of nature, we are told in a passage presumably directed against Hobbes, is not the same as a state of war, but more nearly its opposite. After explaining the right to kill a thief, on the ground that the thief may be deemed to be making war upon me, Locke says:

'And here we have the plain "difference between the state of nature and the state of war", which, however some men have confounded, are as far distant, as a state of peace, goodwill, mutual assistance and preservation, and a state of enmity, malice, violence and mutual destruction are from one another.'

Perhaps the *law* of nature must be regarded as having a wider scope than the *state* of nature, since the former deals with thieves and murderers, while in the latter there are no such malefactors. This, at least, suggests a way out of an apparent inconsistency in Locke, consisting in his sometimes representing the state of nature as one where everyone is virtuous, and at other times discussing what may rightly be done in a state of nature to resist the aggressions of wicked men.

Some parts of Locke's natural law are surprising. For example, he says that captives in a just war are slaves by the law of nature. He says also that by nature every man has a right to punish attacks on himself or his property, even by death. He makes no qualification, so that if I catch a person engaged in petty pilfering I have, apparently, by the law of nature, a right to shoot him.

Property is very prominent in Locke's political philosophy, and is, according to him, the chief reason for the institution of civil government:

'The great and chief end of men uniting into commonwealths, and putting themselves under government, is the preservation of their property; to which in the state of nature there are many things wanting.'

The whole of this theory of the state of nature and natural law is in one sense clear but in another very puzzling. It is clear what Locke thought, but it is not clear how he can have thought it. Locke's ethic, as we saw, is utilitarian, but in his consideration of 'rights' he does not bring in utilitarian considerations. Something of this pervades the whole philosophy of law as taught by lawyers. *Legal* rights can be defined: broadly speaking, a man has a legal right when he can appeal to the law to safeguard him against injury. A man has in general a legal right to his property, but if he has (say) an illicit store of cocaine, he has no legal remedy against a man who steals it. But the lawgiver has to decide what legal rights to create, and falls back naturally on the conception of 'natural' rights, as those which the law should secure.

I am attempting to go as far as is possible towards stating something like Locke's theory in untheological terms. If it is assumed that ethics, and the classification of acts as 'right' and 'wrong', is logically prior to actual law, it becomes possible to restate the theory in terms not involving mythical history. To arrive at the law of nature, we may put the question in this way: in the absence of law and government, what classes of acts by A against B justify B in retaliating against A, and what sort of retaliation is justified in different cases? It is generally held that no man can be blamed for defending himself against a murderous assault, even, if necessary, to the extent of killing the assailant. He may equally defend his wife and children, or, indeed, any member of the general public. In such cases, the existence of the law against murder becomes irrelevant, if, as may easily happen, the man assaulted would be dead before the aid of the police could be invoked; we have, therefore, to fall back on 'natural' right. A man also has a right to defend his property, though opinions differ as to the amount of injury he may justly inflict upon a thief.

In the relations between States, as Locke points out, 'natural' law is relevant. In what circumstances is war justified? So long as no international government exists, the answer to this question is purely ethical, not legal; it must be answered in the same way as it would be for an individual in a state of anarchy.

Legal theory will be based upon the view that the 'rights' of individuals should be protected by the State. That is to say, when a man suffers the kind of injury which would justify retaliation according to the principles of natural law, positive law should enact that the retaliation shall be done by the State. If you see a man making a murderous assault upon your brother, you have a right to kill him, if you cannot otherwise save your brother. In a state of nature —so, at least, Locke holds— if a man has succeeded in killing your brother, you have a right to kill him. But where law exists, you lose this right, which is taken over by the State. And if you kill in self-defence or in defence of another, you will have to prove to a law-court that this was the reason for the killing.

We may then identify 'natural law' with moral rules in so far as they are independent of positive legal enactments. There must be such rules if there is to be any distinction between good and bad laws. For Locke, the matter is simple, since moral rules have been laid down by God, and are to be found in the Bible. When this theological basis is removed, the matter becomes more difficult. But so long as it is held that there is an ethical distinction between right actions and wrong ones, we can say: Natural law decides what actions would be ethically right, and what wrong, in a community that had no government; and positive law ought to be, as far as possible, guided and inspired by natural law.

In its absolute form, the doctrine that an individual has certain inalienable rights is incompatible with utilitarianism, i.e. with the doctrine that right acts are those that do most to promote the general happiness. But in order that a doctrine may be a suitable basis for law, it is not necessary that it should be true in every possible case, but only that it should be true in an overwhelming majority of cases. We can all imagine cases in which murder would be justifiable, but they are rare, and do not afford an argument against the illegality of murder. Similarly it may be—I am not saying that it is—desirable, from a utilitarian point of view, to reserve to each individual a certain sphere of personal liberty. If so, the doctrine of the Rights of Man will be a suitable basis for the appropriate laws, even though these rights be subject to exceptions. A utilitarian will have to examine the doctrine, considered as a basis for laws, from the point of view of its practical effects; he cannot condemn it *ab initio* as contrary to his own ethic.

C. THE SOCIAL CONTRACT

In the political speculation of the seventeenth century, there were two main types of theory as to the origin of government. Of one type we have had an example in Sir Robert Filmer: this type maintained that God had bestowed power on certain persons, and that these persons, or their heirs, constituted the legitimate government, rebellion against which is not only treason, but impiety. This view was sanctioned by sentiments of immemorial antiquity: in almost all early civilizations, the king is a sacred person. Kings, naturally, considered it an admirable theory. Aristocracies had motives for supporting it and motives for opposing it. In its favour was the fact that it emphasized the hereditary principle, and that it gave august support to resistance against the upstart merchant class. Where the middle class was more feared or hated by the aristocracy than the king was, these motives prevailed. Where the contrary was the case, and especially where the aristocracy had a chance of obtaining supreme power itself, it tended to oppose the king, and therefore to reject theories of divine right.

The other main type of theory—of which Locke is a representative—maintained that civil government is the result of a contract, and is an affair purely of this world, not something established by divine authority. Some writers regarded the social contract as a historical fact, others as a legal fiction; the important matter, for all of them, was to find a terrestrial origin for governmental authority. In fact, they could not think of any alternative to divine right except the supposed contract. It was felt by all except rebels that *some* reason must be found for obeying governments, and it was not thought sufficient to say that for most people the authority of government is convenient. Government must, in some sense, have a *right* to exact obedience, and the right conferred by a contract seemed the only alternative to a divine command. Consequently the doctrine that government was instituted by a contract was popular with practically all opponents of the divine right of kings. There is a hint of this theory in Thomas Aquinas, but the first serious development of it is to be found in Grotius.

The contract doctrine was capable of taking forms which justified tyranny. Hobbes, for example, held that there was a contract among the citizens to hand over all power to the chosen sovereign, but the sovereign was not a party to the contract, and therefore necessarily acquired unlimited authority. This theory, at first, might have justified Cromwell's totalitarian State; after the Restoration, it justified Charles II. In Locke's form of the doctrine, however, the government is a party to the contract, and can be justly resisted if it fails to fulfil its part of the bargain. Locke's doctrine is, in essence, more or less democratic, but the democratic element is limited by the view (implied rather than expressed) that those who have no property are not to be reckoned as citizens.

Let us now see just what Locke has to say on our present topic.

There is first a definition of political power:

'Political power I take to be the right of making laws, with penalty of death, and consequently all less penalties for the regulating and preserving of property, and of employing the force of the community in the execution of such laws, and in the defence of the commonwealth from foreign injury, and all this only for the public good.'

Government, we are told, is a remedy for the inconveniences that arise, in the state of nature, from the fact that, in that state, every man is the judge in his own cause. But where the monarch is a party to the dispute, this is no remedy, since the monarch is both judge and plaintiff. These considerations lead to the view that governments should not be absolute, and that the judiciary should be independent of the executive. Such arguments had an important future both in England and in America, but for the moment we are not concerned with them.

By nature, Locke says, every man has the right to punish attacks on himself or his property, even by death. There is political society

607

there, and there only, where men have surrendered this right to the community or to the law.

Absolute monarchy is not a form of civil government, because there is no neutral authority to decide disputes between the monarch and a subject; in fact the monarch, in relation to his subjects, is still in a state of nature. It is useless to hope that being a king will make a naturally violent man virtuous.

'He that would have been insolent and injurious in the woods of America would not probably be much better in a throne, where perhaps learning and religion shall be found out to justify all that he shall do to his subjects, and the sword presently silence all those that dare question it.'

Absolute monarchy is as if men protected themselves against pole-cats and foxes, 'but are content, nay think it safety, to be devoured by lions'.

Civil society involves the rule of the majority, unless it is agreed that a greater number shall be required. (As, for example, in the United States, for a change in the Constitution or the ratification of a treaty.) This sounds democratic, but it must be remembered that Locke assumes the exclusion of women and the poor from the rights of citizenship.

'The beginning of politic society depends upon the consent of the individuals to join into and make one society.' It is argued—somewhat half-heartedly—that such consent must, at some time, have actually taken place, though it is admitted that the origin of government antedates history everywhere except among the Jews.

The civil compact which institutes government binds only those who made it; the son must consent afresh to a compact made by his father. (It is clear how this follows from Locke's principles, but it is not very realistic. A young American who, on attaining the age of twenty-one, announces 'I refuse to be bound by the contract which inaugurated the United States' will find himself in difficulties.)

The power of the government by contract, we are told, never extends beyond the common good. A moment ago I quoted a sentence as to the powers of government, ending 'and all this only for the public good'. It seems not to have occurred to Locke to ask who was to be the judge of the common good. Obviously, if the government is the judge it will always decide in its own favour. Presumably Locke would say that the majority of the citizens is to be the judge. But many questions have to be decided too quickly for it to be possible to ascertain the opinion of the electorate; of these peace and war are perhaps the most important. The only remedy in such cases is to allow to public opinion or its representatives some power—such as impeachment— of subsequently punishing executive officers for acts that are found to have been unpopular. But often this is a very inadequate remedy.

I quoted previously a sentence which I must now quote again:

'The great and chief end of men uniting into commonwealths, and putting themselves under government, is the preservation of their property.'

Consistently with this doctrine Locke declares that:

'The supreme power cannot take from any man any part of his property without his own consent.'

Still more surprising is the statement that, although military commanders have power of life and death over their soldiers, they have no power of taking money. (It follows that, in any army, it would be wrong to punish minor breaches of discipline by fines, but permissible to punish them by bodily injury, such as flogging. This shows the absurd lengths to which Locke is driven by his worship of property.)

The question of taxation might be supposed to raise difficulties for Locke, but he perceives none. The expense of government, he says, must be borne by the citizens, but with their consent, i.e. with that of the majority. But why, one asks, should the consent of the majority suffice? Every man's consent, we were told, is necessary to justify the government in taking any part of his property. I suppose his tacit consent to taxation in accordance with majority decision is presumed to be involved in his citizenship, which, in turn, is presumed to be voluntary. All this is, of course, sometimes quite contrary to the facts. Most men have no effective liberty of choice as to the State to which they shall belong, and none have liberty, nowadays, to belong to no State. Suppose, for example, you are a pacifist, and disapprove of war. Wherever you live, the government will take some of your property for warlike purposes. With what justice can you be compelled to submit to this? I can imagine many answers, but I do not think any of them are consistent with Locke's principles. He thrusts in the maxim of majority rule without adequate consideration, and offers no transition to it from his individualistic premisses, except the mythical social contract.

The social contract, in the sense required, is mythical even when, at some former period, there actually was a contract creating the government in question. The United States is a case in point. At the time when the Constitution was adopted, men had liberty of choice. Even then, many voted against it, and were therefore not parties to the contract. They could, of course, have left the country, and by remaining were deemed to have become bound by a contract to which they had not assented. But in practice it is usually difficult to leave one's country. And in the case of men born after the adoption of the Constitution their consent is even more shadowy.

The question of the rights of the individual as against the government is a very difficult one. It is too readily assumed by democrats that, when the government represents the majority, it has a right to coerce the minority. Up to a point, this must be true, since coercion is of the essence of government. But the divine right of majorities, if pressed too far, may become almost as tyrannical as the divine right of kings. Locke says little on this subject in his *Essays on Government*, but considers it at some length in his *Letters on Toleration*, where he argues that no believer in God should be penalized on account of his religious opinions.

The theory that government was created by a contract is, of course, pre-evolutionary. Government, like measles and whooping-cough, must have grown up gradually, though, like them, it could be introduced suddenly into new regions such as the South Sea Islands. Before men had studied anthropology they had no idea of the psychological mechanisms involved in the beginnings of government, or of the fantastic reasons which lead men to adopt institutions and customs that subsequently prove useful. But as a legal fiction, to *justify* government, the theory of the social contract has *some* measure of truth.

D. PROPERTY

From what has been said hitherto about Locke's views on property, it might seem as though he were the champion of the great capitalists against both their social superiors and their social inferiors, but this would be only a half-truth. One finds in him, side by side and unreconciled, doctrines which foreshadow those of developed capitalism and doctrines which adumbrate a more nearly socialistic outlook. It is easy to misrepresent him by one-sided quotations, on this topic as on most others.

I will put down, in the order in which they occur, Locke's principal dicta on the subject of property.

We are told first that every man has private property in the produce of his own labour—or, at least, should have. In pre-industrial days this maxim was not so unrealistic as it has since become. Urban production was mainly by handicraftsmen who owned their tools and sold their produce. As for agricultural production, it was held by the school to which Locke belonged that peasant proprietorship would be the best system. He states that a man may own as much land as he can till, but not more. He

LOCKE'S POLITICAL PHILOSOPHY

seems blandly unaware that, in all the countries of Europe, the realization of this programme would be hardly possible without a bloody revolution. Everywhere the bulk of agricultural land belonged to aristocrats, who exacted from the farmers either a fixed proportion of the produce (often a half), or a rent which could be varied from time to time. The former system prevailed in France and Italy, the latter in England. Farther East, in Russia and Prussia, the workers were serfs, who worked for the landowner and had virtually no rights. The old system was ended in France by the French Revolution, in northern Italy and Western Germany by the conquests of the French revolutionary armies. Serfdom was abolished in Prussia as a result of defeat by Napoleon, and in Russia as a result of defeat in the Crimean War. But in both countries the aristocrats retained their landed estates. In East Prussia, this system, though drastically controlled by the Nazis, survived till the present day; in Russia and what are now Lithuania, Latvia, and Esthonia, the aristocrats were dispossessed by the Russian Revolution. In Hungary, and Poland they survived; in Eastern Poland they were 'liquidated' by the Soviet Government in 1940. The Soviet Government, however, has done everything in its power to substitute collective farming rather than peasant proprietorship throughout Russia.

In England the development has been more complex. In Locke's day, the position of the rural labourer was mitigated by the existence of commons, on which he had important rights, which enabled him to raise a considerable part of his food himself. This system was a survival from the Middle Ages, and was viewed with disapproval by modern-minded men, who pointed out that from the point of view of production it was wasteful. Accordingly, there was a movement for enclosure of commons, which began under Henry VIII and continued under Cromwell, but did not become strong until about 1750. From that time onward, for about ninety years, one common after another was enclosed and handed over to the local landowners. Each enclosure required an Act of Parliament, and the aristocrats who controlled both Houses of Parliament ruthlessly used their legislative power to enrich themselves, while thrusting agricultural labourers down to the verge of starvation. Gradually, owing to the growth of industry, the position of agricultural labourers improved, since otherwise they could not be prevented from migrating to the towns. At present, as a result of the taxation introduced by Lloyd George, the aristocrats have been compelled to part with most of their rural property. But those who also own urban or industrial property have been able to hang on to their estates. There has been no sudden revolution, but a gradual transition which is still in progress. At present, those aristocrats who are still rich owe their wealth to urban or industrial property.

This long development may be regarded, except in Russia, as in accordance with Locke's principles. The odd thing is that he could announce doctrines requiring so much revolution before they could be put into effect, and yet show no sign that he thought the system existing in his day unjust, or that he was aware of its being different from the system that he advocated.

The labour theory of value—i.e. the doctrine that the value of a product depends upon the labour expended upon it—which some attribute to Karl Marx and others to Ricardo, is to be found in Locke, and was suggested to him by a line of predecessors stretching back to Aquinas. As Tawney says, summarizing scholastic doctrine:

'The essence of the argument was that payment may properly be demanded by the craftsmen who make the goods, or by the merchants who transport them, for both labour in their vocation and serve the common need. The unpardonable sin is that of the speculator or middleman, who snatches private gain by the exploitation of public necessities. The true descendant of the doctrines of Aquinas is the labour theory of value. The last of the schoolmen was Karl Marx.'

The labour theory of value has two aspects, one ethical, the other economic. That is to say, it may assert that the value of a product *ought* to be proportional to the labour expended on it, or that *in fact* the labour regulates the price. The latter doctrine is only approximately true, as Locke recognizes. Nine tenths of value, he says, is due to labour; but as to the other tenth he says nothing. It is labour, he says, that puts the difference of value on everything. He instances land in America occupied by Indians, which has almost no value because the Indians do not cultivate it. He does not seem to realize that land may acquire value as soon as people are *willing* to work on it, and before they have actually done so. If you own a piece of desert land on which somebody else finds oil, you can sell it for a good price without doing any work on it. As was natural in his day, he does not think of such cases, but only of agriculture. Peasant proprietorship, which he favours, is inapplicable to such things as large-scale mining, which require expensive apparatus and many workers.

The principle that a man has a right to the produce of his own labour is useless in an industrial civilization. Suppose you are employed in one operation in the manufacture of Ford cars, how is anyone to estimate what proportion of the total output is due to your labour? Or suppose you are employed by a railway company in the transport of goods, who can decide what share you shall be deemed to have in the production of the goods? Such considerations have led those who wish to prevent the exploitation of labour to abandon the principle of the right to your own produce in favour of more socialistic methods of organizing production and distribution.

The labour theory of value has usually been advocated from hostility to some class regarded as predatory. The Schoolmen, in so far as they held it, did so from opposition to usurers, who were mostly Jews. Ricardo held it in opposition to landowners, Marx to capitalists. But Locke seems to have held it in a vacuum, without hostility to any class. His only hostility is to monarchs, but this is unconnected with his views on value.

Some of Locke's opinions are so odd that I cannot see how to make them sound sensible. He says that a man must not have so many plums that they are bound to go bad before he and his family can eat them; but he may have as much gold and as many diamonds as he can lawfully get, because gold and diamonds do not go bad. It does not occur to him that the man who has the plums might sell them before they go bad.

He makes a great deal of the imperishable character of the precious metals, which, he says, are the source of money and inequality of fortune. He seems, in an abstract and academic way, to regret economic inequality, but he certainly does not think that it would be wise to take such measures as might prevent it. No doubt he was impressed, as all the men of his time were, by the gains to civilization that were due to rich men, chiefly as patrons of art and letters. The same attitude exists in modern America, where science and art are largely dependent upon the benefactions of the very rich. To some extent, civilization is furthered by social injustice. This fact is the basis of what is most respectable in conservatism.

E. CHECKS AND BALANCES

The doctrine that the legislative, executive, and judicial functions of government should be kept separate is characteristic of liberalism; it arose in England in the course of resistance to the Stuarts, and is clearly formulated by Locke, at least as regards the legislature and the executive. The legislative and executive must be separate, he says, to prevent abuse of power. It must, of course, be understood that when he speaks of the legislature he means Parliament, and when he speaks of the executive he means the king; at least this is what he means emotionally, whatever he may logically intend to mean. Accordingly he thinks of the legislature as virtuous, while the executive is usually wicked.

The legislative, he says, must be supreme, except that it must be removable by the community. It is implied that, like the English House of Commons, the legislative is to be elected from time to time by popular vote. The condition that the legislative is to be removable by the people, if taken seriously, condemns the part allowed by the British Constitution in Locke's day to King and Lords as part of the legislative power.

In all well-framed governments, Locke says, the legislative and executive are separate. The question therefore arises: what is to be done when they conflict? If the executive fails to summon the legislative at the proper times, we are told, the executive is at war with the people, and may be removed by force. This is obviously a view suggested by what happened under Charles I. From 1628 to 1640 he tried to govern without Parliament; this sort of thing, Locke feels, must be prevented, by civil war if necessary.

'Force,' he says, 'is to be opposed to nothing but unjust and unlawful force.' This principle is useless in practice unless there exists some body with the legal right to pronounce when force is 'unjust and unlawful'. Charles I's attempt to collect ship-money without the consent of Parliament was declared by his opponents to be 'unjust and unlawful', and by him to be just and lawful. Only the military issue of the Civil War proved that his interpretation of the Constitution was the wrong one. The same thing happened in the American Civil War. Had States the right to secede? No one knew, and only the victory of the North decided the legal question. The belief, which one finds in Locke and in most writers of his time, that any honest man can know what is just and lawful, is one that does not allow for the strength of party bias on both sides, or for the difficulty of establishing a tribunal, whether outwardly or in men's consciences, that shall be capable of pronouncing authoritatively on vexed questions. In practice, such questions, if sufficiently important, are decided simply by power, not by justice and law.

To some degree, though in veiled language, Locke recognizes this fact. In a dispute between legislative and executive, he says there is, in certain cases, no judge under Heaven. Since Heaven does not make explicit pronouncements, this means, in effect, that a decision can only be reached by fighting, since it is assumed that Heaven will give the victory to the better cause. Some such view is essential to any doctrine that divides governmental power. Where such a doctrine is embodied in the Constitution, the only way to avoid occasional civil war is to practise compromise and common sense.

But compromise and common sense are habits of mind, and cannot be embodied in a written constitution.

It is surprising that Locke says nothing about the judiciary, although this was a burning question in his day. Until the Revolution, judges could at any moment be dismissed by the king; consequently they condemned his enemies and acquitted his friends. After the Revolution, they were made irremovable except by an Address from both Houses of Parliament. It was thought that this would cause their decisions to be guided by the law; in fact, in cases involving party spirit, it has merely substituted the judge's prejudice for the king's. However that may be, wherever the principle of checks and balances prevailed the judiciary became a third independent branch of government alongside of the legislative and executive. The most noteworthy example is the United States' Supreme Court.

The history of the doctrine of checks and balances has been interesting.

In England, the country of its origin, it was intended to limit the power of the king, who, until the Revolution, had complete control of the executive. Gradually, however, the executive became dependent upon Parliament, since it was impossible for a ministry to carry on without a majority in the House of Commons. The executive thus became, in effect, a committee chosen in fact, though not in form, by Parliament, with the result that legislative and executive powers became gradually less and less separate. During the last fifty years or so, a further development took place, owing to the Prime Minister's power of dissolution and to the increasing strictness of party discipline. The majority in Parliament now decides which party shall be in power, but, having decided that, it cannot in practice decide anything else. Proposed legislation is hardly ever enacted unless introduced by government. Thus the government is both legislative and executive, and its power is only limited by the need of occasional general elections. This system is, of course, totally contrary to Locke's principles.

In France, where the doctrine was preached with great force by Montesquieu, it was held by the more moderate parties in the French Revolution, but was swept into temporary oblivion by the victory of the Jacobins. Napoleon naturally had no use for it, but it was revived at the Restoration, to disappear again with the rise of Napoleon III. It was again revived in 1871, and led to the adoption of a constitution in which the President had very little power and the government could not dissolve the Chambers. The result was to give great power to the Chamber of Deputies, both as against the government and as against the electorate. There was more division of powers than in modern England, but less than there should be on Locke's principles, since the legislature overshadowed the executive. What the French Constitution will be after the present war it is impossible to foresee.

The country where Locke's principle of the division of powers has found its fullest application is the United States, where the President and Congress are wholly independent of each other, and the Supreme Court is independent of both. Inadvertently, the Constitution made the Supreme Court a branch of the legislature, since nothing is a law if the Supreme Court says it is not. The fact that its powers are nominally only interpretative in reality increases those powers, since it makes it difficult to criticize what are supposed to be purely legal decisions. It says a very great deal for the political sagacity of Americans that this Constitution has only once led to armed conflict.

Locke's political philosophy was, on the whole, adequate and useful until the industrial revolution. Since then, it has been increasingly unable to tackle the important problems. The power of property, as embodied in vast corporations, grew beyond anything imagined by Locke. The necessary functions of the State—for example, in education—increased enormously. Nationalism brought about an alliance, sometimes an amalgamation, of economic and political power, making war the principal means of competition. The single separate citizen has no longer the power and independence that he had in Locke's speculations. Our age is one of organization, and its conflicts are between organizations, not between separate individuals. The state of nature, as Locke says, still exists as between States. A new international Social Contract is necessary before we can enjoy the promised benefits of government. When once an international government has been created, much of Locke's political philosophy will again become applicable, though not the part of it that deals with private property.

Chapter XV

LOCKE'S INFLUENCE

From the time of Locke down to the present day, there have been in Europe two main types of philosophy, and one of these owes both its doctrines and its method to Locke, while the other was derived first from Descartes and then from Kant. Kant himself thought that he had made a synthesis of the philosophy derived from Descartes and that derived from Locke; but this cannot be admitted, at least from a historical point of view, for the followers of Kant were in the Cartesian, not the Lockean, tradition. The heirs of Locke are, first, Berkeley and Hume; second, those of the French *philosophes* who did not belong to the school of Rousseau; third, Bentham and the philosophical Radicals; fourth, with important accretions from Continental philosophy, Marx and his disciples. But Marx's system is eclectic, and any simple statement about it is almost sure to be false; I will, therefore, leave him on one side until I come to consider him in detail.

In Locke's own day, his chief philosophical opponents were the Cartesians and Leibniz. Quite illogically, the victory of Locke's philosophy in England and France was largely due to the prestige of Newton. Descartes' authority as a philosopher was enhanced, in his own day, by his work in mathematics and natural philosophy. But his doctrine of vortices was definitely inferior to Newton's law of gravitation as an explanation of the solar system. The victory of the Newtonian cosmogony diminished men's respect for Descartes and increased their respect for England. Both these causes inclined men favourably towards Locke. In eighteenth-century France, where the intellectuals were in rebellion against an antiquated, corrupt, and effete despotism, they regarded England as the home of freedom, and were predisposed in favour of Locke's philosophy by his political doctrines. In the last times before the Revolution, Locke's influence in France was reinforced by that of Hume, who lived for a time in France and was personally acquainted with many of the leading *savants*.

The chief transmitter of English influence to France was Voltaire.

In England, the philosophical followers of Locke, until the French Revolution, took no interest in his political doctrines. Berkeley was a bishop not much interested in politics; Hume was a Tory who followed the lead of Bolingbroke. England was politically quiescent in their time, and a philosopher could be content to theorize without troubling himself about the state of the world. The French Revolution changed this, and forced the best minds into opposition to the *status quo*. Nevertheless, the tradition in pure philosophy remained unbroken. Shelley's *Necessity of Atheism*, for which he was expelled from Oxford, is full of Locke's influence.[1]

Until the publication of Kant's *Critique of Pure Reason* in 1781, it might have seemed as if the older philosophical tradition of Descartes, Spinoza and Leibniz were being definitely overcome by the newer empirical method. This newer method, however, had never prevailed in German universities, and after 1792 it was held responsible for the horrors of the Revolution. Recanting revolutionaries such as Coleridge found in Kant an intellectual support for their opposition to French atheism. The Germans, in their resistance to the French, were glad to have a German philosophy to uphold them. Even the French, after the fall of Napoleon, were glad of any weapon against Jacobinism. All these factors favoured Kant.

Kant, like Darwin, gave rise to a movement which he would have detested. Kant was a liberal, a democrat, a pacifist, but those who professed to develop his philosophy were none of these things. Or, if they still called themselves Liberals, they were Liberals of a new species. Since Rousseau and Kant, there have been two schools of Liberalism, which may be distinguished as the hard-headed and the soft-hearted. The hard-headed developed, through Bentham, Ricardo, and Marx, by logical stages into Stalin; the soft-hearted, by other logical stages, through Fichte, Byron, Carlyle, and Nietzsche, into Hitler. That statement, of course, is too schematic to be quite true, but it may serve as a map and a mnemonic. The stages in the evolution of ideas have had almost the quality of the Hegelian dialectic: doctrines have developed, by steps that each seem natural, into their opposites. But the developments have not been due solely to the inherent movement of ideas; they have been governed, throughout, by external circumstances and the reflection of these circumstances in human emotions. That this is the case may be made evident by one outstanding fact: that the ideas of liberalism have undergone no part of this development in America, where they remain to this day as in Locke.

Leaving politics on one side, let us examine the differences between the two schools of philosophy, which may be broadly distinguished as the Continental and the British respectively.

There is first of all a difference of method. British philosophy is

---

[1] Take, e.g., Shelley's dictum: 'When a proposition is offered to the mind, it perceives the agreement or disagreement of the ideas of which it is composed.'

more detailed and piecemeal than that of the Continent; when it allows itself some general principle, it sets to work to prove it inductively by examining its various applications. Thus Hume, after announcing that there is no idea without an antecedent impression, immediately proceeds to consider the following objection: suppose you are seeing two shades of colour which are similar but not identical, and suppose you have never seen a shade of colour intermediate between the two, can you, nevertheless, imagine such a shade? He does not decide the question, and considers that a decision adverse to his general principle would not be fatal to him, because his principle is not logical but empirical. When—to take a contrast—Leibniz wants to establish his monadology, he argues, roughly, as follows: Whatever is complex must be composed of simple parts; what is simple cannot be extended; therefore everything is composed of parts having no extension. But what is not extended is not matter. Therefore the ultimate constituents of things are not material, and, if not material, then mental. Consequently a table is really a colony of souls.

The difference of method, here, may be characterized as follows: In Locke or Hume, a comparatively modest conclusion is drawn from a broad survey of many facts, whereas in Leibniz a vast edifice of deduction is pyramided upon a pin-point of logical principle. In Leibniz, if the principle is completely true and the deductions are entirely valid, all is well; but the structure is unstable, and the slightest flaw anywhere brings it down in ruins. In Locke or Hume, on the contrary, the base of the pyramid is on the solid ground of observed fact, and the pyramid tapers upward, not downward; consequently the equilibrium is stable, and a flaw here or there can be rectified without total disaster. This difference of method survived Kant's attempt to incorporate something of the empirical philosophy: from Descartes to Hegel on the one side, and from Locke to John Stuart Mill on the other it remains unvarying.

The difference in method is connected with various other differences. Let us take first metaphysics.

Descartes offered metaphysical proofs of the existence of God, of which the most important had been invented in the eleventh century by St Anselm, Archbishop of Canterbury. Spinoza had a pantheistic God, who seemed to the orthodox to be no God at all; however that may be, Spinoza's arguments were essentially metaphysical, and are traceable (though he may not have realized this) to the doctrine that every proposition must have a subject and a predicate. Leibniz's metaphysics had the same source.

In Locke, the philosophical direction that he inaugurated is not yet fully developed; he accepts as valid Descartes' arguments as to the existence of God. Berkeley invented a wholly new argument; but Hume—in whom the new philosophy comes to completion—rejected metaphysics entirely, and held that nothing can be discovered by reasoning on the subjects with which metaphysics is concerned. This view persisted in the empirical school, while the opposite view, somewhat modified, persisted in Kant and his disciples.

In ethics, there is a similar division between the two schools.

Locke, as we saw, believed pleasure to be the good, and this was the prevalent view among empiricists throughout the eighteenth and nineteenth centuries. Their opponents, on the contrary, despised pleasure as ignoble, and had various systems of ethics which seemed more exalted. Hobbes valued power, and Spinoza, up to a point, agreed with Hobbes. There are in Spinoza two unreconciled views on ethics, one that of Hobbes, the other that the good consists in mystic union with God. Leibniz made no important contribution to ethics, but Kant made ethics supreme, and derived his metaphysics from ethical premisses. Kant's ethic is important, because it is anti-utilitarian, *a priori*, and what is called 'noble'.

Kant says that if you are kind to your brother because you are fond of him, you have no moral merit: an act only has moral merit when it is performed because the moral law enjoins it. Although pleasure is not the good, it is nevertheless unjust—so Kant maintains—that the virtuous should suffer. Since this often happens in this world, there must be another world where they are rewarded after death, and there must be a God to secure justice in the life hereafter. He rejects all the old metaphysical arguments for God and immortality, but considers his new ethical argument irrefutable.

Kant himself was a man whose outlook on practical affairs was kindly and humanitarian, but the same cannot be said of most of those who rejected happiness as the good. The sort of ethic that is called 'noble' is less associated with attempts to improve the world than is the more mundane view that we should seek to make men happier. This is not surprising. Contempt for happiness is easier when the happiness is other people's than when it is our own. Usually the substitute for happiness is some form of heroism. This affords unconscious outlets for the impulse to power, and abundant excuses for cruelty. Or, again, what is valued may be strong emotion; this was the case with the romantics. This led to a toleration of such passions as hatred and revenge; Byron's heroes are typical, and are never persons of exemplary behaviour. The men who did most to promote human happiness were—as might have been expected—those who thought happiness important, not those who despised it in comparison with something more 'sublime'. Moreover, a man's ethic usually reflects his character, and benevolence leads to a desire for the general happiness. Thus the men who thought happiness the end of life tended to be the more benevolent, while those who proposed other ends were often dominated, unconsciously, by cruelty or love of power.

These ethical differences are associated, usually though not invariably, with differences in politics. Locke, as we saw, is tentative in his beliefs, not at all authoritarian, and willing to leave every question to be decided by free discussion. The result, both in his case and in that of his followers, was a belief in reform, but of a gradual sort. Since their systems of thought were piecemeal, and the result of separate investigations of many different questions, their political views tended naturally to have the same character. They fought shy of large programmes all cut out of one block, and preferred to consider each question on its merits. In politics, as in philosophy, they were tentative and experimental. Their opponents, on the other hand, who thought they could 'grasp this sorry scheme of things entire', were much more willing to 'shatter it to bits and then remould it nearer to the heart's desire'. They might do this as revolutionaries, or as men who wished to increase the authority of the powers that be; in either case, they did not shrink from violence in pursuit of vast objectives, and they condemned love of peace as ignoble.

The great political defect of Locke and his disciples, from a modern point of view, was their worship of property. But those who criticized them on this account often did so in the interest of classes that were more harmful than the capitalists, such as monarchs, aristocrats, and militarists. The aristocratic landowner, whose income comes to him without effort and in accordance with immemorial custom, does not think of himself as a money grubber, and is not so thought of by men who do not look below the picturesque surface. The business man, on the contrary, is engaged in the conscious pursuit of wealth, and while his activities were more or less novel they roused a resentment not felt towards the gentlemanly exactions of the landowner. That is to say, this was the case with middle-class writers and those who read them; it was not the case with the peasants, as appeared in the French and Russian Revolutions. But peasants are inarticulate.

Most of the opponents of Locke's school had an admiration for war, as being heroic and involving a contempt for comfort and ease. Those who adopted a utilitarian ethic, on the contrary, tended to regard most wars as folly. This, again, at least in the nineteenth century, brought them into alliance with the capitalists, who disliked wars because they interfered with trade. The capitalists' motive was, of course, pure self-interest, but it led to views more consonant with the general interest than those of militarists and their literary supporters. The attitude of capitalists to war, it is true, has fluctuated. England's wars of the eighteenth century, except the American war, were on the whole profitable, and were supported by business men; but throughout the nineteenth century until its last years, they favoured peace. In modern times, big business, everywhere, has come into such intimate relations with the national State that the situation is greatly changed. But even now, both in England and in America, big business on the whole dislikes war.

Enlightened self-interest is, of course, not the loftiest of motives, but those who decry it often substitute, by accident or design, motives which are much worse, such as hatred, envy, and love of power. On the whole, the school which owed its origin to Locke, and which preached enlightened self-interest, did more to increase human happiness, and less to increase human misery, than was done by the schools which despised it in the name of heroism and self-sacrifice. I do not forget the horrors of early industrialism, but these, after all, were mitigated within the system. And I set against them Russian serfdom, the evils of war and its aftermath of fear and hatred, and the inevitable obscurantism of those who attempt to preserve ancient systems when they have lost their vitality.

Chapter XVI

BERKELEY

GEORGE BERKELEY (1685-1753) is important in philosophy through his denial of the existence of matter—a denial which he supported by a number of ingenious arguments. He maintained that material objects only exist through being perceived. To the objection that, in that case, a tree, for instance, would cease to exist if no one was looking at it, he replied that God always perceives everything; if there were no God, what we take to be material objects would have a jerky life, suddenly leaping into being when we look at them; but as it is, owing to God's perceptions, trees and rocks and stones have an existence as continuous as common sense supposes. This is, in his opinion, a weighty argument for the existence of God. A limerick by Ronald Knox, with a reply, sets forth Berkeley's theory of material objects:

> There was a young man who said, 'God
> Must think it exceedingly odd
>   If he finds that this tree
>   Continues to be
> When there's no one about in the Quad.'

REPLY

> Dear Sir:
>   Your astonishment's odd:
> *I* am always about in the Quad.
>   And that's why the tree
>   Will continue to be,
> Since observed by
>   *Yours faithfully,*
>   GOD.

Berkeley was an Irishman, and became a Fellow of Trinity College, Dublin, at the age of twenty-two. He was presented at court by Swift, and Swift's Vanessa left him half her property. He formed a scheme for a college in the Bermudas, with a view to which he went to America; but after spending three years (1728-31) in Rhode Island, he came home and relinquished the project. He was the author of the well-known line:

623

Westward the course of empire takes its way.

on account of which the town of Berkeley in California was called after him. In 1734 he became Bishop of Cloyne. In later life he abandoned philosophy for tar-water, to which he attributed marvellous medicinal properties. It was concerning tar-water that he wrote: 'These are the cups that cheer, but do not inebriate'— a sentiment more familiar as subsequently applied by Cowper to tea.

All his best work was done while he was still quite young: *A New Theory of Vision* in 1709, *The Principles of Human Knowledge* in 1710. *The Dialogues of Hylas and Philonous* in 1713. His writings after the age of twenty-eight were of less importance. He is a very attractive writer, with a charming style.

His argument against matter is most persuasively set forth in *The Dialogues of Hylas and Philonous*. Of these dialogues I propose to consider only the first and the very beginning of the second, since everything that is said after that seems to me of minor importance. In the portion of the work that I shall consider, Berkeley advances valid arguments in favour of a certain important conclusion, though not quite in favour of the conclusion that he thinks he is proving. He thinks he is proving that all reality is mental; what he is proving is that we perceive qualities, not things, and that qualities are relative to the percipient.

I shall begin with an uncritical account of what seems to me important in the Dialogues; I shall then embark upon criticism; and finally I shall state the problems concerned as they appear to me.

The characters in the Dialogues are two: Hylas, who stands for scientifically educated common sense; and Philonous, who is Berkeley.

After a few amiable remarks, Hylas says that he has heard strange reports of the opinions of Philonous, to the effect that he does not believe in material substance. 'Can anything,' he exclaims, 'be more fantastical, more repugnant to Common Sense, or a more manifest piece of Scepticism, than to believe there is no such thing as *matter?*' Philonous replies that he does not deny the reality of sensible things, i.e. of what is perceived immediately by the senses, but that we do not see the causes of colours or hear the causes of sounds. Both agree that the senses make no inferences. Philonous points out that by sight we perceive only light, colour, and figure; by hearing, only sounds; and so on. Consequently, apart from sensible qualities there is nothing sensible, and sensible things are nothing but sensible qualities or combinations of sensible qualities.

Philonous now sets to work to prove that 'the *reality* of sensible things consists in being perceived', as against the opinion of Hylas, that 'to *exist* is one thing, and to be *perceived* is another'. That sense-data are mental is a thesis which Philonous supports by a detailed examination of the various senses. He begins with heat and cold. Great heat, he says, is a pain, and must be in a mind. Therefore heat is mental; and a similar argument applies to cold. This is reinforced by the famous argument about the lukewarm water. When one of your hands is hot and the other cold, you put both into lukewarm water, which feels cold to one hand and hot to the other; but the water cannot be at once hot and cold. This finishes Hylas, who acknowledges that 'heat and cold are only sensations existing in our minds'. But he points out hopefully that other sensible qualities remain.

Philonous next takes up tastes. He points out that a sweet taste is a pleasure and a bitter taste is a pain, and that pleasure and pain are mental. The same argument applies to odours, since they are pleasant or unpleasant.

Hylas makes a vigorous effort to rescue sound, which, he says, is motion in air, as may be seen from the fact that there are no sounds in a vacuum. We must, he says, 'distinguish between sound as it is perceived by us, and as it is in itself; or between the sound which we immediately perceive and that which exists without us'. Philonous points out that what Hylas calls 'real' sound, being a movement, might possibly be seen or felt, but can certainly not be heard; therefore it is not sound as we know it in perception. As to this, Hylas now concedes that 'sounds too have no real being without the mind'.

They now come to colours, and here Hylas begins confidently: 'Pardon me: the case of colours is very different. Can anything be plainer than that we see them on the objects?' Substances existing without the mind, he maintains, have the colours we see on them. But Philonous has no difficulty in disposing of this view. He begins with the sunset clouds, which are red and golden, and points out that a cloud, when you are close to it, has no such colours. He goes on to the difference made by a microscope, and to the yellowness of everything to a man who has jaundice. And very small insects, he says, must be able to see much smaller objects than we can see. Hylas thereupon says that colour is not in the objects, but in the light; it is, he says, a thin fluid substance. Philonous points out, as in the case of sound, that, according to Hylas, 'real' colours are something different from the red and blue that we see, and that this won't do.

Hereupon Hylas gives way about all secondary qualities, but continues to say that primary qualities, notably figure and motion, are inherent in external unthinking substances. To this Philonous replies that things look big when we are near them and small when we are far off, and that a movement may seem quick to one man and slow to another.

At this point Hylas attempts a new departure. He made a mistake, he says, in not distinguishing the *object* from the *sensation*; the act of perceiving he admits to be mental, but not what is perceived; colours, for example, 'have a real existence without the mind, in some unthinking substance'. To this Philonous replies: 'That any immediate object of the senses—that is, any idea or combination of ideas—should exist in an unthinking substance, or exterior to *all* minds, is in itself an evident contradiction.' It will be observed that, at this point, the argument becomes logical and is no longer empirical. A few pages later, Philonous says: 'Whatever is immediately perceived is an idea; and can any idea exist out of the mind?'

After a metaphysical discussion of substance, Hylas returns to the discussion of visual sensations, with the argument that he sees things at a distance. To this Philonous replies that this is equally true of things seen in dreams, which everyone admits to be mental; further, that distance is not perceived by sight, but judged as the result of experience, and that, to a man born blind but now for the first time able to see, visual objects would not appear distant.

At the beginning of the second Dialogue, Hylas urges that certain traces in the brain are the causes of sensations, but Philonous retorts that 'the brain, being a sensible thing, exists only in the mind'.

The remainder of the Dialogues is less interesting, and need not be considered.

Let us now make a critical analysis of Berkeley's contentions.

Berkeley's argument consists of two parts. On the one hand, he argues that we do not perceive material things, but only colours, sounds, etc., and that these are 'mental' or 'in the mind'. His reasoning is completely cogent as to the first point, but as to the second it suffers from the absence of any definition of the word 'mental'. He relies, in fact, upon the received view that everything must be either material or mental, and that nothing is both.

When he says that we perceive qualities, not 'things' or 'material substances', and that there is no reason to suppose that the different qualities which common sense regards as all belonging to one 'thing' inhere in a substance distinct from each and all of them, his reasoning may be accepted. But when he goes on to say that sensible qualities—including primary qualities—are 'mental', the arguments are of very different kinds, and of very different degrees of validity.

There are some attempting to prove logical necessity, while others are more empirical. Let us take the former first.

Philonous says: 'Whatever is immediately perceived is an idea: and can any idea exist out of the mind?' This would require a long discussion of the word 'idea'. If it were held that thought and perception consist of a relation between subject and object, it would be possible to identify the mind with the subject, and to maintain that there is nothing 'in' the mind, but only objects 'before' it. Berkeley discusses the view that we must distinguish the act of perceiving from the object perceived, and that the former is mental while the latter is not. His argument against this view is obscure, and necessarily so, since, for one who believes in mental substance, as Berkeley does, there is no valid means of refuting it. He says: 'That any immediate object of the senses should exist in an unthinking substance, or exterior to *all* minds, is in itself an evident contradiction.' There is here a fallacy, analogous to the following: 'It is impossible for a nephew to exist without an uncle; now Mr A is a nephew; therefore it is logically necessary for Mr A to have an uncle.' It is, of course, logically necessary given that Mr A is a nephew, but not from anything to be discovered by analysis of Mr A. So, if something is an object of the senses, some mind is concerned with it; but it does not follow that the same thing could not have existed without being an object of the senses.

There is a somewhat analogous fallacy as regards what is conceived. Hylas maintains that he can conceive a house which no one perceives, and which is not in any mind. Philonous retorts that whatever Hylas conceives is in his mind, so that the supposed house is, after all, mental. Hylas should have answered: 'I do not mean that I have in mind the image of a house; when I say that I can conceive a house which no one perceives, what I really mean is that I can understand the proposition "there is a house which no one perceives", or, better still, "there is a house which no one either perceives or conceives".' This proposition is composed entirely of intelligible words, and the words are correctly put together. Whether the proposition is true or false, I do not know; but I am sure that it cannot be shown to be self-contradictory. Some closely similar propositions can be proved. For instance: the number of possible multiplications of two integers is infinite, therefore there are some that have never been thought of. Berkeley's argument, if valid, would prove that this is impossible.

The fallacy involved is a very common one. We can, by means of concepts drawn from experience, construct statements about classes some or all of whose members are not experienced. Take some perfectly ordinary concept, say 'pebble'; this is an empirical concept derived from perception. But it does not follow that all pebbles are perceived, unless we include the fact of being perceived in our definition of 'pebble'. Unless we do this, the concept 'unperceived pebble' is logically unobjectionable, in spite of the fact that it is logically impossible to perceive an instance of it.

Schematically, the argument is as follows. Berkeley says: 'Sensible objects must be sensible. A is a sensible object. Therefore A must be sensible.' But if 'must' indicates logical necessity, the argument is only valid if A *must* be a sensible object. The argument does not prove that, from the properties of A other than its being sensible, it can be deduced that A is sensible. It does not prove, for example, that colours intrinsically indistinguishable from those that we see may not exist unseen. We may believe on physiological grounds that this does not occur, but such grounds are empirical; so far as logic is concerned, there is no reason why there should not be colours where there is no eye or brain.

I come now to Berkeley's empirical arguments. To begin with, it is a sign of weakness to combine empirical and logical arguments, for the latter, if valid, make the former superfluous.[1] If I am contending that a square cannot be round, I shall not appeal to the fact that no square in any known city is round. But as we have rejected the logical arguments, it becomes necessary to consider the empirical arguments on their merits.

The first of the empirical arguments is an odd one: That heat cannot be in the object, because 'the most vehement and intense degree of heat [is] a very great pain' and we cannot suppose 'any unperceiving thing capable of pain or pleasure'. There is an ambiguity in the word 'pain', of which Berkeley takes advantage. It may mean the painful quality of a sensation, or it may mean the sensation that has this quality. We say a broken leg is painful, without implying that the leg is in the mind; it might be, similarly, that heat *causes* pain, and that this is all we ought to mean when we say it *is* a pain. This argument, therefore, is a poor one.

The argument about the hot and cold hands in lukewarm water, strictly speaking, would only prove that what we perceive in that experiment is not hot and cold, but hotter and colder. There is nothing to prove that these are subjective.

In regard to tastes, the argument from pleasure and pain is repeated: Sweetness is a pleasure and bitterness a pain, therefore both are mental. It is also urged that a thing that tastes sweet when I am well may taste bitter when I am ill. Very similar arguments are used about odours: since they are pleasant or unpleasant, 'they

[1] E.g., 'I was not drunk last night. I had only had two glasses: besides, it is well known that I am a teetotaller.'

628

cannot exist in any but a perceiving substance or mind'. Berkeley assumes, here and everywhere, that what does not inhere in matter must inhere in a mental substance, and that nothing can be both mental and material.

The argument in regard to sound is *ad hominem*. Hylas says that sounds are 'really' motions in the air, and Philonous retorts that motions can be seen or felt, not heard, so that 'real' sounds are inaudible. This is hardly a fair argument, since percepts of motion, according to Berkeley, are just as subjective as other percepts. The motions that Hylas requires will have to be unperceived and imperceptible. Nevertheless it is valid in so far as it points out that sound, as heard, cannot be identified with the motions of air that physics regards as its cause.

Hylas, after abandoning secondary qualities, is not yet ready to abandon *primary* qualities, viz. Extension, Figure, Solidity, Gravity, Motion, and Rest. The argument, naturally, concentrates on extension and motion. If things have real sizes, says Philonous, the same thing cannot be of different sizes at the same time, and yet it looks larger when we are near it than when we are far off. And if motion is really in the object, how comes it that the same motion may seem fast to one and slow to another? Such arguments must, I think, be allowed to prove the subjectivity of perceived space. But this subjectivity is physical: it is equally true of a camera, and therefore does not prove that shape is 'mental'. In the second Dialogue Philonous sums up the discussion, so far as it has gone, in the words: 'Besides spirits, all that we know or conceive are our own ideas.' He ought not, of course, to make an exception for spirits, since it is just as impossible to know spirit as to know matter. The arguments, in fact, are almost identical in both cases.

Let us now try to state what positive conclusions we can reach as a result of the kind of argument inaugurated by Berkeley.

Things as we know them are bundles of sensible qualities: a table, for example, consists of its visual shape, its hardness, the noise it emits when rapped, and its smell (if any). These different qualities have certain contiguities in experience, which lead common sense to regard them as belonging to one 'thing', but the concept of 'thing' or 'substance' adds nothing to the perceived qualities, and is unnecessary. So far we are on firm ground.

But we must now ask ourselves what we mean by 'perceiving'. Philonous maintains that, as regards sensible things, their reality consists in their being perceived; but he does not tell us what he means by perception. There is a theory, which he rejects, that perception is a relation between a subject and a percept. Since he believed the ego to be a substance, he might well have adopted this theory; however, he decided against it. For those who reject the notion of a substantial ego, this theory is impossible. What, then, is meant by calling something a 'percept'? Does it mean anything more than that the something in question occurs? Can we turn Berkeley's dictum round, and instead of saying that reality consists in being perceived, say that being perceived consists in being real? However this may be, Berkeley holds it logically possible that there should be unperceived things, since he holds that some real things, viz. spiritual substances, are unperceived. And it seems obvious that, when we say that an event is perceived, we mean something more than that it occurs.

What is this more? One obvious difference between perceived and unperceived events is that the former, but not the latter, can be remembered. Is there any other difference?

Recollection is one of a whole genus of effects which are more or less peculiar to the phenomena that we naturally call 'mental'. These effects are connected with habit. A burnt child fears the fire; a burnt poker does not. The physiologist, however, deals with habit and kindred matters as a characteristic of nervous tissue, and has no need to depart from a physicalist interpretation. In physicalist language, we can say that an occurrence is 'perceived' if it has effects of certain kinds; in this sense we might almost say that a watercourse 'perceives' the rain by which it is deepened, and that a river valley is a 'memory' of former downpours. Habit and memory when described in physicalist terms, are not wholly absent in dead matter; the difference, in this respect, between living and dead matter, is only one of degree.

In this view, to say that an event is 'perceived' is to say that it has effects of certain kinds, and there is no reason, either logical or empirical, for supposing that *all* events have effects of these kinds.

Theory of knowledge suggests a different standpoint. We start, here, not from finished science, but from whatever knowledge is the ground for our belief in science. This is what Berkeley is doing. Here it is not necessary, in advance, to define a 'percept'. The method, in outline, is as follows. We collect the propositions that we feel we know without inference, and we find that most of these have to do with dated particular events. These events we define as 'percepts'. Percepts, therefore, are those events that we know without inference; or at least, to allow for memory, such events were at some time percepts. We are then faced with the question: Can we, from our own percepts, infer any other events? Here four positions are possible, of which the first three are forms of idealism.

(1) We may deny totally the validity of all inferences from my present percepts and memories to other events. This view must be

taken by anyone who confines inference to deduction. Any event, and any group of events, is logically capable of standing alone, and therefore no group of events affords *demonstrative* proof of the existence of other events. If, therefore, we confine inference to deduction, the known world is confined to those events in our own biography that we perceive—or have perceived, if memory is admitted.

(2) The second position, which is solipsism as ordinarily understood, allows some inference from my percepts, but only to other events in my own biography. Take, for example, the view that, at any moment in waking life, there are sensible objects that we do not notice. We see many things without saying to ourselves that we see them; at least, so it seems. Keeping the eyes fixed in an environment in which we perceive no movement, we can notice various things in succession, and we feel persuaded that they were visible before we noticed them; but before we noticed them they were not data for theory of knowledge. This degree of inference from what we observe is made unreflectingly by everybody, even by those who most wish to avoid an undue extension of our knowledge beyond experience.

(3) The third position—which seems to be held, for instance, by Eddington—is that it is possible to make inferences to other events analogous to those in our own experience, and that, therefore, we have a right to believe that there are, for instance, colours seen by other people but not by ourselves, toothaches felt by other people, pleasures enjoyed and pains endured by other people, and so on, but that we have no right to infer events experienced by no one and not forming part of any 'mind'. This view may be defended on the ground that all inference to events which lie outside my observation is by analogy, and that events which no one experiences are not sufficiently analogous to my data to warrant analogical inferences.

(4) The fourth position is that of common sense and traditional physics, according to which there are, in addition to my own experiences and other people's, also events which no one experiences—for example, the furniture of my bedroom when I am asleep and it is pitch dark. G. E. Moore once accused idealists of holding that trains only have wheels while they are in stations, on the ground that passengers cannot see the wheels while they remain in the train. Common sense refuses to believe that the wheels suddenly spring into being whenever you look, but do not bother to exist when no one is inspecting them. When this point of view is scientific, it bases the inference to unperceived events on causal laws.

I do not propose, at present, to decide between these four points of view. The decision, if possible at all, can only be made by an elaborate investigation of non-demonstrative inference and the theory of probability. What I do propose to do is to point out certain logical errors which have been committed by those who have discussed these questions.

Berkeley, as we have seen, thinks that there are logical reasons proving that only minds and mental events can exist. This view, on other grounds, is also held by Hegel and his followers. I believe this to be a complete mistake. Such a statement as 'there was a time before life existed on this planet', whether true or false, cannot be condemned on grounds of logic, any more than 'there are multiplication sums which no one will have ever worked out'. To be observed, or to be a percept, is merely to have effects of certain kinds, and there is no logical reason why all events should have effects of these kinds.

There is, however, another kind of argument, which, while it does not establish idealism as a metaphysic, does, if valid, establish it as a practical policy. It is said that a proposition which is unverifiable has no meaning; that verification depends upon percepts; and that, therefore, a proposition about anything except actual or possible percepts is meaningless. I think that this view, strictly interpreted, would confine us to the first of the above four theories, and would forbid us to speak about anything that we have not ourselves explicitly noticed. If so, it is a view that no one can hold in practice, which is a defect in a theory that is advocated on practical grounds. The whole question of verification, and its connection with knowledge, is difficult and complex; I will, therefore, leave it on one side for the present.

The fourth of the above theories, which admits events that no one perceives, may also be defended by invalid arguments. It may be held that causality is known *a priori*, and that causal laws are impossible unless there are unperceived events. As against this, it may be urged that causality is not *a priori*, and that whatever regularity can be observed must be in relation to percepts. Whatever there is reason to believe in the laws of physics must, it would seem, be capable of being stated in terms of percepts. The statement may be odd and complicated; it may lack the characteristic of continuity which, until lately, was expected of a physical law. But it can hardly be impossible.

I conclude that there is no *a priori* objection to any one of our four theories. It is possible, however, to say that all truth is pragmatic, and that there is no pragmatic difference between the four theories. If this is true, we can adopt whichever we please, and the difference between them is only linguistic. I cannot accept this view; but this, also, is a matter for discussion at a later stage.

It remains to be asked whether any meaning can be attached to the words 'mind' and 'matter'. Everyone knows that 'mind' is what an idealist thinks there is nothing else but, and 'matter' is what a materialist thinks the same about. The reader knows also, I hope, that idealists are virtuous and materialists are wicked. But perhaps there may be more than this to be said.

My own definition of 'matter' may seem unsatisfactory; I should define it as what satisfies the equations of physics. There may be nothing satisfying these equations; in that case either physics, or the concept 'matter', is a mistake. If we reject substance, 'matter' will have to be a logical construction. Whether it can be any construction composed of events—which may be partly inferred— is a difficult question, but by no means an insoluble one.

As for 'mind', when substance has been rejected a mind must be some group or structure of events. The grouping must be effected by some relation which is characteristic of the sort of phenomena we wish to call 'mental'. We may take memory as typical. We might—though this would be rather unduly simple—define a 'mental' event as one which remembers or is remembered. Then the 'mind' to which a given mental event belongs is the group of events connected with the given event by memory-chains, backwards or forwards.

It will be seen that, according to the above definitions, a mind and a piece of matter are, each of them, a group of events. There is no reason why every event should belong to a group of one kind or the other, and there is no reason why some events should not belong to both groups; therefore some events may be neither mental nor material, and other events may be both. As to this, only detailed empirical considerations can decide.

Chapter XVII

HUME

D AVID HUME (1711-76) is one of the most important among philosophers, because he developed to its logical conclusion the empirical philosophy of Locke and Berkeley, and by making it self-consistent made it incredible. He represents, in a certain sense, a dead end: in his direction, it is impossible to go further. To refute him has been, ever since he wrote, a favourite pastime among metaphysicians. For my part, I find none of their refutations convincing; nevertheless, I cannot but hope that something less sceptical than Hume's system may be discoverable.

His chief philosophical work, the *Treatise of Human Nature*, was written while he was living in France during the years 1734 to 1737. The first two volumes were published in 1739, the third in 1740. He was a very young man, not yet in his thirties; he was not well known, and his conclusions were such as almost all schools would find unwelcome. He hoped for vehement attacks, which he would meet with brilliant retorts. Instead, no one noticed the book; as he says himself, 'it fell dead-born from the press'. 'But,' he adds, 'being naturally of a cheerful and sanguine temper, I very soon recovered from the blow.' He devoted himself to the writing of essays, of which he produced the first volume in 1741. In 1744 he made an unsuccessful attempt to obtain a professorship at Edinburgh; having failed in this, he became first tutor to a lunatic and then secretary to a general. Fortified by these credentials, he ventured again into philosophy. He shortened the *Treatise* by leaving out the best parts and most of the reasons for his conclusions; the result was the *Inquiry into Human Understanding*, for a long time much better known than the *Treatise*. It was this book that awakened Kant from his 'dogmatic slumbers'; he does not appear to have known the *Treatise*.

He wrote also *Dialogues Concerning Natural Religion*, which he kept unpublished during his lifetime. By his direction, they were published posthumously in 1779. His *Essay on Miracles*, which became famous, maintains that there can never be adequate historical evidence for such events.

His *History of England*, published in 1755 and following years, devoted itself to proving the superiority of Tories to Whigs and of Scotchmen to Englishmen; he did not consider history worthy of philosophic detachment. He visited Paris in 1763, and was made much of by the *philosophes*. Unfortunately, he formed a friendship with Rousseau, and had a famous quarrel with him. Hume behaved with admirable forbearance, but Rousseau, who suffered from persecution mania, insisted upon a violent breach.

Hume has described his own character in a self-obituary, or 'funeral oration', as he calls it: 'I was a man of mild dispositions, of command of temper, of an open, social and cheerful humour, capable of attachment, but little susceptible of enmity, and of great moderation in all my passions. Even my love of literary fame, my ruling passion, never soured my temper, notwithstanding my frequent disappointments.' All this is borne out by everything that is known of him.

Hume's *Treatise of Human Nature* is divided into three books, dealing respectively with the understanding, the passions, and morals. What is important and novel in his doctrines is in the first book, to which I shall confine myself.

He begins with the distinction between 'impressions' and 'ideas'. These are two kinds of perceptions, of which *impressions* are those that have more force and violence. 'By ideas I mean the faint images of these in thinking and reasoning.' Ideas, at least when simple, are like impressions, but fainter. 'Every simple idea has a simple impression, which resembles it; and every simple impression a correspondent idea.' 'All our simple ideas in their first appearance are derived from simple impressions, which are correspondent to them, and which they exactly represent.' Complex ideas, on the other hand, need not resemble impressions. We can imagine a winged horse without having ever seen one, but the *constituents* of this complex idea are all derived from impressions. The proof that impressions come first is derived from experience; for example, a man born blind has no ideas of colours. Among ideas, those that retain a considerable degree of the vivacity of the original impressions belong to *memory*, the others to *imagination*.

There is a section (Book I, part i, sec. vii) 'Of Abstract Ideas', which opens with a paragraph of emphatic agreement with Berkeley's doctrine that 'all general ideas are nothing but particular ones, annexed to a certain term, which gives them a more extensive significance, and makes them recall upon occasion other individuals, which are similar to them.' He contends that, when we have an idea of a man, it has all the particularity that the impression of a man has. 'The mind cannot form any notion of quantity or quality without forming a precise notion of degrees of each.' 'Abstract ideas are in themselves individual, however they may become general in their representation.' This theory, which is a modern form of nominalism, has two defects, one logical, the other psychological. To begin with the logical objection: 'When we have found a resemblance among several objects,' Hume says, 'we apply the same name to all of them.' Every nominalist would agree. But in fact a common name, such as 'cat', is just as unreal as the universal CAT is. The nominalist solution of the problem of universals thus fails through being insufficiently drastic in the application of its own principles; it mistakenly applies these principles only to 'things', and not also to words.

The psychological objection is more serious, at least in connection with Hume. The whole theory of ideas as copies of impressions, as he sets it forth, suffers from ignoring *vagueness*. When, for example, I have seen a flower of a certain colour, and I afterwards call up an image of it, the image is lacking in precision, in this sense, that there are several closely similar shades of colour of which it might be an image, or 'idea', in Hume's terminology. It is not true that 'the mind cannot form any notion of quantity or quality without forming a precise notion of degrees of each.' Suppose you have seen a man whose height is six feet one inch. You retain an image of him, but it probably would fit a man half an inch taller or shorter. Vagueness is different from generality, but has some of the same characteristics. By not noticing it, Hume runs into unnecessary difficulties, for instance, as to the possibility of imagining a shade of colour you have never seen, which is intermediate between two closely similar shades that you have seen. If these two are sufficiently similar, any image you can form will be equally applicable to both of them and to the intermediate shade. When Hume says that ideas are derived from impressions which they *exactly* represent he goes beyond what is psychologically true.

Hume banished the conception of *substance* from psychology, as Berkeley had banished it from physics. There is, he says, no *impression* of self, and therefore no idea of self (Book I, part iv, sec. vi). 'For my part, when I enter most intimately into what I call *myself*, I always stumble on some particular perception or other, of heat or cold, light or shade, love or hatred, pain or pleasure. I never catch *myself* at any time without a perception, and never can observe anything but the perception.' There may, he ironically concedes, be some philosophers who can perceive their selves; 'but setting aside some metaphysicians of this kind, I may venture to affirm of the rest of mankind, that they are nothing but a bundle or collection of different perceptions, which succeed each other with inconceivable rapidity, and are in a perpetual flux and movement'.

This repudiation of the idea of the Self is of great importance.

Let us see exactly what it maintains, and how far it is valid. To begin with, the Self, if there is such a thing, is never perceived, and therefore we can have no idea of it. If this argument is to be accepted, it must be carefully stated. No man perceives his own brain, yet, in an important sense, he has an 'idea' of it. Such 'ideas', which are inferences from perceptions, are not among the logically basic stock of ideas; they are complex and descriptive—this must be the case if Hume is right in his principle that all simple ideas are derived from impressions, and if this principle is rejected, we are forced back on 'innate' ideas. Using modern terminology, we may say: Ideas of unperceived things or occurrences can always be defined in terms of perceived things or occurrences, and therefore, by substituting the definition for the term defined, we can always state that we know empirically without introducing any unperceived things or occurrences. As regards our present problem, all psychological knowledge can be stated without introducing the 'Self'. Further, the 'Self', as defined can be nothing but a bundle of perceptions, not a new simple 'thing'. In this I think that any thoroughgoing empiricist must agree with Hume.

It does not follow that there is no simple Self; it only follows that we cannot know whether there is or not, and that the Self, except as a 'bundle' of perceptions, cannot enter into any part of our knowledge. This conclusion is important in metaphysics, as getting rid of the last surviving use of 'substance'. It is important in theology, as abolishing all supposed knowledge of the 'soul'. It is important in the analysis of knowledge, since it shows that the category of subject and object is not fundamental. In this matter of the ego Hume made an important advance on Berkeley.

The most important part of the whole *Treatise* is the section called 'Of Knowledge and Probability'. Hume does not mean by 'probability' the sort of knowledge contained in the mathematical theory of probability, such as that the chance of throwing double sixes with two dice is one thirty-sixth. This knowledge is not itself probable in any special sense; it has as much certainty as knowledge can have. What Hume is concerned with is uncertain knowledge, such as is obtained from empirical data by inferences that are not demonstrative. This includes all our knowledge as to the future, and as to unobserved portions of the past and present. In fact, it includes everything except, on the one hand, direct observation, and, on the other, logic and mathematics. The analysis of such 'probable' knowledge led Hume to certain sceptical conclusions, which are equally difficult to refute and to accept. The result was a challenge to philosophers, which, in my opinion, has still not been adequately met.

Hume begins by distinguishing seven kinds of philosophical relation: resemblance, identity, relations of time and place, proportion in quantity or number, degrees in any quality, contrariety, and causation. These, he says, may be divided into two kinds: those that depend only on the ideas, and those that can be changed without any change in the ideas. Of the first kind are resemblance, contrariety, degrees in quality, and proportions in quantity or number. But spatio-temporal and causal relations are of the second kind. Only relations of the first kind give *certain* knowledge; our knowledge concerning the others is only *probable*. Algebra and arithmetic are the only sciences in which we can carry on a long chain of reasoning without losing certainty. Geometry is not so certain as algebra and arithmetic, because we cannot be sure of the truth of its axioms. It is a mistake to suppose, as many philosophers do, that the ideas of mathematics 'must be comprehended by a pure and intellectual view, of which the superior faculties of the soul are alone capable'. The falsehood of this view is evident, says Hume, as soon as we remember that 'all our ideas are copied from our impressions'.

The three relations that depend not only on ideas are identity, spatio-temporal relations, and causation. In the first two, the mind does not go beyond what is immediately present to the senses. (Spatio-temporal relations, Hume holds, can be perceived, and can form parts of impressions.) Causation alone enables us to infer some thing or occurrence from some other thing or occurrence: " 'Tis only *causation*, which produces such a connexion, as to give us assurance from the existence or action of one object, that 'twas followed or preceded by any other existence or action.'

A difficulty arises from Hume's contention that there is no such thing as an *impression* of a causal relation. We can perceive, by mere observation of A and B, that A is above B, or to the right of B, but not that A causes B. In the past, the relation of causation had been more or less assimilated to that of ground and consequent in logic, but this, Hume rightly perceived, was a mistake.

In the Cartesian philosophy, as in that of the Scholastics, the connection of cause and effect was supposed to be necessary, as logical connections are necessary. The first really serious challenge to this view came from Hume, with whom the modern philosophy of causation begins. He, in common with almost all philosophers down to and including Bergson, supposes the law to state that there are propositions of the form 'A causes B', where A and B are classes of events; the fact that such laws do not occur in any well-developed science appears to be unknown to philosophers. But much of what they have said can be translated so as to be applicable to causal laws such as do occur; we may, therefore, ignore this point for the present.

Hume begins by observing that the power by which one subject produces another is not discoverable from the ideas of the two objects, and that we can therefore only know cause and effect from experience, not from reasoning or reflection. The statement 'what begins must have a cause', he says, is not one that has intuitive certainty, like the statements of logic. As he puts it: 'There is no object, which implies the existence of any other if we consider these objects in themselves, and never look beyond the ideas which we form of them.' Hume argues from this that it must be experience that gives knowledge of cause and effect, but that it cannot be merely the experience of the two events A and B which are in a causal relation to each other. It must be experience, because the connection is not logical; and it cannot be merely the experience of the particular events A and B, since we can discover nothing in A by itself which should lead to produce B. The experience required, he says, is that of the constant conjunction of events of the kind A with events of the kind B. He points out that when, in experience, two objects are constantly conjoined, we do *in fact* infer one from the other. (When he says 'infer', he means that perceiving the one makes us expect the other; he does not mean a formal or explicit inference.) 'Perhaps, the necessary connection depends on the inference,' not vice versa. That is to say, the sight of A causes the expectation of B, and so leads us to believe that there is a necessary connection between A and B. The inference is not determined by reason, since that would require us to assume the uniformity of nature, which itself is not necessary, but only inferred from experience.

Hume is thus led to the view that, when we say 'A causes B', we mean only that A and B are constantly conjoined in fact, not that there is some necessary connection between them. 'We have no other notion of cause and effect, but that of certain objects, which have been *always conjoined* together. . . . We cannot penetrate into the reason of the conjunction.'

He backs up his theory with a definition of 'belief', which is, he maintains, 'a lively idea related to or associated with a present impression'. Through association, if A and B have been constantly conjoined in past experience, the impression of A produces that lively idea of B which constitutes belief in B. This explains why we believe A and B to be connected: the percept of A *is* connected with the idea of B, and so we come to think that A is connected with B, though this opinion is really groundless. 'Objects have no discoverable connexion together; nor is it from any other principle but custom operating upon the imagination, that we can draw any

inference from the appearance of one to the experience of another.'
He repeats many times the contention that what appears to us as
necessary connection among *objects* is really only connection among
the ideas of those objects: the mind is *determined* by custom, and
' 'tis this impression, or *determination*, which affords me the idea
of necessity'. The repetition of instances, which leads us to the
belief that A causes B, gives nothing new in the object, but in the
mind leads to an association of ideas; thus 'necessity is something
that exists in the mind, not in objects'.

Let us now ask ourselves what we are to think of Hume's
doctrine. It has two parts, one objective, the other subjective. The
objective part says: When we judge that A causes B, what has in
fact happened, so far as A and B are concerned, is that they have
been frequently observed to be conjoined, i.e. A has been immediately, or very quickly, followed by B; we have no right to say
that A *must* be followed by B, or will be followed by B on future
occasions. Nor have we any ground for supposing that, however
often A is followed by B, any relation beyond sequence is involved.
In fact, causation is definable in terms of sequence, and is not an
independent notion.

The subjective part of the doctrine says: The frequently observed
conjunction of A and B *causes* the impression of A to *cause* the idea
of B. But if we are to define 'cause' as is suggested in the objective
part of the doctrine, we must reword the above. Substituting the
definition of 'cause', the above becomes:

'It has been frequently observed that the frequently observed
conjunction of two objects A and B has been frequently followed
by occasions on which the impression of A was followed by the
idea of B.'

This statement, we may admit, is true, but it has hardly the
scope that Hume attributes to the subjective part of his doctrine.
He contends, over and over again, that the frequent conjunction
of A and B gives no *reason* for expecting them to be conjoined in
the future, but is merely a *cause* of this expectation. That is to say:
Experience of frequent conjunction is frequently conjoined with
a habit of association. But, if the objective part of Hume's doctrine
is accepted, the fact that, in the past, associations have been
frequently formed in such circumstances, is no reason for supposing that they will continue, or that new ones will be formed in
similar circumstances. The fact is that, where psychology is concerned, Hume allows himself to believe in causation in a sense,
which, in general, he condemns. Let us take an illustration. I see
an apple, and expect that, if I eat it, I shall experience a certain
kind of taste. According to Hume, there is no reason why I should

experience this kind of taste: the law of habit explains the existence of my expectation, but does not justify it. But the law of habit is itself a causal law. Therefore if we take Hume seriously we must say: Although in the past the sight of an apple has been conjoined with expectation of a certain kind of taste, there is no reason why it should continue to be so conjoined: perhaps the next time I see an apple I shall expect it to taste like roast beef. You may, at the moment, think this unlikely; but that is no reason for expecting that you will think it unlikely five minutes hence. If Hume's objective doctrine is right, we have no better reason for expectations in psychology than in the physical world. Hume's theory might be caricatured as follows: 'The proposition "A causes B" means "the impression of A causes the idea of B".' As a definition, this is not a happy effort.

We must therefore examine Hume's objective doctrine more closely. This doctrine has two parts: (1) When we say 'A causes B', all that we have a *right* to say is that, in past experience, A and B have frequently appeared together or in rapid succession, and no instance has been observed of A not followed or accompanied by B. (2) However many instances we may have observed of the conjunction of A and B, that gives no *reason* for expecting them to be conjoined on a future occasion, though it is a *cause* of this expectation, i.e. it has been frequently observed to be conjoined with such an expectation. These two parts of the doctrine may be stated as follows: (1) in causation there is no indefinable relation except conjunction or succession; (2) induction by simple enumeration is not a valid form of argument. Empiricists in general have accepted the first of these theses and rejected the second. When I say they have rejected the second, I mean that they have believed that, given a sufficiently vast accumulation of instances of a conjunction, the likelihood of the conjunction being found in the next instance will exceed a half; or, if they have not held exactly this, they have maintained some doctrine having similar consequences.

I do not wish, at the moment, to discuss induction, which is a large and difficult subject; for the moment, I am content to observe that, if the first half of Hume's doctrine is admitted, the rejection of induction makes all expectation as to the future irrational, even the expectation that we shall continue to feel expectations. I do not mean merely that our expectations *may* be mistaken; that, in any case, must be admitted. I mean that, taking even our firmest expectations, such as that the sun will rise tomorrow, there is not a shadow of reason, for supposing them more likely to be verified than not. With this proviso, I return to the meaning of 'cause'.

Those who disagree with Hume maintain that 'cause' is a specific relation, which entails invariable sequence, but is not entailed by it. To revert to the clocks of the Cartesians: two perfectly accurate chronometers might strike the hours one after the other invariably, without either being the cause of the other's striking. In general, those who take this view maintain that we can sometimes *perceive* causal relations, though in most cases we are obliged to infer them, more or less precariously, from constant conjunction. Let us see what arguments there are for and against Hume on this point.

Hume summarizes his argument as follows:

'I am sensible, that of all the paradoxes, which I have had, or shall hereafter have occasion to advance in the course of this treatise, the present one is the most violent, and that 'tis merely by dint of solid proof and reasoning I can ever hope it will have admission, and overcome the inveterate prejudices of mankind. Before we are reconcil'd to this doctrine, how often must we repeat to ourselves, *that* the simple view of any two objects or actions, however related, can never give us any idea of power, or of a connexion betwixt them: *that* this idea arises from a repetition of their union: *that* the repetition neither discovers nor causes anything in the objects, but has an influence only on the mind, by that customary transition it produces: *that* this customary transition is, therefore, the same with the power and necessity, which are consequently felt by the soul, and not perceiv'd externally in bodies?'

Hume is commonly accused of having too atomic a view of perception, but he allows that certain relations can be perceived. 'We ought not,' he says, 'to receive as reasoning any of the observations we make concerning *identity*, and the relations of *time* and *place*; since in none of them the mind can go beyond what is immediately present to the senses.' Causation, he says, is different in that it takes us beyond the impressions of our senses, and informs us of unperceived existences. As an argument, this seems invalid. We believe in many relations of time and place which we cannot perceive: we think that time extends backwards and forwards, and space beyond the walls of our room. Hume's real argument is that, while we sometimes perceive relations of time and place, we never perceive causal relations, which must therefore, if admitted, be inferred from relations that can be perceived. The controversy is thus reduced to one of empirical fact: Do we, or do we not, sometimes perceive a relation which can be called causal? Hume says no, his adversaries say yes, and it is not easy to see how evidence can be produced by either side.

I think perhaps the strongest argument on Hume's side is to be derived from the character of causal laws in physics. It appears that simple rules of the form 'A causes B' are never to be admitted in science, except as crude suggestions in early stages. The causal laws by which such simple rules are replaced in well-developed sciences are so complex that no one can suppose them given in perception; they are all, obviously, elaborate inferences from the observed course of nature. I am leaving out of account modern quantum theory, which reinforces the above conclusion. So far as the physical sciences are concerned, Hume is *wholly* in the right; such propositions as 'A causes B' are never to be accepted, and our inclination to accept them is to be explained by the laws of habit and association. These laws themselves, in their accurate form, will be elaborate statements as to nervous tissue—primarily its physiology, then its chemistry, and ultimately its physics.

The opponent of Hume, however, even if he admits the whole of what has just been said about the physical sciences, may not yet admit himself decisively defeated. He may say that in psychology we have cases where a causal relation can be perceived. The whole conception of cause is probably derived from volition, and it may be said that we can perceive a relation, between a volition and the consequent act, which is something more than invariable sequence. The same might be said of the relation between a sudden pain and a cry. Such views, however, are rendered very difficult by physiology. Between the will to move my arm and the consequent movement there is a long chain of causal intermediaries consisting of processes in the nerves and muscles. We perceive only the end terms of this process, the volition and the movement, and if we think we see a direct causal connection between these we are mistaken. This argument is not conclusive on the general question, but it shows that it is rash to suppose that we perceive causal relations when we think we do. The balance, therefore, is in favour of Hume's view that there is nothing in *cause* except invariable succession. The evidence, however, is not so conclusive as Hume supposed.

Hume is not content with reducing the evidence of a causal connection to experience of frequent conjunction; he proceeds to argue that such experience does not justify the expectation of similar conjunctions in the future. For example: when (to repeat a former illustration) I see an apple, past experience makes me expect that it will taste like an apple, and not like roast beef; but there is no rational justification for this expectation. If there were such a justification, it would have to proceed from the principle 'that those instances, of which we have had no experience, resemble those of which we have had experience'. This principle is not logically necessary, since we can at least conceive a change in the course of nature. It should therefore be a principle of probability. But all probable arguments assume this principle, and therefore it cannot itself be proved by any probable argument, or even rendered probable by any such argument. 'The supposition, *that the future resembles the past*, is not founded on arguments of any kind, but is derived entirely from habit.'[1] The conclusion is one of complete scepticism:

'All probable reasoning is nothing but a species of sensation. 'Tis not solely in poetry and music, we must follow our taste and sentiment, but likewise in philosophy. When I am convinced of any principle, 'tis only an idea, which strikes more strongly upon me. When I give the preference to one set of arguments above another, I do nothing but decide from my feeling concerning the superiority of their influence. Objects have no discoverable connexion together; nor is it from any other principle but custom operating upon the imagination, that we can draw any inference from the appearance of one to the existence of another.'[2]

The ultimate outcome of Hume's investigation of what passes for knowledge is not what we must suppose him to have desired. The sub-title of his book is: 'An attempt to introduce the experimental method of reasoning into moral subjects.' It is evident that he started out with a belief that scientific method yields the truth, the whole truth, and nothing but the truth; he ended, however, with the conviction that belief is never rational, since we know nothing. After setting forth the arguments for scepticism (Book I, part iv, sec. i), he goes on, not to refute the arguments, but to fall back on natural credulity.

'Nature, by an absolute and uncontrollable necessity, has determined us to judge as well as to breathe and feel; nor can we any more forbear viewing certain objects in a stronger and fuller light, upon account of their customary connexion with a present impression, than we can hinder ourselves from thinking as long as we are awake, or seeing the surrounding bodies, when we turn our eyes towards them in broad sunshine. Whoever has taken the pains to refute this *total* scepticism, has really disputed without an antagonist, and endeavoured by arguments to establish a faculty, which nature has antecedently implanted in the mind, and rendered unavoidable. My intention then in displaying so carefully the arguments of that fantastic sect, is only to make the reader sensible of the truth of my hypothesis, *that all our reasonings concerning causes and effects are derived from nothing but custom; and that belief is more properly an act of the sensitive, than of the cogitative part of our natures.*'

'The sceptic,' he continues (Book I, part iv, sec. ii), 'still continues

---

[1] Book I, part iii, sec. iv.   [2] Book I, part iii, sec. viii.

to reason and believe, even though he asserts that he cannot defend his reason by reason; and by the same rule he must assent to the principle concerning the existence of body, tho' he cannot pretend by any arguments of philosophy to maintain its veracity . . . We may well ask, *what causes us to believe in the existence of body?* But 'tis vain to ask, *whether there be body or not?* That is a point, which we must take for granted in all our reasonings.'

The above is the beginning of a section 'Of scepticism with regard to the senses.' After a long discussion, this section ends with the following conclusion:

'This sceptical doubt, both with respect to reason and the senses, is a malady, which can never be radically cured, but must return upon us every moment, however we may chase it away, and sometimes may seem entirely free from it. . . . Carelessness and inattention alone can afford us any remedy. For this reason I rely entirely upon them; and take it for granted, whatever may be the reader's opinion at this present moment, that an hour hence he will be persuaded there is both an external and internal world.'

There is no reason for studying philosophy—so Hume maintains—except that, to certain temperaments, this is an agreeable way of passing the time. 'In all the incidents of life we ought still to preserve our scepticism. If we believe, that fire warms, or water refreshes, 'tis only because it costs us too much pains to think otherwise. Nay, if we are philosophers, it ought only to be upon sceptical principles, and from an inclination which we feel to be employing ourselves after that manner.' If he abandoned speculation, 'I *feel* I should be a loser in point of pleasure; and this is the origin of my philosophy.'

Hume's philosophy, whether true or false, represents the bankruptcy of eighteenth-century reasonableness. He starts out, like Locke, with the intention of being sensible and empirical, taking nothing on trust, but seeking whatever instruction is to be obtained from experience and observation. But having a better intellect than Locke's, a greater acuteness in analysis, and a smaller capacity for accepting comfortable inconsistencies, he arrives at the disastrous conclusion that from experience and observation nothing is to be learnt. There is no such thing as a rational belief: 'If we believe that fire warms, or water refreshes, 'tis only because it costs us too much pains to think otherwise.' We cannot help believing, but no belief can be grounded in reason. Nor can one line of action be more rational than another, since all alike are based upon irrational convictions. This last conclusion, however, Hume seems not to have drawn. Even in his most sceptical chapter, in which he sums up the conclusions of Book I, he says: 'Generally speaking, the errors in religion are dangerous; those in philosophy only ridiculous.' He has no right to say this. 'Dangerous' is a causal word, and a sceptic as to causation cannot know that anything is 'dangerous'.

In fact, in the later portions of the Treatise, Hume forgets all about his fundamental doubts, and writes much as any other enlightened moralist of his time might have written; he applies to his doubts the remedy that he recommends, namely 'carelessness and inattention'. In a sense, his scepticism is insincere, since he cannot maintain it in practice. It has, however, this awkward consequence, that it paralyses every effort to prove one line of action better than another.

It was inevitable that such a self-refutation of rationality should be followed by a great outburst of irrational faith. The quarrel between Hume and Rousseau is symbolic: Rousseau was mad but influential, Hume was sane but had no followers. Subsequent British empiricists rejected his scepticism without refuting it; Rousseau and his followers agreed with Hume that no belief is based on reason, but thought the heart superior to reason, and allowed it to lead them to convictions very different from those that Hume retained in practice. German philosophers, from Kant to Hegel, had not assimilated Hume's arguments. I say this deliberately, in spite of the belief which many philosophers share with Kant, that his *Critique of Pure Reason* answered Hume. In fact, these philosophers—at least Kant and Hegel—represent a pre-Humian type of rationalism, and can be refuted by Humian arguments. The philosophers who cannot be refuted in this way are those who do not pretend to be rational, such as Rousseau, Schopenhauer, and Nietzsche. The growth of unreason throughout the nineteenth century and what has passed of the twentieth is a natural sequel to Hume's destruction of empiricism.

It is therefore important to discover whether there is any answer to Hume within the framework of a philosophy that is wholly or mainly empirical. If not, there is no intellectual difference between sanity and insanity. The lunatic who believes that he is a poached egg is to be condemned solely on the ground that he is in a minority, or rather—since we must not assume democracy—on the ground that the government does not agree with him. This is a desperate point of view, and it must be hoped that there is some way of escaping from it.

Hume's scepticism rests entirely upon his rejection of the principle of induction. The principle of induction, as applied to causation, says that, if A has been found very often accompanied or followed by B, and no instance is known of A not being accompanied or followed by B, then it is probable that on the next occasion on which A is observed it will be accompanied or followed by B. If the principle is to be adequate, a sufficient number of instances must make the probability not far short of certainty. If this principle, or any other from which it can be deduced, is true, then the causal inferences which Hume rejects are valid, not indeed as giving certainty, but as giving a sufficient probability for practical purposes. If this principle is not true, every attempt to arrive at general scientific laws from particular observations is fallacious, and Hume's scepticism is inescapable for an empiricist. The principle itself cannot, of course, without circularity, be inferred from observed uniformities, since it is required to justify any such inference. It must therefore be, or be deduced from, an independent principle not based upon experience. To this extent, Hume has proved that pure empiricism is not a sufficient basis for science. But if this one principle is admitted, everything else can proceed in accordance with the theory that all our knowledge is based on experience. It must be granted that this is a serious departure from pure empiricism, and that those who are not empiricists may ask why, if one departure is allowed, others are to be forbidden. These, however, are questions not directly raised by Hume's arguments. What these arguments prove—and I do not think the proof can be controverted—is, that induction is an independent logical principle, incapable of being inferred either from experience or from other logical principles, and that without this principle science is impossible.

Chapter XVIII

THE ROMANTIC MOVEMENT

FROM the latter part of the eighteenth century to the present day, art and literature and philosophy, and even politics, have been influenced, positively or negatively, by a way of feeling which was characteristic of what, in a large sense, may be called the romantic movement. Even those who were repelled by this way of feeling were compelled to take account of it, and in many cases were more affected by it than they knew. I propose in this chapter to give a brief description of the romantic outlook, chiefly in matters not definitely philosophical; for this is the cultural background of most philosophic thought in the period with which we are now to be concerned.

The romantic movement was not, in its beginnings, connected with philosophy, though it came before long to have connections with it. With politics, through Rousseau, it was connected from the first. But before we can understand its political and philosophical effects we must consider it in its most essential form, which is as a revolt against received ethical and aesthetic standards.

The first great figure in the movement is Rousseau, but to some extent he only expressed already existing tendencies. Cultivated people in eighteenth-century France greatly admired what they called *la sensibilité*, which meant a proneness to emotion, and more particularly to the emotion of sympathy. To be thoroughly satisfactory, the emotion must be direct and violent and quite uninformed by thought. The man of sensibility would be moved to tears by the sight of a single destitute peasant family, but would be cold to well-thought-out schemes for ameliorating the lot of peasants as a class. The poor were supposed to possess more virtue than the rich; the sage was thought of as a man who retires from the corruption of courts to enjoy the peaceful pleasures of an unambitious rural existence. As a passing mood, this attitude is to be found in poets of almost all periods. The exiled Duke in *As You Like It* expresses it, though he goes back to his dukedom as soon as he can; only the melancholy Jaques sincerely prefers the life of the forest. Even Pope, the perfect exemplar of all that the romantic movement rebelled against, says:

Happy the man whose wish and care
A few paternal acres bound,
Content to breathe his native air
On his own ground.

The poor, in the imaginations of those who cultivated sensibility, always had a few paternal acres, and lived on the produce of their own labour without the need of external commerce. True, they were always losing the acres in pathetic circumstances, because the aged father could no longer work, the lovely daughter was going into a decline, and the wicked mortgagee or the wicked lord was ready to pounce either on the acres or on the daughter's virtue. The poor, to the romantics, were never urban and never industrial; the proletariat is a nineteenth-century conception, perhaps equally romanticized, but quite different.

Rousseau appealed to the already existing cult of sensibility, and gave it a breadth and scope that it might not otherwise have possessed. He was a democrat, not only in his theories, but in his tastes. For long periods of his life, he was a poor vagabond, receiving kindness from people only slightly less destitute than himself. He repaid this kindness, in action, often with the blackest ingratitude, but in emotion his response was all that the most ardent devotee of sensibility could have wished. Having the tastes of a tramp, he found the restraints of Parisian society irksome. From him the romantics learnt a contempt for the trammels of convention—first in dress and manners, in the minuet and the heroic couplet, then in art and love, and at last over the whole sphere of traditional morals.

The romantics were not without morals; on the contrary, their moral judgments were sharp and vehement. But they were based on quite other principles than those that had seemed good to their predecessors. The period from 1660 to Rousseau is dominated by recollections of the wars of religion and the civil wars in France and England and Germany. Men were very conscious of the danger of chaos, of the anarchic tendencies of all strong passions, of the importance of safety and the sacrifices necessary to achieve it. Prudence was regarded as the supreme virtue; intellect was valued as the most effective weapon against subversive fanatics; polished manners were praised as a barrier against barbarism. Newton's orderly cosmos, in which the planets unchangingly revolve about the sun in law-abiding orbits, became an imaginative symbol of good government. Restraint in the expression of passion was the chief aim of education, and the surest mark of a gentleman. In the Revolution, pre-romantic French aristocrats died quietly; Madame

Roland and Danton, who were romantics, died rhetorically.

By the time of Rousseau, many people had grown tired of safety, and had begun to desire excitement. The French Revolution and Napoleon gave them their fill of it. When in 1815, the political world returned to tranquillity, it was a tranquillity so dead, so rigid, so hostile to all vigorous life, that only terrified conservatives could endure it. Consequently there was no such intellectual acquiescence in the *status quo* as had characterized France under the Roi Soleil and England until the French Revolution. Nineteenth-century revolt against the system of the Holy Alliance took two forms. On the one hand, there was the revolt of industrialism, both capitalist and proletarian, against monarchy and aristocracy; this was almost untouched by romanticism, and reverted, in many respects, to the eighteenth century. This movement is represented by the philosophical radicals, the free-trade movement, and Marxian socialism. Quite different from this was the romantic revolt, which was in part reactionary, in part revolutionary. The romantics did not aim at peace and quiet, but at vigorous and passionate individual life. They had no sympathy with industrialism because it was ugly, because money-grubbing seemed to them unworthy of an immortal soul, and because the growth of modern economic organizations interfered with individual liberty. In the post-revolutionary period they were led into politics, gradually, through nationalism: each nation was felt to have a corporate soul, which could not be free so long as the boundaries of States were different from those of nations. In the first half of the nineteenth century, nationalism was the most vigorous of revolutionary principles, and most romantics ardently favoured it.

The romantic movement is characterized, as a whole, by the substitution of aesthetic for utilitarian standards. The earth-worm is useful, but not beautiful; the tiger is beautiful, but not useful. Darwin (who was not a romantic) praised the earth-worm; Blake praised the tiger. The morals of the romantics have primarily aesthetic motives. But in order to characterize the romantics, it is necessary to take account, not only of the importance of aesthetic motives, but also of the change of taste which made their sense of beauty different from that of their predecessors. Of this, their preference for Gothic architecture is one of the most obvious examples. Another is their taste in scenery. Dr Johnson preferred Fleet Street to any rural landscape, and maintained that a man who is tired of London must be tired of life. If anything in the country was admired by Rousseau's predecessors, it was a scene of fertility, with rich pastures and lowing kine. Rousseau, being Swiss, naturally admired the Alps. In his disciples' novels and stories, we find wild torrents, fearful precipices, pathless forests, thunder-storms, tempests at sea, and generally what is useless, destructive, and violent. This change seems to be more or less permanent: almost everybody, nowadays, prefers Niagara and the Grand Canyon to lush meadows and fields of waving corn. Tourist hotels afford statistical evidence of taste in scenery.

The temper of the romantics is best studied in fiction. They liked what was strange: ghosts, ancient decayed castles, the last melancholy descendants of once-great families, practitioners of mesmerism and the occult sciences, falling tyrants and levantine pirates. Fielding and Smollett wrote of ordinary people in circumstances that might well have occurred; so did the realists who reacted against romanticism. But to the romantics such themes were too pedestrian; they felt inspired only by what was grand, remote, and terrifying. Science, of a somewhat dubious sort, could be utilized if it led to something astonishing; but in the main the Middle Ages, and what was most medieval in the present, pleased the romantics best. Very often they cut loose from actuality, either past or present, altogether. *The Ancient Mariner* is typical in this respect, and Coleridge's *Kubla Khan* is hardly the historical monarch of Marco Polo. The geography of the romantics is interesting: from Xanadu to 'the lone Chorasamian shore', the places in which it is interested are remote, Asiatic, or ancient.

The romantic movement, in spite of owing its origin to Rousseau, was at first mainly German. The German romantics were young in the last years of the eighteenth century, and it was while they were young that they gave expression to what was most characteristic in their outlook. Those who had not the good fortune to die young, in the end allowed their individuality to be obscured in the uniformity of the Catholic Church. (A romantic could become a Catholic if he had been born a Protestant, but could hardly be a Catholic otherwise, since it was necessary to combine Catholicism with revolt.) The German romantics influenced Coleridge and Shelley, and independently of German influence the same outlook became common in England during the early years of the nineteenth century. In France, though in a weakened form, it flourished after the Restoration, down to Victor Hugo. In America it is to be seen almost pure in Melville, Thoreau, and Brook Farm, and, somewhat softened, in Emerson and Hawthorne. Although romantics tended towards Catholicism, there was something ineradicably Protestant in the individualism of their outlook, and their permanent successes in moulding customs, opinions, and institutions were almost wholly confined to Protestant countries.

The beginnings of romanticism in England can be seen in the

writings of the satirists. In Sheridan's *Rivals* (1775), the heroine is determined to marry some poor man for love rather than a rich man to please her guardian and his parents; but the rich man whom they have selected wins her love by wooing her under an assumed name and pretending to be poor. Jane Austen makes fun of the romantics in *Northanger Abbey* and *Sense and Sensibility* (1797-8). *Northanger Abbey* has a heroine who is led astray by Mrs Radcliffe's ultra-romantic *Mysteries of Udolpho*, which was published in 1794. The first *good* romantic work in England—apart from Blake, who was a solitary Swedenborgian and hardly part of any 'movement'—was Coleridge's *Ancient Mariner*, published in 1799. In the following year, having unfortunately been supplied with funds by the Wedgwoods, he went to Göttingen and became engulfed in Kant, which did not improve his verse.

After Coleridge, Wordsworth, and Southey had become reactionaries, hatred of the Revolution and Napoleon put a temporary brake on English romanticism. But it was soon revived by Byron, Shelley, and Keats, and in some degree dominated the whole Victorian epoch.

Mary Shelley's *Frankenstein*, written under the inspiration of conversations with Byron in the romantic scenery of the Alps, contains what might almost be regarded as an allegorical prophetic history of the development of romanticism. Frankenstein's monster is not, as he has become in proverbial parlance, a *mere* monster: he is, at first, a gentle being, longing for human affection, but he is driven to hatred and violence by the horror which his ugliness inspires in those whose love he attempts to gain. Unseen, he observes a virtuous family of poor cottagers, and surreptitiously assists their labours. At length he decides to make himself known to them:

'The more I saw of them, the greater became my desire to claim their protection and kindness; my heart yearned to be known and loved by these amiable creatures; to see their sweet looks directed towards me with affection, was the utmost limit of my ambition. I dared not think that they would turn from me with disdain and horror.'

But they did. So he first demanded of his creator the creation of a female like himself, and, when that was refused, devoted himself to murdering, one by one, all whom Frankenstein loved. But even then, when all his murders are accomplished, and while he is gazing upon the dead body of Frankenstein, the monster's *sentiments* remain noble:

'That also is my victim! in his murder my crimes are consummated; the miserable genius of my being is wound to its close!

Oh, Frankenstein! generous and self-devoted being! What does it avail that I now ask thee to pardon me? I, who irretrievably destroyed thee by destroying all that thou lovedst. Alas! he is cold, he cannot answer me. . . . When I run over the frightful catalogue of my sins, I cannot believe that I am the same creature whose thoughts were once filled with sublime and transcendent visions of the beauty and the majesty of goodness. But it is even so; the fallen angel becomes a malignant devil. Yet even that enemy of God and man had friends and associates in his desolation; I am alone.'

Robbed of its romantic form, there is nothing unreal in this psychology, and it is unnecessary to search out pirates or Vandal kings in order to find parallels. To an English visitor, the ex-Kaiser, at Doorn, lamented that the English no longer loved him. Dr Burt, in his book on the juvenile delinquent, mentions a boy of seven who drowned another boy in the Regent's Canal. His reason was that neither his family nor his contemporaries showed him affection. Dr Burt was kind to him, and he became a respectable citizen; but no Dr Burt undertook the reformation of Frankenstein's monster.

It is not the psychology of the romantics that is at fault: it is their standard of values. They admire strong passions, of no matter what kind, and whatever may be their social consequences. Romantic love, especially when unfortunate, is strong enough to win their approval, but most of the strongest passions are destructive—hate and resentment and jealousy, remorse and despair, outraged pride and the fury of the unjustly oppressed, martial ardour and contempt for slaves and cowards. Hence the type of man encouraged by romanticism, especially of the Byronic variety, is violent and anti-social, an anarchic rebel or a conquering tyrant.

This outlook makes an appeal for which the reasons lie very deep in human nature and human circumstances. By self-interest Man has become gregarious, but in instinct he has remained to a great extent solitary; hence the need of religion and morality to reinforce self-interest. But the habit of foregoing present satisfactions for the sake of future advantages is irksome, and when passions are roused the prudent restraints of social behaviour become difficult to endure. Those who, at such times, throw them off, acquire a new energy and sense of power from the cessation of inner conflict, and, though they may come to disaster in the end, enjoy meanwhile a sense of godlike exaltation which, though known to the great mystics, can never be experienced by a merely pedestrian virtue. The solitary part of their nature reasserts itself, but if the intellect survives the reassertion must clothe itself in myth. The mystic becomes one with God, and in the contemplation of the Infinite feels himself absolved from duty to his neighbour. The anarchic rebel does even better: he feels himself not one with God, but God. Truth and duty, which represent our subjection to matter and to our neighbours, exist no longer for the man who has become God; for others, truth is what *he* posits, duty what *he* commands. If we could all live solitary and without labour, we could all enjoy this ecstasy of independence; since we cannot, its delights are only available to madmen and dictators.

Revolt of solitary instincts against social bonds is the key to the philosophy, the politics, and the sentiments, not only of what is commonly called the romantic movement, but of its progeny down to the present day. Philosophy, under the influence of German idealism, became solipsistic, and self-development was proclaimed as the fundamental principle of ethics. As regards sentiment, there has to be a distasteful compromise between the search for isolation and the necessities of passion and economics. D. H. Lawrence's story, 'The Man Who Loved Islands', has a hero who disdained such compromise to a gradually increasing extent and at last died of hunger and cold, but in the enjoyment of complete isolation; but this degree of consistency has not been achieved by the writers who praise solitude. The comforts of civilized life are not obtainable by a hermit, and a man who wishes to write books or produce works of art must submit to the ministrations of others if he is to survive while he does his work. In order to continue to *feel* solitary, he must be able to prevent those who serve him from impinging upon his ego, which is best accomplished if they are slaves. Passionate love, however, is a more difficult matter. So long as passionate lovers are regarded as in revolt against social trammels, they are admired; but in real life the love-relation itself quickly becomes a social trammel, and the partner in love comes to be hated, all the more vehemently if the love is strong enough to make the bond difficult to break. Hence love comes to be conceived as a battle, in which each is attempting to destroy the other by breaking through the protecting walls of his or her ego. This point of view has become familiar through the writings of Strindberg, and, still more, of D. H. Lawrence.

Not only passionate love, but every friendly relation to others, is only possible, to this way of feeling, in so far as the others can be regarded as a projection of one's own Self. This is feasible if the others are blood-relations, and the more nearly they are related the more easily it is possible. Hence an emphasis on race, leading, as in the case of the Ptolemys, to endogamy. How this affected Byron, we know; Wagner suggests a similar sentiment in the love of Siegmund and Sieglinde. Nietzsche, though not scandalously, preferred his sister to all other women: 'How strongly I feel,' he writes to her, 'in all that you say and do, that we belong to the same stock. You understand more of me than others do, because we come of the same percentage. This fits in very well with my "philosophy".'

The principle of nationality, of which Byron was a protagonist, is an extension of the same 'philosophy'. A nation is assumed to be a race, descended from common ancestors, and sharing some kind of 'blood-consciousness'. Mazzini, who constantly found fault with the English for their failure to appreciate Byron, conceived nations as possessed of a mystical individuality, and attributed to them the kind of anarchic greatness that other romantics sought in heroic men. Liberty, for nations, came to be regarded, not only by Mazzini, but by comparatively sober statesmen, as something absolute, which, in practice, made international co-operation impossible.

Belief in blood and race is naturally associated with anti-semitism. At the same time, the romantic outlook, partly because it is aristocratic, and partly because it prefers passion to calculation, has a vehement contempt for commerce and finance. It is thus led to proclaim an opposition to capitalism which is quite different from that of the socialist who represents the interest of the proletariat, since it is an opposition based on dislike of economic preoccupations, and strengthened by the suggestion that the capitalist world is governed by Jews. This point of view is expressed by Byron on the rare occasions when he condescends to notice anything so vulgar as economic power:

> Who hold the balance of the world? Who reign
>   O'er conquerors, whether royalist or liberal?
> Who rouse the shirtless patriots of Spain?
>   (That make old Europe's journals squeak and gibber all.)
> Who keep the world, both Old and New, in pain
>   Or pleasure? Who make politics run glibber all?
> The shade of Buonaparte's noble daring?
> Jew Rothschild, and his fellow Christian Baring.

The verse is perhaps not very musical, but the sentiment is quite of our time, and has been re-echoed by all Byron's followers.

The romantic movement, in its essence, aimed at liberating human personality from the fetters of social convention and social morality. In part, these fetters were a mere useless hindrance to desirable forms of activity, for every ancient community has developed rules of behaviour for which there is nothing to be said except that they are traditional. But egoistic passions, when once let loose, are not easily brought again into subjection to the needs of society. Christianity has succeeded, to some extent, in taming the Ego, but economic, political, and intellectual causes stimulated revolt against the Churches, and the romantic movement brought the revolt into the sphere of morals. By encouraging a new lawless Ego it made social co-operation impossible, and left its disciples faced with the alternative of anarchy or despotism. Egoism, at first, made men expect from others a parental tenderness; but when they discovered, with indignation, that others had their own Ego, the disappointed desire for tenderness turned to hatred and violence. Man is not a solitary animal, and so long as social life survives, self-realization cannot be the supreme principle of ethics.

Chapter XIX

ROUSSEAU

JEAN JACQUES ROUSSEAU (1712-78), though a *philosophe* in the eighteenth-century French sense, was not what would now be called a 'philosopher'. Nevertheless he had a powerful influence on philosophy, as on literature and taste and manners and politics. Whatever may be our opinion of his merits as a thinker, we must recognize his immense importance as a social force. This importance came mainly from his appeal to the heart, and to what, in his day, was called 'sensibility'. He is the father of the romantic movement, the initiator of systems of thought which infer non-human facts from human emotions, and the inventor of the political philosophy of pseudo-democratic dictatorships as opposed to traditional absolute monarchies. Ever since his time, those who considered themselves reformers have been divided into two groups, those who followed him and those who followed Locke. Sometimes they co-operated, and many individuals saw no incompatibility. But gradually the incompatibility has become increasingly evident. At the present time, Hitler is an outcome of Rousseau; Roosevelt and Churchill, of Locke.

Rousseau's biography was related by himself in his *Confessions* in great detail, but without any slavish regard for truth. He enjoyed making himself out a great sinner, and sometimes exaggerated in this respect; but there is abundant external evidence that he was destitute of all the ordinary virtues. This did not trouble him, because he considered that he always had a warm heart, which, however, never hindered him from base actions towards his best friends. I shall relate only so much of his life as is necessary in order to understand his thought and his influence.

He was born in Geneva, and educated as an orthodox Calvinist. His father, who was poor, combined the professions of watch-maker and dancing-master, his mother died when he was an infant, and he was brought up by an aunt. He left school at the age of twelve, and was apprenticed to various trades, but hated them all, and at the age of sixteen fled from Geneva to Savoy. Having no means of subsistence, he went to a Catholic priest and represented himself as wishing to be converted. The formal conversion took place at Turin, in an institution for catechumens; the process lasted nine days. He represents his motives as wholly mercenary: 'I could not dissemble from myself that the holy deed I was about to do was at bottom the act of a bandit.' But this was written after he had reverted to Protestantism, and there is reason to think that for some years he was a sincerely believing Catholic. In 1742 he testified that a house in which he was living in 1730 had been miraculously saved from a fire by a bishop's prayers.

Having been turned out of the institution at Turin with twenty francs in his pocket, he became lackey to a lady named Madame de Vercelli, who died three months later. At her death, he was found to be in possession of a ribbon which had belonged to her, which in fact he had stolen. He asserted that it had been given him by a certain maid, whom he liked; his assertion was believed, and she was punished. His excuse is odd: 'Never was wickedness further from me than at this cruel moment; and when I accused the poor girl, it is contradictory and yet it is true that my affection for her was the cause of what I did. She was present to my mind, and I threw the blame from myself on the first object that presented itself.' This is a good example of the way in which, in Rousseau's ethic, 'sensibility' took the place of all the ordinary virtues.

After this incident, he was befriended by Madame de Warens, a convert from Protestantism like himself, a charming lady who enjoyed a pension from the king of Savoy in consideration of her services to religion. For nine or ten years, most of his time was spent in her house; he called her 'maman' even after she became his mistress. For a while he shared her with her factotum; all lived in the greatest amity, and when the factotum died Rousseau felt grief, but consoled himself with the thought: 'Well, at any rate I shall get his clothes.'

During his early years there were various periods which he spent as a vagabond, travelling on foot, and picking up a precarious livelihood as best he could. During one of these interludes, a friend, with whom he was travelling, had an epileptic fit in the streets of Lyons; Rousseau profited by the crowd which gathered to abandon his friend in the middle of the fit. On another occasion he became secretary to a man who represented himself as an archimandrite on the way to the Holy Sepulchre; on yet another, he had an affair with a rich lady, by masquerading as a Scotch Jacobite named Dudding.

However, in 1743, through the help of a great lady, he became secretary to the French Ambassador to Venice, a sot named Montaigu, who left the work to Rousseau but neglected to pay his salary. Rousseau did the work well, and the inevitable quarrel was not his fault. He went to Paris to try to obtain justice; everybody admitted that he was in the right, but for a long time nothing was done. The vexations of this delay had something to do with turning Rousseau against the existing form of government in France, although, in the end, he received the arrears of salary that were due to him.

It was at about this time (1745) that he took up with Thérèse le Vasseur, who was a servant at his hotel in Paris. He lived with her for the rest of his life (not to the exclusion of other affairs); he had five children by her, all of whom he took to the Foundling Hospital. No one has ever understood what attracted him to her. She was ugly and ignorant; she could neither read nor write (he taught her to write, but not to read); she did not know the names of the months, and could not add up money. Her mother was grasping and avaricious; the two together used Rousseau and all his friends as sources of income. Rousseau asserts (truly or falsely) that he never had a spark of love for Thérèse; in later years she drank, and ran after stable-boys. Probably he liked the feeling that he was indubitably superior to her, both financially and intellectually, and that she was completely dependent upon him. He was always uncomfortable in the company of the great, and genuinely preferred simple people; in this respect his democratic feeling was wholly sincere. Although he never married her, he treated her almost as a wife, and all the grand ladies who befriended him had to put up with her.

His first literary success came to him rather late in life. The Academy of Dijon offered a prize for the best essay on the question: Have the arts and sciences conferred benefits on mankind? Rousseau maintained the negative, and won the prize (1750). He contended that science, letters, and the arts are the worst enemies of morals, and, by creating wants, are the sources of slavery; for how can chains be imposed on those who go naked, like American savages? As might be expected, he is for Sparta, and against Athens. He had read Plutarch's *Lives* at the age of seven, and been much influenced by them; he admired particularly the life of Lycurgus. Like the Spartans, he took success in war as the test of merit; nevertheless, he admired the 'noble savage', whom sophisticated Europeans could defeat in war. Science and virtue, he held, are incompatible, and all sciences have an ignoble origin. Astronomy comes from the superstition of astrology; eloquence from ambition; geometry from avarice; physics from vain curiosity; and even ethics has its source in human pride. Education and the art of printing are to be deplored; everything that distinguishes civilized man from the untutored barbarian is evil.

Having won the prize and achieved sudden fame by this essay, Rousseau took to living according to its maxims. He adopted the simple life, and sold his watch, saying that he would no longer need to know the time.

The ideas of the first essay were elaborated in a second, a 'Discourse on Inequality' (1754), which, however, failed to win a prize. He held that 'man is naturally good, and only by institutions is he made bad'—the antithesis of the doctrine of original sin and salvation through the Church. Like most political theorists of his age, he spoke of a state of nature, though somewhat hypothetically, as 'a state which exists no longer, perhaps never existed, probably never will exist, and of which none the less it is necessary to have just ideas, in order to judge well our present state'. Natural law should be deduced from the state of nature, but as long as we are ignorant of natural man it is impossible to determine the law originally prescribed or best suited to him. All we can know is that the wills of those subject to it must be conscious of their submission, and it must come directly from the voice of nature. He does not object to *natural* inequality, in respect of age, health, intelligence, etc., but only to inequality resulting from privileges authorized by convention.

The origin of civil society and of the consequent social inequalities is to be found in private property. 'The first man who, having enclosed a piece of land, bethought himself of saying "this is mine", and found people simple enough to believe him, was the real founder of civil society.' He goes on to say that a deplorable revolution introduced metallurgy and agriculture; grain is the symbol of our misfortune. Europe is the unhappiest Continent, because it has the most grain and the most iron. To undo the evil, it is only necessary to abandon civilization, for man is naturally good, and savage man, *when he has dined*, is at peace with all nature and the friend of all his fellow-creatures (my italics).

Rousseau sent this essay to Voltaire, who replied (1755): 'I have received your new book against the human race, and thank you for it. Never was such a cleverness used in the design of making us all stupid. One longs, in reading your book, to walk on all fours. But as I have lost that habit for more than sixty years, I feel unhappily the impossibility of resuming it. Nor can I embark in search of the savages of Canada, because the maladies to which I am condemned render a European surgeon necessary to me; because war is going on in those regions; and because the example of our actions has made the savages nearly as bad as ourselves.'

It is not surprising that Rousseau and Voltaire ultimately quarrelled; the marvel is that they did not quarrel sooner.

In 1754, having become famous, he was remembered by his native city, and invited to visit it. He accepted, but as only Calvinists could be citizens of Geneva, he had himself reconverted to his original faith. He had already adopted the practice of speaking of himself as a Genevan puritan and republican, and after his reconversion he thought of living in Geneva. He dedicated his *Discourse on Inequality* to the City Fathers, but they were not pleased; they had no wish to be considered only the equals of ordinary citizens. Their opposition was not the only drawback to life in Geneva; there was another, even more grave, and this was that Voltaire had gone to live there. Voltaire was a writer of plays and an enthusiast for the theatre, but Geneva, on puritan grounds, forbade all dramatic representations. When Voltaire tried to get the ban removed, Rousseau entered the lists on the Puritan side. Savages never act plays; Plato disapproves of them; the Catholic Church refuses to marry or bury actors; Bossuet calls the drama a 'school of concupiscence'. The opportunity for an attack on Voltaire was too good to be lost, and Rousseau made himself the champion of ascetic virtue.

This was not the first public disagreement of these two eminent men. The first was occasioned by the earthquake of Lisbon (1755), about which Voltaire wrote a poem throwing doubt on the Providential government of the world. Rousseau was indignant. He commented: 'Voltaire, in seeming always to believe in God, never really believed in anybody but the devil, since his pretended God is a maleficent Being who according to him finds all his pleasure in working mischief. The absurdity of this doctrine is especially revolting in a man crowned with good things of every sort, and who from the midst of his own happiness tries to fill his fellow-creatures with despair, by the cruel and terrible image of the serious calamities from which he is himself free.'

Rousseau, for his part, saw no occasion to make such a fuss about the earthquake. It is quite a good thing that a certain number of people should get killed now and then. Besides, the people of Lisbon suffered because they lived in houses seven stories high; if they had been dispersed in the woods, as people ought to be, they would have escaped uninjured.

The questions of the theology of earthquakes and of the morality of stage plays caused a bitter enmity between Voltaire and Rousseau, in which all the *philosophes* took sides. Voltaire treated Rousseau as a mischievous madman; Rousseau spoke of Voltaire as 'that trumpet of impiety, that fine genius, and that low soul'. Fine sentiments, however, must find expression, and Rousseau wrote to Voltaire (1760): 'I hate you, in fact, since you have so willed it; but I hate you like a man still worthier to have loved you, if you had willed it. Of all the sentiments with which my heart was full towards you, there only remain the admiration that we cannot refuse to your fine genius, and love for your writings. If there is nothing in you that I can honour but your talents, that is no fault of mine.'

We come now to the most fruitful period of Rousseau's life. His novel *La nouvelle Héloïse* appeared in 1760; *Emile* and *The Social Contract* both in 1762. *Emile*, which is a treatise on education according to 'natural' principles, might have been considered harmless by the authorities if it had not contained 'The Confession of Faith of a Savoyard Vicar', which set forth the principles of natural religion as understood by Rousseau, and was irritating to both Catholic and Protestant orthodoxy. *The Social Contract* was even more dangerous, for it advocated democracy and denied the divine right of kings. The two books, while they greatly increased his fame, brought upon him a storm of official condemnation. He was obliged to fly from France; Geneva would have none of him;[1] Bern refused him asylum. At last Frederick the Great took pity on him, and allowed him to live at Motiers, near Neuchatel, which was part of the philosopher-king's dominions. There he lived for three years; but at the end of that time (1765) the villagers of Motiers, led by the pastor, accused him of poisoning, and tried to murder him. He fled to England, where Hume, in 1762, had proffered his services.

In England, at first, all went well. He had a great social success, and George III granted him a pension. He saw Burke almost daily, but their friendship soon cooled to the point where Burke said: 'He entertained no principle, either to influence his heart, or guide his understanding, but vanity.' Hume was longest faithful, saying he loved him much, and could live with him all his life in mutual friendship and esteem. But by this time Rousseau, not unnaturally, had come to suffer from the persecution mania which ultimately drove him insane, and he suspected Hume of being the agent of plots against his life. At moments he would realize the absurdity of such suspicions, and would embrace Hume, exclaiming 'No, no, Hume is no traitor,' to which Hume (no doubt much embarrassed) replied, '*Quoi, mon cher Monsieur!*' But in the end his delusions won the day and he fled. His last years were spent in Paris in great poverty, and when he died suicide was suspected.

After the breach, Hume said: 'He has only *felt* during the whole course of his life, and in this respect his sensibility rises to a pitch beyond what I have seen any example of; but it still gives him a

---

[1] The Council of Geneva ordered the two books to be burnt, and gave instructions that Rousseau was to be arrested if he came to Geneva. The French Government had ordered his arrest: the Sorbonne and the Parlement of Paris condemned *Emile*.

more acute feeling of pain than of pleasure. He is like a man who was stripped not only of his clothes, but of his skin, and turned out in this situation to combat with the rude and boisterous elements.'

This is the kindest summary of his character that is in any degree compatible with truth.

There is much in Rousseau's work which, however important in other respects, does not concern the history of philosophical thought. There are only two parts of his thinking that I shall consider in any detail; these are, first, his theology, and second, his political theory.

In theology he made an innovation which has now been accepted by the great majority of Protestant theologians. Before him, every philosopher from Plato onwards, if he believed in God, offered intellectual arguments in favour of his belief.[1] The arguments may not, to us, seem very convincing, and we may feel that they would not have seemed cogent to anyone who did not already feel sure of the truth of the conclusion. But the philosopher who advanced the arguments certainly believed them to be logically valid, and such as should cause certainty of God's existence in any unprejudiced person of sufficient philosophical capacity. Modern Protestants who urge us to believe in God, for the most part, despise the old 'proofs', and base their faith upon some aspect of human nature—emotions of awe or mystery, the sense of right and wrong, the feeling of aspiration, and so on. This way of defending religious belief was invented by Rousseau. It has become so familiar that his originality may easily not be appreciated by a modern reader, unless he will take the trouble to compare Rousseau with (say) Descartes or Leibniz.

'Ah, Madame!' Rousseau writes to an aristocratic lady, 'sometimes in the privacy of my study, with my hands pressed tight over my eyes or in the darkness of the night, I am of opinion that there is no God. But look yonder: the rising of the sun, as it scatters the mists that cover the earth, and lays bare the wondrous glittering scene of nature, disperses at the same moment all cloud from my soul. I find my faith again, and my God, and my belief in Him. I admire and adore Him, and I prostrate myself in His presence.'

On another occasion he says: 'I believe in God as strongly as I believe any other truth, because believing and not believing are the last things in the world that depend on me.' This form of argument has the drawback of being private; the fact that Rousseau

[1] We must except Pascal. 'The heart has its reasons, of which reason is ignorant' is quite in Rousseau's style.

cannot help believing something affords no ground for another person to believe the same thing.

He was very emphatic in his theism. On one occasion he threatened to leave a dinner party because Saint Lambert (one of the guests), expressed a doubt as to the existence of God. '*Moi Monsieur*,' Rousseau exclaimed angrily, '*je crois en Dieu!*' Robespierre, in all things his faithful disciple, followed him in this respect also. The 'Fête de l'Etre Suprême' would have had Rousseau's whole-hearted approval.

'The Confession of Faith of a Savoyard Vicar', which is an interlude in the fourth book of *Emile*, is the most explicit and formal statement of Rousseau's creed. Although it professes to be what the voice of nature has proclaimed to a virtuous priest, who suffers disgrace for the wholly 'natural' fault of seducing an unmarried woman,[1] the reader finds with surprise that the voice of nature, when it begins to speak, is uttering a hotch-pot of arguments derived from Aristotle, St Augustine, Descartes, and so on. It is true that they are robbed of precision and logical form; this is supposed to excuse them, and to permit the worthy Vicar to say that he cares nothing for the wisdom of the philosophers.

The later parts of 'The Confession of Faith' are less reminiscent of previous thinkers than the earlier parts. After satisfying himself that there is a God. the Vicar goes on to consider rules of conduct. 'I do not deduce these rules,' he says, 'from the principles of a high philosophy, but I find them in the depths of my heart, written by Nature in ineffaceable characters.' From this he goes on to develop the view that conscience is in all circumstances an infallible guide to right action. 'Thanks be to Heaven,' he concludes this part of his argument, 'we are thus freed from all this terrifying apparatus of philosophy; we can be men without being learned; dispensed from wasting our life in the study of morals, we have at less cost a more assured guide in this immense labyrinth of human opinions.' Our natural feelings, he contends, lead us to serve the common interest, while our reason urges selfishness. We have therefore only to follow feeling rather than reason in order to be virtuous.

Natural religion, as the Vicar calls his doctrine, has no need of a revelation; if men had listened to what God says to the heart, there would have been only one religion in the world. If God has revealed Himself specially to certain men, this can only be known by human testimony, which is fallible. Natural religion has the advantage of being revealed directly to each individual.

There is a curious passage about hell. The Vicar does not know

[1] 'Un prêtre en bonne règle ne doit faire des enfants qu'aux femmes mariées,' he elsewhere reports a Savoyard priest as saying.

whether the wicked go to eternal torment, and says, somewhat loftily, that the fate of the wicked does not greatly interest him; but on the whole he inclines to the view that the pains of hell are not everlasting. However this may be, he is sure that salvation is not confined to the members of any one Church.

It was presumably the rejection of revelation and of hell that so profoundly shocked the French government and the Council of Geneva.

The rejection of reason in favour of the heart was not, to my mind, an advance. In fact, no one thought of this device so long as reason appeared to be on the side of religious belief. In Rousseau's environment, reason, as represented by Voltaire, was opposed to religion, therefore away with reason! Moreover reason was abstruse and difficult; the savage, even when he has dined, cannot understand the ontological argument, and yet the savage is the repository of all necessary wisdom. Rousseau's savage—who was not the savage known to anthropologists—was a good husband and a kind father; he was destitute of greed, and had a religion of natural kindliness. He was a convenient person, but if he could follow the good Vicar's reasons for believing in God he must have had more philosophy than his innocent naïveté would lead one to expect.

Apart from the fictitious character of Rousseau's 'natural man', there are two objections to the practice of basing beliefs as to objective fact upon the emotions of the heart. One is that there is no reason whatever to suppose that such beliefs will be true; the other is, that the resulting beliefs will be private, since the heart says different things to different people. Some savages are persuaded by the 'natural light' that it is their duty to eat people, and even Voltaire's savages, who are led by the voice of reason to hold that one should only eat Jesuits, are not wholly satisfactory. To Buddhists, the light of nature does not reveal the existence of God, but does proclaim that it is wrong to eat the flesh of animals. But even if the heart said the same thing to all men, that could afford no evidence for the existence of anything outside our own emotions. However ardently I, or all mankind, may desire something, however necessary it may be to human happiness, that is no ground for supposing this something to exist. There is no law of nature guaranteeing that mankind should be happy. Everybody can see that this is true of our life here on earth, but by a curious twist our very sufferings in this life are made into an argument for a better life hereafter. We should not employ such an argument in any other connection. If you had bought ten dozen eggs from a man, and the first dozen were all rotten, you would not infer that the remaining nine dozen must be of surpassing excellence; yet that is the kind of reasoning that 'the heart' encourages as a consolation for our sufferings here below.

For my part, I prefer the ontological argument, the cosmological argument, and the rest of the old stock-in-trade, to the sentimental illogicality that has sprung from Rousseau. The old arguments at least were honest: if valid, they proved their point; if invalid, it was open to any critic to prove them so. But the new theology of the heart dispenses with argument; it cannot be refuted, because it does not profess to prove its points. At bottom, the only reason offered for its acceptance is that it allows us to indulge in pleasant dreams. This is an unworthy reason, and if I had to choose between Thomas Aquinas and Rousseau, I should unhesitatingly choose the Saint.

Rousseau's political theory is set forth in his *Social Contract*, published in 1762. This book is very different in character from most of his writing; it contains little sentimentality and much close intellectual reasoning. Its doctrines, though they pay lip-service to democracy, tend to the justification of the totalitarian State. But Geneva and antiquity combined to make him prefer the City State to large empires such as those of France and England. On the title-page he calls himself 'citizen of Geneva', and in his introductory sentences he says: 'As I was born a citizen of a free State, and a member of the Sovereign, I feel that, however feeble the influence of my voice may have been on public affairs, the right of voting on them makes it my duty to study them.' There are frequent laudatory references to Sparta, as it appears in Plutarch's Life of Lycurgus. He says that democracy is best in small States, aristocracy in middle-sized ones, and monarchy in large ones. But it is to be understood that, in his opinion, small States are preferable, in part because they make democracy more practicable. When he speaks of democracy, he means, as the Greeks meant, direct participation of every citizen; representative government he calls 'elective aristocracy'. Since the former is not possible in a large State, his praise of democracy always implies praise of the City State. This love of the City State is, in my opinion, not sufficiently emphasized in most accounts of Rousseau's political philosophy.

Although the book as a whole is much less rhetorical than most of Rousseau's writing, the first chapter opens with a very forceful piece of rhetoric: 'Man is born free, and everywhere he is in chains. One man thinks himself the master of others, but remains more of a slave than they are.' Liberty is the nominal goal of Rousseau's thought, but in fact it is equality that he values, and that he seeks to secure even at the expense of liberty.

His conception of the Social Contract seems, at first, analogous to Locke's, but soon shows itself more akin to that of Hobbes. In the development from the state of nature, there comes a time when individuals can no longer maintain themselves in primitive independence; it then becomes necessary to self-preservation that they should unite to form a society. But how can I pledge my liberty without harming my interests? 'The problem is to find a form of association which will defend and protect with the whole common force the person and goods of each associate, and in which each, while uniting himself with all, may still obey himself alone, and remain as free as before. This is the fundamental problem of which the Social Contract provides the solution.'

The Contract consists in 'the total alienation of each associate, together with all his rights, to the whole community; for, in the first place, as each gives himself absolutely, the conditions are the same for all; and this being so, no one has any interest in making them burdensome to others'. The alienation is to be without reserve. 'If individuals retained certain rights, as there would be no common superior to decide between them and the public, each, being on one point his own judge, would ask to be so on all; the state of nature would thus continue, and the association would necessarily become inoperative or tyrannical.'

This implies a complete abrogation of liberty and a complete rejection of the doctrine of the rights of man. It is true that, in a later chapter, there is some softening of this theory. It is there said that, although the social contract gives the body politic absolute power over all its members, nevertheless human beings have natural rights as men. 'The sovereign cannot impose upon its subjects any fetters that are useless to the community, nor can it even wish to do so.' But the sovereign is the sole judge of what is useful or useless to the community. It is clear that only a very feeble obstacle is thus opposed to collective tyranny.

It should be observed that the 'sovereign' means, in Rousseau, not the monarch or the government, but the community in its collective and legislative capacity.

The Social Contract can be stated in the following words. 'Each of us puts his person and all his power in common under the supreme direction of the general will, and, in our corporate capacity, we receive each member as an indivisible part of the whole.' This act of association creates a moral and collective body, which is called the 'State' when passive, the 'Sovereign' when active, and a 'Power' in relation to other bodies like itself.

The conception of the 'general will', which appears in the above wording of the Contract, plays a very important part in Rousseau's system. I shall have more to say about it shortly.

It is argued that the Sovereign need give no guarantees to its subjects, for, since it is formed of the individuals who compose it, it can have no interest contrary to theirs. 'The Sovereign, merely by virtue of what it is, is always what it should be.' This doctrine is misleading to the reader who does not note Rousseau's somewhat peculiar use of terms. The Sovereign is not the government, which, it is admitted, may be tyrannical; the Sovereign is a more or less metaphysical entity, not fully embodied in any of the visible organs of the State. Its impeccability, therefore, even if admitted, has not the practical consequences that it might be supposed to have.

The will of the Sovereign, which is always right, is the 'general will'. Each citizen, *quâ* citizen, shares in the general will, but he may also, as an individual, have a particular will running counter to the general will. The Social Contract involves that whoever refuses to obey the general will shall be forced to do so. 'This means nothing less than that he will be forced to be free.'

This conception of being 'forced to be free' is very metaphysical. The general will in the time of Galileo was certainly anti-Copernican; was Galileo 'forced to be free' when the Inquisition compelled him to recant? Is even a malefactor 'forced to be free' when he is put in prison? Think of Byron's Corsair:

> O'er the glad waters of the deep blue sea,
> Our thoughts as boundless and our hearts as free.

Would this man be more 'free' in a dungeon? The odd thing is that Byron's noble pirates are a direct outcome of Rousseau, and yet, in the above passage, Rousseau forgets his romanticism and speaks like a sophistical policeman. Hegel, who owed much to Rousseau, adopted his misuse of the word 'freedom', and defined it as the right to obey the police, or something not very different.

Rousseau has not that profound respect for private property that characterizes Locke and his disciples. 'The State, in relation to its members, is master of all their goods.' Nor does he believe in division of powers, as preached by Locke and Montesquieu. In this respect, however, as in some others, his later detailed discussions do not wholly agree with his earlier general principles. In Book III, chapter i, he says that the part of the Sovereign is limited to making laws, and that the executive, or government, is an intermediate body set up between the subjects and the Sovereign to secure their mutual correspondence. He goes on to say: 'If the Sovereign desires to govern, or the magistrate to give laws, or if the subjects refuse to obey, disorder takes the place of regularity, and . . . the State falls into despotism or anarchy.' In this sentence, allowing for the difference of vocabulary, he seems to agree with Montesquieu.

I come now to the doctrine of the general will, which is both important and obscure. The general will is not identical with the will of the majority, or even with the will of all the citizens. It seems to be conceived as the will belonging to the body politic as such. If we take Hobbes's view, that a civil society is a person, we must suppose it endowed with the attributes of personality, including will. But then we are faced with the difficulty of deciding what are the visible manifestations of this will, and here Rousseau leaves us in the dark. We are told that the general will is always right and always tends to the public advantage; but that it does not follow that the deliberations of the people are equally correct, for there is often a great deal of difference between the will of all and the general will. How, then, are we to know what is the general will? There is, in the same chapter, a sort of answer:

'If, when the people, being furnished with adequate information, held its deliberations, the citizens had no communication one with another, the grand total of the small differences would always give the general will, and the decision would always be good.'

The conception in Rousseau's mind seems to be this: every man's political opinion is governed by self-interest, but self-interest consists of two parts, one of which is peculiar to the individual, while the other is common to all the members of the community. If the citizens have no opportunity of striking logrolling bargains with each other, their individual interests, being divergent, will cancel out, and there will be left a resultant which will represent their common interest; this resultant is the general will. Perhaps Rousseau's conception might be illustrated by terrestrial gravitation. Every particle in the earth attracts every other particle in the universe towards itself; the air above us attracts us upward while the ground beneath us attracts us downward. But all these 'selfish' attractions cancel each other out in so far as they are divergent, and what remains is a resultant attraction towards the centre of the earth. This might be fancifully conceived as the act of the earth considered as a community, and as the expression of its general will.

To say that the general will is always right is only to say that, since it represents what is in common among the self-interests of the various citizens, it must represent the largest collective satisfaction of self-interest possible to the community. This interpretation of Rousseau's meaning seems to accord with his words better than any other that I have been able to think of.[1]

[1] E.g., 'There is often much difference between the will of all and the general will: the latter considers only the common interest: the former looks to private interest, and is only a sum of particular wills: but take away from these same wills the more and the less which destroy each other, and the general will remains as the sum of the differences.'

In Rousseau's opinion, what interferes in practice with the expression of the general will is the existence of subordinate associations within the State. Each of these will have its own general will, which may conflict with that of the community as a whole. 'It may then be said that there are no longer as many votes as there are men, but only as many as there are associations.' This leads to an important consequence: 'It is therefore essential, if the general will is to be able to express itself, that there should be no partial society within the State, and that each citizen should think only his own thoughts: which was indeed the sublime and unique system established by the great Lycurgus.' In a footnote, Rousseau supports his opinion with the authority of Machiavelli.

Consider what such a system would involve in practice. The State would have to prohibit churches (except a State Church), political parties, trade-unions, and all other organizations of men with similar economic interests. The result is obviously the Corporate or Totalitarian State, in which the individual citizen is powerless. Rousseau seems to realize that it may be difficult to prohibit all associations, and adds, as an afterthought, that, if there *must* be subordinate associations, then the more there are the better, in order that they may neutralize each other.

When, in a later part of the book, he comes to consider government, he realizes that the executive is inevitably an association having an interest and a general will of its own, which may easily conflict with that of the community. He says that while the government of a large State needs to be stronger than that of a small one, there is also more need of restraining the government by means of the Sovereign. A member of the government has three wills: his personal will, the will of the government, and the general will. These three should form a *crescendo*, but usually in fact form a *diminuendo*. Again: 'Everything conspires to take away from a man who is set in authority over others the sense of justice and reason.'

Thus in spite of the infallibility of the general will, which is 'always constant, unalterable, and pure', all the old problems of eluding tyranny remain. What Rousseau has to say on these problems is either a surreptitious repetition of Montesquieu, or an insistence on the supremacy of the legislature, which, if democratic, is identical with what he calls the Sovereign. The broad general principles with which he starts, and which he presents as if they solved political problems, disappear when he condescends to detailed considerations, towards the solution of which they contribute nothing.

The condemnation of the book by contemporary reactionaries

leads a modern reader to expect to find in it a much more sweeping revolutionary doctrine than it in fact contains. We may illustrate this by what is said about democracy. When Rousseau uses this word, he means, as we have already seen, the direct democracy of the ancient City State. This, he points out, can never be completely realized, because the people cannot be always assembled and always occupied with public affairs. 'Were there a people of gods, their government would be democratic. So perfect a government is not for men.'

What we call democracy he calls elective aristocracy; this, he says, is the best of all governments, but it is not suitable to all countries. The climate must be neither very hot nor very cold; the produce must not much exceed what is necessary, for, where it does, the evil of luxury is inevitable, and it is better that this evil should be confined to a monarch and his Court than diffused throughout the population. In virtue of these limitations, a large field is left for despotic government. Nevertheless his advocacy of democracy, in spite of its limitations, was no doubt one of the things that made the French Government implacably hostile to the book; the other presumably, was the rejection of the divine right of kings, which is implied in the doctrine of the Social Contract as the origin of government.

The Social Contract became the Bible of most of the leaders in the French Revolution, but no doubt, as is the fate of Bibles, it was not carefully read and was still less understood by many of its disciples. It reintroduced the habit of metaphysical abstractions among the theorists of democracy, and by its doctrine of the general will it made possible the mystic identification of a leader with his people, which has no need of confirmation by so mundane an apparatus as the ballot-box. Much of its philosophy could be appropriated by Hegel[1] in his defence of the Prussian autocracy. Its first-fruits in practice were the reign of Robespierre; the dictatorships of Russia and Germany (especially the latter) are in part an outcome of Rousseau's teaching. What further triumphs the future has to offer to his ghost I do not venture to predict.

---

[1] Hegel selects for special praise the distinction between the general will and the will of all. He says; 'Rousseau would have made a sounder contribution towards a theory of the State, if he had always kept this distinction in sight' (*Logic*, sec. 163).

Chapter XX

KANT

A. GERMAN IDEALISM IN GENERAL

PHILOSOPHY in the eighteenth century was dominated by the British empiricists, of whom Locke, Berkeley, and Hume may be taken as the representatives. In these men there was a conflict, of which they themselves appear to have been unaware, between their temper of mind and the tendency of their theoretical doctrines. In their temper of mind they were socially minded citizens, by no means self-assertive, not unduly anxious for power, and in favour of a tolerant world where, within the limits of the criminal law, every man could do as he pleased. They were good-natured, men of the world, urbane and kindly.

But while their temper was social, their theoretical philosophy led to subjectivism. This was not a new tendency; it had existed in late antiquity, most emphatically in St Augustine; it was revived in modern times by Descartes's *cogito*, and reached a momentary culmination in Leibniz's windowless monads. Leibniz believed that everything in his experience would be unchanged if the rest of the world were annihilated; nevertheless he devoted himself to the reunion of the Catholic and Protestant Churches. A similar inconsistency appears in Lock, Berkeley, and Hume.

In Locke, the inconsistency is still in the theory. We saw in an earlier chapter that Locke says, on the one hand: 'Since the mind, in all its thoughts and reasonings, hath no other immediate object but its own ideas, which it alone does or can contemplate, it is evident that our knowledge is only conversant about them.' And: 'Knowledge is the perception of the agreement or disagreement of two ideas.' Nevertheless, he maintains that we have three kinds of knowledge of real existence: intuitive, of our own; demonstrative, of God's; and sensitive, of things present to sense. *Simple* ideas, he maintains, are 'the product of things operating on the mind in a natural way'. How he knows this, he does not explain; it certainly goes beyond 'the agreement or disagreement of two ideas'.

Berkeley took an important step towards ending this inconsistency. For him, there are only minds and their ideas; the *physical* external world is abolished. But he still failed to grasp *all* the consequences of the epistemological principles that he took over from

Locke. If he had been completely consistent, he would have denied knowledge of God and ot all minds except his own. From such denial he was held back by his feelings as a clergyman and as a social being.

Hume shrank from nothing in pursuit of theoretical consistency, but felt no impulse to make his practice conform to his theory. Hume denied the Self, and threw doubt on induction and causation. He accepted Berkeley's abolition of matter, but not the substitute that Berkeley offered in the form of God's ideas. It is true that, like Locke, he admitted no simple idea without an antecedent impression, and no doubt he *imagined* an 'impression' as a state of mind directly caused by something external to the mind. But he could not admit this as a *definition* of 'impression', since he questioned the notion of 'cause'. I doubt whether either he or his disciples were ever clearly aware of this problem as to impressions. Obviously, on his view, an 'impression' would have to be defined by some intrinsic character distinguishing it from an 'idea', since it could not be defined causally. He could not therefore argue that impressions give knowledge of things external to ourselves, as had been done by Locke, and, in a modified form, by Berkeley. He should, therefore, have believed himself shut up in a solipsistic world, and ignorant of everything except his own mental states and their relations.

Hume, by his consistency, showed that empiricism, carried to its logical conclusion, led to results which few human beings could bring themselves to accept, and abolished, over the whole field of science, the distinction between rational belief and credulity. Locke had foreseen this danger. He puts into the mouth of a supposed critic the argument: 'If knowledge consists in agreement of ideas, the enthusiast and the sober man are on a level.' Locke, living at a time when men had grown tired of 'enthusiasm', found no difficulty in persuading men of the validity of his reply to this criticism. Rousseau, coming at a moment when people were, in turn, getting tired of reason, revived 'enthusiasm', and, accepting the bankruptcy of reason, allowed the heart to decide questions which the head left doubtful. From 1750 to 1794, the heart spoke louder and louder; at last Thermidor put an end, for a time, to its ferocious pronouncements, so far at least as France was concerned. Under Napoleon, heart and head were alike silenced.

In Germany, the reaction against Hume's agnosticism took a form far more profound and subtle than that which Rousseau had given to it. Kant, Fichte, and Hegel developed a new kind of philosophy, intended to safeguard both knowledge and virtue from the subversive doctrines of the late eighteenth century. In Kant, and still more in Fichte, the subjectivist tendency that begins with Descartes was carried to new extremes; in this respect there was at first no reaction against Hume. As regards subjectivism, the reaction began with Hegel, who sought, through his logic, to establish a new way of escape from the individual into the world.

The whole of German idealism has affinities with the romantic movement. These are obvious in Fichte, and still more so in Schelling; they are least so in Hegel.

Kant, the founder of German idealism, is not himself politically important, though he wrote some interesting essays on political subjects. Fichte and Hegel, on the other hand, both set forth political doctrines which had, and still have, a profound influence upon the course of history. Neither can be understood without a previous study of Kant, whom we shall consider in this chapter.

There are certain common characteristics of the German idealists, which can be mentioned before embarking upon detail.

The critique of knowledge, as a means of reaching philosophical conclusions, is emphasized by Kant and accepted by his followers. There is an emphasis upon mind as opposed to matter, which leads in the end to the assertion that only mind exists. There is a vehement rejection of utilitarian ethics in favour of systems which are held to be demonstrated by abstract philosophical arguments. There is a scholastic tone which is absent in the earlier French and English philosophers; Kant, Fichte, and Hegel were university professors, addressing learned audiences, not gentlemen of leisure addressing amateurs. Although their effects were in part revolutionary, they themselves were not intentionally subversive; Fichte and Hegel were very definitely concerned in the defence of the State. The lives of all of them were exemplary and academic; their views on moral questions were strictly orthodox. They made innovations in theology, but they did so in the interests of religion.

With these preliminary remarks, let us turn to the study of Kant.

B. OUTLINE OF KANT'S PHILOSOPHY

Immanuel Kant (1724-1804) is generally considered the greatest of modern philosophers. I cannot myself agree with this estimate, but it would be foolish not to recognize his great importance.

Throughout his whole life, Kant lived in or near Königsberg, in East Prussia. His outer life was academic and wholly uneventful, although he lived through the Seven Years' War (during part of which the Russians occupied East Prussia), the French Revolution, and the early part of Napoleon's career. He was educated in the

Wolfian version of Leibniz's philosophy, but was led to abandon it by two influences: Rousseau and Hume. Hume, by his criticism of the concept of causality, awakened him from his dogmatic slumbers so at least he says, but the awakening was only temporary, and he soon invented a soporific which enabled him to sleep again. Hume, for Kant, was an adversary to be refuted, but the influence of Rousseau was more profound. Kant was a man of such regular habits that people used to set their watches by him as he passed their doors on his constitutional, but on one occasion his time-table was disrupted for several days; this was when he was reading *Emile*. He said that he had to read Rousseau's books several times, because, at a first reading, the beauty of the style prevented him from noticing the matter. Although he had been brought up as a pietist, he was a Liberal both in politics and in theology; he sympathized with the French Revolution until the Reign of Terror, and was a believer in democracy. His philosophy, as we shall see, allowed an appeal to the heart against the cold dictates of theoretical reason, which might, with a little exaggeration, be regarded as a pedantic version of the Savoyard Vicar. His principle that every man is to be regarded as an end in himself is a form of the doctrine of the Rights of Man; and his love of freedom is shown in his saying (about children as well as adults) that 'there can be nothing more dreadful than that the actions of a man should be subject to the will of another'.

Kant's early works are more concerned with science than with philosophy. After the earthquake of Lisbon he wrote on the theory of earthquakes; he wrote a treatise on wind, and a short essay on the question whether the west wind in Europe is moist because it has crossed the Atlantic Ocean. Physical geography was a subject in which he took great interest.

The most important of his scientific writings is his *General Natural History and Theory of the Heavens* (1755), which anticipates Laplace's nebular hypothesis, and sets forth a possible origin of the solar system. Parts of this work have a remarkable Miltonic sublimity. It has the merit of inventing what proved a fruitful hypothesis, but it does not, as Laplace did, advance serious arguments in its favour. In parts it is purely fanciful, for instance in the doctrine that all planets are inhabited, and that the most distant planets have the best inhabitants—a view to be praised for its terrestrial modesty, but not supported by any scientific grounds.

At a time when he was more troubled by the arguments of sceptics than he was earlier or later, he wrote a curious work called *Dreams of a Ghost-seer, Illustrated by the Dreams of Metaphysics* (1766). The 'ghost-seer' is Swedenborg, whose mystical system had been presented to the world in an enormous work of which four copies were sold, three to unknown purchasers and one to Kant. Kant, half serious and half in jest, suggests that Swedenborg's system, which he calls 'fantastic', is perhaps no more so than orthodox metaphysics. He is not, however, wholly contemptuous of Swedenborg. His mystical side, which existed though it did not much appear in his writings, admired Swedenborg, whom he calls 'very sublime'.

Like everybody else at that time, he wrote a treatise on the sublime and the beautiful. Night is sublime, day is beautiful; the sea is sublime, the land is beautiful; man is sublime, woman is beautiful; and so on.

The *Encyclopaedia Britannica* remarks that 'as he never married, he kept the habits of his studious youth to old age'. I wonder whether the author of this article was a bachelor or a married man.

Kant's most important book is *The Critique of Pure Reason* (first edition, 1781; second edition, 1787). The purpose of this work is to prove that, although none of our knowledge can transcend experience, it is, nevertheless, in part *a priori* and not inferred inductively from experience. The part of our knowledge which is *a priori* embraces, according to him, not only logic, but much that cannot be included in logic or deduced from it. He separates two distinctions which, in Leibniz, are confounded. On the one hand there is the distinction between 'analytic' and 'synthetic' propositions; on the other hand, the distinction between '*a priori*' and 'empirical' propositions. Something must be said about each of these distinctions.

An 'analytic' proposition is one in which the predicate is part of the subject; for instance, 'a tall man is a man', or 'an equilateral triangle is a triangle'. Such propositions follow from the law of contradiction; to maintain that a tall man is not a man would be self-contradictory. A 'synthetic' proposition is one that is not analytic. All the propositions that we know only through experience are synthetic. We cannot, by a mere analysis of concepts, discover such truths as 'Tuesday was a wet day' or 'Napoleon was a great general'. But Kant, unlike Leibniz and all other previous philosophers, will not admit the converse, that all synthetic propositions are only known through experience. This brings us to the second of the above distinctions.

An 'empirical' proposition is one which we cannot know except by the help of sense-perception, either our own or that of someone else whose testimony we accept. The facts of history and geography are of this sort; so are the laws of science, whenever our knowledge of their truth depends on observational data. An '*a priori*' proposition, on the other hand, is one which, though it may be *elicited* by experience, is seen, when known, to have a basis other than experience. A child learning arithmetic may be helped by experiencing two marbles and two other marbles, and observing that altogether he is experiencing four marbles. But when he has grasped the general proposition 'two and two are four' he no longer requires confirmation by instances; the proposition has a certainty which induction can never give to a general law. All the propositions of pure mathematics are in this sense *a priori*.

Hume had proved that the law of causality is not analytic, and had inferred that we could not be certain of its truth. Kant accepted the view that it is synthetic, but nevertheless maintained that it is known *a priori*. He maintained that arithmetic and geometry are synthetic, but are likewise *a priori*. He was thus led to formulate his problem in these terms:

How are synthetic judgments *a priori* possible?

The answer to this question, with its consequences, constitutes the main theme of *The Critique of Pure Reason*.

Kant's solution of the problem was one in which he felt great confidence. He had spent twelve years in looking for it, but took only a few months to write his whole long book after his theory had taken shape. In the preface to the first edition he says: 'I venture to assert that there is not a single metaphysical problem which has not been solved, or for the solution of which the key at least has not been supplied.' In the preface to the second edition he compares himself to Copernicus, and says that he has effected a Copernican revolution in philosophy.

According to Kant, the outer world causes only the matter of sensation, but our own mental apparatus orders this matter in space and time, and supplies the concepts by means of which we understand experience. Things in themselves, which are the causes of our sensations, are unknowable; they are not in space or time, they are not substances, nor can they be described by any of those other general concepts which Kant calls 'categories'. Space and time are subjective, they are part of our apparatus of perception. But just because of this, we can be sure that whatever we experience will exhibit the characteristics dealt with by geometry and the science of time. If you always wore blue spectacles, you could be sure of seeing everything blue (this is not Kant's illustration). Similarly, since you always wear spatial spectacles in your mind, you are sure of always seeing everything in space. Thus geometry is *a priori* in the sense that it must be true of everything experienced, but we have no reason to suppose that anything analogous is true of things in themselves, which we do not experience.

Space and time, Kant says, are not concepts; they are forms of 'intuition'. (The German word is '*Anschauung*', which means literally 'looking at' or 'view'. The word 'intuition', though the accepted translation, is not altogether a satisfactory one.) There are also, however, *a priori* concepts; these are the twelve 'categories', which Kant derives from the forms of the syllogism. The twelve categories are divided into four sets of three: (1) of quantity unity, plurality, totality; (2) of quality: reality, negation, limitation; (3) of relation: substance-and-accident, cause-and-effect, reciprocity; (4) of modality: possibility, existence, necessity. These are subjective in the same sense in which space and time are—that is to say, our mental constitution is such that they are applicable to whatever we experience, but there is no reason to suppose them applicable to things in themselves. As regards cause, however, there is an inconsistency, for things in themselves are regarded by Kant as causes of sensations, and free volitions are held by him to be causes of occurrences in space and time. This inconsistency is not an accidental oversight; it is an essential part of his system.

A large part of *The Critique of Pure Reason* is occupied in showing the fallacies that arise from applying space and time or the categories to things that are not experienced. When this is done, so Kant maintains, we find ourselves troubled by 'antinomies'—that is to say, by mutually contradictory propositions each of which can apparently be proved. Kant gives four such antinomies, each consisting of thesis and antithesis.

In the first, the thesis says: 'The world has a beginning in time, and is also limited as regards space.' The antithesis says: 'The world has no beginning in time, and no limits in space; it is infinite as regards both time and space.'

The second antinomy proves that every composite substance both is, and is not, made up of simple parts.

The thesis of the third antinomy maintains that there are two kinds of causality, one according to the laws of nature, the other that of freedom; the antithesis maintains that there is only causality according to the laws of nature.

The fourth antinomy proves that there is, and is not, an absolutely necessary Being.

This part of the *Critique* greatly influenced Hegel, whose dialectic proceeds wholly by way of antinomies.

In a famous section, Kant sets to work to demolish all the purely intellectual proofs of the existence of God. He makes it clear that he has other reasons for believing in God; these he was to set forth later in *The Critique of Practical Reason*. But for the time being his purpose is purely negative.

There are, he says, only three proofs of God's existence by pure reason; these are the ontological proof, the cosmological proof, and the physico-theological proof.

The ontological proof, as he sets it forth, defines God as the *ens realissimum*, the most real being; i.e. the subject of all predicates that belong to being absolutely. It is contended, by those who believe the proof valid, that, since 'existence' is such a predicate, this subject must have the predicate 'existence', i.e. must exist. Kant objects that existence is not a predicate. A hundred thalers that I merely imagine may, he says, have all the same predicates as a hundred real thalers.

The cosmological proof says: If anything exists, then an absolutely necessary Being must exist; now I know that I exist; therefore an absolutely necessary Being exists, and this must be the *ens realissimum*. Kant maintains that the last step in this argument is the ontological argument over again, and that it is therefore refuted by what has been already said.

The physico-theological proof is the familiar argument from design, but in a metaphysical dress. It maintains that the universe exhibits an order which is evidence of purpose. This argument is treated by Kant with respect, but he points out that, at best, it proves only an Architect, not a Creator, and therefore cannot give an adequate conception of God. He concludes that 'the only theology of reason which is possible is that which is based upon moral laws or seeks guidance from them'.

God, freedom, and immortality, he says, are the three 'ideas of reason'. But although pure reason leads us to *form* these ideas, it cannot itself prove their reality. The importance of these ideas is practical, i.e. connected with morals. The purely intellectual use of reason leads to fallacies; its only right use is directed to moral ends.

The practical use of reason is developed briefly near the end of *The Critique of Pure Reason*, and more fully in *The Critique of Practical Reason* (1786). The argument is that the moral law demands justice, i.e. happiness proportional to virtue. Only Providence can insure this, and has evidently not insured it in *this* life. Therefore there is a God and a future life; and there must be freedom, since otherwise there would be no such thing as virtue.

Kant's ethical system, as set forth in his *Metaphysic of Morals* (1785), has considerable historical importance. This book contains the 'categorical imperative', which, at least as a phrase, is familiar outside the circle of professional philosophers. As might be expected, Kant will have nothing to do with utilitarianism, or with any doctrine which gives to morality a purpose outside itself. He wants, he says, 'a completely isolated metaphysic of morals, which is not mixed with any theology or physics or hyperphysics'. All moral concepts, he continues, have their seat and origin wholly *a priori* in the reason. Moral worth exists only when a man acts from a sense of duty; it is not enough that the act should be such as duty *might* have prescribed. The tradesman who is honest from self-interest, or the man who is kind from benevolent impulse, is not virtuous. The essence of morality is to be derived from the concept of law; for, though everything in nature acts according to laws, only a rational being has the power of acting according to the idea of law; i.e. by Will. The idea of an objective principle in so far as it is compelling to the will, is called a command of the reason, and the formula of the command is called an *imperative*.

There are two sorts of imperative: the *hypothetical* imperative which says 'You must do so-and-so if you wish to achieve such-and-such an end'; and the *categorical* imperative, which says that a certain kind of action is objectively necessary, without regard to any end. The categorical imperative is synthetic and *a priori*. Its character is deduced by Kant from the concept of Law:

'If I think of a categorical imperative, I know at once what it contains. For as the imperative contains, besides the Law, only the necessity of the maxim to be in accordance with this law, but the Law contains no condition by which it is limited, nothing remains over but the generality of a law in general, to which the maxim of the action is to be conformable, and which conforming alone presents the imperative as necessary. Therefore the categorical imperative is a single one, and in fact this: *Act only according to a maxim by which you can at the same time will that it shall become a general law.* Or: '*Act as if the maxim of your action were to become through your will a general natural law.*'

Kant gives as an illustration of the working of the categorical imperative that it is wrong to borrow money, because if we all tried to do so there would be no money left to borrow. One can in like manner show that theft and murder are condemned by the categorical imperative. But there are some acts which Kant would certainly think wrong but which cannot be shown to be wrong by his principles, for instance suicide; it would be quite possible for a melancholic to wish that everybody should commit suicide. His maxim seems, in fact, to give a necessary but not a sufficient criterion of virtue. To get a *sufficient* criterion, we should have to abandon Kant's purely formal point of view, and take some account of the effects of actions. Kant, however, states emphatically that virtue does not depend upon the intended result of an action, but only on the principle of which it is itself a result; and if this is conceded, nothing more concrete than his maxim is possible.

Kant maintains, although his principle does not seem to entail this consequence, that we ought so to act as to treat every man as an end in himself. This may be regarded as an abstract form of the doctrine of the rights of man, and it is open to the same objections. If taken seriously, it would make it impossible to reach a decision whenever two people's interests conflict. The difficulties are particularly obvious in political philosophy, which requires some principle, such as preference for the majority, by which the interests of some can, when necessary, be sacrificed to those of others. If there is to be any ethic of government, the end of government must be one, and the only single end compatible with justice is the good of the community. It is possible, however, to interpret Kant's principle as meaning, not that each man is an absolute end, but that all men should count equally in determining actions by which many are affected. So interpreted, the principle may be regarded as giving an ethical basis for democracy. In this interpretation, it is not open to the above objection.

Kant's vigour and freshness of mind in old age are shown by his treatise on *Perpetual Peace* (1795). In this work he advocates a federation of free States, bound together by a covenant forbidding war. Reason, he says, utterly condemns war, which only an international government can prevent. The civil constitution of the component States should, he says, be 'republican', but he defines this word as meaning that the executive and the legislative are separated. He does not mean that there should be no king; in fact, he says that it is easiest to get a perfect government under a monarchy. Writing under the impact of the Reign of Terror, he is suspicious of democracy; he says that it is of necessity despotism, since it establishes an executive power. 'The "whole people", so-called, who carry their measures are really not all, but only a majority: so that here the universal will is in contradiction with itself and with the principle of freedom.' The phrasing shows the influence of Rousseau, but the important idea of a world federation as the way to secure peace is not derived from Rousseau.

Since 1933, this treatise has caused Kant to fall into disfavour in his own country.

C. KANT'S THEORY OF SPACE AND TIME

The most important part of *The Critique of Pure Reason* is the doctrine of space and time. In this section I propose to make a critical examination of this doctrine.

To explain Kant's theory of space and time clearly is not easy, because the theory itself is not clear. It is set forth both in *The*

Critique of Pure Reason and in the *Prolegomena;* the latter exposition is the easier, but is less full than that in the *Critique.* I will try first to expound the theory, making it as plausible as I can; only after exposition will I attempt criticism.

Kant holds that the immediate objects of perception are due partly to external things and partly to our own perceptive apparatus. Locke had accustomed the world to the idea that the secondary qualities—colours, sounds, smells, etc.—are subjective, and do not belong to the object as it is in itself. Kant, like Berkeley and Hume, though in not quite the same way, goes further, and makes the primary qualities also subjective. Kant does not at most times question that our sensations have causes, which he calls 'things-in-themselves' or '*noumena*'. What appears to us in perception, which he calls a 'phenomenon', consists of two parts: that due to the object, which he calls the 'sensation', and that due to our subjective apparatus, which, he says, causes the manifold to be ordered in certain relations. This latter part he calls the *form* of the phenomenon. This part is not itself sensation, and therefore not dependent upon the accident of environment; it is always the same, since we carry it about with us, and it is *a priori* in the sense that it is not dependent upon experience. A pure form of sensibility is called a 'pure intuition' (*Anschauung*); there are two such forms, namely space and time, one for the outer sense, one for the inner.

To prove that space and time are *a priori* forms, Kant has two classes of arguments, one metaphysical, the other epistemological, or, as he calls it, transcendental. The former class of arguments are taken directly from the nature of space and time, the latter indirectly from the possibility of pure mathematics. The arguments about space are given more fully than those about time, because it is thought that the latter are essentially the same as the former.

As regards space, the metaphysical arguments are four in number.

(1) Space is not an empirical concept, abstracted from outer experiences, for space is presupposed in referring sensations to something *external*, and external experience is only possible through the presentation of space.

(2) Space is a necessary presentation *a priori*, which underlies all external perceptions; for we cannot imagine that there should be no space, although we can imagine that there should be nothing in space.

(3) Space is not a discursive or general concept of the relations of things in general, for there is only *one* space, of which what we call 'spaces' are parts, not instances.

(4) Space is presented as an infinite *given* magnitude, which holds

685

within itself all the parts of space; this relation is different from that of a concept to its instances, and therefore space is not a concept but an *Anschauung*.

The transcendental argument concerning space is derived from geometry. Kant holds that Euclidean geometry is known *a priori*, although it is synthetic, i.e. not deducible from logic alone. Geometrical proofs, he considers, depend upon the figures; we can *see*, for instance, that, given two intersecting straight lines at right angles to each other, only one straight line at right angles to both can be drawn through their point of intersection. This knowledge, he thinks, is not derived from experience. But the only way in which my intuition can anticipate what will be found in the object is if it contains only the form of my sensibility, antedating in my subjectivity all the actual impressions. The objects of sense must obey geometry, because geometry is concerned with our ways of perceiving, and therefore we cannot perceive otherwise. This explains why geometry, though synthetic, is *a priori* and apodeictic.

The arguments with regard to time are essentially the same, except that arithmetic replaces geometry with the contention that counting takes time.

Let us now examine these arguments one by one.

The first of the metaphysical arguments concerning space says: 'Space is not an empirical concept abstracted from external experiences. For in order that certain sensations may be referred to something outside me [i.e. to something in a different position in space from that in which I find myself], and further in order that I may be able to perceive them as outside and beside each other, and thus as not merely different, but in different places, the presentation of space must already give the foundation [*zum Grunde liegen*].' Therefore external experience is only possible through the presentation of space.

The phrase 'outside me [i.e. in a different place from that in which I find myself]' is a difficult one. As a thing-in-itself, I am not anywhere, and nothing is spatially outside me; it is only my body as a phenomenon that can be meant. Thus all that is really involved is what comes in the second part of the sentence, namely that I perceive different objects as in different places. The image which arises in one's mind is that of a cloak-room attendant who hangs different coats on different pegs; the pegs must already exist, but the attendant's subjectivity arranges the coats.

There is here, as throughout Kant's theory of the subjectivity of space and time, a difficulty which he seems to have never felt. What induces me to arrange objects of perception as I do rather than otherwise? Why, for instance, do I always see people's eyes above their mouths and not below them? According to Kant, the eyes and the mouth exist as things in themselves, and cause my separate percepts, but nothing in them corresponds to the spatial arrangement that exists in my perception. Contrast with this the physical theory of colours. We do not suppose that in matter there are colours in the sense in which our percepts have colours, but we do think that different colours correspond to different wave-lengths. Since waves, however, involve space and time, there cannot, for Kant, be waves in the causes of our percepts. If, on the other hand, the space and time of our percepts have counterparts in the world of matter, as physics assumes, then geometry is applicable to these counterparts, and Kant's arguments fail. Kant holds that the mind orders the raw material of sensation, but never thinks it necessary to say why it orders it as it does and not otherwise.

In regard to time this difficulty is even greater, because of the intrusion of causality. I perceive the lightning before I perceive the thunder; a thing-in-itself A caused my perception of lightning, and another thing-in-itself B caused my perception of thunder, but A was not earlier than B, since time exists only in the relations of percepts. Why, then, do the two timeless things A and B produce effects at different times? This must be wholly arbitrary if Kant is right, and there must be no relation between A and B corresponding to the fact that the percept caused by A is earlier than that caused by B.

The second metaphysical argument maintains that it is possible to imagine nothing in space, but impossible to imagine no space. It seems to me that no serious argument can be based upon what we can or cannot imagine; but I should emphatically deny that we can imagine space with nothing in it. You can imagine looking at the sky on a dark cloudy night, but then you yourself are in space, and you imagine the clouds that you cannot see. Kant's space, as Vaihinger pointed out, is absolute, like Newton's, and not merely a system of relations. But I do not see how absolute empty space can be imagined.

The third metaphysical argument says: 'Space is not a discursive, or, as is said, general concept of the relations of things in general, but a pure intuition. For, in the first place, we can only imagine [sich vorstellen] one single space, and if we speak of 'spaces' we mean only parts of one and the same unique space. And these parts cannot precede the whole as its parts . . . but can only be thought as in it. It [space] is essentially unique, the manifold in it rests solely on limitations.' From this it is concluded that space is an a priori intuition.

The gist of this argument is the denial of plurality in space itself.

What we call 'spaces' are neither instances of a general concept 'a space', nor parts of an aggregate. I do not know quite what, according to Kant, their logical status is, but in any case they are logically subsequent to space. To those who take, as practically all moderns do, a relational view of space, this argument becomes incapable of being stated, since neither 'space' nor 'spaces' can survive as a substantive.

The fourth metaphysical argument is chiefly concerned to prove that space is an intuition, not a concept. Its premiss is 'space is imagined [or presented, *vorgestellt*] as an infinite *given* magnitude'. This is the view of a person living in a flat country, like that of Königsberg; I do not see how an inhabitant of an Alpine valley could adopt it. It is difficult to see how anything infinite can be 'given'. I should have thought it obvious that the part of space that is given is that which is peopled by objects of perception, and that for other parts we have only a feeling of possibility of motion. And if so vulgar an argument may be intruded, modern astronomers maintain that space is in fact not infinite, but goes round and round, like the surface of the globe.

The transcendental (or epistemological) argument, which is best stated in the *Prolegomena*, is more definite than the metaphysical arguments, and is also more definitely refutable. 'Geometry', as we now know, is a name covering two different studies. On the one hand, there is pure geometry, which deduces consequences from axioms, without inquiring whether the axioms are 'true'; this contains nothing that does not follow from logic, and is not 'synthetic', and has no need of figures such as are used in geometrical textbooks. On the other hand, there is geometry as a branch of physics, as it appears, for example, in the general theory of relativity; this is an empirical science, in which the axioms are inferred from measurements, and are found to differ from Euclid's. Thus of the two kinds of geometry one is *a priori* but not synthetic, while the other is synthetic but not *a priori*. This disposes of the transcendental argument.

Let us now try to consider the questions raised by Kant as regards space in a more general way. If we adopt the view, which is taken for granted in physics, that our percepts have external causes which are (in some sense) material, we are led to the conclusion that all the actual qualities in percepts are different from those in their unperceived causes, but that there is a certain structural similarity between the system of percepts and the system of their causes. There is, for example, a correlation between colours (as perceived) and wave-lengths (as inferred by physicists). Similarly there must be a correlation between space as an ingredient in percepts and space as an ingredient in the system of unperceived causes of percepts. All this rests upon the maxim 'same cause, same effect', with its obverse, 'different effects, different causes'. Thus, e.g. when a visual percept A appears to the left of a visual percept B, we shall suppose that there is some corresponding relation between the cause of A and the cause of B.

We have, on this view, two spaces, one subjective and one objective, one known in experience and the other merely inferred. But there is no difference in this respect between space and other aspects of perception, such as colours and sounds. All alike, in their subjective forms, are known empirically; all alike, in their objective forms, are inferred by means of a maxim as to causation. There is no reason whatever for regarding our knowledge of space as in any way different from our knowledge of colour and sound and smell.

With regard to time, the matter is different, since, if we adhere to the belief in unperceived causes of percepts, the objective time must be identical with the subjective time. If not, we get into the difficulties already considered in connection with lightning and thunder. Or take such a case as the following: You hear a man speak, you answer him, and he hears you. His speaking, and his hearing of your reply, are both, so far as you are concerned, in the unperceived world; and in that world the former precedes the latter. Moreover his speaking precedes your hearing in the objective world of physics; your hearing precedes your reply in the subjective world of percepts; and your reply precedes his hearing in the objective world of physics. It is clear that the relation 'precedes' must be the same in all these propositions. While, therefore, there is an important sense in which perceptual space is subjective, there is no sense in which perceptual time is subjective.

The above arguments assume, as Kant does, that percepts are caused by 'things in themselves', or, as we should say, by events in the world of physics. This assumption, however, is by no means logically necessary. If it is abandoned, percepts cease to be in any important sense 'subjective', since there is nothing with which to contrast them.

The 'thing-in-itself' was an awkward element in Kant's philosophy, and was abandoned by his immediate successors, who accordingly fell into something very like solipsism. Kant's inconsistencies were such as to make it inevitable that philosophers who were influenced by him should develop rapidly either in the empirical or in the absolutist direction; it was, in fact, in the latter direction that German philosophy moved until after the death of Hegel.

Kant's immediate successor, Fichte (1762-1814), abandoned 'things in themselves', and carried subjectivism to a point which seems almost to involve a kind of insanity. He holds that the Ego is the only ultimate reality, and that it exists because it posits itself; the non-Ego, which has a subordinate reality, also exists only because the Ego posits it. Fichte is not important as a pure philosopher, but as the theoretical founder of German nationalism, by his *Addresses to the German Nation* (1807-8), which were intended to rouse the Germans to resistance to Napoleon after the battle of Jena. The Ego as a metaphysical concept easily became confused with the empirical Fichte; since the Ego was German, it followed that the Germans were superior to all other nations. 'To have character and to be a German,' says Fichte, 'undoubtedly mean the same thing.' On this basis he worked out a whole philosophy of nationalistic totalitarianism, which had great influence in Germany.

His immediate successor Schelling (1775-1854) was more amiable but not less subjective. He was closely associated with the German romantics; philosophically, though famous in his day, he is not important. The important development from Kant's philosophy was that of Hegel.

Chapter XXI

CURRENTS OF THOUGHT
IN THE NINETEENTH CENTURY

THE intellectual life of the nineteenth century was more complex than that of any previous age. This was due to several causes. First: the area concerned was larger than ever before; America and Russia made important contributions, and Europe became more aware than formerly of Indian philosophies, both ancient and modern. Second: science, which had been a chief source of novelty since the seventeenth century, made new conquests, especially in geology, biology, and organic chemistry. Third: machine production profoundly altered the social structure, and gave men a new conception of their powers in relation to the physical environment. Fourth: a profound revolt, both philosophical and political, against traditional systems in thought, in politics, and in economics, gave rise to attacks upon many beliefs and institutions that had hitherto been regarded as unassailable. This revolt had two very different forms, one romantic, the other rationalistic. (I am using these words in a liberal sense.) The romantic revolt passes from Byron, Schopenhauer, and Nietzsche to Mussolini and Hitler; the rationalistic revolt begins with the French philosophers of the Revolution, passes on, somewhat softened, to the philosophical radicals in England, then acquires a deeper form in Marx and issues in Soviet Russia.

The intellectual predominance of Germany is a new factor, beginning with Kant. Leibniz, though a German, wrote almost always in Latin or French, and was very little influenced by Germany in his philosophy. German idealism after Kant, as well as later German philosophy, was, on the contrary, profoundly influenced by German history; much of what seems strange in German philosophical speculation reflects the state of mind of a vigorous nation deprived, by historical accidents, of its natural share of power. Germany had owed its international position to the Holy Roman Empire, but the Emperor had gradually lost control of his nominal subjects. The last powerful Emperor was Charles V, and he owed his power to his possessions in Spain and the Low Countries. The Reformation and the Thirty Years' War destroyed what had been left of German unity, leaving a number of petty principalities which were at the mercy of France. In the eighteenth century only one German state, Prussia, had successfully resisted the French; that is why Frederick was called the Great. But Prussia itself had failed to stand against Napoleon, being utterly defeated in the battle of Jena. The resurrection of Prussia under Bismarck appeared as a revival of the heroic past of Alaric, Charlemagne, and Barbarossa. (To Germans, Charlemagne is a German, not a Frenchman). Bismarck showed his sense of history when he said, 'We will not go to Canossa.'

Prussia, however, though politically predominant, was culturally less advanced than much of Western Germany; this explains why many eminent Germans, including Goethe, did not regret Napoleon's success at Jena. Germany, at the beginning of the nineteenth century, presented an extraordinary cultural and economic diversity. In East Prussia serfdom still survived; the rural aristocracy were largely immersed in bucolic ignorance, and the labourers were completely without even the rudiments of education. Western Germany, on the other hand, had been in part subject to Rome in antiquity; it had been under French influence since the seventeenth century; it had been occupied by French revolutionary armies, and had acquired institutions as liberal as those of France. Some of the princes were intelligent, patrons of the arts and sciences, imitating Renaissance princes in their courts; the most notable example was Weimar, where the Grand Duke was Goethe's patron. The princes were, naturally, for the most part opposed to German unity, since it would destroy their independence. They were therefore anti-patriotic, and so were many of the eminent men who depended on them, to whom Napoleon appeared the missionary of a higher culture than that of Germany.

Gradually, during the nineteenth century, the culture of Protestant Germany became increasingly Prussian. Frederick the Great, as a free-thinker and an admirer of French philosophy, had struggled to make Berlin a cultural centre; the Berlin Academy had as its perpetual President an eminent Frenchman, Maupertuis, who, however, unfortunately became the victim of Voltaire's deadly ridicule. Frederick's endeavours, like those of the other enlightened despots of the time, did not include economic or political reform; all that was really achieved was a claque of hired intellectuals. After his death, it was again in Western Germany that most of the men of culture were to be found.

German philosophy was more connected with Prussia than were German literature and art. Kant was a subject of Frederick the Great; Fichte and Hegel were professors at Berlin. Kant was little influenced by Prussia; indeed he got into trouble with the Prussian Government for his liberal theology. But both Fichte and Hegel were philosophic mouthpieces of Prussia, and did much to prepare the way for the later identification of German patriotism with admiration for Prussia. Their work in this respect was carried on by the great German historians, particularly by Mommsen and Treitschke. Bismarck finally persuaded the German nation to accept unification under Prussia, and thus gave the victory to the less internationally minded elements in German culture.

Throughout the whole period after the death of Hegel, most academic philosophy remained traditional, and therefore not very important. British empiricist philosophy was dominant in England until near the end of the century, and in France until a somewhat earlier time; then, gradually, Kant and Hegel conquered the universities of France and England, so far as their teachers of technical philosophy were concerned. The general educated public, however, was very little affected by this movement, which had few adherents among men of science. The writers who carried on the academic tradition—John Stuart Mill on the empiricist side, Lotze, Sigwart, Bradley, and Bosanquet on the side of German idealism—were none of them quite in the front rank among philosophers, that is to say, they were not the equals of the men whose systems they, on the whole, adopted. Academic philosophy has often before been out of touch with the most vigorous thought of the age, for instance, in the sixteenth and seventeenth centuries, when it was still mainly scholastic. Whenever this happens, the historian of philosophy is less concerned with the professors than with the unprofessional heretics.

Most of the philosophers of the French Revolution combined science with beliefs associated with Rousseau. Helvetius and Condorcet may be regarded as typical in their combination of rationalism and enthusiasm.

Helvetius (1715-71) had the honour of having his book *De l'Esprit* (1758) condemned by the Sorbonne and burnt by the hangman. Bentham read him in 1769 and immediately determined to devote his life to the principles of legislation, saying: 'What Bacon was to the physical world, Helvetius was to the moral. The moral world has therefore had its Bacon, but its Newton is still to come.' James Mill took Helvetius as his guide in the education of his son John Stuart.

Following Locke's doctrine that the mind is a *tabula rasa*, Helvetius considered the differences between individuals entirely due to differences of education: in every individual, his talents and his virtues are the effect of his instruction. Genius, he maintains, is often due to chance: if Shakespeare had not been caught poaching, he would have been a wool merchant. His interest in legislation

693

comes from the doctrine that the principal instructors of adolescence are the forms of government and the consequent manners and customs. Men are born ignorant, not stupid; they are made stupid by education.

In ethics, Helvetius was a utilitarian; he considered pleasure to be the good. In religion, he was a deist, and vehemently anticlerical. In theory of knowledge, he adopted a simplified version of Locke: 'Enlightened by Locke, we know that it is to the sense-organs we owe our ideas, and consequently our mind.' Physical sensibility, he says, is the sole cause of our actions, our thoughts, our passions, and our sociability He strongly disagrees with Rousseau as to the value of knowledge, which he rates very highly.

His doctrine is optimistic, since only a perfect education is needed to make men perfect. There is a suggestion that it would be easy to find a perfect education if the priests were got out of the way.

Condorcet (1743-94) has opinions similar to those of Helvetius, but more influenced by Rousseau. The rights of man, he says, are all deduced from this one truth, that he is a sensitive being, capable of making reasonings and acquiring moral ideas, from which it follows that men can no longer be divided into rulers and subjects, liars and dupes. 'These principles, for which the generous Sidney gave his life and to which Locke attached the authority of his name, were afterwards developed more precisely by Rousseau.' Locke, he says, first showed the limits of human knowledge. His 'method soon became that of all philosophers, and it is by applying it to morals, politics, and economics, that they have succeeded in pursuing in these sciences a road almost as sure as that of the natural sciences.'

Condorcet much admires the American Revolution. 'Simple common sense taught the inhabitants of the British Colonies that Englishmen born on the other side of the Atlantic Ocean had precisely the same rights as those born on the meridian of Greenwich.' The United States Constitution, he says, is based on natural rights, and the American Revolution made the rights of man known to all Europe, from the Neva to the Guadalquivir. The principles of the French Revolution, however, are 'purer, more precise, deeper than those that guided the Americans'. These words were written while he was in hiding from Robespierre; shortly afterwards, he was caught and imprisoned. He died in prison, but the manner of his death is uncertain.

He was a believer in the equality of women. He was also the inventor of Malthus's theory of population, which, however, had not for him the gloomy consequences that it had for Malthus, because he coupled it with the necessity of birth control. Malthus's father was a disciple of Condorcet, and it was in this way that Malthus came to know of the theory.

Condorcet is even more enthusiastic and optimistic than Helvetius. He believes that, through the spread of the principles of the French Revolution, all the major social ills will soon disappear. Perhaps he was fortunate in not living beyond 1794.

The doctrines of the French revolutionary philosophers, made less enthusiastic and much more precise, were brought to England by the philosophical radicals, of whom Bentham was the recognized chief. Bentham was, at first, almost exclusively interested in law; gradually, as he grew older, his interests widened and his opinions became more subversive. After 1808, he was a republican, a believer in the equality of women, an enemy of imperialism, and an uncompromising democrat. Some of these opinions he owed to James Mill. Both believed in the omnipotence of education. Bentham's adoption of the principle of 'the greatest happiness of the greatest number' was no doubt due to democratic feeling, but it involved opposition to the doctrine of the rights of man, which he bluntly characterized as 'nonsense'.

The philosophical radicals differed from men like Helvetius and Condorcet in many ways. Temperamentally, they were patient and fond of working out their theories in practical detail. They attached great importance to economics, which they believed themselves to have developed as a science. Tendencies to enthusiasm which existed in Bentham and John Stuart Mill, but not in Malthus or James Mill, were severely held in check by this 'science', and particularly by Malthus's gloomy version of the theory of population, according to which most wage-earners must always, except just after a pestilence, earn the smallest amount that will keep them and their families alive. Another great difference between the Benthamites and their French predecessors was that in industrial England there was violent conflict between employers and wage-earners, which gave rise to trade-unionism and socialism. In this conflict the Benthamites, broadly speaking, sided with the employers against the working class. Their last representative, John Stuart Mill, however, gradually ceased to give adherence to his father's stern tenets, and became, as he grew older, less and less hostile to socialism, and less and less convinced of the eternal truth of classical economics. According to his autobiography, this softening process was begun by the reading of the romantic poets.

The Benthamites, though at first revolutionary in a rather mild way, gradually ceased to be so, partly through success in converting the British government to some of their views, partly through opposition to the growing strength of socialism and trade-unionism. Men who were in revolt against tradition, as already mentioned, were of two kinds, rationalistic and romantic, though in men like Condorcet both elements were combined. The Benthamites were almost wholly rationalistic, and so were the Socialists who rebelled against them as well as against the existing economic order. This movement does not acquire a complete philosophy until we come to Marx, who will be considered in a later chapter.

The romantic form of revolt is very different from the rationalist form, though both are derived from the French Revolution and the philosophers who immediately preceded it. The romantic form is to be seen in Byron in an unphilosophical dress, but in Schopenhauer and Nietzsche it has learnt the language of philosophy. It tends to emphasize the will at the expense of the intellect, to be impatient of chains of reasoning, and to glorify violence of certain kinds. In practical politics it is important as an ally of nationalism. In tendency, if not always in fact, it is definitely hostile to what is commonly called reason, and tends to be anti-scientific. Some of its most extreme forms are to be found among Russian anarchists, but in Russia it was the rationalist form of revolt that finally prevailed. It was Germany, always more susceptible to romanticism than any other country, that provided a governmental outlet for the anti-rational philosophy of naked will.

So far, the philosophies that we have been considering have had an inspiration which was traditional, literary, or political. But there were two other sources of philosophical opinion, namely science and machine production. The second of these began its theoretical influence with Marx, and has grown gradually more important ever since. The first has been important since the seventeenth century, but took new forms during the nineteenth century.

What Galileo and Newton were to the seventeenth century, Darwin was to the nineteenth. Darwin's theory had two parts. On the one hand, there was the doctrine of evolution, which maintained that the different forms of life had developed gradually from a common ancestry. This doctrine, which is now generally accepted, was not new. It had been maintained by Lamarck and by Darwin's grandfather Erasmus, not to mention Anaximander. Darwin supplied an immense mass of evidence for the doctrine, and in the second part of his theory believed himself to have discovered the cause of evolution. He thus gave to the doctrine a popularity and a scientific force which it had not previously possessed, but he by no means originated it.

The second part of Darwin's theory was the struggle for existence and the survival of the fittest. All animals and plants multiply faster than nature can provide for them; therefore in each generation many perish before the age for reproducing themselves. What determines which will survive? To some extent, no doubt, sheer luck, but there is another cause of more importance. Animals and plants are, as a rule, not exactly like their parents, but differ slightly by excess or defect in every measurable characteristic. In a given environment, members of the same species compete for survival, and those best adapted to the environment have the best chance. Therefore among chance variations those that are favourable will preponderate among adults in each generation. Thus from age to age deer run more swiftly, cats stalk their prey more silently, and giraffes' necks become longer. Given enough time, this mechanism, so Darwin contended, could account for the whole long development from the protozoa to *homo sapiens*.

This part of Darwin's theory has been much disputed, and is regarded by most biologists as subject to many important qualifications. That, however, is not what most concerns the historian of nineteenth-century ideas. From the historical point of view, what is interesting is Darwin's extension to the whole of life of the economics that characterized the philosophical radicals. The motive force of evolution, according to him, is a kind of biological economics in a world of free competition. It was Malthus's doctrine of population, extended to the world of animals and plants, that suggested to Darwin the struggle for existence and the survival of the fittest as the source of evolution.

Darwin himself was a liberal, but his theories had consequences in some degree inimical to traditional liberalism. The doctrine that all men are born equal, and that the differences between adults are due wholly to education, was incompatible with his emphasis on congenital differences between members of the same species. If, as Lamarck held, and as Darwin himself was willing to concede up to a point, acquired characteristics were inherited, this opposition to such views as those of Helvetius could have been somewhat softened; but it has appeared that only congenital characteristics are inherited, apart from certain not very important exceptions. Thus the congenital differences between men acquire fundamental importance.

There is a further consequence of the theory of evolution, which is independent of the particular mechanism suggested by Darwin. If men and animals have a common ancestry, and if men developed by such slow stages that there were creatures which we should not know whether to classify as human or not, the question arises: at what stage in evolution did men, or their semi-human ancestors, begin to be all equal? Would *Pithecanthropus erectus*, if he had been properly educated, have done work as good as Newton's?

697

Would the Piltdown Man have written Shakespeare's poetry if there had been anybody to convict him of poaching? A resolute egalitarian who answers these questions in the affirmative will find himself forced to regard apes as the equals of human beings. And why stop with apes? I do not see how he is to resist an argument in favour of Votes for Oysters. An adherent of evolution should maintain that not only the doctrine of the equality of all men, but also that of the rights of man, must be condemned as unbiological, since it makes too emphatic a distinction between men and other animals.

There is, however, another aspect of liberalism which was greatly strengthened by the doctrine of evolution, namely the belief in progress. So long as the state of the world allowed optimism, evolution was welcomed by liberals, both on this ground and because it gave new arguments against orthodox theology. Marx himself, though his doctrines are in some respects pre-Darwinian, wished to dedicate his book to Darwin.

The prestige of biology caused men whose thinking was influenced by science to apply biological rather than mechanistic categories to the world. Everything was supposed to be evolving, and it was easy to imagine an immanent goal. In spite of Darwin, many men considered that evolution justified a belief in cosmic purpose. The conception of organism came to be thought the key to both scientific and philosophical explanations of natural laws, and the atomic thinking of the eighteenth century came to be regarded as out of date. This point of view has at last influenced even theoretical physics. In politics it leads naturally to emphasis upon the community as opposed to the individual. This is in harmony with the growing power of the State; also with nationalism, which can appeal to the Darwinian doctrine of survival of the fittest applied, not to individuals, but to nations. But here we are passing into the region of extra-scientific views suggested to a large public by scientific doctrines imperfectly understood.

While biology has militated against a mechanistic view of the world, modern economic technique has had an opposite effect. Until about the end of the eighteenth century, scientific technique, as opposed to scientific doctrines, had no important effect upon opinion. It was only with the rise of industrialism that technique began to affect men's thought. And even then, for a long time, the effect was more or less indirect. Men who produce philosophical theories are, as a rule, brought into very little contact with machinery. The romantics noticed and hated the ugliness that industrialism was producing in places hitherto beautiful, and the vulgarity (as they considered it) of those who had made money in 'trade'. This led them into an opposition to the middle class which sometimes brought them into something like an alliance with the champions of the proletariat. Engels praised Carlyle, not perceiving that what Carlyle desired was not the emancipation of wage-earners, but their subjection to the kind of masters they had had in the Middle Ages. The Socialists welcomed industrialism, but wished to free industrial workers from subjection to the power of employers. They were influenced by industrialism in the problems that they considered, but not much in the ideas that they employed in the solution of their problems.

The most important effect of machine production on the imaginative picture of the world is an immense increase in the sense of human power. This is only an acceleration of a process which began before the dawn of history, when men diminished their fear of wild animals by the invention of weapons and their fear of starvation by the invention of agriculture. But the acceleration has been so great as to produce a radically new outlook in those who wield the powers that modern technique has created. In old days, mountains and waterfalls were natural phenomena; now, an inconvenient mountain can be abolished and a convenient waterfall can be created. In old days, there were deserts and fertile regions; now, the desert can, if people think it worth while, be made to blossom like the rose, while fertile regions are turned into deserts by insufficiently scientific optimists. In old days, peasants lived as their parents and grandparents had lived, and believed as their parents and grandparents had believed; not all the power of the Church could eradicate pagan ceremonies, which had to be given a Christian dress by being connected with local saints. Now the authorities can decree what the children of peasants shall learn in school, and can transform the mentality of agriculturists in a generation; one gathers that this has been achieved in Russia.

There thus arises, among those who direct affairs or are in touch with those who do so, a new belief in power: first, the power of man in his conflicts with nature, and then the power of rulers as against the human beings whose beliefs and aspirations they seek to control by scientific propaganda, especially education. The result is a diminution of fixity; no change seems impossible. Nature is raw material; so is that part of the human race which does not effectively participate in government. There are certain old conceptions which represent men's belief in the limits of human power; of these the two chief are God and truth. (I do not mean that these two are *logically* connected.) Such conceptions tend to melt away; even if not explicitly negated, they lose importance, and are retained only superficially. This whole outlook is new, and it is impossible to say how mankind will adapt itself to it. It has already produced immense cataclysms, and will no doubt produce others in the future. To frame a philosophy capable of coping with men intoxicated with the prospect of almost unlimited power and also with the apathy of the powerless is the most pressing task of our time.

Though many still sincerely believe in human equality and theoretical democracy, the imagination of modern people is deeply affected by the pattern of social organization suggested by the organization of industry in the nineteenth century, which is essentially undemocratic. On the one hand there are the captains of industry, and on the other the mass of workers. This disruption of democracy from within is not yet acknowledged by ordinary citizens in democratic countries, but it has been a preoccupation of most philosophers from Hegel onwards, and the sharp opposition which they discovered between the interests of the many and those of the few has found practical expression in Fascism. Of the philosophers, Nietzsche was unashamedly on the side of the few, Marx whole-heartedly on the side of the many. Perhaps Bentham was the only one of importance who attempted a reconciliation of conflicting interests; he therefore incurred the hostility of both parties.

To formulate any satisfactory modern ethic of human relationships, it will be essential to recognize the necessary limitations of men's power over the non-human environment, and the desirable limitations of their power over each other.

Chapter XXII

HEGEL

HEGEL (1770-1831) was the culmination of the movement in German philosophy that started from Kant; although he often criticized Kant, his system could never have arisen if Kant's had not existed. His influence, though now diminishing, has been very great, not only or chiefly in Germany. At the end of the nineteenth century, the leading academic philosophers, both in America and in Great Britain, were largely Hegelians. Outside of pure philosophy, many Protestant theologians adopted his doctrines, and his philosophy of history profoundly affected political theory. Marx, as everyone knows, was a disciple of Hegel in his youth, and retained in his own finished system some important Hegelian features. Even if (as I myself believe) almost all Hegel's doctrines are false, he still retains an importance which is not merely historical, as the best representative of a certain kind of philosophy which, in others, is less coherent and less comprehensive.

His life contained few events of importance. In youth he was much attracted to mysticism, and his later views may be regarded, to some extent, as an intellectualizing of what had first appeared to him as mystic insight. He taught philosophy, first as *Privatdozent* at Jena—he mentions that he finished his *Phenomenology of Mind* there the day before the battle of Jena—then at Nuremberg, then as professor at Heidelberg (1816-1818), and finally at Berlin from 1818 to his death. He was in later life a patriotic Prussian, a loyal servant of the State, who comfortably enjoyed his recognized philosophical pre-eminence; but in his youth he despised Prussia and admired Napoleon, to the extent of rejoicing in the French victory at Jena.

Hegel's philosophy is very difficult—he is, I should say, the hardest to understand of all the great philosophers. Before entering on any detail, a general characterization may prove helpful.

From his early interest in mysticism he retained a belief in the unreality of separateness: the world, in his view, was not a collection of hard units, whether atoms or souls, each completely self-subsistent. The apparent self-subsistence of finite things appeared to him to be an illusion; nothing, he held, is ultimately and completely real except the whole. But he differed from Parmenides and Spinoza in conceiving the whole, not as a simple substance, but as a complex system, of the sort that we should call an organism. The apparently separate things of which the world seems to be composed are not simply an illusion; each has a greater or lesser degree of reality, and its reality consists in an aspect of the whole, which is what it is seen to be when viewed truly. With this view goes naturally a disbelief in the reality of time and space as such, for these, if taken as completely real, involve separateness and multiplicity. All this must have come to him first as mystic 'insight'; its intellectual elaboration, which is given in his books, must have come later.

Hegel asserts that the real is rational, and the rational is real. But when he says this he does not mean by 'the real' what an empiricist would mean. He admits, and even urges, that what to the empiricist appear to be facts are, and must be, irrational; it is only after their apparent character has been transformed by viewing them as aspects of the whole that they are seen to be rational. Nevertheless, the identification of the real and the rational leads unavoidably to some of the complacency inseparable from the belief that 'whatever is, is right'.

The whole, in all its complexity, is called by Hegel 'the Absolute'. The Absolute is spiritual; Spinoza's view, that it has the attribute of extension as well as that of thought, is rejected.

Two things distinguish Hegel from other men who have had a more or less similar metaphysical outlook. One of these is emphasis on logic: it is thought by Hegel that the nature of Reality can be deduced from the sole consideration that it must be not self-contradictory. The other distinguishing feature (which is closely connected with the first) is the triadic movement called the 'dialectic'. His most important books are his two *Logics*, and these must be understood if the reasons for his views on other subjects are to be rightly apprehended.

Logic, as Hegel understands the word, is declared by him to be the same thing as metaphysics; it is something quite different from what is commonly called logic. His view is that any ordinary predicate, if taken as qualifying the whole of Reality, turns out to be self-contradictory. One might take as a crude example the theory of Parmenides, that the One, which alone is real, is spherical. Nothing can be spherical unless it has a boundary, and it cannot have a boundary unless there is something (at least empty space) outside of it. Therefore to suppose the Universe as a whole to be spherical is self-contradictory. (This argument might be questioned by bringing in non-Euclidean geometry, but as an illustration it will serve.) Or let us take another illustration, still more crude—far too much so to be used by Hegel. You may say, without apparent contradiction, that Mr A is an uncle; but if you were to say that the Universe is an uncle, you would land yourself in difficulties. An uncle is a man who has a nephew, and the nephew is a separate person from the uncle; therefore an uncle cannot be the whole of Reality.

This illustration might also be used to illustrate the dialectic, which consists of thesis, antithesis, and synthesis. First we say: 'Reality is an uncle.' This is the thesis. But the existence of an uncle implies that of a nephew. Since nothing really exists except the Absolute, and we are now committed to the existence of a nephew, we must conclude: 'The Absolute is a nephew.' This is the anti-thesis. But there is the same objection to this as to the view that the Absolute is an uncle; therefore we are driven to the view that the Absolute is the whole composed of uncle and nephew. This is the synthesis. But this synthesis is still unsatisfactory, because a man can be an uncle only if he has a brother or sister who is a parent of the nephew. Hence we are driven to enlarge our universe to include the brother or sister, with his wife or her husband. In this sort of way, so it is contended, we can be driven on, by the mere force of logic, from any suggested predicate of the Absolute to the final conclusion of the dialectic, which is called the 'Absolute Idea'. Throughout the whole process, there is an underlying assumption that nothing can be really true unless it is about Reality as a whole.

For this underlying assumption there is a basis in traditional logic, which assumes that every proposition has a subject and a predicate. According to this view, every fact consists in something having some property. It follows that relations cannot be real, since they involve *two* things, not one. 'Uncle' is a relation, and a man may become an uncle without knowing it. In that case, from an empirical point of view, the man is unaffected by becoming an uncle; he has no quality which he did not have before, if by 'quality' we understand something necessary to describing him as he is in himself, apart from his relations to other people and things. The only way in which the subject-predicate logic can avoid this difficulty is to say that the truth is not a property of the uncle alone, or of the nephew alone, but of the whole composed of uncle-and-nephew. Since everything, except the Whole, has relations to out-side things, it follows that nothing quite true can be said about separate things, and that in fact only the Whole is real. This follows more directly from the fact that 'A and B are two' is not a subject-predicate proposition, and therefore, on the basis of the traditional logic, there can be no such proposition. Therefore there are not as many as two things in the world; therefore the Whole, considered as a unity, is alone real.

The above argument is not explicit in Hegel, but is implicit in his system, as in that of many other metaphysicians.

A few examples of Hegel's dialectic method may serve to make it more intelligible. He begins the argument of his logic by the assumption that 'the Absolute is Pure Being'; we assume that it just *is*, without assigning any qualities to it. But pure being without any qualities is nothing; therefore we are led to the antithesis: 'The Absolute is Nothing'. From this thesis and antithesis we pass on to the synthesis: the union of Being and Not-Being is Becoming, and so we say: 'The Absolute is Becoming.' This also, of course, won't do, because there has to be something that becomes. In this way our views of Reality develop by the continual correction of previous errors, all of which arose from undue abstraction, by taking something finite or limited as if it could be the whole. 'The limitations of the finite do not come merely from without; its own nature is the cause of its abrogation, and by its own act it passes into its counterpart.'

The process, according to Hegel, is essential to the understanding of the result. Each later stage of the dialectic contains all the earlier stages, as it were in solution; none of them is *wholly* superseded, but is given its proper place as a moment in the Whole. It is therefore impossible to reach the truth except by going through all the steps of the dialectic.

Knowledge as a whole has its triadic movement. It begins with sense-perception, in which there is only awareness of the object. Then, through sceptical criticism of the senses, it becomes purely subjective. At last, it reaches the stage of self-knowledge, in which subject and object are no longer distinct. Thus self-consciousness is the highest form of knowledge. This, of course, must be the case in Hegel's system, for the highest kind of knowledge must be that possessed by the Absolute, and as the Absolute is the Whole there is nothing outside itself for it to know.

In the best thinking, according to Hegel, thoughts become fluent and interfuse. Truth and falsehood are not sharply defined opposites, as is commonly supposed; nothing is wholly false, and nothing that *we* can know is wholly true. 'We can know in a way that is false'; this happens when we attribute absolute truth to some detached piece of information. Such a question as 'Where was Caesar born?' has a straightforward answer, which is true in a sense, but not in the philosophical sense. For philosophy, 'the truth is the whole', and nothing partial is *quite* true.

'Reason,' Hegel says, 'is the conscious certainty of being all reality.' This does not mean that a separate person is all reality; in his separateness he is not quite real, but what is real in him is his participation in Reality as a whole. In proportion as we become more rational, this participation is increased.

The Absolute Idea, with which the *Logic* ends, is something like Aristotle's God. It is thought thinking about itself. Clearly the Absolute cannot think about anything but itself, since there *is* nothing else, except to our partial and erroneous ways of apprehending Reality. We are told that Spirit is the only reality, and that its thought is reflected into itself by self-consciousness. The actual words in which the Absolute Idea is defined are very obscure. Wallace translates them as follows:

'*The Absolute Idea*. The idea, as unity of the Subjective and Objective Idea, is the notion of the Idea—a notion whose object (*Gegenstand*) is the Idea as such, and for which the objective (*Objekt*) is Idea—an Object which embraces all characteristics in its unity.'

The original German is even more difficult.[1] The essence of the matter is, however, somewhat less complicated than Hegel makes it seem. The Absolute Idea is pure thought thinking about pure thought. This is all that God does throughout the ages—truly a Professor's God. Hegel goes on to say: 'This unity is consequently the absolute and all truth, the Idea which thinks itself.'

I come now to a singular feature of Hegel's philosophy, which distinguishes it from the philosophy of Plato or Plotinus or Spinoza. Although ultimate reality is timeless, and time is merely an illusion generated by our inability to see the Whole, yet the time-process has an intimate relation to the purely logical process of the dialectic. World history, in fact, has advanced through the categories, from Pure Being in China (of which Hegel knew nothing except that it was) to the Absolute Idea, which seems to have been nearly, if not quite, realized in the Prussian State. I cannot see any justification, on the basis of his own metaphysic, for the view that world history repeats the transitions of the dialectic, yet that is the thesis which he developed in his *Philosophy of History*. It was an interesting thesis, giving unity and meaning to the revolutions of human affairs. Like other historical theories, it required, if it was to be made plausible, some distortion of facts and considerable ignorance. Hegel, like Marx and Spengler after him, possessed both these qualifications. It is odd that a process which is represented as cosmic should all have taken place on our planet, and most of it near the

---

[1] The definition in German is: '*Der Begriff der Idee, dem die Idee als solche der Gegenstand, dem das Objekt sie ist.*' Except in Hegel, *Gegenstand* and *Objekt* are synonyms.

Mediterranean. Nor is there any reason, if reality is timeless, why the later parts of the process should embody higher categories than the earlier parts—unless one were to adopt the blasphemous supposition that the Universe was gradually learning Hegel's philosophy.

The time-process, according to Hegel, is from the less to the more perfect, both in an ethical and in a logical sense. Indeed these two senses are, for him, not really distinguishable, for logical perfection consists in being a closely-knit whole, without ragged edges, without independent parts, but united, like a human body, or still more like a reasonable mind, into an organism whose parts are interdependent and all work together towards a single end; and this also constitutes ethical perfection. A few quotations will illustrate Hegel's theory:

'Like the soul-conductor Mercury, the Idea is, in truth, the leader of peoples and of the world; and Spirit, the rational and necessitated will of that conductor, is and has been the director of the events of the world's history. To become acquainted with Spirit in this its office of guidance, is the object of our present undertaking.'

'The only thought which philosophy brings with it to the contemplation of history is the simple conception of Reason; that Reason is the sovereign of the world; that the history of the world, therefore, presents us with a rational process. This conviction and intuition is a hypothesis in the domain of history as such. In that of philosophy it is no hypothesis. It is there proved by speculative cognition, that Reason—and this term may here suffice us, without investigating the relation sustained by the universe to the Divine Being—is *Substance*, as well as *Infinite Power*; its own *infinite material* underlying all the natural and spiritual life which it originates, as also the *Infinite Form*, that which sets the material in motion. Reason is the *substance* of the universe.'

'That this "Idea" or "Reason" is the *True*, the *Eternal*, the absolutely *powerful* essence; that it reveals itself in the world, and that in that world nothing else is revealed but this and its honour and glory—is the thesis which, as we have said, has been proved in philosophy, and is here regarded as demonstrated.'

'The world of intelligence and conscious volition is not abandoned to chance, but must show itself in the light of the self-cognizant Idea.'

This is 'a result which happens to be known to *me*, because I have traversed the entire field'.

All these quotations are from the introduction to *The Philosophy of History*.

Spirit, and the course of its development, is the substantial object

of the philosophy of history. The nature of Spirit may be understood by contrasting it with its opposite, namely Matter. The
essence of matter is gravity; the essence of Spirit is Freedom. Matter
is outside itself, whereas Spirit has its centre in itself. Spirit is self-
contained existence.' If this is not clear, the following definition
may be found more illuminating:

'But what is Spirit? It is the one immutably homogeneous Infinite
—pure Identity—which in its second phase separates itself from
itself and makes this second aspect its own polar opposite, namely
as existence for and in Self as contrasted with the Universal.'

In the historical development of Spirit there have been three
main phases: The Orientals, the Greeks and Romans, and the
Germans. 'The history of the world is the discipline of the un-
controlled natural will, bringing it into obedience to a universal
principle and conferring subjective freedom. The East knew, and
to the present day knows, only that *One* is free; the Greek and
Roman world, that *some* are free; the German world knows that
All are free.' One might have supposed that democracy would be
the appropriate form of government where all are free, but not so.
Democracy and aristocracy alike belong to the stage where some
are free, despotism to that where one is free, and *monarchy* to that
in which all are free. This is connected with the very odd sense in
which Hegel uses the word 'freedom'. For him (and so far we may
agree) there is no freedom without law; but he tends to convert
this, and to argue that wherever there is law there is freedom. Thus
'freedom', for him, means little more than the right to obey the law.

As might be expected, he assigns the highest role to the Germans
in the terrestrial development of Spirit. 'The German spirit is the
spirit of the new world. Its aim is the realization of absolute Truth
as the unlimited self-determination of freedom—*that* freedom
which has its own absolute form itself as its purport.'

This is a very superfine brand of freedom. It does not mean that
you will be able to keep out of a concentration camp. It does not
imply democracy, or a free press,[1] or any of the usual Liberal watch-
words, which Hegel rejects with contempt. When Spirit gives laws
to itself, it does so freely. To our mundane vision, it may seem
that the Spirit that gives laws is embodied in the monarch, and the
Spirit to which laws are given is embodied in his subjects. But from
the point of view of the Absolute the distinction between monarch
and subjects, like all other distinctions, is illusory, and when the
monarch imprisons a liberal-minded subject, that is still Spirit freely

[1] Freedom of the Press, he says, does not consist in being allowed to write
what one wants: this view is crude and superficial. For instance, the Press
should not be allowed to render the Government or the police contemptible.

determining itself. Hegel praises Rousseau for distinguishing between the general will and the will of all. One gathers that the monarch embodies the general will, whereas a parliamentary majority only embodies the will of all. A very convenient doctrine.

German history is divided by Hegel into three periods: the first, up to Charlemagne; the second, from Charlemagne to the Reformation; the third, from the Reformation onwards. These three periods are distinguished as the Kingdoms of the Father, the Son, and the Holy Ghost, respectively. It seems a little odd that the Kingdom of the Holy Ghost should have begun with the bloody and utterly abominable atrocities committed in suppressing the Peasants' War, but Hegel, naturally, does not mention so trivial an incident. Instead, he goes off, as might be expected, into praises of Machiavelli.

Hegel's interpretation of history since the fall of the Roman Empire is partly the effect, and partly the cause, of the teaching of world history in German schools. In Italy and France, while there has been a romantic admiration of the Germans on the part of a few men such as Tacitus and Machiavelli, they have been viewed, in general, as the authors of the 'barbarian' invasion, and as enemies of the Church, first under the great Emperors, and later as the leaders of the Reformation. Until the nineteenth century the Latin nations looked upon the Germans as their inferiors in civilization. Protestants in Germany naturally took a different view. They regarded the late Romans as effete, and considered the German conquest of the Western Empire an essential step towards revivification. In relation to the conflict of Empire and Papacy in the Middle Ages, they took a Ghibelline view: to this day, German schoolboys are taught a boundless admiration of Charlemagne and Barbarossa. In the times after the Reformation, the political weakness and disunity of Germany was deplored, and the gradual rise of Prussia was welcomed as making Germany strong under Protestant leadership, not under the Catholic and somewhat feeble leadership of Austria. Hegel, in philosophizing about history, has in mind such men as Theodoric, Charlemagne, Barbarossa, Luther, and Frederick the Great. He is to be interpreted in the light of their exploits, and in the light of the then recent humiliation of Germany by Napoleon.

So much is Germany glorified that one might expect to find it the final embodiment of the Absolute Idea, beyond which no further development would be possible. But this is not Hegel's view. On the contrary, he says that America is the land of the future, 'where, in the ages that lie before us, the burden of the world's history shall reveal itself—perhaps [he adds characteristically] in a contest between North and South America'. He seems to think that everything important takes the form of war. If it were suggested to him that the contribution of America to world history might be the development of a society without extreme poverty, he would not be interested. On the contrary, he says that, as yet, there is no real State in America, because a real State requires a division of classes into rich and poor.

Nations, in Hegel, play the part that classes play in Marx. The principle of historical development, he says, is national genius. In every age, there is some one nation which is charged with the mission of carrying the world through the stage of the dialectic that it has reached. In our age, of course, this nation is Germany. But in addition to nations, we must also take account of world-historical individuals; these are men in whose aims are embodied the dialectical transitions that are due to take place in their time. These men are heroes, and may justifiably contravene ordinary moral rules. Alexander, Caesar, and Napoleon are given as examples. I doubt whether, in Hegel's opinion, a man could be a 'hero' without being a military conqueror.

Hegel's emphasis on nations, together with his peculiar conception of 'freedom', explains his glorification of the State—a very important aspect of his political philosophy, to which we must now turn our attention. His philosophy of the State is developed both in his *Philosophy of History* and in his *Philosophy of Law*. It is in the main compatible with his general metaphysic, but not necessitated by it; at certain points, however—e.g., as regards the relations between States—his admiration of the national State is carried so far as to become inconsistent with his general preference of wholes to parts.

Glorification of the State begins, so far as modern times are concerned, with the Reformation. In the Roman Empire, the Emperor was deified, and the State thereby acquired a sacred character; but the philosophers of the Middle Ages, with few exceptions, were ecclesiastics, and therefore put the Church above the State. Luther, finding support in Protestant princes, began the opposite practice; the Lutheran Church, on the whole, was Erastian. Hobbes, who was politically a Protestant, developed the doctrine of the supremacy of the State, and Spinoza, on the whole, agreed with him. Rousseau, as we have seen, thought the State should not tolerate other political organizations. Hegel was vehemently Protestant, of the Lutheran section; the Prussian State was an Erastian absolute monarchy. These reasons would make one expect to find the State highly valued by Hegel, but, even so, he goes to lengths which are astonishing.

We are told in *The Philosophy of History* that 'the State is the actually existing realized moral life', and that all the spiritual reality possessed by a human being he possesses only through the State. 'For his spiritual reality consists in this, that his own essence—Reason—is objectively present to him, that it possesses objective immediate existence for him. . . . For truth is the unity of the universal and subjective Will, and the universal is to be found in the State, in its laws, its universal and rational arrangements. The State is the Divine Idea as it exists on earth.' Again: 'The State is the embodiment of rational freedom, realizing and recognizing itself in an objective form . . . . The State is the Idea of Spirit in the external manifestation of human Will and its Freedom.'

The Philosophy of Law, in the section on the State, develops the same doctrine somewhat more fully. 'The State is the reality of the moral idea—the moral spirit, as the visible substantial will, evident to itself, which thinks and knows itself, and fulfils what it knows in so far as it knows it.' The State is the rational in and for itself. If the State existed only for the interests of individuals (as Liberals contend), an individual might or might not be a member of the State. It has, however, a quite different relation to the individual: since it is objective Spirit, the individual only has objectivity, truth, and morality in so far as he is a member of the State, whose true content and purpose is union as such. It is admitted that there may be bad States, but these merely exist, and have no true reality, whereas a rational States is infinite in itself.

It will be seen that Hegel claims for the State much the same position as St Augustine and his Catholic successors claimed for the Church. There are, however, two respects in which the Catholic claim is more reasonable than Hegel's. In the first place, the Church is not a chance geographical association, but a body united by a common creed, believed by its members to be of supreme importance; it is thus in its very essence the embodiment of what Hegel calls the 'Idea'. In the second place, there is only one Catholic Church, whereas there are many States. When each State, in relation to its subjects, is made as absolute as Hegel makes it, there is difficulty in finding any philosophical principle by which to regulate the relations between different States. In fact, at this point Hegel abandons his philosophical talk, falling back on the state of nature and Hobbes's war of all against all.

The habit of speaking of '*the* State', as if there were only one, is misleading so long as there is no world State. Duty being, for Hegel, solely a relation of the individual to his State, no principle is left by which to moralize the relations between States. This Hegel recognizes. In external relations, he says, the State is an individual, and each State is independent as against the others. 'Since in this independence the being-for-self of real spirit has its existence, it is the first freedom and highest honour of a people.' He goes on to argue against any sort of League of Nations by which the independence of separate States might be limited. The duty of a citizen is entirely confined (so far as the external relations of his State are concerned) to upholding the substantial individuality and independence and sovereignty of his own State. It follows that war is not wholly an evil, or something that we should seek to abolish. The purpose of the State is not merely to uphold the life and property of the citizens, and this fact provides the moral justification of war, which is not to be regarded as an absolute evil or as accidental, or as having its cause in something that ought not to be.

Hegel does not mean only that, in some situations, a nation cannot rightly avoid going to war. He means much more than this. He is opposed to the creation of institutions—such as a world government—which would prevent such situations from arising, because he thinks it a good thing that there should be wars from time to time. War, he says, is the condition in which we take seriously the vanity of temporal goods and things. (This view is to be contrasted with the opposite theory, that all wars have economic causes.) War has a positive moral value. 'War has the higher significance that through it the moral health of peoples is preserved in their indifference towards the stabilizing of finite determinations.' Peace is ossification; the Holy Alliance, and Kant's League for Peace, are mistaken, because a family of States needs an enemy. Conflicts of States can only be decided by war; States being towards each other in a state of nature, their relations are not legal or moral. Their rights have their reality in their particular wills, and the interest of each State is its own highest law. There is no contrast of morals and politics, because States are not subject to ordinary moral laws.

Such is Hegel's doctrine of the State—a doctrine which, if accepted, justifies every internal tyranny and every external aggression that can possibly be imagined. The strength of his bias appears in the fact that his theory is largely inconsistent with his own metaphysic, and that the inconsistencies are all such as tend to the justification of cruelty and international brigandage. A man may be pardoned if logic compels him regretfully to reach conclusions which he deplores, but not for departing from logic in order to be free to advocate crimes. Hegel's logic led him to believe that there is more reality or excellence (the two for him are synonyms) in wholes than in their parts, and that a whole increases in reality and excellence as it becomes more organized. This justified him in preferring a State to an anarchic collection of individuals, but it should equally have led him to prefer a world State to an anarchic collection of States. Within the State, his general philosophy should have led him to feel more respect for the individual than he did feel, for the wholes of which his *Logic* treats are not like the One of Parmenides, or even like Spinoza's God; they are wholes in which the individual does not disappear, but acquires fuller reality through his harmonious relation to a larger organism. A State in which the individual is ignored is not a small-scale model of the Hegelian Absolute.

Nor is there any good reason, in Hegel's metaphysic, for the exclusive emphasis on the State, as opposed to other social organizations. I can see nothing but Protestant bias in his preference of the State to the Church. Moreover, if it is good that society should be as organic as possible, as Hegel believes, then many social organizations are necessary, in addition to the State and the Church. It should follow from Hegel's principles that every interest which is not harmful to the community, and which can be promoted by co-operation, should have its appropriate organization, and that every such organization should have its quota of limited independence. It may be objected that ultimate authority must reside somewhere, and cannot reside elsewhere than in the State. But even so it may be desirable that this ultimate authority should not be irresistible when it attempts to be oppressive beyond a point.

This brings us to a question which is fundamental in judging Hegel's whole philosophy. Is there more reality, and is there more value, in a whole than in its parts? Hegel answers both questions in the affirmative. The question of reality is metaphysical, the question of value is ethical. They are commonly treated as if they were scarcely distinguishable, but to my mind it is important to keep them apart. Let us begin with the metaphysical question.

The view of Hegel, and of many other philosophers, is that the character of any portion of the universe is so profoundly affected by its relations to the other parts and to the whole, that no true statement can be made about any part except to assign it its place in the whole. Since its place in the whole depends upon all the other parts, a true statement about its place in the whole will at the same time assign the place of every other part in the whole. Thus there can be only one true statement; there is no truth except the whole truth. And similarly nothing is quite real except the whole, for any part, when isolated, is changed in character by being isolated, and therefore no longer appears quite what it truly is. On the other hand, when a part is viewed in relation to the whole, as it should be, it is seen to be not self-subsistent, and to be incapable of existing

712

except as part of just that whole which alone is truly real. This is the metaphysical doctrine.

The ethical doctrine, which maintains that value resides in the whole rather than in the parts, must be true if the metaphysical doctrine is true, but need not be false if the metaphysical doctrine is false. It may, moreover, be true of some wholes and not of others. It is obviously true, in some sense, of a living body. The eye is worthless when separated from the body; a collection of *disjecta membra*, even when complete, has not the value that once belonged to the body from which they were taken. Hegel conceives the ethical relation of the citizen to the State as analogous to that of the eye to the body : in his place the citizen is part of a valuable whole, but isolated he is as useless as an isolated eye. The analogy, however, is open to question; from the ethical importance of some wholes, that of all wholes does not follow.

The above statement of the ethical problem is defective in one important respect, namely, that it does not take account of the distinction between ends and means. An eye in a living body is *useful*, that is to say, it has value as a means; but it has no more *intrinsic* value than when detached from the body. A thing has intrinsic value when it is prized for its own sake, not as a means to something else. We value the eye as a means of seeing. Seeing may be a means or an end; it is a means when it shows us food or enemies, it is an end when it shows us something that we find beautiful. The State is obviously valuable as a means : it protects us against thieves and murderers, it provides roads and schools, and so on. It may, of course, also be bad as a means, for example by waging an unjust war. The real question we have to ask in connection with Hegel is not this, but whether the State is good *per se*, as an end : do the citizens exist for the sake of the State, or the State for the sake of the citizens? Hegel holds the former view; the liberal philosophy that comes from Locke holds the latter. It is clear that we shall only attribute intrinsic value to the State if we think of it as having a life of its own, as being in some sense a person. At this point, Hegel's metaphysic becomes relevant to the question of value. A person is a complex whole, having a single life; can there be a super-person, composed of persons as the body is composed of organs, and having a single life which is not the sum of the lives of the component persons? If there can be such a super-person, as Hegel thinks, then the State may be such a being, and it may be as superior to ourselves as the whole body is to the eye. But if we think this super-person a mere metaphysical monstrosity, then we shall say that the intrinsic value of a community is derived from that of its members, and that the State is a means, not an end.

We are thus brought back from the ethical to the metaphysical question. The metaphysical question itself, we shall find, is really a question of logic.

The question at issue is much wider than the truth or falsehood of Hegel's philosophy; it is the question that divides the friends of analysis from its enemies. Let us take an illustration. Suppose I say 'John is the father of James.' Hegel, and all who believe in what Marshal Smuts calls 'holism', will say: 'Before you can understand this statement, you must know who John and James are. Now to know who John is, is to know all his characteristics, for apart from them he would not be distinguishable from any one else. But all his characteristics involve other people or things. He is characterized by his relations to his parents, his wife, and his children, by whether he is a good or a bad citizen, and by the country to which he belongs. All these things you must know before you can be said to know whom the word "John" refers to. Step by step, in your endeavour to say what you mean by the word "John", you will be led to take account of the whole universe, and your original statement will turn out to be telling you something about the universe, not about two separate people, John and James.'

Now this is all very well, but it is open to an initial objection. If the above argument were sound, how could knowledge ever begin? I know numbers of propositions of the form 'A is the father of B', but I do not know the whole universe. If all knowledge were knowledge of the universe as a whole, there would be no knowledge. This is enough to make us suspect a mistake somewhere.

The fact is that, in order to use the word 'John' correctly and intelligently, I do not need to know *all* about John, but only enough to recognize him. No doubt he has relations, near or remote, to everything in the universe, but he can be spoken of truly without taking them into account, except such as are the direct subject-matter of what is being said. He may be the father of Jemima as well as of James, but it is not necessary for me to know this in order to know that he is the father of James. If Hegel were right, we could not state fully what is meant by 'John is the father of James' without mentioning Jemima: we ought to say 'John, the father of Jemima, is the father of James.' This would still be inadequate; we should have to go on to mention his parents and grandparents, and a whole Who's Who. But this lands us in absurdities. The Hegelian position might be stated as follows: The word "John" means all that is true of John.' But as a definition this is circular, since the word 'John' occurs in the defining phrase. In fact, if Hegel were right, no word could begin to have a meaning, since we should need to know already the meanings of all other words in order to state all the properties of what the word designates, which, according to the theory, are what the word means.

To put the matter abstractly: we must distinguish properties of different kinds. A thing may have a property not involving any other thing; this sort is called a *quality*. Or it may have a property involving one other thing; such a property is being married. Or it may have one involving two other things, such as being a brother-in-law. If a certain thing has a certain collection of qualities, and no other thing has just this collection of qualities, then it can be defined as 'the thing having such-and such qualities'. From its having these qualities, nothing can be deduced by pure logic as to its relational properties. Hegel thought that, if enough was known about a thing to distinguish it from all other things, then all its properties could be inferred by logic. This was a mistake, and from this mistake arose the whole imposing edifice of his system. This illustrates an important truth, namely, that the worse your logic, the more interesting the consequences to which it gives rise.

Chapter XXIII

BYRON

THE nineteenth century, in comparison with the present age, appears rational, progressive, and satisfied; yet the opposite qualities of our time were possessed by many of the most remarkable men during the epoch of liberal optimism. When we consider men, not as artists or discoverers, not as sympathetic or antipathetic to our own tastes, but as forces, as causes of change in the social structure, in judgments of value, or in intellectual outlook, we find that the course of events in recent times has necessitated much readjustment in our estimates, making some men less important than they had seemed, and others more so. Among those whose importance is greater than it seemed, Byron deserves a high place. On the Continent, such a view would not appear surprising, but in the English-speaking world it may be thought strange. It was on the Continent that Byron was influential, and it is not in England that his spiritual progeny is to be sought. To most of us, his verse seems often poor and his sentiment often tawdry, but abroad his way of feeling and his outlook on life were transmitted and developed and transmuted until they became so wide-spread as to be factors in great events.

The aristocratic rebel, of whom Byron was in his day the exemplar, is a very different type from the leader of a peasant or proletarian revolt. Those who are hungry have no need of an elaborate philosophy to stimulate or excuse discontent, and anything of the kind appears to them merely an amusement of the idle rich. They want what others have, not some intangible and metaphysical good. Though they may preach Christian love, as the medieval communist rebels did, their real reasons for doing so are very simple: that the lack of it in the rich and powerful causes the sufferings of the poor, and that the presence of it among comrades in revolt is thought essential to success. But experience of the struggle leads to a despair of the power of love, leaving naked hate as the driving force. A rebel of this type, if, like Marx, he invents a philosophy, invents one solely designed to demonstrate the ultimate victory of his party, not one concerned with values. His values remain primitive: the good is enough to eat, and the rest is talk. No hungry man is likely to think otherwise.

The aristocratic rebel, since he has enough to eat, must have other causes of discontent. I do not include among rebels the mere leaders of factions temporarily out of power; I include only men whose philosophy requires some greater change than their own personal success. It may be that love of power is the underground source of their discontent, but in their conscious thought there is criticism of the government of the world, which, when it goes deep enough, takes the form of Titanic cosmic self-assertion or, in those who retain some superstition, of Satanism. Both are to be found in Byron. Both, largely through men whom he influenced, became common in large sections of society which could hardly be deemed aristocratic. The aristocratic philosophy of rebellion, growing, developing, and changing as it approached maturity, has inspired a long series of revolutionary movements, from the Carbonari after the fall of Napoleon to Hitler's *coup* in 1933; and at each stage it has inspired a corresponding manner of thought and feeling among intellectuals and artists.

It is obvious that an aristocrat does not become a rebel unless his temperament and circumstances are in some way peculiar. Byron's circumstances were very peculiar. His earliest recollections were of his parents' quarrels; his mother was a woman whom he feared for her cruelty and despised for her vulgarity; his nurse combined wickedness with the strictest Calvinist theology; his lameness filled him with shame, and prevented him from being one of the herd at school. At ten years old, after living in poverty, he suddenly found himself a Lord and the owner of Newstead. His great-uncle the 'wicked Lord', from whom he inherited, had killed a man in a duel thirty-three years ago, and been ostracized by his neighbours ever since. The Byrons had been a lawless family, and the Gordons, his mother's ancestors, even more so. After the squalor of a back street in Aberdeen, the boy naturally rejoiced in his title and his Abbey, and was willing to take on the character of his ancestors in gratitude for their lands. And if, in recent years, their bellicosity had led them into trouble, he learnt that in former centuries it had brought them renown. One of his earliest poems, 'On Leaving Newstead Abbey', relates his emotions at this time, which are of admiration for his ancestors who fought in the Crusades, at Crecy, and at Marston Moor. He ends with the pious resolve:

Like you will he live, or like you will he perish:
When decay'd, may he mingle his dust with your own.

This is not the mood of a rebel, but it suggests 'Childe' Harold, the modern peer who imitates medieval barons. As an undergraduate, when for the first time he had an income of his own, he wrote that he felt as independent as 'a German Prince who coins his own cash, or a Cherokee Chief who coins no cash at all, but enjoys what is more precious, Liberty. I speak in raptures of that Goddess because my amiable Mama was so despotic'. He wrote, in later life, much noble verse in praise of freedom, but it must be understood that the freedom he praised was that of a German Prince or a Cherokee Chief, not the inferior sort that might conceivably be enjoyed by ordinary mortals.

In spite of his lineage and his title, his aristocratic relations fought shy of him, and he was made to feel himself socially not of their society. His mother was intensely disliked, and he was looked on with suspicion. He knew that she was vulgar, and darkly feared a similar defect in himself. Hence arose that peculiar blend of snobbery and rebellion that characterized him. If he could not be a gentleman in the modern style, he would be a bold baron in the style of his crusading ancestors, or perhaps in the more ferocious but even more romantic style of the Ghibelline chiefs, cursed of God and Man as they trampled their way to splendid downfall. Medieval romances and histories were his etiquette books. He sinned like the Hohenstaufen, and like the crusaders he died fighting the Moslem.

His shyness and sense of friendlessness made him look for comfort in love affairs, but as he was unconsciously seeking a mother rather than a mistress, all disappointed him except Augusta. Calvinism, which he never shook off—to Shelley, in 1816, he described himself as 'Methodist, Calvinist, Augustinian'—made him feel that his manner of life was wicked; but wickedness, he told himself, was a hereditary curse in his blood, an evil fate to which he was predestined by the Almighty. If that were indeed the case, since he *must* be remarkable, he would be remarkable as a sinner, and would dare transgressions beyond the courage of the fashionable libertines whom he wished to despise. He loved Augusta genuinely because she was of his blood—of the Ishmaelite race of the Byrons—and also, more simply, because she had an elder sister's kindly care for his daily welfare. But this was not all that she had to offer him. Through her simplicity and her obliging good-nature, she became the means of providing him with the most delicious self-congratulatory remorse. He could feel himself the equal of the greatest sinners—the peer of Manfred, of Cain, almost of Satan himself. The Calvinist, the aristocrat, and the rebel were all equally satisfied; and so was the romantic lover, whose heart was broken by the loss of the only earthly being still capable of rousing in it the gentler emotions of pity and love.

Byron, though he felt himself the equal of Satan, never quite ventured to put himself in the place of God. This next step in the growth of pride was taken by Nietzsche, who says: 'If there were Gods, how could I endure it to be not God! *Therefore* there are no Gods.' Observe the suppressed premiss of this reasoning: 'Whatever humbles my pride is to be judged false.' Nietzsche, like Byron, and even to a greater degree, had a pious upbringing, but having a better intellect, he found a better escape than Satanism. He remained, however, very sympathetic to Byron. He says:

'The tragedy is that we cannot believe the dogmas of religion and metaphysics if we have the strict methods of truth in heart and head, but on the other hand, we have become through the development of humanity so tenderly sensitively suffering that we need the highest kind of means of salvation and consolation: whence arises the danger that man may bleed to death through the truth that he recognizes. Byron expresses this in immortal lines:

> Sorrow is knowledge: they who know the most
> Must mourn the deepest o'er the fatal truth,
> The Tree of Knowledge is not that of Life.'

Sometimes, though rarely, Byron approaches more nearly to Nietzsche's point of view. But in general Byron's ethical theory, as opposed to his practice, remains strictly conventional.

The great man, to Nietzsche, is godlike, to Byron, usually, a Titan at war with himself. Sometimes, however, he portrays a sage not unlike Zarathustra—the Corsair, in his dealings with his followers,

> Still sways their souls with that commanding art
> That dazzles, leads, yet chills the vulgar heart.

And this same hero 'hated man too much to feel remorse'. A footnote assures us that the Corsair is true to human nature, since similar traits were exhibited by Genseric, King of the Vandals, by Ezzelino the Ghibelline tyrant, and by a certain Louisiana pirate.

Byron was not obliged to confine himself to the Levant and the Middle Ages in his search for heroes, since it was not difficult to invest Napoleon with a romantic mantle. The influence of Napoleon on the imagination of nineteenth-century Europe was very profound; he inspired Clausewitz, Stendhal, Heine, the thought of Fichte and Nietzsche, and the acts of Italian patriots. His ghost stalks through the age, the only force which is strong enough to stand up against industrialism and commerce, pouring scorn on pacifism and shop-keeping. Tolstoy's *War and Peace* is an attempt to exorcize the ghost, but a vain one, for the spectre has never been more powerful than at the present day.

During the Hundred Days, Byron proclaimed his wish for Napoleon's victory, and when he heard of Waterloo he said, 'I'm damned sorry for it.' Only once, for a moment, did he turn against his hero: in 1814, when (so he thought) suicide would have been more seemly than abdication. At this moment, he sought consolation in the virtue of Washington, but the return from Elba made this effort no longer necessary. In France, when Byron died, 'It was remarked in many newspapers that the two greatest men of the century, Napoleon and Byron, had disappeared almost at the same time.'[1] Carlyle, who, at the time, considered Byron 'the noblest spirit in Europe', and felt as if he had 'lost a brother', came afterwards to prefer Goethe, but still coupled Byron with Napoleon:

'For your nobler minds, the publishing of some such Work of Art, in one or the other dialect, becomes almost a necessity. For what is it properly but an altercation with the Devil, before you begin honestly Fighting him? Your Byron publishes his *Sorrows of Lord George*, in verse and in prose, and copiously otherwise: your Bonaparte presents his *Sorrows of Napoleon* Opera, in an all too-stupendous style; with music of canon-volleys, and murder shrieks of a world; his stage-lights are the fires of Conflagration; his rhyme and recitative are the tramp of embanded Hosts and the sound of falling Cities.'[2]

It is true that, three chapters further on, he gives the emphatic command: 'Close thy *Byron*; open thy *Goethe*.' But Byron was in his blood, whereas Goethe remained an aspiration.

To Carlyle, Goethe and Byron were antitheses; to Alfred de Musset, they were accomplices in the wicked work of instilling the poison of melancholy into the cheerful Gallic soul. Most young Frenchmen of that age knew Goethe, it seems, only through *The Sorrows of Werther*, and not at all as the Olympian. Musset blamed Byron for not being consoled by the Adriatic and Countess Guiccioli—wrongly, for after he knew her he wrote no more *Manfreds*. But *Don Juan* was as little read in France as Goethe's more cheerful poetry. In spite of Musset, most French poets, ever since, have found Byronic unhappiness the best material for their verses.

To Musset, it was only after Napoleon that Byron and Goethe were the greatest geniuses of the century. Born in 1810, Musset was one of the generation whom he describes as '*conçus entre deux batailles*' in a lyrical description of the glories and disasters of the Empire. In Germany, feeling about Napoleon was more divided.

[1] Maurois, *Life of Byron*.
[2] *Sartor Resartus*, Book II, chap. vi.

There were those who, like Heine, saw him as the mighty missionary of liberalism, the destroyer of serfdom, the enemy of legitimacy, the man who made hereditary princelings tremble; there were others who saw him as Antichrist, the would-be destroyer of the noble German nation, the immoralist who had proved once for all that Teutonic virtue can only be preserved by unquenchable hatred of France. Bismarck effected a synthesis: Napoleon remained Antichrist, but an Antichrist to be imitated, not merely to be abhorred. Nietzsche, who accepted the compromise, remarked with ghoulish joy that the classical age of war is coming, and that we owe this boon, not to the French Revolution, but to Napoleon. And in this way nationalism, Satanism, and hero-worship, the legacy of Byron, became part of the complex soul of Germany.

Byron is not gentle, but violent like a thunderstorm. What he says of Rousseau is applicable to himself. Rousseau was, he says

> He who threw
> Enchantment over passion, and from woe
> Wrung overwhelming eloquence . . .
> yet he knew
> How to make madness beautiful, and cast
> O'er erring deeds and thoughts, a heavenly hue.

But there is a profound difference between the two men. Rousseau is pathetic, Byron is fierce; Rousseau's timidity is obvious, Byron's is concealed; Rousseau admires virtue provided it is simple, while Byron admires sin provided it is elemental. The difference, though it is only that between two stages in the revolt of unsocial instincts, is important, and shows the direction in which the movement is developing.

Byron's romanticism, it must be confessed, was only half sincere. At times, he would say that Pope's poetry was better than his own, but this judgment, also, was probably only what he thought in certain moods. The world insisted on simplifying him, and omitting the element of pose in his cosmic despair and professed contempt for mankind. Like many other prominent men, he was more important as a myth than as he really was. As a myth, his importance, especially on the Continent, was enormous.

Chapter XXIV

SCHOPENHAUER

SCHOPENHAUER (1788-1860) is in many ways peculiar among philosophers. He is a pessimist, whereas almost all the others are in some sense optimists. He is not fully academic, like Kant and Hegel, nor yet completely outside the academic tradition. He dislikes Christianity, preferring the religions of India, both Hinduism and Buddhism. He is a man of wide culture, quite as much interested in art as in ethics. He is unusually free from nationalism, and as much at home with English and French writers as with those of his own country. His appeal has always been less to professional philosophers than to artistic and literary people in search of philosophy that they could believe. He began the emphasis on Will which is characteristic of much nineteenth- and twentieth-century philosophy; but for him Will, though metaphysically fundamental, is ethically evil—an opposition only possible for a pessimist. He acknowledges three sources of his philosophy, Kant, Plato, and the Upanishads, but I do not think he owes as much to Plato as he thinks he does. His outlook has a certain temperamental affinity with that of the Hellenistic age; it is tired and valetudinarian, valuing peace more than victory, and quietism more than attempts at reform, which he regards as inevitably futile.

Both his parents belonged to prominent commercial families in Danzig, where he was born. His father was a Voltairian, who regarded England as the land of liberty and intelligence. In common with most of the leading citizens of Danzig, he hated the encroachments of Prussia on the independence of the free city, and was indignant when it was annexed to Prussia in 1793—so indignant that he removed to Hamburg, at considerable pecuniary loss. Schopenhauer lived there with his father from 1793 to 1797; then he spent two years in Paris, at the end of which his father was pleased to find that the boy had nearly forgotten German. In 1803 he was put in a boarding-school in England, where he hated the cant and hypocrisy. Two years later, to please his father, he became a clerk in a commercial house in Hamburg, but he loathed the prospect of a business career, and longed for a literary and academic life. This was made possible by his father's death, probably by suicide; his mother was willing that he should abandon commerce for school and university. It might be supposed that he would, in consequence, have preferred her to his father, but the exact opposite happened: he disliked his mother, and retained an affectionate memory of his father.

Schopenhauer's mother was a lady of literary aspirations, who settled in Weimar two weeks before the battle of Jena. There she kept a literary salon, wrote books, and enjoyed friendships with men of culture. She had little affection for her son, and a keen eye for his faults. She warned him against bombast and empty pathos; he was annoyed by her philanderings. When he came of age he inherited a modest competence; after this, he and his mother gradually found each other more and more intolerable. His low opinion of women is no doubt due, at least in part, to his quarrels with his mother.

Already at Hamburg he had come under the influence of the romantics, especially Tieck, Novalis, and Hoffmann, from whom he learnt to admire Greece and to think ill of the Hebraic elements in Christianity. Another romantic, Friedrich Schlegel, confirmed him in his admiration of Indian philosophy. In the year in which he came of age (1809), he went to the university of Göttingen, where he learnt to admire Kant. Two years later he went to Berlin, where he studied mainly science; he heard Fichte lecture, but despised him. He remained indifferent throughout the excitement of the war of liberation. In 1819 he became a *Privatdozent* at Berlin, and had the conceit to put his lectures at the same hour as Hegel's; having failed to lure away Hegel's hearers, he soon ceased to lecture. In the end he settled down to the life of an old bachelor in Frankfurt. He kept a poodle named Atma (the world-soul) walked two hours every day, smoked a long pipe, read the London *Times*, and employed correspondents to hunt up evidences of his fame. He was anti-democratic, and hated the revolution of 1848; he believed in spiritualism and magic; in his study he had a bust of Kant and a bronze of Buddha. In his manner of life he tried to imitate Kant except as regards early rising.

His principal work, *The World as Will and Idea*, was published at the end of 1818. He believed it to be of great importance, and went so far as to say that some paragraphs in it had been dictated by the Holy Ghost. To his great mortification it fell completely flat. In 1844 he persuaded the publisher to bring out a second edition; but it was not till some years later that he began to receive some of the recognition for which he longed.

Schopenhauer's system is an adaptation of Kant's, but one that emphasizes quite different aspects of the *Critique* from those emphasized by Fichte or Hegel. They got rid of the thing-in-itself, and thus made knowledge metaphysically fundamental. Schopenhauer retained the thing-in-itself, but identified it with will. He held that what appears to perception as my body is really my will. There was more to be said for this view as a development of Kant than most Kantians were willing to recognize. Kant had maintained that a study of the moral law can take us behind phenomena, and give us knowledge which sense-perception cannot give; he also maintained that the moral law is essentially concerned with the will. The difference between a good man and a bad man is, for Kant, a difference in the world of things-in-themselves, and is also a difference as to volitions. It follows that, for Kant, volitions must belong to the real world, not to the world of phenomena. The phenomenon corresponding to a volition is a bodily movement; that is why, according to Schopenhauer, the body is the appearance of which will is the reality.

But the will which is behind phenomena cannot consist of a number of different volitions. Both time and space, according to Kant—and in this Schopenhauer agrees with him—belong only to phenomena; the thing-in-itself is not in space or time. My will, therefore, in the sense in which it is real, cannot be dated, nor can it be composed of separate acts of will, because it is space and time that are the source of plurality—the 'principle of individuation', to use the scholastic phrase which Schopenhauer prefers. My will, therefore, is one and timeless. Nay, more, it is to be identified with the will of the whole universe; my separateness is an illusion, resulting from my subjective apparatus of spatio-temporal perception. What is real is one vast will, appearing in the whole course of nature, animate and inanimate alike.

So far, we might expect Schopenhauer to identify his cosmic will with God, and teach a pantheistic doctrine not unlike Spinoza's, in which virtue would consist in conformity to the divine will. But at this point his pessimism leads to a different development. The cosmic will is wicked; will, altogether, is wicked, or at any rate is the source of all our endless suffering. Suffering is essential to all life, and is increased by every increase of knowledge. Will has no fixed end, which if achieved would bring contentment. Although death must conquer in the end, we pursue our futile purposes, 'as we blow out a soap-bubble as long and as large as possible, although we know perfectly well that it will burst'. There is no such thing as happiness, for an unfulfilled wish causes pain, and attainment brings only satiety. Instinct urges men to procreation, which brings into existence a new occasion for suffering and death; that is why shame is associated with the sexual act. Suicide is useless; the doctrine of transmigration, even if not literally true, conveys truth in the form of a myth.

All this is very sad, but there is a way out, and it was discovered in India.

The best of myths is that of Nirvana (which Schopenhauer interprets as extinction). This, he agrees, is contrary to Christian doctrine, but 'the ancient wisdom of the human race will not be displaced by what happened in Galilee'. The cause of suffering is intensity of will; the less we exercise will, the less we shall suffer. And here knowledge turns out to be useful after all, provided it is knowledge of a certain sort. The distinction between one man and another is part of the phenomenal world, and disappears when the world is seen truly. To the good man, the veil of Maya (illusion) has become transparent; he sees that all things are one, and that the distinction between himself and another is only apparent. He reaches this insight by love, which is always sympathy, and has to do with the pain of others. When the veil of Maya is lifted, a man takes on the suffering of the whole world. In the good man, knowledge of the whole quiets all volition; his will turns away from life and denies his own nature. 'There arises within him a horror of the nature of which his own phenomenal existence is an expression, the kernel and inner nature of that world which is recognized as full of misery.'

Hence Schopenhauer is led to complete agreement, at least as regards practice, with ascetic mysticism. Eckhart and Angelus Silesius are better than the New Testament. There are some good things in orthodox Christianity, notably the doctrine of original sin as preached, against 'the vulgar Pelagianism', by St Augustine and Luther; but the Gospels are sadly deficient in metaphysics. Buddhism, he says, is the highest religion; and his ethical doctrines are orthodox throughout Asia, except where the 'detestable doctrine of Islam' prevails.

The good man will practise complete chastity, voluntary poverty, fasting, and self-torture. In all things he will aim at breaking down his individual will. But he does not do this, as do the Western mystics, to achieve harmony with God; no such positive good is sought. The good that is sought is wholly and entirely negative:

'We must banish the dark impression of that nothingness which we discern behind all virtue and holiness as their final goal, and which we fear as children fear the dark; we must not even evade it like the Indians, through myths and meaningless words, such as reabsorption in Brahma or the Nirvana of the Buddhists. Rather do we freely acknowledge that what remains after the entire abolition of will is for all those who are still full of will certainly nothing; but, conversely, to those in whom the will has turned and has denied itself, this our world, which is so real, with all its suns and milky ways—is nothing.'

There is a vague suggestion here that the saint sees something positive which other men do not see, but there is nowhere a hint as to what this is, and I think the suggestion is only rhetorical. The world and all its phenomena, Schopenhauer says, are only the objectification of will. With the surrender of the will,

'all those phenomena are also abolished; that constant strain and effort without end and without rest at all the grades of objectivity in which and through which the world consists; the multifarious forms succeeding each other in gradation; the whole manifestation of the will; and, finally, also the universal forms of this manifestation, time and space, and also its last fundamental form, subject and object; all are abolished. No will: no idea, no world. Before us there is certainly only nothingness'.

We cannot interpret this except as meaning that the saint's purpose is to come as near as possible to non-existence, which, for some reason never clearly explained, he cannot achieve by suicide. Why the saint is to be preferred to a man who is always drunk is not very easy to see; perhaps Schopenhauer thought the sober moments were bound to be sadly frequent.

Schopenhauer's gospel of resignation is not very consistent and not very sincere. The mystics to whom he appeals believed in contemplation; in the Beatific Vision the most profound kind of knowledge was to be achieved, and this kind of knowledge was the supreme good. Ever since Parmenides, the delusive knowledge of appearance was contrasted with another kind of knowledge, not with something of a wholly different kind. Christianity teaches that in *knowledge* of God standeth our eternal life. But Schopenhauer will have none of this. He agreed that what commonly passes for knowledge belongs to the realm of Maya, but when we pierce the veil, we behold not God, but Satan, the wicked omnipotent will, perpetually busied in weaving a web of suffering for the torture of its creatures. Terrified by the Diabolic Vision, the sage cries 'Avaunt!' and seeks refuge in non-existence. It is an insult to the mystics to claim them as believers in this mythology. And the suggestion that, without achieving complete non-existence, the sage may yet live a life having some value, is not possible to reconcile with Schopenhauer's pessimism. So long as the sage exists, he exists because he retains will, which is evil. He may diminish the quantity of evil by weakening his will, but he can never acquire any positive good.

Nor is the doctrine sincere, if we may judge by Schopenhauer's

726

life. He habitually dined well, at a good restaurant; he had many trivial love-affairs, which were sensual but not passionate; he was exceedingly quarrelsome and unusually avaricious. On one occasion he was annoyed by an elderly seamstress who was talking to a friend outside the door of his apartment. He threw her downstairs, causing her permanent injury. She obtained a court order compelling him to pay her a certain sum (15 thalers) every quarter as long as she lived. When at last she died, after twenty years, he noted in his account-book: 'Obit anus, abit onus.'[1] It is hard to find in his life evidences of any virtue except kindness to animals, which he carried to the point of objecting to vivisection in the interests of science. In all other respects he was completely selfish. It is difficult to believe that a man who was profoundly convinced of the virtue of asceticism and resignation would never have made any attempt to embody his convictions in his practice.

Historically, two things are important about Schopenhauer: his pessimism, and his doctrine that will is superior to knowledge. His pessimism made it possible for men to take to philosophy without having to persuade themselves that all evil can be explained away, and in this way, as an antidote, it was useful. From a scientific point of view, optimism and pessimism are alike objectionable: optimism assumes, or attempts to prove, that the universe exists to please us, and pessimism that it exists to displease us. Scientifically, there is no evidence that it is concerned with us either one way or the other. The belief in either pessimism or optimism is a matter of temperament, not of reason, but the optimistic temperament has been much commoner among Western philosophers. A representative of the opposite party is therefore likely to be useful in bringing forward considerations which would otherwise be overlooked.

More important than pessimism was the doctrine of the primacy of the will. It is obvious that this doctrine has no necessary logical connection with pessimism, and those who held it after Schopenhauer frequently found in it a basis for optimism. In one form or another, the doctrine that will is paramount has been held by many modern philosophers, notably Nietzsche, Bergson, James, and Dewey. It has, moreover, acquired a vogue outside the circles of professional philosophers. And in proportion as will has gone up in the scale, knowledge has gone down. This is, I think, the most notable change that has come over the temper of philosophy in our age. It was prepared by Rousseau and Kant, but was first proclaimed in its purity by Schopenhauer. For this reason, in spite of inconsistency and a certain shallowness, his philosophy has considerable importance as a stage in historical development.

[1] 'The old woman dies, the burden departs.'

Chapter XXV

NIETZSCHE

NIETZSCHE (1844-1900) regarded himself, rightly, as the successor of Schopenhauer, to whom, however, he is superior in many ways, particularly in the consistency and coherence of his doctrine. Schopenhauer's oriental ethic of renunciation seems out of harmony with his metaphysic of the omnipotence of will; in Nietzsche, the will has ethical as well as metaphysical primacy. Nietzsche, though a professor, was a literary rather than an academic philosopher. He invented no new technical theories in ontology or epistemology; his importance is primarily in ethics, and secondarily as an acute historical critic. I shall confine myself almost entirely to his ethics and his criticism of religion, since it was this aspect of his writing that made him influential.

His life was simple. His father was a Protestant pastor, and his upbringing was very pious. He was brilliant at the university as a classicist and student of philology, so much so that in 1869, before he had taken his degree, he was offered a professorship of philology at Basel, which he accepted. His health was never good, and after periods of sick leave he was obliged to retire finally in 1879. After this, he lived in Switzerland and Italy; in 1888 he became insane, and remained so until his death. He had a passionate admiration for Wagner, but quarrelled with him, nominally over *Parsifal* which he thought too Christian and too full of renunciation. After the quarrel he criticized Wagner savagely, and even went so far to accuse him of being a Jew. His general outlook, however, remained very similar to that of Wagner in the *Ring*; Nietzsche's superman is very like Siegfried, except that he knows Greek. This may seem odd, but that is not my fault.

Nietzsche was not consciously a romantic; indeed he often severely criticizes the romantics. Consciously his outlook was Hellenic, but with the Orphic component omitted. He admired the pre-Socratics, except Pythagoras. He has a close affinity to Heraclitus. Aristotle's magnanimous man is very like what Nietzsche calls the 'noble man', but in the main he regards the Greek philosophers from Socrates onwards as inferior to their predecessors. He cannot forgive Socrates for his humble origin; he calls him a 'roturier', and accuses him of corrupting the noble Athenian youth with a democratic moral bias. Plato, especially, is condemned on account of his taste for edification. Nietzsche, however, obviously does not quite like condemning him, and suggests, to excuse him, that perhaps he was insincere, and only preached virtue as a means of keeping the lower classes in order. He speaks of him on one occasion as 'a great Cagliostro'. He likes Democritus and Epicurus, but his affection for the latter seems somewhat illogical, unless it is interpreted as really an admiration for Lucretius.

As might be expected, he has a low opinion of Kant, whom he calls 'a moral fanatic à la Rousseau'.

In spite of Nietzsche's criticism of the romantics, his outlook owes much to them; it is that of aristocratic anarchism, like Byron's, and one is not surprised to find him admiring Byron. He attempts to combine two sets of values which are not easily harmonized: on the one hand he likes ruthlessness, war, and aristocratic pride; on the other hand, he loves philosophy and literature and the arts, especially music. Historically, these values coexisted in the Renaissance; Pope Julius II, fighting for Bologna and employing Michelangelo, might be taken as the sort of man whom Nietzsche would wish to see in control of governments. It is natural to compare Nietzsche with Machiavelli, in spite of important differences between the two men. As for the differences: Machiavelli was a man of affairs, whose opinions had been formed by close contact with public business, and were in harmony with his age; he was not pedantic or systematic, and his philosophy of politics scarcely forms a coherent whole; Nietzsche, on the contrary, was a professor an essentially bookish man, and a philosopher in conscious opposition to what appeared to be the dominant political and ethical trends of his time. The similarities, however, go deeper. Nietzsche's political philosophy is analogous to that of *The Prince* (not *The Discourses*), though it is worked out and applied over a wider field. Both Nietzsche and Machiavelli have an ethic which aims at power and is deliberately anti-Christian, though Nietzsche is more frank in this respect. What Caesar Borgia was to Machiavelli, Napoleon was to Nietzsche: a great man defeated by petty opponents.

Nietzsche's criticism of religions and philosophies is dominated entirely by ethical motives. He admires certain qualities which he believes (perhaps rightly) to be only possible for an aristocratic minority; the majority, in his opinion, should be only means to the excellence of the few, and should not be regarded as having any independent claim to happiness or well-being. He alludes habitually to ordinary human beings as the 'bungled and botched', and sees no objection to their suffering if it is necessary for the production of a great man. Thus the whole importance of the period from 1789 to 1815 is summed up in Napoleon: 'The Revolution

729

made Napoleon possible: that is its justification. We ought to desire the anarchical collapse of the whole of our civilization if such a reward were to be its result. Napoleon made nationalism possible: that is the latter's excuse.' Almost all of the higher hopes of this century, he says, are due to Napoleon.

He is fond of expressing himself paradoxically and with a view to shocking conventional readers. He does this by employing the words 'good' and 'evil' with their ordinary connotations, and then saying that he prefers 'evil' to 'good'. His book, *Beyond Good and Evil*, really aims at changing the reader's opinion as to what is good and what is evil, but professes, except at moments, to be praising what is 'evil' and decrying what is 'good'. He says, for instance, that it is a mistake to regard it as a duty to aim at the victory of good and the annihilation of evil; this view is English, and typical of 'that blockhead, John Stuart Mill,' a man for whom he has a specially virulent contempt. Of him he says:

'I abhor the man's vulgarity when he says "What is right for one man is right for another"; "Do not to others that which you would not that they should do unto you."[1] Such principles would fain establish the whole of human traffic *upon mutual services*, so that every action would appear to be a cash payment for something done to us. The hypothesis here is ignoble to the last degree: it is taken for granted that there is some sort of *equivalence in value between my actions and thine.*'[2]

True virtue, as opposed to the conventional sort, is not for all, but should remain the characteristic of an aristocratic minority. It is not profitable or prudent; it isolates its possessor from other men; it is hostile to order, and does harm to inferiors. It is necessary for higher men to make war upon the masses, and resist the democratic tendencies of the age, for in all directions mediocre people are joining hands to make themselves masters. 'Everything that pampers, that softens, and that brings the "people" or "woman" to the front, operates in favour of universal suffrage—that is to say, the dominion of "inferior" men.' The seducer was Rousseau, who made woman interesting; then came Harriet Beecher Stowe and the slaves; then the Socialists with their championship of workmen and the poor. All these are to be combated.

Nietzsche's ethic is not one of self-indulgence in any ordinary sense; he believes in Spartan discipline and the capacity to endure as well as inflict pain for important ends. He admires strength of will above all things. 'I test the *power of a will*,' he says, 'according to the amount of resistance it can offer and the amount of pain

[1] I seem to remember that someone anticipated Mill in this dictum.
[2] In all quotations from Nietzsche, the italics are in the original.

and torture it can endure and know how to turn to its own advantage; I do not point to the evil and pain of existence with the finger of reproach, but rather entertain the hope that life may one day become more evil and more full of suffering than it has ever been.' He regards compassion as a weakness to be combated. 'The object is to attain that enormous *energy of greatness* which can model the man of the future by means of discipline and also by means of the annihilation of millions of the bungled and botched, and which can yet avoid *going to ruin* at the sight of the suffering created thereby, the like of which has never been seen before.' He prophesied with a certain glee an era of great wars; one wonders whether he would have been happy if he had lived to see the fulfilment of his prophecy.

He is not, however, a worshipper of the State; far from it. He is a passionate individualist, a believer in the hero. The misery of a whole nation, he says, is of less importance than the suffering of a great individual: 'The misfortunes of all these small folk do not together constitute a sum-total, except in the feelings of *mighty* men.'

Nietzsche is not a nationalist, and shows no excessive admiration for Germany. He wants an international ruling race, who are to be the lords of the earth: 'a new vast aristocracy based upon the most severe self-discipline, in which the will of philosophical men of power and artist-tyrants will be stamped upon thousands of years.'

He is also not definitely anti-Semitic, though he thinks Germany contains as many Jews as it can assimilate, and ought not to permit any further influx of Jews. He dislikes the New Testament, but not the Old, of which he speaks in terms of the highest admiration. In justice to Nietzsche it must be emphasized that many modern developments which have a certain connection with his general ethical outlook are contrary to his clearly expressed opinions.

Two applications of his ethic deserve notice: first, his contempt for women; second, his bitter critique of Christianity.

He is never tired of inveighing against women. In his pseudo-prophetical book. *Thus Spake Zarathustra*, he says that women are not, as yet, capable of friendship; they are still cats, or birds, or at best cows. 'Man shall be trained for war and woman for the recreation of the warrior. All else is folly.' The recreation of the warrior is to be of a peculiar sort if one may trust his most emphatic aphorism on this subject: 'Thou goest to woman? Do not forget thy whip.'

He is not always quite so fierce, though always equally contemptuous. In the *Will to Power* he says: 'We take pleasure in woman as in a perhaps daintier, more delicate, and more ethereal kind of creature. What a treat it is to meet creatures who have only dancing and nonsense and finery in their minds! They have always been the delight of every tense and profound male soul.' However, even these graces are only to be found in women so long as they are kept in order by manly men; as soon as they achieve any independence they become intolerable. 'Woman has so much cause for shame; in woman there is so much pedantry, super-ficiality, schoolmasterliness, petty presumption, unbridledness, and indiscretion concealed . . . which has really been best restrained and dominated hitherto by the *fear* of man.' So he says in *Beyond Good and Evil*, where he adds that we should think of women as property, as Orientals do. The whole of his abuse of women is offered as self-evident truth; it is not backed up by evidence from history or from his own experience, which, so far as women were concerned, was almost confined to his sister.

Nietzsche's objection to Christianity is that it caused acceptance of what he calls 'slave morality'. It is curious to observe the contrast between his arguments and those of the French *philosophes* who preceded the Revolution. They argued that Christian dogmas are untrue; that Christianity teaches submission to what is deemed to be the will of God, whereas self-respecting human beings should not bow before any higher Power; and that the Christian Churches have become the allies of tyrants, and are helping the enemies of democracy to deny liberty and continue to grind the faces of the poor. Nietzsche is not interested in the metaphysical truth of either Christianity or any other religion; being convinced that no religion is really true, he judges all religions entirely by their social effects. He agrees with the *philosophes* in objecting to submission to the supposed will of God, but he would substitute for it the will of earthly 'artist-tyrants'. Submission is right, except for these super-men, but not submission to the Christian God. As for the Christian Churches' being allies of tyrants and enemies of democracy, that, he says, is the very reverse of the truth. The French Revolution and Socialism are, according to him, essentially identical in spirit with Christianity; to all alike he is opposed, and for the same reason: that he will not treat all men as equal in any respect whatever.

Buddhism and Christianity, he says, are both 'nihilistic' religions, in the sense that they deny any ultimate difference of value between one man and another, but Buddhism is much the less objectionable of the two. Christianity is degenerative, full of decaying and excremental elements; its driving force is the revolt of the bungled and botched. This revolt was begun by the Jews, and brought into Christianity by 'holy epileptics' like St Paul, who had no honesty.

'The New Testament is the gospel of a completely *ignoble* species of man.' Christianity is the most fatal and seductive lie that ever existed. No man of note has ever resembled the Christian ideal; consider for instance the heroes of Plutarch's *Lives*. Christianity is to be condemned for denying the value of 'pride, pathos of distance, great responsibility, exuberant spirits, splendid animalism, the instincts of war and of conquest, the deification of passion, revenge, anger, voluptuousness, adventure, knowledge'. All these things are good, and all are said by Christianity to be bad—so Nietzsche contends.

Christianity, he argues, aims at taming the heart in man, but this is a mistake. A wild beast has a certain splendour, which it loses when it is tamed. The criminals with whom Dostoevsky associated were better than he was, because they were more self-respecting. Nietzsche is nauseated by repentance and redemption, which he calls a *folie circulaire*. It is difficult for us to free ourselves from this way of thinking about human behaviour: 'we are heirs to the conscience-vivisection and self-crucifixion of two thousand years.' There is a very eloquent passage about Pascal, which deserves quotation, because it shows Nietzsche's objections to Christianity at their best:

'What is it that we combat in Christianity? That it aims at destroying the strong, at breaking their spirit, at exploiting their moments of weariness and debility, at converting their proud assurance into anxiety and conscience-trouble; that it knows how to poison the noblest instincts and to infect them with disease, until their strength, their will to power, turns inwards, against themselves—until the strong perish through their excessive self-contempt and self-immolation: that gruesome way of perishing, of which Pascal is the most famous example.'

In place of the Christian saint Nietzsche wishes to see what he calls the 'noble' man, by no means as a universal type, but as a governing aristocrat. The 'noble' man will be capable of cruelty, and, on occasion, of what is vulgarly regarded as crime; he will recognize duties only to equals. He will protect artists and poets and all who happen to be masters of some skill, but he will do so as himself a member of a higher order than those who only know how to do something. From the example of warriors he will learn to associate death with the interests for which he is fighting; to sacrifice numbers, and take his cause sufficiently seriously not to spare men; to practise inexorable discipline; and to allow himself violence and cunning in war. He will recognize the part played by cruelty in aristocratic excellence: 'almost everything that we call "higher culture" is based upon the spiritualizing and intensifying of *cruelty*'. The 'noble' man is essentially the incarnate will to power.

What are we to think of Nietzsche's doctrines? How far are they true? Are they in any degree useful? Is there in them anything objective, or are they the mere power-phantasies of an invalid?

It is undeniable that Nietzsche has had a great influence, not among technical philosophers, but among people of literary and artistic culture. It must also be conceded that his prophecies as to the future have, so far, proved more nearly right than those of liberals or Socialists. If he is a mere symptom of disease, the disease must be very widespread in the modern world.

Nevertheless there is a great deal in him that must be dismissed as merely megalomaniac. Speaking of Spinoza he says: 'How much of personal timidity and vulnerability does this masquerade of a sickly recluse betray!' Exactly the same may be said of him, with the less reluctance since he has not hesitated to say it of Spinoza. It is obvious that in his day-dreams he is a warrior, not a professor; all the men he admires were military. His opinion of women, like every man's, is an objectification of his own emotion towards them, which is obviously one of fear. 'Forget not thy whip'—but nine women out of ten would get the whip away from him, and he knew it, so he kept away from women, and soothed his wounded vanity with unkind remarks.

He condemns Christian love because he thinks it is an outcome of fear: I am afraid my neighbour may injure me, and so I assure him that I love him. If I were stronger and bolder, I should openly display the contempt for him which of course I feel. It does not occur to Nietzsche as possible that a man should genuinely feel universal love, obviously because he himself feels almost universal hatred and fear, which he would fain disguise as lordly indifference. His 'noble' man—who is himself in day-dreams—is a being wholly devoid of sympathy, ruthless, cunning, cruel, concerned only with his own power. King Lear, on the verge of madness, says:

> I will do such things—
> What they are yet I know not—but they shall be
> The terror of the earth.

This is Nietzsche's philosophy in a nutshell.

It never occurred to Nietzsche that the lust for power, with which he endows his superman, is itself an outcome of fear. Those who do not fear their neighbours see no necessity to tyrannize over them. Men who have conquered fear have not the frantic quality of Nietzsche's 'artist-tyrant' Neros, who try to enjoy music and massacre while their hearts are filled with dread of the inevitable palace revolution. I will not deny that, partly as a result of his teaching, the real world has become very like his nightmare, but that does not make it any the less horrible.

It must be admitted that there is a certain type of Christian ethic to which Nietzsche's strictures can be justly applied. Pascal and Dostoevsky—his own illustrations—have both something abject in their virtue. Pascal sacrificed his magnificent mathematical intellect to his God, thereby attributing to Him a barbarity which was a cosmic enlargement of Pascal's morbid mental tortures. Dostoevsky would have nothing to do with 'proper pride'; he would sin in order to repent and to enjoy the luxury of confession. I will not argue the question how far such aberrations can justly be charged against Christianity, but I will admit that I agree with Nietzsche in thinking Dostoevsky's prostration contemptible. A certain uprightness and pride and even self-assertion of a sort, I should agree, are elements in the best character; no virtue which has its roots in fear is much to be admired.

There are two sorts of saints: the saint by nature, and the saint from fear. The saint by nature has a spontaneous love of mankind; he does good because to do so gives him happiness. The saint from fear, on the other hand, like the man who only abstains from theft because of the police, would be wicked if he were not restrained by the thought of hell-fire or of his neighbours' vengeance. Nietzsche can only imagine the second sort of saint; he is so full of fear and hatred that spontaneous love of mankind seems to him impossible. He has never conceived of the man who, with all the fearlessness and stubborn pride of the superman, nevertheless does not inflict pain because he has no wish to do so. Does anyone suppose that Lincoln acted as he did from fear of hell? Yet to Nietzsche Lincoln is abject, Napoleon magnificent.

It remains to consider the main ethical problem raised by Nietzsche, namely: should our ethic be aristocratic, or should it, in some sense, treat all men alike? This is a question which, as I have just stated it, has no very clear meaning, and obviously, the first step is to try to make the issue more definite.

We must in the first place try to distinguish an aristocratic *ethic* from an aristocratic *political theory*. A believer in Bentham's principle of the greatest happiness of the greatest number has a democratic ethic, but he may think that the general happiness is best promoted by an aristocratic form of government. This is not Nietzsche's position. He holds that the happiness of common people is no part of the good *per se*. All that is good or bad in itself exists only in the superior few; what happens to the rest is of no account.

The next question is: How are the superior few defined? In practice, they have usually been a conquering race or a hereditary aristocracy—and aristocracies have usually been, at least in theory, descendants of conquering races. I think Nietzsche would accept this definition. 'No morality is possible without good birth,' he tells us. He says that the noble caste is always at first barbarian, but that every elevation of Man is due to aristocratic society.

It is not clear whether Nietzsche regards the superiority of the aristocrat as congenital or as due to education and environment. If the latter, it is difficult to defend the exclusion of others from advantages for which, *ex hypothesi*, they are equally qualified. I shall therefore assume that he regards conquering aristocracies and their descendants as biologically superior to their subjects, as men are superior to domestic animals, though in a lesser degree.

What shall we mean by 'biologically superior'? We shall mean, when interpreting Nietzsche, that individuals of the superior race, and their descendants, are more likely to be 'noble' in Nietzsche's sense: they will have more strength of will, more courage, more impulse towards power, less sympathy, less fear, and less gentleness.

We can now state Nietzsche's ethic. I think what follows is a fair analysis of it:

Victors in war, and their descendants, are usually biologically superior to the vanquished. It is therefore desirable that they should hold all the power, and should manage affairs exclusively in their own interests.

There is here still the word 'desirable' to be considered. What is 'desirable' in Nietzsche's philosophy? From the outsider's point of view, what Nietzsche calls 'desirable' is what Nietzsche desires. With this interpretation, Nietzsche's doctrine might be stated more simply and honestly in the one sentence: 'I wish I had lived in the Athens of Pericles or the Florence of the Medici.' But this is not a philosophy; it is a biographical fact about a certain individual. The word 'desirable' is not synonymous with 'desired by me'; it has some claim, however shadowy, to legislate universally. A theist may say that what is desirable is what God desires, but Nietzsche cannot say this. He could say that he knows what is good by an ethical intuition, but he will not say this, because it sounds too Kantian. What he can say, as an expansion of the word 'desirable', is this: 'If men will read my works, a certain percentage of them will come to share my desires as regards the organization of society; these men, inspired by the energy and determination which my philosophy will give them, can preserve and restore aristocracy, with themselves as

736

aristocrats or (like me) sycophants of aristocracy. In this way they will achieve a fuller life than they can have as servants of the people.'

There is another element in Nietzsche, which is closely akin to the objection urged by 'rugged individualists' against trade-unions. In a fight of all against all, the victor is likely to possess certain qualities which Nietzsche admires, such as courage, resourcefulness, and strength of will. But if the men who do not possess these aristocratic qualities (who are the vast majority) band themselves together, they may win in spite of their individual inferiority. In this fight of the collective *canaille* against the aristocrats, Christianity is the ideological front, as the French Revolution was the fighting front. We ought therefore to oppose every kind of union among the individually feeble, for fear lest their combined power should outweigh that of the individually strong; on the other hand, we ought to promote union among the tough and virile elements of the population. The first step towards the creation of such a union is the preaching of Nietzsche's philosophy. It will be seen that it is not easy to preserve the distinction between ethics and politics.

Suppose we wish—as I certainly do—to find arguments against Nietzsche's ethics and politics, what arguments can we find?

There are weighty practical arguments, showing that the attempt to secure his ends will in fact secure something quite different. Aristocracies of birth are nowadays discredited; the only practicable form of aristocracy is an organization like the Fascist or the Nazi party. Such an organization rouses opposition, and is likely to be defeated in war; but if it is not defeated it must, before long, become nothing but a police State, where the rulers live in terror of assassination, and the heroes are in concentration camps. In such a community faith and honour are sapped by delation, and the would-be aristocracy of supermen degenerates into a clique of trembling poltroons.

These, however, are arguments for our time; they would not have held good in past ages, when aristocracy was unquestioned. The Egyptian government was conducted on Nietzschean principles for several millennia. The governments of almost all large States were aristocratic until the American and the French Revolutions. We have therefore to ask ourselves whether there is any good reason for preferring democracy to a form of government which has had such a long and successful history—or rather, since we are concerned with philosophy, not politics, whether there are objective grounds for rejecting the ethic by which Nietzsche supports aristocracy.

The ethical, as opposed to the political, question is one as to

737

sympathy. Sympathy, in the sense of being made unhappy by the suffering of others, is to some extent natural to human beings; young children are troubled when they hear other children crying. But the development of this feeling is very different in different people. Some find pleasure in the infliction of torture; others, like Buddha, feel that they cannot be completely happy so long as any living thing is suffering. Most people divide mankind emotionally into friends and enemies, feeling sympathy for the former, but not for the latter. An ethic such as that of Christianity or Buddhism has its emotional basis in universal sympathy; Nietzsche's, in a complete absence of sympathy. (He frequently preaches against sympathy, and in this respect one feels that he has no difficulty in obeying his own precepts.) The question is: If Buddha and Nietzsche were confronted, could either produce any argument that ought to appeal to the impartial listener? I am not thinking of political arguments. We can imagine them appearing before the Almighty, as in the first chapter of the Book of Job, and offering advice as to the sort of world He should create. What could either say?

Buddha would open the argument by speaking of the lepers, outcast and miserable; the poor, toiling with aching limbs and barely kept alive by scanty nourishment; the wounded in battle, dying in slow agony; the orphans, ill-treated by cruel guardians; and even the most successful haunted by the thought of failure and death. From all this load of sorrow, he would say, a way of salvation must be found, and salvation can only come through love.

Nietzsche, whom only Omnipotence could restrain from interrupting, would burst out when his turn came: 'Good heavens, man, you must learn to be of tougher fibre. Why go about snivelling because trivial people suffer? Or, for that matter, because great men suffer? Trivial people suffer trivially, great men suffer greatly, and great sufferings are not to be regretted, because they are noble. Your ideal is a purely negative one, absence of suffering, which can be completely secured by non-existence. I, on the other hand, have positive ideals: I admire Alcibiades, and the Emperor Frederick II, and Napoleon. For the sake of such men, any misery is worth while. I appeal to You, Lord, as the greatest of creative artists, do not let Your artistic impulses be curbed by the degenerate fear-ridden maunderings of this wretched psychopath.'

Buddha, who in the courts of Heaven has learnt all history since his death, and has mastered science with delight in the knowledge and sorrow at the use to which men have put it, replies with calm urbanity: 'You are mistaken, Professor Nietzsche, in thinking my ideal a purely negative one. True, it includes a negative element, the absence of suffering; but it has in addition quite as much that is positive as is to be found in your doctrine. Though I have no special admiration for Alcibiades and Napoleon, I, too, have my heroes: my successor Jesus, because he told men to love their enemies; the men who discovered how to master the forces of nature and secure food with less labour; the medical men who have shown how to diminish disease; the poets and artists and musicians who have caught glimpses of the Divine beatitude. Love and knowledge and delight in beauty are not negations; they are enough to fill the lives of the greatest men that have ever lived.'

'All the same,' Nietzsche replies, 'your world would be insipid. You should study Heraclitus, whose works survive complete in the celestial library. Your love is compassion, which is elicited by pain; your truth, if you are honest, is unpleasant, and only to be known through suffering; and as to beauty, what is more beautiful than the tiger, who owes his splendour to his fierceness? No, if the Lord should decide for your world, I fear we should all die of boredom.'

'*You* might,' Buddha replies, 'because you love pain, and your love of life is a sham. But those who really love life would be happy as no one can be happy in the world as it is.'

For my part, I agree with Buddha as I have imagined him. But I do not know how to prove that he is right by any arguments such as can be used in a mathematical or a scientific question. I dislike Nietzsche because he likes the contemplation of pain, because he erects conceit into a duty, because the men whom he most admires are conquerors, whose glory is cleverness in causing men to die. But I think the ultimate argument against his philosophy, as against any unpleasant but internally self-consistent ethic, lies not in an appeal to facts, but in an appeal to the emotions. Nietzsche despises universal love; I feel it the motive power to all that I desire as regards the world. His followers have had their innings, but we may hope that it is coming rapidly to an end.

Chapter XXVI

THE UTILITARIANS[1]

THROUGHOUT the period from Kant to Nietzsche, professional philosophers in Great Britain remained almost completely unaffected by their German contemporaries, with the sole exception of Sir William Hamilton, who had little influence. Coleridge and Carlyle, it is true, were profoundly affected by Kant, Fichte, and the German Romantics, but they were not philosophers in the technical sense. Somebody seems to have once mentioned Kant to James Mill, who, after a cursory inspection, remarked: 'I see well enough what poor Kant would be at.' But this degree of recognition is exceptional; in general, there is complete silence about the Germans. Bentham and his school derived their philosophy, in all its main outlines, from Locke, Hartley, and Helvetius; their importance is not so much philosophical as political, as the leaders of British radicalism, and as the men who unintentionally prepared the way for the doctrines of socialism.

Jeremy Bentham, who was the recognized leader of the 'Philosophical Radicals', was not the sort of man one expects to find at the head of a movement of this sort. He was born in 1748, but did not become a Radical till 1808. He was painfully shy, and could not without great trepidation endure the company of strangers. He wrote voluminously, but never bothered to publish; what was published under his name had been benevolently purloined by his friends. His main interest was jurisprudence, in which he recognized Helvetius and Beccaria as his most important predecessors. It was through the theory of law that he became interested in ethics and politics.

He bases his whole philosophy on two principles, the 'association principle', and the 'greatest-happiness principle'. The association principle had been emphasized by Hartley in 1749; before him, though association of ideas was recognized as occurring, it was regarded, for instance by Locke, only as a source of trivial errors. Bentham, following Hartley, made it the basic principle of psychology. He recognizes association of ideas and language, and also association of ideas and ideas. By means of this principle he aims at a deterministic account of mental occurrences. In essence the

[1] For a fuller treatment of this subject, as also of Marx, see Part II of my *Freedom and Organization, 1814-1914.*

doctrine is the same as the more modern theory of the 'conditioned reflex', based on Pavlov's experiments. The only important difference is that Pavlov's conditioned reflex is physiological, whereas the association of ideas was purely mental. Pavlov's work is therefore capable of a materialistic explanation, such as is given to it by the behaviourists, whereas the association of ideas led rather towards a psychology more or less independent of physiology. There can be no doubt that, scientifically, the principle of the conditioned reflex is an advance on the older principle. Pavlov's principle is this: Given a reflex according to which a stimulus B produces a reaction C, and given that a certain animal has frequently experienced a stimulus A at the same time as B, it often happens that in time the stimulus A will produce the reaction C even when B is absent. To determine the circumstances under which this happens is a matter of experiment. Clearly, if we substitute ideas for A, B, and C, Pavlov's principle becomes that of the association of ideas.

Both principles, indubitably, are valid over a certain field; the only controversial question is as to the extent of this field. Bentham and his followers exaggerated the extent of the field in the case of Hartley's principle, as certain behaviourists have in the case of Pavlov's principle.

To Bentham, determinism in psychology was important, because he wished to establish a code of laws—and, more generally, a social system—which would automatically make men virtuous. His second principle, that of the greatest happiness, became necessary at this point in order to define 'virtue'.

Bentham maintained that what is good is pleasure or happiness —he used these words as synonyms—and what is bad is pain. Therefore one state of affairs is better than another if it involves a greater balance of pleasure over pain, or a smaller balance of pain over pleasure. Of all possible states of affairs, that one is best which involves the greatest balance of pleasure over pain.

There is nothing new in this doctrine, which came to be called 'utilitarianism'. It had been advocated by Hutcheson as early as 1725. Bentham attributes it to Priestley, who, however, had no special claim to it. It is virtually contained in Locke. Bentham's merit consisted, not in the doctrine, but in his vigorous application of it to various practical problems.

Bentham held not only that the good is happiness in general, but also that each individual always pursues what he believes to be his own happiness. The business of the legislator, therefore, is to produce harmony between public and private interests. It is to the interest of the public that I should abstain from theft, but it is not to my interest except where there is an effective criminal law. Thus the criminal law is a method of making the interests of the individual coincide with those of the community; that is its justification.

Men are to be punished by the criminal law in order to prevent crime, not because we hate the criminal. It is more important that the punishment should be certain than that it should be severe. In his day, in England, many quite minor offences were subject to the death penalty, with the result that juries often refused to convict because they thought the penalty excessive. Bentham advocated abolition of the death penalty for all but the worst offences, and before he died the criminal law had been mitigated in this respect.

Civil law, he says, should have four aims: subsistence, abundance, security, and equality. It will be observed that he does not mention liberty. In fact, he cared little for liberty. He admired the benevolent autocrats who preceded the French Revolution—Catherine the Great and the Emperor Francis. He had a great contempt for the doctrine of the rights of man. The rights of man, he said, are plain nonsense; the imprescriptible rights of man, nonsense on stilts. When the French revolutionaries made their 'Déclaration des droits de l'homme,' Bentham called it 'a metaphysical work—the *ne plus ultra* of metaphysics'. Its articles, he said, could be divided into three classes: (1) Those that are unintelligible, (2) those that are false, (3) those that are both.

Bentham's ideal, like that of Epicurus, was security, not liberty. 'Wars and storms are best to read of, but peace and calms are better to endure.'

His gradual evolution towards Radicalism had two sources: on the one hand, a belief in equality, deduced from the calculus of pleasures and pains; on the other hand, an inflexible determination to submit everything to the arbitrament of reason as he understood it. His love of equality early led him to advocate equal division of a man's property among his children, and to oppose testamentary freedom. In later years it led him to oppose monarchy and hereditary aristocracy, and to advocate complete democracy, including votes for women. His refusal to believe without rational grounds led him to reject religion, including belief in God; it made him keenly critical of absurdities and anomalies in the law, however venerable their historical origin. He would not excuse anything on the ground that it was traditional. From early youth he was opposed to imperialism, whether that of the British in America, or that of other nations; he considered colonies a folly.

It was through the influence of James Mill that Bentham was induced to take sides in practical politics. James Mill was twenty-five years younger than Bentham, and an ardent disciple of his doctrines, but he was also an active Radical. Bentham gave Mill a house (which had belonged to Milton), and assisted him financially while he wrote a history of India. When this history was finished, the East India Company gave James Mill a post, as they did afterwards to his son until their abolition as a sequel to the Mutiny. James Mill greatly admired Condorcet and Helvetius. Like all Radicals of that period, he believed in the omnipotence of education. He practised his theories on his son John Stuart Mill, with results partly good, partly bad. The most important bad result was that John Stuart could never quite shake off his influence, even when he perceived that his father's outlook had been narrow.

James Mill, like Bentham, considered pleasure the only good and pain the only evil. But like Epicurus he valued moderate pleasure most. He thought intellectual enjoyments the best, and temperance the chief virtue. 'The intense was with him a bye-word of scornful disapprobation,' says his son, who adds that he objected to the modern stress laid upon feeling, Like the whole utilitarian school, he was utterly opposed to every form of romanticism. He thought politics could be governed by reason, and expected men's opinions to be determined by the weight of evidence. If opposing sides in a controversy are presented with equal skill, there is a moral certainty—so he held—that the greater number will judge right. His outlook was limited by the poverty of his emotional nature, but within his limitations he had the merits of industry, disinterestedness, and rationality.

His son John Stuart Mill, who was born in 1806, carried on a somewhat softened form of the Benthamite doctrine to the time of his death in 1873.

Throughout the middle portion of the nineteenth century, the influence of the Benthamites on British legislation and policy was astonishingly great, considering their complete absence of emotional appeal.

Bentham advanced various arguments in favour of the view that the general happiness is the *summum bonum*. Some of these arguments were acute criticisms of other ethical theories. In his treatise on political sophisms he says, in language which seems to anticipate Marx, that sentimental and ascetic moralities serve the interests of the governing class, and are the product of an aristocratic régime. Those who teach the morality of sacrifice, he continues, are not victims of error: they want others to sacrifice to them. The moral order, he says, results from equilibrium of interests. Governing corporations pretend that there is already identity of interests between the governors and the governed, but reformers make it clear that this identity does not yet exist, and try to bring it about. He maintains that only the principle of utility can give a criterion in morals and legislation, and lay the foundation of a social science. His main positive argument in favour of his principle is that it is really implied by apparently different ethical systems. This, however, is only made plausible by a severe restriction of his survey.

There is an obvious lacuna in Bentham's system. If every man always pursues his own pleasure, how are we to secure that the legislator shall pursue the pleasure of mankind in general? Bentham's own instinctive benevolence (which his psychological theories prevented him from noticing) concealed the problem from him. If he had been employed to draw up a code of laws for some country, he would have framed his proposals in what he conceived to be the public interest, not so as to further his own interests or (consciously) the interests of his class. But if he had recognized this fact, he would have had to modify his psychological doctrines. He seems to have thought that, by means of democracy combined with adequate supervision, legislators could be so controlled that they could only further their private interests by being useful to the general public. There was in his day not much material for forming a judgment as to the working of democratic institutions, and his optimism was therefore perhaps excusable, but in our more disillusioned age it seems somewhat naïve.

John Stuart Mill, in his *Utilitarianism*, offers an argument which is so fallacious that it is hard to understand how he can have thought it valid. He says: Pleasure is the only thing desired; therefore pleasure is the only thing desirable. He argues that the only things visible are things seen, the only things audible are things heard, and similarly the only things desirable are things desired. He does not notice that a thing is 'visible' if it *can* be seen, but 'desirable' if it *ought* to be desired. Thus 'desirable' is a word presupposing an ethical theory; we cannot infer what is desirable from what is desired.

Again: if each man in fact and inevitably pursues his own pleasure, there is no point in saying he *ought* to do something else. Kant urged that 'you ought' implies 'you can'; conversely, if you cannot, it is futile to say you ought. *If* each man must always pursue his own pleasure, ethics is reduced to prudence: you may do well to further the interests of others in the hope that they in turn will further yours. Similarly in politics all co-operation is a matter of log-rolling. From the premisses of the utilitarians no other conclusion is validly deducible.

There are two distinct questions involved. First, does each man pursue his own happiness? Second, is the general happiness the right end of human action?

When it is said that each man desires his own happiness, the statement is capable of two meanings, of which one is a truism and the other is false. Whatever I may happen to desire, I shall get some pleasure from achieving my wish; in this sense, whatever I desire is *a* pleasure, and it may be said, though somewhat loosely, that pleasures are what I desire. This is the sense of the doctrine which is a truism.

But if what is meant is that, when I desire anything, I desire it because of the pleasure that it will give me, that is usually untrue. When I am hungry I desire food, and so long as my hunger persists food will give me pleasure. But the hunger, which is a desire, comes first; the pleasure is a consequence of the desire. I do not deny that there are occasions when there is a direct desire for pleasure. If you have decided to devote a free evening to the theatre, you will choose the theatre that you think will give you the most pleasure. But the actions thus determined by the direct desire for pleasure are exceptional and unimportant. Everybody's main activities are determined by desires which are anterior to the calculation of pleasures and pains.

Anything whatever may be an object of desire; a masochist may desire his own pain. The masochist, no doubt, derives pleasure from the pain that he has desired, but the pleasure is because of the desire, not *vice versa*. A man may desire something that does not affect him personally except because of his desire—for instance, the victory of one side in a war in which his country is neutral. He may desire an increase of general happiness, or a mitigation of general suffering. Or he may, like Carlyle, desire the exact opposite. As his desires vary, so do his pleasures.

Ethics is necessary because men's desires conflict. The primary cause of conflict is egoism: most people are more interested in their own welfare than in that of other people. But conflicts are equally possible where there is no element of egoism. One man may wish everybody to be Catholic, another may wish everybody to be Calvinist. Such non-egoistic desires are frequently involved in social conflicts. Ethics has a twofold purpose: first, to find a criterion by which to distinguish good and bad desires; second, by means of praise and blame, to promote good desires and discourage such as are bad.

The ethical part of the utilitarian doctrine, which is logically independent of the psychological part, says: Those desires and those actions are good which in fact promote the general happiness. This need not be the *intention* of an action, but only its *effect*. Is there any valid theoretical argument either for or against this doctrine? We found ourselves faced with a similar question in relation to Nietzsche. His ethic differs from that of the utilitarians, since it holds that only a minority of the human race have ethical importance—the happiness or unhappiness of the remainder should be ignored. I do not myself believe that this disagreement can be dealt with by theoretical arguments such as might be used in a scientific question. Obviously those who are excluded from the Nietzschean aristocracy will object, and thus the issue becomes political rather than theoretical. The utilitarian ethic is democratic and anti-romantic. Democrats are likely to accept it, but those who like a more Byronic view of the world can, in my opinion, be refuted only practically, not by considerations which appeal only to facts as opposed to desires.

The Philosophical Radicals were a transitional school. Their system gave birth to two others, of more importance than itself, namely Darwinism and Socialism. Darwinism was an application to the whole of animal and vegetable life of Malthus's theory of population, which was an integral part of the politics and economics of the Benthamites—a global free competition, in which victory went to the animals that most resembled successful capitalists. Darwin himself was influenced by Malthus, and was in general sympathy with the Philosophical Radicals. There was, however, a great difference between the competition admired by orthodox economists and the struggle for existence which Darwin proclaimed as the motive force of evolution. 'Free competition', in orthodox economics, is a very artificial conception, hedged in by legal restrictions. You may undersell a competitor, but you must not murder him. You must not use the armed forces of the State to help you to get the better of foreign manufacturers. Those who have not the good fortune to possess capital must not seek to improve their lot by revolution. 'Free competition', as understood by the Benthamites, was by no means really free.

Darwinian competition was not of this limited sort; there were no rules against hitting below the belt. The framework of law does not exist among animals, nor is war excluded as a competitive method. The use of the State to secure victory in competition was against the rules as conceived by the Benthamites, but could not be excluded from the Darwinian struggle. In fact, though Darwin himself was a Liberal, and though Nietzsche never mentions him except with contempt, Darwin's 'Survival of the Fittest' led, when thoroughly assimilated, to something much more like Nietzsche's philosophy than like Bentham's. These developments, however, belong to a later period, since Darwin's *Origin of Species* was published in 1859, and its political implications were not at first perceived.

Socialism, on the contrary, began in the heyday of Benthamism, and as a direct outcome of orthodox economics. Ricardo, who was intimately associated with Bentham, Malthus, and James Mill, taught that the exchange value of a commodity is entirely due to the labour expended in producing it. He published this theory in 1817, and eight years later Thomas Hodgskin, an ex-naval officer, published the first Socialist rejoinder, *Labour Defended Against the Claims of Capital*. He argued that if, as Ricardo taught, all value is conferred by labour, then all the reward ought to go to labour; the share at present obtained by the landowner and the capitalist must be mere extortion. Meanwhile Robert Owen, after much practical experience as a manufacturer, had become convinced of the doctrine which soon came to be called Socialism. (The first use of the word 'Socialist' occurs in 1827, when it is applied to the followers of Owen.) Machinery, he said, was displacing labour, and *laisser-faire* gave the working classes no adequate means of combating mechanical power. The method which he proposed for dealing with the evil was the earliest form of modern Socialism.

Although Owen was a friend of Bentham, who had invested a considerable sum of money in Owen's business, the Philosophical Radicals did not like his new doctrines; in fact, the advent of Socialism made them less Radical and less philosophical than they had been. Hodgskin secured a certain following in London, and James Mill was horrified. He wrote:

'Their notions of property look ugly; . . . they seem to think that it should not exist, and that the existence of it is an evil to them. Rascals, I have no doubt, are at work among them. . . . The fools, not to see that what they madly desire would be such a calamity to them as no hands but their own could bring upon them.'

This letter, written in 1831, may be taken as the beginning of the long war between Capitalism and Socialism. In a later letter, James Mill attributes the doctrine to the 'mad nonsense' of Hodgskin, and adds: 'These opinions if they were to spread, would be the subversion of civilized society; worse than the overwhelming deluge of Huns and Tartars.'

Socialism, in so far as it is only political or economic, does not come within the purview of a history of philosophy. But in the hands of Karl Marx Socialism acquired a philosophy. His philosophy will be considered in the next chapter.

Chapter XXVII

KARL MARX

KARL MARX is usually thought of as the man who claimed to have made Socialism scientific, and who did more than anyone else to create the powerful movement which, by attraction and repulsion, has dominated the recent history of Europe. It does not come within the scope of the present work to consider his economics, or his politics except in certain general aspects; it is only as a philosopher, and an influence on the philosophy of others, that I propose to deal with him. In this respect he is difficult to classify. In one aspect, he is an outcome, like Hodgskin, of the Philosophical Radicals, continuing their rationalism and their opposition to the romantics. In another aspect he is a revivifier of materialism, giving it a new interpretation and a new connection with human history. In yet another aspect he is the last of the great system-builders, the successor of Hegel, a believer, like him, in a rational formula summing up the evolution of mankind. Emphasis upon any one of these aspects at the expense of the others gives a false and distorted view of his philosophy.

The events of his life in part account for this complexity. He was born in 1818, at Treves, like St Ambrose. Treves had been profoundly influenced by the French during the revolutionary and Napoleonic era, and was much more cosmopolitan in outlook than most parts of Germany. His ancestors had been rabbis, but his parents became Christian when he was a child. He married a gentile aristocrat, to whom he remained devoted throughout his life. At the university he was influenced by the still prevalent Hegelianism, as also by Feuerbach's revolt against Hegel towards materialism. He tried journalism, but the *Rheinische Zeitung*, which he edited, was suppressed by the authorities for its radicalism. After this, in 1843, he went to France to study Socialism. There he met Engels, who was the manager of a factory in Manchester. Through him he came to know English labour conditions and English economics. He thus acquired, before the revolutions of 1848, an unusually international culture. So far as Western Europe was concerned, he showed no national bias. This cannot be said of Eastern Europe, for he always despised the Slavs.

He took part in both the French and the German revolutions of 1848, but the reaction compelled him to seek refuge in England

748

in 1849. He spent the rest of his life, with a few brief intervals, in London, troubled by poverty, illness, and the deaths of children, but nevertheless indefatigably writing and amassing knowledge. The stimulus to his work was always the hope of the social revolution, if not in his lifetime, then in some not very distant future.

Marx, like Bentham and James Mill, will have nothing to do with romanticism; it is always his intention to be scientific. His economics is an outcome of British classical economics, changing only the motive force. Classical economists, consciously or unconsciously, aimed at the welfare of the capitalist, as opposed both to the landowner and to the wage-earner; Marx, on the contrary, set to work to represent the interest of the wage-earner. He had in youth—as appears in the Communist Manifesto of 1848—the fire and passion appropriate to a new revolutionary movement, as liberalism had had in the time of Milton. But he was always anxious to appeal to evidence, and never relied upon any extra-scientific intuition.

He called himself a materialist, but not of the eighteenth-century sort. His sort, which, under Hegelian influence, he called 'dialectical', differed in an important way from traditional materialism, and was more akin to what is now called instrumentalism. The older materialism, he said, mistakenly regarded sensation as passive, and thus attributed activity primarily to the object. In Marx's view, all sensation or perception is an interaction between subject and object; the bare object, apart from the activity of the percipient, is a mere raw material, which is transformed in the process of becoming known. Knowledge in the old sense of passive contemplation is an unreal abstraction; the process that really takes place is one of *handling* things. 'The question whether objective truth belongs to human thinking is not a question of theory, but a practical question,' he says. 'The truth, i.e. the reality and power, of thought must be demonstrated in practice. The contest as to the reality or non-reality of a thought which is isolated from practice, is a purely scholastic question. . . . Philosophers have only *interpreted* the world in various ways, but the real task is to *alter* it.'[1]

I think we may interpret Marx as meaning that the process which philosophers have called the pursuit of knowledge is not, as has been thought, one in which the object is constant while all the adaptation is on the part of the knower. On the contrary, both subject and object, both the knower and the thing known, are in a continual process of mutual adaptation. He calls the process 'dialectical' because it is never fully completed.

[1] *Eleven Theses on Feuerbach*, 1845.

749

It is essential to this theory to deny the reality of 'sensation' as conceived by British empiricists. What happens, when it is most nearly what they mean by 'sensation', would be better called 'noticing', which implies activity. In fact—so Marx would contend —we only notice things as part of the process of acting with reference to them, and any theory which leaves out action is a misleading abstraction.

So far as I know, Marx was the first philosopher who criticized the notion of 'truth' from this activist point of view. In him this criticism was not much emphasized, and I shall therefore say no more about it here, leaving the examination of the theory to a later chapter.

Marx's philosophy of history is a blend of Hegel and British economics. Like Hegel, he thinks that the world develops according to a dialectical formula, but he totally disagrees with Hegel as to the motive force of this development. Hegel believed in a mystical entity called 'Spirit', which causes human history to develop according to the stages of the dialectic as set forth in Hegel's *Logic*. Why Spirit has to go through these stages is not clear. One is tempted to suppose that Spirit is trying to understand Hegel, and at each stage rashly objectifies what it has been reading. Marx's dialectic has none of this quality except a certain inevitableness. For Marx, matter, not spirit, is the driving force. But it is a matter in the peculiar sense that we have been considering, not the wholly dehumanized matter of the atomists. This means that, for Marx, the driving force is really man's relation to matter, of which the most important part is his mode of production. In this way Marx's materialism, in practice, becomes economics.

The politics, religion, philosophy, and art of any epoch in human history are, according to Marx, an outcome of its methods of production, and, to a lesser extent, of distribution. I think he would not maintain that this applies to all the niceties of culture, but only to its broad outlines. The doctrine is called the 'materialist conception of history'. This is a very important thesis; in particular, it concerns the historian of philosophy. I do not myself accept the thesis as it stands, but I think that it contains very important elements of truth, and I am aware that it has influenced my own views of philosophical development as set forth in the present work. Let us, to begin with, consider the history of philosophy in relation to Marx's doctrine.

Subjectively, every philosopher appears to himself to be engaged in the pursuit of something which may be called 'truth'. Philosophers may differ as to the definition of 'truth', but at any rate it is something objective, something which, in some sense, everybody ought to accept. No man would engage in the pursuit of philosophy if he thought that *all* philosophy is *merely* an expression of irrational bias. But every philosopher will agree that many other philosophers have been actuated by bias, and have had extra-rational reasons, of which they were usually unconscious, for many of their opinions. Marx, like the rest, believes in the truth of his own doctrines; he does not regard them as nothing but an expression of the feelings natural to a rebellious middle-class German Jew in the middle of the nineteenth century. What can be said about this conflict between the subjective and objective views of a philosophy?

We may say, in a broad way, that Greek philosophy down to Aristotle expresses the mentality appropriate to the City State; that Stoicism is appropriate to a cosmopolitan despotism; that scholastic philosophy is an intellectual expression of the Church as an organization; that philosophy since Descartes, or at any rate since Locke, tends to embody the prejudices of the commercial middle class; and that Marxism and Fascism are philosophies appropriate to the modern industrial State. This, I think, is both true and important. I think, however, that Marx is wrong in two respects. First, the social circumstances of which account must be taken are quite as much political as economic; they have to do with power, of which wealth is only one form. Second, social causation largely ceases to apply as soon as a problem becomes detailed and technical. The first of these objections I have set forth in my book *Power*, and I shall therefore say no more about it. The second more intimately concerns the history of philosophy, and I will give some examples of its scope.

Take, first, the problem of universals. This problem was first discussed by Plato, then by Aristotle, by the Schoolmen, by the British empiricists, and by the most modern logicians. It would be absurd to deny that bias has influenced the opinions of philosophers on this question. Plato was influenced by Parmenides and Orphism; he wanted an eternal world, and could not believe in the ultimate reality of the temporal flux. Aristotle was more empirical, and had no dislike of the every-day world. Thorough-going empiricists in modern times have a bias which is the opposite of Plato's: they find the thought of a super-sensible world unpleasant, and are willing to go to great lengths to avoid having to believe in it. But these opposing kinds of bias are perennial, and have only a somewhat remote connection with the social system. It is said that love of the eternal is characteristic of a leisure class, which lives on the labour of others. I doubt if this is true. Epictetus and Spinoza were not gentlemen of leisure. It might be urged, on the contrary, that the conception of heaven as a place where nothing is done is that of weary toilers who want nothing but rest. Such argumentation can be carried on indefinitely, and leads nowhere.

On the other hand, when we come to the detail of the controversy about universals, we find that each side can invent arguments which the other side will admit to be valid. Some of Aristotle's criticisms of Plato on this question have been almost universally accepted. In quite recent times, although no decision has been reached, a new technique has been developed, and many incidental problems have been solved. It is not irrational to hope that, before very long, a definite agreement may be reached by logicians on this question.

Take, as a second example, the ontological argument. This, as we have seen, was invented by Anselm, rejected by Thomas Aquinas, accepted by Descartes, refuted by Kant, and reinstated by Hegel. I think it may be said quite decisively that, as a result of analysis of the concept 'existence', modern logic has proved this argument invalid. This is not a matter of temperament or of the social system; it is a purely technical matter. The refutation of the argument affords, of course, no ground for supposing its conclusion, namely the existence of God, to be untrue; if it did, we cannot suppose that Thomas Aquinas would have rejected the argument.

Or take the question of materialism. This is a word which is capable of many meanings; we have seen that Marx radically altered its significance. The heated controversies as to its truth or falsehood have largely depended, for their continued vitality, upon avoidance of definition. When the term is defined, it will be found that, according to some possible definitions, materialism is demonstrably false; according to certain others, it may be true, though there is no positive reason to think so; while according to yet other definitions there are some reasons in its favour, though these reasons are not conclusive. All this, again, depends upon technical considerations, and has nothing to do with the social system.

The truth of the matter is really fairly simple. What is conventionally called 'philosophy' consists of two very different elements. On the one hand, there are questions which are scientific or logical; these are amenable to methods as to which there is general agreement. On the other hand, there are questions of passionate interest to large numbers of people, as to which there is no solid evidence either way. Among the latter are practical questions as to which it is impossible to remain aloof. When there is a war, I must support my own country or come into painful conflict both with friends and with the authorities. At many times there has been no middle course between supporting and opposing the official religion. For one reason or another, we all find it impossible to maintain an attitude of sceptical detachment on many issues as to which pure reason is silent. A 'philosophy', in a very usual sense of the word, is an organic whole of such extra-rational decisions. It is in regard to 'philosophy' in this sense that Marx's contention is largely true. But even in this sense a philosophy is determined by other social causes as well as by those that are economic. War, especially, has its share in historical causation; and victory in war does not always go to the side with the greatest economic resources.

Marx fitted his philosophy of history into a mould suggested by Hegelian dialectic, but in fact there was only one triad that concerned him: feudalism, represented by the landowner; capitalism, represented by the industrial employer; and Socialism, represented by the wage-earner. Hegel thought of nations as the vehicles of dialectic movement; Marx substituted classes. He disclaimed always all ethical or humanitarian reasons for preferring Socialism or taking the side of the wage-earner; he maintained, not that this side was ethically better, but that it was the side taken by the dialectic in its wholly deterministic movement. He might have said that he did not advocate Socialism, but only prophesied it. This, however, would not have been wholly true. He undoubtedly believed every dialectical movement to be, in some impersonal sense, a progress, and he certainly held that Socialism, once established, would minister to human happiness more than either feudalism or capitalism have done. These beliefs, though they must have controlled his life, remained largely in the background so far as his writings are concerned. Occasionally, however, he abandons calm prophecy for vigorous exhortation to rebellion, and the emotional basis of his ostensibly scientific prognostications is implicit in all he wrote.

Considered purely as a philosopher, Marx has grave shortcomings. He is too practical, too much wrapped up in the problems of his time. His purview is confined to this planet, and, within this planet, to Man. Since Copernicus, it has been evident that Man has not the cosmic importance which he formerly arrogated to himself. No man who has failed to assimilate this fact has a right to call his philosophy scientific.

There goes with this limitation to terrestrial affairs a readiness to believe in progress as a universal law. This readiness characterized the nineteenth century, and existed in Marx as much as in his contemporaries. It is only because of the belief in the inevitability of progress that Marx thought it possible to dispense with ethical considerations. If Socialism was coming, it must be an improvement. He would have readily admitted that it would not seem to be an improvement to landowners or capitalists, but that only showed that they were out of harmony with the dialectic movement of the time. Marx professed himself an atheist, but retained a cosmic optimism which only theism could justify.

Broadly speaking, all the elements in Marx's philosophy which are derived from Hegel are unscientific, in the sense that there is no reason whatever to suppose them true.

Perhaps the philosophic dress that Marx gave to his Socialism had really not much to do with the basis of his opinions. It is easy to restate the most important part of what he had to say without any reference to the dialectic. He was impressed by the appalling cruelty of the industrial system as it existed in England a hundred years ago, which he came to know thoroughly through Engels and the reports of Royal Commissions. He saw that the system was likely to develop from free competition towards monopoly, and that its injustice must produce a movement of revolt in the proletariat. He held that, in a thoroughly industrialized community, the only alternative to private capitalism is State ownership of land and capital. None of these propositions are matters for philosophy, and I shall therefore not consider their truth or falsehood. The point is that, if true, they suffice to establish what is practically important in his system. The Hegelian trappings might therefore be dropped with advantage.

This history of Marx's reputation has been peculiar. In his own country his doctrines inspired the programme of the Social Democratic Party, which grew steadily until, in the general election of 1912, it secured one third of all the votes cast. Immediately after the first world war, the Social Democratic Party was for a time in power, and Ebert, the first president of the Weimar Republic, was a member of it; but by this time the Party had ceased to adhere to Marxist orthodoxy. Meanwhile, in Russia, fanatical believers in Marx had acquired the government. In the West, no large working-class movement has been quite Marxist; the British Labour Party, at times, has seemed to move in that direction, but has nevertheless adhered to an empirical type of Socialism. Large numbers of intellectuals, however, have been profoundly influenced by him, both in England and in America. In Germany all advocacy of his doctrines has been forcibly suppressed, but may be expected to revive when the Nazis are overthrown.[1]

Modern Europe and America have thus been divided, politically and ideologically, into three camps. There are Liberals, who still, as far as may be, follow Locke or Bentham, but with varying degrees of adaptation to the needs of industrial organization. There are Marxists, who control the Government in Russia, and are likely

[1] I am writing in 1943.

754

to become increasingly influential in various other countries. These two sections of opinion are philosophically not very widely separated, both are rationalistic, and both, in intention, are scientific and empirical. But from the point of view of practical politics the division is sharp. It appears already in the letter of James Mill quoted in the preceding chapter, saying 'their notions of property look ugly'.

It must, however, be admitted that there are certain respects in which the rationalism of Marx is subject to limitations. Although he holds that his interpretation of the trend of development is true, and will be borne out by events, he believes that the argument will only appeal (apart from rare exceptions) to those whose class interest is in agreement with it. He hopes little from persuasion, everything from the class war. He is thus committed in practice to power politics, and to the doctrine of a master class, though not of a master race. It is true that, as a result of the social revolution, the division of classes is expected ultimately to disappear, giving place to complete political and economic harmony. But this is a distant ideal, like the Second Coming; in the meantime, there is war and dictatorship, and insistence upon ideological orthodoxy.

The third section of modern opinion, represented politically by Nazis and Fascists, differs philosophically from the other two far more profoundly than they differ from each other. It is anti-rational and anti-scientific. Its philosophical progenitors are Rousseau, Fichte, and Nietzsche. It emphasizes will, especially will to power; this it believes to be mainly concentrated in certain races and individuals, who therefore have a right to rule.

Until Rousseau, the philosophical world had a certain unity. This has disappeared for the time being, but perhaps not for long. It can be recovered by a rationalistic reconquest of men's minds, but not in any other way, since claims to mastery can only breed strife.

Chapter XXVIII

BERGSON

Henri Bergson was the leading French philosopher of the present century. He influenced William James and Whitehead, and had a considerable effect upon French thought. Sorel, who was a vehement advocate of syndicalism and the author of a book called *Reflections on Violence*, used Bergsonian irrationalism to justify a revolutionary labour movement having no definite goal. In the end, however, Sorel abandoned syndicalism and became a royalist. The main effect of Bergson's philosophy was conservative, and it harmonized easily with the movement which culminated in Vichy. But Bergson's irrationalism made a wide appeal quite unconnected with politics, for instance to Bernard Shaw, whose *Back to Methuselah* is pure Bergsonism. Forgetting politics, it is in its purely philosophical aspect that we must consider it. I have dealt with it somewhat fully as it exemplifies admirably the revolt against reason which, beginning with Rousseau, has gradually dominated larger and larger areas in the life and thought of the world.

The classification of philosophies is effected, as a rule, either by their methods or by their results: 'empirical' and 'a priori' is a classification by methods, 'realist' and 'idealist' is a classification by results. An attempt to classify Bergson's philosophy in either of these ways is hardly likely to be successful, since it cuts across all the recognized divisions.

But there is another way of classifying philosophies, less precise, but perhaps more helpful to the non-philosophical; in this way, the principle of division is according to the predominant desire which has led the philosopher to philosophize. Thus we shall have philosophies of feeling, inspired by the love of happiness; theoretical philosophies, inspired by the love of knowledge; and practical philosophies, inspired by the love of action.

Among philosophies of feeling we shall place all those which are primarily optimistic or pessimistic, all those that offer schemes of salvation or try to prove that salvation is impossible; to this class belong most religious philosophies. Among theoretical philosophies we shall place most of the great systems; for though the desire for knowledge is rare, it has been the source of most of what is best in philosophy. Practical philosophies, on the other hand, will be those which regard action as the supreme good, considering happiness an effect and knowledge a mere instrument of successful activity. Philosophies of this type would have been common among Western Europeans if philosophers had been average men; as it is, they have been rare until recent times; in fact their chief representatives are the pragmatists and Bergson. In the rise of this type of philosophy we may see, as Bergson himself does, the revolt of the modern man of action against the authority of Greece, and more particularly of Plato; or we may connect it, as Dr Schiller apparently would, with imperialism and the motor-car. The modern world calls for such a philosophy, and the success which it has achieved is therefore not surprising.

Bergson's philosophy, unlike most of the systems of the past, is dualistic: the world, for him, is divided into two disparate portions, on the one hand life, on the other matter, or rather that inert something which the intellect views as matter. The whole universe is the clash and conflict of two opposite motions: life, which climbs upward, and matter, which falls downward. Life is one great force, one vast vital impulse, given once for all from the beginning of the world, meeting the resistance of matter, struggling to break a way through matter, learning gradually to use matter by means of organization; divided by the obstacles it encounters into diverging currents, like the wind at a street-corner; partly subdued by matter through the very adaptations which matter forces upon it; yet retaining always its capacity for free activity, struggling always to find new outlets, seeking always for greater liberty of movement amid the opposing walls of matter.

Evolution is not primarily explicable by adaptation to environment; adaptation explains only the turns and twists of evolution, like the windings of a road approaching a town through hilly country. But this simile is not quite adequate; there is no town, no definite goal, at the end of the road along which evolution travels. Mechanism and teleology suffer from the same defect: both suppose that there is no essential novelty in the world. Mechanism regards the future as implicit in the past, and teleology, since it believes that the end to be achieved can be known in advance, denies that any essential novelty is contained in the result.

As against both these views, though with more sympathy for teleology than for mechanism, Bergson maintains that evolution is truly *creative*, like the work of an artist. An impulse to action, an undefined want, exists beforehand, but until the want is satisfied it is impossible to know the nature of what will satisfy it. For example, we may suppose some vague desire in sightless animals to be able to be aware of objects before they were in contact with them. This led to efforts which finally resulted in the creation of eyes. Sight satisfied the desire, but could not have been imagined beforehand. For this reason, evolution is unpredictable, and determinism cannot refute the advocates of free will.

This broad outline is filled in by an account of the actual development of life on the earth. The first division of the current was into plants and animals; plants aimed at storing up energy in a reservoir, animals aimed at using energy for sudden and rapid movements. But among animals, at a later stage, a new bifurcation appeared: *instinct* and *intellect* became more or less separated. They are never wholly without each other, but in the main intellect is the misfortune of man, while instinct is seen at its best in ants, bees, and Bergson. The division between intellect and instinct is fundamental in his philosophy, much of which is a kind of Sandford and Merton, with instinct as the good boy and intellect as the bad boy.

Instinct at its best is called *intuition*. 'By *intuition*,' he says, 'I mean instinct that has become disinterested, self-conscious, capable of reflecting upon its object and of enlarging it indefinitely.' The account of the doings of intellect is not always easy to follow, but if we are to understand Bergson we must do our best.

Intelligence or intellect, 'as it leaves the hands of nature, has for its chief object the inorganic solid'; it can only form a clear idea of the discontinuous and immobile; its concepts are outside each other like objects in space, and have the same stability. The intellect separates in space and fixes in time; it is not made to think evolution, but to represent *becoming* as a series of states. 'The intellect is characterized by a natural inability to understand life'; geometry and logic, which are its typical products, are strictly applicable to solid bodies, but elsewhere reasoning must be checked by common sense, which, as Bergson truly says, is a very different thing. Solid bodies, it would seem, are something which mind has created on purpose to apply intellect to them, much as it has created chessboards in order to play chess on them. The genesis of intellect and the genesis of material bodies, we are told, are correlative; both have been developed by reciprocal adaptation. 'An identical process must have cut out matter and the intellect, at the same time, from a stuff that contained both.'

This conception of the simultaneous growth of matter and intellect is ingenious, and deserves to be understood. Broadly, I think, what is meant is this: Intellect is the power of seeing things as separate one from another, and matter is that which is separated into distinct things. In reality there are no separate solid things, only an endless stream of becoming, in which nothing becomes and there is nothing that this nothing becomes. But becoming may be a movement up or a movement down: when it is a movement up it is called life, when it is a movement down it is what, as misapprehended by the intellect, is called matter. I suppose the universe is shaped like a cone, with the Absolute at the vertex, for the movement up brings things together, while the movement down separates them, or at least seems to do so. In order that the upward motion of mind may be able to thread its way through the downward motion of the falling bodies which hail upon it, it must be able to cut out paths between them; thus as intelligence was formed, outlines and paths appeared, and the primitive flux was cut up into separate bodies. The intellect may be compared to a carver, but it has the peculiarity of imagining that the chicken always was the separate pieces into which the carving-knife divides it.

As intellect is connected with space, so instinct or intuition is connected with time. It is one of the noteworthy features of Bergson's philosophy that, unlike most writers, he regards time and space as profoundly dissimilar. Space, the characteristic of matter, arises from a dissection of the flux which is really illusory, useful, up to a certain point, in practice, but utterly misleading in theory. Time, on the contrary, is the essential characteristic of life or mind. 'Wherever anything lives,' he says, 'there is, open somewhere, a register in which time is being inscribed.' But the time here spoken of is not mathematical time, the homogeneous assemblage of mutually external instants. Mathematical time, according to Bergson, is really a form of space; the time which is of the essence of life is what he calls *duration*. This conception of duration is fundamental in his philosophy; it appears already in his earliest book *Time and Free Will*, and it is necessary to understand it if we are to have any comprehension of his system. It is, however, a very difficult conception. I do not fully understand it myself, and therefore I cannot hope to explain it with all the lucidity which it doubtless deserves.

'Pure duration,' we are told, 'is the form which our conscious states assume when our ego lets itself *live*, when it refrains from separating its present state from its former states'. It forms the past and the present into one organic whole, where there is mutual penetration, succession without distinction. 'Within our ego, there is succession without mutual externality; outside the ego, in pure space, there is mutual externality without succession.'

'Questions relating to subject and object, to their distinction and their union, should be put in terms of time rather than of space.' In the duration in which we *see ourselves acting*, there are dissociated elements; but in the duration in which we *act*, our states melt into each other. Pure duration is what is most removed from externality and least penetrated with externality, a duration in which the past is big with a present absolutely new. But then our

759

will is strained to the utmost; we have to gather up the past which is slipping away, and thrust it whole and undivided into the present. At such moments we truly possess ourselves, but such moments are rare. Duration is the very stuff of reality, which is perpetual becoming, never something made.

It is above all in *memory* that duration exhibits itself, for in memory the past survives in the present. Thus the theory of memory becomes of great importance in Bergson's philosophy. *Matter and Memory* is concerned to show the relation of mind and matter, of which both are affirmed to be real, by an analysis of memory, which is 'just the intersection of mind and matter'.

There are, he says, two radically different things, both of which are commonly called *memory*; the distinction between these two is much emphasized by Bergson. 'The past survives,' he says, 'under two distinct forms: first, in motor mechanisms; secondly, in independent recollections.' For example, a man is said to remember a poem if he can repeat it by heart, that is to say, if he has acquired a certain habit or mechanism enabling him to repeat a former action. But he might, at least theoretically, be able to repeat the poem without any recollection of the previous occasions on which he has read it; thus there is no consciousness of past events involved in this sort of memory. The second sort, which alone really deserves to be called memory, is exhibited in recollections of separate occasions when he has read the poem, each unique and with a date. Here, he thinks, there can be no question of *habit*, since each event only occurred once, and had to make its impression immediately. It is suggested that in some way everything that has happened to us is remembered, but as a rule only what is useful comes into consciousness. Apparent failures of memory, it is argued, are not really failures of the mental part of memory, but of the motor mechanism for bringing memory into action. This view is supported by a discussion of brain physiology and the facts of amnesia, from which it is held to result that true memory is not a function of the brain. The past must be *acted* by matter, *imagined* by mind. Memory is not an emanation of matter; indeed the contrary would be nearer the truth if we mean matter as grasped in concrete perception, which always occupies a certain duration.

'Memory must be, in principle, a power absolutely independent of matter. If, then, spirit is a reality, it is here, in the phenomena of memory, that we may come into touch with it experimentally.'

At the opposite end from pure memory Bergson places pure perception, in regard to which he adopts an ultra-realist position. 'In pure perception,' he says, 'we are actually placed outside ourselves, we touch the reality of the object in an immediate intuition.'

So completely does he identify perception with its object that he almost refuses to call it mental at all. 'Pure perception,' he says, 'which is the lowest degree of mind—mind without memory—is really part of matter, as we understand matter.' Pure perception is constituted by dawning action, its actuality lies in its activity. It is in this way that the brain becomes relevant to perception, for the brain is not an instrument of action. The function of the brain is to limit our mental life to what is practically useful. But for the brain, one gathers, everything would be perceived, but in fact we only perceive what interests us. 'The body, always turned towards action, has for its essential function to limit, with a view to action, the life of the spirit.' It is, in fact, an instrument of choice.

In the above outline, I have in the main endeavoured merely to state Bergson's views, without giving the reasons adduced by him in favour of their truth. This is easier than it would be with most philosophers, since as a rule he does not give reasons for his opinions, but relies on their inherent attractiveness, and on the charm of an excellent style. Like advertisers, he relies upon picturesque and varied statement, and on apparent explanation of many obscure facts. Analogies and similes, especially, form a very large part of the whole process by which he recommends his views to the reader. The number of similes for life to be found in his works exceeds the number in any poet known to me. Life, he says, is like a shell bursting into fragments which are again shells. It is like a sheaf. Initially, it was 'a tendency to accumulate in a reservoir, as do especially the green parts of vegetables'. But the reservoir is to be filled with boiling water from which steam is issuing; 'jets must be gushing out unceasingly, of which each, falling back, is a world'. Again 'life appears in its entirety as an immense wave which, starting from a centre, spreads outwards, and which on almost the whole of its circumference is stopped and converted into oscillation: at one single point the obstacle has been forced, the impulsion has passed freely'. Then there is the great climax in which life is compared to a cavalry charge. 'All organized beings, from the humblest to the highest, from the first origins of life to the time in which we are, and in all places as in all times, do but evidence a single impulsion, the inverse of the movement of matter, and in itself indivisible. All the living hold together, and all yield to the same tremendous push. The animal takes its stand on the plant, man bestrides animality, and the whole of humanity, in space and in time, is one immense army galloping beside and before and behind each of us in an overwhelming charge able to beat down every resistance and to clear many obstacles, perhaps even death.'

But a cool critic, who feels himself a mere spectator, perhaps an unsympathetic spectator, of the charge in which man is mounted upon animality, may be inclined to think that calm and careful thought is hardly compatible with this form of exercise. When he is told that thought is a mere means of action, the mere impulse to avoid obstacles in the field, he may feel that such a view is becoming in a cavalry officer, but not in a philosopher, whose business, after all, is with thought: he may feel that in the passion and noise of violent motion there is no room for the fainter music of reason, no leisure for the disinterested contemplation in which greatness is sought, not by turbulence, but by the greatness of the universe which is mirrored. In that case, he may be tempted to ask whether there are any reasons for accepting such a restless view of the world. And if he asks this question, he will find, if I am not mistaken, that there is no reason whatever for accepting this view, either in the universe or in the writings of M. Bergson.

One of the bad effects of an anti-intellectual philosophy, such as that of Bergson, is that it thrives upon the errors and confusions of the intellect. Hence it is led to prefer bad thinking to good, to declare every momentary difficulty insoluble, and to regard every foolish mistake as revealing the bankruptcy of intellect and the triumph of intuition. There are in Bergson's works many allusions to mathematics and science, and to a careless reader these allusions may seem to strengthen his philosophy greatly. As regards science, especially biology and physiology, I am not competent to criticize his interpretations. But as regards mathematics, he has deliberately preferred traditional errors in interpretation to the more modern views which have prevailed among mathematicians for the last eighty years. In this matter, he has followed the example of most philosophers. In the eighteenth and early nineteenth centuries, the infinitesimal calculus, though well developed as a method, was supported, as regards its foundations, by many fallacies and much confused thinking. Hegel and his followers seized upon these fallacies and confusions, to support them in their attempt to prove all mathematics self-contradictory. Thence the Hegelian account of these matters passed into the current thought of philosophers, where it has remained long after the mathematicians have removed all the difficulties upon which the philosophers rely. And so long as the main object of philosophers is to show that nothing can be learned by patience and detailed thinking, but that we ought rather to worship the prejudices of the ignorant under the title of 'reason' if we are Hegelians, or of 'intuition' if we are Bergsonians, so long philosophers will take care to remain ignorant of what mathematicians have done to remove the errors by which Hegel profited.

Apart from the question of number, which we have already

considered, the chief point at which Bergson touches mathematics is his rejection of what he calls the 'cinematographic' representation of the world. Mathematics conceives change, even continuous change, as constituted by a series of states; Bergson, on the contrary, contends that no series of states can represent what is continuous, and that in change a thing is never in any state at all. The view that change is constituted by a series of changing states he calls cinematographic; this view, he says, is natural to the intellect, but is radically vicious. True change can only be explained by true duration; it involves an interpenetration of past and present, not a mathematical succession of static states. This is what is called a 'dynamic' instead of a 'static' view of the world. The question is important, and in spite of its difficulty we cannot pass it by.

Bergson's theory of duration is bound up with his theory of memory. According to this theory, things remembered survive in memory, and thus interpenetrate present things: past and present are not mutually external, but are mingled in the unity of consciousness. Action, he says, is what constitutes being; but mathematical time is a mere passive receptacle, which does nothing and therefore is nothing. The past, he says, is that which acts no longer, and the present is that which is acting. But in this statement, as indeed throughout his account of duration, Bergson is unconsciously assuming the ordinary mathematical time; without this, his statements are unmeaning. What is meant by saying 'the past is essentially *that which acts no longer*' (his italics), except that the past is that of which the action is past? the words 'no longer' are words expressive of the past; to a person who did not have the ordinary notion of the past as something outside the present, these words would have no meaning. Thus his definition is circular. What he says is, in effect, 'the past is that of which the action is in the past'. As a definition, this cannot be regarded as a happy effort. And the same applies to the present. The present, we are told, is '*that which is acting*' (his italics). But the word 'is' introduces just that idea of the present which was to be defined. The present is that which *is* acting as opposed to that which *was* acting or *will be* acting. That is to say, the present is that whose action is in the present, not in the past or in the future. Again the definition is circular. An earlier passage on the same page will illustrate the fallacy further. 'That which constitutes our pure perception,' he says, 'is our dawning action. . . . The *actuality* of our perception thus lies in its *activity*, in the movements which prolong it, and not in its greater intensity: the past is only idea, the present is ideo-motor.' This passage makes it quite clear that, when Bergson speaks of the past, he does not mean the past, but our present memory of the past. The past when it existed was just as active as the present is now; if Bergson's account were correct, the present moment ought to be the only one in the whole history of the world containing any activity. In earlier times there were other perceptions, just as active, just as actual in their day, as our present perceptions; the past, in its day, was by no means only idea, but was in its intrinsic character just what the present is now. This real past, however, Bergson simply forgets; what he speaks of is the present idea of the past. The real past does not mingle with the present, since it is not part of it; but that is a very different thing.

The whole of Bergson's theory of duration and time rests throughout on the elementary confusion between the present occurrence of a recollection and the past occurrence which is recollected. But for the fact that time is so familiar to us, the vicious circle involved in his attempt to deduce the past as what is no longer active would be obvious at once. As it is, what Bergson gives is an account of the difference between perception and recollection—both *present* facts—and what he believes himself to have given is an account of the difference between the present and the past. As soon as this confusion is realized, his theory of time is seen to be simply a theory which omits time altogether.

Of course a large part of Bergson's philosophy, probably the part to which most of its popularity is due, does not depend upon argument, and cannot be upset by argument. His imaginative picture of the world, regarded as a poetic effort, is in the main not capable of either proof or disproof. Shakespeare says life's but a walking shadow, Shelley says it is like a dome of many-coloured glass, Bergson says it is a shell which bursts into parts that are again shells. If you like Bergson's image better, it is just as legitimate.

The good which Bergson hopes to see realized in the world is action for the sake of action. All pure contemplation he calls 'dreaming', and condemns by a whole series of uncomplimentary epithets: static, Platonic, mathematical, logical, intellectual. Those who desire some prevision of the end which action is to achieve are told that an end foreseen would be nothing new, because desire, like memory, is identified with its object. Thus we are condemned, in action, to be the blind slaves of instinct: the life-force pushes us on from behind, restlessly and unceasingly. There is no room in this philosophy for the moment of contemplative insight when, rising above the animal life, we become conscious of the greater ends that redeem man from the life of the brutes. Those to whom activity without purpose seems a sufficient good will find in Bergson's books a pleasing picture of the universe. But those to whom action, if it is to be of any value, must be inspired by some vision, by some imaginative foreshadowing of a world less painful, less unjust, less full of strife than the world of our everyday life, those, in a word, whose action is built on contemplation, will find in this philosophy nothing of what they seek, and will not regret that there is no reason to think it true.

Chapter XXIX

WILLIAM JAMES

WILLIAM JAMES (1842-1910) was primarily a psychologist, but was important in philosophy on two accounts: he invented the doctrine which he called 'radical empiricism', and he was one of the three protagonists of the theory called 'pragmatism' or 'instrumentalism'. In later life he was, as he deserved to be, the recognized leader of American philosophy. He was led by the study of medicine to the consideration of psychology; his great book on the subject, published in 1890, had the highest possible excellence. I shall not, however, deal with it, since it was a contribution to science rather than to philosophy.

There were two sides to William James's philosophical interests, one scientific, the other religious. On the scientific side, the study of medicine had given his thoughts a tendency towards materialism, which, however, was held in check by his religious emotions. His religious feelings were very Protestant, very democratic, and very full of the warmth of human kindness. He refused altogether to follow his brother Henry into fastidious snobbishness. 'The prince of darkness,' he said, 'may be a gentleman, as we are told he is, but whatever the God on earth and heaven is, he can surely be no gentleman.' This is a very characteristic pronouncement.

His warm-heartedness and his delightful humour caused him to be almost universally beloved. The only man I know of who did not feel any affection for him was Santayana, whose doctor's thesis William James had described as 'the perfection of rottenness'. There was between these two men a temperamental opposition which nothing could have overcome. Santayana also liked religion, but in a very different way. He liked it aesthetically and historically, not as a help towards a moral life; as was natural, he greatly preferred Catholicism to Protestantism. He did not intellectually accept any of the Christian dogmas, but he was content that others should believe them, and himself appreciated what he regarded as the Christian myth. To James, such an attitude could not but appear immoral. He retained from his Puritan ancestry a deep-seated belief that what is of most importance is good conduct, and his democratic feeling made him unable to acquiesce in the notion of one truth for philosophers and another for the vulgar. The temperamental opposition between Protestant and Catholic persists among the unorthodox;

Santayana was a Catholic free thinker, William James a Protestant, however heretical.

James's doctrine of radical empiricism was first published in 1904, in an essay called 'Does "Consciousness" Exist?' The main purpose of this essay was to deny that the subject-object relation is fundamental. It had, until then, been taken for granted by philosophers that there is a kind of occurrence called 'knowing', in which one entity, the knower or subject, is aware of another, the thing known, or the object. The knower was regarded as a mind or soul; the object known might be a material object, an eternal essence, another mind, or, in self-consciousness, identical with the knower. Almost everything in accepted philosophy was bound up with the dualism of subject and object. The distinction of mind and matter, the contemplative ideal, and the traditional notion of 'truth', all need to be radically reconsidered if the distinction of subject and object is not accepted as fundamental.

For my part, I am convinced that James was partly right on this matter, and would, on this ground alone, deserve a high place among philosophers. I had thought otherwise until he, and those who agreed with him, persuaded me of the truth of his doctrine. But let us proceed to his arguments.

Consciousness, he says, 'is the name of a nonentity, and has no right to a place among first principles. Those who still cling to it are clinging to a mere echo, the faint rumour left behind by the disappearing "soul" upon the air of philosophy'. There is, he continues, 'no aboriginal stuff or quality of being, contrasted with that of which material objects are made, out of which our thoughts of them are made'. He explains that he is not denying that our thoughts perform a function which is that of knowing, and that this function may be called 'being conscious'. What he is denying might be put crudely as the view that consciousness is a 'thing'. He holds that there is 'only one primal stuff or material', out of which everything in the world is composed. This stuff he calls 'pure experience'. Knowing, he says, is a particular sort of relation between two portions of pure experience. The subject-object relation is derivative: 'experience, I believe, has no such inner duplicity'. A given undivided portion of experience can be in one context a knower, and in another something known.

He defines 'pure experience' as 'the immediate flux of life which furnishes the material to our later reflection'.

It will be seen that this doctrine abolishes the distinction between mind and matter, if regarded as a distinction between two different kinds of what James calls 'stuff'. Accordingly those who agree with James in this matter advocate what they call 'neutral monism', according to which the material of which the world is constructed is neither mind nor matter, but something anterior to both. James himself did not develop this implication of his theory; on the contrary, his use of the phrase 'pure experience' points to a perhaps unconscious Berkeleian idealism. The word 'experience' is one often used by philosophers, but seldom defined. Let us consider for a moment what it can mean.

Common sense holds that many things which occur are not 'experienced', for instance, events on the invisible side of the moon. Berkeley and Hegel, for different reasons, both denied this, and maintained that what is not experienced is nothing. Their arguments are now held by most philosophers to be invalid—rightly, in my opinion. If we are to adhere to the view that the 'stuff' of the world is 'experience', we shall find it necessary to invent elaborate and unplausible explanations of what we mean by such things as the invisible side of the moon. And unless we are able to infer things not experienced from things experienced, we shall have difficulty in finding grounds for belief in the existence of anything except ourselves. James, it is true, denies this, but his reasons are not very convincing.

What do we mean by 'experience'? The best way to find an answer is to ask: What is the difference between an event which is not experienced and one which is? Rain seen or felt to be falling is experienced, but rain falling in the desert where there is no living thing is not experienced. Thus we arrive at our first point: there is no experience except where there is life. But experience is not coextensive with life. Many things happen to me which I do not notice; these I can hardly be said to experience. Clearly I experience whatever I remember, but some things which I do not explicitly remember may have set up habits which still persist. The burnt child fears the fire, even if he has no recollection of the occasion on which he was burnt. I think we may say that an event is 'experienced' when it sets up a habit. (Memory is one kind of habit.) Broadly speaking, habits are only set up in living organisms. A burnt poker does not fear the fire, however often it is made red-hot. On common-sense grounds, therefore, we shall say that 'experience' is not coextensive with the 'stuff' of the world. I do not myself see any valid reason for departing from common sense on this point.

Except in this matter of 'experience', I find myself in agreement with James's radical empiricism.

It is otherwise with his pragmatism and 'will to believe'. The latter, especially, seems to me to be designed to afford a specious but sophistical defence of certain religious dogmas—a defence, moreover, which no whole-hearted believer could accept.

The Will to Believe was published in 1896; *Pragmatism, a New Name for Some Old Ways of Thinking* was published in 1907. The doctrine of the latter is an amplification of that of the former.

The Will to Believe argues that we are often compelled, in practice, to take decisions where no adequate theoretical grounds for a decision exist, for even to do nothing is still a decision. Religious matters, James says, come under this head; we have, he maintains, a right to adopt a believing attitude although 'our merely logical intellect may not have been coerced'. This is essentially the attitude of Rousseau's Savoyard vicar, but James's development is novel.

The moral duty of veracity, we are told, consists of two coequal precepts: 'believe truth', and 'shun error'. The sceptic wrongly attends only to the second, and thus fails to believe various truths which a less cautious man will believe. If believing truth and avoiding error are of equal importance, I may do well, when presented with an alternative, to believe one of the possibilities at will, for then I have an even chance of believing truth, whereas I have none if I suspend judgment.

The ethic that would result if this doctrine were taken seriously is a very odd one. Suppose I meet a stranger in the train, and I ask myself: 'Is his name Ebenezer Wilkes Smith?' If I admit that I do not know, I am certainly not believing truly about his name: whereas, if I decide to believe that that is his name, there is a chance that I may be believing truly. The sceptic, says James, is afraid of being duped, and through his fear may lose important truth; 'what proof is there', he adds, 'that dupery through hope is so much worse than dupery through fear?' It would seem to follow that, if I have been hoping for years to meet a man called Ebenezer Wilkes Smith, positive as opposed to negative veracity should prompt me to believe that this is the name of every stranger I meet, until I acquire conclusive evidence to the contrary.

'But,' you will say, 'the instance is absurd, for, though you do not know the stranger's name, you do know that a very small percentage of mankind are called Ebenezer Wilkes Smith. You are therefore not in that state of complete ignorance that is pre-supposed in your freedom of choice.' Now strange to say, James throughout his essay, never mentions probability, and yet there is almost always some discoverable consideration of probability in regard to any question. Let it be conceded (though no orthodox believer would concede it) that there is no evidence either for or against any of the religions of the world. Suppose you are a Chinese, brought into contact with Confucianism, Buddhism, and Christianity. You are precluded by the laws of logic from supposing that each of the three is true. Let us suppose that Buddhism and Christianity each has an even chance, then, given that both cannot be true, one of them must be, and therefore Confucianism must be false. If all three are to have equal chances, each must be more likely to be false than true. In this sort of way James's principle collapses as soon as we are allowed to bring in considerations of probability.

It is curious that, in spite of being an eminent psychologist, James allowed himself at this point a singular crudity. He spoke as if the only alternatives were complete belief or complete disbelief, ignoring all shades of doubt. Suppose, for instance, I am looking for a book in my shelves. I think, 'It *may be* in this shelf,' and I proceed to look; but I do not think, 'It *is* in this shelf' until I see it. We habitually act upon hypotheses, but not precisely as we act upon what we consider certainties; for when we act upon an hypothesis we keep our eyes open for fresh evidence.

The precept of veracity, it seems to me, is not such as James thinks. It is, I should say: 'Give to any hypothesis which is worth your while to consider just that degree of credence which the evidence warrants.' And if the hypothesis is sufficiently important there is the additional duty of seeking further evidence. This is plain common sense, and in harmony with the procedure in the law courts, but it is quite different from the procedure recommended by James.

It would be unfair to James to consider his will to believe in isolation; it was a transitional doctrine, leading by a natural development to pragmatism. Pragmatism, as it appears in James, is primarily a new definition of 'truth'. There were two other protagonists of pragmatism, F. C. S. Schiller and Dr John Dewey. I shall consider Dr Dewey in the next chapter; Schiller was of less importance than the other two. Between James and Dr Dewey there is a difference of emphasis. Dr Dewey's outlook is scientific, and his arguments are largely derived from an examination of scientific method, but James is concerned primarily with religion and morals. Roughly speaking, he is prepared to advocate any doctrine which tends to make people virtuous and happy; if it does so, it is 'true' in the sense in which he uses that word.

The principle of pragmatism, according to James, was first enunciated by C. S. Peirce, who maintained that, in order to attain clearness in our thoughts of an object, we need only consider what conceivable effects of a practical kind the object may involve. James, in elucidation, says that the function of philosophy is to find out what difference it makes to you or me if this or that world-formula is true. In this way theories become instruments, not answers to enigmas.

Ideas, we are told by James, become true in so far as they help us to get into satisfactory relations with other parts of our experience: 'An idea is "true" so long as to believe it is profitable to our lives.' Truth is one species of good, not a separate category. Truth happens to an idea; it is *made* true by events. It is correct to say, with the intellectualists, that a true idea must agree with reality, but 'agreeing' does not mean 'copying'. 'To "agree" in the widest sense with a reality can only mean to be guided either straight up to it or into its surroundings, or to be put into such working touch with it as to handle either it or something connected with it better than it we disagreed.' He adds that 'the true is only the expedient in the way of our thinking . . . in the long run and on the whole of course'. In other words, 'our obligation to seek truth is part of our general obligation to do what pays'.

In a chapter on pragmatism and religion he reaps the harvest. 'We cannot reject any hypothesis if consequences useful to life flow from it.' 'If the hypothesis of God works satisfactorily in the widest sense of the word, it is true.' 'We may well believe, on the proofs that religious experience affords, that higher powers exist and are at work to save the world on ideal lines similar to our own.'

I find great intellectual difficulties in this doctrine. It assumes that a belief is 'true' when its effects are good. If this definition is to be useful— and if not it is condemned by the pragmatist's test—we must know (*a*) what is good. (*b*) what are the effects of this or that belief, and we must know these things before we can know that anything is 'true', since it is only after we have decided that the effects of a belief are good that we have a right to call it 'true'. The result is an incredible complication. Suppose you want to know whether Columbus crossed the Atlantic in 1492. You must not, as other people do, look it up in a book. You must first inquire what are the effects of this belief, and how they differ from the effects of believing that he sailed in 1491 or 1493. This is difficult enough, but it is still more difficult to weigh the effects from an ethical point of view. You may say that obviously 1492 has the best effects, since it gives you higher marks in examinations. But your competitors, who would surpass you if you said 1491 or 1493, may consider your success instead of theirs ethically regrettable. Apart from examinations, I cannot think of any practical effects of the belief except in the case of a historian.

But this is not the end of the trouble. You must hold that your estimate of the consequences of a belief, both ethical and factual, is true, for if it is false your argument for the truth of your belief is mistaken. But to say that your belief as to consequences is true is, according to James, to say that *it* has good consequences, and this in turn is only true if it has good consequences, and so on *ad infinitum*. Obviously this won't do.

There is another difficulty. Suppose I say there was such a person as Columbus, everyone will agree that what I say is true. But why is it true? Because of a certain man of flesh and blood who lived 450 years ago— in short, because of the causes of my belief, not because of its effects. With James's definition, it might happen that 'A exists' is true although in fact A does not exist. I have always found that the hypothesis of Santa Claus 'works satisfactorily in the widest sense of the word'; therefore 'Santa Claus exists' is true, although Santa Claus does not exist. James says (I repeat): 'If the hypothesis of God works satisfactorily in the widest sense of the word, it is true.' This simply omits as unimportant the question whether God really is in His heaven; if He is a useful hypothesis, that is enough. God the Architect of the Cosmos is forgotten; all that is remembered is belief in God, and its effects upon the creatures inhabiting our petty planet. No wonder the Pope condemned the pragmatic defence of religion.

We come here to a fundamental difference between James's religious outlook and that of religious people in the past. James is interested in religion as a human phenomenon, but shows little interest in the objects which religion contemplates. He wants people to be happy, and if belief in God makes them happy let them believe in Him. This, so far, is only benevolence, not philosophy; it becomes philosophy when it is said that if the belief makes them happy it is 'true'. To the man who desires an object of worship this is unsatisfactory. He is not concerned to say, 'If I believed in God I should be happy'; he is concerned to say, 'I believe in God and therefore I am happy.' And when he believes in God, he believes in Him as he believes in the existence of Roosevelt or Churchill or Hitler; God, for him, is an actual Being, not merely a human idea which has good effects. It is this genuine belief that has the good effects, not James's emasculate substitute. It is obvious that if I say 'Hitler exists' I do not mean 'the effects of believing that Hitler exists are good'. And to the genuine believer the same is true of God.

James's doctrine is an attempt to build a superstructure of belief upon a foundation of scepticism, and like all such attempts it is dependent on fallacies. In his case the fallacies spring from an attempt to ignore all extra-human facts. Berkeleian idealism combined with scepticism causes him to substitute belief in God for God, and to pretend that this will do just as well. But this is only

a form of the subjectivistic madness which is characteristic of most
modern philosophy.

Chapter XXX

JOHN DEWEY

JOHN DEWEY, who was born in 1859, is generally admitted to be the leading living philosopher of America. In this estimate I entirely concur. He has had a profound influence, not only among philosophers, but on students of education, aesthetics, and political theory. He is a man of the highest character, liberal in outlook, generous and kind in personal relations, indefatigable in work. With many of his opinions I am in almost complete agreement. Owing to my respect and admiration for him, as well as to personal experience of his kindness, I should wish to agree completely, but to my regret I am compelled to dissent from his most distinctive philosophical doctrine, namely the substitution of 'inquiry' for 'truth' as the fundamental concept of logic and theory of knowledge.

Like William James, Dewey is a New Englander, and carries on the tradition of New England liberalism, which has been abandoned by some of the descendants of the great New Englanders of a hundred years ago. He has never been what might be called a 'mere' philosopher. Education, especially, has been in the forefront of his interests, and his influence on American education has been profound. I, in my lesser way, have tried to have an influence on education very similar to his. Perhaps he, like me, has not always been satisfied with the practice of those who professed to follow his teaching, but any new doctrine, in practice, is bound to be subject to some extravagance and excess. This, however, does not matter so much as might be thought, because the faults of what is new are so much more easily seen than those of what is traditional.

When Dewey became professor of philosophy at Chicago in 1894, pedagogy was included among his subjects. He founded a progressive school, and wrote much about education. What he wrote at this time was summed up in his book *The School and Society* (1899), which is considered the most influential of all his writings. He has continued to write on education throughout his life, almost as much as on philosophy.

Other social and political questions have also had a large share of his thought. Like myself, he was much influenced by visits to Russia and China, negatively in the first case, positively in the second. He was reluctantly a supporter of the first World War. He

774

had an important part in the inquiry as to Trotsky's alleged guilt, and, while he was convinced that the charges were unfounded, he did not think that the Soviet régime would have been satisfactory if Trotsky instead of Stalin had been Lenin's successor. He became persuaded that violent revolution leading to dictatorship is not the way to achieve a good society. Although very liberal in all economic questions, he has never been a Marxist. I heard him say once that, having emancipated himself with some difficulty from the traditional orthodox theology, he was not going to shackle himself with another. In all this his point of view is almost identical with my own.

From the strictly philosophical point of view, the chief importance of Dewey's work lies in his criticism of the traditional notion of 'truth', which is embodied in the theory that he calls 'instrumentalism'. Truth, as conceived by most professional philosophers, is static and final, perfect and eternal; in religious terminology, it may be identified with God's thoughts, and with those thoughts which, as rational beings, we share with God. The perfect model of truth is the multiplication table, which is precise and certain and free from all temporal dross. Since Pythagoras, and still more since Plato, mathematics has been linked with theology, and has profoundly influenced the theory of knowledge of most professional philosophers. Dewey's interests are biological rather than mathematical, and he conceives thought as an evolutionary process. The traditional view would, of course, admit that men gradually come to know more, but each piece of knowledge, when achieved, is regarded as something final. Hegel, it is true, does not regard human knowledge in this way. He conceives human knowledge as an organic whole, gradually growing in every part, and not perfect in any part until the whole is perfect. But although the Hegelian philosophy influenced Dewey in his youth, it still has its Absolute and its eternal world which is more real than the temporal process. These can have no place in Dewey's thought, for which all reality is temporal, and process, though evolutionary, is not, as for Hegel, the unfolding of an eternal Idea.

So far, I am in agreement with Dewey. Nor is this the end of my agreement. Before embarking upon discussion of the points as to which I differ, I will say a few words as to my own view of 'truth'.

The first question is: What sort of thing is 'true' or 'false'? The simplest answer would be: a sentence. 'Columbus crossed the ocean in 1492' is true; 'Columbus crossed the ocean in 1776' is false. This answer is correct, but incomplete. Sentences are true or false as the case may be, because they are 'significant', and their significance depends upon the language used. If you were translating an account of Columbus into Arabic, you would have to alter '1492' into the corresponding year of the Mohammedan era. Sentences in different languages may have the same significance, and it is the significance, not the words, that determines whether the sentence is 'true' or 'false'. When you assert a sentence, you express a 'belief', which may be equally well expressed in a different language. The 'belief' whatever it may be, is what is 'true' or 'false' or 'more or less true'. Thus we are driven to the investigation of 'belief'.

Now a belief, provided it is sufficiently simple, may exist without being expressed in words. It would be difficult, without using words, to believe that the ratio of the circumference of a circle to the diameter is approximately 3.14159, or that Caesar, when he decided to cross the Rubicon, sealed the fate of the Roman republican constitution. But in simple cases unverbalized beliefs are common. Suppose, for instance, in descending a staircase, you make a mistake as to when you have got to the bottom: you take a step suitable for level ground, and come down with a bump. The result is a violent shock or surprise. You would naturally say, 'I thought I was at the bottom', but in fact you were not thinking about the stairs, or you would not have made the mistake. Your muscles were adjusted in a way suitable to the bottom, when in fact you were not yet there. It was your body rather than your mind that made the mistake—at least that would be a natural way to express what happened. But in fact the distinction between mind and body is a dubious one. It will be better to speak of an 'organism', leaving the division of its activities between the mind and the body undetermined. One can say, then: your organism was adjusted in a manner which would have been suitable if you had been at the bottom, but in fact was not suitable. This failure of adjustment constituted error, and one may say that you were entertaining a false belief.

The *test* or error in the above illustration is *surprise*. I think this is true generally of beliefs that can be tested. A *false* belief is one which, in suitable circumstances, will cause the person entertaining it to experience surprise, while a *true* belief will not have this effect. But although surprise is a good criterion when it is applicable, it does not give the *meaning* of the words 'true' and 'false', and is not always applicable. Suppose you are walking in a thunderstorm, and you say to yourself, 'I am not at all likely to be struck by lightning'. The next moment you are struck, but you experience no surprise, because you are dead. If one day the sun explodes, as Sir James Jeans seems to expect, we shall all perish instantly, and therefore not be surprised, but unless we expect the catastrophe we shall all have been mistaken. Such illustrations suggest objectivity in truth and falsehood: what is true (or false) is a state of the organism, but it is true (or false), in general, in virtue of occurrences outside the organism. Sometimes experimental tests are possible to determine truth and falsehood, but sometimes they are not; when they are not, the alternative nevertheless remains, and is significant.

I will not further develop my view of truth and falsehood, but will proceed to the examination of Dewey's doctrine.

Dewey does not aim at judgments that shall be absolutely 'true', or condemn their contradictories as absolutely 'false'. In his opinion there is a process called 'inquiry', which is one form of mutual adjustment between an organism and its environment. If I wished, from my point of view, to go as far as possible towards agreeing with Dewey, I should begin by an analysis of 'meaning' or 'significance'. Suppose for example you are at the Zoo, and you hear a voice through a megaphone saying, 'A lion has just escaped.' You will, in that case, act as you would if you saw the lion—that is to say, you will get away as quickly as possible. The sentence 'a lion has escaped' *means* a certain occurrence, in the sense that it promotes the same behaviour as the occurrence would if you saw it. Broadly : a sentence S 'means' an event E if it promotes behaviour which E would have promoted. If there has in fact been no such occurrence, the sentence is false. Just the same applies to a belief which is not expressed in words. One may say : a belief is a state of an organism promoting behaviour such as a certain occurrence would promote if sensibly present; the occurrence which would promote this behaviour is the 'significance' of the belief. This statement is unduly simplified, but it may serve to indicate the theory I am advocating. So far, I do not think that Dewey and I would disagree very much. But with his further developments I find myself in very definite disagreement.

Dewey makes *inquiry* the essence of logic, not truth or knowledge. He defines inquiry as follows : 'Inquiry is the controlled or directed transformation of an indeterminate situation into one that is so determinate in its constituent distinctions and relations as to convert the elements of the original situation into a unified whole.' He adds that 'inquiry is concerned with objective transformations of objective subject-matter'. This definition is plainly inadequate. Take for instance the dealings of a drill-sergeant with a crowd of recruits, or of a bricklayer with a heap of bricks; these exactly fulfil Dewey's definition of 'inquiry'. Since he clearly would not include them, there must be an element in his notion of 'inquiry' which he has forgotten to mention in his definition. What this element is, I shall attempt to determine in a moment. But let us first consider what emerges from the definition as it stands.

It is clear that 'inquiry', as conceived by Dewey, is part of the general process of attempting to make the world more organic. 'Unified wholes' are to be the outcome of inquiries. Dewey's love of what is organic is due partly to biology, partly to the lingering influence of Hegel. Unless on the basis of an unconscious Hegelian metaphysic, I do not see why inquiry should be expected to result in 'unified wholes'. If I am given a pack of cards in disorder, and asked to inquire into their sequence, I shall, if I follow Dewey's prescription, first arrange them in order, and then say that this was the order resulting from inquiry. There will be, it is true, an 'objective transformation of objective subject-matter' while I am arranging the cards, but the definition allows for this. If, at the end, I am told: 'We wanted to know the sequence of the cards when they were given to you, not after you had re-arranged them,' I shall, if I am a disciple of Dewey, reply. 'Your ideas are altogether too static. I am a dynamic person, and when I inquire into any subject-matter I first alter it in such a way as to make the inquiry easy.' The notion that such a procedure is legitimate can only be justified by a Hegelian distinction of appearance and reality: the appearance may be confused and fragmentary, but the reality is always orderly and organic. Therefore when I arrange the cards I am only revealing their true eternal nature. But this part of the doctrine is never made explicit. The metaphysic of organism underlies Dewey's theories, but I do not know how far he is aware of this fact.

Let us now try to find the supplement to Dewey's definition which is required in order to distinguish inquiry from other kinds of organizing activity, such as those of the drill-sergeant and the bricklayer. Formerly it would have been said that inquiry is distinguished by its purpose, which is to ascertain some truth. But for Dewey 'truth' is to be defined in terms of 'inquiry', not *vice versa*; he quotes with approval Peirce's definition: 'Truth' is 'the opinion which is fated to be ultimately agreed to by all who investigate.' This leaves us completely in the dark as to what the investigators are doing, for we cannot, without circularity, say that they are endeavouring to ascertain the truth.

I think Dr Dewey's theory might be stated as follows. The relations of an organism to its environment are sometimes satisfactory to the organism, sometimes unsatisfactory. When they are unsatisfactory, the situation may be improved by mutual adjustment. When the alterations by means of which the situation is improved are mainly on the side of the organism—they are never *wholly* on either side—the process involved is called 'inquiry'. For example: during a battle you are mainly concerned to alter the environment, i.e. the enemy; but during the preceding period of reconnaissance you are mainly concerned to adapt your own forces to his dispositions. This earlier period is one of 'inquiry'.

The difficulty of this theory, to my mind, lies in the severing of the relation between a belief and the fact or facts which would commonly be said to 'verify' it. Let us continue to consider the example of a general planning a battle. His reconnaissance planes report to him certain enemy preparations, and he, in consequence, makes certain counter-preparations. Common sense would say that the reports upon which he acts are 'true' if, in fact, the enemy have made the moves which they are said to have made, and that, in that case, the reports remain true even if the general subsequently loses the battle. This view is rejected by Dr Dewey. He does not divide beliefs into 'true' and 'false', but he still has two kinds of beliefs, which we will call 'satisfactory' if the general wins, and 'unsatisfactory' if he is defeated. Until the battle has taken place, he cannot tell what to think about the reports of his scouts.

Generalizing, we may say that Dr Dewey, like everyone else, divides beliefs into two classes, of which one is good and the other bad. He holds, however, that a belief may be good at one time and bad at another; this happens with imperfect theories which are better than their predecessors but worse than their successors Whether a belief is good or bad depends upon whether the activities which it inspires in the organism entertaining the belief have consequences which are satisfactory or unsatisfactory to it. Thus a belief about some event in the past is to be classified as 'good' or 'bad', not according to whether the event really took place, but according to the future effects of the belief. The results are curious. Suppose somebody says to me: 'Did you have coffee with your breakfast this morning?" If I am an ordinary person, I shall try to remember. But if I am a disciple of Dr Dewey I shall say: 'Wait a while; I must try two experiments before I can tell you.' I shall then first make myself believe that I had coffee, and observe the consequences, if any; I shall then make myself believe that I did not have coffee, and again observe the consequences, if any. I shall then compare the two sets of consequences, to see which I found the more satisfactory. If there is a balance on one side I shall decide for that answer. If there is not, I shall have to confess that I cannot answer the question.

But this is not the end of our troubles. How am I to know the consequences of believing that I had coffee for breakfast? If I say 'the consequences are such-and-such', this in turn will have to be tested by its consequences before I can know whether what I have said was a 'good' or a 'bad' statement. And even if this difficulty were overcome, how am I to judge which set of consequences is the more satisfactory? One decision as to whether I had coffee may fill me with contentment, the other with determination to further the war effort. Each of these may be considered good, but until I have decided which is better I cannot tell whether I had coffee for breakfast. Surely this is absurd.

Dewey's divergence from what has hitherto been regarded as common sense is due to his refusal to admit 'facts' into his metaphysic, in the sense in which 'facts' are stubborn and cannot be manipulated. In this it may be that common sense is changing, and that his view will not seem contrary to what common sense is becoming.

The main difference between Dr Dewey and me is that he judges a belief by its effects, whereas I judge it by its causes where a past occurrence is concerned. I consider such a belief 'true', or as nearly 'true' as we can make it, if it has a certain kind of relation (sometimes very complicated) to its causes. Dr Dewey holds that it has 'warranted assertability'—which he substitutes for 'truth'—if it has certain kinds of effects. This divergence is connected with a difference of outlook on the world. The past cannot be affected by what we do, and therefore, if truth is determined by what has happened, it is independent of present or future volitions; it represents, in logical form, the limitations on human power. But if truth, or rather 'warranted assertability', depends upon the future, then, in so far as it is in our power to alter the future, it is in our power to alter what should be asserted. This enlarges the sense of human power and freedom. Did Caesar cross the Rubicon? I should regard an affirmative answer as unalterably necessitated by a past event. Dr Dewey would decide whether to say yes or no by an appraisal of future events, and there is no reason why these future events could not be arranged by human power so as to make a negative answer the more satisfactory. If I find the belief that Caesar crossed the Rubicon very distasteful, I need not sit down in dull despair; I can, if I have enough skill and power, arrange a social environment in which the statement that he did not cross the Rubicon will have 'warranted assertability'.

Throughout this book, I have sought, where possible, to connect philosophies with the social environment of the philosophers concerned. It has seemed to me that the belief in human power, and the unwillingness to admit 'stubborn facts', were connected with the hopefulness engendered by machine production and the scientific manipulation of our physical environment. This view is shared by many of Dr Dewey's supporters. Thus George Raymond Geiger, in a laudatory essay, says that Dr Dewey's method 'would mean a revolution in thought just as middle-class and unspectacular, but just as stupendous, as the revolution in industry of a century ago'. It seemed to me that I was saying the same thing when I wrote 'Dr Dewey has an outlook which, where it is distinctive, is in harmony with the age of industrialism and collective enterprise. It is natural that his strongest appeal should be to Americans, and also that he should be almost equally appreciated by the progressive elements in countries like China and Mexico.'

To my regret and surprise, this statement, which I had supposed completely innocuous, vexed Dr Dewey, who replied: 'Mr Russell's confirmed habit of connecting the pragmatic theory of knowing with obnoxious aspects of American industrialism . . . is much as if I were to link his philosophy to the interests of the English landed aristocracy.'

For my part, I am accustomed to having my opinions explained (especially by Communists) as due to my connection with the British aristocracy, and I am quite willing to suppose that my views, like other men's, are influenced by social environment. But if, in regard to Dr Dewey, I am mistaken as to the social influences concerned, I regret the mistake. I find, however, that I am not alone in having made it. Santayana, for instance, says: 'In Dewey, as in current science and ethics, there is a pervasive quasi-Hegelian tendency to dissolve the individual into his social functions, as well as everything substantial and actual into something relative and transitional.'

Dr Dewey's world, it seems to me, is one in which human beings occupy the imagination; the cosmos of astronomy, though of course acknowledged to exist, is at most times ignored. His philosophy is a power philosophy, though not, like Nietzsche's, a philosophy of individual power; it is the power of the community that is felt to be valuable. It is this element of social power that seems to me to make the philosophy of instrumentalism attractive to those who are more impressed by our new control over natural forces than by the limitations to which that control is still subject.

The attitude of man towards the non-human environment has differed profoundly at different times. The Greeks, with their dread of hubris and their belief in a Necessity or Fate superior even to Zeus, carefully avoided what would have seemed to them insolence towards the universe. The Middle Ages carried submission much further: humility towards God was a Christian's first duty. Initiative was cramped by this attitude, and great originality was scarcely possible. The Renaissance restored human pride, but carried it to the point where it led to anarchy and disaster. Its work was largely undone by the Reformation and the Counter-reformation. But modern technique, while not altogether favourable to the lordly individual of the Renaissance, has revived the sense of the collective power of human communities. Man, formerly too humble, begins to think of himself as almost a God. The Italian pragmatist Papini urges us to substitute the 'Imitation of God' for the 'Imitation of Christ'.

In all this I feel a grave danger, the danger of what might be called cosmic impiety. The concept of 'truth' as something dependent upon facts largely outside human control has been one of the ways in which philosophy hitherto has inculcated the necessary element of humility. When this check upon pride is removed, a further step is taken on the road towards a certain kind of madness —the intoxication of power which invaded philosophy with Fichte, and to which modern men, whether philosophers or not, are prone. I am persuaded that this intoxication is the greatest danger of our time, and that any philosophy which, however unintentionally, contributes to it is increasing the danger of vast social disaster.

Chapter XXXI

THE PHILOSOPHY OF LOGICAL ANALYSIS

I N philosophy ever since the time of Pythagoras there has been
an opposition between the men whose thought was mainly
inspired by mathematics and those who were more influenced
by the empirical sciences. Plato, Thomas Aquinas, Spinoza, and Kant
belong to what may be called the mathematical party; Democritus,
Aristotle, and the modern empiricists from Locke onwards, belong
to the opposite party. In our day a school of philosophy has arisen
which sets to work to eliminate Pythagoreanism from the principles
of mathematics, and to combine empiricism with an interest in the
deductive parts of human knowledge. The aims of this school are
less spectacular than those of most philosophers in the past, but
some of its achievements are as solid as those of the men of science.

The origin of this philosophy is in the achievements of mathematicians who set to work to purge their subject of fallacies and
slipshod reasoning. The great mathematicians of the seventeenth
century were optimistic and anxious for quick results; consequently
they left the foundations of analytical geometry and the infinitesimal calculus insecure. Leibniz believed in actual infinitesimals,
but although this belief suited his metaphysics it had no sound
basis in mathematics. Weierstrass, soon after the middle of
the nineteenth century, showed how to establish the calculus
without infinitesimals, and thus at last made it logically secure.
Next came Georg Cantor, who developed the theory of continuity
and infinite number. 'Continuity' had been, until he defined it, a
vague word, convenient for philosophers like Hegel, who wished to
introduce metaphysical muddles into mathematics. Cantor gave a
precise significance to the word, and showed that continuity, as he
defined it, was the concept needed by mathematicians and physicists. By this means a great deal of mysticism, such as that of
Bergson, was rendered antiquated.

Cantor also overcame the long-standing logical puzzles about
infinite number. Take the series of whole numbers from 1 onwards;
how many of them are there? Clearly the number is not finite. Up
to a thousand, there are a thousand numbers; up to a million, a
million. Whatever finite number you mention, there are evidently
more numbers than that, because from 1 up to the number in
question there are just that number of numbers, and then there are

others that are greater. The number of finite whole numbers must, therefore, be an infinite number. But now comes a curious fact: The number of even numbers must be the same as the number of all whole numbers. Consider the two rows:

$$1, \quad 2, \quad 3, \quad 4, \quad 5, \quad 6, \ldots$$
$$2, \quad 4, \quad 6, \quad 8, \quad 10, \quad 12, \ldots$$

There is one entry in the lower row for every one in the top row; therefore the number of terms in the two rows must be the same, although the lower row consists of only half the terms in the top row. Leibniz, who noticed this, thought it a contradiction, and concluded that, though there are infinite collections, there are no infinite numbers. Georg Cantor, on the contrary, boldly denied that it is a contradiction. He was right; it is only an oddity.

Georg Cantor defined an 'infinite' collection as one which has parts containing as many terms as the whole collection contains. On this basis he was able to build up a most interesting mathematical theory of infinite numbers, thereby taking into the realm of exact logic a whole region formerly given over to mysticism and confusion.

The next man of importance was Frege, who published his first work in 1879, and his definition of 'number' in 1884; but, in spite of the epoch-making nature of his discoveries, he remained wholly without recognition until I drew attention to him in 1903. It is remarkable that, before Frege, every definition of number that had been suggested contained elementary logical blunders. It was customary to identify 'number' with 'plurality'. But an instance of 'number' is a particular number, say 3, and an instance of 3 is a particular triad. The triad is a plurality, but the class of all triads—which Ferge identified with the number 3—is a plurality of pluralities, and number in general, of which 3 is an instance, is a plurality of pluralities of pluralities. The elementary grammatical mistake of confounding this with the simple plurality of a given triad made the whole philosophy of number, before Frege, a tissue of nonsense in the strictest sense of the term 'nonsense'.

From Frege's work it followed that arithmetic, and pure mathematics generally, is nothing but a prolongation of deductive logic. This disproved Kant's theory that arithmetical propositions are 'synthetic' and involve a reference to time. The development of pure mathematics from logic was set forth in detail in *Principia Mathematica*, by Whitehead and myself.

It gradually became clear that a great part of philosophy can be reduced to something that may be called 'syntax', though the word has to be used in a somewhat wider sense than has hitherto been customary. Some men, notably Carnap, have advanced the theory that all philosophical problems are really syntactical, and that, when errors in syntax are avoided, a philosophical problem is thereby either solved or shown to be insoluble. I think, and Carnap now agrees, that this is an overstatement, but there can be no doubt that the utility of philosophical syntax in relation to traditional problems is very great.

I will illustrate its utility by a brief explanation of what is called the theory of descriptions. By a 'description' I mean a phrase such as 'The present President of the United States', in which a person or thing is designated, not by name, but by some property which is supposed or known to be peculiar to him or it. Such phrases had given a lot of trouble. Suppose I say, 'The golden mountain does not exist', and suppose you ask 'What is it that does not exist?' It would seem that, if I say 'It is the golden mountain,' I am attributing some sort of existence to it. Obviously I am not making the same statement as if I said, 'The round square does not exist.' This seemed to imply that the golden mountain is one thing and the round square is another, although neither exists. The theory of descriptions was designed to meet this and other difficulties.

According to this theory, when a statement containing a phrase of the form 'the so-and-so' is rightly analysed, the phrase 'the so-and-so' disappears. For example, take the statement 'Scott was the author of *Waverley*.' The theory interprets this statement as saying

'One and only one man wrote *Waverley*, and that man was Scott.' Or, more fully:

'There is an entity c such that the statement "x wrote *Waverley*" is true if x is c and false otherwise; moreover c is Scott.'

The first part of this, before the word 'moreover', is defined as meaning: 'The author of *Waverley* exists (or existed or will exist).' Thus 'The golden mountain does not exist' means:

'There is no entity c such that "x is golden and mountainous" is true when x is c, but not otherwise.'

With this definition the puzzle as to what is meant when we say 'The golden mountain does not exist' disappears.

'Existence,' according to this theory, can only be asserted of descriptions. We can say 'The author of *Waverley* exists,' but to say 'Scott exists' is bad grammar, or rather bad syntax. This clears up two millennia of muddle-headedness about 'existence', beginning with Plato's *Theaetetus*.

One result of the work we have been considering is to dethrone mathematics from the lofty place that it has occupied since Pythagoras and Plato, and to destroy the presumption against empiricism which has been derived from it. Mathematical knowledge, it is true, is not obtained by induction from experience; our reason for believing that 2 and 2 are 4 is not that we have so often found, by observation, that one couple and another couple together make a quartet. In this sense, mathematical knowledge is still not empirical. But it is also not *a priori* knowledge about the world. It is, in fact, merely verbal knowledge. '3' means '2 + 1', and '4' means '3 + 1'. Hence it follows (though the proof is long) that '4' means the same as '2 + 2'. Thus mathematical knowledge ceases to be mysterious. It is all of the same nature as the 'great truth' that there are three feet in a yard.

Physics, as well as pure mathematics, has supplied material for the philosophy of logical analysis. This has occurred especially through the theory of relativity and quantum mechanics.

What is important to the philosopher in the theory of relativity is the substitution of space-time for space and time. Common sense thinks of the physical world as composed of 'things' which persist through a certain period of time and move in space. Philosophy and physics developed the notion of 'thing' into that of 'material substance', and thought of material substance as consisting of particles, each very small, and each persisting throughout all time. Einstein substituted events for particles; each event had to each other a relation called 'interval', which could be analysed in various ways into a time-element and a space-element. The choice between these various ways was arbitrary, and no one of them was theoretically preferable to any other. Given two events A and B, in different regions, it might happen that according to one convention they were simultaneous, according to another A was earlier than B, and according to yet another B was earlier than A. No physical facts correspond to these different conventions.

From all this it seems to follow that events, not particles, must be the 'stuff' of physics. What has been thought of as a particle will have to be thought of as a series of events. The series of events that replaces a particle has certain important physical properties, and therefore demands our attention; but it has no more substantiality than any other series of events that we might arbitrarily single out. Thus 'matter' is not part of the ultimate material of the world, but merely a convenient way of collecting events into bundles.

Quantum theory reinforces this conclusion, but its chief philosophical importance is that it regards physical phenomena as possibly discontinuous. It suggests that, in an atom (interpreted as above), a certain state of affairs persists for a certain time, and then suddenly is replaced by a finitely different state of affairs. Continuity of motion, which had always been assumed, appears to have been a mere prejudice. The philosophy appropriate to quantum theory, however, has not yet been adequately developed. I suspect that it will demand even more radical departures from the traditional doctrine of space and time than those demanded by the theory of relativity.

While physics has been making matter less material, psychology has been making mind less mental. We had occasion in a former chapter to compare the association of ideas with the conditioned reflex. The latter, which has replaced the former, is obviously much more physiological. (This is only one illustration; I do not wish to exaggerate the scope of the conditioned reflex.) Thus from both ends physics and psychology have been approaching each other, and making more possible the doctrine of 'neutral monism' suggested by William James's criticism of 'consciousness'. The distinction of mind and matter came into philosophy from religion, although, for a long time, it seemed to have valid grounds. I think that both mind and matter are merely convenient ways of grouping events. Some single events, I should admit, belong only to material groups, but others belong to both kinds of groups, and are therefore at once mental and material. This doctrine effects a great simplification in our picture of the structure of the world.

Modern physics and physiology throw a new light upon the ancient problem of perception. If there is to be anything that can be called 'perception', it must be in some degree an effect of the object perceived, and it must more or less resemble the object if it is to be a source of knowledge of the object. The first requisite can only be fulfilled if there are causal chains which are, to a greater or less extent, independent of the rest of the world. According to physics, this is the case. Light-waves travel from the sun to the earth, and in doing so obey their own laws. This is only roughly true. Einstein has shown that light-rays are affected by gravitation. When they reach our atmosphere, they suffer refraction, and some are more scattered than others. When they reach a human eye, all sorts of things happen which would not happen elsewhere, ending up with what we call 'seeing the sun'. But although the sun of our visual experience is very different from the sun of the astronomer, it is still a source of knowledge as to the latter, because 'seeing the sun' differs from 'seeing the moon' in ways that are causally connected with the difference between the astronomer's sun and the astronomer's moon. What we can know of physical objects in this way, however, is only certain abstract properties of structure. We can know that the sun is round in a sense, though not quite the sense in which what we see is round; but we have no reason to suppose that it is bright or warm, because physics can account for its seeming so without supposing that it is so. Our knowledge of the physical world, therefore, is only abstract and mathematical.

Modern analytical empiricism, of which I have been giving an outline, differs from that of Locke, Berkeley, and Hume by its incorporation of mathematics and its development of a powerful logical technique. It is thus able, in regard to certain problems, to achieve definite answers, which have the quality of science rather than of philosophy. It has the advantage, as compared with the philosophies of the system-builders, of being able to tackle its problems one at a time, instead of having to invent at one stroke a block theory of the whole universe. Its methods, in this respect, resemble those of science. I have no doubt that, in so far as philosophical knowledge is possible, it is by such methods that it must be sought; I have also no doubt that, by these methods, many ancient problems are completely soluble.

There remains, however, a vast field, traditionally included in philosophy, where scientific methods are inadequate. This field includes ultimate questions of value; science alone, for example, cannot prove that it is bad to enjoy the infliction of cruelty. Whatever can be known, can be known by means of science; but things which are legitimately matters of feeling lie outside its province.

Philosophy, throughout its history, has consisted of two parts inharmoniously blended: on the one hand a theory as to the nature of the world, on the other an ethical or political doctrine as to the best way of living. The failure to separate these two with sufficient clarity has been a source of much confused thinking. Philosophers, from Plato to William James, have allowed their opinions as to the constitution of the universe to be influenced by the desire for edification: knowing, as they supposed, what beliefs would make men virtuous, they have invented arguments, often very sophistical, to prove that these beliefs are true. For my part I reprobate this kind of bias, both on moral and on intellectual grounds. Morally, a philosopher who uses his professional competence for anything except a disinterested search for truth is guilty of a kind of treachery. And when he assumes, in advance of inquiry, that certain beliefs, whether true or false, are such as to promote good behaviour, he is so limiting the scope of philosophical speculation as to make philosophy trivial; the true philosopher is prepared to examine *all* preconceptions. When any limits are placed, consciously or unconsciously, upon the pursuit of truth, philosophy becomes paralysed by fear, and the ground is prepared for a government censorship punishing those who utter 'dangerous thoughts'—in fact, the philosopher has already placed such a censorship over his own investigations.

Intellectually, the effect of mistaken moral considerations upon philosophy has been to impede progress to an extraordinary extent. I do not myself believe that philosophy can either prove or disprove the truth of religious dogmas, but ever since Plato most philosophers have considered it part of their business to produce 'proofs' of immortality and the existence of God. They have found fault with the proofs of their predecessors—St Thomas rejected St Anselm's proofs, and Kant rejected Descartes'—but they have supplied new ones of their own. In order to make their proofs seem valid, they have had to falsify logic, to make mathematics mystical, and to pretend that deep-seated prejudices were heaven-sent intuitions.

All this is rejected by the philosophers who make logical analysis the main business of philosophy. They confess frankly that the human intellect is unable to find conclusive answers to many questions of profound importance to mankind, but they refuse to believe that there is some 'higher' way of knowing, by which we can discover truths hidden from science and the intellect. For this renunciation they have been rewarded by the discovery that many questions, formerly obscured by the fog of metaphysics, can be answered with precision, and by objective methods which introduce nothing of the philosopher's temperament except the desire to understand. Take such questions as: What is number? What are space and time? What is mind, and what is matter? I do not say that we can here and now give definitive answers to all these ancient questions, but I do say that a method has been discovered by which, as in science, we can make successive approximations to the truth, in which each new stage results from an improvement, not a rejection, of what has gone before.

In the welter of conflicting fanaticisms, one of the few unifying forces is scientific truthfulness, by which I mean the habit of basing our beliefs upon observations and inferences as impersonal, and as much divested of local and temperamental bias, as is possible for human beings. To have insisted upon the introduction of this virtue into philosophy, and to have invented a powerful method by which it can be rendered fruitful, are the chief merits of the philosophical school of which I am a member. The habit of careful veracity acquired in the practice of this philosophical method can be extended to the whole sphere of human activity, producing, wherever it exists, a lessening of fanaticism with an increasing capacity of sympathy and mutual understanding. In abandoning a part of its dogmatic pretensions, philosophy does not cease to suggest and inspire a way of life.

contempt, 58, 60

Continental philosophy, 618-19, 531, 548

continuity, 783, 786-7

Contra Celsum. See Against Celsus

contradiction, law of, 93, 573, 679

convention, and romanticism, 652

co-ordinate geometry, 55, 522, 544-5, 529

Copernican hypothesis, 233, 266, 480; in antiquity, 223-5; and human pride, 18, 523

Copernicus, Nikolaus, 216, 226, 465, 475, 412-15, 680; and Aristarchus of Samos, 145-6, 223-5; disposes of man's cosmic importance, 513, 753; and Galileo, 519, 520; and Kepler, 516, 517; and Newton, 87, 520, 524

Cordova, 324, 418, 420

Corinth, 34; League of, 235, 343

Cornford, F. M., 42, 51, 52, 59 *n.*, 60, 93, 157 *n.*, 159 *n.*, 161

Corporate State, 673

corporation lawyers, 91

Corsair, Byron's, 271, 719

Cortes, 539

Cos, 236

cosmic impiety, 782

cosmic justice, 46, 60, 62, 63, 152

cosmic strife, 60, 130

cosmogony, of Descartes, 546; and Plato, 122, 157-62

cosmological argument, 568-9, 682

cosmology, in ancient philosophy, 72, 80, 85, 88-9

cosmopolitan point of view, 230, 751

Cotes, Roger, 546

councils of the Church, 329-30, 365-6, 373, 422, 461, 472

Council of Elders, 114

Counter-Reformation, 481, 487, 509-11, 781

courage, 109

Couturat, Louis, 568, 571

Cowper, William, 624

creation, 32, 157-8, 161, 297-8, 331, 419, 449, 464, 574-5; and St Augustine, 351-3, 355, 356; and Jews, 311, 421; and theology, 47, 144, 149, 298, 400, 401

creative evolution, 757-8

Creator, 84, 85, 144, 145, 149, 295, 352, 369, 565

Crecy, 717

credibility and consistency, 592

Crete, 27-9, 30, 37, 38, 118

Crimean War, 611

criminal law, 36, 114, 115, 508, 742

Critias, 97, 102

critique of knowledge, 677

Critique of Practical Reason, The (Kant), 681, 682

Critique of Pure Reason, The (Kant), 576, 618, 646, 679-82, 684-5, 723

Crito (Plato), 147, 148, 155

Croesus, 44

Cromwell, Oliver, 21, 510, 532, 538, 582, 583, 584, 596, 607, 611

Croton, 49

Crucifixion, 147

cruelty, 150, 262, 269, 562, 620-1, 733-4, 788

Crusades, 324, 422, 427, 436, 438, 717, 718; and Albigenses, 435; first, 422, 423, 427, 431; second, 431; third, 426, 427; fourth, 434-5, 436, 484

culture, and Athens, 76-8; in Carolingian period, 389, 391; in later antiquity, 204, 284; Mohammedan, 413-22; and Roman Empire, 277-88

Cumont, 285 *n.*, 355 *n.*, 466 *n.*

cycle of fire, 261

Cymbeline, 509

Cynics, -ism, 109, 240-2, 260, 357, 555, 579

Cyprian, St, 277

Cyril of Alexandria, St, 365-6, 370

Cyrus, 33, 44, 312, 491

d'Ailly, 463 *n.*

daimon, 107

Damascus, 415

Damasus I, St, Pope, 337, 341

Damian, St Peter, 404, 405, 407-8, 410

damnation, 357, 359, 362, 524, 554; of unbaptized infants, 362-3

Danes, 16, 306, 391, 395

Daniel, 319

Dante, 18, 182, 216, 290, 304, 367, 427, 460, 493

Danton, 653

England—*contd.*
ution, 583, 584; and romanticism, 654-5; and Rome, 277, 390; in seventeenth century, 521, 539, 581; Victorian age in, 92, 722; universities in, 474; and wealth in fourteenth century, 468

England, Bank of, 578, 583

England, Church of, 581, 598-9

Enneads (Plotinus), 292, 294-5, 297, 416

ens realissimum, 682

entelechy, 551

enthusiasm, 21, 36, 39, 586-7, 676

environment, 757, 778

envy, 150

Ephesians, 26, 59

Ephesus, 27, 59, 165, 365-6, 373, 380

Ephors, 114-15, 117

Epictetus, 249 *n*, 260, 261, 267-71, 282, 751

Epicureanism, 182, 229, 240, 249-59, 260, 282, 283, 292, 300, 367, 522

Epicurus, 82, 83, 249-59, 356, 387, 729; and utilitarians, 742, 743

epicycles, 513, 514, 516-17

Epimenides, 326

epistemology, 686, 688. *See also* theory of knowledge

equality, 153; of man, in ancient philosophy, 130-1, 186, 194, 200, 201, 202, 276; of man, in modern philosophy, 505, 578, 603, 663, 669, 697-8, 700, 732, 742; of women, 694, 695, 742

Erasmus, 499-504, 509

Erastianism, 360, 709

Eratosthenes, 225, 233

Erigena, Johannes Scotus *See* John the Scot

Erinyes, 62

Eros, 39

error(s), 769; in Aristotle, 175, 208-12; in Platonic theory of ideas, 141

eschatology, 360, 361

Essais philosophiques (Descartes), 545

Essay Concerning Human Understanding (Locke), 584-95

Essay on Man (Pope), 368

Essay on Miracles (Hume), 634

Essays on Government (Locke), 610

Essence, 141, 158, 297, 458, 459, 567, 569, 590; and Aquinas, 446, 447, 448, 453; and Aristotle, 177, 210-11

essences, 151, 153, 159, 574

Essenes, 316 *n*.

Essex, Robert Devereux, Earl of, 526

Este family, 564

Esthonia, 611

eternity, 56, 63, 158, 272, 296, 352, 556

ethic(s), 287, 415; and Aquinas, 450-1; aristocratic, 735; and Aristotle, 146, 185-95, 215; and Bentham, 742-3; Christian, 109, 300, 307, 322; contemplative ideal in, 53; and differences between Continental and British philosophy, 620-1; and Epicurus, 254; and good of community, 191, 683; Greek, 89, 109, 130; in Hellenistic world, 238; and Helvétius, 694; and James, 769, 770, 771, 772; Jewish, 321-2; and Kant, 677, 682-4; and Locke, 592-5, 604-5; and Marx, 753; and More, 507; and Nietzsche, 728, 729-30, 735-9; "noble", 733-4; and Plato, 93, 123, 132-3, 134, 356; romantic, 657, 659; and Rousseau, 481, 661, 662, 667; and Schopenhauer, 722, 728; and Socrates, 90, 109, 147; and Spinoza, 552, 560-2; and Stoicism, 260, 265, 272-5; and utilitarians, 677, 745

Ethics (Spinoza), 552, 553-9, 564

Etna, 71, 359

Eton, 232 *n*.

Euclid, 54, 55, 160, 219, 220-1, 234, 244, 275, 431, 455, 532, 554, 686, 688

Eudoxus, 219, 220

Eugene, Prince, 564

Eugenics, 128

Eugenius IV, Pope, 472-3, 485

Eugenius, usurper in Roman Empire, 338

eunuchs, 173, 328

Euphrates, 25, 277

Euripides, 38, 39, 40, 76, 79, 96, 97, 105, 196

Eustochium, 341-2

Latin language—*contd.*
Hymns, 431; and Ireland, 396-7;
and philosophy, 288, 347; and
Roman Empire, 280; and translations, 221, 323, 358, 417, 419, 420
Latin world, and Alexander, 466
Latvia, 611
Laud, Archbishop, 532, 581
laurel leaves, 74
law(s), legislation, 36, 116, 210,
605-6, 614; and Aristotle, 197,
201; in Athens, 92, 147-8; and
Bentham, 592-3, 741, 742, 746; of
causality, 529; of gravitation,
517, 520-1, 523, 525; and Greeks,
130, 134; of Hammurabi, 27;
Hebrew, Jewish or Mosaic, 311,
315, 319, 322, 345; and Hegel,
707, 710; and Helvétius, 693; of
inertia, 518, 519; and Kant, 683;
of motion, 217, 518, 520, 522-3,
524-5; natural, 46, 130, 254, 601-6,
663; of nature, 32, 95; philosophy of, 36, 604; of planetary
motion, 516, 517, 520; and Protagoras, 93, 94; and Stoics, 273
Lawrence, D. H., 657
Laws (Plato), 219
Lea, Henry C., 129 *n.*, 404 *n.*, 470
League for Peace, Kant's, 711
League of Cambrai, 484
League of Nations, 711
Lear, King, 734
Lee, Joseph, quoted, 602
Leeuwenhoek, Anton van, 521
legal fictions, 388-9, 610
legal rights, 604-5
legal theory of war, 605
legislative function, legislature,
613-16, 673, 684, 741
Legnano, 426
Leibniz, 56, 563-76; and calculus,
522, 564, 783; and ethics, 620;
and Germany, 563, 691; and God,
411, 550, 565, 566-75, 619, 666;
and infinite number, 784; influence of, 618; and Kant, 678,
679; and knowledge, 589; and
Locke, 589, 617; method of, 619;
and plenum, 87, 88; and principle of individuation, 459; and
Spinoza, 552, 563, 564, 566, 567;
and subjectivism, 431, 675; and

Leibniz—*contd.*
substance, 565
Leipzig, 563
leisure, 123, 192
Lenin, 775
Leo I, the Great, St, Pope, 365
Leo III, St, Pope, 388
Leo IX, St, Pope, 406
Leo X, Pope, 485, 486, 493
Leo XIII, Pope, 444
Leo III, the Isaurian, Emperor, 386
Leonardo, see Vinci
Leontia, Empress, 381
Leopardi, 239
Lesbos, 30
Lethe, 39
Letter of Aristeas, 317 *n.*
Lettres philosophiques (Voltaire),
585
Leucippus, 82-5, 88, 215, 251
Leuctra, 116
Levant, 719
Leviathan, (Hobbes), 532-41
Leviticus, 315
Leyden, University of, 544
liberal culture, 479
liberalism, liberals, 348, 754; and
Darwin, 697-8, 746; and Dewey,
774, 775; in eighteenth and nine-
teenth centuries, 118, 510, 618;
and Hegel, 707, 710, 713; in Holland, 552, 577; and Kant, 618;
and Locke, 21, 593, 613; and Milton, 749; and More, 507-8; and
Napoleon, 721; New England,
774; and Nietzsche, 733; philosophical, 21, 22, 577-83; and
State, 203, 539; in Western Germany 692
liberty, 226, 425, 718; and Bentham,
742; and Churches, 732; and
Filmer, 597; and Hobbes, 535,
537, 538; and Locke, 592, 593-4,
603; and Machiavelli, 495; for
nations, 580, 658; and Rousseau,
669, 670; and utilitarianism, 606
life, 768; and Bergson, 757, 761-2,
764; elixir of, 61
light-waves, 72, 87, 787
Lincoln, Abraham, 735
Lippershey, Hans, 521
Lisbon, earthquake of, 664, 678
Lithuania, 611

Luther, Martin—*contd.*
philosophy, 708; and State, 510,
709
Lutheran Church, 709
Lutterworth, 473, 474
Lycurgus, 112, 113, 115, 117, 118-20,
495, 497, 662, 669, 673
Lydia, 30, 40, 44, 45
Lykon, 103
Lyons, 469, 661; Poor men of, 440,
441
Lysis (Plato), 109

Macbeth, 561
Maccabaeus, John Hyrcanus, 321
Maccabaeus, Jonathan and Judas,
317
Maccabees, 231, 233, 317-19, 320,
361
Macedonia, -ns, 173, 229, 232, 233,
240; and barbarians, 343; and
City State, 134, 203, 229; bring
disorder, 229, 234-5, 258, 279; and
Greek culture, 15, 279; and
Rome, 277
Machiavelli, Niccolò, 18, 202, 481,
490, 491-8, 531, 540, 673, 708, 729
machine production, 480, 691, 696,
699, 747, 780
McKenna, Stephen, 293
madness, 164, 782
Maenads, 37, 40
magic, 27, 32, 237, 247, 255, 299,
329, 450, 457; black, 455, 466; in
Renaissance, 489, 522; and
Science, 455
Magna Carta, 434
Magna Graecia, 66, 76
Magnanimous man, 187-8, 194, 728
Magnet, 45, 521, 529
Maimonides, 324, 420-1
majority, 608, 609, 610
Malchus, *see* Porphyry
Malebranche, 444, 545, 564
Malthus, Thomas Robert, 694-5,
697, 746, 747
man, brotherhood of, 241, 269, 271,
272, 287; and Copernicus, 223,
753; measure of all things, 94,
163-5, 166, 170-1; place of, in
universe, 223, 523; undue emphasis on, 753. *See also* Rights of
man

Manchester, 748
Manchester School, 580
Manfred, King of Naples and
Sicily, 486, 718
Manichaeism, 149, 325-6, 344, 347-8,
349, 350, 351, 357, 439, 571
Manichaeus, 348
Manilius, 246
Mansur, Al, 418
many, the, 73, 86
Marathon, 76, 96
Marcion, 439-40
Marcomanni, 285
Marcus Aurelius, 16, 204, 249, 260,
261, 267, 268, 269, 271-6, 280, 282,
283, 285, 439
Marduk, 26, 27
Mark Antony, *see* Antonius,
Marcus
Marozia, 393-4
marriage, 113, 114, 119, 128, 149,
187, 196, 241, 314, 391-2, 404,
450, 453, 506
Mars, 516, 517
Marseilles, 236, 266, 380
Marsiglio of Padua, 459-61, 470, 474
Marston Moor, 717
Martel, Charles, *see* Charles Martel
Martin I, St, Pope, 386
Martin V, Pope, 472
Martin of Tours, St, 373
Marx, Karl, 653, 691, 696, 700,
740 *n.*, 747, 748-55; and Bentham,
696, 743; and class struggle, 540,
755; and Darwinism, 698; and
Dewey, 775; eclecticism of, 617;
and Hegel, 701, 709, 748, 753, 754;
and history, 361, 705, 748, 750,
753; and labour theory of value,
612, 613; and liberalism, 581, 618;
and revolt, 716, 748; and Plato,
152; and State, 754
Mary, Queen of England, 598
Mary, Queen of Scots, 597
Master of Animals, 28
Masuccio di Salerno, 489
materialism, 86 *n.*, 89, 254, 258, 291,
356, 533, 551, 564, 633, 766; and
Marx, 748, 749, 750, 752; in psychology, 741; and Stoics, 260,
261, 262, 265, 292
mathematical logic, 572-3, 576
mathematics, 365, 410, 431; in

metaphysics—*contd.*
559-60; and Zeno, 261
Metaphysics (Aristotle), 216, 417
Metapontion, 50, 52
Methodism, 42, 257
Methuselah, 358
metre, 153
Metrodorus, 251
Mexico, 26, 598, 781
Michael II, 398
Michael III, 392, 399
Michael of Cesena, 459
Michelangelo, 490, 517, 729
microscope, 110, 521
Middle Ages, 31, 335, 395, 699; and
Aristotle, 244, 412, 463; and St
Augustine, 360; and Boethius,
367, 370; and Byron, 717, 718,
719; and Church, 17-18, 385, 392,
482, 597; and City of God, 353-4;
communist rebels in, 716;
despised in fifteenth century,
475; die hard, 475; and Donation
of Constantine, 387; dualism of,
239, 304; and economics, 303-4;
and Gregory the Great, 378; and
individualism, 579, 580; and
Italian cities, 196; Jew in, 324,
326; and kings, 305, 340 *n.*; and
landholding, 611; and law of
nature, 601; legal fictions in,
388-9; and logic, 206; and Lucretius, 256; Mohammedan civilization in, 324; originality and
archaism in, 422-3; and philosophy, 56, 434, 709; and Plato,
157, 412; and Plotinus, 290; and
politics, 18, 196; and pseudo
Dionysius, 398, 401; and romanticism, 654; and sin, 362, 523;
submissive toward non-human
environment, 523, 781; and superstition, 514; and Stoics, 275; and
transubstantiation, 403; universality of Church and Empire in,
287; unscientific, 512, 514, 523.
See also Church, Holy Roman
Empire, Papacy
middle class, 475, 577, 621, 606, 699,
751, 780
Mikado, 129, 598
Milan, 335, 338, 339, 344, 347, 349,
404, 409; in conflict of Emperor

Milan—*contd.*
and Pope, 423, 425, 426; Patarine
movement in, 407-8, 424; in
Renaissance, 483, 487
Milesian school, 47-8, 59, 231
Miletus, 44, 45, 46, 47, 49, 50, 79,
82, 115
Milhaud, Gaston, 85 *n.*
Milky Way, 520
Mill, James, 693, 695, 740, 742-3,
747, 749, 755
Mill, John Stuart, 529, 619, 693, 695,
730, 743, 744-5
millenium, 361
Milton, John, 150, 234-5, 340 *n.*,
440, 743, 749
mind, 632; and Anaxagoras, 79, 80;
and Aristotle, 182-3; and Locke,
590-1; and Plato, 159, 166; and
Plotinus, 293-4, 298; and Spinoza,
253-4; and Zeno, 264
mind and matter, 194, 626; and
Bergson, 760; and Cartesians,
545-6, 548, 550-1; defined, 787;
and James, 767-8; and Kant, 677;
and Leibniz, 565-6; and logical
analysis, 787, 789
Minoan age of culture, 27-9, 30,
286
miracle(s), 50, 71, 328, 331, 340,
375-6, 450, 634; of the mass, 403
missionaries, 372, 390, 396-7, 427,
441, 510
Mistress of Animals, 28, 247
Mithraism, 286
Mitylene, 250
Mnemosyne, 39
Mnesarchos, 49
modality, 681
moderation, 89, 581, 583
moderns, 500
Mohammed, 326, 382, 413, 414, 436.
See also Prophet
Mohammedan(s), 232, 366, 718;
Africa and Spain become, 281;
and Algebra, 288; and Aristotle,
288, 445; and chemistry, 61, 288,
420; and Christian philosophy,
305, 468; and Church, 287; conquests of, 233, 287-8, 333, 387,
394; and culture, 420; and Frederick II, 436-7; and Greek culture,
281, 414, 416; and Hellenistic